THE SECRET MIDDLE AGES

Ça rime comme
hallebarde et miséricorde

Hit nys nout as men wenet

THE SECRET
MIDDLE AGES

MALCOLM JONES

SUTTON PUBLISHING

First published in the United Kingdom in 2002 by
Sutton Publishing Limited · Phoenix Mill
Thrupp · Stroud · Gloucestershire · GL5 2BU

This paperback edition first published in 2004.

British Library Cataloguing in Publication Data
A catalogue record for this book is available from the British Library.

ISBN 0-7509-3874-9

*For my parents
and all my other teachers*

Typeset in 11/14pt New Baskerville.
Typesetting and origination by
Sutton Publishing Limited.
Printed and bound in England by
J.H. Haynes & Co. Ltd, Sparkford.

CONTENTS

LiSt of iLLustrations

Figures and Ornaments

Ornament to half-title and pages v, vi, xiv, xxii, xxv, 295, 300, 366: bronze roundel with enamelled inscription, *hyt nys nout as men wenet*, English, ?15thC. (Present whereabouts unknown: photograph © The British Museum)

Ornament to Chapter 1: elderly man in bath with young woman fool: lead lid, ?Dutch, 15thC. (Photograph courtesy of Brian Spencer)

1.1 Lovers (woman naked) beside fountain: cast of biscuit-mould, German, first half 15thC. (© Städtisches Museum in Andreasstift, Worms)

1.2 Lovers (woman naked) seated on bed playing instruments: cast of biscuit-mould, German, first half 15thC. (Museum Wiesbaden)

1.3 Man threshes chicks out of eggs: misericord, Emmerich, late 15thC. (Photograph courtesy of Elaine Block)

1.4 All ride the ass: woodcut, German, early 16thC. (Bodleian Library, Oxford, Douce Prints W.2.2b (25). Photograph from E. Diederichs, *Deutsches Leben der Vergangenheit*, Abb. 666, Jena, 1908)

1.5 Fox/wolf preaches to sheep: stained and painted glass, English mid-15thC. (© Burrell Collection, Glasgow)

1.6 Dildo-pedlar (and dog running off with one): cast of biscuit-mould, German, first half 15thC. (© MAK Österreichisches Museum für Angewandte Kunst, Vienna)

Ornament to Chapter 2: four-leaf clover inscribed 't': lead badge, English 14th/15thC. (Photograph courtesy of Brian Spencer)

2.1 Christ-child caressing parrot with New Year's greeting: woodcut-sheet, German, mid-15thC. (© Staatlichen Museen Preußischer Kulturbesitz, Berlin)

2.2 St Gertrude and mice: woodcut-sheet, German, mid-15thC. (© Staatlichen Museen Preußischer Kulturbesitz, Berlin)

2.3 Quatrefoil replaces head of God the Father: manuscript miniature, English, early 13thC. (By permission of the Master and Fellows of Trinity College, Cambridge. Ref: Trinity College Library, MS B.11.4, f. 119r)

2.4 St Werburgh's geese in pen: misericord supporter, Chester Cathedral, late 14thC. (© University of Manchester: photograph courtesy of Christa Grössinger)

FOREWORD

In the Royal Society of Antiquaries, a lofty hall off the courtyard of the Royal Academy, Malcolm Jones was showing slides of winged penises, flying vulvas, belled cocks, pudenda on stilts, and other symbols of vigour and fertility; he was accompanying the slides with a learned commentary on the emblems, on their associated puns, proverbs, and possible significance and uses. From this material, he then moved on to sows and donkeys spinning thread, to lubricious widows, and other misogynist motifs; this was followed by a look at some capering wild men or wodehouses, and a short enquiry into fantasies associated with their hairy bodies.

It was the first time I had heard Malcolm Jones speak, and I was there because I'd read an extraordinarily rich and surprising article on sexual culture in the Middle Ages published in the journal, *Folklore*. The evidence he was presenting to his audience of Antiquaries focused on medieval lead badges, die-cast metal artefacts, which have been buried for centuries: many of his examples have recently been dredged up from the tidal Schelde estuary in the Netherlands. The invention of the metal detector, and the perseverance of anoraked enthusiasts in the mudflats, have made possible the discovery of a new contemporary treasure hoard. These cheap souvenirs from pilgrimage sites, akin to the contemporary lapel or hitchhiker's rucksack badge, these emblems have revealed new depths to the fantastical, bold, rude and secular *mentalité* of the ordinary medieval man and woman.

The talk Malcolm was giving that day was scholarly, serious, and highly original. But it was also, inevitably, funny: there is no other response to these images and punning devices than laughter. Laughter is interesting in its complexity of response: a release from embarrassment, a recognition of rudeness and outrageousness, as well as a kind of shock that the unspeakable has been spoken, the obscene brought in from the wings to take centre stage. In this packed and fascinating book, *The Secret Middle Ages*, Malcolm Jones has mustered a crowd of many more star witnesses, an exuberant and outspoken host of characters – burlesque saints, wise fools (and ribald ones), hairy anchorites, Englishmen with tails, donkey-headed dunces, and a huge and entertaining cast of animal characters who bridge the world of the classical fable and the Victorian children's tale. These figures are compacted of stories, and communicate symbolically, through sign, gesture, allegory, wordplay, and dense, literary allusion. They provide an iconic thesaurus of 'the other Middle Ages', as the author calls his focus of interest (*c.* 1100–1500). Together they colour in a picture of a less repressed, less courtly, less institutionalised, more eclectic, and above all less Christian complex of thinking and feeling, connecting to non-Christian antecedents. What Chaucer in English, Boccaccio in Italian, and, later, Rabelais in French, explore through their storytelling, comic vision and verbal virtuosity, many artists using every kind of form – biscuit moulds, misericords, valentines, crockery, leather, mirrors and body language – also contain and communicate through these quotidian artefacts; social historians who see only the heavenward-reaching spires of Gothic cathedrals, penitential liturgical paraphernalia, and morbid rituals for the dead, let alone pervasive superstition and ignorance, are shutting their faculties to a lively, and very different history.

Traditionally, the overlooked margin has been the place where the subversive gesture, the impious (often devilish) doodle, the blasphemous vignette have been confined, but Malcolm Jones sweeps them into plain sight, as part of a larger record of imaginative order imposed on experience. Also, unlike analysts who use the psychological model of repression to explain medieval secular imagery, he finds impious energies expanding throughout the social sphere, nor only fuelling a counter culture identified with the plebeian, lower orders. Mikhail Bakhtin's celebrated study of Rabelais developed the idea of the carnivalesque in order to understand popular forms of expression that involve unruliness, mockery, and insubordination. The generous and wide-ranging repertory of motifs and objects offered here by Malcolm Jones effectively puts a question mark against this model of inversion, of occasional eruptions and explosions of the people's voice. His wonderful mass of lore, from the language of flowers to the vision of Cockaigne, from the encoding of sexual knowledge to the dirty jokes shifts the secular temper of the times from the periphery and spreads it more widely. His material consequently also disturbs easy acceptance of the carnivalesque as medieval authority's method of containing rebellion and maintaining social cohesion. It reveals the plurality of means of expression in medieval society, a looser political stranglehold on the tendencies and pleasures of the imaginary, and widespread and deeply embedded ways of meaning and communication held in common.

Much of the imagery has become unfamiliar to contemporary receivers, because we are ignorant of the sources, and cut off from the circulation of their ideas – partly as a result of aesthetic patrolling of medieval profanity. But recovering these meanings, discovering the things that aroused a man or a woman in fifteenth-century York, or that made them laugh, or stirred their derision, can reconnect us to the past, even if we do not experience the same things in the same way. As Malcolm Jones points out, it is very odd indeed that in this country, which is so rich in different local traditions, and so committed to historical understanding, so little research into the vernacular cultures of the past is being done (his university, Sheffield, being one of the very few to offer a course of study into folklore).

'Folklore' was the term coined in 1846 to describe the common stockpot of customs, beliefs, images, songs and sayings of a place and the people who live there.

In an age so riven by questions of belonging and unbelonging, these elements – these *commonplaces* of a culture – give texture, distinctiveness and vitality to memory, individually and socially. But to be a folklorist in these islands somehow condemns you to be seen as a kind of train-spotter, jigging in Morris bells, and quaffing Real Ale. Yet the stories, images, proverbial wisdom collected and discussed here could never be described as nostalgic or cosy, but go to the heart of many matters, including difficult, disturbing areas of mistrust, xenophobia, intolerance, misanthropy, as well as sexual conflict.

The Secret Middle Ages contains a unique and remarkable archive of illustrations, of unfamiliar artefacts and pictures, never gathered together before, and the result of years of unrivalled intellectual archaeology. It really would be impossible to credit the complexity and duration of the work involved in such a record – it requires finding, travelling, noticing, identifying, collecting and obtaining a photograph of every item. The publishers are also to be congratulated, along with the author, on these generous reproductions in colour and black and white. Every image here counts: each one gives rise to a journey, a journey through stories, fantasies, assumptions, values; throughout, Malcolm Jones is a most learned and spirited guide, a vivid storyteller and a lexicographer, an iconographic decipherer and a widely versed translator. He's a living descendant of those prodigal narrative information gatherers of the Middle Ages, those indefatigable chroniclers and encyclopaedists like Bartholomaeus Anglicus, Honorius of Autun, Gervase of Tilbury, and Petrus Comestor ('Peter the Eater', so called because he consumed such mighty helpings of knowledge), who also produced books of wonders and curiosities and of lost knowledge of flora and fauna, and made sticks and stones come alive and speak across time.

Marina Warner
June 2002

PREFACE

This book deliberately sets out to present only half the picture, or half the story, of late medieval art. But it is a half that has been missing, very much the *other* half. It was born of my frustration with existing general books on medieval art, which seemed to me only ever to present a partial picture consisting of the selfsame artworks that I had seen in all the other 'art' books, if arranged in a slightly different order – clearly the stock of medieval art was both very religious, and very limited. The reasons for this curious imbalance are bound up with the history of art history. At the risk of gross oversimplification, the history of the discipline is the history of connoisseurship, and connoisseurs were traditionally interested in 'Old Masters' and the Renaissance which, of course, 'began' in Italy, and sounded the death-knell of the benighted Middle Ages. It was the Italians who were first classified as Old Masters (and so it has largely remained) although later, and grudgingly, certain Northern European artists were admitted to the charmed circle, mainly the Flemish and the German, but by now, if, as conventionally, we end the Middle Ages in 1500, these 'parvenus' were for the most part, safely post-medieval.

While mainly concerned with paintings, connoisseurs were also interested in a mysterious, ill-defined (but always expensive) class of item known as the 'object of vertù,' examples of which they sold to each other from time to time (and still do) via the salerooms of the major auction houses. The connoisseur reserved the extreme of his contempt for objects which could only be called 'archaeological', unless, of course, they were 'classical', or – at a pinch – if not classical, at least fashioned from gold or silver. It would be all too possible (but too depressing) to reconstruct the traditional art-historical hierarchy of medieval art. At the very pinnacle of the pyramid would be paintings – preferably on panel – of the Italian Renaissance – preferably Florentine – and at the bottom, slithering around in the slime (for is it not, after all, quite literally their provenance?) the badges of lead to which I devote so much space here.

This is, of course, a caricature, but such historically-derived attitudes to medieval art, however unconscious, still underlie much of the modern perception of the art of the European Middle Ages. Not only have certain periods and regions been unthinkingly privileged in past decades, but, so too, have particular media, and particular subjects – as if, absurdly, a Florentine painting of the Virgin and Child by a named artist is somehow intrinsically more valuable to art history, than a German clay cake-mould of a peasant 'brooding' eggs by an anonymous artist. A recent magnificently produced and authoritative book on medieval jewellery omitted to discuss the bulk of the humblest lead jewellery which is, as I suggest here, both of disproportionate importance to our understanding of medieval culture as a whole, and all but unstudied, and would have benefited especially from being studied by an author so plainly familiar with the more pretentious pieces. Gems and precious metals may dazzle the eye – as, indeed, they do in that book's sumptuous colour plates – but often advertise little more than the predictable, conspicuous consumption of the elite; a lead badge or brooch, on the other hand, though it may look like some tawdry fairing, may be of more iconographic significance than a cofferful of royal jewels. In the study of the applied arts of the Middle Ages, and sad to say, in England above all, one is still too often forced to the conclusion that ancient snobberies, of the sort which have historically divorced the connoisseur's *objet d'art* from the archaeologist's *artefact*, and *high art* from *folk art*, are still alive and well and living in our national museums and galleries.

In this light, it is entirely predictable that although the personal seals of relatively humble English men and women (including some known to have been of villein status) make up some 80 per cent of all known seals surviving from medieval England, 'they have been far less studied than the other one-fifth' of aristocratic type.[1] And yet the situation is not quite so bleak as the influential Dutch cultural historian of the *Waning of the Middle Ages*, Johan Huizinga, believed, writing just after the First World War:

> . . . we only possess a very special fraction of it [sc. art]. Outside ecclesiastical art very little remains. Profane art and applied art have only been preserved in rare specimens. This is a serious want, because these are just the forms of art which would have most revealed to us the relation of artistic productions to social life.[2]

Like so many such generalisations, this is both true and untrue, true only in part, but not even entirely true at the date that it was written. 'Profane' and applied art have *not* only been preserved in rare specimens, European museums are full of such specimens, but art historians have only rarely deemed them worthy of study, and therefore the great bulk of such material remained unpublished – certainly at the period in which Huizinga was writing – though it is to be hoped that now, at long last, the situation is being somewhat redressed, not least by the publication of catalogues of the lead badges which feature so prominently in the present book and which, ironically, were later to surface in such profusion from Huizinga's native soil.

In 1988, writing 'On the State of Medieval Art History' in *The Art Bulletin*, Herbert Kessler devoted a mere five lines (in an article running to some twenty pages) to 'secular art', the subject of this book:

Even in the secular realm, medieval art was forcefully conventional. Although considerably greater freedom for innovation existed there than in religious production, secular art, too, was governed by the requirement of accuracy in recording secular history.

Admittedly, this generalisation was written by a specialist in medieval religious art, but the absurdly thin coverage of studies of medieval secular art to 1988 – only one book and two articles being footnoted – speaks volumes. It is my hope that this book will take its place alongside those written both before and since 1988, so that never again will it be possible for anyone purportedly reviewing 'The State of Medieval Art History' to have done with 'the secular realm' in five lines!

I suggest that it is not only that religious art has been privileged for historical and even less worthy reasons, but that – if I dare put it thus baldly – many writers on this period simply do not know the range of visual material that is out there. I hope there are many illustrations in the present book that are unfamiliar to most readers, and even a few that are unknown to experts in the field. Of course, there must be some that are familiar, when the argument requires them – I am not trying to present novelties for novelty's sake – but I trust the previously unknown images reproduced here will, by their very publication, become better known to students working in this area, and I look forward to seeing them reappear in others' books.

Hence my title. This material is not really 'secret', of course, though one might be forgiven for thinking that much of it was. With the exception of those items literally kept secret from us by the ground which has covered them until their recent excavation, all this material has long been available in museum, archive, and gallery collections – nor, for the most part, can we hide behind the excuse that it was uncatalogued. But there is a sense in which that side of the Middle Ages I write about here *has* been 'secret', for it has not been made public, not been published, and thus remained, as it were, always in shadow – even suspect. With this book I hope to have cast a little light on some neglected aspects of the era.

Nor is this entirely a book about art. There are many aspects of medieval, as of modern, art which are part of the visual culture of the period, though they may rarely ever have been consciously depicted. We hear, for example, of humiliating punishments to which enemies of the nation or of society were subjected, punishments whose visual impact was often an important component of their efficacy – such evidence from chroniclers and others is made use of in Chapter 5. But much art (by anyone's definition) has simply not survived the passage of the intervening centuries, and so, to recover some of this 'lost' material, this book makes full use of inventories and other descriptions of lost work.

In what follows, I have deliberately avoided using such terms as 'popular art' or 'folk art' in my attempt to redress what I see as an imbalance in the modern representation of medieval art, because such terms seem to me to be just as potentially damaging in the opposite direction, implying that such art was not also visible to the upper echelons of society. Similarly, although I concern myself principally with art which is not overtly religious in its subject matter, it would be foolish and betray a deeply erroneous understanding of medieval realities, to style such work 'secular', however oddly the depiction of genitals and buttocks, for instance, may sit with our early twenty-first-century understanding of what is appropriate to church decoration. It is perhaps needless to add, that the aesthetic appeal of any of the items I discuss, I regard as accidental, and would ideally purge myself of all such irrelevant estimations – if I could.

I think it only right to define some of the parameters of my subject. Chronologically, by 'medieval', I normally mean late medieval, say, roughly 1200–1500 *and somewhat beyond* – 'medieval' attitudes and motifs are not all swept away in one cleansing rush of Renaissance fresh air, of course, so I feel free to extend my Middle Ages well into the sixteenth century. Geographically, I focus on England, as it is the English material with which I am most familiar, but I am also anxious to show that England was by no means as much an island culturally as has sometimes been assumed, but shared in many European fashions. Occasionally I treat of continental motifs for which I know of no medieval English reflex, if they seem to me to be of sufficient intrinsic interest in illuminating medieval *mentalité*.

In terms of genre, I have tried not to privilege manuscripts and other graphic works at the expense of artefacts. On leaving university a formative year spent in what was then the British Museum's Department of Medieval and Later Antiquities, has left me with an enduring affection for objects. The lead badges, in particular, constitute a major 'new' category of material that cannot be ignored by historians of this era any longer.

I must also admit, however, that, for all the foregoing, this is a book without a thesis – unless it is that I claim there is a wealth of fascinating material that needs to be considered before we think – let alone dare to declare – we know what medieval art is. It is my hope that I have presented as much, and as representative a sample, of that 'secret' art as my knowledge, and my indulgent publishers, will allow. I feel no shame in submitting to the world a survey of 'the rest of' medieval art, without arguing any sort of case beyond its necessary publication – indeed, I believe that the case of medieval art has been argued hitherto with only a very partial and unrepresentative sampling of the evidence. I have read rather too many books which have taken a 'global' overview of the Middle Ages or medieval art, and shown us a Brocéliande, magical only in so far as it is extraordinarily more than the sum of its trees. I shall not be unhappy if this present book identifies rather too many trees than might be happily accommodated in any self-respecting wood. And if my wood should prove invisible, I flatter myself that the questing reader may at least make out some of its major denizens through the gloom of trees too densely packed – I leave it to others to discern the wood in its entirety. I am very suspicious of over-arching 'unified field' theories of anything – let alone medieval art. Where is our humility? Is it reasonable for any modern to claim sufficient knowledge of the medieval era as to be able to 'pluck out the heart of its mystery'? We are all gropers in the darkness, and if all our little illuminations should coalesce so far as to cast an uncertain light on the subject of our study, that is the best we may reasonably hope for.

Any book that purports to be about culture must also to some degree be about the language in which that culture expresses itself. I write as a student of language and of the English language in particular. One cannot study the English language without becoming familiar with the *Oxford English Dictionary (OED)*, and that deepening familiarity can breed only awe. One cannot use the *OED* over the decades, as I have done, without becoming aware of what a great monument it is, both to our language and to English nineteenth- and twentieth-century scholarship. That it was first compiled in a pre-computer age is hard for us now to believe. That it is now already available on searchable CD-ROM, and increasingly so on the Internet, makes it easily the single most important resource for the study of our language. The *OED* is an anthology of English literature too, of course, and, if I have beautified myself with its feathers freely, I hope I have remembered to acknowledge their origin – discerning readers will at least be clear that what may appear as my own encyclopedic reading is, in fact, that of the *OED*'s many readers, past and present. Without this passe-partout to our (and many other people's) language, the present book would be a poorer thing than it is.

Lastly, I hope this is a book with 'attitude' – doubtless one which, with the passing of time, I shall wish I had tempered – but a book in which, though I pay lip-service to a proper stylistic objectivity, I have managed to forget my scholarly pretensions sufficiently often to seem like a person interested in what he is writing about. While I trust I have not abandoned *gravitas* completely, I believe it should be possible to write interestingly and seriously, and still sound like a human being trying to get to grips, however imperfectly, with the puzzles and contradictions of an era that is both so like and so unlike our own.

ACKNOWLEDGEMENTS

The proper acknowledgement of my debt to others' work would make a chapter in itself. We moderns are all pygmies standing on the shoulders of giants, and I take this opportunity to name a few of the giants in my own pygmyhood.

This is a book which has had an unnaturally long gestation. It should have been written ten years ago – though would, of course, have been rather different if it had. The industry of friends and colleagues has frequently put me to shame over the past decade, and frequently, in response to their polite enquiries, led to embarrassing mumblings about working on a book. I hope that the present volume will to some extent absolve me in their eyes for this shocking indolence.

Seminal in the development of my own understanding of the areas discussed in this book, was Lilian Randall's *Images in the Margins of Gothic Manuscripts* – an eye-opener, if ever there was one – and it is no exaggeration to say that my discovery of that book's riches some thirty years ago, led directly to the present book, and to establishing my interests in iconographic investigation *per se*. More recently, another American scholar, Ruth Mellinkoff, has published a superb and handsome volume, *Outcasts: Signs of Otherness in Northern European Art of the Late Middle Ages* (Berkeley, 1993), which I wish I had written, and I thank her for her friendship and generous sharing of her knowledge.

The late Michael Camille's books, which have anticipated some of the areas addressed here, have been a constant inspiration, and not least for their written style – a breath of fresh air! – and I have been grateful for his continued encouragement of my own work. *The Medieval Art of Love* (London, 1998) is typical of his ability to surprise us with new and significant images of artefacts especially, and it is an example I have tried to adopt here. It is a matter of deep regret his tragically early death means I can no longer present him with a copy of this book, but I am hopeful that it would have earned his approval.

It will be clear from what follows that two media in particular have engaged my attention, the misericord and the lead badge. Any book I might once have written on misericords has now been rendered superfluous by the appearance of Christa Grössinger's excellent and superbly illustrated survey, *The World Turned Upside Down. English Misericords* (London, 1997), and I am grateful both to her and to my fellow 'misericordians' who have gathered around the indefatigable Elaine Block and her journal *The Profane Arts*, and especially to Kenneth Varty, doyen of *renardiens* – and one of the two people professionally obliged to read my doctoral thesis. On first moving to my present home in Derbyshire, it was to Charles Tracy's expertise I turned for advice on the identification and date of a piece of carved woodwork that I had noticed, and his willing assistance soon led to a joint article and an enduring friendship, and I thank him for his continued faith in me.

In this country, lead badges have been the province of one man, Brian Spencer, and his generous friendship and scholarship down the years have taught me so much, and revealed so many embarrassing gaps in my own knowledge. In the Netherlands, H.J.E. Van Beuningen has been the pre-eminent collector and promoter of the importance of these artefacts and it is thanks to his kindness and enthusiasm that I have had the privilege of working with the badges in his collection and access to the many photographs of them reproduced here.

It is no accident that during the unconscionably delayed appearance of this book I have become acquainted (and sometimes friends, indeed) more with museum curators than with librarians. John Cherry, who has just retired as Keeper of what was the British Museum's Department of Medieval and Later Antiquities (now 'rebranded' as Medieval and Modern Europe), has been unfailingly helpful and friendly to my often naive enquiries. I have frequently envied and sought to emulate his modestly priced, yet profusely illustrated, *Medieval Decorative Art* (London, 1991).

Latterly, my footsteps have bent towards the Museum's Department of Prints and Drawings, where Sheila O'Connell has patiently explained the nuances of print-production to me and facilitated access to that Department's rich holdings. It is rare that an entirely original work appears, but such indeed was *The Popular Print in England 1550–1850*, and it was my privilege to have become acquainted with her during the preparation of that ground-breaking volume. It is a sorry indictment of previous English scholarship in this area, but perhaps not so surprising given the shameful tradition of the denigration of the vernacular in English art history, that we had to wait until the final year of the twentieth century for such a necessary survey.

In case I may appear churlishly dismissive of librarians, I want to single out here the Derbyshire County Library Service which, before I had regular access to a university library, supplied me with untold volumes from all over the world – though the Director of Library Services was once moved to tell this particular rate-payer precisely how many books and articles he had on order. The friendly staff of my local public library in Matlock were always indulgent to my requests and I am happy to be able to thank them here in print.

When I first came across J.B. Smith's article, 'Whim-whams for a goose's bridle' in the journal *Lore and Language*, I knew at last that I was not alone, and was confirmed in my belief that it was indeed possible to pursue the sort of thing I was interested in at a serious level, and I have spent the time between trying, however inadequately, to approach the level of his scholarship.

On first looking into Lutz Röhrich's *Lexikon der sprichwörtlichen Redensarten*, the scales dropped from my eyes, and I understood in a flash the significance of the proverbial in medieval art, and a growing acquaintance with that magisterial work led me to a proper appreciation of the proverb – an appreciation that quite inevitably introduced me to my friend, Wolfgang Mieder, whose own industry is as proverbial as his generosity.

In what often seems the all-too-insular world of English scholarship, I am especially happy to have this opportunity to acknowledge a general debt to Dutch and German cultural historians, who have had the breadth of vision that has been granted to few English scholars (with the honourable exception of Peter Burke). I refer, in particular, to Herman Pleij, and the encyclopedic Paul Vandenbroeck and Christoph Gerhardt, to name only the most important to my own researches. I wish I had more room to expatiate on their individual contributions to the history of European culture, but their monuments are their works and they do not need my poor praise.

Finally, as one who aspires to be worthy of the title of folklorist and as perhaps the only individual in England employed full time to pursue that calling, I cannot close these Acknowledgements without allowing myself some observations on the state of folklore in England, for my native country is surely unique among the nations of Europe, of the world indeed, in officially despising its folklore. With all too few exceptions, certainly in recent decades, its intelligentsia have disdained to acknowledge this discipline at all, in fact have sought to belittle and ridicule it. Notwithstanding this establishment onslaught, a number of independent-minded spirits have found succour in the arms of the Folklore Society, and my membership of that brave organisation has introduced me to many experts in subjects for which bibliographies do not yet exist, and whose constant support and encouragement bolstered my determination to bring the present project to fruition.

When every other nation in the world has a centrally funded institute of its national folklore, I marvel that the country of my birth should be so scornful of its indigenous, immemorial culture that it has none. But here – inevitably – I come to acknowledge my debt to the University of Sheffield, and more particularly to my colleague and friend, John Widdowson, founder of the university's National Centre for English Cultural Tradition, a title which, however – sadly, if predictably – does not imply national funding (I avoid using the weasel-word 'heritage' which has now been hijacked as the current establishment euphemism for theme-park Britain).

It behoves me too to commend the enlightened policies of both Sheffield University, which granted me a semester's Study Leave in order to finish this long unfinished book, and of the Arts and Humanities Research Board, which was prepared to double it. I am also most grateful to the British Academy for awarding me a Small Research Grant, which has subsidised the publication of the greater part of the images reproduced here.

Matlock, April 2002.

CONVENTIONS AND ABBREVIATIONS

I adopt the archaeologist's useful – though it seems far from universally recognised – convention that a medial 'x' between two dates indicates that the item was manufactured (or event occurred) at some unknown date between those termini – where a similarly positioned hyphen indicates duration of composition or occurrence. Frequently cited reference works, some of which appear in the body of the text, are abbreviated thus:

DMLBS   ed. R.E. Latham *et al.*, *Dictionary of Medieval Latin from British Sources* (Oxford, 1975 –).

EPNS   English Place Name Society.

Geisberg   M. Geisberg, *Der deutsche Einblatt-Holzschnitt in der ersten Hälfte des 16. Jahrhunderts* (Munich, 1923–30; rev. W.L. Strauss, New York, 1974).

HP1   ed. H.J.E. Van Beuningen and A.M. Koldeweij, *Heilig en Profaan. 1000 Laat-middeleeuwse insignes uit de collectie H.J.E. Van Beuningen* (Cothen, 1993).

HP2   ed. H.J.E. Van Beuningen, A.M. Koldeweij and D. Kicken, *Heilig en Profaan 2. 1200 Laat-middeleeuwse insignes uit openbare en particuliere collecties* (Cothen, 2001).

IMEV   ed. C. Brown and R.H. Robins, *The Index of Middle English Verse* (New York, 1943).

LSR   ed. L. Röhrich, *Das große Lexikon der sprichwörtlichen Redensarten* (Freiburg, 1991).

MED   ed. H. Kurath *et al.*, *Middle English Dictionary* (Ann-Arbor, 1952–2002).

Motif-Index   S. Thompson, *Motif Index of Folk Literature* (Bloomington, 1966).

MOL   B. Spencer, *Pilgrim Souvenirs and Secular Badges* (London, 1998).

ODEP   F.P. Wilson (ed.), *The Oxford Dictionary of English Proverbs* (3rd ed., Oxford, 1970).

OED   *The Oxford English Dictionary*, second ed. CD (Oxford, 1994).

PMLA   Proceedings of the Modern Languages Association (of America).

Randall   L. Randall, *Images in the Margins of Medieval Manuscripts* (Berkeley, 1966).

Schreiber   W.L. Schreiber, *Handbuch des Holz- und Metallschnittes des xv Jahrhunderts* (Leipzig, 1926–30).

TPMA   ed. Kuratorium Singer der Schweizerischen Akademie der Geistes- und Sozialwissenschaften, *Thesaurus Proverbiorum Medii Aevi. Lexikon der Sprichwörter des romanisch-germanischen Mittelalters* (Berlin and New York, 1995–).

Whiting   B.J. and H.W. Whiting, *Proverbs, Sentences and Proverbial Sayings from English Writings, Mainly before 1500* (Cambridge, Mass., 1958).

ONE

LOVE, DEATH AND BISCUITS

One day in 1521 the Mayor of Frankfurt, Claus Stalburg, known as 'The Rich', sat down at a table in his elegant town house and drew up an inventory of all the biscuit-moulds he owned. There is something decidedly odd to our modern sensibilities at the thought of a wealthy businessman concerning himself with such domestic trivia, but the forty stone moulds Stalburg possessed were evidently something of an enthusiasm with him – had he not, indeed, commissioned them, and from one of the city's most accomplished engravers, the assay-master Hartmann Kistener? And, ironically, perhaps, the six biscuit-moulds that survive are all that has come down to us of Kistener's work.

> These are my, Claus Stalburg's, engraved biscuit-moulds, that I myself caused to be engraved by Hartmann Kistener, assay-master, dwelling at the Kante . . .

Stalburg then went on to describe the forty-eight scenes depicted on his moulds, and their great variety serves almost as an anthology of late medieval iconography, both sacred and profane, and includes many of the topics to be treated more fully later. Here is the list, somewhat edited, with the date of manufacture, where recorded.

1. 1512   A large round [St] Christopher
    1518   and on the other side, the story of Romulus and Remus
2. 1515   Joust between Bechtold vom Rin and Seiffrid Folcker
3. 1519   The story of Thisbe, how they both stabbed themselves in love
    1519   and on the other side, the chaste Lucretia's pitiful death
4. 1510   How the king's son's horse trampled the widow's son dead, on whom the king pronounced the judgment of the law
5. 1512   How Christ was baptised in the Jordan by John the Baptist
6.   The goddess Venus with the little child and the old man

7.   The story of David, how he took pleasure in Bathsheba washing her feet
8.   1517   Nobody with his household utensils and a rhyme above
               on the other side, the Peasants' Dance
9.   1514   Women and fools together having fun with one another
10.   A peasant and his wife who thresh young chickens out of eggs
11.   A young fellow having fun with a girl sitting on a bed *stenlings*
12.   Our Lady with her child on her arm under a tabernacle
13.   Our Lady with Joseph sitting in contemplation surrounded by angels
14.   A young man with a girl in his arms seen by the town crier
15.   A girl with an old bald man whom hornets sting and a fool who drives them away from him
16.   1517   Riding the Ass, and everyone wants to be next
17.   St Sebastian shot by the heathens with bows
18.   1511   Three naked women fishing with rods and bringing up eel pots
19.   1511   A girl sitting alone, and a young fellow opens the door, meaning to come to her
20.   1512   A girl sitting in a rose-garden making a garland
21.   1510   Our Lady in childbed and Joseph with the shepherds and the ass
22.   1519   St Margaret having vanquished the devil with him under her feet
23.   A peasant and a girl having a sack full of Fidelity for sale
24.   1513   Two naked goddesses, one standing in fire, the other in water
25.   1510   Adam and Eve naked with the snake in the tree in the middle
26.   1510   Samson the strong sleeping while the woman cuts off his hair
27.   Four naked children above a gushing fountain
28.   A young fellow and a girl by a gushing fountain with a little rhyme
29.   1517   A naked Jesus standing in the sun
30.   1511   A girl catching birds with a *Klobe* [cleft stick for trapping birds' feet]
31.   A fool in a basket who is dragged along by an old woman
32.   An old hermit whom a girl invites to drink/offers a drink

               [Old Franconian]
33.   Christ's Passion
34.   Morris Dance
35.   Our Lady's Coronation
36.   St Anne with her child
37.   Offering of the Three Kings
               on the other side, Our Lady's greeting [the Annunciation]
38.   St Christopher walking in the water
               on the other side, the Christ child
39.   St Mary Magdalene's Ascension
               on the other side, St John the Rough [the Baptist in camel-skin]
40.   a *beckert* [? hermit] praying,
               on the other side, the Knight St George

The Vagaries of Survival

From Stalburg's collection of thirty-two moulds engraved by Kistener, only four or 12.5 per cent have survived (nos 4, 26, 27, and 32),[1] but representing only 11 per cent of the subjects listed above. If we depend for our knowledge of late medieval art only on what has physically survived we cannot but have a totally false impression of what there once was. A survival rate of 12.5 per cent for these evidently treasured items belonging to one of the most important men in one of Germany's most important cities should give us pause when we are tempted to draw conclusions about medieval art from the body of works which have come down to us; and in an attempt to counteract the accidents of survival, I intend to draw on inventories and wills throughout this book.

But let us now take a closer look at the contents of this miniature gallery. Whatever view one takes of David spying on Bathsheba bathing and of Delilah cutting Samson's hair,[2] three-quarters of the subjects Stalburg commissioned from Kistener may fairly be termed non-religious. If we now try to state broadly to what areas these images belong, it soon becomes apparent that roughly half the scenes belong to what may broadly be termed the erotic (though not the pornographic). Just as the ostensibly biblical subject of Bathsheba bathing (no. 7) allows the male viewer the same voyeuristic pleasure in spying on the naked female body that King David was unable to resist, so too, scenes of the virtuous heroines of antiquity stabbing themselves were peculiarly popular, offering up as they did, vulnerable female bosoms to the pointed male gaze, including Lucretia's suicide and Thisbe's (in reaction to that of her lover, Pyramus – both on no. 3). Contemporary engravings whether in wood or metal frequently show these women naked: Hans Baldung Grien's *Lucretia* (*c.* 1522) shown only from the waist upwards, stabs herself between the breasts, while Hans Sebald Beham's full-length frontal nude is on the very point of piercing her nipple with a stiletto,[3] and in Wechtlin's woodcut of about 1515, both Pyramus and Thisbe are displayed naked (though it is not clear why) – one cannot help suspecting that there is some sado-erotic *frisson* here, even on the miniature scale of a biscuit-mould. All the female nudes mentioned so far are, as it were, sanctioned by history, though they may look like contemporary early sixteenth-century women, their historicity protects the contemporary owner of such images from the suspicion of eroticism.

Figure 1.1

There are four other pairs of lovers in this collection: again there is a voyeuristic feel to no. 14, for the young man and the girl in his arms are observed by the town crier. What a pity Stalburg did not see fit to transcribe the little rhyme accompanying the youth and his girl beside the babbling fountain (no. 28), but although his example of the motif has not come down to us, no fewer than four others have survived, and the rhyme on the example in Worms (Figure 1.1) is reasonably legible:

| Youth: | *Ach wae frawe war wollent yr* | [Oh, alas lady, where are you going?] |
| Girl: | *in daz bat ist min begir.* | [Into the 'bath' is my longing.] |

And true to her word, the young woman is naked but for the customary strategic veil; but the word used for 'longing' here (*begir*) is also used for sexual longing or lust (see, especially, no. 32, the hermit and the girl, discussed below) and we must surely suspect that innuendo here.

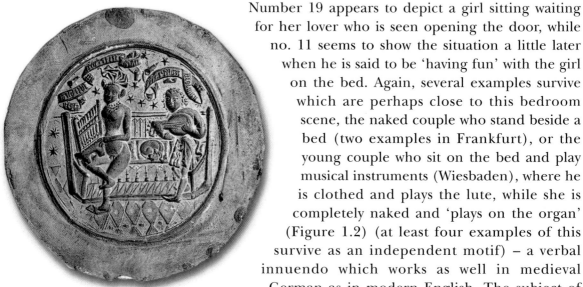

Figure 1.2

Number 19 appears to depict a girl sitting waiting for her lover who is seen opening the door, while no. 11 seems to show the situation a little later when he is said to be 'having fun' with the girl on the bed. Again, several examples survive which are perhaps close to this bedroom scene, the naked couple who stand beside a bed (two examples in Frankfurt), or the young couple who sit on the bed and play musical instruments (Wiesbaden), where he is clothed and plays the lute, while she is completely naked and 'plays on the organ' (Figure 1.2) (at least four examples of this survive as an independent motif) – a verbal innuendo which works as well in medieval German as in modern English. The subject of no. 9 is said to be women and fools (jesters) who are 'having fun' together – the same verb is used as in no. 11, and it seems likely that there is the same suggestion of flirtatious play. There are two surviving examples of a clay mould in which one or two naked women in a bath try to drag a fool in with them; the woman on the mould in Seligenstadt says 'come here to me!', but the fool as he struggles to escape replies, 'there's my exit!'. There is a clear relationship between these moulds and an engraving of *c.* 1470 by the Master of the Banderoles which shows a fool resisting the temptations of three bathing women who try to drag him in with them.[4] It is clear from the banderole inscriptions – albeit in Latin – that this is a sexual invitation; the fool whose limp condition is exposed by the women who pull at his tunic protests:

'Though I'd like to stay with you lady my penis doesn't want to rise just now so I don't want to continue.'

But the women will not be so easily denied:

'Come into the bath with us good Johan then the little thing will stand for us and not . . .'

Contrast the voyeuristic fool (perhaps shown in a state of sexual arousal) who draws aside the curtain to spy on an evidently elderly man enjoying a bath with a young woman (see chapter ornament) from a fifteenth-century lead lid of probably foreign origin (several Dutch examples being known) found on the Thames foreshore. Is this mere titillation, or is this, rather, an example of what in Chapter 6 I term the 'commentary' fool, who points out for us the folly of an old man chasing young women?

One of the two surviving moulds by Kistener not owned by Stalburg, dated 1530, shows a sort of anti-Fountain of Youth in which four naked women bathe and similarly attempt to entice four men in with them, but the men flee, claiming that the hot waters had previously given them the stone. The point we should note, however, is that such scenes are predicated on the lasciviousness attributed to women in the late Middle Ages (see Chapter 11).

Two of Stalburg's moulds concern relationships between old men and young women and in no. 32 there is the added *frisson* that the old man is a religious. As this is one of Stalburg's four surviving moulds (dated 1523),[5] we are able to quote the dialogue between the aged forest-dwelling hermit (*Waldbruder*) and the girl (who holds up a cup) as they stand either side of a seemingly ornamental fountain:

> Hermit: 'I have a desire for you'
> Girl: 'Brother, take this drink for it.'

While the old hermit's words seem unequivocal, there are two possible interpretations of the girl's words, depending on what view we take of her reaction: either she is almost literally pouring cold water on his intentions, saying 'Take this glass of spring water to cool your ardour', or – if the spring has something of the Fountain of Youth[6] about it – she means, 'Take this glass of spring water, it will endow you with a young man's capabilities!' The content of the banderoles on a similar scene in Mainz, however, shows that young woman to be disappointed in love: 'Infidelity has done me such hurt that I want to die . . .', and the hermit offers proper spiritual consolation, 'Maiden, pure fidelity is only found in God.' The other related composition (no. 15) is described as 'A girl with an old bald man whom hornets sting and a fool who drives them away from him.' This is undoubtedly another example of an 'unequal couple' (see Chapter 11) and the artist's criticism of their relationship is signalled both by the presence of the swarm of hornets – as discussed in Chapter 5 – and by the 'commentary' fool (see Chapter 6).

The final motif, which may be described as 'erotic' in a less overtly sexual sense, belongs rather to the milieu of courtly love (see Chapter 10), for – despite what we know of rose symbolism (see Chapter 12) – it depicts an innocent-sounding girl sitting in a rose-garden making a garland (of roses, presumably).

The remaining secular images do not fall into any obvious category. Number 4, one of the few moulds to have come down to us, figures the *exemplum* of the death of the widow's son, 'How the king's son's horse trampled the widow's son dead, on whom the king pronounced the judgment of the law' – a popular motif in the decoration of late medieval German law-courts and other civic buildings, as an example of disinterested justice.[7] The reference is to a late classical story told of the Emperor Trajan whose son rode down a widow's son, killing him, and when the widow appealed to the Emperor for justice, he gave his judgment that he renounced his own son and that he should henceforth become the widow's son. Stalburg's original mould survives in a private collection so that we know that the banderoles (it is the Emperor's son who speaks) read:

> I wanted to give my steed his head
> and thus the widow's son was ridden down.

Another classical subject is the 'Romulus and Remus' (no. 1), presumably showing the twins being suckled by the wolf, while the joust of 'Bechtold vom Rin' and 'Seiffrid Folcker' (no. 2) would appear to be a commemoration of a recent historical event. The 'Peasants' Dance' (no. 8) was a subject popular at this period and much ink has been spilled in recent years debating whether such images are critical of such festivities and the peasants who indulge in them or, on the other hand, approving, and symptomatic of an urban nostalgia for the simple life of the rustic. The morris dance (no. 34) is an early example of the motif, while no. 23 sounds allegorical: 'a peasant and a girl having a sack full of Fidelity [*Treue*] for sale' – (see the 'hunt' for Fidelity, pp. 9–10).

Of the remaining subjects, three or four may be considered broadly humorous. According to Stalburg's description, no. 31 featured 'a fool in a basket who is dragged along by an old woman' – in the context of the bathing women's apparent desire for fools (no. 9), this might not seem unreasonable, and yet I believe this is a slip of the mayoral pen, and that he meant to write 'an old woman in a basket who is dragged along by a fool', for this is the subject of a popular engraving by the Master bxg (active *c.* 1470–*c.* 1490), copied by Israhel van Meckenem (died ante-1503).[8]

Figure 1.3

The subject of no. 10, 'a peasant and his wife who thresh young chickens out of eggs',[9] is a well-known proverbial folly, as carved on the late fifteenth-century misericord at Emmerich reproduced here (Figure 1.3) – for the depiction of other such follies see Chapter 7. The 'four naked children' disporting themselves 'above' a gushing fountain (no. 27) survives (dated 1517) in the Württembergischen Landesmuseum in Stuttgart, and is a Germanic attempt at rendering the essentially alien Italianate Renaissance concept of *putti*, newly fashionable in Germany.

The final Kistener mould to be discussed (no. 30) featured a girl catching birds with a *Kloben* (a cleft stick for trapping the birds' legs when they alighted on the stick which would have been held out by the fowler from within a hide, the birds being attracted by the presence of some decoy, usually an owl). The precise mechanics, however, are not the point here, for it is clear that, in the present instance, we are concerned with entrapment of a sexual kind. The fact that the fowler is female should instantly alert us to the fact that this can hardly be a real-life scene – fowling was not a female pastime. Woodcuts by Niklas Stoer (*Die Ewlen Bays, c.* 1532 [G1356]) and Urs Graf (in Murner's *Geuchmatt,* 1519) show a young man caught within the *Kloben* held by a young woman or an old woman who has used the young woman as a decoy.[10]

It is likely that no. 18, the 'Three naked women fishing with rods and bringing up eel-pots' [*Reusen*] – clearly no ordinary fishing expedition – also belongs in this milieu. The women are themselves the bait for the (unmentioned) men who are the fish, and there are several sixteenth-century examples of naked women sitting within lobster-pots while men dressed as fools clamour to enter.[11] Early in the century the fashion for *décolletage* was the complaint of the anonymous author of the *Klag wyplicher scham,* the title-page of which is illustrated by a woodcut of a chastely dressed matron evidently reproving a younger woman in a very low-cut bodice who has an owl on her wrist – clearly another reference to woman as fowler of men. As late as 1683, however, the eponymous London Bully stole a picture of 'A lady with her breasts half-naked and petticoats up as high as her knees, wielding a net for the trawling of men' – a rare reference to what was evidently a late seventeenth-century English popular print in much the same vein (woman as fisher of men) as Stalburg's much earlier biscuit-mould.

Several of these designs will have depended on earlier engravings in metal or wood, and the proverbial no. 16, 'Riding the Ass', will certainly have borne a close relationship to a contemporary German woodcut (Figure 1.4), which seems also to

Figure 1.4

have been the model for 'All doe ride the asse', a sheet engraved by Renold Elstrack and issued in London in 1607.[12]

If we compare Stalburg's collection of moulds with the remainder of the extant corpus of these fascinating objects, we find that erotic motifs, both courtly and more overtly sexual, again predominate. The Classical Judgment of Paris again provides the opportunity for watching a nude beauty contest in miniature. But there are also couples in a garden, in the open air, by a well, and playing a board game; one such couple out walking – he, finely dressed, she, naked except for a veil – are 'surprised by Death' in his familiar skeletal form. The following conversation takes place:

> He: Death, take it easy!
>   we want to live for many a day yet
> She: I am in great shape
>   and will live longer for sure
> Death: Long life is not given
>   just because you want it.

If Death manages to remain civil in this chilling exchange, in his confrontation with a lone naked woman on another mould, his manner is far from courtly. The girl repeats the same line:

> I am young and in great shape
> and will live longer for sure.

To which Death responds with a brutal, if traditional, insult:

> Ah! You poor sack of earth!
> What I am you must become!

Another version of the same encounter has the girl saying:

> Your grisly shape
> makes me old and grey

as if the mere sight of Death turns her into an aged woman, but Death responds in his traditional manner:

> Whether you look poor or rich
> You will become like me.

Death does not only delight in frightening young semi-naked women, however; the scholar need not think he will escape. On another mould a man sits at a table immersed in his books while behind him, like some grisly pantomime, a skeletal death creeps up with his scythe; the banderole reads, in equally traditional manner:

> Think on your end
> Death comes behind.

But let us leave these *memento mori* motifs and return to the lovers. On a relatively early mould a young man, hands raised and together in the familiar gesture of prayer, stands before his lady and makes a declaration of his love in typically extravagant fashion:

> Lady of otherworldly radiance
> my heart shall be yours alone.

To which she responds graciously and simply:

> Then I give you this garland
> whose roots lie in my heart.

We have seen that one of Stalburg's moulds dated 1512 depicted the classic courtly love scene of a maiden sitting in a garden making just such a garland, while another mould shows two rival young men fighting over one, in front of a castle from which their lady looks down.

The pains of love from the male point of view are vividly symbolised on another mould in which the woman holds a heart in a pair of tongs on an anvil and beats it with a hammer (also found on a carved wooden *Minnekästchen*). He complains:

> Oh! The terrible pains
> you give me in my heart!

But she is pitiless:

> To the unfaithful heart
> one gives such pain.

There is even the possibility that such depictions may be more than a charming convention, that they may have some relation with late medieval rituals of sympathetic love magic, and in the context of heart symbolism, the extraordinary late fifteenth-century panel painting in Leipzig is discussed in Chapter 10.

Another early mould depicts a young woman holding two dogs on a lead who meets a young man; her banderole opens 'I am hunting with my hounds . . .' but unfortunately the rest of her speech and his reply are fragmentary, so that we cannot be sure of the import of this meeting, but another engraving by Van Meckenem depicts a young woman who also has two hounds on a leash and whose banderole reads:

> I travel with bird and hounds
> that I might find true fidelity.

A hermit replies:

> Maiden tender and pure
> they are found in God alone.

Figure 1.5

This is the same response which we have heard him give to the young woman whom 'Infidelity' had done 'such hurt' and who sought consolation from him on the mould in Mainz mentioned above (p. 5) – indeed, knowledge of the Van Meckenem print's engraved banderole allows us to reconstruct the damaged Mainz text. A variant composition is found on a late fifteenth-century tapestry of Strasbourg manufacture. Here the young woman with the hounds on a leash is in conversation with another, older, woman. The young woman's banderole reads:

> I have searched with my hounds
> I can find no fidelity in the world.

To which the older woman responds sententiously:

> temporal love has no permanence
> think on the end at the beginning.

Men's infidelity is also the complaint of another woman on a biscuit-mould whom we overhear lamenting in a garden:

> The longer I am alone the better,
> when fidelity and belief are so diminished.

Her conclusions are in stark contrast to the young woman who is seen literally sieving fools on a late mould (dated 1541), who proclaims:

> fools who are single
> must pass through the sieve.

Why this should be so is not clear. Is it to sieve them of the undesirable foolish vices that prevent them from being wanted as husbands by any right-minded woman?[13] The fool on another mould who links arms with the seated woman spinning (and who is thus shown as properly, indeed virtuously, occupied) is mysterious and, not being provided with banderoles, will probably remain so. A different kind of fool – ultimately an impotent, complaisant husband who allows himself to be dominated by his wife, is the man shown sitting on (that is, brooding) a basket of eggs, while his wife holds one up to the light to see if it is ready to hatch (see Chapter 11). The woman who leads a lion on a leash, evidently another strong woman, is perhaps allegorical, possibly a Virtue such as Fortitudo.

A unique surviving fable representation is that of the fox and stork (one of the most popular fables in all media); both the original invitation and the 'return match' are depicted, and the banderole inscription applies equally to both: 'Eat dear neighbour, I invite you. . .'. The rascally fox is also the subject of another mould which survives in two versions, while the motif itself was also hugely popular and is represented in every conceivable medium, such as the stained-glass panel reproduced here (Figure 1.5). On the mould the fox stands in a pulpit and preaches to a congregation of four (proverbially foolish) geese, who have presumably not noticed that he already has two dead geese safely stored in his cowl! The banderole is not legible in its entirety but ends with the ominous word, *krag* (craw).

We must not forget that, to some extent at least, these moulds really were intended for the production of biscuits and other sweetmeats (such as marzipan), and the giving of such pictorial biscuits as seasonal gifts explains the young man who has doffed his hat to wish a lady (?), now broken off, 'Happy New Year!', on an early but, sadly, fragmentary fifteenth-century mould.

The Kunstgewerbemuseum in Berlin possesses a circular mould of a pedlar displaying his tray of wares to a young customer; despite the fact that he is shown playing a pipe, he still manages to announce, 'I am a pedlar fine', while the boy, clearly impressed by this dexterity, says, 'Give me the pipe, man!' Another salesman is the subject of what must surely be the most coarse of all the moulds described: an elderly bearded man has set down his back-basket and has lifted the lid sufficiently to show the two elegantly clad women, their page, and one old lady, that he is selling dildoes (Figure 1.6) – perhaps for once we should

Figure 1.6

be grateful that the banderoles are blank! And yet even this image is not without parallels. A Flemish woodcut sheet of sixteen miscellaneous images (?c. 1520), in addition to a paired cock and hen with suggestive banderoles, includes a pedlar dressed as a fool with the usual eared hood and *marotte* (fool's bauble), bearing a tray of dildoes and the inscription:

> I have here wares that serve me (well)
> everybody loves them.

And much earlier, in a frankly pornographic twelfth-century Latin comedy, the *Alda*, the naive heroine having been deflowered by a man who has pretended to be a woman, is told that s/he acquired the instrument of defloration from a pedlar (*institor*), who had arrived in the village market-place with a large display of such 'tails' (*caudas*), priced according to size, and that a crowd of girls had gathered round, and s/he had been the first to buy one, but only a small one, as s/he had not had much money.[14]

I hope enough evidence has been brought forward here to convince readers both of the value of inventories, and of this particular humble domestic artefactual medium, but there are a number of other genres of applied art that have been just as completely neglected by traditional historians of medieval art as these moulds have been – the most obvious and most significant example, finally being appreciated at long last for the enormous light it can shed on the truly popular iconography of the era, is the lead badge, currently emerging in considerable quantities from riverine deposits in the Netherlands, Paris and London. But misericords – though they have enjoyed a somewhat higher profile, especially in recent decades – are still *terra incognita* to the traditional historian of medieval art; and yet they have so very much iconographic information to convey. The evidence afforded by other so-called minor media – often dismissed in the past as the concern of that lowly creature, the antiquary – personal seals and floor tiles, for example – will also be fully exploited in what follows.

For too long we have been presented with an over-religious picture of medieval life and art wholly dominated by the Church. Overtly religious imagery was ubiquitous, of course, but not to the exclusion of everything else. The era has been misrepresented by a concentration on Christian iconography at the expense of non-religious or neutral imagery. As Claus Stalburg's inventory demonstrates, by the early sixteenth century – even in the cradle of the Reformation – there was plenty of interest in the representation of subjects not deriving from the Bible or Christian teaching, and they are what this book is about.

TWO

MAGICAL METAL, SILLY SAINTS AND RISIBLE RELICS: THE ART AND ARTEFACTS OF POPULAR RELIGION

For the reasons given in the Preface, this book focuses almost exclusively on the non-religious art of the Middle Ages, but there are a number of motifs which, while not necessarily being part of mainstream Christianity or having some biblical prompt, might yet be said to belong to the area of popular religion, and it is some of these which are the subject of the present chapter.

Official religion seems always to have been somewhat equivocal regarding the orthodoxy of charms and we begin with a consideration of some of these amulets of more or less overtly Christian iconography. The cult of the saints had an enormous influence on the lives of late medieval Christians, and the little lead badges they wore as souvenirs of pilgrimages made to saints' shrines seem to have soon taken on a similarly protective function, even though some of these so-called saints were as suspect as their popularly celebrated miracles. Also considered here is the iconography of such often bizarre and, on the eve of the Reformation, frequently burlesqued saints and their relics, as are some of the more colourful episodes in their Lives, especially those which relate to motifs familiar in international folktale.

Coral and Sharks' Teeth: Charms and Talismans

For the theologically unsophisticated (the great bulk of the population), official Christianity was perhaps not the all-sufficient doctrine it was understood to be by authority, but one that might be usefully supplemented by sundry magical practices given a Christian colouring. When even the Christ Child dandled on the Virgin's knee is shown in Italian painting of the fourteenth and fifteenth centuries wearing a little red coral branch amulet round his neck, how could such a thing not be Christian?[1] The inventory of the stock of a Dijon goldsmith taken in 1453 included three such little branches of coral mounted in silver, doubtless intended as baptismal gifts for children.[2] In a contemporary painting by Petrus Christus of St Eligius anachronistically plying his trade as a mid-fifteenth-century Flemish goldsmith, a branch of red coral is plainly visible as part of his stock on display, as well as fossilised sharks' teeth (identified by modern scholarship as belonging to a species found in the black crag of Boom near Antwerp)![3] These triangular fossil teeth were known in the vernacular as 'serpent's' or 'adder's tongues': the French King Jean le Bon had such a 'serpent's tongue' mounted in silver according to the inventory of his goods taken at his death in London in 1364, and in 1488 James III of Scotland owned four such 'serpent tonguis', and his wife, Margaret of Denmark, 'a serpent toung & one unicorne horne set in gold', while the future Henry VIII of England had 'a unicornes bone and a serpente tonge hang[ing] be a cheyne', according to an inventory of his possessions made in 1504 when Prince Henry was thirteen.[4] Just such a pendent *Natternzunge* on which a heart has been superimposed may be seen worn on a chain by a prostitute in an early sixteenth-century German woodcut.[5]

GOOD LUCK CARDS AND PICTURES

We perhaps think of greetings cards as a modern phenomenon and yet some of the earliest known single-sheet woodcuts of the fifteenth century might legitimately be considered to fall into this category. As still today, in the Middle Ages the New Year

Figure 2.1

Figure 2.2

was the time to pass on one's good wishes to friends and relations for the year ahead. Some twenty-five such German sheets survive from the latter part of the fifteenth century;[6] one type depicts the naked Christ Child sitting in the grass on a cushion caressing a parrot. From the double-strand of beads around his neck hang two pendent amulets, one of which is unmistakably a coral-branch. The banderole reads '(have a) very good year' and some versions continue 'and long life' (Figure 2.1).

There can be no doubt that the pasting up in dwelling-houses of individual saints' pictures was tantamount to asking for their protection, either in general or for the specific disease or other misfortune which was their speciality. The plague, which periodically devastated large parts of Europe, was an ever-present nightmare and woodcut sheets of Saint Sebastian or St Roch, or even St Valentine, are really a form of pictorial prayer, asking the saint in question to intercede with God on behalf of fragile humanity.

St Gertrude, on the other hand, was invoked against a very specific type of plague – mice and rats. One of the charming mid-fifteenth-century sheets of the saint spinning while mice play with her spindle, climb up her distaff and attempt to bite through her thread (Figure 2.2),[7] includes a two-line banderole to which she points and which reads:

> Whoever honours her with a Paternoster and an Ave Maria
> they will be safe from mice. St Gertrude.[8]

Against the dangers of childbirth women prayed to St Margaret for assistance. According to the legendary life of this virgin saint, when she was devoured by a dragon she burst unharmed from its belly – and it is clearly to this mimetic miracle, frequently depicted in art, that she owes her popularity. In 1977 the Musée des Arts et Traditions Populaires in Paris acquired a leaf of mid-fourteenth-century parchment which folds, map-like, into twenty-five small squares; they are covered on one side with the text of a verse legend of St Margaret. On the other side are written passages from the Gospels (including the words reported by Luke of the woman who said to Jesus, 'Blessed is the womb that bore you'), followed by the names of the Magi, Caspar, Melchior, Balthazar, various well-known prayers, and less well-known charms (one of which includes the magic letters AGLA), and some rather crude drawings of the saint and the tyrant who persecuted her.[9] Other examples are known, and such amuletic parchments were folded up and worn on the person of the pregnant woman, perhaps sewn into a bag or enclosed in some other container like a phylactery attached by means of a lace.

The Magical Magi

The very names of the Magi were regarded as magical, and countless brooches and other items of personal jewellery are inscribed with the potent triad (*IASPAR* or) *CASPAR MELCHIOR BALTHAZAR*, often in garbled form (but usually in that order). Significantly, these range from pieces in gold such as the ring-brooch of *c.* 1400 so inscribed in the Victoria and Albert Museum, or the contemporary Glenlyon brooch in the British Museum on which the prophylactic virtue of the names of the Magi is augmented by Christ's dying CONSUMATUM, to the many similar brooches in lead, such as the solid example with a central floral ornament in the Museum of London dated to *c.* 1360 and inscribed *CASPER: MELCHIOR: BPTIS.* Of particular interest are the lead crowns which seem to be exclusively French and which, it has been suggested, may have been worn during Epiphany festivities. The best-preserved example depicts the named Magi frontally, standing one after the other with their gifts before a seated Virgin and Child (who carries an orb) and followed by an angel.[10]

A more workaday object in the collection of the Museum of London is the pendent needlecase made of tin on which are inscribed in Latin, 'Mother of God, remember me', the names of the Magi, and an *Agnus Dei* [image of a lamb bearing a cross or flag]. Like the Glenlyon brooch, a blue-enamelled gold brooch bequeathed in 1380 by Charles V similarly augmented the names of the Magi with another 'magical' inscription on the other side, in this case, *AVE MARIA*; there was clearly the feeling that 'the more the magicer', that such 'words of power' had a cumulative effect.

Other Words of Power

Another English fifteenth-century gold ring illustrates this cumulative principle:

> The five wounds of Christ are my medicine, the holy cross and Christ's passion are my
> medicine Jasper Melchior Balthazar ananyzapta tetragrammaton.[11]

Also employing Christ's dying words is another English ring of thirteenth-century date inscribed CONSUMATUM E[ST] inside the hoop, while on the outside are engraved the magical words *Buro Berto Berneto*, said to be a charm for toothache; it is thus singularly appropriate, if we apply the logic of sympathetic magic, that the ring's heart-shaped bezel is set with a wolf's tooth.[12]

Other magical words include the *ananizapta* found on the Middleham reliquary pendant (1425x50) and, according to the early sixteenth-century Spaniard Martín de Arles, standing for *antidotum Nazareni auferat necem intoxicationis sanctificet alimenta pocula trinitas alma* (May the antidote of Jesus avert death by poisoning and the Trinity sanctify my food and drink) – which, to me at least, sounds very much like an explanation invented long after the reason behind the initial coinage had been forgotten!

Other Luck-bringers

A lengthy inscription in similar vein adorns a lead reliquary of the Virgin in the Musée National du Moyen Age in Paris, 'May he who makes me have good luck, he who sells me, he who wears me',[13] and two ring-brooches in the British Museum's collection bear similarly protective messages: 'Blessed be he who wears me', and 'This which you have fastened on saves you either by sea ?or in battle',[14] while a fifteenth-century finger-ring found at Eltham Castle, Kent, reads 'He who wears me will be successful and come back in great joy'.[15] The belief in the efficacy of such amulets, whether inscribed or not, was strong, and the English chronicler Matthew Paris tells the story of an aged knight named Robert Fitzwalter who, on his deathbed in 1235, told his wife to take the gemstone he wore round his neck and give it to his eldest son and heir, 'for while I wear it, I cannot die, neither will he die nor anyone else who chances to wear it'.[16]

The fourteenth-century romance of *Percyvelle of Galles*, preserved uniquely in the mid-fifteenth-century Thornton manuscript, attests to a similar life-preserving ring:

> Siche a vertue es in the stane,
> In alle this werlde wote I nane
> Siche stone in a rynge;
> A man that had it in were
> One his body for to bere
> There scholde no dyntys hym dere,
> Ne to the dethe brynge.[17]

Reinforcement: the Lucky Four-leaf Clover

Other jewellery seems to be hedging its bets. England's premier saint, St Thomas à Becket, the 'blisful hooly martir', whose Canterbury shrine Chaucer's pilgrims set out to seek, easily enjoyed most-favoured-saint status, to judge from the surviving examples of lead badges and other items cast in his honour, but the most interesting in the present context are the tiny fourteenth- or fifteenth-century badges in the form of a four-leaf clover with a Lombardic 't' at their centres (see chapter ornament). This letter 't' is probably the saint's initial, for these badges are of proven Canterbury provenance, but Thomas is not known to have had any connexion with the quatrefoil.[18] Despite their tiny dimensions (only 23 mm wide) these badges clearly depict the veined leaves of the clover plant, the rare four-leaved specimens of which are still regarded as tokens of great good fortune to this day. It seems to me, therefore, that the only way to explain this conjunction is to see it as an example of 'reinforcement', a deliberate amalgamation of religious and secular good luck, the lucky four-leaf clover enhanced by being consecrated or 'signed' with Saint Thomas's initial. The earliest reference to the four-leaved clover as lucky is found in the *Gospelles of Dystaues* printed by de Worde in London *c.* 1510:

> He that fyndeth the trayfle [trefoil] with foure leues, and kepe it in reuerence knowe for also true as the gospell yt [that] he shall be ryche all his lyfe.[19]

Figure 2.3

But contemporaneously the same printer had also issued *The .iiii. leues of the trueloue*,[20] a Christian moralisation of the courtly lovers' interpretation of the true love plant (*Paris quadrifolia*), which identifies the four leaves of this other quatrefoil as representing the three persons of the Trinity plus the Virgin. I suggest that it is in this context that the extraordinary replacement of the head of God the Father by a veined quatrefoil in the censored image of the Trinity to be found in an early thirteenth-century English psalter must be seen (Figure 2.3).[21]

There is, however, another intriguing possibility with regard to the 't' on the little lead badges: it might, rather, stand for *Truelove*, the common name of the similarly four-leaved *Paris quadrifolia*, and might additionally be a charm to bring good luck in love, and have nothing to do with the saint!

Just this sort of fertile ambiguity is evident in an early fourteenth-century gold brooch from Devizes in the shape of an 'A' ornamented with five stones and bearing inscriptions on both sides.[22] Between the five stones are the letters *AGLA*, a magical word said to be formed from the initial letters of the Hebrew *ATHA GEBRI LEILAN ADONAI* 'Thou art mighty for ever, O Lord', while on the back is the French inscription 'I cause men to love and I give the gift of love', alluding to love between earthly lovers. Indeed, the letter 'A' of the brooch's shape may well stand for the intial letter of *Amor* or *Amour* given the inscription on the reverse, or, or also, *AVE [MARIA]*. A portrait of a young man painted by Jan Mostaert of Haarlem *c.* 1520[23] shows him wearing rows of letter 'A' badges or brooches on his costume which could conceivably relate to the name of his beloved, but his hat-brooch portrays the Annunciation with the encircling inscription *AVE GRACIA PLENA* [sic]. The Van Beuningen collection in Rotterdam includes four lead brooches in the form of the letter 'A', all surmounted by a crown,[24] and Chaucer's Prioress had a gold brooch attached to her rosary, 'On which ther was first write a crowned A, And after 'Amor vincit omnia".[25] This motto usually, of course, refers to worldly love between lovers, not divine love, though Madame Eglantine would doubtless have claimed otherwise if challenged!

Pentangle and Other Magical Devices

Other amuletic devices drew vaguely on the authority of the Old Testament for their sanction, such as the 'Solomon's seal', variously described as a star of five points (and thus a *pentagram* or *pentangle*) or six (*hexagram, Star of David*). The protective pentangle device was borne on the shield of the English hero Sir Gawain, and the fourteenth-century poet attributes it to the authority of Solomon who, he notes, used it to betoken 'Truth',[26] but it may also be seen protecting the baby, incised into the footboard of his cradle, in Schäuffelein's woodcut sheet of *Death and the Ages of Man* (*c.* 1517).[27] Surprisingly, however, pentangular jewellery is not common, whereas six-pointed stars *are* well represented in the lead badge corpus. If we consider the published Dutch material alone, there are certainly fourteen such, including three with male busts at their centres, two with initials (one of which is 'm'), and another three within circular frames (making them conceivably Jewish symbols?).[28]

From a site in London comes a mould for casting six badges of the crowned letter 'm': it therefore seems almost certain that these multiple badges commemorate, and for their wearers beseech the protection of, the Virgin Mary as the Queen of Heaven.[29] Whether or not the 'm' in the late fourteenth-century six-pointed star badge from Dordrecht alludes to the Virgin Mary, and may thus be interpreted as another example of 'reinforcement',[30] contemporaries were quite clear that badges from Marian shrines could confer good fortune on wearers. Early in the sixteenth century, one Elizabeth Newhouse, who had just been to Walsingham on pilgrimage, wrote to her newly unemployed son in London: 'Look wisely to yourself . . . and for good luck I send you a Walsynggam brooch.'[31] The shrine of Our Lady of Walsingham, at Walsingham Priory in Norfolk, was England's premier pilgrimage site after Canterbury, and even surpassed Becket's shrine in the early sixteenth century. Little badges of the type which depicts the Virgin and Child within a crescent moon – a non-Christian luck-bringer in its own right, of course – have been identified as souvenirs of visits to the shrine of Our Lady of Willesden.[32] Nothing better reflects the 'waning of the Middle Ages' than the change in attitude to such popular devotions.

Tawdry Pilgrim Tat

Apart from badges as souvenirs of visits to various real saints' shrines, pilgrims might also bear away with them various noise-making items such as horns, whistles, rattles and bells. The miniature horn-shaped whistles known from London and Salisbury bear various inscriptions: bla me (blow me), ave maria (as also one in the Dutch corpus), and be mari (be merry' – or garbled version of previous?).[33] In the contemporary morality play *Mankind* (*c.* 1465–70) of East Anglian provenance, the character Nought says 'I kan pype in a Walsyngham wystyll',[34] which suggests that such souvenir whistles were available from the shrine of Our Lady of Walsingham too, and that already such 'tourist' trinkets were regarded as a proverbial type of worthlessness, 'not worth a whistle', indeed.[35] In much the same way the thin silk (neck-)laces sold at the fair held in honour of St Audrey in Oxford, known as 'tawdry laces' (and an example of linguistic 'false division'), gave rise to the adjective used to describe any cheap and nasty fairing, that is, 'tawdry'. These necklaces were apparently a somewhat macabre commemoration of the saint who, according to Bede and Aelfric, died of a tumour in her throat, which she considered to be a just retribution because in her youth she had out of vanity adorned her neck with many splendid necklaces.[36]

There is an interesting list of 'superstitious' trinkets found in the Preface to William Patten's *The Expedicion into Scotlande of Prince Edward, Duke of Soomerset* (1548): 'Pardon Beades, Tanthonie belles, Tauthrie laces, Rosaries, Collets'. The *Tauthrie laces* we have already met, and we might guess that *Tanthonie belles* must be St Antony's bells, which the *OED* defines, s.v. *tantony*, as hand-bells or small church-bells, though I do not believe that can be Patten's meaning. The dictionary rightly points out that St Antony's traditional attributes in art are his pig (hence English dialect 'tantony' for the runt of the litter, again, via 'false division'), his tau-staff or crutch[37] (a 'St Antony's cross') and his bell. Surviving examples of fifteenth-century tau-cross badges made in England and the Netherlands have a suspension loop at the base of the 'T' from which, as the sole survivor in Rotterdam shows, hung a little bell with its own tiny clapper[38] – these are surely Patten's 'Tanthonie belles'. Spencer notes that Canterbury pilgrims in Chaucer's period were accustomed to wear similarly tiny bells suspended round the neck (as was also the practice at continental pilgrimage sites), and some of the surviving examples are inscribed CAMPANA THOME (Thomas's bell). William Thorpe, a Lollard preacher contemporary with Chaucer, refers to them in a complaint about the general rowdiness of Canterbury pilgrims:

> what with the noise of their singing, and with the sound of their piping and with the *jangling of their Canterbury bells,* and with the barking out of dogs after them, they make more noise than if the king came thereaway, with all his clarions and other minstrels.[39]

SAINTS' LIVES – PIOUS FOLKTALES?

If the late medieval imagination could dream up such patently absurd saints as those discussed below, it should come as no surprise to find similarly absurd episodes in the purported 'Lives' of more orthodox saints. While the absurd saints were hardly taken seriously, I turn now to a consideration of certain narrative motifs in the lives of some of the 'real', if less-well-known, British saints that are represented in art and have a particular folkloric resonance.

Whatever the actual details of their lives (and that assumes that they had a real existence, which even some orthodox medieval saints patently did not),[40] the saint's life as a narrative genre, especially in the later Middle Ages, when the Age of Saints was already located in the remote past, is a rich source of international folktale motifs familiar from non-religious sources. For those saints about whom few historical details were preserved, it was the pious duty of the hagiographer to invent suitable and usually miraculous incidents which could be seen to confirm the special status conferred on his hero by divine power. The number of such truly 'invented' motifs, in the sense of original incidents unique to a given saint, is few, however. Like the teller of any avowedly secular story, the hagiographer freely borrowed appropriate suggestive details from similar non-religious hero-tales. A motif which proved popular, whether borrowed from secular story or not, would soon find itself borrowed into other saintly biographies.

Saint Confines Birds in Roofless Barn

One fifteenth-century lead badge shows five birds in what looks like a wide low basket, but is in fact a circular enclosure made from panels of wattle fencing, a scene relating to a miracle reported in the Life of St Werburg of Chester (d. 699). According to her late medieval *Life* by Henry Bradshaw (d. 1513), when St Werburg's tenants complained to her that wild geese were devastating their crops, she:

> . . . commaunded a seruaunt go hastely
> To dryve those wylde gees & brynge home to her place
> There to be pynned . . .　　　　　　　　　　　　　[penned]
> The messanger, merueyled and mused in his mynde
> Of this straunge message, stode styll in a study
> Knowynge that well it passed course of kynde　　[that it was quite against nature]
> Wylde gees for to pynne by any mannes polycy
> Syth nature hath ordeyned suche byrdes to fly
> Supposynge his lady had ben unreasonable　　　[mad]
> Commaundynge to do a thynge unpossyble.[41]

But the 'miracle' is also recorded on a late fourteenth-century misericord in Chester Cathedral, where the left-hand supporter depicts the saint and her incredulous servant either side of the penned geese (Figure 2.4), and the badges were clearly sold as souvenirs to those who had made the pilgrimage to her shrine in the cathedral.[42] In the present instance, of course, the significant fact is that the saint is able to achieve what for any ordinary mortal would be a proverbial folly to attempt, for the saint is a 'fool for God's sake'. The same motif is found in the Lives of Sts Cadog, David, Gildas, Illtud and Samson.[43]

Unofficial Saints

Some 'pilgrim' badges commemorate 'saints' who were never officially canonised but seem to have enjoyed great popularity locally, such as Richard Caister of Norwich, and more attractively, John Schorn (d. 1315) of North Marston, who was also honoured at Windsor. There are six surviving rood-screen paintings of Schorn

Figure 2.4

and a number of lead badges which concentrate on one of his more spectacular miracles, showing the occasion on which he conjured the Devil into a boot. In 1537 the Bishop of London, acting as a commissioner for the removal of superstitious images, reported that:

> at Merston Mr Johan Schorn stondith blessing a bote [boot], whereunto they do say he conveyed the devill. He is mough [much] sought for the agow [ague]. If it be your lordeschips pleasur, I schall sett that botyd [booted] ymage in a nother place.[44]

Two royal 'saints' who similarly never quite made the grade were Thomas of Lancaster, who was beheaded as a rebel by his cousin Edward II in 1322, and King Henry VI. Despite a remarkable lack of traditional attributes of sainthood while alive, after Lancaster's ignominious death, 'pilgrims' began to flock to his tomb and claims of miraculous cures circulated widely, much to King Edward's displeasure, and to such an extent that he was moved to write to the Bishop of London regarding 'painted images' of Lancaster that surrounded a commemorative tablet in St Paul's Cathedral, and which 'many persons . . . victims of infernal trickery . . . venerate and worship . . . and affirm that it there works miracles'. When Edward was overthrown in 1327 and the boy-king Edward III set on the throne, the new faction continued to champion Thomas's cause, for political reasons, and on the eve of the Reformation his hat and belt were still being kept as remedies for headaches and the hazards of childbirth respectively. We hear of a London merchant who sold a covered cup in 1338 which was adorned with a 'print' of 'St Thomas of Lancaster', but the more truly popular images were once again cast in lead, and a remarkable devotional panel depicting six scenes from the 'saint's' 'passion' survives (in the British Museum) flanked by Sts Peter, Paul and others, and surmounted by a Crucifixion.

Brian Spencer has plausibly argued that a number of small lead panel badges which depict a youth in a subservient attitude, sometimes kneeling and with hands raised in supplication, before a standing queen who threatens him with a cudgel or stick, are satirical of the earliest years of Edward III's reign, during which period his mother, Queen Isabella, in practice, ruled in his name, and that such badges would have been worn by opponents of the new regime, led for a time by Henry, brother of 'St' Thomas of Lancaster. That reproduced here from the British Museum bears the ironic legend *MOTHERE* at the foot of the badge (Figure 2.5).

Figure 2.5

Spencer has also memorably characterised Henry VI as a man 'whose true holiness was as apparent to everyone as his exasperating incompetence as monarch'. Like Thomas of Lancaster, he too was put to death by the victorious Yorkist faction who succeeded him and who were anxious to squash any popular veneration, but after their defeat at the Battle of Bosworth in 1485, the way was open for mass veneration of Henry, centred round his miracle-working tomb at Windsor. He is often shown on the badges with his personal device the heraldic antelope or yale, with its distinctive saw-tooth horns and tusks, as also on a unique, large but damaged woodcut printed in the final decade of the fifteenth century.[45] Here the king is shown standing in all his regalia adored by kneeling supplicants who are presumably praying to him for relief from their wounds (for example, the woman with a knife through her throat and the man pierced by an arrow). In the background we glimpse a pair of manacles, two crutches, a shirt and a model ship suspended within the saint's shrine, all votives left behind by grateful pilgrims cured or relieved (freed from prison or saved from shipwreck, perhaps) by virtue of the royal 'saint's' intercession.

A *bona fide* officially canonised royal saint was Edward the Confessor. According to an inventory of the possessions of Henry V drawn up in 1422, the King had a tapestry featuring King Edward the Confessor, a saintly king understandably popular with the monarchy.[46] A rare panel painting of St Edward giving his ring to a needy pilgrim executed *c.* 1370 survives in a private collection at Forthampton,[47] and the same scene is found on Chertsey tiles in Westminster Abbey made 1250x70. Saint Edward's shrine was located in Westminster Abbey, but despite the best efforts of Henry III, who rebuilt the choir of the abbey in his honour and translated his relics to a magnificent new shrine in 1269, the Confessor never achieved widespread popular devotion, and relatively few pilgrim badges survive that can be unequivocally identified as his.[48]

The Hairy Anchorite: St John of Beverley and Other Saintly Wild Men

Another distinct sub-species of medieval saint is the 'hairy anchorite', the man or woman who goes out into the wilderness and whose hair grows long and shaggy, a sort of holy wodehouse (Wild Man). Influence from the biblical story of Nebuchadnezzar must be presumed in the formation of the type, but probably the best-known and most influential early Christian example is St John Chrysostom. Other hairy anchorites include the medieval French saint, St Jehan Paulus (*poilu*, 'hairy'), clearly based on Chrysostom, St Macarius the Roman, Saint James the Penitent, and the female St Mary of Egypt. In Middle English literature even the essentially secular heroes of the Romances Sir Gowther and Sir Orfeo partake of this popular motif, but the best-known English example is probably St John of Beverley (d. 721).

The historical eighth-century John of Beverley, Bishop of York, was canonised in 1037, and the earliest Latin Life was written in the 1060s by Fulcard of St Omer. By the middle of the following century there existed a compilation of his miracles which incidentally shows that his tomb at Beverley was already drawing pilgrims from as far afield within Britain as East Anglia and Scotland. In the early fifteenth century, his fame enjoyed a sudden increase due to the fact that the Battle of Agincourt (1415) was won on the feast of his translation, 25 October[49] – a grateful Henry V ordered the day to be observed nationally, enlisted the saint as one of the patrons of the royal house, and visited the shrine himself in 1420, as did his pious successor, Henry VI, in 1448.

If little is known for certain about Beverley's early Anglo-Saxon patron saint, his life story is still most unlikely to have been anything like that recorded in the early printed Flemish 'Life', in which his biography is made to conform to the folktale type of the 'hairy anchorite'. It seems at first sight extraordinary that the Belgian printer Thomas Van der Noot should issue a Flemish 'Life of St John of Beverley' in Brussels *c.* 1512.[50] Why should he believe a Flemish readership should be at all interested in the life of an English saint of only local interest even in England? Equally puzzling, there is no extant antecedent English edition from which Van der Noot's could be translated; however – especially in the light of what we know of the bilingual practice of the contemporary printer, Jan van Doesborch – the Brussels volume entitles us to posit a lost English *Life of St John of Beverley*, perhaps printed locally in York, where the first known printed book appeared in 1509, and where we know of two printers of Flemish origin working *c.* 1510, Hugo Goes and Frederick Freez, or even – as we know that the former printed at least one item there – in Beverley itself.

In fact, the attraction of the *Life* to Van der Noot must have been in part its intrinsic notoriety. According to the title-page of *Jan van Beverley*, the saintly hermit, after forcing himself on his sister, murdered and buried her, and then fled into the wilds living like a wild man. The book is illustrated with woodcuts (that on the title-page is suitably lurid) depicting John's sister resisting his advances in the foreground, her murder in the middle distance and her burial in the background. Of particular iconographical interest is the cut depicting the capture of the hermit by huntsmen, who is portrayed as a wild man on all fours, which presumably owes something to Dürer's *c.* 1496 engraving of the hermit *St John Chrysostom* in the wilderness, also on all fours, in the background, behind a *Madonna lactans*.[51] Immediately, however, it perhaps owes more to the woodcut tradition,[52] a similar scene of St John Chrysostom captured by the hunter and his dogs illustrates his 'Life' in Fyner's *Heiligenleben* (Urach, 1481).[53]

There was, however, another reason why the Flemish reading-public might be interested in the 'Life' of St John of Beverley, and that was the late medieval passion 'to goon on pilgrimages'. But pilgrimage was not only undertaken by the pious:

> In the towns and cities of Flanders, Brabant and Hainault it was common practice for courts of law to mete out pilgrimages as punishments for particular crimes. The pilgrimages were assigned from penitential tariffs established by local custom.[54]

A list of a hundred pilgrimage shrines compiled at Dendremonde (Belgium) at the beginning of the fifteenth century names the shrine of St John at Beverley as one of the group which were assessed at the maximum tariff (a group which also includes the shrine of Our Lady at Salisbury).

Pilgrims, whether pious or penitential, would have hoped to return home with some souvenir of their visit to St John's shrine, especially a lead badge – indeed, for a penitential pilgrim from Flanders, for example, such a token might be considered essential proof that the pilgrimage had been successfully completed. Small lead *ampullae* filled with thaumaturgic water from the holy shrine or a nearby spring were another common type of souvenir; the excavation of a moated site at Arnold near Beverley recently yielded such an *ampulla* decorated with a compass-drawn flower on the obverse, and a crown above a shield bearing the letter 'I' (for *Iohn*), probably another souvenir of a pilgrimage to the shrine of Beverley's patron saint.[55]

It has been argued that the series of eleven illustrations in the *bas-de-page* of the early fourteenth-century English *Smithfield Decretals*[56] reflects knowledge of a version of the hairy anchorite story very close to that told in *Jan van Beverley*, as, it seems, does a fourteenth-century wall-painting featuring John the Baptist at Idsworth.[57] An attractive mid-fifteenth-century hand-coloured woodcut sheet uniquely preserved in the National Gallery of Art, Washington, depicts another hairy anchorite, St Onuphrius.

Animal Runs Round the Bounds Defining the Saint's Precinct

One method of miraculously defining the site of a saint's church was for an animal to run round the bounds, its course marking the extent of the sacred precinct. In the medieval Welsh tradition there are two early instances of this motif: St Cybi's goat and St Oudoceus's stag. In the latter story, a stag hunted by King Einion of Glywysing sought refuge in St Oudoceus's cloak, and on seeing the animal's trust in the holy man, the King gave Oudoceus all the territory around which the stag had run.

A similar story, though not identically motivated, is told of the foundation of the abbey at Minster-in-Thanet, Kent. According to the tale, Queen Domneva, *alias* Eormenburgh of Mercia, was given by King Ecgberht of Kent all the land her pet hind could encompass in a single run, in compensation for the murder of her

Figure 2.6

brothers by one of his councillors. About the year 1410 Thomas of Elmham, a monk at St Augustine's Abbey, Canterbury, drew a map of the Isle of Thanet – one of the earliest extant English local maps[58] – on which a zigzag line in green ink which runs roughly north–south across the island is labelled *cursus cerve* (the hind's run/course)[59] and above the label the outline of Domneva's pet deer is still just visible (Figure 2.6).

Animal Helps Saint to Construct his Cell

Having determined the site, sometimes animals would help the saint build his cell. A stag which had been granted sanctuary by the Welsh saint Illtud used voluntarily to draw the loads of timber he needed to build his church.[60] Another Celtic saint, the Irishman Alto, who founded the monastery of Altomünster in Bavaria in the eighth century, was also the beneficiary of animal help as a mark of special divine favour: in the forest in which he chose to build his cell the birds brought him what twigs and branches they could. This avian assistance is portrayed in a charmingly naive woodcut sheet now in the National Gallery of Art, Washington, probably issued *c.* 1500 (Figure 2.7).

Stags Draw Saint's Plough

Once the site was located and the church built, the saint's next task was to cultivate the earth. The Welsh saints were fortunate enough to receive assistance from wild animals that offered themselves for drawing the plough.

Sts Cadog and Deiniol were able to use stags to pull their ploughs who returned to the woods after their day's work. When the tyrant Maelgwn stole Tydecho's oxen they were replaced by stags and, as if further to drive home the futility of thinking to hinder God's annointed, while the stags ploughed, a wolf did the harrowing.[61] At St Neot in Cornwall the eponymous saint's life is told in a series of painted glass windows in the nave made *c.* 1528.[62] One window depicts the saint ploughing with the two yoked stags above a caption which reads: 'Here a yoke was put on stags in place of the cattle'. The same story is also told of his compatriot St Kea,[63] and of the holy hermit, Robert of Knaresborough, the latter again memorialised in a glass window of *c.* 1482 from Darley Abbey in Derbyshire, but now installed in St Matthew's Church, Morley (Colour Plate 1).[64]

Another fascinating artefact which commemorates the importance of more workaday ploughing in traditional societies is a little lead badge, which takes the form of a plough surmounted by a crown, and is presumably associated with the traditional English folk-religious celebration of Plough Monday. It is inscribed with the proverbial exhortation, part of the Plough Monday prayer, 'God sped de ploue', and was perhaps worn by the teams of young men (later known as plough-bullocks/-jags, etc.) who drew the decorated plough around the village on that day, asking for alms and sometimes performing a rudimentary folk-play.[65] A beam in the late fourteenth-century plough gallery of Cawston Church, Norfolk, is inscribed:

> God spede the plow
> And send us all corne enow
> our purpose for to mak
> at crow of cok
> of the plowlete of Sygate
> Be mery and glade
> Wat Goodale this work mad.[66]

The opening couplet is found in a contemporary manuscript of *Piers Plowman*: 'God spede ye plouz and sende us korne inoug' inscribed above a painting of a ploughing scene which prefaces the text.[67]

Figure 2.7

Phallic and Other Burlesque Saints and their Relics

In the opening speech of Heywood's *Playe Called the Foure PP* (*c.* 1520), the Palmer (the pilgrim returned from the Holy Land, as a sign of which he carried a palm-branch or leaf), gives a long list of the shrines he has visited.[68] The fact that St Trunnion should be paired with St Uncumber in the Palmer's list, seems to imply that both had something in common in Heywood's mind, and that, I suggest, was their bizarre sexuality, transsexuality in the case of the latter, and blatant phallicism in the former case. Saint Trunnion's name is yet another example of false division, being earlier known (in *The Canterbury Tales*) and later (in Nashe's pornographic *Choice of Valentines*) as St Runyon. The 'Saint Pintle the Apostle' by whom Free Will swears in the interlude *Hickscorner*, written in 1514,[69] is another such burlesque phallic saint.

In another of Heywood's plays, *The Pardoner and the Frere, the Curate and Neybour Pratte* (published in 1533), some of the list of burlesque relics from his earlier *Playe Called the Foure PP* are repeated.[70] Here again we see on display All Hallows' jawbone and the big toe of the Trinity, to which are added St Michael's skull, the arm of St Sunday[71] and – clearly deriving from Chaucer's Pardoner – a holy Jew's hip-bone,[72] plus a mitten, and a relic of Our Lady:

> Her bongrace which she ware, with her French hood,
> When she went out always, for sun-burning.

The other source for his absurd relics was the early sixteenth-century French farce he also drew on in the earlier play, in which the Pardoner exhibits relics of several burlesque saints, including the skull of St Pion (St Boozer), patron saint of heavy drinkers, and other pieces of burlesque sexual saints (see below), as well as the splendidly insubstantial grunt of St Anthony's sow, and the wing of one of the seraphim who surround the Godhead (denounced by the Triacleur, the French Pothecary, as a feather from the goose the Pardoner had for his dinner!), and many more of a similar nature.[73]

The absurd relics topos was very popular in the English theatre of the earlier part of the sixteenth century, to judge from the number of such lists we have. John Bale includes a similar list in his *King Johan* of the late 1530s:[74] a feather of St Michael's wing, one of Adam's toenails, the 'huckyll bone of a Jewe' (which looks like it harks back to Chaucer's Pardoner again), St Thomas à Becket's shoe-latchet, a bone of the blessed Trinity (again), and a number of deliberately disgusting items, one of 'St Job's scabs',[75] one of Moses' maggots, a louse from St Francis, a fart of St Fandigo – a probably imaginary saint – and a dram of the turd of St Barnabas. A century later the anti-Catholic polemicist, Thomas Scott, a man very familiar with the Netherlands and preacher to the English garrison at Utrecht, published *The Second Part of Vox Populi* in 1624, in which he included a discussion on the credibility of miracles, including the popular belief that:

> . . . a young married wife shall have a child in the same yeare if she can stride ouer at once Saint Rombauts breeches at Mechlin.[76]

A perfectly ordinary late medieval pilgrim badge, souvenir of a visit to the shrine of St Rombout of Mechelen in Belgium is known, showing a stylised saint with the arms of the city,[77] but in view of the fame of the saint's wonder-working nether garments, I am disposed to suggest that a little fifteenth-century badge excavated in Bruges may indeed celebrate this very relic (Figure 2.8). At first inclined to see it in terms of the well-known anti-feminist motif, so popular in the Middle Ages, of the 'Battle for the Breeches' (see Chapter 11), I now think it is perhaps a Protestant badge satirising credulous Catholic belief in the fecundating power of such absurd relics. It is at precisely this period, in the late medieval/early modern era, that a sub-species of burlesque saint, the sexual, but preeminently the phallic, saint reaches its climax.

Figure 2.8

In Rabelais' *Pantagruel*, published in 1532, Panurge boasts in typically extravagant fashion that his codpiece alone will sweep down the thousands of enemy warriors and that St Balletrou, who lies inside it, will account for the similar numbers of their female camp-followers.[78] The notion of the codpiece as the resting-place of the phallic saint did not originate with Rabelais; *c.* 1500, in the *Sermon Joyeux de Saint Velu* (Hairy)[79] the parodic preacher, as the climax to a phallic farrago purporting to give the 'Life' of the saint, martyred in *Vite*rbo by *un connu*, that is 'a certain person', but punning on *un con nu* (a naked cunt), holds aloft the biggest part of the saint's 'tomb', which the stage direction tells us is a codpiece (*brayette*)![80]

Protestant polemicists were keen to publish to the world their scandalised reports of the existence of *real* phallic saints among especially rural Catholic communities. In his *Traité des Reliques* of 1543, for example, when he came to discussing the relics of St Bartholomew, Calvin revealed that at Trier, '*il y en a je ne sais quel membre*' (They have I don't know what member of his there), which was his delicate way of saying that the cathedral claimed to have the saint's penis – but so too did the cathedral at Augsburg![81] It was said to be of an extraordinary length and to have the property of making women conceive, a power also claimed for Christ's foreskin – one of the few bodily relics of Christ for which there was at least some biblical authority – by the several churches which claimed to possess it.[82]

In his imaginative *Confession de Sancy* (1597–1617) Agrippa d'Aubigné recorded the continuing devotion to St Foutin at several places in France, and Marnix refers to his ithyphallic image in a nunnery at Fontaine in Perigeux (euphemistically known as *Saint Chose*, that is, Saint Thing), where women unable to conceive were accustomed to offer to the saint wax votives in the form of the sexual organs of both sexes, and to watch votive candles planted on the saint's member until they burned down to it.[83] Whether or not the various French St Foutins derive from St Photinus, the first Bishop of Lyons (and the phallicism attributed to him only via a folk-etymological connexion of his name with the verb *foutre*), it is certain that similar sexual organs in wax were offered at a number of other saints' shrines. In his *Dialogue Concerning Heresies* of 1529, Sir Thomas More retails an anecdote concerning a newly married English couple who visit the shrine of St Valéry-sur-Somme in Picardy, where to their astonishment they report that:

> lyke as in other pylgrymages [= pilgrimage sites] ye se hanged vp legges of waxe or armes or such other partes, so was in that chapell all theyr offrynges yt [that] honge aboute the walles none other thynge but mennes gere & womens gere made in waxe.[84]

Both Viret[85] and Estienne mention St Greluchon/Guerlichon, whose phallic image in an abbey in the Berri area was also part of a ritual by which barren women hoped to conceive: they drank a powder made from scrapings of the statue's penis, a member with which – in Estienne's words – it was '*horriblement bien fourni*' (horribly well furnished).[86] A similar ritual is related by d'Aubigné, the manufacture of *saint vinaigre* (saintly vinegar) from the wine-reddened penis of another such image allegedly discovered by the Huguenots who took the town of Embrun in 1585 in the main church there; the similarly well-endowed image of St Eutropius was publicly burned in the market-place by Protestants at Orange in 1562.[87]

Figure 2.9

The nearest thing I am aware of to this sort of practice in England, though less overtly phallic, is a 'relic' of St Leonard that was kept in the parish church at Bromley in Essex, though how long it had been there before the earliest mention of it is uncertain. According to James Howell's *Paroimiographia. Proverbs, or Old sayed sawes and adages . . .* of 1659, the expression, 'Go ride upon St Leonard's saddle', was 'A speech used to be spoken to barren women; this saddle was kept at Bromley'. Note that this saddle implies the well-known sexual metaphor of 'riding' (see Chapter 12).

Marnix noted that at St Auban, barren women would visit the image of St Arnaud (also, facetiously, the patron saint of cuckolds in medieval French literature),[88] who would lift the apron it wore for the sake of modesty, and this exposure would suffice to make them fertile thereafter.[89] Estienne mentions St René of Anjou as another of these phallic saints:

> `but how the women conducted themselves around it (who also showed them his fine priapic weapons), just as I would be ashamed to describe it, so would readers be ashamed to read about it.[90]

It seems clear that St René's fecundating power is due to the folk-etymological connexion of his name with the kidneys or loins (*reins*), in an age which regarded these organs as the seat of sexual potency: Montaigne, for example, rendered the phrase, '*Diaboli virtus in lumbis est*', of St Jerome's misogynist classic, the *Adversus contra Joviniam*, as '*Car la vertu du diable est aux roignons*' (for the power of the Devil is in the kidneys – compare the English phallic St *Runyon* (above)).[91]

Another and startling Dutch image of a burlesque saint is this broadsheet published in Amsterdam *c.* 1520 of St Aelwaer, a name etymologically meaning All-true, but by this time tantamount to Quarrelsome (Figure 2.9). The inscription above the woodcut by Cornelis Anthonisz reads 'Everyone serves St Quarrelsome with great desire, who is honoured by many people'. The text makes it clear that she is the patron saint of squabblers and arguers from all ranks of society. This parodic image becomes more than a little shocking when we realise it is based unmistakably on the standard iconography of the Flight into Egypt, indeed, one recent scholar has seen the ass on which St Aelwaer is mounted as 'an exact (if reversed) quotation of the ass in *The Flight into Egypt* from Dürer's *Life of the Virgin* series'.[92] Thus the ill-omened magpie perched on Aelwaer's head within her halo, quite probably parodies the dove which represents the Holy Ghost seen hovering directly over the Virgin's head in standard representations of the gift of tongues at Pentecost – clearly appropriate to our quarrelsome squabblers' saint. The pig under her arm, by the same token, must with equally astonishing irreverence – not to say blasphemy – parallel the infant Jesus as held by the Virgin in standard images of The Flight. The lengthy text makes similarly irreverent references to the text of the Gospels.

As the image of this burlesque saint seems to poke deliberate fun at a well-known contemporary image of the Virgin Mary, it does not seem too speculative to see it as an attack on what Protestants saw as Mariolatry – it is, after all, arguably not as offensive as the contemporary small lead badge (Figure 12.2) which depicts three phalli bearing a litter on which a phallus-crowned vulva sits, and which I suggest in Chapter 12 is to be interpreted as a proto-Protestant satirical attack on Marian processions.

The Decline of the Saints' Power

On Holy Rood Day, 14 September 1465, John Paston, anxious to see his sister safely married off, wrote to his wife from Norwich:

> I pray yow voysyt [visit] the Rood of Northedor and Seynt Savyour, at Barmonsey, amonge whyll ye abyd in London, and lat my sustyr Margery goo with yow to pray to them that sche may have a good hosbond or [ere] sche com hom agen.[93]

The two roods mentioned by John Paston were famous in their day (shortly before they were destroyed in the Reformation in 1547) as wonder-working crosses, but it is not difficult to see why, to a Reformer, praying to a cross that one may obtain a good husband would be regarded as sheer idolatry. The two roods in question were those at the north door of St Paul's Cathedral, and that at St Saviour in Bermondsey Abbey. The Lollard, Elizabeth Sampson, was so unimpressed by the Bermondsey rood and the quality, presumably, of its carved Christ, that she dubbed it 'Sym Sawyer with kyt lyppe' (Sim Sawyer with the cut lip).[94]

Despite its general dependence on the French *Farce d'un pardonneur d'un triacleur et d'une taverniere*, Heywood's *Playe Called the Foure PP* opens with a long list of the shrines his Palmer has visited in which he clearly betrays his London origins. He tells us he was:

> At Saint Tuncumber and St Trunnion
> At Saint Botolph and St Anne of Buxton
> . . . and St George in Southwark
> At Waltham and at Walsingham
> And at the good rood of Dagenham
> . . . And at Saint Winefride's well in Wales
> At our Lady of Boston at Saint Edmund's burgh
> . . . At Redbourn and at the blood of Hales
> . . . At Saint David's . . .
> At Master John Shorn at Canterbury
> The great God of Catwade, at King Henry
> At Saint Saviour's, at Our Lady of Southwell
> At Crome, at Willesden, and at Muswell
> At Saint Richard . . .
> And at Our Lady that standeth in the oak.   [between Highgate and Islington]

Heywood's purpose is certainly satirical, but even he is not quite as forthright as Elizabeth Sampson in her denunciation of the shrines at *Crome* (Crome's Hill, Greenwich) and Willesden, who admitted repeatedly saying that:

> Our Lady of Willesdon was a burnt arse elf and a burnt arse stock [block of wood], and if she might have helpen men and women which go to her of pilgrimage she would not have suffered her tail [genitals] to have been burnt, and what [why] should folk worship Our Lady of Willesdon or Our Lady of Crome, for the one is but a burnt arse stock and the other is but a puppet [doll].[95]

Note that 'burnt' means here infected with venereal disease. The Reformers seem to have had it in for Our Lady of Willesden; *c.* 1530 Thomas Bilney abused her 'as a stewed whore' (a whore from the Bankside 'Stews' or brothels), and one of the earliest printed works of the English Reformation, Roye and Barlowe's *Rede Me And Be Nott Wrothe*, published in Strasbourg in 1528, condemned women's pilgrimages to her shrine: 'Wyves to deceave their husbandes Make to her many errandes Vnder coloure of devocion . . .' (a motivation to which Chaucer's Wife of Bath cheerfully admits, by the way!), going so far as to denounce the Virgin herself: 'As for whordom and letcherousnes She is the chefe lady mastres.'[96]

As for Heywood's Saint Tuncomber, she too is the result of 'false division' and is more usually known in English as Uncomber, the saintly bearded lady of questionable sexuality – also known as Wilgefortis or Kummernis in German.[97] A statue of 'her' still exists in Westminster Abbey, and Thomas More derided the custom of women offering oats at it:

> Whereof I cannot perceive the reason, but if it be because she should provide a horse for an evil husband to ride to the devil upon, for that is the thing that she is so sought for, as they say. Insomuch that women have therefore changed her name and instead of Saint Wilgeforte call her Saint Uncumber, because that they reckon that for a peck of oats she will not fail to uncumber them of their husbands.[98]

This was one saint Margery Paston should not be praying to!

This chapter – this entire book, indeed – is predicated on my feeling that the motifs of mainstream Christian art are too well known to need further rehearsal, and indeed, that further rehearsal becomes positively stultifying. I am not so self-deluding as to believe that the quasi-religious subjects discussed in this chapter are of equal significance with those mainstream motifs, but I am unabashed in contending that these often tawdry yet sometimes poetic manifestations of popular religion are yet of real significance for the proper understanding of late medieval culture as a whole – and not just of 'popular culture'. For too long, a radical misunderstanding of popular culture has been abroad – as if the constituents of this popular culture were only available to the great unwashed and were quite unknown or inaccessible to the elite. Economic and social pre-eminence were no bar to a recognition of the power of charms, talismans and divinatory practices frowned upon by the Church, and the highest-born in the land, as we have noted, wore jewellery bearing prophylactic inscriptions or devices of which theologians would certainly have disapproved.

And even before that revolution in the established order that marks the end of our period, and which we moderns term the Reformation, bolder spirits were already poking fun at a belief in the efficacious power of saints' relics, and indeed, in the very reality of the saint, an insolence later eagerly seized upon by Protestant polemicists.

THREE

LICKED INTO SHAPE:
ANIMAL SYMBOLISM

The range of animal imagery displayed in late medieval art is vast and it is not possible to treat it comprehensively in a single chapter. Instead of attempting such a survey, I have settled on discussing dogs, cats, and rats and some Bestiary imagery, including bears and unicorns, as well as the use made of animals in sexual imagery, and in some areas of real life; but many other motifs which involve animals are discussed elsewhere, for example, those which involve the trickster figure Reynard, under proverbial follies in Chapter 7.

Sometimes a dog is just a dog. Not a symbol of anything else, just a dog going about its doggy business. The ever-present danger for iconographers is – in the words of Horatio's reproach to Hamlet – 'to consider too curiously'. Not every item in a painting, for example, is there for some emblematic purpose, some are just everyday *realia* (though many would doubtless consider that a purposeful presence too). And we err if we always try to project some significance onto every constituent image. That said, this chapter is indeed concerned with the purposeful presence in medieval art of the symbolic animal!

Dogs

The little dog at the feet of the couple in the celebrated *Arnolfini Wedding*, painted by Jan van Eyck in 1434, is clearly there as a symbol of fidelity. Was not Fido once a popular name for dogs? – the faithful hound, 'man's best friend'? And here he is undeniably a symbol of their plighted troth, the fidelity they swear to each other. In fact, 'Love me, love my dog', is a sentiment of surprising antiquity. In a late fifteenth-century poem, 'Jak and his Stepdame', we are told that:

> 'In olde termys it is fownd,   [In an old expression]
> "He that lovythe me lovythe my hound".'

But as long ago as the mid-twelfth century, St Bernard of Clairvaux had said the same in a Latin sermon: *Qui me amat, amat et canem meum.*

Pet dogs, whether ladies' lap-dogs or gentlemen's hunting-hounds are often seen sitting at the feet of effigies, especially female effigies, on tombs. These dogs are symbolic of fidelity, to be sure, but that these animals were often held in real affection is evident from the significant fact that they are sometimes named on the funerary monument. On the effigial slab of Sir Jehan de Seure (d. 1391) at Ozouer-le-Repos, a greyhound wearing a collar on which is the Arthurian name Parceval, appears at his master's feet, while a far less lithe-looking beast, with the name Dyamant (Diamond) on his collar, is seen at the feet of Sir John's lady. In England, at Deerhurst, on the contemporary brass of Lord and Lady Cassy (d. 1400), a real dog, identified as Terri, lies at the feet of his mistress, while as so often at this period, a 'heraldic' lion reclines at her husband's feet. Formerly in the church at Ingham, the brass of Sir Bryan de Stapleton (d. 1438) labelled his dog as plain Jakke.

In a more amorous context there are now two examples known of a shield-shaped lead pendant of late fourteenth-century date on which a dog appears with upraised paw which barks out the message *AMOVRS*, and the locket – if that is what it is – is further ornamented with the talismanic names of the Magi (see Chapter 1).[1] The type of dog portrayed here, however, is not the greyhound, so well represented in the inventories of princely jewels,[2] but the lap-dog type, and the implication may well be that the lover hopes to enjoy the same sort of intimacy with his beloved as her favourite pet, that he also hopes, as it were, to lie in her lap.[3]

THE POLYSEMY OF SYMBOLISM

But if animals are being used symbolically, it is still simplistic to assume, for example, that dog = fidelity. Fidelity is only one of the nine significances listed for the dog in one of the best handbooks of iconography.[4] Indeed, we should expect most symbols to be polyvalent or polysemous, and we are dependent on the context to determine which is the appropriate significance. The first significance in the above handbook entry shows that sometimes the dog represents Envy – and nowhere more obviously than when it is the animal attribute of that Vice in depictions of the Seven. Curiously, the handbook omits to mention the common motif – indeed it is the proverbial 'bone of contention' – of two dogs disputing over a bone, found, for example, in fourteenth-century manuscript margins,[5] on fifteenth-century choir-stalls,[6] and in engraved work, such as the 3-of-Dogs playing-card designed by the Master ES (*c.* 1463). By the time of Baude's verses 'for making tapestry', the two different species of dog quarrelling over the bone have interestingly become representatives of different social classes; the aristocratic greyhound believes he is entitled to have the bone 'on account of lineage', while the plebeian mastiff believes it is rightly his by dint of 'virtue with courage'. An early pictorial example of two shaggy dogs fighting over a bone at his feet was to be seen, somewhat inappropriately perhaps, on the brass of Laurence de St Maur (d. 1337), rector of Higham Ferrers.

Gelert, the Faithful Hound

But just occasionally a dog is more than just a dog, is a super-dog, an Animal Hero First Class, and such is Prince Llywelyn's dog Gelert. I still remember being taken, aged eight, on a grey, drizzly day to visit Gelert's grave at Bedd-gelert (Gelert's Grave) in North Wales by my Welsh father. I recall being told the story and, like many another young hearer before and since, finding it so unbearably poignant that tears were the inevitable response. It would be another thirty years before I would realise that this 'grave' was just a cynical late eighteenth-century ploy to exploit the 'Romantic' tourist, and that rather than 'Gelert', Llywelyn's dog might more appropriately have been named 'Motif No. B524.1.4.1'. But, according to the folktale, returning from the hunt, Prince Llywelyn found the dog covered with gore, and assuming it had killed his baby son, whom it had been left to protect, slew the animal, only subsequently to discover that it had killed a wolf that had entered the house, and that beneath the overturned cradle his son was safely asleep. In fact, this is an international folktale concerning a Faithful Hound, which appears, for example, in a thirteenth-century *exemplum* of Etienne de Bourbon, but which in these islands is best known in this Welsh version, in which the dog's owner is Llywelyn the Great (1173–1240), and an early text of the tale is indeed to be found in the mid-fourteenth-century Welsh version of the *Seven Wise Masters of Rome*. In illustrative contexts, the story is the subject of woodcuts in the 1533 edition of Pauli's *Schimpf und Ernst*,[7] and executed by Erhard Schoen, in a contemporary broadsheet of Hans Sachs's *Historia. Der ritter mit dem getrewen hund*,[8] as well as in editions of other *exempla* collections in which the tale occurs.[9]

The new received wisdom – as most recently retailed by *The Oxford Companion to the Literature of Wales*[10] – is that this version of the story associated with the village of Beddgelert was unknown there before 1784, in which year it was fabricated by David Prichard, landlord of the local pub: 'The cromlech which is said to be Gelert's grave, like the well-known poem by W.R. Spencer which Joseph Haydn set to music, was based on details supplied by Prichard.' Be that as it may, exactly 300 years earlier, in 1484, the heraldic *Rous Roll* gives the arms of Wales as a helm on which the crest is a dog and cradle, which surely suggests that some version of the tale was indeed already associated with the Welsh royal line at this date.

One bizarre reflex of the folktale motif of the Faithful Hound is to be found in the story of St Guinefort, by means of which a human saint local to the Lyon area, whose aid was especially sought in the healing of children, became transmogrified into a saintly greyhound! At least three examples of a small lead badge of fourteenth-century date in the form of a greyhound and bearing a legend which declares the badge to be amuletic exist; as the greyhound is not otherwise known to be traditionally lucky, these might well, in my opinion, be considered to be an off-shoot of St Guinefort's cult. The legend reads, 'May he who wears me have good luck'.[11]

THE BESTIARY

The first port of call for anyone interested in animal symbolism in the Middle Ages should be the Bestiary, indeed, the importance of the Bestiary as a source for medieval

Figure 3.1

knowledge and belief about animals cannot be overstated. But it should not be confused with a zoological textbook, nor even a work of 'moralised' natural history. Medieval clerics were quite indifferent as to whether the habits ascribed to the animals were actually true, what mattered was that these details could be read analogically as so many lessons in the Book of Nature, promoting Christian virtues and discouraging vice. The Bestiary text, which continued to evolve throughout the course of the Middle Ages, seems to have begun its career in late antiquity as a collection of observations and folklore about real and imaginary creatures, subsequently to be 'moralised' by a Christian and probably English redactor. The earliest extant illustrated Bestiary is the ninth-century Bern manuscript, but its style of illustration shows that it derives from a late antique model of the fourth century or earlier. Otherwise, the extant English Bestiaries begin in the twelfth century, though there is evidence for illustrated manuscripts of the work available to the Anglo-Saxons.[12]

Unless some particularly specific quirk of Bestiary-lore is depicted – such as the sentinel crane with the pebble clutched in its claw which will drop on its foot and wake it, should it fall asleep, carved on a misericord at Denston – it is not always easy to decide whether an image is likely to derive immediately from the Bestiary, or only possibly, at some remove. It has recently been shown that Bestiary manuscripts functioned primarily as handy sources of sermon anecdotes (*exempla*) for preachers, especially among the Cistercians.[13] It is thus no surprise to find under the entry *canis* that:

> They gladly dash out hunting with Master, and will even guard his body when dead and not leave it. In sum, it is part of their nature that they cannot live without men. So much do dogs adore their owners that one can read how when King Garamantes was captured by his enemies and sold into slavery, two hundred of his hounds, having made up a party rescued him from exile out of the middle of the whole battle-line of his foes, and fought those who resisted.[14]

This story was not included in the original late classical Latin *Physiologus* text on which the English Bestiaries are based, but seems to have been first introduced and illustrated in the so-called Second Family manuscripts, appearing first in the late twelfth century. The manuscript reproduced here dates from the 1220s or '30s and shows the capture of the King on the left and the rescue by his dogs on the right (Figure 3.1). Something very like this story was painted in Henry III's palace at Westminster according to a document dated 30 June 1256, which authorises payment to Master William of Westminster for having painted:

> at Westminster, in the wardrobe where the King is wont to wash his head, a certain picture of the King who was rescued by his dogs from the sedition plotted against the same King by his subjects.[15]

Ross believed that the subject was 'no doubt an unusual one for a wall-painting', but as it happens, we can now cite explicit evidence to the contrary, for the Master of the Game, translating some twenty years later, the *Livre de Chasse* (1387–9) of Gaston Phebus, notes that 'men may se painted in the reaume of France' in many places, the story of Aubrey's faithful greyhound and the murderer Maquaire (compare the international folktale of that other faithful hound Gelert, above).[16]

Cats and Cat-skinning

The Bestiary, that compendium of unnatural history, is uncharacteristically laconic in its entry on the cat.[17] The usual popular etymologies are perpetrated, including the suggestion that the name *catus* derives from the Latin verb *captare*, 'to catch', but they are clearly set in the context of catching mice, and there is no doubt that it is in relation to the mouse and its usefulness as a mouser, that the cat was valued in medieval life and thought. The tenth-century Welsh *Law of Hywel Dda*, for example, says about the cat:

> The value of a kitten from the night it is born until it opens its eyes, one legal penny; and from then until it kills mice, two legal pence; and after it kills mice, four legal pence, and at that it remains for ever. Her properties are to see and hear and kill mice.

Certainly it is in relation to the mouse that the cat is most often depicted in art; typical is an early fourteenth-century misericord carving in Winchester Cathedral

1 Robert of Knaresborough Ploughs with stags: stained glass window (detail), St Matthew's Church, Morley, *c.* 1482.

here layut rob ert plos rth wyth the deere

2 Flemish Proverbs: tapestry fragment, Flemish, late 15thC.

3 Composite phallic head, inscribed in retrograde *TESTA DE CAZI*:
maiolica plate, Casteldurante, 1536.

4 Landgraf Ludwig I von Hessen and his arms hanged upside down: painted manuscript *Schandbild*, German, 1438.

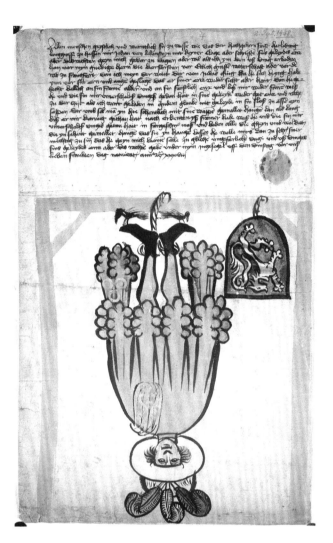

5 Sow soils seal of Herzog Johann von Bayern-Holland: painted manuscript *Schandbild*, German, *c.* 1420.

6 *Netherlandish Proverbs*, Bruegel the Elder, oil on canvas, 1557.

which shows the cat with a mouse dangling from its jaws. As always with this kind of apparently representational art, we cannot be certain whether there might not be some metaphorical meaning behind it. An *exemplum* in Arnold of Liège's *Alphabetum Narrationum*, composed originally in 1308, for example, and thus exactly contemporary with the Winchester misericord, compares the Devil and the human soul to a cat playing with a mouse, or, as Caxton puts it in his *Royal Book* published in 1484: 'The devyl playeth ofte with the synnar, lyke as the catte doth with the mous.'

But as we have already noted with dogs, there is evidence that domestic cats also inspired the affection of their owners. A particularly popular name for a domestic cat in late medieval England, a 'pet-name' indeed, was Gibbe, the pet-form of Gilbert. It is almost a type-name, significantly chosen to anglicise *Tiberz* in the English translation of the *Roman de la Rose*,[18] and 'Gyb our cat' is the animal responsible for killing Jane Scrope's pet sparrow (also type-named) in Skelton's elegiac 'Phyllyp Sparowe' (*a.* 1509),[19] as he is also the hero-villain of the Tudor comedy *Gammer Gurton's Needle*. He makes what is apparently his earliest appearance, however, on the personal seal of one Gilbert Stone attached to a document in the Public Record Office dated 1392;[20] it depicts a cat with a mouse in its mouth and the perimeter legend *GRET: WEL: GIBBE: OURE: CAT* (see chapter ornament).[21]

The cat is also renowned for her cunning, of course – and in this she is akin to the fox. An amusing inhabited initial in an early thirteenth-century English psalter shows a cat standing behind a lectern reading, or perhaps preaching, to a mouse – the similarity to the Preaching Fox who, having lulled his congregation into a sense of false security will pounce and devour them, is striking (see Chapter 9).[22] The tables are turned, however, on a capital in Tarragona Cathedral, carved *c.* 1210; here one face of the capital depicts the apparently dead cat being carried by a large number of rodent bearers on a bier, but turning the corner of the capital, the sculptor has shown the cat suddenly come alive and pouncing on the foolish mice – another of Renard's exploits. But the cat does not have it all her own way, as in one of the fables told by the thirteenth-century English preacher Odo of Cheriton, 'The Mouse in the Beer-jug'. A mouse who has fallen into a jug of beer is rescued from drowning by a cat, but only after the promise has been extracted from her that she will come again to the cat when she is called. When the cat does call, the mouse declares her promise worthless, as not only was it sworn under duress, but when she was drunk![23]

Like most symbols in art, the cat can potentially be interpreted *in bono* and *in malo*. We have already noted the tendency to allegorise the way the cat plays with its prey in which it may symbolise the Devil. This potential for devilish interpretation may account for the oft-rehearsed allegation that heretical sects such as the Waldensians and Paterini paid homage to their god in the form of a monstrous black cat by administering an anal kiss, the so-called *osculum infame*, as rendered by the artist who illuminated the frontispiece to a fifteenth-century French translation of Tinctoris, *Tractatus Contra Sectum Valdensium*, in which one of the manifestations of the god is distinctly feline.[24] The Waldensians were also popularly known by the name Cathars, and it seems to have been Alain de Lille who first had the bright idea of identifying the initial element of the name with the devilish cat, in the popular etymologising vein that came naturally to medieval clerics. The late twelfth-century *Winchester Bible*

Figure 3.2

illustrates Mattathias beheading the idolatrous Jew by a drawing which shows his decapitated head left on the altar of what is clearly a cat idol (Figure 3.2).[25]

In this context, and given their status as a favourite pet with elderly women, it is hardly surprising that the animal should often figure as the witch's familiar. As early as 1324 one of the forms in which the incubus appeared to the Irish witch Alice Kyteler was that of a cat. In fact, the cat might be the witch herself in one of her shape-shifting manifestations; as early as the *Otia Imperialia* of Gervase of Tilbury (*c.* 1211), we read that 'women have been seen and wounded in the shape of cats by persons who were secretly on watch'; they were wounded while in feline guise, and subsequently these same wounds were noticed on the women after they had reverted to human form.[26] It is a story repeated in the infamous *Malleus Maleficarum* (*c.* 1486). Two supporters to a misericord in Winchester Cathedral carved *c.* 1305 have been interpreted as depicting just such an episode, but there are several difficulties in the way of this.[27] By the time of the late fifteenth-century depictions of witches by Hans Baldung Grien, however, they are often accompanied by cats.

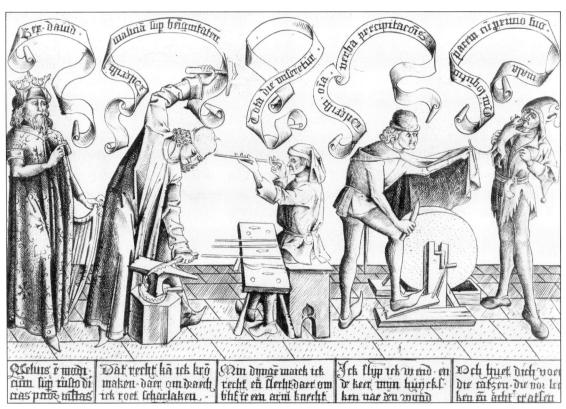

Figure 3.3

As for the proverbial cat, there seem to be more unfavourable than favourable representations in medieval art. Popular in Germanic lands is 'Beware of cats who lick your face but scratch your back'. It is found on a late fifteenth-century woodcut-illustrated single sheet, though the cut of a cat bringing a mouse back to its kitten does not seem especially apposite to the caption. The same proverb is inscribed on the fourteenth-century choir-stalls of St Leonhardskirche in Basel, in the form 'Cursed be the cats who lick your face but scratch your back', which may, in fact, antedate all the known literary examples.[28] It also features as one of the four proverbs engraved on a single sheet by Israhel Van Meckenem *c.* 1495 (Figure 3.3).

A rather curious idiom which seems to be restricted to English, and of which I know of only one illustration, is 'to turn the cat in the pan', which means 'to reverse the order of things so dexterously as to make them appear the very opposite of what they really are; to turn a thing right about' (*OED*). It is first found in a text attributed to Wyclif and dated 1383: 'Many men of lawe . . . bi here suteltes turnen the cat in the panne'. Curiously the proverb dictionaries can cite no fifteenth-century instances, and yet only a generation after Wyclif's use the idiom is actually illustrated by an ink drawing in the margin of a legal manuscript known as the Muschamp Moot Book (Figure 3.4).[29] The legal context is interesting and – *pace* later attempts at rationalising etymologies – the early fifteenth-century artist clearly envisaged a real cat in a real (frying-)pan!

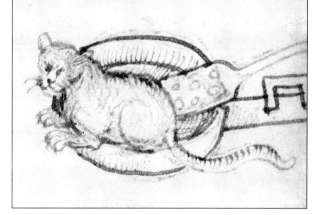

Figure 3.4

A more popular and European-wide proverbial idiom is that of 'belling the cat', deriving from the Aesopic fable; it is found as one of the proverbs depicted on the fragmentary Flemish tapestry now in the Isabella Stewart Gardner Museum and Art Gallery in Boston (Colour Plate 2), and on a contemporary misericord at Kempen on the Lower Rhine near the Dutch border carved in 1493.

The one idiom in which the cat seems to come off worse, is the story behind the English word *cat's-paw*, in the sense, 'A person used as a tool by another to accomplish a purpose' (*OED*). The *OED* notes that the earlier form is *cat's-foot*, and under the entry for that word explains, 'used . . . in reference to the fable or tale of a monkey . . . using the foot or paw of a cat to rake roasted chestnuts out of the burning coals. The story is told by some of a monkey belonging to Pope Julius II.'[30] An emblem in Sambucus's *Emblemata* (Antwerp, 1564) was recently described as 'the earliest known written version of this fable',[31] but, in fact, the dupe here is a dog. The earliest unequivocal feline version of the anecdote I am aware of, however, is found (and illustrated) in *De Warachtighe Fabulen Der Dieren*, a Flemish paraphrase of Aesop's *Fables*, published with Dutch verses by Eduard de Dene in Bruges in 1567, and illustrated with 108 small etchings by Marcus Gheeraerts the Elder.[32]

Catskins

Having rehearsed some of the symbolic uses of the cat in the art of the late Middle Ages, and at the risk of offending all cat-loving readers, I turn now to one particular actual use of the animal – the skinning of domestic cats for their fur.

The forlorn tabby-catskin hanging down from the back-basket carried by the man in the Bosch painting now in Rotterdam's Museum Boijmans-van-Beuningen had long puzzled me as, indeed, it seems to have puzzled most commentators. This *tondo* shows us Bosch in his 'realist' mode, not the more notorious (and thus inevitably better-known) Bosch of the hellish nightmare. The man at the centre of the composition has been variously described by art historians as – neutrally – a Wayfarer, or specifically, as The Prodigal Son.[33] Curiously, I believe the catskin is actually one of those diagnostic details which enables us to identify this man for certain.

It is scarcely possible to set about trying to research a topic like cat-skinning in the late Middle Ages in any systematic way, and so I suppose the detail of the tabby-catskin hanging sadly from the back-basket must have lain dormant in my subconscious for some years, until brought to the surface again by one of those moments of serendipity for which all researchers must be grateful.

The English encyclopedist known as Bartholomeus Anglicus closed his description of the cat in his mid-thirteenth-century *De Proprietatibus Rerum* on this somewhat elegiac note: 'The catte is ofte for his fayre skynne ytake of the skynnere and yslayne and yhulde' (flayed) – as translated by Trevisa in 1398.[34] But it is the matter-of-factness of this statement that should impress us – there was nothing unusual in the thirteenth century about skinning domestic cats! The identical sentiment is expressed proverbially in that curious composition, The Dialogue of Solomon and Marcolf in which Marcolf says, 'A cat that has a good skin shall be flayed.'

Late medieval literature provides evidence that catskins were precisely the sort of wares carried around by the lowest classes of itinerant tradesmen – by pedlars, indeed – but scorned by higher-class salesmen. In the B-text of *Piers Plowman* (*c.* 1377) Langland has Covetousness say:

> I have as much pite of povere men as pedlere hath of cattes,
> That wolde kille hem, if he cacche hem myghte, for coveitise of hir skynnes.[35]

But closer to the date of Bosch's painting, there is another significant citation in a fifteenth-century English carol:

> *We ben chapmen lyght of fote,*   [We are chapmen light of foot
> *The fowle weyis for to fle*   the foul ways we avoid
> *We bern abowtyn non cattes skynnys,*   we don't carry around catskins
> *Pursis, perlis, syluer pynnis . . .*[36]   purses, pearls, silver pins . . .]

The chapmen are anxious that we should realise that they are superior to the pedlars, that they do not carry around with *them* such pedlars' wares as purses, pins and catskins! Throughout Europe cats were skinned for their fur, but only for the humblest customers – it is this association with relatively impoverished wearers which explains why a number of monastic rules from the eleventh century onwards specify that even senior members of the order are not permitted to trim their hoods, for example, with fur of any higher grade than cat.[37]

A German literary reference attests to the ignominy associated with skinning cats – skinners, tanners, knackers and any artisans obliged to work with animal carcases were always bound to be considered 'Ignoble People' as Danckert calls them[38] – but in a society which arranged its animals as well as its professions hierarchically, a cat-skinner was pretty near the bottom of the heap; indeed, *Katzenschinder* (cat-flayer) was used as a derogatory term for furriers in the German-speaking world from at least the fifteenth century. It is so used in Michael Beheim's *Buch von den Wienern* (1462), for example, and in 1519 we hear of a group of Leipzig students who got into a slanging-match with a group of furriers' apprentices who they abused as *katzen-schynder*.[39]

But to return to Bosch's painting: where does all this get us? Well, it seems to me that we have found that cat-skinning was regarded as one of the lowliest, if not actually one of the most disreputable, occupations it was possible to pursue, that catskins constituted one of the lowest grades of fur it was possible to buy in the late Middle Ages, and furthermore, that they were one of the typical wares carried from village to village by pedlars, and that this strongly suggests that the man painted by Bosch is not intended to be a symbolic Prodigal Son as de Tolnay would have it – he is not even a neutral Wayfarer as Walter Gibson styles him – he is a Pedlar, and personally, I am not disposed to read anything more symbolic than that into the catskin hanging from his back-basket.

Unicorn

On one of the misericords of Beverley Minster carved in 1520 a lion confronts a stag, while on the 'supporters' which – as uniquely in the English corpus, flank the central subject – a crowned lion opposes a unicorn which is nonchalantly scratching its head with a hind hoof.[40] Another confrontation, which, it seems, cannot be fortuitous, is afforded by the unicorn that occupies the central carving on another Beverley misericord, while opposite its pointing horn, carved in low relief in the stall-division spandrel, is a positively provocative lion-mask with sticking-out tongue. It is difficult not to see in this opposition a deliberate confrontation of these two heraldic beasts on the part of the carver, but what evidence is there for our unthinking modern linking of the lion and the unicorn?

Long before the lion and the unicorn came to be heraldically confronted as 'royal beasts' in the arms of England at the Act of Union in 1603, they had appeared opposite each other, as heraldic supporters of the Valois arms, for example, on the famous late fifteenth-century *Dame à la Licorne* tapestries, and they also support the shield of the early sixteenth-century Parisian bookseller Olivier Senant.[41] The lion and the unicorn, flanking respectively a man and a woman, are also found on two fifteenth-century *Minnekästchen*, one German, the other French,[42] 'the lion symbolizing the strength and courage of the man and the unicorn the chastity of the lady'.[43] There is further an interesting record of a vestment 'powdered' with lions and unicorns in an English inventory of 1530.[44]

The history of this iconographical confrontation between the lion and the unicorn, however, goes back much further, to the earliest illustrations of the words of Psalm 22:21 (AV), in which the Psalmist prays: 'Save me from the lion's mouth: for thou hast heard me, from the horns of the unicorns.'

Exactly contemporary with the carving of the Beverley stalls, a non-biblical reference which also mentions this by now traditional opposition between the lion and the unicorn is found in *Of the newe landes and of ye people founde by the messengers of the kynge of portyngale named Emanuel*, the first book printed in English (albeit in Antwerp) to include a report of the discovery of America. In the tradition of associating mysterious beasts, and indeed races, with far-off lands, in one of the five accounts of voyages of exploration contained in this volume, there is mention of the deadly feud between the two animals: 'These vnicornes slee many Lyons, and the Lyon sleeth the vnicorne with subtylnes.'[45]

That the unicorn did not exist was no hindrance to the medieval imagination; after all, its existence is vouched for by the Bible (as above), and the Bestiary, of course, which reports that it:

> can be trapped by the following stratagem. A virgin girl is led to where it lurks, and there she is sent off by herself into the wood. He soon leaps into her lap when he sees her, and embraces her, and hence he gets caught.

The illustrations make it clear that the way the unicorn 'gets caught' is that, in a highly unsporting manner, a man previously hidden behind a tree, jumps out and spears it! The scene itself, with the unicorn's horn buried in the lap of the virgin, is clearly a gift for amateur psychologists, but for the moment at least, I resist that temptation. A distinct sub-type of this motif, doubtless motivated by the Bestiary's moralisation, 'Our Lord Jesus Christ is also a unicorn spiritually', replaces the virgin with the Virgin, an allegorical hunt particularly popular at the end of the fifteenth century and existing in several tapestries, paintings and other versions.[46]

Another unicorn scene which enjoyed some popularity was that in which it is shown dipping its horn into a pool to purify it, as on a misericord from Cartmel Priory and on one of the superb set of *Unicorn Hunt* tapestries (*c.* 1500) now in the Metropolitan Museum in New York. Several examples of unicorn horns are listed in medieval inventories of princely collections and cathedral treasuries, and of two extant examples in San Marco in Venice, one bears the name of a Byzantine Emperor, John V or VI Palaeologus, as well as biblical passages and a Greek text extolling the unicorn's efficacy against poison.[47] This reputation the unicorn had from late antiquity as an antidote for poison, as mentioned by Aelian, for example, led to a demand for unicorn horns which the market was happy to supply. As Earl Rivers remarked in his *Dictes* (1477), 'Ther is summe contre that a litil yuory or vnycorne bone is bought for a grete somme of gold' – presumably only the original salesman knew that the horn was in fact that of a narwhal, as was the example sold in 1994 at Christie's in London for £400,000. Together with a close relation in the Victoria and Albert Museum, this is an intricately carved piece of twelfth-century date.

It was clearly this aspect of the fabulous beast that was uppermost in the mind of King James I of Scotland when in his book *The Kingis Quair* (1423) he referred to 'The lufare vnicorne, That voidis venym with his euoure horne' (The friendly unicorn that renders venom harmless with his ivory horn). It is perhaps not surprising that European monarchs should be most concerned with the possibility of being poisoned, and in 1488 Margaret of Denmark, wife of James III of Scotland, owned 'a serpent toung & one unicorne horne set in gold', while the King himself owned four 'serpent tonguis' (that is, the fossilised shark's teeth we have already observed for sale in the jeweller's shop painted by Petrus Christus in Chapter 2). In 1451 in England we hear of a 'ryng of vnicorn horne',[48] while the future Henry VIII of England had 'a unicornes bone and a serpente tonge hang[ing] be a cheyne', according to an inventory of his possessions made in 1504 when Prince Henry was thirteen.[49]

Licked into Shape

This is what the Bestiary has to say about the bear:

> they say that these creatures produce a formless foetus, giving birth to something like a bit of pulp, and this the mother-bear arranges into the proper legs and arms by licking it.

Or as the author of the *Pilgrimage of the Sowle* (1413), printed seventy years later by Caxton, puts it:

> Beres ben brought forthe al fowle and transformyd [misshapen] and after that, by lyckynge of the fader and the moder, they ben brought in to theyr kyndely [natural] shap.[50]

It would thus appear that the perfectly normal post-parturition process among mammals of the expulsion of the after-birth and the licking of the new-born clean, has, in the case of this particular mammal, given rise to the bizarre story that the she-bear literally 'licks her cubs into shape', as we still say in everyday English, while no longer recognising the origin of the expression, and the French and German vernaculars similarly still use the expression 'an unlicked bear' to refer to a coarse, ill-bred person.[51] This Bestiary-derived belief was known to Shakespeare, however, who in *Henry VI Part Three* (1593), alludes to an 'vn-lick'd Beare-whelpe, That carryes no impression like the Damme' (III.ii.161), and reference to the notion became something of a commonplace among Jacobean authors, in their conventional expressions of modesty for their works.[52] Like so many other Bestiary motifs it was illustrated in the earliest emblem-books, appearing, for example, as the 98th emblem in Guillaume de la Perrière's *Théâtre des bons engins* (Paris, 1539). At much the same time, with typical Renaissance hubris, the painter Titian adopted it as his personal device, together with the motto, 'Art is stronger than Nature', perhaps after having seen it in that strange work purporting to decipher ancient Egyptian pictograms, the *Hieroglyphica of Horapollo*, first published in Venice in 1505.[53]

The Rat-porteur/Rapporteur

The late fifteenth-century misericord at Vendôme illustrated here (Figure 3.5) shows a man wearing a basket on his back and carrying a stick. He seems to be

Figure 3.5

running or at least walking very fast – we might imagine he is a pedlar but, if so, closer examination reveals that he is peddling small animals with long tails; two are clearly visible in the top of the basket and one pokes its head through a hole in the wickerwork halfway down. Like all such representations, this is quite mysterious if one does not recognise that it is the pictorialisation of a pun. One famous iconographer suggested this motif symbolised humanity burdened by the falsity of the world – providing another useful lesson for us; late medieval art is not always as portentous as art-historians seem naturally to believe.[54] There are further sixteenth-century examples of this motif on misericords at St Chamant (Cantal) and at Montbenoit Abbey (Doubs) on the border with Switzerland, where a fool with his bauble follows the mysterious man.[55]

In fact, this is the visualisation of a pun. The rat-carrier is a *rat-porteur = rapporteur* and this sort of 'reporter' is a tale-bearer, a bearer of false reports (a 'tail-bearer' perhaps!), and two *rats-porteurs* of this kind are depicted whispering in the ears of a king in a *Proverbes en rimes* manuscript in the British Library,[56] and in a fascinating illustrated manuscript in Paris, closely related to Henri Baude's *Ditz moraux pour faire tapisserie* (for which see Chapter 7).[57] Interestingly, this visual pun was also represented on stage, in the late fifteenth-century fool-play, the *Sottie nouvelle du Roy des Sotz* in which the sot Coquibus enters wearing a back-basket (hotte) so that the Roy des Sotz (King of the Fools) enquires, 'Qu'esse qu'il porte en ceste hotte?' Coquibus replies, 'Ce sont ratz', supplying the 'feed' for Sottinet to say, 'C'est un rapporteur!' And there are at least two further instances of this pun represented in art, for it was painted *c.* 1500 on one of the wooden ceiling panels of the Salle des Gardes at the château of Plessis-Bourré (Maine-et-Loire), and was also formerly to be found at the château of Branzac at Loupiac (Cantal) painted in 1571.[58]

Aubailly termed the genre to which the *Sottie nouvelle du Roy des Sotz* belongs, the *sottie-rébus*, and I add another similar animal example relevant to our misericord iconography. In the *Sottie des sots qui corrigent le Magnificat*, the pedant Dando enters carrying a goose in his arms, for his speciality is said to be *ferrer les oies* (shoeing geese),[59] as depicted on misericords at St Martin-aux-Bois in late fifteenth-century France, and at Walcourt in Belgium *c.* 1520, at Whalley in Lancashire (*c.* 1445) (Figure 7.11), and again on one of the ceiling panels of the château at Plessis-Bourré. A further example of this motif appears on one of the fascinating early sixteenth-century *monnaies des innocents*, figuring in a rebus of the surname

DAVERLOIS (as if <*davier l'oie* meaning 'frame the goose').[60] In much the same spirit, Jacques Ferre-bouc (literally, 'Shoe-the-goat'), a Parisian printer active 1492–1530, made use of a rebus device depicting a blacksmith shoeing a goat (*bouc*) in a shoeing-frame.[61] In the context of the presentation of proverbs on stage, Aubailly also refers to the obscure piece of the 'Wakers of the sleeping cat', for which see Chapter 7.[62]

ANIMALS AS SEXUAL SYMBOLS

A still under-researched area of animal iconography is that of sexual animal symbolism. Joyce Salisbury draws attention to the hitherto apparently unremarked (or, at least, uncommented upon) erection, with which William the Conqueror's horse is depicted on the Bayeux Tapestry:

> the man and his stallion were linked in a complex tie that metaphorically associated sexuality with power. In the tapestry, William's power was expressed by his horse's erection.[63]

Elsewhere in the same book she notes that in the *Laws and Customs of England* as codified by the thirteenth-century lawyer Bracton, it is stated that the horse belonging to a man found guilty of rape (who will himself suffer the loss of his own life and members), 'By the law of the Romans, the Franks and the English . . . shall to his [that is, the rapist's] disgrace, be dishonoured upon its scrotum and its tail, which shall be cut off as close as possible to the buttocks.'[64]

Clearly the man and beast were closely identified in their sexuality, in life as in art – it will come as no surprise to the modern reader, used to the term 'stud', defined by the *OED* as 'A man of (reputedly) great sexual potency or accomplishments', but the use of some other animals or animal parts to signify the sexuality of a man or woman, or more specifically, their respective sexual organs, may.

The Ass

But not the ass, surely. During a vacation job on a building site in 1973 I found myself working alongside a painter known familiarly to his workmates as 'Donkey-prick'. I was not still so naive as not to be able to guess why, but with some relish, the sobriquet was explained to me anyway – it is curious, how persons of a perceived academic bent are popularly supposed to be entirely ignorant of sexual matters! But it was only long after graduating that I discovered that the ass had long enjoyed this particular reputation, a piece of 'low' folk-culture that can be traced as far back as the burlesque medieval Latin *Testamentum domini asini* in which the ass leaves to widows in his will his *priapum . . . una cum testiculis*.[65] The popular currency of this reputation is confirmed by the contemporary twelfth-century Catalan *trobador* Guilhem de Bergueda, described the Bishop of Urgel as having 'a bigger "hammer" than a Spanish mule'.[66] The only representation of such asinine endowment in late medieval art that I am aware of, however, is to be seen on one of the fascinating lead badges recently excavated from the drowned villages of the Schelde estuary, which depicts an ithyphallic ass wearing a cape over its shoulders sitting spinning at a distaff. What can this mean? I suggest that – as spinning is quintessentially a feminine occupation, conducted even in the *monde renversé* by a female animal, the sow – this is a World Turned Upside Down motif with a vengeance!

The Baboon

The baboon does not perhaps any longer spring to the modern mind in this context, but it certainly did in the fifteenth and sixteenth centuries. In a list of animal insults in his poem 'Agenst Garnesche' (1514), Skelton calls Sir Christopher Garnesche, 'Thou rammysche [like a ram] stynkyng gote' – another traditionally lascivious animal, of course – but also, 'Thow bawdy babyone'.[67] A century later, when performing baboons were enjoying a certain vogue on the stage, Shakespeare and Fletcher in their co-production, *The Two Noble Kinsmen* (1613), brought a country morris troupe on stage, one of whose members is dressed as a *bavian*, that is, a baboon. The schoolmaster who leads the team warns this actor, 'My friend, carry your tail without offense Or scandal to the ladies . . .',[68] in which *tail* probably means 'penis', as commonly in the drama of this period – the admonition was presumably necessary, to guard against what was doubtless all too predictable comic business for an actor dressed as a proverbially lustful animal. When introducing his troupe, indeed, the pedant refers unequivocally to what must have been the 'animal's' very apparent genital endowment: 'The Bavian, with long tail and eke long tool' (and also long penis/and penis just as long).

Visual proof that the baboon was, indeed, considered a notably phallic animal is afforded by a Florentine sheet of twenty-four roundels engraved with animals, probably as patterns for a set of playing-pieces, *c.* 1460; the baboon is unique in being the only animal to be identified by name (*BABVINO*) and the only one shown in a state of evident sexual arousal (Figure 3.6).[69]

Figure 3.6

Figure 3.7

Cockerel

It is often said that the cockerel 'symbolises lust', as if this symbolism were well known and copiously attested, but proofs of this assertion are rarely offered and are, in fact, by no means as common as such formulations might seem to suggest.

Particularly useful are those relatively few instances where the abstract Vices are represented and allotted particular animals as attributes, heraldic badges, and so on. On the famous Regensburg tapestry (*c.* 1390), for example, Luxuria wears a rose garland on her head surmounted by a long-tailed cockerel as her crest.[70] In a contemporary German manuscript, Bloomfield noted that Lechery appears in the form of a beautifully clothed woman with loose and disordered hair, carrying a cockerel,[71] while on a chimney-piece of the first half of the fifteenth century on which St Magdalena and six animal-headed Vices are depicted, it is presumably the cock-headed figure that is intended as Luxuria.[72] Unequivocal evidence is afforded by the late fifteenth-century Bavarian emblematic catechism, in which both the sixth of the Seven Deadly Sins, Lechery, and the seventh of the Ten Commandments, 'Thou shalt not commit adultery', are symbolised by a cockerel(Figure 3.7).[73]

These are firmly established examples in late medieval art of the equivalence, cockerel = lust/lechery, but it should be noted both that they are all relatively late, and that all hail from the Germanic area. Be that as it may, there is evidence of a non-iconographic type which seems to confirm this symbolism, both in Germany and elsewhere. Its sexual connotations are confirmed by the appearance of the bird perched on the shoulders of mercenaries' whores in German prints of the 1530s,[74] and in such similarly equivocal contexts as the seal matrix depicting a naked man and woman with a helm and shield between them on both of which stand cockerels.[75] Thus, when in a drawing of 1529 by Pieter Coecke van Aelst, the young man reaches into his basket to pull out a live cock as an offering to the girl with whom he has been gaming in the tavern, the artist is surely signalling the young man's true intentions.[76]

We come next to a consideration of a multiple erotic pun in one of Dürer's engravings and its implications for understanding the specifically phallic symbolism of the bird. In *The Men's Bath* (*c.* 1500) the artist has placed one of the bathers standing behind the tap in such a way that its spout is on a level with his breech-cloth, an obviously suggestive positioning, and moreover the tap handle is itself in the form of a cockerel.[77] A fascinating network of semantic relationships is thus alluded to by the artist, as well as antedating by a century the earliest recorded literary attestation in the Grimms' German dictionary of the word *hahn* (cock) in the sense 'penis'. In the sense 'tap, stopcock' it is attested as early as 1503 in German, 'if the child turns a cock, all the wine runs out', and as the *OED* remarks for this 'stopcock' sense of English *cock*, 'the resemblance of some stop-cocks to a cock's head with its comb, readily suggests itself'. Indeed, there are at least two such cockerel-shaped taps to be found on aquamanili (bronze vessels from which water was poured for washing one's hands prior to a meal) cast in Nürnberg *c.* 1400, as well as a fifteenth-century tap found on the Thames foreshore (Figure 3.8), in addition to the tap in Dürer's engraving. I suggest, therefore, that the use of German *hahn*, and English *cock* for a stopcock or tap reflects another late medieval *realium* (see pp. 58–60 for others). The fact that a stopcock is the key which controls the emission of fluid, but one which in the late Middle Ages often took the form of a cockerel, that proverbially lascivious bird, can only have reinforced the phallic symbolism of the bird in art.

Figure 3.8

Confirmation that the word *coc* could indeed also mean 'penis' as early as *c.* 1300 is provided – in the most extraordinarily graphic manner – by, to my knowledge, a uniquely explicit depiction of the sex organs engaged in intercourse on a bronze seal matrix found recently at Wicklewood in Norfolk (Figure 3.9). According to the perimeter legend (*IAS:TIDBAVLCOC*) it is the personal seal of one 'James Tidbaulcoc', whose surname is composed of a Middle English form of the personal name Theobald, plus -coc, which also functions as a diminutive at this period in such surnames as Simcock (that is, 'little Simon'), Wilcocks

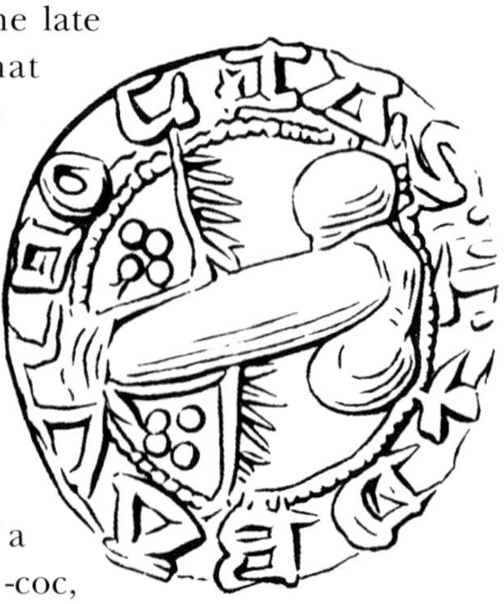

Figure 3.9

(that is, 'little William'), etc., but here the designer is clearly punning on the penile sense of *cock* (as attested in the contemporary *pilkoc* – see the *OED* s.v. *pillicock*, 'penis'), and on *ball* in the still current sense, 'testicle', and – perhaps – on the Middle English adverb *tid*, 'quickly', or *astid*, 'immediately, urgently'.

There is reason to believe the equivoque was also a literary commonplace for there is an early fifteenth-century English poem which opens, 'I haue a gentil cook' (I have a noble cockerel), in which the cockerel/penis *double entendre* is also clearly present, as after describing this magnificent bird in some detail, the burden carries a sting in the tail: 'and every night he perches in my lady's chamber'.[78]

It was undoubtedly observation of the strutting lord of the barnyard harem that led naturally to this symbolism, and it is surely significant that among the many and often bizarre lead badges of sexual content which are emerging in increasing numbers from riverine deposits throughout Europe, that of the cock treading the hen should figure as one of the few to have been found in England.[79] Further significant testimony is afforded by a very 'primitive'-seeming ritual which at the beginning of the thirteenth century could be witnessed in Rome every first Sunday in Lent. After watching a play and witnessing the death of a bear which represented the Devil, the Pope and his retinue would go to Mount Testaccio, where, according to the contemporary account, a cock would be killed, the act representing 'the lasciviousness of our loins, so that from then on, we might live chastely and our souls should be worthy to receive the body of Christ at Easter'.[80]

Nor can it be an accident that fifteenth-century folk-medicine prescribes 'to make a woman love you, the two testicles of a cockerel', powdered and given in a drink.[81] In the same way, the extraordinary *Evangiles de Quenouilles* (translated into English and published by de Worde as *The Gospelles of Dystaues* in 1507) prohibits the young girl from eating sheeps' heads, cocks' combs or eels – all, presumably, phallic symbols, if by 'sheeps' heads' we infer the horned ram's head. Eating such 'foods' – if the list is anything other than mere fantasy (it seems unlikely cocks' combs were eaten at all!) – would give her epilepsy, but this condition was also popularly known as the 'falling sickness' in several vernaculars (as a translation of the Latin *morbus caducus*) and this term was also used as a popular pun to denote the seduction of a girl who had 'fallen' in the sexual sense.[82]

Rabbit (Coney) and Other Lovers' Pet Names

If the cockerel may at times stand for the penis (as in English *cock* and German *hahn*), the rabbit often stands for the vulva (*coney* in English, that is, *cunny*, and compare *connin* in French).

By the seventeenth century, in popular drama and broadside ballads, the convention that the vagina is a *coney-burrow*, the penis a *coney-burrow ferret* and the sexual pursuit a *coney hunt* has become a commonplace of erotic diction.[83] But it seems likely that the *double entendre* was available much earlier, as in this passage from Heywood's *Proverbs and Epigrams* of 1562:

> Jane, thou sellest sweete conies in this pultry shoppe
> But none so sweete as thy selfe, sweete conye moppe.[84]

In the list of endearments contemporary with this from the interlude *The Trial of Treasure* (1567), *cony* again appears with *swete*:

> My dere lady.
> My mouse, my nobs and cony swete,
> My hope and ioye, my whole delight.[85]

But this is very reminiscent of a similar passage of lovers' endearments in Skelton's *Tunnyng of Elynour Rummyng*, half a century earlier (*c.* 1517), where Elynour tells one of her gossips the pet names her husband calls her:

> Whan we kys and play
> In lust and in lykyng.
> He calleth me his whytyng,
> His mullyng and his mytyng,
> His nobbes and his conny,
> His swetyng and his honny,
> With, 'Bas, my prety bonny.'[86]

Interestingly, the rhyme with *honny* (honey) shows that *bonny* is our modern 'bunny', or 'bunny-rabbit', and thus antedates by almost a century the *OED*'s first citation of *bunny* in this sense from *Wily Beguiled* (1602): 'Sweet Peg . . . my honey, my *bunny*, my duck, my dear'.[87]

It is clear from the above that the use of pet names by lovers is no recent fashion, and it has been rightly said that it is preponderantly 'small furry animals [which] belong to the iconography of sensuality'.[88] The word *mouse* is used as such an endearment in English early in the Elizabethan period (1567) as above, and at times it too takes on an equivocal sense. In Shakespeare, for example, Capulet had been a *mouse-hunt*, that is, a hunter of 'mice', in his rakish youth, and Hamlet counsels his mother not to:

> Let the bloat King tempt you to bed,
> Pinch wanton on your cheek, call you his mouse,[89]

where the sexual overtones seem very much to the fore. But we can cite several much earlier medieval examples of this symbolism. In a *fabliau* entitled *La sorisete des estopes*, the bride tells her naive bridegroom that she has left her *con* at her mother's house. Understandably alarmed, he hurries off to retrieve it, and on arriving at the house, is given a mouse in a basket by the bride's mother.[90] Another illustration of this equation can be found in what seems at first sight a bizarre drawing by the Swiss artist Urs Graf (dated 1529), which depicts a prostitute taking a mouse for a walk on a lead, thereby constituting a sort of walking advertisement of her services.[91]

Love's Hunt

Much more frequently than a 'mouse-hunt', in medieval French (as we have already noticed for later English), the male lover's pursuit of the woman is referred to as a 'rabbit-hunt', the *chace du connin* as it is termed in Jean de Meung's immensely influential *Roman de la Rose* (*c.* 1275). This conceit is, indeed, a commonplace of medieval erotic thought. In his *Libro de Buen Amor* (1330), for example, the Spanish Archpriest of Hita, Juan Ruiz, refers to the lover as a 'rabbiter' (*conejero*),[92] while in the General Prologue to the *Canterbury Tales* Chaucer employs essentially the same image as part of the characterisation of his very worldly Monk: 'Of prikyng and of hunting for the hare Was al his lust . . .'[93] The two English words spelled 'venery' are etymologically distinct, but Spenser was certainly not the only English writer unable to resist the coincidence:

> To the wood she goes, to
> seeke her spouse,
> That from her still does fly,
> And followes other game and venery.[94]

In the art of courtly love the male lover is sometimes symbolised by the hound leaping onto the rabbit/hare, as on an ivory mirror case of *c.* 1300 in the Victoria and Albert Museum.[95] In this sort of wish-fulfilment, the animals' actions foreshadow those of the human actors (here on horseback above them): the lover chucks the lady under the chin, a gesture which at this period was considered erotic rather than avuncular. A particularly eloquent example of the way in which the rabbit symbolises the physical goal of the lover's quest, is to be found in the upper margin of a Flemish psalter illuminated some time in the first quarter of the fourteenth century,[96] where we see the lady's head framed within the opening initial of the text, on top of which sits a rabbit, and opposite, as a line-ending, a male figure extends his hands in the familiar gesture of prayer. In the lower margin we see how the lover's prayers have been answered, as the lady is shown leading him to her bedchamber, pointing through an imposing doorway to the bed within, in which we are shown the consummation of their love. The text which these very secular drawings accompany is Isaiah 38, beginning at verse 10: 'I said, in the midst of my days I shall go to the gates of hell', the *portas inferni* (gates of hell) being playfully interpreted by the illuminator – superficially at least – as the doorway to the bedchamber whither the lover is drawn by the deadly sin of lust; but the image of a gate or doorway, of course, is itself an ancient sexual metaphor.

The rabbit has always been famed in the popular mind for its reproductive capacity and the depiction of pairs of rabbits in the margins of medieval manuscripts must often allude to the activity which, it is assumed, rabbits spend much of their time engaged in. It is significant, for example, that in the illustrations to a late thirteenth-century manuscript of Aristotle's *De Historiis Animalium* which depicts the copulation of the various animals discussed, the human coupling is observed by a pair of rabbits.[97] Similarly, in a fresco painted *c.* 1470 by Francesco del Cossa in the Palazzo Schifanoia in Ferrara, the courtly courting couples dallying in a rocky landscape dominated by the naked figures of the Three Graces, are surrounded by pairs of rabbits, which also accompany the chariot of Venus.[98] More explicitly, a drawing known as *Allegory of Lust* by Pisanello (d. 1455/6) depicts a naked woman on a bed of flames with a rabbit/hare at her feet.

Figure 3.10

Cockles and Mussels

We now know of two examples of fascinating lead amulets – if that is what they are – deposited *c.* 1400 and excavated in Rotterdam and Amsterdam. The Rotterdam piece is in the form of the two halves of a mussel shell, with an unmistakable vulva symbol incised on the inside of one of the valves (Figure 3.10). Clearly, the hidden or secret nature of the interior engraving is an important aspect of the piece. The Amsterdam piece, on the other hand, is a variant design in which a vulva peeps out through the opened shell (cast in one with the valve).[99] The best contemporary parallel to these late medieval amulets is to be found on the central panel of Bosch's *Garden of Earthly Delights*, probably painted *c.* 1510.[100] In the central foreground of this panel we are shown a naked couple copulating inside an outsize mussel shell, open sufficiently to expose the man's bare buttocks, scrotum and legs viewed from behind, and his partner's bare feet. A very similar detail (quite likely a deliberate quotation of the Bosch) is the naked couple within a transparent globe (?pearl) inside a mussel shell in Bruegel's *Luxuria* drawing of 1557. The English word *mussel* (ultimately from the Latin *muscula*), and its cognates in the Germanic and Romance languages, seems to be oddly devoid of erotic associations, but another bivalve, the cockle, and its immediate French original, *coquille*,[101] are indeed used to represent the female genitals. The word is so used, for example, in Villon's jargon,[102] and, *c.* 1505, in this passage from Roger de Collereye's parodic *Sermon pour une Nopce* [Sermon for a Wedding]:

> And thus, my young girls,
> do not proffer your 'cockles'
> to lords or to fools
> unless they offer you money![103]

and would appear to be first attested in this sense in the fourteenth century.[104]

For all its late date, there is a suggestive passage in John Aubrey's fascinating late seventeenth-century *Remaines of Gentilisme and Judaisme*:

> Young Wenches have a wanton sport, which they call 'moulding of Cocklebread': viz. they gett upon a Table-board, and then gather-up their knees and their Coates with their hands as high as they can, and then they wabble to and fro with their Buttocks as if they were kneading of Dowgh with their Arses, and say these words, viz. . . .

> My Dame is sick and gonne to bed
> And I'le go mowld my Cockle-bread.

Aubrey wrote that he had some reason to believe that 'the word cockle is an old antiquated Norman word, which signifies "arse" . . .',[105] but writing in 1892 concerning this passage, Northall noted that 'it is significant that the *labia minora* are still termed *cockles* in vulgar parlance',[106] a usage attested from at least the eighteenth century.[107] The seventeenth-century antiquary was surely correct, however, in citing as *comparandum*, a passage from Burchard of Worms' penitential manual of *c.* 1010, in which parish priests are exhorted to demand of the female parishioner at confession, whether she has ever kneaded bread with her buttocks, baked it, and then given it to a man she loved, in order that it might increase his love for her, and in his conclusion that, therefore, 'this practice is a relique of Naturall Magick: an unlawful Philtrum' (philtre).[108] Kittredge, the historian of witchcraft, noted that the same practice is alluded to in the *Arundel Penitential*, an English work of *c.* 1300.[109]

Foxtail

A popular secular attribute during the late Middle Ages was Reynard's quintessential badge, the foxtail. But like most such attributes it was far from univalent, perhaps the fetishism which still adheres to it as a hunting trophy today – and by the seventeenth century, in England and in Germany, it had already been allotted a name of its own (English *brush* or *drag*; German *Rute*)[110] – merely continues a singularity perceived since time immemorial. Most commonly, the tail functions as a *pars pro toto* so that when attached to a person, it connotes cunning, trickery, hypocrisy, and any other negative quality traditionally attributed to the fox.

One of its most important functions is as an attribute of the professional fool, as discussed in Chapter 6, but it seems also to have been felt appropriate as an insult, whether verbal or actual. About 1000, a monk in one of Aelfric Bata's *Colloquies* says to another, 'You are a fox tail'; it was presumably a meaningful insult,[111] and certainly, the attaching of a foxtail to a person's garment was considered an insult. Rabelais several times mentions the attachment of a foxtail for this purpose; one of Panurge's tricks is to mock academics he meets out walking in this manner.[112] But even in classical times Lactantius reports that boys in Rome would pin (cattle-)tails on passers-by in mockery, and, according to St Augustine's Anglo-Norman biographer Goscelin, writing around 1100, the inhabitants of Rochester mocked the saint by attaching fish tails to his garments – they were punished for this insult by themselves growing tails, the origin of the Kentish Longtails and popular medieval *Angli caudati* gibes (see Chapter 5).

Unequivocal evidence in art of the foxtail as an erotic (and, indeed, phallic) symbol is particularly plentiful in the sixteenth century, beginning with a South German drawing of about 1530 (Figure 3.11) which depicts a young seated woman whose fingers are nibbled by a fox, to which she says, 'little fox, present me your little tail'. From later in the century there are several examples of the motif of a naked woman with a fox trapped by the tail, which she holds (as if) to comb, between her legs;[113] by the seventeenth century, this motif is even found engraved on the front plate of an iron chastity belt, together with the inscription:

Figure 3.11

Stop little fox, I
have caught you.
You have often
wiped/rubbed me through there.[114]

In German this innuendo is undoubtedly motivated by the fact that *Rute* is a 'term of art' for the fox's tail specifically, but literally the word means 'rod' and is also a common euphemism for 'penis'. It is this same erotic foxtail motif which lies behind a curious fable that Rabelais relates in Chapter XV of *Pantagruel* (1532), the nub of which involves a *faux-naïf* lion exhorting a fox to wipe well an old woman's 'wound', both inside and out with his tail, in which the fox is clearly introduced for the sake of the visual innuendo of the foxtail between the woman's legs.[115]

A significant late medieval instance of a particular foxtail motif in art[116] is to be found on a brass dish of late fifteenth-century German manufacture depicting the popular scene of the dominant wife humiliating her husband (Figure 3.12). She sits astride him and thrashes his bared buttocks with a foxtail switch[117] – he is further humiliated by being portrayed holding the reel on which he has been winding the yarn spun by his wife – quintessentially women's work, of course (see Chapter 11). A contemporary *exemplum* from a German Latin collection, the *Mensa Philosophica* (*c.* 1470), involves nuns being punished by being struck three times with a foxtail; clearly this is not a physically painful punishment,

Figure 3.12

though it may have been considered particularly demeaning or dishonourable, but neither, one suspects, especially given the 'erotic foxtail' motif discussed above, can a suggestive element be entirely absent.[118]

But it seems that foxtails were also a genuine fashion accessory in the thirteenth century. In 'Der Jüngling' the Austrian poet Konrad von Haslau complains of the habit of some young dandies of hanging foxtails from their hats,[119] while in Edward II's early fourteenth-century England, the chronicler John of Reading wrote that '[Women's] bizarre clothing is so tight that they wear the tails of foxes hanging under their skirts at the back to hide their arses.'[120] Is Deschamps, writing around 1385, *à propos d'une femme débauchée*, alluding to the same fashion in France?

> What does she need? What does she need?
> A foxtail, of course,
> so that nothing should enter her body
> to give her 'belly-ache'.[121]

But sexual innuendo is also presumably present (compare with the 'erotic foxtail' discussed above). Or was there possibly some belief in the contraceptive power of the foxtail? The complex of associations and practices is quite bewildering!

Squirrel Nutcracker and the Nuthatch

On the left shoulder of a woodcut print known as *The Mercenary's Whore* (*c.* 1530), opposite the cock sitting on her right shoulder, sits a squirrel.[122] Is it sheer coincidence that on an English die-piece of the 1330s/40s for stamping out metal foil spangles to adorn garments and so on, the cockerel and the squirrel also appear to be a pair?[123]

I am far from suggesting that every depiction in medieval art of a woman holding, feeding and caressing a squirrel must necessarily carry a sexual connotation; there are many cases where that would be patently absurd, as squirrels were kept as pets by noblewomen (see, for example, one of the elaborate Chertsey tile royal portraits of the 1290s, on which Queen Eleanor is depicted holding a pet squirrel).[124] But equally, there are some contexts – especially given what we know of squirrel symbolism elsewhere in European art – where the animal's presence is equivocal. In his study of courtly love iconography, D.W. Robertson concluded that the squirrel sometimes 'represents the object of the lover's quest', and cited an ivory mirror-back in the Victoria and Albert Museum on which 'a lover leads away a lady who holds in her arm one of the "wigte gent and smale" which are symbols for the centre of feminine attractiveness, at least from the young lover's point of view'.[125] In similar vein, the ring-giving scene in the *bas-de-page* of the early fourteenth-century *Ormesby Psalter* in which the lady also holds a squirrel in one hand, has been interpreted as a 'bawdy betrothal',[126] while in a church context, such as the sedilia corbel in the church at Heckington depicting a woman feeding a squirrel, the woman is perhaps to be seen as an emblem of Luxuria.[127] The British Museum has a fifteenth-century ring bearing a *figura grammatica* erotic inscription, together with the engraved design of a woman holding a squirrel on a chain (Figure 3.13) – with which we

Figure 3.13

might compare the Urs Graf drawing of the woman with the mouse on a lead discussed on p. 52.[128]

A number of English personal seals also feature squirrels, at least six such bearing some version of the legend, I CRACK NUTS. This seems to me to be one of those equivocal inscriptions; indeed, I believe that this is another piece of sexual innuendo, though here the squirrel plays, as it were, a male role. The literary evidence in English to support this conclusion is admittedly late: the earliest I have been able to find is the passage of innuendo in Lyly's *Mother Bombie* (*c.* 1589):

A.   I love a nutbrowne lasse, tis good to recreate.
B.   Thou meanest, a browne nut is good to crack.
A.   Why wold it not do thee good to crack such a nut?[129]

In French, on the other hand, the evidence is early and unequivocal: in the thirteenth-century *fabliau* known as *L'Esquiriel*, Robin's 'squirrel' searches for the nuts eaten the day before by the heroine, in her 'belly'; elsewhere, in response to her interest in the commotion under his clothes, Robin explains that the squirrel is coming up out of its hole. It is in another *fabliau*, however, that the expression 'to crack nuts', meaning 'to have intercourse', occurs three times, and the *Roman de la Rose*, a work enormously influential on medieval European literature as a whole, goes so far as to refer to a *con crossue*, as if it were a 'nut' that had been 'cracked'.[130]

To return to the seal-legend I CRACK NUTS, the three dated examples (from charters) belong to the early years of the fourteenth century. It is always possible that these seals were used by people bearing appropriate surnames, such as Adam *Crackenot* (1296), William *Casnot* (1327),[131] and the several attested *Notehakes* (1220–1379), but of the half-dozen examples known, the two belonging to persons whose surnames are recorded do not bear this theory out. In view of the 'off the peg' appearance of these fairly stereotyped seals, it seems most unlikely that they were personalised for use only by those with suitable surnames, but had a wider appeal; there seems to me to be a jocular feel about them, which suggests they were designed for the medieval Jack-the-lad market, for the would-be man-of-the-medieval-world who fancied himself as a bit of a Don Juan, or at least, who was not averse to others thinking he was.

REALIA

Just as we still use words such as 'cat's paw', or idioms such as 'lick into shape' or 'curry favour' (for which see Chapter 7), which depend on stories we no longer know, a number of words that are still part of our vocabulary similarly owe their origins to medieval *realia* – long since obsolete, but depictions of which may be found in late medieval art. In English we still seem to lack a term corresponding to the German *Realienkunde* for the study of everyday objects from the distant past, whether in art or as archaeological material but I continue this chapter with a couple of examples of 'dead metaphors' which originate in such *realia* of medieval life.

Stalking-horse

In 1279 Almeric le Despenser, lord of Holsborough in Morton Underhill, and Ralf Bagot, the parson of Morton Underhill (both of whom should have known better) went poaching in the King's forest 'with a certain device made in the form of a horse, and beneath this device they went and poached two hinds'.[132] This is clearly the earliest reference to what we now term, though we do not use the term literally any more, a stalking-horse. The *OED* explains that a stalking-horse is:

> A horse trained to allow a fowler to conceal himself behind it or under its coverings in order to get within easy range of the game without alarming it. Hence, a portable screen of canvas or other light material, made in the figure of a horse (or sometimes of other animals), similarly used for concealment in pursuing game.

The first citation for the word in 1519 refers to a real horse so used, but as Markham explains in his *Fowling* (1621):

> Now forasmuch as these Stalking horses are not euer in readinesse. In this case he [the fowler] may take any pieces of oulde Canuasse, and hauing made it in the shape or proportion of a Horse, let it be painted as neere the colour of a Horse as you can deuise.

In fact, as the *OED*'s bracket rightly states, in Chapter 76 of *Le Livre de Chasse* (1387–9) Gaston Phebus describes a 'stalking cow', a sort of canvas screen in the form of a bovine silhouette (*une toile qui semble a un buef*), which is carried in front of the hunter and then rammed into the ground before making the shot, but the artist of an early fifteenth-century manuscript[133] has painted a sort of pantomime-horse, at the bottom of which we can just see the feet of the men hidden within it, and which can thus walk to the required vantage point on its own four feet!

Bell-wether

Exceptionally, because in conflict with the dictionary's practice which, being 'arranged on historical principles', presents the earliest attested sense of a word first, and the other senses in chronological order of attestation, the first sense of the word bell-wether in the *OED* is given as 'The leading sheep of a flock, on whose neck a bell is hung', from the *Promptorium Parvulorum*, here dated 1440, followed by a second sense, the figurative sense, 'A chief or leader', first attested in Lydgate's *Bochas*, here dated *c.* 1430.

In the nature of things, the figurative sense of a word can only evolve subsequent to the literal sense, and it is thus merely an accident of survival (or of the organisation of the *OED*'s reading programme) that in the recorded history of the word, the figurative sense appears to antedate the literal. The visual record can

Figure 3.14

come to the lexicographer's aid here, however, proving that the *realium*, the wether with the bell round his neck, is no mere etymologist's fancy, but was formerly to be seen in medieval English sheep pastures. The celebrated *Luttrell Psalter*[134] compiled a century before the earliest attestation of the word, includes a detailed depiction of a sheep-fold with just such a 'bell-wether' at its centre (Figure 3.14).

EXEMPLARY ANIMALS? – SYMBOLS OR PURE DECORATION?

It is often a problem to know whether or not a given representation was intended by the artist to be symbolic, of some Christian or other moral message perhaps, or merely ornamental. In interpreting such subjects the context – the type of adjacent subject, for instance – can sometimes be decisive, but often there can be no such certainty. It is also often assumed – mistakenly in my opinion – that because a subject appears, say, in a church building, it necessarily conveys some moral message, and much Procrustean ingenuity has been shown in moralising quite amoral decoration.

It is rarely possible to identify, in isolation, whether any particular carving was intended symbolically or merely decoratively, but taken in context, it should usually be possible to pronounce one way or the other. The mobbed owl is a case in point.

The Mobbed Owl

Curiously, the Bestiary does not mention the mobbing of the owl by small birds, but Bestiary artists seem often to have chosen to depict this behaviour despite having no textual prompt, though it does state that owls are symbolic of the Jews.[135] As the author of *Birds in Medieval Manuscripts* wrote, however, images of owls attacked by small birds are not necessarily symbolic, since such scenes would have been familiar from everyday observation.[136]

A late Dürer woodcut which depicts an owl mobbed by four smaller birds, has been related to a passage in a sermon by Geiler von Kaisersberg, delivered *c.* 1500, in which the famous preacher alludes to a man who, though ridiculed by his neighbours, is yet a useful member of society, by means of a comparison with the mobbed owl: 'Among them he is like nothing else but a howlet or owl among other birds.'[137]

Whatever the metaphorical possibilities of such a representation, however, I suspect the motif of the owl attacked from all sides by smaller birds simply afforded the artist the opportunity of executing an aesthetically satisfying composition – a composition especially well suited to the circular roof boss, as at Sherborne,[138] or the misericord at Norwich, generally agreed to be a particularly successful carving.

H-J. Raupp, in his superb study, summarised the history of modern scholarly interpretation of the 'profane' images in churches, a category into which the great bulk of misericord carvings fit.[139] Two earlier attitudes he saw as now superseded are the mainly nineteenth-century attempt to see all such apparently secular images as symbols within an all-inclusive theological programme, and the opposite extreme position, which he identified with the views of Emil Mâle, that such imagery was pure decoration, an expression only of the free play of the artist's imagination.

Thanks largely to the debate these earlier scholars' opinions generated, we are now in a position to accept that, for example, by the date of the carving of the Beverley Minster stalls (1520), their 'secular' imagery might be capable of either interpretation: an individual motif that is not overtly religious might theoretically be symbolic or purely decorative, but once again, the context should usually enable us to come down on one side or the other. A particular case in which the context suggests a symbolic reading of the image in question, and that, *in malo*, is the owl supporter to the misericord which depicts the Preaching Fox. Similarly, a 'rabbit trinity' carved on a misericord supporter in Beverley Minster is capable of the most abstruse interpretation, as a symbol of the eternal cyclicity of creation or time, but this erudite theological symbolism of the earlier Middle Ages – the device is found from the ninth century on – had probably waned by the time of its carving in 1520. It is difficult to believe that an earlier artist would have allowed a sacrilegious bowman, as on the opposite supporter at Beverley, to take a pot-shot at his rabbit triad – which usefully raises another key issue in the interpretation of such potentially 'equivocal' scenes – that of date. For all its apparent continuity, the Middle Ages is not the unchanging continuum which cultural and art historians have sometimes too readily assumed: there are differences between the attitudes of 1000 and 1500, and an image may well be figural without being figurative. Sometimes a dog is just a dog.

The range of animal imagery displayed in late medieval art is vast and we have inevitably been able only to consider a few examples of the use made of it in medieval life and thought, but further aspects of animal imagery, proverbial animals and the topsy-turvy fauna of the World Turned Upside Down, for example, are discussed in later chapters.

FOUR

why englishmen have tails: the iconography of nationality and race and the uses of monstrosity

Monstrosity in the late Middle Ages came in every conceivable shape and size and covered a multitude of beings. One way through the almost infinite possibilities of monstrosity is to attempt to construct a taxonomy, as if we were nineteenth-century zoologists of the bizarre.

GROTESQUES – SERIOUS OR JUST PLAIN SILLY?

I begin with what I shall term grotesques, those animal-human hybrids typically found as 'Images In the Margins of Gothic Manuscripts', and so amply and expertly anthologised in Lilian Randall's seminal book of that title.[1] Scholarly opinion as to how we should interpret these literally marginal creatures has fluctuated over the years, from the nineteenth-century view which saw them all as merely amusing, however regrettable, *drôleries*, to a late twentieth-century stance which saw them as far more subversive, detecting coded messages in their postures and compositions, in deliberate allusion to or rejection of the (mainly religious) texts they accompanied.[2] While acknowledging the possibility of certain specific types and occasional examples having a wry or other commentary function, I, too, see the great majority of them as indeed 'emptily' humorous, as no more than mere *jeux d'esprit*, exercises in the artistic imagination.

And yet we must not think that being comic is not itself one of the uses of monstrosity – if tumblers and 'girners' could afford amusement at even the most noble of festivities we should not be too surprised at a misericord supporter carved in the late fourteenth century in the parish church at Nantwich. It takes the form of a hybrid creature that has a human face where its bottom should be, thus making a behind of its front, a paradoxical reversal similar to those little lead badges which depict a bottom or a phallic 'nose' protruding from a hood where the face should be.[3] The little misericord supporter at Ripon a century later, however, is little more than a face on legs (Figure 4.1) but is probably intended to be one of the Monstrous Races.

Figure 4.1

ON THE EDGE OF THE KNOWN WORLD: THE MONSTROUS RACES

Located somewhere between animals and humans were the so-called 'Monstrous Races',[4] humanoid 'marginal' beings believed to inhabit the furthest corners of the medieval world, quite literally, as depicted in the borders of early *mappaemundi*, like the celebrated late thirteenth-century Hereford example, or, on a miniature scale, at the edge of the world map in a thirteenth-century English psalter.[5] The extent to which they were entitled to claim human status was hotly contested by medieval theologians, for if they counted as humans and were therefore endowed with God-given souls, then it was Christian duty to despatch missionaries to make contact with them, convert them, and thus save those souls. Being an era in which respect for authority – in this case, that of the classical world – far outweighed empirical evidence (how many medievals had actually seen a *sciapod* in its native habitat, I wonder?), their existence was for the most part accepted as fact on the authority of Greek and Roman authors.

One of the later English Bestiary manuscripts opens with a whole page illustrating nine of these Monstrous Races, whose inclusion in a book of beasts is justified by a quotation from the eighth-century encyclopedist Isidore of Seville, in which he argues that monsters are not unnatural, but the creation of God's will, following the divine scheme in ways that our limited human understanding cannot comprehend.[6]

As Elizabethan explorers expanded the horizons of the medieval world, travellers' tales relocated these fabulous humanoids in the New World, and it is in this context that Shakespeare places Caliban in the brave New World, and while Othello does not say where he came across the 'men whose heads Do grow beneath their shoulders' [I.iii.144–5], just such a 'man' – or *blemya* to give him his proper name – is depicted (together with a rather fetching, though two-breasted, Amazon) as inhabiting the map of Guiana engraved by Jodocus Hondius, *c.* 1599.[7]

Monsters perhaps more familiar to us, and which thus, unreasonably, we feel somehow more acceptable, more as it were 'canonical', are the similar animal-human hybrids of classical antiquity which the Middle Ages inherited: the centaur and the satyr, for example, or the somewhat more exotic manticore. All found their way into those extravagant handbooks of unnatural history which are one of the artistic high-points of the English late Middle Ages, the Bestiaries. As we saw in the previous chapter, the compilers of these superb twelfth- to fourteenth-century manuscripts were really not that bothered as to the reality or otherwise of these creatures, all that mattered was that these details could be read analogically as so many lessons in the Book of Nature, promoting Christian virtues and discouraging vice.

MONSTROUS BIRTHS

In his *Essay on Human Understanding* (1690) Locke wrote, 'I do not know how they can be excused from Murther, who kill monstrous Births (as we call them) because of an unordinary shape.'[8] Before embarking on the taxonomy of monsters proper, we should note in passing that real *human* abnormalities, especially abnormal births, were the subject of woodcut sheets as early as Wolf Traut's woodcut-illustrated broadside of female conjoined twins born in Spalt in December 1512, or Hans Burgkmaier's 1516 engraving of the twins born at Tettnang in Germany, or the Italian Master N.A. DAT's contemporary portrait of those born in Trebizond.[9] In England, from the single decade of the 1560s, we know of nine woodcut-illustrated sheets depicting what are termed 'monstrous children'. The earliest extant English sheet of this type, however, was issued in 1552 and depicts conjoined twins born at Middleton Stony, Oxfordshire. The publication of such sheets – despite whatever suspicions we may have about contemporary prurience – had an ostensibly monitory function: the 1552 twins, for instance, are accompanied by a verse which ends, 'The Lorde hath sent us in these dayes, An image for you all.'

Monstrous Exaggeration: Devils, Giants and Woodwoses

One of the uses of monstrosity, as exemplified by the several Elizabethan pamphlets concerning children born with 'ruffs' or growths around the neck, was to chastise pride in appearance, and specifically, the extravagance of women's fashions. But this was already an old theme, and an early example of its deployment opens our taxonomy of monstrosity proper.

One of the major forms monstrosity can take is the sheer exaggeration of human features. A wholesale exaggeration of features, facial and bodily, is one of the obvious ways in which we recognise devils in medieval art.[10] The diabolical physique is still recognisably a distortion of the human body to which animal parts, horns, claws and a tail have been added. The devil who tempts Christ in the mid-twelfth-century *Winchester Psalter* (see chapter ornament) has interestingly been presented by the artist as a 'bearded lady', and dressed as a woman in the height of contemporary fashion in a tightly laced gown slit up the side (a so-called *fenêtre d'enfer*), and a train and sleeve so extravagantly long that they have had to be knotted. In a literal *travesty*, this monster traverses the boundaries of both humanity and gender.

A different sort of exaggeration, of size, results in the giant, a monstrously large and coarse humanoid. He is also the bogeyman, who was used to frighten children, such as the terrifying ogre depicted in a woodcut by Hans Weiditz *c.* 1521 portrayed in the act of eating small children.

A third kind of exaggeration takes the natural human attribute of hair and covers the entire body with a shaggy blanket of it, resulting in the Wild Man (and Woman), also known in English as the *woodwose* or *wodehouse*. These figures, whom we first glimpse as somewhat sinister denizens of the primeval Germanic forest with a disturbing penchant for abducting human females, have, by the close of the fifteenth century, become a kind of medieval 'noble savage', pursuing an idyllic sylvan lifestyle.

In his earlier manifestation, however, his nature was more animal than human, more savage than 'noble savage', and he is a creature of assorted ignoble appetites. The Middle English version of *The Wars of Alexander*, for example, probably composed in the late fourteenth century, is a translation of the Medieval Latin *Historia Alexandri Magni de Preliis*, and at one point in it Alexander is confronted by the sudden appearance of a wild man, described in the Latin text merely as hairy, of great size and having a voice like that of a boar. The modern editor of the vernacular rendering points out that 'the description in the English text is much amplified' and, indeed, one of these amplifications for which there is no hint in the original, is that we are informed that 'large was his odd lome the lengthe of a yerde' (his 'extra limb' was huge, a yard in length); clearly one aspect of the Wild Man's inhuman monstrosity is the extravagant sexual appetite implied by the outsize dimensions of his penis (for which *yard* was itself a contemporary euphemism).[11] In a manner reminiscent of the Bestiary mode of trapping the long-horned unicorn (see previous chapter), Alexander orders a naked maiden to be set before the Wild Man, who is then swiftly bound by the King's men while still drooling over his prospective prey. Just such a Wild Man abducting a human female is the subject of a Dutch openwork lead roundel of fifteenth-century date. Before an impressive castle, a Wild Man brandishing a club leads a woman in chains, her hands upraised in prayer, while a banderole above her opens *GOT HELPE O. . . .* Clearly, she fears for her life – and chastity too, no doubt. On a slightly earlier badge, however, the tables are turned, for here the Wild Man, again with his characteristic club, is chained to a tree, with above him a banderole, the first three letters of which (*OVE*) represent the exclamation, 'Oh, woe!' Is he a 'prisoner of love' pining for his Lady? A late fifteenth-century Swiss tapestry shows a seated Lady who holds a chain which is attached to the ankle of a standing Wild Man; their banderoles explain that he is only too happy to give up his wild life and be tamed by such a Lady, and that she will be gentle with him.[12] A *Minnekästchen* now in Basel contemporary with the badge also depicts a Lady holding a Wild Man on a leash who declares 'A Lady[13] makes me both tame and wild'. In this present motif there is clearly an implication about the civilising force of the love of a good woman but also, perhaps, of the conquest of a darker aggressive male sexual drive.

In the late Middle Ages Wild Men become a highly popular decorative motif, impersonated in pageants, and represented in every artistic medium, such as this pair accompanied by dragons on a mid-fifteenth-century misericord in Beverley parish church (Figure 4.2). The Wild Man even becomes a constituent of religious folktale in the story-motif known to folklorists as 'The Hairy Anchorite'. The future saint, usually after committing some heinous crime (such as raping and murdering his

Figure 4.2

sister), flees in his crazed state to the woods where he becomes a wild man reverting to a state of *savagery* (in its etymological sense, the *salvage man* of the Elizabethans, *homo sylvaticus*) and grows the characteristic all-over shaggy hair (see Chapter 2).

The appearance of two Wild Men together with two mermaids as heraldic supporters of the arms of Jacques d'Armagnac in a late fifteenth-century manuscript exemplifies the decorative function of the wodewose and introduces another contemporary 'monster', rather more his counterpart, in terms of iconographic popularity, than the wild woman – the mermaid (whose proper masculine partner, the merman, is similarly a rather artificial construct).

Mermaids

Taxonomically, the mermaid will serve to introduce the classes of animal-human hybrids which are composed of human torso plus animal part – in this case, a fish-tail, of course. Her 'classic' essential attributes are the comb and mirror (Figure 3.6). There is no doubt that these tools of the seductive siren are to be interpreted negatively as the tools of vanity, and thus it is no surprise to find them in the hands of the Whore of Babylon seated on the waters in the Apocalypse tapestries in Angers (1370s), or in the hands of Oiseuse (Idleness) in illustrated manuscripts of the *Roman de la Rose*.[14] The *Melusine* written by Jean d'Arras c. 1387 is a bizarre 'foundation legend' of a family dynasty (that of the Lusignan in Poitou) whose progenitor is seduced by a mermaid whose true identity is unknown to him; not just popular in France, it was soon translated into other vernaculars. Tinged with an obvious voyeurism, the climactic woodcut in early printed illustrated copies of the romance (such as that printed in Paris, c. 1530), shows the husband, Raimond, spying on his wife in the bath. Her real nature discovered, the spell is broken and the mermaid-wife, reverting to the earlier bird-type of siren, flies off.

The Tailed English (Angli caudati)

Another type of caudal appendage added to the human figure results in the strange figure of the 'tailed Englishman' (*Anglus caudatus*). This was a popular European gibe directed against the English throughout the late Middle Ages. The fifteenth-century English mystic Margery Kempe who, it must be said, can never have been the easiest of travelling companions, records in her spiritual autobiography how fellow pilgrims were at one point in 1433, somewhere between Wilsnack and Aachen, so moved as to call her an English *sterte*, an obsolete word for 'tail' (still preserved in the bird name, *redstart*, and – now disguised – in the phrase *stark naked*).[15]

The original slur was applied only to the inhabitants of Kent ('Kentish longtails') who were said to have been cursed with long tails after having insulted St Augustine by docking the tail of his horse.[16] This incident is also depicted in medieval art as part of the legend of St Thomas à Becket.[17] On Christmas Eve 1170, according to several reliable contemporary chroniclers writing independently of each other, Robert de Broc of Saltwood, near Hythe in Kent, sent out his nephew John who, in the middle of the king's highway, cut off the tail of the horse upon which the shortly to be martyred Thomas à Becket was riding. William of Canterbury relates that so aggrieved was the saint by this attack on his mare that he complained of the insult in his last interview with his murderers: 'A mare in my service has, in contempt of my name, had its tail cut off – as though I could be put to shame by the mutilation of a beast!' Note especially the automatic identification made by Thomas with his horse, and compare what we have said about the Conqueror's horse in Chapter 3. At some point after the date of Becket's martyrdom, a popular tradition grew up to the effect that the descendants of the de Brocs, and subsequently all Kentishmen – even, finally, all Englishmen – were born with tails, as a perpetual reminder of their ancestor's crime. This particular motivation for the well-known *Angli caudati* gibe, however, is not found before Bower's continuation of Fordun's *Scotichronicon c.* 1440, and even here, it follows on from the much commoner and, indeed, earlier-attested story antedating Becket's martyrdom, which attributes the curse to St Augustine, on whom the people of Rochester were said to have hung rays' tails, in derision of his mission, a tale evidenced as early as Gocelin's biography of the saint, *c.* 1100.[18]

It was only to be expected that the motif of the tailed English should have been mercilessly exploited by England's enemies, most notably the Scots, who made use of the gibe as early as 1217, and, of course, the French, who had taken it up as early as the mid-twelfth century, though the earliest attestation known to me occurs in the Flemish Latin beast-fable, the *Ysengrimus* written *c.* 1148. According to the thirteenth-century Middle English romance of *Richard Coer de Lyon* (based on a lost Anglo-Norman romance of *c.* 1230–50), the Lionheart himself is insulted as *taylard* and

tayled king, and in Robert of Brunne's *Chronicle* composed in *c.* 1330 there is also a reference to the *Inglis tayled kyng.*

Given the popularity of this gibe, I believe it can be recognised in what must be one of the earliest-known political cartoons, aimed at another 'Inglis tayled kyng'. This extraordinary miniature (Figure 4.3) painted in the margins of a late thirteenth-century Picard manuscript[19] shows a figure, naked except for a crown and gauntlets, who is clearly depicted with a long tail which wraps round his leg; some kind of raptor perches on his left wrist and in his right hand he holds a falconry lure. I believe the French painter intended this image to represent the English King Edward I (who was devoted to falconry and built a mews for his birds in Charing Cross)[20] and, crucially, declared war on France in 1293.

Figure 4.3

There is every reason to believe the incident with Becket's horse to have been historical, not least because there are other avowedly historical instances. In the records of early trailbaston proceedings from the Lincoln Roll of 1305, for example, a certain Philip Darcy was convicted of having removed the wheels from some carts belonging to the Prior of Nocton in Lincolnshire, and further, of having cut off the tail of the horse on which one of the canons was riding. Adding insult to injury, he then forced one of the Priory's grooms to kiss the mutilated horse's hindquarters (see Chapter 13).[21]

Such malicious tail-docking was a visible sign of an insult given, but – as routinely – the worldling's humiliation is the proud badge of the saint. The *Institutes of Sempringham* were codified for the monastic community founded by Gilbert of Sempringham in 1147, and the rubric to canon 19 reads 'Concerning the docking of horses', and the canon itself begins:

> All our horses destined for waggons and carts shall be docked. Their manes shall also be cut short and their tails clipped about, so that they look contemptible and disfigured.[22]

Here, Gilbert deliberately sets out to make the horses used by his Order look 'contemptible and disfigured', the antithesis of proud warriors' steeds, and significantly this is to be effected by docking their tails and manes.

The Horns of the Cuckold (and the Hen-pecked Husband)

Adding animal horns to a man could make him into a devil, of course, but it could also identify him as a cuckold, that is, the husband (occasionally the lover), of a woman who was sexually unfaithful to him. A traditional figure of fun, the cuckold's humiliation – in these traditional societies which regarded the wife as firmly under the husband's control, especially in sexual matters – was the mainspring of countless *fabliaux* and other comic works. Without the classic horned cuckold, indeed, Elizabethan and Jacobean comic drama and pamphlets would be unthinkable, but medieval representations are not common.

A man with goat's horns is depicted in a late fifteenth-century Florentine engraving satirising cuckolds which goes by the title, *The King of the Goats*,[23] from which it is apparent that this artist, at least, envisaged the cuckold's horns as those of the goat. A mid-thirteenth-century account by Boncompagno, however, implies that almost any horned animal might figure in this convention, noting that Italian women referred to their deceived husbands as 'goats', 'bulls' and 'stags', as well as 'cuckoos', and in addition used various jocular phrases involving words beginning with the syllables *cucu-* (such as *cucurbita*, 'gourd') alluding, of course, to the word *cuculus* which must therefore have already acquired the sense 'cuckold' by this time.[24]

The earliest representation known to me, however, is a remarkable miniature (Figure 4.4) adorning a French manuscript of canon law illuminated *c.* 1300.[25] In the illustration to *Causa* XXIX of Gratian's *Decretals*, the priest is shown in the process of joining the right hands of the betrothed in wedlock,[26] seemingly oblivious of the magnificent pair of four-tined stag's antlers rising from the groom's head!

The nobleman, identified as such by the falcon perched on his wrist, who is presumably the man responsible for making the groom a cuckold, stands aloof to the right of the 'happy' couple.

Figure 4.4

In Germany and England, certainly in vernacular literature, the evidence for this convention is relatively late, however. The first English citations unequivocally linked to cuckold imagery are from the fifteenth-century works of Lydgate (*c.* 1370–*c.* 1450). Nevertheless, British Latin authors do evince a familiarity with the cuckold's horns, as early as *c.* 1200, in one of the fables of Walter of England, for example, but, more significantly, in Geoffrey of Monmouth's *Vita Merlini* (*c.* 1148). In this work, Merlin is portrayed as a Wild Man who, riding on a stag, the Wild Man's favourite mount, arrives at the house of his former mistress. He finds her enjoying the night of her wedding to his rival, and in a fit of jealous rage, tears off the stag's antlers and hurls them at the couple. Contemporary continental literature in the vernacular also features references to the horns of the rejected lover – in a late twelfth-century poem by the troubadour Bernart de Ventadour, for instance – and there is reason to believe that the convention evolved in the Middle Ages, in regions where Romance languages were spoken. The earliest reference of all, however, is the expression, 'to wear the horned hat', which appears in Artemidorus's Latin dream-manual of *c.* AD 200, and later appears in the Provençal poetry of the twelfth-century troubadours Guilhem de Bergueda (*porta cofa cornuda*) and Marcabru (*porta capel cornut*). I compare this expression with the punishment meted out to a fourteenth-century Italian who pimped for his wife (thus by definition cuckolding himself), and was subsequently forced to wear a two-horned cap.

Once again, nicknames provide significant early evidence for the existence of the words concerned and thus, presumably, of the popular conception behind such usage. While it is not possible to say for certain whether the various medieval nicknames involving the element *horn* allude to this convention, since horns were common instruments and trophies, possible English candidates include *Panhorn* (1251 – for the first element, compare brain-*pan*), and more obliquely perhaps, *Bukenheved* (buck's head, 1301) and *Herteheued* (hart's head, 1332); the nicknames of two late thirteenth-century Parisians, Guille and Guillaume *le Cornu* (1292 – 'the horned') were probably similarly motivated.

The term *cuckold* is usually accepted as deriving from the bird name *cuckoo*, despite semantic difficulties – for it is not the cuckoo that raises the offspring of others, but they hers – but the connection was certainly made by medieval people. The cuckoo was the cuckold's bird long before the closing song in Shakespeare's *Love's Labours Lost*:

> The cuckoo then, on every tree,
> Mocks married men; for thus sings he,
> Cuckoo;
> Cuckoo, cuckoo: O word of fear,
> Unpleasing to a married ear!

Chaucer's *Knight's Tale*, for example, iconographically describes 'Jalousye with a cukkow sittynge on his hand', but in his *Fulgens and Lucrece* (*c.* 1497), Medwall appears to record an interesting superstition clearly related to the Shakespearian song:

> . . . men say amonge
> He that throwyth stone or stycke
> At such a byrde he is lycke   [likely]
> To synge that byrdes songe.

The hood seems also to have been part of the folklore of the cuckold (as in the expression 'wered a cukwold hoode' in the fifteenth-century manuscript of *Ipomadon*), for which the coincidence of Latin *cucullus* (hood) with *cuculus* (cuckoo) probably bears some responsibility. Bruegel's famous *Netherlandish Proverbs* painting of 1559 (Colour Plate 6) is alternatively known as *The Blue Hood* (a phrase attested from the late fourteenth century), from its central motif, which shows a young wife pulling a hooded cape over her husband's head, clearly symbolising her intention to hoodwink or deceive him. This particular iconographic motif can certainly be traced back to a late fifteenth-century stall-elbow carved by a Flemish craftsman in Toledo Cathedral, but from at least the late fourteenth century, English sources also record various *hood* expressions in a cuckoldry context. Note, for example, that in this phrase from the poet Lydgate, 'With such a metyerde she hathe shape him an hoode' (with such a 'meat-yard' she has made him a hood), *metyerde* (literally, 'measuring-rod') puns on 'meat' + 'yard' in the sense 'penis'.

In a Latin–English glossary of *c.* 1440 the word *cockney*, literally 'cock's-egg' (*coken* + *ey*), is defined as *cornutus* (literally 'horned one', that is, cuckold), and probably already has this sense in Chaucer's *Reeve's Tale*. The German name for the cuckold, *Hahnrei*, might also seem to be composed of *hahn* (cock) + *ei* (egg), but the second element is *-rei*, meaning 'castrated,' so that the word means 'castrated cock', 'capon'. But by the common semantic process of metaphoric transfer, *capon* is itself similarly used to mean 'eunuch' in thirteenth-century English, and a most interesting early fifteenth-century gloss on the Latin word *gallinacius* reads: *homo debilis* (impotent man), a *malkyn* (otherwise a nickname for a promiscuous young woman) and a *capoun*. This is of particular interest as Konrad Gesner records in his *Vogelbuch* of 1557 that one method of contemporary caponisation was to excise the cock's testicles, comb and one of its spurs, grafting the spur in place of the comb where it continued to grow resembling a small horn – this grafting of a 'horn', it is suggested, then served as a sign by which to identify the caponised birds, and this practice may have reinforced the notion of the horned cuckold, that is, the 'caponised' husband.

The cuckold is naturally assimilated to the 'hen-pecked' husband or effeminate man. The *hennetaster* (hen-groper), a type of the effeminate man, was carved *c.* 1500 in stallwork at Emmerich, Kempen and Aarschot. The earliest English literary reference to this motif (contemporary with his appearing in Bruegel's *Dutch Proverbs*) is Dame Chat's insulting insinuation that Hodge came '. . . creeping into my pens, / And there was caught within my house groping among my hens' (*Gammer Gurton's Needle, c.* 1563). It is notable how so many of these terms concerning dominant and subservient sexual roles revolve around the barnyard relations of the cock and hen (see the discussion of *cock* in Chapter 3).

A late but interesting instance of the public ridicule of cuckolds is recorded in Henry Machyn's *Diary* for 15 May 1562: 'The same day was set up at the Cuckold Haven a great May-pole by butchers and fisher-men, full of horns; and they made great cheer.' That derisive horns were a constituent of the mocking rituals known as *charivaris*, when aimed at cuckolds, may be gathered from early depictions (such as Hoefnagel's drawing of 1569) and descriptions. The apprentices of a goldsmith insulted their master by 'making a horned head upon his dore sett betwene the lettres of his name and other lyke villanyes' in London in 1558 and, throughout the Elizabethan era, court records make frequent allusion to the setting up of horns at the doors of houses where the husband was believed to be a cuckold. An especially elaborate instance occurred in Wiltshire in 1616 when a 'buck's horn stuck with a wisp of hay and a picture of a woman's privities' was used. The wisp of hay is perhaps to be understood in the sense of *wisp* defined by the *OED* as 'A twist or figure of straw for a scold to rail at', and well illustrated for the fifteenth century by the dictionary's first citation from Caxton's translation, *The Knight of the Tower*:

> He writhed a litell wipse of strawe, and sette it afore her, and saide, ladi, yef that ye will chide more, chide with that straw.

The message of the strange composite Wiltshire device would then be that the cuckolded husband was not only a cuckold, whose wife openly advertised her sexual availability, but also a *cotquean*, subservient to his scolding wife.[27]

Animal Heads

But to resume our taxonomy of monstrosity: adding the distinctive ears of the ass to a man's head (or the comb of a cock, for that matter >*coxcomb*) makes him a fool, the ass being a proverbially foolish beast, of course,[28] and in a miniature from the margins of the *Psalter of Humphrey de Bohun*, illuminated before 1373, we see what appears to be the earliest depiction of a jester wearing an ass-eared hood[29] (see also Chapter 6).

But to go a stage further and put an entire ass's head onto a person carried the same connotations of stupidity, and in the German Middle Ages, as well as being

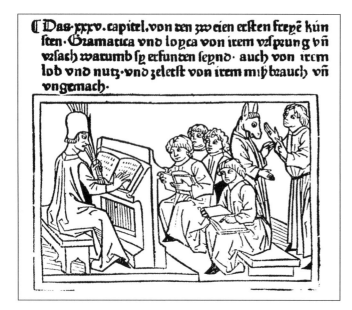

Figure 4.5

called the *asinus,* a Latin term afforded official status by being mentioned in several late medieval school ordinances, the incompetent student was more drastically made an ass of by being obliged to wear an ass's head. Such a scene is depicted in Figure 4.5, which illustrates Rodericus Zamorensis, *Spiegel des menschlichen Lebens* issued in Augsburg in the 1470s.[30] It may well be that something of this schoolboy humiliation lies behind the transformation of Bottom in Shakespeare's *Midsummer Night's Dream* (*c.* 1595), who declares, all unconsciously, 'This is to make an asse of me!' (III.i.115).

The device of demonising or, rather, 'bestialising' one's opponents became the stock-in-trade of the Reformation polemicist. German Protestant controversialists had satirised the Catholic writer Thomas Murner in the shape of a cat, by punningly analysing his surname as if it were composed of the elements *murren* (purr) and *narr* (fool), but surprisingly, Murner turned this intended etymological insult to his own advantage, by adopting the persona of a heroic cat-headed defender of the faith, as seen in the woodcuts in his *Von dem grossen Lutherischen Narren,* published in Strasbourg in 1522.

But for the most part, iconographically at least, it was the Protestants who had the better of it. They seized upon the familiar Gospel verse in which Matthew warned against 'false prophets, which come to you in sheep's clothing, but inwardly they are ravening wolves' (8.15), to characterise the Catholic clergy, and, given the pastoral metaphor of the shepherd caring for his flock, there was something peculiarly satisfying in depicting that shepherd as a predatory wolf temporarily disguised as a sheep, lulling his flock into a false sense of security with his hypocritical words, only to prey on them at the last. Perhaps, too, as the fearsome denizen of the primeval Germanic forest, as the Big Bad Wolf, indeed, some memory lingered on of the old Germanic term for an outlaw,[31] one who was to be hunted down like a wolf, as a menace to society, the 'wolf's head', as he is named in *The Laws of Edward the Confessor* (*c.* 1000),[32] for, as the thirteenth-century *Mirror for Justices* explains, *lou est beste haie de tote gent* (the wolf is a beast hated by everyone). The striking woodcut

(Figure 4.6) which illustrates the title-page to Urbanus Rhegius, *Wie man die falschen propheten . . .* (Wittenberg and Brunswick, 1539), seems to have given the hint to the engraver of the vicious illustration inserted into William Turner's *The Hunting of the Romish Wolf*, published from the safety of Emden *c.* 1555, during 'Bloody' Mary's persecutions of Protestants in England.[33]

Wie man die falschen Propheten erkennen / ja greiffen mag / Ein predig zu Mynden jnn Westphalen gethan / durch D. Vrbanum Rhegium.

Jeremie 10. Die Hirten sind zu narren worden / vnd fragen nichts nach Gott / Darumb können sie auch nichts rechts leren / sondern zerstrewet die Herd.

Wittemberg. M. D. XXXIX.

Figure 4.6

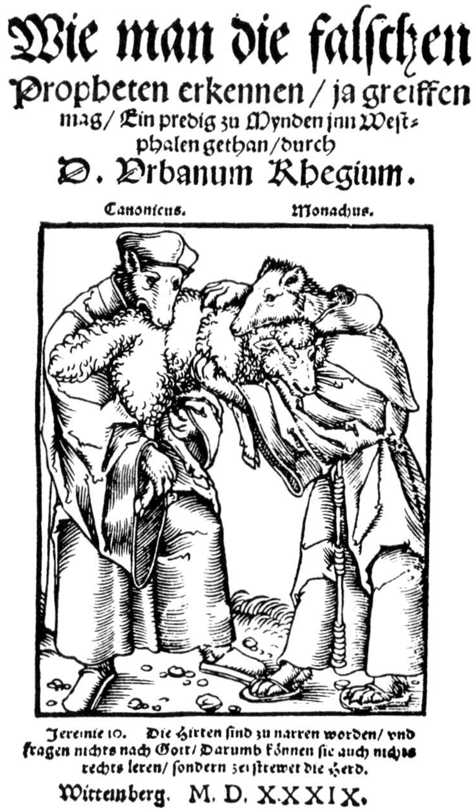

Multiple Heads

If an animal's head added to a human body is to be interpreted as monstrous, so too is any number of heads greater than one. The literally treated *tricephalos* with foliate stems emerging from its mouths on a misericord at Cartmel, Lancashire, carved *c.* 1430, was perhaps intended by the carver as a symbolic image of the Trinity. The triple-headed Pope paying a German mercenary, on the other hand, engraved by Melchior Lorch and dated 1555, was clearly intended as a sort of anti-Trinity. Two cuts illustrating pamphlets against Luther by Hans Brosamer issued in Leipzig in 1529, show him as two-headed (compare the connotations of English 'two-faced') and seven-headed, the latter an undoubted allusion to the Beast of the Apocalypse as described in Revelations 13.

Other variations rung on the theme of the human head by the artists of the Reformation include the striking image of the head as bagpipe, as the 'Devil's instrument', in an anti-Catholic sheet with woodcut by Erhard Schoen (Nürnberg, *c.* 1530), in which the Devil has animal claws and a (?)cockerel's head, and the bag of his instrument is the head of a tonsured monk. A similar degree of abstraction applied to the same monastic target is to be seen in a Spanish misericord in the cathedral at Ciudad Rodrigo executed *c.* 1500 by the 'Germanic' carver Rodrigo Aleman. Here the tonsured monks' heads are placed on bodies which are no more than wineskins, and they sing from a piece of music labelled *vino puro* – they sing in praise of good, undiluted wine (Figure 4.7)!

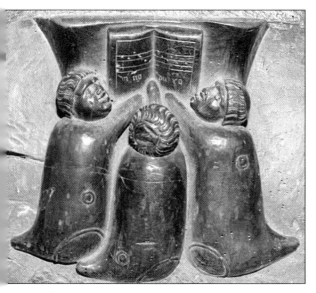

Figure 4.7

THE PAPAL ASS AND THE MONK-CALF

We cannot leave the visual polemic of the Reformation, the era in which visual satire may be said to have finally come of age, without mentioning two of the most famous monsters of their day, one doubtless entirely fabricated, the other real, but considerably 'improved'. Both monsters appeared in cuts attributed to Cranach that illustrate Luther's anti-Papal pamphlet, *Deutung der czwo grewlichen Figuren, Bapstesel zu Rom vnd Mvnchskalb zu Freyberg* (1523). The 'Papal Ass' (*Bapstesel*) with its ass's head, scaly limbs, hooves, claws and monster-headed tail had allegedly been found in the Tiber in 1496, whereas 'The Monk-Calf' (*Mvnchskalb*) was a misbirth born in December 1522 in Freiberg near Dresden. The original woodcut sheet of this latter, issued early in 1523, was labelled 'The Monster of Saxony', but was very soon adapted by being moved through ninety degrees so that the original quadruped now assumed a bipedal, and thus more apparently human, stance. Finally, in Cranach's version, the human features of the 'monster' are accentuated. Ironically, we see here the reverse of the usual process of distorting the human form, here the artist has been at pains to render the 'monster' more human!

Figure 4.8

MONSTROUS SEXUALITY

As we have seen already with Alexander's Wild Man, sexuality – in as much as it was troublesome to humanity – was always likely to be a facet of monstrosity too, and the monster a proxy on which human concerns about sex, conscious or unconscious, could be projected. Continuing our taxonomic approach, monstrous sexuality may be simply conveyed by exaggeration of the sex organs, and the crudely carved stone sculptures known as *sheelagh-na-gigs* – of which the example from Llandrindod in Wales (Figure 4.8) is typical – are perhaps some of the best examples of this strategy. Often to be found built into what are assumed to be later churches and secular houses, to my mind they are best seen as amuletic, as *apotropaia*, warding off the attentions of the Evil Eye by employing the shock tactic of genital exposure. The hands of these schematic figures are frequently depicted pulling apart the labia of the vulva, presumably in order to exaggerate the size and amplify the repellent effect. The breasts of these female figures are noticeably minimal, but often the ribs are indicated, as on the Llandrindod example and on the tiny Dutch lead badges too, a feature which I take to allude to the crone-like aspect of the type, as with the Scots Gaelic *cailleach.*

If, to exaggerated male sexual organs, we add an animal head – in this case that of a cock (and, as argued in the previous chapter, this semantics is not accidental) – then we might end up with a monster of the type represented by the late Roman bronze *priapi gallinacei,* or the notorious Albani bronze said to be held in the Vatican Museum. A stage more bizarre, perhaps, is the sexual monster which is no more than an icon of the male or female sex organs, which seems, as it were, to have a life of its own in its literal dismemberment from its human body; but these are treated fully in Chapter 12.

COMPOSITION

A further strategy for the production of monstrosity is that of composition, that is, the making of a figure from many constituent parts (whether the same object or different objects) which fill in the outline of the usually human form. In as much as the head stands for the whole, the reverse of a bronze medal cast in Italy in the 1530s or 1540s depicts a head composed entirely of phalli – some have argued that it was intended to be a satyr, that proverbially lascivious classical monster, others that it was intended as a satire, aimed at the notorious contemporary pornographer, Pietro Aretino. Of the same period (dated 1536 on the reverse) is an extraordinary Italian maiolica plate painted in Casteldurante (Colour Plate 3), again showing a head composed entirely of phalli, but this time bearing a label inscribed (in mirror-writing) *OGNI HOMO ME GVARDA COME FOSSE VNA TESTA DE CAZI* (People look at me as if I were a dickhead)!

Composite heads of the type later made famous by the painter Arcimboldo are for the most part merely ingeniously executed design ideas, but from at least a century earlier, composite monsters were created in an intentionally symbolic or emblematic fashion. One such emblematically composite head is a pen-and-ink drawing of the Wise Man made by Hermann Bote as an illustration to the manuscript of his *Weltchronik,* (Hamburg, *a.* 1518),[34] but we shall examine him, together with the similar Ideal Servant (Figure 9.7), in more detail in Chapter 9.

The Picture of Nobody

I close this brief survey of monstrosity, which has involved the combination and composition, recombination and distortion, of so many animal and human figures and parts of figures, for a variety of uses – but frequently with some satiric purpose – with what must surely be the ultimate dissolution, the Picture of Nobody (Figure 4.9). In this curiously post-modern title-page woodcut to a mock-sermon printed in Germany *c.* 1510, the empty frame is captioned 'The picture of nobody because nobody is depicted in it'!

Figure 4.9

FIVE

SIGNS OF INFAMY: THE ICONOGRAPHY OF HUMILIATION AND INSULT

The punishments that any society metes out to those who transgress its rules vary enormously according to time, place, age and sex of the perpetrator, gravity of offence, and so on, but, like any other aspect of a particular culture, they will usually have something to tell us about the symbolic system of that culture; and the great variety of late medieval punishments is no exception to this general rule. At the root of many punishments is the notion of humiliation or ridicule, often via inversion, whether literal, in the case of hanging upside down or riding facing the tail, or metaphorical, as in forcing a man to carry a distaff, the attribute appropriate to a woman.

Other iconographic peculiarities are what I am calling here 'signs of infamy', that signal to the viewer that the individual so marked is reprehensible in some way. The first such to be considered is an insect-swarm shown around a person's head.

Insect-swarm Round the Head

Before the end of the fifteenth century, and growing ever more popular throughout the following century, we encounter the motif of a swarm of insects surrounding a human head. In the half-century between *c.* 1480 and *c.* 1530 I have noted some fifteen examples, all except the very earliest from the Germanic area. Two versions of book title-page frames of *c.* 1520 by Cranach,[1] for example, depict a drunken, semi-naked or tattered peasant boozing and surrounded by flies,[2] but otherwise the earlier instances of the swarm are associated with those unequivocally identified as fools by their costume (see below),[3] including the woodcut of the eponymous *Nemo* (Nobody) on the title-page of the edition issued in Leipzig in 1518 (Figure 5.1). Even the great god Mars in Botticelli's famous painting of *Venus and Mars* (*a.* 1510) is, in Calman's words, 'not only mocked by satyr children but . . . his folly [is] made plain by the swarm of hornets around his

Figure 5.1

head',[4] though others have detected an allusion to the love of Julius de Medici for Simonetta *Vespucci*.

The earliest example, however, probably dating from the early 1480s, is a significant one: it occurs as the *bas-de-page* illustration for September in the Calendar of the *Hours of Charles d'Angoulême*,[5] and depicts an elderly man with long, straggly hair offering fruit and wine to a girl whose hand he holds, and who with the other hand uses a leafy branch to drive away four large flies which surround his head. The French illuminator has closely modelled this scene on an engraving by Israhel van Meckenem, but added the flies and branch, an all the more deliberate addition in that elsewhere in this manuscript he has merely pasted in the actual van Meckenem prints and painted over them! The most recent commentator confessed that the implications of these additions were not entirely clear to her, but given the evident disparity in age of the couple, that is they are 'Unequal Lovers', it seems certain that the critical addition of the flies is to point up the old man's folly. We have an apparent proof of this in the description of one of the forty biscuit-moulds listed in Claus Stalburg's inventory of 1521 with which we began, where the fifteenth item is 'an old bald-headed man whom hornets sting beside a young woman, and a fool who drives them away from him'.

The earliest related English idiom I am aware of is the Scots *heid full of beis* (compare the still current English idiom, 'to have a bee in one's bonnet') from

Gavin Douglas's 1513 translation of the *Aeneid*.[6] But it is perhaps possible to trace the origins of the bee-form of this motif further back in time. In an Austrian manuscript of the *Etymachia* illustrated in Vorau in 1330, Invidia (Envy)'s helmet is a beehive surrounded by bees, presumably symbolising the stings of the envious. A century later in a manuscript of South German provenance, it is a basket of bees, and by 1460 it has become a nest of bees in the Augsburg manuscript depiction which lies behind the woodcut illustration to *Ein schone materi vo den siben todsunden . . .* printed by Baemler in the same city in 1474.[7]

But perhaps we can take this bee-swarm motif back further still, to the ninth-century *Stuttgart Psalter* illustration of Psalm 117 (AV 118), verse 12: 'they

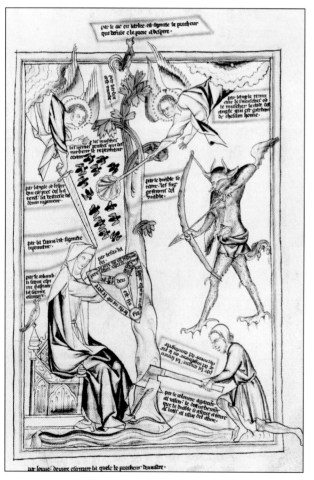

Figure 5.2

surrounded me like bees', in which 'they' are all the people hostile to the Psalmist, where the bees would appear, on the face of it, to symbolise no more than the stinging attacks of one's enemies. In their biblical commentaries, however, Gregory and Eucherius of Lyon interpreted the Psalmist's bees as those hypocrites or backbiting flatterers who have honey in their mouths but stings in their tails,[8] and it is presumably in this tradition that Luther described flattering courtiers as like 'bumble-bees, those virtueless, idle ravening vermin'.

Perhaps one of the most significant occurrences of our motif, however, is to be found in a drawing which supplements the usual cycle in the *Lambeth/De Quincy Apocalypse* (?London, *c.* 1260), and constitutes a pictorial allegory of penitence, in which a repentant woman is attacked by the Devil, but fends him off with the shield of faith (Figure 5.2).[9] She is also attacked by an ominous swarm of thirteen flies,[10] but defended by a guardian angel who plies a fly-swat. The illustrator has helpfully added explicit labels in Anglo-Norman to each component of his unique composition, so that next to the fly-swarm we read, 'By the flies [are signified] the idle thoughts which disturb the penitent at prayer', and next to the angel, 'by the angel driving away the flies with the fly-swat is signified the help of the angel who is the guardian of every man'.

To sum up: the presence of a swarm of flies/bees/insects round a person's head indicates that that person is either a fool or (fatally) prone to be distracted by idle, flattering or perhaps even homicidal thoughts.

A <u>VERY</u> BAD HAIR DAY: THE BIRD'S NEST ON THE HEAD

As we shall see below, the hair of a fool's head is usually in some way extravagant: he may be completely shaven-headed, or he may have various styles of bizarre tonsure – all of which must be regarded as marks of his humiliation – but too much wild, unruly hair was clearly considered just as disfiguring and, again, was accorded to those figures of whom we are clearly meant to disapprove.

The ultimate 'bad hair day' must surely be attributed to those characters who are depicted with birds nesting in their hair. The appearance of the motif at the very end of the Middle Ages seems to coincide with the popularity of the insect-swarm motif and, though rarer, may well be synonymous. The earliest example I know of is untypical in not being Germanic, but otherwise quite typical in being applied to the *mato*, the 'joker'[11] of the Italian tarot pack, and can be dated no more closely than the second half of the fifteenth century.[12] Perhaps the most significant example, however, in that it occurs together with the insect-swarm, is the same woodcut of *Nemo* we have just mentioned above, whose scallop-edged costume shows that the engraver intended to portray him as something of a fool (Figure 5.1). One of Leonhard Beck's typically bold woodcut sheets which Geisberg entitled 'The cook and her lover', shows the latter dressed in fool's costume and addressed by his mate as *Wiedhopff Henslin*, that is, 'Hoopoe Hänslein', the crested bird nesting on his head presumably being intended as a hoopoe – an identification not without significance.

In English the proverbial 'Ill bird that fouls its own nest' is non-specific, but in German the species in question is agreed to be the hoopoe – this piece of Bestiary-derived lore was equally available to the English, of course, but the bird itself is too rare a visitor for its insanitary domestic habits to be popularly known in this country (though for the reader of English, Caxton noted that 'the hoop is found moche in mareys [marsh] and fylthes').[13] In a contemporary woodcut illustrating Murner's *Schelmenzunft* (1512) the *Unnutzvogel* (literally, 'useless bird') is depicted as a hoopoe and shown fouling its own nestlings.[14]

Goitres and Gestures

In accordance with the principle of visually stigmatising all 'undesirables', certain types are marked out by a prominent and sometimes multiple nodular goitre, especially in those Alpine lands in which the condition was formerly prevalent.[15] If the fool is merely foolish – though as we have said, late medieval moralists would not have regarded his folly as harmlessly humorous – the mockers and executioners of Christ and his saints are by definition vicious. The man who has brought St Catherine to her wheel to be put to death in the Milanese *Sforza Hours* (*c.* 1490) has been given a sharply scalloped edge to his tunic not unlike that of the contemporary fool, but also a multiple goitre.[16] The hideously grotesque kneeling man with the prominent goitre on a fresco in a church in the Southern Tirol, painted by a Swabian artist in 1487, further identifies himself as one of the Mockers of Christ by 'biting his thumb' at the Saviour, an insulting gesture that Shakespeare accurately alludes to in the Italian setting of *Romeo and Juliet*'s opening scene.

Insulting Gestures

The Teeth-flick

This gesture was probably never an English one, and it is noticeable that Shakespeare seems to feel the need to gloss the fact that it is insulting, for his English audience, by having Sampson say, 'I will bite my thumb at them, which is disgrace to them if they bear it.' In an exactly contemporary play, *Wits Misery*, Lodge has one of his characters refer to 'Giuing me the Fico with his thombe in his mouth', which again sounds as if these Elizabethan dramatists were somewhat uncertain about the gesture, as the 'fig' is a different form of gestural insult.

The Fig

The use of the Italian form of English 'fig' in Lodge's play, and Pistol's reference to *figo* and the *fig of Spain*[17] show that this was another continental gesture unfamiliar to the English before the sixteenth century. The 'fig', as *OED* defines it, is 'a contemptuous gesture which consisted in thrusting the thumb between two of the closed fingers or into the mouth', but it is one which may frequently be seen in medieval art, especially in the common Mocking of Christ – a very valuable scene for the study of medieval insulting gesture, as Ruth Mellinkoff has so amply documented.[18] Jet amulets in the form of a hand making the fig gesture, still popular in Spain, have been found there from as early as the second half of the thirteenth century,[19] and an early instance of the gesture represented in art is to be seen in a thirteenth-century copy of the *Institutes of Justinian*.[20]

Waggling the Fingers in the Ears

In 1542 the Eton schoolmaster Nicholas Udall published a partial translation of Erasmus's *Apophthegms* in which the following passage is found:

> when men doe mocke any body, thei wagge their handes vp and doune by their eares at the sides of their hed and doe counterfeact the facion of an Asses eares. So then the asse also appereth by waggyng his eares vp and doun, to mocke & skorne folkes. . . .

Of course, in origin, these are the words of the Dutch humanist, not the English schoolteacher, but Udall was no slavish translator, and at the very least, this gesture must have been familiar to him.

Cocking a Snook

Ruth Mellinkoff has pushed back the earliest known depiction of the gesture we term 'thumbing the nose' or 'cocking a snook', and the Germans 'making a long nose', some three centuries before the formerly earliest-noted instance in Bruegel's mid-sixteenth-century *Feast of Fools* engraving, to a German parchment roll of *c.* 1230, in which a black man (one of Ham's cursed descendants) directs the gesture against the Egyptians. She also reproduces two examples from the typological

Figure 5.3

miniatures of the Mocking of Hur and the Mocking of Christ in a fourteenth-century German *Speculum Salvationis* about the signification of which there can be no doubt.[21] I am able to add a thirteenth-century example from the *Oscott Psalter* (*c.* 1265),[22] again in a Mocking of Christ context, and two further fourteenth-century examples, one Swiss and one English. In the *Smithfield Decretals* (*c.* 1330) the gesture is directed by a hare – in so far as that animal may be said to have a thumb – at a hanged dog,[23] while painted in a window-niche of the Unterhof at Diessenhofen near Schaffhausen is a man who directs the double-handed version of the gesture at passers-by![24] Back in England, on one of the misericords in Beverley Minster carved in 1520, in a playful piece of self-reference, a carver depicted in one supporter thumbs his nose at his colleague on the opposite one (Figure 5.3).[25]

As a parting shot, I cite the case of Robert de Suttone who, on being suspended from his office by the sheriff's court in 1291, is recorded as having insulted the court by repeating the exclamation *Tprurt!* five times and 'at the same time raising his thumb in contempt for his suspension'. It is clear from other examples of this onomatopoeic outburst that it is intended to imitate the sound of a fart;[26] Robert was in effect telling the members of the court that he 'didn't give a fart' for them, but I know of no good parallel for the presumably upward thrusting of the thumb, a gesture clearly understood by those present to be contemptuous – unless the gladiatorial 'thumbs up', of which the modern interpretation, as the *OED* remarks, is 'the reverse of that in the ancient amphitheatre'.

SCHANDBILDER: IMAGES AND RITUALS OF INVERSION

> But wee hoope we shalle do the a pryve thyng;
> A roope, a ladder, and a ring,[27]
> Heigh on gallowes for to henge
> And thus shalle be your endyng.
> And He that made the, be ther to helpyng,
> And we on our behalfe shalle be welle willyng.
> For thy lettre is knowlechyng[28]   [acknowledges (your guilt)].

Intriguing testimony to the power of images in the Middle Ages is provided by the defamatory or shaming picture which seems first to appear in Italy in the late thirteenth century,[29] and had spread to Northern Europe by the early fifteenth century. It seems to have been in France, during the Hundred Years War, that the English first became aware of the practice.[30] MS Harley 53 of the English *Brut* chronicle records an incident during the Duke of Burgundy's siege of (English) Calais in 1436:

> They of Brigges [Bruges] made payntet clothes, howe the Flemmynges were att seege att Caleis, and howe thai wann the toune; and hanget out Englisshe men by the helis out at lopes:[31] and well was hym that myght by of thes clothes! And thai made entirludes and plaies in Brigges, of the Cardynall of Wynchester And of the Dolfyn, of thaire purposyng and Ansuaryng att the trety of Arras, And all in dispite and hoker [mockery/derision] of Englissh men. . . .[32]

Two years later, according to a Parisian chronicler, three English lords, the Earl of Suffolk, Lord Willoughby and Sir Thomas Blount, were also depicted on painted cloths, hung out at the four gates of Paris, each:

> knight was hanged by his feet from a gallows with his spurs on, completely armed except for his head, at each side a devil binding him with chains, and at the bottom of the picture, by his face, two hideous ugly crows made to look as if they were pecking out his eyes.[33]

Coincidentally, a German *Schandbild* painted in the same year depicts the malefactor similarly hanged upside down, the rope attached to his feet, with beside him his coat of arms also hanging inverted from the gallows, and as if to emphasise the inversion, instead of pecking out his eyes, two ravens peck at his feet (Colour Plate 4). Similarly, 'when Dunois besieged the castle of Harcourt in 1449, he had its captain, Richard Frognall, "hanged by the feet in painting at the door", because he had broken his oath by taking up arms against the French and so was "gravely dishonoured"'.

By 1453 the English had caught on, and at the Battle of Castillon in that year, the English leader, Talbot, carried:

> several standards knowingly and deliberately made false and deceptive, carrying inscriptions and devices intended to be insulting and disdainful to good Frenchmen.

Sadly, not a single one of these paintings, English or French, survives. In Germany, however, a fascinating collection of such enforcing pictures from the fifteenth and sixteenth centuries does survive, together with the accompanying threatening and insulting letters (*Scheltbriefe*), written by some very poisonous pens indeed.[34] These offensive images are painted and drawn on large sheets of paper and were displayed somewhat like 'Wanted' posters in public places (town hall, church, but also places of ill-repute such as brothels and the pillory), to the great shame of the persons complained of; indeed, sometimes the mere threat of the imminent posting of such an image was enough for the malefactor (often a debtor) to make reparation. The practice is alluded to as German in Marston's *Malcontent* (1604):

> they . . . execute her in pictures as they do in Germany, and hang her in their shops. By this means is she better known . . . than if she had been five times carted [V.i.29ff.].

It is interesting to note, however, that the legal writer Michael Dalton in his *Countrey Justice* (1618) specifies that a libel could also be committed by pictures or signs of shame, as pictures of the gallows, pillory, cucking-stool, horns or such like. (See p. 71 for the horns.)

In 1454, in an attempt to reassure his creditors that he and his associates would indeed repay the money he owed them, Archbishop Dietrich of Cologne wrote:

> And if it be the case that we . . . default on the aforementioned payment, then may Johann Lord of Gemen . . . thereupon denounce us to our heirs . . . and cause our images, coats of arms and so on, to be painted as he sees fit, as scathingly as he can conceive.

It is to be hoped that he and his associates paid up on time.

It is instructive to analyse the pictorial motifs of the German *Schandbilder*. From the first century of their appearance in Germany, *c.* 1420–*c.* 1520, I am aware of ten such images. The earliest image depicts the miscreant Herzog Johann von Bayern-Holland lifting up a sow's tail in order to imprint his worthless seal (painted outsize so that we may the more readily identify him) with the animal's dung (Colour Plate 5), a gesture repeated in pictures painted in 1468 and 1525 (Figure 5.4), except that the animal in the former is a mare (later sixteenth-century images add the she-ass and the bitch in this role), but in both the malefactors are shown mounted backwards on the animals. The *Schandbild* of *c.* 1500 which was pasted on the door of the Ingolstadt council house merely depicts a cow, but she shits over the outsize seal, labelled in type, of Heinz von Guttenberg, and the image is accompanied by a printed *Scheltbrief* in the same face, which is that used in the earliest books known to have been printed in the town. The besmirching of the miscreant's seal or coat of arms in this manner, is also attested from Italy.[35]

Figure 5.4

The exclusive use of female animals in this role is notable, and has been attributed – somewhat inadequately, one might think – to a general feeling that contact with female animals is somehow intrinsically more demeaning than similar contact with the male would be.

A special case, and an especially ominous one, is this defamatory German fifteenth-century single sheet which is undoubtedly related to the imagery of the *Schandbild*, the so-called *Judensau* (Jews' Sow) (Figure 5.5). Unlike those specific painted images designed to enforce reparation from a named individual, however, this is a generic insult aimed at an entire community, and being a woodcut, one with the potential for mass-produced multiple copies. With the figure who sits backwards above the hindquarters of the sow and sucks her tail (according to the banderole), compare the similarly mounted man in Figure 5.4, while the man below him is apparently preparing to blow up her arse – again, the same concentration on the anus of the animal that is found in the painted images.

It was inevitable that sooner or later the defamatory image would include a sexual element, and in a *Schandbild* dated 1545 now in the Lippischen Landesarchiv, Detmold, two of the thirteen debtors complained against are shown buggering a she-ass and a bitch – their treachery to the lender is further emphasised by the presence of a yellow-robed Judas, the arch-traitor, clutching his purse.

The images of 1438 (Colour Plate 4) and *c.* 1490 depict the malefactor hanged upside down, the rope attached to his feet, with beside him his coat of arms also hanging inverted from the gallows. In the earlier picture, instead of pecking out his eyes two ravens peck at his feet, as if to emphasise the inversion, while in the later picture a little devil with a spiked club belabours the unfortunate hanging man. The

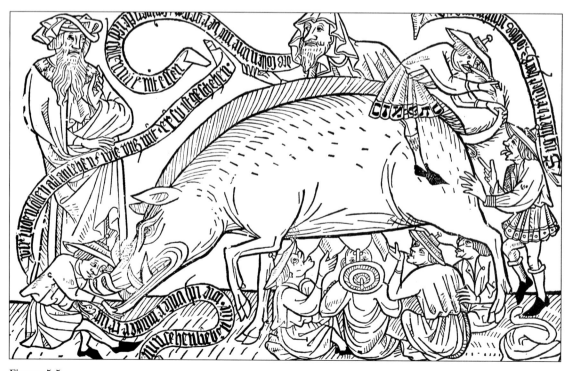

Figure 5.5

hanged man of the tarot pack, about which such a lot of modern nonsense has been (and continues to be) written, is named in early sources *il traditore* (the traitor), and is nothing more than a standard *pittura infamante* which would have been recognised as such by any late medieval Italian.[36] A preparatory drawing for another such *pittura* made in 1530 by Andrea del Sarto shows the traitor hanging by his right foot, though the Tarot man hangs by his left, as did Rodolfo da Varano painted on the façade of the Palazzo del Podestà for his treachery to the Florentines in 1377. No less a figure than Botticelli painted the traitors involved in the Florentine Pazzi conspiracy on the Bargello in 1478, also hanging by their feet, and we have already noted above instances of the French portraying their English enemies in this fashion.

Other German *Schandbilder* show judicially lopped-off limbs dangling from the gallows and the wheel (1464,[37] 1523), as well as the malefactors themselves broken on the wheel (1490, 1525 (Figure 5.4)). In an idiosyncratic picture executed shortly before 1500 the miscreant, a nobleman by the name of Heinrich von Veltheim, is depicted skinning a dead horse (Colour Plate 7) – the banderole above the scene includes the remark that this 'greatly defames the Knightly Order', and that because of his false words Heinrich is now enrolled in the 'Order of Nag-skinners'! Any occupation that dealt with such things as dead animals was felt to be fatally ignoble, and no greater ignominy could be imagined for a knight than to soil his hands in such a dishonourable occupation (see the discussion of cat-skinning in Chapter 3).

Despite the evidence that artists who were (later to become) 'big names' were involved in the production of these images in Italy, it is evident that it was considered a particularly demeaning commission – at the outset of his career in 1440, Andrea del Castagno painted the Albizzi conspirators (who behaved treacherously at the Battle of Anghiari) on the Florentine Palazzo del Podestà and quickly acquired the nickname *degli impiccati* (of the hanged men) for his pains. Andrea del Sarto went to the extreme of constructing a sort of shed inside which he hid to paint his *pitture* of 1530, precisely in order to avoid acquiring such an unflattering sobriquet, and it is hardly surprising, for of the 112 such paintings of criminals made between 1274 and 1303, just over half were done by painters who were themselves accused of murder.[38]

There is no doubt either, of course, of the extreme shame such a painting visited on the miscreant and his family; at least one man preferred to be hanged in reality, rather than in image, to avoid having his reputation so publicly and enduringly sullied in paint.

Freedberg singled out two late fourteenth-century Florentine paintings which were described in some detail and will thus bear some comparison with our surviving German *Schandbilder*.[39] In 1377 the traitor Rodolfo da Varano was painted hanging by his left foot with a siren on one side of him and a basilisk on the other, a devil gripping him by the throat, and in addition, was shown with arms splayed and making the insulting 'fig' gesture at the Church and the Commune. As we have seen above, hanging up by the heels is a common feature of such French and German images too, while devils appear also in the notices of the Parisian painted cloths of 1438 and on the German *Schandbild* of *c.* 1490.

In the other Florentine *pittura* of 1388/9 Bonaccorso di Lapo di Giovanni was painted standing:

with his feet in water, and on his head a large 'mitre', and at his throat an iron collar. This is attached to a chain that a devil holds in his hand as he drags him. In his right hand he holds a basilisk, and in his left a [word missing]. At his side at the bottom, there is a she-wolf standing upright and leaning against him at one side, and on the other a pig, also upright and leaning against his clothing. Under his feet there was written in large letters:

> Arrogant, avaricious, traitor, liar,
> Lustful, thankless, full of deceits,
> I am Bonaccorso di Lapo di Giovanni.

Edgerton claims that having one's feet represented in water is a traditional symbol of inconstancy and perhaps also avarice. The basilisk clearly denotes evil, and the she-wolf and pig are perhaps best seen as insulting quasi-heraldic supporters.[40] We may add that (as Edgerton himself notes elsewhere) *la (ver)gogna* (significantly, the word itself means 'shame, dishonour') was the term for the iron collar by which miscreants were chained to the pillory in the public square and there left exposed to public ridicule.

Baffling!

That the practice of manufacturing *Schandbilder* was indeed foreign to the English, seems to be confirmed by the earliest citations for the word *baffle*.[41] In his *Chronicle*, not published until 1548 but completed *c.* 1532, Edward Hall relates the following, concerning an incident which occurred prior to the Battle of Flodden in 1513:

> He was content that the Scottes should Baffull hym, which is a great reproache among the Scottes, and is used when a man is openly perjured, and then they make of him an Image paynted reuersed with hys heles upwarde, with hys name, wonderynge [wandering about], cryenge and blowing out of hym with hornes.[42]

Such an 'image' was undoubtedly a *Schandbild*, and is mentioned again in a 1551 description by Sir Robert Bowes, as well as in a real life incident in which a warden of the West March was expelled from office and degraded in this manner, 'his pictor hung at the crosse with his heid downwart, and with the words Infamy and Perjurie written across his legs, and all this done verie solemnly by trumpetts and harrolds of armes'.[43]

The Scottish connexion is reinforced by the *OED*'s citation from *Churchyard's Chippes* (1575) in which a Scotsman declares:

> I will baffull your good name, sounde with the trumpet your dishonour, and paint your pictor with the heeles vpward, and beate it in despight of yourselfe.[44]

Another such visual ritual took place at a meeting in the Borders between the Scots and English in 1519 when a Scottish ambassador 'bare at his speres pointe a glove, and above the same a litell pauper being therin written the name of Sir Roger Gray', by way of reproving Sir Roger for breaking his word. In return, the Grays 'bearing gloves and blawne hornes came into Scotland by day light and blawne out apoun Scottismen'.[45]

Derisive Headgear ('Mitre')

One feature to be found in Italian *pitture* but not in the French and German images, is the depiction of the malefactors wearing 'mitres'. When John Hus was burned at the stake in person, rather than merely in effigy, at Konstanz in 1415, he was forced to wear a paper *mitra* painted with devils and the word *haeresiarcha* (arch-heretic), as can be seen in the several contemporary and later representations of his martyrdom. Very similar to Hus's are the *mitre* worn by the condemned heretics in the painting of St Dominic presiding over a Spanish *auto-da-fé* painted by Pedro Berrugete, *c.* 1495.[46]

In the English *Apology for Lollard Doctrines* of *c.* 1400 occurs a jibe which could have been aimed at many contemporary prelates: 'Than is an hornid asse born ther in.' The reference was clearly to the resemblance of the episcopal horned mitre[47] to the upstanding ears of an ass, and in a Flemish psalter of a generation later, a mitred ass actually appears.[48] The shape of the mitre lends itself to joking allusions, not only to ears, but to horns – always a fascinating topic to the late medieval and early modern mind (see Chapter 11) – and it may be because of these associations that it was frequently used in penances and punishments at this period, both as a humiliating device and as an emblem of sinfulness.

Paper hats inscribed with the sundry sins of the damned, are shown in Taddeo di Bartolo's late fourteenth-century hell frescoes in the Duomo of San Gimignano.[49] Historical examples from Italy include an occasion in 1184 when the people of Rome seized a number of clerks in the service of Pope Lucius III and put out the eyes of all except one, setting derisive mitres on their heads, mounting them nose to tail on asses, and making them swear to present themselves to the Pope in this condition. According to the records, the antipope Burdinus, who styled himself Gregory VIII, was captured in 1121 by Pope Calixtus II at Sutri, mounted backwards on a camel whose tail he was forced to hold in place of reins, and led thus to Rome. When this event was portrayed in a miniature in the fourteenth-century *Saxony World Chronicle*, however, Burdinus was shown seated naked on an ass, facing forwards, and with a mitre on his head,[50] in much the same way as prescribed in a decree of Gian Galeazzo Visconti, Duke of Milan, issued in 1393, which ordained that anyone convicted of forgery, poisoning, or murder:

> is to be led on an ass, with a paper mitre on his head, through the high-street and other public places of this city or state.[51]

These *mitre* might also be decorated with visual depictions of the wearer's crimes. In the fifteenth-century Île-de-France, a dishonest chicken farmer was led to his punishment wearing a mitre with chickens and other fowl painted on it, and 'an abundance of writing'; while in 1511, a lax forest ranger was paraded around in a paper mitre decorated with standing and fallen trees.[52] In 1444, at Sibenik in

Dalmatia, an elderly woman reputed to be a witch was accused of using spells to lure rich lovers to her daughter. An ecclesiastical court condemned her 'to be led through the town by her daughter, seated on a donkey but turned backwards to face its tail, and smeared with excrement . . . both must wear paper mitres and pictures of the Devil'.[53] Very similar usage is recorded by Bruegel, in the bizarre charivari which forms part of his illustration of *Luxuria* (1557). The monstrous procession is led, appropriately, by a bagpiper,[54] and the rider, naked and with hands tied behind his back as he is scourged by the mob, wears a paper *mitra* to which is affixed the history of his lust.[55] A woodcut in the first (1563) edition of Foxe's *Actes and Monuments* (popularly known as the *Book of Martyrs*) depicts the martyrdom of Nicholas Burton before the Spanish Inquisition; he is seated backwards on an ass and wears an over-tunic and tall hat decorated with devils. A woodcut in the third edition (1576) depicts the martyrdom of four men of Windsor in 1543, and includes a picture of two men mounted backwards on horses who, the caption informs us, are 'riding about the market place with papers on their heades for periurie'. As late as 1587 at Elgin in Scotland one Hindrye Kaye was sentenced for incest with his mother-in-law to stand at the church door for three Sundays, barefoot, in sackcloth, and with 'ane myter upon his heid'.[56]

Sometimes, it seems, the offender might be obliged to wear more than a paper hat: in 1465 a man named Chamberlain who lived in the sanctuary of Westminster Abbey confessed to an intention to murder William, Lord Berkeley, also at that time living in sanctuary. John Smyth of Nibley, the Jacobean chronicler of the family's history, records in his *Lives of the Berkeleys* that the Abbot of Westminster:

> decreed him to bee had to an open place in the sanctuary of punishment and reproofe, And made him to be arayed in papires painted with signes of untroth, sedition, and doublenesse, And was made to goe before the procession in that aray, and afterwards soe set in the stocks, that the people might behold him.[57]

Sadly, we have no further details of the appearance of those 'signes of untroth, sedition, and doublenesse' that were painted on the various papers in which Chamberlain was arrayed.

The practice of marking out malefactors by obliging them to wear some sort of ridiculous headgear is an ancient tradition which perhaps ultimately even underlies the old-fashioned dunce's cap of the schoolroom. In the German Middle Ages, however, the incompetent student was literally made an ass of, not only by being known as the *asinus*, a Latin term afforded official status by being mentioned in several late medieval school ordinances,[58] but more drastically by being obliged to wear an ass's head (Figure 4.5), as we noted in Chapter 4.

The insult value of the word 'ass' is incidentally confirmed for the English Middle Ages by an unremarked marginal 'speech-bubble' in the mid-thirteenth-century *Rutland Psalter*: in the *bas-de-page* of f. 37 one cleric says to another as he draws his dagger, 'You are an ass', but curiously, the inscription is in mirror-writing.

Those thought to have regal ambitions might be humbled in their punishment by being given the trappings of royalty – most obviously the crown – in burlesque form. The archetype, of course, is the crown of thorns, purple robe, reed sceptre and mocking inscription, 'King of the Jews', that were forced on Christ (and see the crown of nettles, below). A remarkable late medieval English burlesquing of a man with real regal ambitions, subjecting the victim to an involuntary *imitatio Christi*, is recorded in the *Chronicle* written by John of Wheathamsted, as having been visited on Richard Plantagenet, Duke of York, executed after the Battle of Wakefield in 1460. Wheathamsted explicitly makes 'the comparison of Richard with Christ by representing the Duke's execution as an analogue of the crucifixion':[59]

> They stood him on a little anthill and put on his head a base garland made of marsh-grass [?reeds/rushes] in the manner of a crown, just like the Jews before Our Lord, and they bent their knees before him, saying in mockery – 'Hail king without rule! Hail king without a kingdom! Hail duke and prince totally without people or possessions!'[60]

A similar mock-crown was one of the details of the public humiliation (prior to execution) imposed by the King of Sweden on two of his enemies in 1526 when they were forced to enter Stockholm:

> Clad in old, threadbare tattered cloaks, riding backwards on famished horses, Peder Sunnänvader with a coronet of straw on his head and a broken sword by his side, Master Knut with a crosier of birch-bark.[61]

Displaying the Attributes of Dishonest Trade

The nature of the offender's crime might, in some cases, be conveyed by the display of objects, rather than by writings or pictures. Since the urinal was the unmistakable attribute of the medieval doctor, in allusion to his almost exclusive diagnostic technique of urinalysis,[62] a quack named Roger Clerk who was subjected to a charivari in London in 1382, was paraded through the city seated backwards on a horse, holding the tail as reins, and with 'two urinals called "jordans" in the vernacular' tied round his neck, together with a whetstone, the latter being the proverbial prize for a prodigious liar.[63]

Another English example involved one John Watte, a spurious pardoner, who was forced to ride through Cheapside seated backwards on his horse, the forged Indulgences dangling round his neck, and wearing a tall paper hat suitably inscribed.[64] As many such crimes involve lying, the punishment of the 'pillory and whetstone' is frequent. In 1364 John de Hakford was found guilty of making a false charge of conspiracy against the chief men of the City of London, and was given a year's prison sentence, and in addition, obliged once each quarter to stand in the pillory without hood or girdle, barefoot, with a whetstone hung by a chain from his neck and lying on his breast, and to be accompanied to the pillory, where his crime was solemnly proclaimed by a pair of trumpets, the whetstone being described in the document as 'the sign/badge of a false liar'.[65]

A more drastic punishment for lying was to have one's tongue bored through; and a woodcut in de Worde's edition of Hawes's *Passetyme of Pleasure* (1509) shows a man with his feet in the stocks and a woman performing a very business-like operation on his tongue with a hand-drill. The cut is also found in the same printer's *The Example of Euyll Tongues* to which it is far more appropriate; although the earliest extant edition of this work is dated *c.* 1525, the existence of this cut must surely presuppose a lost earlier edition *ante* 1509.

The English Dominican preacher John Bromyard in his massive *Summa Predicantium* (1325x50) deplored the prevalence of swearing and blasphemy in his day, and quoted approvingly the measures against such excesses taken by St Louis of France, which included cutting the tongues of blasphemers, branding them on the face with a hot iron, and at a later date the King ordained that:

> they should be set in a public place in the high stocks, which in their tongue are called escale, similar in form and in mode of punishment to that inflicted upon cutpurses in the realm of England.[66]

Figure 5.6

Such an *escale* or 'ladder' is to be seen in one of the stone quatrefoils of the Martyrs' Portal of Nôtre-Dame Cathedral in Paris, carved in the early 1260s.[67]

The Dishonest Baker

As we have seen, the dishonest trader was punished by humiliation, and he or she paraded through the town to the pillory together with their fraudulent wares. Illustrations of three fourteenth-century dishonest bakers are known to me, two in the expected legal context, but the third occupying the *bas-de-page* of the iconographically extraordinarily rich *Smithfield Decretals* (*c.* 1330).[68] This last is very similar to another such Metropolitan depiction, that represented in a *c.* 1320 manuscript of the *Assisa Panis*, the regulations concerning the proper weights and qualities of various breads: both show the baker bound seated, but barefoot, to a horse-drawn hurdle, with the underweight loaf pierced and hanging like a giant pendant from a rope round his neck. The third such image occupying the lower half of the decorated intial E of a Royal Charter granted to Bristol in 1347 is similar, except for the addition of a pair of scales symbolising the short weight for which the baker is being punished in this humiliatingly public manner (Figure 5.6). Adam Fox cites an instance of a similar popular ritual surviving in Essex as late as 1768: when a local painter was paid by an aggrieved corn chandler to portray a farmer, believed to be selling short measures of barley, riding backwards upon a donkey holding its tail and with his false measure round his neck.[69]

In 1382 we hear of a fascinating divination ritual practised by one Robert Berewold, by means of which he claimed to discover the thief of a mazer bowl: he fixed a round wooden peg in the top of a loaf of bread and four knives in the form of a cross, and 'did soothsaying and the magic art over them': like any other fraudster, he was put in the pillory with the 'magic' loaf hung from his neck.[70]

The Dishonest Alewife

The alewife, or brewster, seems to have been the other notoriously dishonest tradesperson to judge from contemporary complaints and satires and, like some post-lapsarian Adam and Eve, both a baker with peel and scales (as on the Bristol charter), and an alewife with short-measure tankard on her head, may be seen carried on the shoulders of devils towards the hell-mouth in the *Holkham Bible Picture Book* illuminated *c.* 1325.[71] Piers Plowman wanted the pillory to be more strictly applied as a punishment for:

> brewsters and bakers, butchers and cooks . . .
> For they poison people privily and oft . . .

and in the Doom play of the late medieval Chester mystery-cycle, the alewife damned for adulterating her beer is deemed fit to become Satan's bride. A real-life example of such a fraudulent alewife was Alice, wife of Robert de Caustone, who put a false bottom in her quart measuring-tankard, raising it by an inch and a half, so that not even six such measures yielded a true gallon; she was punished with the pillory in 1364 and had her false measure cut in half, one half tied to the pillory and the other half kept for reference purposes, presumably, in London's Guildhall.[72]

The fraudulent alewife was a popular target in the visual arts too: she may be seen naked, except for her fashionable horned headdress (another constant target of the moralists' attack), still clinging onto her fraudulent tankard, and thrown over the back of a devil who is heading for a yawning hell-mouth, carved *c.* 1420 on a misericord in Ludlow (Figure 5.7). She is presented similarly naked on a roof boss

Figure 5.7

in Norwich Cathedral, but the fiend who carries her here, as she shamelessly waves her tankard on his shoulders, also wheels a barrow. In the late medieval Doom painted over the chancel arch in St Thomas's Church, Salisbury, she takes centre-stage, once again cheerily waving her cheating measure in a gesture of seeming unrepentance.

FEMALE CRIMES

The Mortar

One of the judicial punishments thought suitable for a scold in late medieval England was the hanging of a heavy wooden mortar round the offender's neck. 'John Morris's wife is a common scold and shall wear the mortar' reads a legal pronouncement of 1423 from Maldon, Essex.[73] The vessel in question is not without its symbolic associations, but is probably best seen here as comparable with the Germanic custom of the *Laster-* or *Bagstein* (MHG *bâgen*, 'scold, squabble'),[74] that is, of hanging a heavy stone round the offender's neck and making him or her walk thus weighed down through the town. A marginal illustration from the *Hours of Catherine of Cleves* (Utrecht, *c.* 1440) depicts a woman wearing a heavy stone slab hanging from shoulder straps before and behind her, and a paper mitre inscribed with her sins. The Orléans Museum still possesses a Gossips' Stone of sixteenth-century date, a bald head of stone with bulging, staring eyes and tongue sticking out. In addition to carrying the stone(s), the unfortunate female gossip might also be driven through the town in her shift, prodded by a goad wielded by her victim[75] (see, further, the 'stones of justice' which formed part of the punishment of adulterers below). The punishment was also accorded those who blasphemed, and such a sinner may be seen hanging from the gallows in the hell-scene sculpted on the tympanum at Conques, *c.* 1130.

Ducking Stool

From the thirteenth century onwards, the ducking stool was used as a humiliating punishment for the scold, later defined, in Tudor law, as:

> a troublesome and angry woman who, by her brawling and wrangling amongst her neighbours, doth break the public peace and beget, cherish and increase public discord.[76]

The *Rutland Psalter* of *c.* 1260 includes a unique marginal image of a woman in a ducking stool and a man with a look of unmistakably malicious glee, about to activate the ducking mechanism.[77]

Scold's Bridle and the Wisp

The bridle was another traditional punishment for the scold's tongue. A misericord of the fifteenth century in Stratford-upon-Avon Church (see chapter ornament), shows what I interpret as three stages in the savage taming of a shrew. Most unusually, the supporters are the same size as the central motif, which seems to demand a serial reading of the carvings. The head on the left sticks out its tongue (insultingly?), the central head grins widely, while that on the right is shown with a sausage-like gag in its mouth.[78]

An altogether less vicious and apparently domestic reproof to the scold was the following curious gesture, as described in Caxton's translation, *The Knight of the Tower* (Chapter xiv):

> But now for al that she wolde not be stylle but chode more than to fore And when the knyght sawe that she wolde not leue ne be stylle for no thyng he took a lytell wyspe of strawe that he fond And set it to fore her And saide to her Madame yf ye chyde more so chyde to this wyspe of strawe For I leue it here for me And wente his way and lefte hyr there.[79]

A German manuscript containing the fifteenth-century poem *Der Böse Weib und die Teufel* (The Evil Wife and the Devil) contains the couplet:

> an evil woman and a wisp of straw
> they are surely both the Devil's

which seems to attest to the same or a similar practice in contemporary Germany. (A discussion of the buck's horn stuck with a wisp of hay and a picture of a woman's privities left as an insulting message in Jacobean Wiltshire is referred to on p. 71.

Punishing the Spinster

Plough-pulling

The woman who 'failed' to marry in late medieval and early modern society was the subject of special scorn (unless, of course, her celibacy was as a result of religious vows); various humiliating fates were promised her in the next life, and sometimes forced on her in this.[80] An apparently historical practice was the German custom of obliging unmarried women to pull a plough, illustrated *c.* 1530 by Erhard Schoen for a poem by Hans Sachs, and it seems to have been particularly at Carnival time that the unmarried women were most in danger from such communal disapproval and ridicule.[81]

Leading Apes in Hell (post-mortem punishment)

The best-known of the fates awaiting the spinster was to lead apes in hell, as Kate fears she will have to do in Shakespeare's *Taming of the Shrew* (*c.* 1590).[82] The earliest written reference to this proverbial motif in English dates from around 1560, but this is one of several such interesting cases where a representation of the speech idiom in art antedates its earliest literary attestation, for one of the Bristol misericords carved in 1520 depicts a devil in the jaws of hell receiving a naked woman leading four apes on a leash (Figure 5.8).[83]

Figure 5.8

Man Humiliated by Carrying Distaff

So strong were the female associations of the distaff, the female implement *par excellence*, that they were exploited as the basis for another characteristic medieval punishment by humiliation in which, on occasions, men convicted of crimes of sex and violence were paraded in public carrying a distaff.[84] (For other examples of men thus 'feminised' and – in the world of orthodox late medieval gender roles – thereby humiliated, see Chapter 11.)

Sexual Punishment for Adulterers

On a now censored misericord at Walcourt in Flanders carved in 1531, a woman led a man by a rope attached to his penis – not surprisingly, he advances with a 'hands up' gesture;[85] one possible explanation of this unusual scene is that it represents the punishment of adulterers. A very similar scene may be seen painted in a fourteenth-century manuscript known as the *Custumal of Toulouse*, except that the punitive context is much clearer in that both are entirely naked and are preceded by a trumpeter and followed by an armed guard.[86] Under the title 'carry the chained stones', the great eighteenth-century lexicographer Ducange – a surprisingly underused, though quite invaluable source – cites a passage from Book I of Jan Stiernhook's *De Jure Sveonum et Gothorum vetusto* (Stockholm, 1672) entitled 'De Poena Adulterii', describing how these 'stones of justice' are placed on the shoulders of the adulteress, and then:

> a rope is tied to the adulterer's genital member, in order that she (the adulteress) thus burdened should publicly lead her 'rider' round the town.[87]

But when, in a French manuscript of the mid-fourteenth century, a nun is depicted leading a man by a string tied to his genitals, in the context of the other *bas-de-page* miniatures in this extraordinarily decorated *Roman de la Rose* manuscript, it seems certain that this is intended satirically.[88]

Carting

Similarly and necessarily genital in its focus is the image from a fifteenth-century illustrated manuscript of the *Cent Nouvelles Nouvelles* (Figure 5.9). The 45th *nouvelle* concerns a Scot living in Rome who pretends to be a washerwoman, calling himself Donna Margarita, thereby enabling him to gain access to many households where, as a normal part of the payment for 'her' services, (s)he is allowed to sleep over after 'her' day's work. It seems that the Roman ladies

Figure 5.9

are for the most part only too willing to go along with this deception, until she is finally discovered for what he is, and then paraded through the thoroughfares of Rome in a cart:

> So the justices ordered that he should be put on a cart and led through the city of Rome, stopping at every crossroads, and there he would be displayed for all to see his genitals. And thus it was done.[89]

The Glasgow University Library manuscript shows him in women's clothes, accompanied by an officer of the law in the act of raising the false washerwoman's skirts for all to see the evidence of his manhood.[90]

Carting was certainly the punishment meted out to convicted bawds in Elizabethan England, and probably much earlier: what is important is the spectacle made of the offender, the public humiliation. Two further ways of summoning and expressing public disapproval were ringing with basins, that is, making 'rough music' by bashing and clanging metal household utensils as the whore was led through the town, or being whipped 'at the cart's tail' or 'arse' (while tied to the cart as it was driven through the streets), both of which are punishments commonly attested from the same period.

Barrowing of Hell

There is evidence to show that being wheeled in a barrow was regarded as a sort of ignominious punishment, perhaps popular rather than official, but considered demeaning in the folk mind. In hell scenes, from at least the thirteenth century, artists are accustomed to depict one or more persons (sometimes identified by their headgear

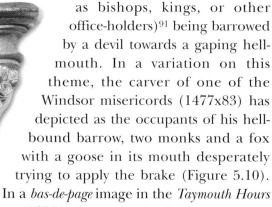

Figure 5.10

as bishops, kings, or other office-holders)[91] being barrowed by a devil towards a gaping hell-mouth. In a variation on this theme, the carver of one of the Windsor misericords (1477x83) has depicted as the occupants of his hell-bound barrow, two monks and a fox with a goose in its mouth desperately trying to apply the brake (Figure 5.10). In a *bas-de-page* image in the *Taymouth Hours* of about 1325 a fearsome devil barrows seven naked souls towards hell.[92]

There is no doubt that such barrowings were enacted on stage in the mystery plays: in the *Mystère de Ste. Barbe* played at Laval in 1493, for instance, stage-devils used carts and wheelbarrows to carry off the damned souls,[93] and in *L'Empereur Justinian au Liban*, the devil barrowing the Emperor says:

> My barrow will take him there
> where we will throw him,
> we'll drag him to hell
> without more ado.[94]

There are hints that such barrowings might also imply sexual misdemeanours. In the *bas-de-page* of the celebrated Bodleian *Romance of Alexander* manuscript, illuminated in Flanders *c.* 1340, a naked man conveys four nuns in a large wheelbarrow towards their convent.[95] In a roughly contemporary manuscript in Douai we see a man barrowing a woman, while beside them a devil sits astride a naked man beating him with a scourge,[96] and in another contemporary book probably illuminated in Maastricht, a cleric pursued by a devil is pushing a barrow in which one of his fellows is embracing a woman.[97] Certainly barrowing, in person or in effigy, could form part of the charivari, as is seen, for example, in the famous illustrations to the early fourteenth-century *Roman de Fauvel*.[98]

In Rome in 1525 the poet Maestro Andrea constructed a sort of mobile exhibition in the form of a barrow (*caretta*) containing *papier mâché* effigies of all the older Roman courtesans, each inscribed with the name. Disguised as a crippled beggar he wheeled it through the streets emptying the lot into the Tiber in front of the Pope as his finale. It is somehow satisfying to be able to report that he was later beaten through the city by the vengeful courtesans he had thus ridiculed, but a few years later his *Pvrgatorio delle cortegiane di Roma* (*c.* 1530) appeared, with its title-page illustrated by the woodcut of a diseased prostitute round whose legs the flies buzz. Although wheelbarrows were a normal means of conveyance for all invalids and cripples,[99] this image cannot help but suggest that these women are 'rubbish'.[100] A most significant record is that of Olivier de la Marche who witnessed, *c.* 1440, what Huizinga called 'a theatrical display of hyperbolic humility', when the titular King of Naples, who had renounced the world because of the exhortations of St Colette, entered a town 'carried in a sort of wheelbarrow not differing from the barrows in which dung and ordure are usually carried'.[101]

In the light of the above there is further the suspicion that the barrowing motif belongs, too, to the iconography of misogyny: on one of the late fifteenth-century desk fronts in St George's Chapel, Windsor, for instance, a man is shown barrowing a woman towards a hell-mouth,[102] as is another on a Bruges misericord carved in the second quarter of the century.[103] The suspicion – it can be no more – is that these are husbands wheeling their scolding wives off to hell. In a late thirteenth-century French miniature, a man barrowing a woman off to the left, seems to be deliberately contrasted with a younger man on the right, kneeling before Lady Love, who strikes him to the heart with the arrow of love.[104]

The Deceived Lover's Punishment

That the lover should be deceived by the object of his love might be thought punishment enough, but further iconographic humiliation awaited him. The dragging of a heavy log across ploughed ground to break up the clods of earth was originally an agricultural practice, but certainly by the sixteenth century, references show that the action had become proverbial for conveying the wasted labour of a man whose wife/mistress deceived or rejected him. The motif appears several times in art around 1500: in an engraving attributed to Israhel van Meckenem (where the banderole above the *Bloksleper* is inscribed 'all wasted effort'); and carved on misericords at Kappenberg (1509x20) and Toledo (1489x95).[105] I have suggested elsewhere that on one of the Beverley Minster misericords carved in 1520, the man lifting a beam while his wife has nothing better to do than to de-flea her dog – a known idleness motif[106] – may be a somewhat garbled version of this Flemish motif in England.

Riding Backwards

A punishment that was particularly popular (we have already noticed several instances in passing), attested in a wide variety of contexts, is that of riding backwards; that is, the culprit is seated on a horse or, preferably, a donkey, so as to face the animal's tail, which he is sometimes made to hold in his hand in place of reins.[107] In France in the fourteenth century, this was the penalty inflicted 'on men who showed cowardice and particularly on husbands whose wives used to beat them'.[108] Throughout the Middle Ages and the Renaissance, instances occur of the penalty being imposed on political or religious enemies and on various wrong-doers, and after it had been abandoned by official courts it still appeared as an element in traditional acts of popular justice. In the English charivari rituals of the seventeenth century, a 'feeble' husband was sometimes mocked by a 'rough-music' procession in which one of the participants rode backwards on a horse or donkey, holding a distaff, while another, enacting the role of the 'wife', beat him with a ladle.[109]

The earliest depiction of the motif found by Mellinkoff is the figure of Death, the Fourth Rider of the Apocalypse, mounted backwards on his pale horse in an early twelfth-century German manuscript.[110] Another, this time skeletal, Death appears mounted backwards on an ass at the end of the Middle Ages, in the woodcut to Chapter 94 of Brant's *Narrenschiff.* If figures of evil such as the Fourth Rider should be thus mounted, it should come as no surprise to find the human representatives of evil, such as witches and other unbelievers so portrayed. In the first decade of the sixteenth century Dürer engraved a small picture of a witch riding backwards on a goat accompanied by four *putti*;[111] similarly, a figure whom Mellinkoff identifies as a Jew, is carved seated backwards on a goat-like beast and holding its tail on a fifteenth-century misericord at Aarschot.[112]

English medieval misericords offer four examples of this motif, from the fourteenth century onwards, in Wells, Hereford and Bristol Cathedrals, and it also occurs on a carving believed to have come from a stall in Bangor Cathedral.[113] The fourteenth-century carvings show the man to be naked or almost so, and in the Wells example it is difficult to see how he is managing to cling on, whereas the early sixteenth-century Bristol rider is clothed and, as well as having one hand on the reins, like his Hereford predecessor, also grasps the animal's tail – as does the contemporary backwards-rider at Wells. The Wells rider's precarious position forces his face uncomfortably close to the horse's anal cleft, a detail for which there is literary precedent. In the *Lay of Havelok the Dane* (*c.* 1300), the traitor Godard is punished by being bound hand and foot and beaten like a bear, after which the king's men:

> . . . *keste him on a scabbed mere,*   [. . . flung him onto a mangy mare,
> *Hise nose went unto the crice.* . . .   his nose against the anal cleft. . . .]

In the case of the Hereford carving (1340x1355)[114] there is an intriguing possibility that the choice of motif was inspired by memories of a similarly bizarre humiliation imposed on a political offender in that city some years previously. In 1326, Hugh Despenser the Younger was captured while trying to escape to Wales and brought back to Bristol in the custody of Thomas Wake, who mounted him on 'the smallest, skinniest and most wretched horse' and forced him to wear a tabard with his arms reversed,[115] and a crown of nettles on his head. In this manner, he was led behind the royal train as it wended its way from Bristol to Hereford, attention being drawn to his plight by the sound of trumpets. This spectacle caused great commotion in the city, as Henry Knighton reports in his Latin *Chronicle.* Despenser was greeted not only with insults and yells but with the blowing of horns, summed up by Knighton as a *horridus sonus*, all of which suggests what would later come to be known as the 'rough music' associated with a charivari.[116] Finally, the wretched man was condemned and executed. Admittedly, Despenser was not described as being mounted backwards, and the rider on the Hereford misericord wears neither tabard nor nettle-crown; nevertheless, the impact that Despenser's humiliation obviously had on the populace, and the fact that we do know that such punishments with the victim on horseback, his face towards the horse tail were still being meted out in Hereford some two centuries later (1535),[117] lend the suggestion a certain plausibility.

Clerics were not immune from this type of punishment, and we have already described the sorry case of the antipope Burdinus above; another instance is a *Schandbild* of *c.* 1540 sent by Heinrich Reling, vicar of St John's Church in Minden, to the abbot and monastery of Sts Simeon and Mauritius in Minden, to shame them into paying the rents they owed him (Colour Plate 8). It depicts one of the brethren hanging from a gallows with lolling tongue, while towards him walks an ass on which the abbot is mounted backwards, one hand grasping the animal's tail and the other his crozier; his cowl has ass's ears attached.[118]

Mellinkoff also cites the case of the German mercenary soldiers who in 1198 and for no apparent reason seized a nun, stripped her naked, spread her with honey and rolled her in feathers, then mounted her backwards on a horse which they led about while mocking her.[119] This sort of humiliation, reflecting many a real-life charivari no doubt, is to be found in imaginative literature too; the ladies who judge the tale of Jehan de Santré's treacherous mistress recommend various similar punishments for her:

> I say that she should be tied on an ass, her face towards the tail, and led about the town to great derision.
> I say that such a woman should be stripped completely naked above the belt and [have her head] completely shaved, then be anointed with honey and led about the town so that the flies run after her and sting her.[120]

One suspects, however, that this is more the male author's own dubious fantasy than that of his fictional female judge.

As we pursue the interpretation of these varied but related iconographical motifs, we find the themes of reversal and ridicule, of folly and sin, of carnival and punishment, echoing one another, even blending together. In a strictly hierarchical society and one in which the sense of status and honour was so powerful, any reversal of the 'natural' and 'seemly' assumed explosive force. In some cases, as in the motifs of folly and topsy-turvydom discussed elsewhere, the reversals were merely humorous; in others, such as the alleged unruliness and violence of scolds and viragos, they were perceived as simultaneously ludicrous and threatening. In the many punishments by ridicule and humiliation, the aim was to exploit reversal in order to degrade the offender and, by implication, reassert right order in the community, which assembled to mock him or her. Once again, the little images in manuscript margins and the carvings inconspicuously tucked away under misericords lead unexpectedly deep into the psychology and social attitudes of the Middle Ages.

six

The FOOL AND The ATTRIBUTES OF FOLLY

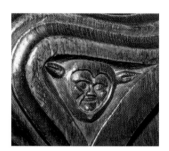

The fool is not only one of the most important cultural figures of the late Middle Ages, he is also perhaps the most interesting: a paradoxical figure who, at his most servile, merely entertains the society which patronises him with empty, puerile buffoonery, but who, at his most heroic, challenges the very assumptions on which that society is founded. The meaning of the term 'fool' vacillates between simpleton and satirist, drooling village idiot and *morosophe*, between Vice and 'fool for Christ's sake', whipping-boy and scourge; he is both the problem and the commentary on that problem – all these possibilities are encompassed in the term 'fool'.

He is especially a key figure for understanding the transitional period between the end of the Middle Ages and the beginning of the early modern era, and this is nowhere better demonstrated than in the Germanic region, where Sebastian Brant's *Narrenschiff* (Basel, 1494) rapidly became a Europe-wide best-seller, being translated into Latin, the *lingua franca* of scholarship, in 1497, and into the various vernaculars in the years following (two English translations appeared in 1509, one in prose), and inspiring various imitative ships-of-fools, such as the English *Cock Lorelles Bote* (1518). It is important to note, however, that Brant's innumerable ocean-going fools – 'the number of fools is infinite' is a favourite quotation in folly literature [*Ecclesiastes* I.15] – are not funny men (despite the funny costume and other comic attributes given to them by the illustrator), but a company of Vices; and they are sailing to perdition.

GENERAL APPEARANCE: COSTUME

Historically, the particular fool to whom we owe much of our knowledge of fool iconography is the *insipiens* who, in the opening words of Psalm 52 (AV 53), 'hath said in his heart, There is no God', and from the early thirteenth century on, the illuminated D of the first Latin word of the Psalm becomes a circular frame in which we are shown the atheistic fool, often disputing with King David, the reputed author of the Psalms, so that in later manuscripts he is visualised very much as David's court jester.

Sometimes he is completely naked, a madman who has thrown off his clothes in his frenzy, and carries only a club for his own protection, and chews on a round loaf or stone, and many of the earliest Psalter fools are of this type. Interesting evidence that nudity might play a part in real-life fooling is afforded by the Wardrobe Accounts of Edward I, which record a payment made to Bernard the Fool and fifty-four of his companions who came before the King at Pontoise near Paris, 'naked and with dancing revelry', about the year 1300.

Where he is dressed, however, nothing in the costume of the fool – including the various accessories – is accidental, everything is symbolic of his folly, his derangement, and not least, the familiar motley or *mi-parti*. Mellinkoff notes that the fiddlers in the mid-thirteenth-century French *Morgan Old Testament Bible* are the only characters, from a figure-stock of several hundred, to be dressed in parti-coloured tunics with deeply dagged skirts,[1] and similarly in the Heidelberg manuscript of the *Sachsenspiegel* (*c.* 1330), the fiddler is the only figure depicted with a violently dagged hem to his parti-coloured tunic. It is also perhaps significant that in early fifteenth-century London, prostitutes, another class of disreputable entertainer, as part of their public humiliation, were forced to wear hoods of *ray*, the name of a striped cloth (see below).

Like others before her, Mellinkoff derives the pointed headgear, bells, shaved heads, and grotesque physical features of the fool ultimately from Roman mime actors,[2] as well as his parti-coloured and dagged costume, drawing attention to a most striking late antique bronze statuette of a mime actress dancing, found in Syria, whose costume includes extravagant dagging with each strip of material terminating in a bell, bells on her jacket and on one ankle-band, and a floppy peaked hat which is also adorned with bells.[3] In similar vein, I should like to note in this connexion an extraordinary little Gallo-Roman bronze head from a securely dated second-century stratum in a villa at Mathay near Angoulême, which was called a fool's head by the excavators, for he does, indeed, appear to be wearing some sort of peaked and eared hood astonishingly like that which becomes standard in the late Middle Ages, and another not dissimilar recently found at Great Walsingham.[4]

In the late Middle Ages and early modern era there is always a tension between the literally weak-minded 'natural' fool, the unfortunate whose unconscious antics provided amusement for a society that had radically different attitudes to mental illness from our own, and the 'artificial' fool or jester, who made his living aping the bizarre behaviour and inconsequential speech of the deranged. This derangement is reflected in the very costume of the 'artificial' fool – the motley (from *mote*, speck, spot, blemish, stain),[5] the check, the extravagant dagging giving a tattered effect, the clash of bright colours (especially the yellow and green which Pastoureau has termed the *couleurs du désordre*),[6] the absurdly elongated footwear and headgear. We shall see below how Robert of Sicily successfully adopted the disguise of a fool, so that 'He semyd a fole, that queynt syre, Bothe by hede and by atyre', pointing up the two most important elements of the fool's appearance, his hairstyle and his costume.

Figure 6.1

Thanks largely to the long and very full sequence of *Dixit insipiens* initials, we can trace the gradual evolution of what we may call the 'standard' fool's costume (the image we conjure up even today of the 'typical' court jester) sufficiently well to be able to say that it had crystallised by about 1430. The standard late medieval fool wears a costume of two contrasting colours including a short tunic with scalloped or dagged edges and baggy sleeves, leggings usually of different colours, extravagantly long pointed shoes, and a hood with ass's ears, cock's comb and one or more peaks, sometimes in the form of a cockerel's head and neck (in the latest period). The whole costume and hood are hung with bells, and he carries either a *marotte* (often a miniature representation of himself) or a bladder-stick, or sometimes a ladle (Figure 6.1), which may well have served as a collecting-box for alms.

All the elements that went to make up this bizarre costume can be traced in the artistic record, and seem to derive in the main either from the clothes of the lowest ranks of society, or to be symbolic of the true madman's appearance – tattered, ragged, extravagantly inappropriate, or otherwise 'deranged' dress.

We should beware of making too sharp a distinction between the various species of medieval entertainer of which the fool was but one. His function and his costume had obvious connexions with the other relatively lowly employees of the nobility: he too was a retainer and thus, in some degree, also wore his master's livery. But he was also a musician in the period before that profession became respectable and had much in common with the itinerant entertainers of the Middle Ages known in Latin as *joculatores*, a term which embraces the etymologically and semantically related English terms *joker* and *juggler*, and the French *jongleur*, with its musical and narrative associations. A Robert *le Fol* is significantly listed among the minstrels of Edward III's Queen Philippa in the Wardrobe Accounts for 1333,[7] and he may well be the same as the King's fool who is again listed with the minstrels in 1363/4, and in the latter year seemingly transferred to the Abbey of St Albans, with maintenance for life at royal expense. This same Robert Fool is otherwise called William *Cheupayn*, suggesting perhaps that 'Robert the Fool' may be something of a generic or traditional name for the English court fool, but his presumably original surname is also of interest, for it looks as if it

7 Heinrich von Veltheim depicted flaying a dead horse: painted manuscript *Schandbild*, German, 1490s.

8 Abbot of Minden in fool's hood rides backwards on ass, another monk hangs from gallows: painted manuscript *Schandbild*, German, *c.* 1540.

9 Fool embraces woman: painted wooden towel-rail, Arnt van Tricht, Kalkar, 1530s.

10 Fool-bishop inside initial 'D': manuscript miniature, English, first half of 13thC.

11 Der Busant: tapestry fragment, Strasbourg, late 15thC.

12 Man Grimacing: oil on panel, Flemish, early 16thC.

13 Exemplum of man, fox, serpent: manuscript miniature, *Rutland Psalter*, English, *c.* 1260.

is a hybrid Anglo-French nickname composed of the English verb 'chew' and the French word for 'bread' – could there be a reference here to the depiction of the atheistic fool of Psalm 52, commonly shown gnawing on a round loaf?

Although more archival research into the lives of real-life fools still remains to be done, much of significance has already been uncovered, especially regarding costume and other 'props', but a certain amount may be gleaned from the very names of particular household fools. One such was the 'John Goose, my lord of Yorks fole', recorded in the Privy Purse Expenses of Henry VII's queen, Elizabeth of York, or the earliest known 'Tom-fool', whose funeral expenses are recorded in the Durham Cathedral Accounts of 1356 – for abbeys considered themselves households in much the same way as great secular establishments. The Cathedral Accounts for 1338–9 record the purchase of four ells of checked 'burel' (*burelli scacciati*) for clothing Thome Fole, and on f. 84 of the precisely contemporary *Luttrell Psalter* (Figure 6.2) a most interesting entertainer is depicted making his

Figure 6.2

little dog jump through a hoop – he wears a long tunic of red and blue check, and on his head what looks like a bishop's mitre (see below) of the same pattern.

It is probable that another common trait of the fool's costume, the often very scant or short gown/tunic, is also in origin – like the shaven head – a sign of his humiliation. Some medieval legal codes (German and Welsh, for example) prescribe the cutting short of a malefactor's garment for certain offences as a punishment by humiliation. According to the spiritual autobiography of the English mystic, Margery Kempe, while en route for the Holy Land on her pilgrimage of 1413, she managed so to irritate her travelling companions in the neighbourhood of Konstanz that:

> They cut her gown so short that it came only a little below her knee and made her put on a white canvas like a sackcloth apron, so that she should be taken for a fool.[8]

Tonsure/Hair

Fools' heads seem either to have been completely shaven – 'lette the madde persons hed be shauen ones a moneth' recommends Boorde's *Dyetary of Helth* (1542) – or to have been shaved in some special manner: double and triple tonsures are commonly illustrated. There can be little doubt that whatever pseudo-medical reasons might be given for completely shaving the fool's head, the result was seen as a mark of infamy, of humiliation, of a similar if less positive humiliation, to the tonsure voluntarily undergone by the priest. Compare the punishment meted out to convicted brothel-keepers of both sexes in late medieval London, according to the *Liber Albus* (compiled in 1419): for the man '. . . let all the hair and beard be shaved, except a fringe on the head two inches in breadth . . .', and for the woman, '. . . let her hair be cut round about her head . . .', and the same punishment for a common whore's third offence – for her first offence she was forced to wear a hood of ray and carry a white wand.[9]

Entirely shaven fools' heads are commonly seen in thirteenth-century psalters, and the shaven head may have been felt particularly appropriate to the atheistic *insipiens*, in that, as early as the seventh-century *Lex Visigothorum* the shaving of the head was part of the punishment for blasphemy.[10] Single, double and even triple tonsures can be seen in fourteenth-century psalters – an interesting example is to be found within the Psalm 52 initial 'D' of a manuscript in Oxford,[11] which depicts the triple-tonsured fool disputing the existence of God with a tonsured priest. The fool sits on the floor wearing a very scant tunic (compare above), extravagant shoes of the *poulaines* type, and holds his bladder-stick, proclaiming 'There is no God', while the fully robed cleric, who sits on a stool holding his Bible responds, 'It is obvious you lie', thus incidentally alluding to the head of God which appears from the heavens addressing him with, 'See what the fool says'.

Medieval literature also amply attests to the fool's tonsure. The following is from the late fourteenth-century Vernon manuscript's version of *Robert of Cicyle* (the subject, incidentally, of a lost English 'painted cloth'):[12]

He heet a barbur him before	[summoned]
That as a fool he schulde be schore	
Al around, lich a frere,	[like a friar]
An honde-brede boue either ere,	[hand's breadth above]
And on his croune make a crois.	

Here we see the comparison deliberately made with the clerical tonsure (wrongly denied by some scholars) and further, reference to a cross left on the crown of the fool's head – whether of hair or bare scalp is not certain, but the former is more probable (compare the discussion of Tristan's *croiz*).[13] Something very like this arrangement of circular tonsure plus cross seems to be depicted on the head of the late thirteenth-century *insipiens* in the English *Huth Psalter*.[14] Once again, s.v. *tondere ad modum crucis* and *tondere in crucem*, the invaluable Ducange gives fourteenth-century examples of such cruciform tonsure as a punishment for adultery and other crimes, in which it is manifestly a sign of infamy – a striking modern parallel is provided by the shaving of the heads of women who collaborated with the Nazis after Paris was relieved. The sexual 'crimes' of women seem often to have been punished by targeting their hair or heads in some way (note the prostitutes' hoods of ray above), and carved 1464x1478 on the upper stall frieze of the choir in Seville Cathedral, a devil assists in cutting off the hair of adulterous women.[15]

Ipomedon, according to the late Middle English *Lyfe of Ipomydon*, like other Romance heroes – Tristan most notably – chooses to disguise himself as a fool, so:

> A barbor he callyd . . .
> And shove hym bothe byhynd and byfore,
> Queyntly endentyd oute and in,   [quaintly indented]
> And also he shove halfe his chynne.   [shaved]
> He semyd a fole, that queynt syre,
> Bothe by hede and by atyre.[16]

Here, the half-shaving of the fool's chin is an interesting detail, and is found elsewhere: in Wace's *Roman de Brut*, for example, we hear of Baldulf who disguised himself as a *jongleur* and so:

> had half his beard shaved
> and his head similarly
> and just one of his moustaches
> he looked a very ?rogue and fool.[17]

The same was true of the German fool. The author of the late thirteenth-century *Des Teufels Netz* complains that people who were not born fools – incidentally confirming that it was the practice to mark out 'natural' fools in this manner – were falsely adopting the fool's tonsure:

> And were not born fools/ And yet have
> themselves shorn around the head.[18]

Another aspect of the fool's foolishness is his very preparedness to allow himself to be shaved at all, that is, by a foolish or inexperienced barber, a spectacle which occurred as part of the public Fête des Fous in Sens in 1494,[19] and is also depicted in both the late fifteenth-century *Proverbes en Rimes* manuscripts and Bruegel's *Netherlandish Proverbs* painting (1559) (Colour Plate 6), and survives, indeed, in modern German carnivals.

Cock's Comb

By the Elizabethan period the English word *coxcomb* (merely a different spelling for *cock's comb*) had come to mean 'fool', as well as the fool's characteristic headgear in the form of a cock's crest or its entire head and neck, and the attribute itself as an addition to the fool's hood is also relatively late – at least, I know of no examples earlier than about 1450. The ass who bequeathed his ears to the fool's hood had long been associated with foolishness, of course, but where did the notion of adorning the fool's head with the comb or head and neck of a cockerel come from? The rather idiosyncratic fool carved on a bench-end at St Levan in Cornwall sports a beard and carries a *marotte* whose head is also bearded and is uniquely topped by a horseshoe.

Ass-eared Hood

The ass-eared hood was certainly in evidence by 1250. Although the earliest known depiction is a little fool in the margin of the *Dixit insipiens* page of the *Psalter of*

Humphrey de Bohun,[20] Mezger was able to cite an unequivocal reference to such a fool's hood from a mid-thirteenth-century German poem by Meister Stolle.[21] It is yet another motif for which ultimate classical origin has been claimed, albeit on very flimsy evidence, citing one of Martial's epigrams written late in the first century AD, in which he describes the son of the fool Cyrta as having a pointed head and long ears which move like those of an ass, a description which has been connected with the ass-eared and peaked hood worn by a Roman terracotta, now known only from an eighteenth-century drawing.[22]

Marotte *or Bauble*

The earliest psalter fools, appearing shortly after 1200, carry what is undeniably a simple stick, lopped branch, club or cudgel. This simple stick-type of club was perhaps a staff allowed the fool for his own protection as much as anything else, in an age which exposed many genuine unfortunates, 'natural' as opposed to 'artificial' fools, to the rigours of public humiliation. In the *Prose Tristan*, for example, the hero having lost his reason on becoming a real fool (in other versions of the story he merely disguises himself as a fool), takes a shepherd's cudgel in order to fend off those who annoy and torment him. The fool's club is perhaps also implicit in the matronymic of Edward II's court fool, Robert, who is named in the royal accounts for 1310–11 as the son of one Dulcia *Withastaf* (With-a-staff), if we can assume that the post may have been hereditary!

In a cauterisation diagram for the treatment of four psychopathologies – mania, epilepsy, melancholy and frenzy – the maniac, despite the secular context, is rendered as the *insipiens* of Psalm 52. He is shown shaven-headed, only partially clothed (and hence exposing his genitals), grasping a club with a curved end, and – a significant clue to his origin – with pointing finger, which some psalter fools use to point at God looming out of a cloud above their heads. When the popular Dutch poet Jacob van Maerlant compiled his encyclopedia *Der naturen bloeme, c.* 1275, he interpolated into his description of the Monstrous Races, a note to the effect that very many of the people of Burgundy suffered from goitrous growths at the throat. When the fourteenth-century illuminator came to portray the Burgundian, however, he depicted something very like the psalter fool – Jacob does not say that these Burgundians afflicted with goitre are all bald, nor that they wield enormous clubs, but this is how the illuminator saw him, even the pointing finger is retained, but now drawing our attention to his deformity.

But the club is very soon (certainly by the late thirteenth century) transformed into the familiar fool's-head-on-a-stick, often a miniature representation of the fool who wields it, technically termed the *marotte*, which is sometimes made to deliver the fool's speeches.

Herman Pleij, the Dutch historian who has taught us so much about the popular culture of the late Middle Ages in Northern Europe, has called the fool-with-his-*marotte* 'the central figure of the medieval folk-festival'.[23] The *marotte* or, to use the English technical term, the 'bauble', is the one attribute above all others which identifies the medieval fool for us. Classically, we perhaps visualise it as the little fool's-head-on-a-stick which the fool, especially the 'all-licens'd fool' of a Lear,[24] converses with in much the same way as a modern ventriloquist uses his dummy. Typically the *marotte* is made the originator of all the remarks felt too critical to be spoken by the fool-figure himself. In a Dutch play of about 1500, for example, the fool repeatedly punches his *marotte* whenever it comes out with criticism directed against abuses committed by the clergy and the better-off burghers, thus ostensibly dissociating himself from the criticisms of these powerful groups voiced by his bauble.

Actual examples of the 'classic' *marotte* survive from the late medieval era in the collections of several major European museums.[25] But the 'fool's-head-on-a-stick' is only one type of bauble and a relatively late one at that – the earliest known illustrations of the type go back no later than the late thirteenth century, while the *alter ego* type in which the *marotte*-head mirrors that of its owner, is a later development still.[26] The unique bronze *marotte*-head reproduced here (Figure 6.3) was found at Ellesmere in Shropshire and has an aperture in the neck to receive the stick.

Figure 6.3

Another type of bauble, obviously related to a certain degree to the club type, is what Mezger has styled the *Narrenwurst* (fool's sausage). In the earliest instances – the *Dixit insipiens* initials of such mid-thirteenth-century manuscripts as the *York*, *Rutland* and *Wilton Psalters*, we see a pendulous and probably stuffed leather protuberance attached to a wooden handle. In the important non-psalter image from the contemporary illuminated *Apocalypse* manuscripts, it is even possible to make out the swivel-mechanism of such a *marotte* belonging to Domitian's anachronistic court fool. In later examples, such as that borne by the *insipiens* from the *Psalter of Stephen of Derby* (1350x1375), the handle has been abandoned; but as early as *c.* 1270–80,[27] and commonly in fifteenth- and sixteenth-century examples, it is provided with a wrist strap.

Phallic Marotte and Fool Phallicism

Other types of *marotte* are also represented in art, the bladder-on-a-stick, for example, and the sometimes distinctly phalliform padded leather cosh. The editor of the thirty or so extant late medieval French *sermons joyeux* has posited the use of a phallic *marotte* by the parodic preacher of the *Sermon joyeux de Saint Velu* (Burlesque sermon of St Hairy), the eponymous saint being one of the popular late medieval genre of burlesque phallic saints we discussed in Chapter 2. In addition to exhibiting to his 'congregation' the 'tomb' of the martyred St Velu (that is, a codpiece), the modern editor suggests that at the climax of his sermon the fool-preacher held aloft the pseudo-saint himself in the form of his phallic *marotte*. In his *Treatise against masks* issued in 1608, Savaron recorded that in Clermont during the end-of-year festivals, young men, masked and disguised as fools, ran through the streets armed with clubs in the form of a codpiece stuffed with straw or padding, striking men and women.

It is frequently said in both general and specific works, that the fool's *marotte* is obviously phallic, but evidence for this assertion is rarely given and is, in fact, far

Figure 6.4

from being as self-evident as such statements imply. In what follows I shall try to provide that evidence from art and literature for the phallic associations of the fool-figure as a whole – not just of his *marotte*. In particular, I shall hope to demonstrate an iconographic link with late antiquity, though once again, I am far from suggesting that this constitutes a case for continuity – it may rather be that we are witnessing the surfacing of certain deep-seated notions (such as the perceived link between folly and the expression of human sexuality) which are semantic universals, at least in Western culture.

It is possible that the type of phallic *marotte* which the Elizabethan writer Nashe described as a 'leathern pudding' attached to a wooden handle (where *pudding* means what we should now call 'sausage', the sense preserved in 'black pudding'), and which seems to be found in manuscript illuminations from the mid-thirteenth century, may have a rather more august ancestry than one might expect, and may, indeed, never have quite died out in Western Europe. A late tenth-century lexicon of Greek, known traditionally as *Suidas*, glosses the word *phalloi* as 'oblong pieces of wood ending in a penis made of skins', such as are known to have been used in Rome during the celebration of the Bacchanalia. In the 1940s a magnificent hoard of fourth-century late Roman silver objects was turned up by a ploughman near Mildenhall in Suffolk and is now in the British Museum. The Great Dish depicts a Bacchic *thiasos* or revel-rout and includes a dancing satyr and maenad on the right, while on the left, an elderly Silenus approaches Bacchus with a wine-cup in one hand and what looks very like the ancestor of our medieval *Narrenwurst*, precisely as in the *Suidas* description, in the other.

In fact, relatively few *marottes* represented in art – unless one is prepared to see a phallic symbol in every stick – can be termed unequivocally phallic, but one such, about which there can be no argument, is to be seen in an engraving by Hans Sebald Beham of a male and female fool in conversation, dating probably to the 1530s (Figure 6.4). The pot by her side on which she rests her hand and the position in which he holds the wine flask are also both provocative.[28] In English art, a little earlier than the Beham engraving, a small dancing fool on one of the supporters of a misericord in Beverley Minster, carved in 1520, sports a little phalliform pudding attached to a stick handle (see below). More often, however, this *Narrenwurst* type of *marotte* is less overtly phallic, lacking the testicular appendages of the Beham engraving, but may nonetheless be suggestively placed, as for example, in an O-initial from an alphabet said to be by Dürer and appearing in books by the humanist Cervicornus (Eucharius Hirtzhorn) printed in Cologne. On other occasions the fool bestrides his staff or the handle of his *marotte* so that its end projects from between his legs in an indelicate manner,[29] although a connexion with the hobby-horse, that other fool-attribute, also comes to mind.

Phallic Hood and Bagpipe

There is a type of late medieval English ceramic whistle made in the shape of a fool's head, in which the arrangement of the two bells at the base of the hood, especially when considered in conjunction with the peak, must surely be seen as a deliberate phallic allusion (Figure 6.5).[30] What relationship, if any, these have with the small late Roman bronze heads surmounted by a phallus found in Britain and France – if any, indeed – is unclear.[31]

Figure 6.5

Another widely represented aspect of fool-phallicism is the suggestive use he makes of the bagpipe. The bagpiping fool carved by the Rhenish master Rodrigo Aleman on a stall-elbow in the cathedral of Plasencia in Spain around 1500, for example, is of particular iconographical interest in that, in tune with the erotic connotations of the instrument itself, his genitals are prominently if 'accidentally' exposed.[32] Another fool fingers his erect penis in a direct parallel to the way in which the boar beside him fingers the chanter of his bagpipe in a marginal drawing in a fourteenth-century English Aristotle manuscript (Figure 6.6).

Foxtail

We have already noted some of the several significances of the foxtail in Chapter 3, but deferred discussion of its role in the fool's costume to here.[33] Sometimes the fool appears to brandish a foxtail like an alternative *marotte*, sometimes it appears as a costume accessory, hanging from his belt or hood, but as we have seen, in the nature of things, the foxtail is unlikely to have positive symbolic associations.[34]

Figure 6.6

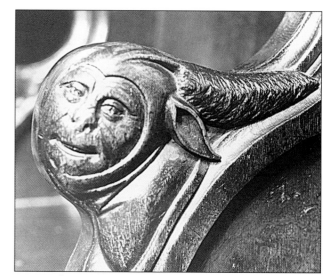

Figure 6.7a   Figure 6.7b

There is a remarkable, though hitherto quite unremarked, elbow-rest in the shape of a fool's head carved on the Manchester Cathedral stalls, *c.* 1506. Both sides of the Manchester carving show the fool's head in traditional close-fitting (ass-)eared hood, but with a different adornment to each side of it. On one side the hood terminates – as commonly enough – in a bell (Figure 6.7a), while the other side of the hood has no point as such, but bears an attached bushy tail, clearly intended as that of a fox (Figure 6.7b). This is a most interesting iconographic detail for an English fool representation, and in England, at any rate, is unique.[35]

Despite earlier English literary attestations – none of which, however, specifies exactly where the fool's foxtail is worn – the Manchester elbow is the only English fool to show the tail attached to the hood, known otherwise only from the continental instances cited above. In the earliest English literary reference to this costume accessory, the late fourteenth-century *Robert of Cicyle*,[36] there is mention of several such tails, presumably attached to the fool's tunic:

> The fole Roberd . . .
> Clad in a fulle sympulle garment
> Withe foxe tayles to renne abowte.[37]

The most interesting *exemplum*, editorially entitled *The Sage Fool's Testament*,[38] in which a household fool pointedly bequeaths his many attributes to the various members of his lord's household and then explains the relevance of each in the hope of their reformation, has been shown to derive ultimately from the English Franciscan collection of *exempla* known as the *Fasciculus Morum*, compiled in the opening years of the fourteenth century. In the 'standard' and earliest version found in all manuscripts of the *Fasciculus*, the fool bequeaths his bauble to his master's steward, his bowl to the butler, and his own soul to hell – in order to be with that of his master! In the nature of such 'mock testaments' (a popular

European genre, only sparsely represented in English),[39] the basic Latin story was soon subject to elaboration and variation, so that by the time of the fifteenth-century English vernacular translations, we hear in addition, for example, of the fool's hood being left to his lord's steward. Later still we find an example of the bequest of his coxcomb, in a most interesting piece of real-life popular theatre, which took place in Lincolnshire in 1601 as part of the Dymoke case, and which, though beyond our chronological limits, strictly speaking, is of such great intrinsic interest, but still so surprisingly little known, that it merits quoting in full here:

> Roger Baiard in annother part of the plaie Did . . . represent . . . the parte of the foole, and the part of the vice [NB the apparent synonymy of these two roles] . . . and theire acting the . . . parte did declare his last will and testiment and . . . did bequeathe his wodden Dagger to . . . the Earle of Lincoln, and his Cockscome and bable unto all those that would not go to Horncastle with . . . Sir Edward Dimocke against him.[40]

The version of the tale which most concerns us here, however, is found in one of the fifteenth-century Latin manuscripts of the *Fasciculus*. Writing in 1477, the scribe, a chaplain named Thomas Olyphant, improved on his original by adding the following two items to the fool's bequest in the margin of his copy:

> I further bequeath my foxtail to your servants, that is, those who cover their faces with their hair, etc. And I bequeath my bells to the keepers of your horses who are so proud, etc.[41]

Clearly, in 1477, Olyphant regarded a foxtail (*caudam vulpis*) as a characteristic part of the fool's costume.

There is an almost contemporary vernacular English reference to the fool's single foxtail, though no detail as to its precise location, in the description of Godfrey Gobelyve in Stephen Hawes's *Passetyme of Pleasure* (1508):

> A folysshe dwarf . . .
> . . . with a hood, a bell,
> a foxtayle and a bagge,
> in a pyed cote he rode
> brygge a bragge.

Presumably he carried the bag, but perhaps the foxtail hung from his belt, as is the case with the astrologising fool in Dürer's woodcut illustration to cap. 65 of Brant's *Narrenschiff* (1494). In a fragmentary Tudor play of mid-sixteenth-century date entitled *Albion Knight*, the Vice figure, Injury, has a foxtail (as is attested – admittedly, much later – for the fool in the morris dance). As Godfrey's bell was presumably on the tip of his hood, as on the Manchester stall-elbow, perhaps the foxtail also attached to Injury's hood?

The earliest illustration of a foxtail in connexion with the fool is that found dangling from a stick held by the *insipiens* in a mid-fifteenth-century English psalter,[42] while in a contemporary French manuscript, an illuminated translation of Boccaccio's *De casibus virorum illustrium*, a hairy male figure (?Wild Man) wears a hood, at the tip of which is a bell, and to the back of which is attached a foxtail, thus demonstrating precisely the same dual hood decoration as the Manchester stall-elbow.[43] Closely contemporary with the Manchester stall-elbow are two depictions of the tail attached to the fool's hood in the work of Bosch (d. 1516). In the Albertina version of his *Shaving the Fool* drawing, the barber wears a foxtail attached to his head,[44] while a drawing in Brussels now attributed to Bosch,[45] which depicts a number of beggars and cripples, includes a fool with a foxtail hanging from his eared hood, and an ass's tail hanging behind him[46] – in addition he wears only one shoe (see further below), and appears to be carrying a pair of scissors the wrong way round, that is, by the blades. A Bruegel painting (dated 1568) of a group of cripples shows them wearing simple overshirts to which several foxtails are hung, and modern carnival fools also seem to favour a number of tails.[47]

But the German fool's foxtail should also be seen in the context of the expression, 'stroke [someone] with the foxtail',[48] the equivalent, presumably, and of likely equivalent import, to the contemporary English idiom, 'to give a flap with a foxtail'. A most interesting substitution can be observed in the way in which Peter Floetner adapted the original illustration to Chapter 33 of Brant's *Narrenschiff* (1494), 'Of Adultery', for his own single-leaf print of the same title issued *c.* 1532.[49] Brant's illustration depicts the complaisant, cuckolded husband in the fool's ass-eared hood looking through his fingers, while his adulterous wife draws a straw through his mouth.[50] Floetner replaces the straw through the mouth with the semantically equivalent gesture of the foxtail being stroked across the foolish husband's coxcomb. But an anti-Catholic print issued in 1546 known as *The Shop of Foxtails* similarly employs the expression from which it is clear that it signifies 'to deceive'.[51] The friar pinned to the ground by the knight in armour who hits him with two foxtails, says 'Ah, why do you knock me down and strike me with the foxtail . . .', to which the knight replies, 'Ah, you have long deceived us,/drawn the foxtail through our mouths. . . .'[52]

Hobby-horsing Around

The hobby-horse is another of the fool's attributes seen in psalter illuminations and elsewhere.[53] The Wardrobe Accounts of 1334–5 for the court of Edward III interestingly make mention of *xiiij hobihorses pro ludo Regis*.[54] In 1347–8 the Christmas revels in which these hobby-horses may have been used in a mock joust, mention a similar number of *viseres* and *crestes* as part of the entertainers' festive costume, including a set of the latter in the form of upended legs wearing shoes – compare the arms of the Foljambe family, as seen on an English alabaster panel of the 1370s, which includes a helmet with just such a crest, that is, in 'canting heraldry', a *folle jambe*, the leg being 'mad' or 'foolish' because, in classic *monde renversé* fashion, it springs from the head! In similar topsy-turvy fashion, in one of the *Proverbes en Rimes* manuscripts of about 1500, the illustrated proverb depicts a fool with *marotte* in one hand, but wearing only one shoe – the other he holds on his head with his free hand (Figure 8.3)! Wearing one's shoes backwards is doubtless a synonymous trait: in the woodcut to the first Latin edition of Brant, *Stultifera Navis* (Basel, 1497), the fool wears his pattens (undershoes) back to front.

Monosandalism: One Shoe On, One Shoe Off

Another version of the Middle English *Robert of Cicyle* records that as part of the disguise he adopted, 'that all men hym a fole shuld hold', Robert wore 'Vpon the to legge a brokyn bote/A rente hose on the other foote . . .' (A broken boot on one leg, a torn stocking on the other foot), he thus wears only one shoe, and this is an important though rarely remarked trait of fool iconography.

As early as 1209 a goliard named Surianus, who styled himself 'long-favoured with the fools' dementia, bishop and archpriest of the wandering scholars of Austria, Styria and Bavaria', composed a parodic Indulgence in which he describes how all the members of that 'sect', 'impelled by sheer simplicity and sluggish folly' wander about 'always with one foot bare'.[55] Another highly revealing example, from the altarpiece originally made for the Karmeliterkirche in Cologne, depicts a Downs Syndrome child playing with a chained ape in a court setting;[56] whether the clothes he is dressed in constitute a fool's costume or not, the child who toys with the ape's clog as it searches for fleas in his hair, wears only one boot while his other foot is naked.

The Psalm 52 *insipiens* depicted in the woodcut to the Venetian *Malermi Bible* printed in 1490 (and in Holbein's copies of this image for his biblical illustrations, though he improves on his original by also having the fool ride his hobby-horse back to front) wears only one shoe, and at the same point in a mid-fourteenth-century French Bible, the fool is similarly only half-shod, albeit with a rather fancy openwork leather shoe.[57] In an *Etymologia* manuscript illuminated *c.* 1300, the word *cachinor* (laugher) is illustrated by a fool, here naked, except for his hood and one shoe, and the sword and *marotte* he carries.[58] A fine bronze statue of a fool who wears only one shoe and sits on a wineskin playing his bagpipe, part of an ornamental fountain made in Germany around 1480, is in a private collection in the USA;[59] the Metropolitan Museum in New York has another half-shod fool, this time playing the recorder and acting as one of the supporting feet for a silver covered beaker made at much the same time in Ingoldstadt.[60] Around the year 1500 the Flemish artist Arnt van Tricht cast a superb bronze candleholder in the shape of a fool, now in the Bargello Museum, Florence; not only does his fool wear only one shoe, he also stands with his finger in his mouth.[61]

Remarkably, in one of the very rare departures from the close copies of the German woodcuts that Pynson had done for his English translation of Brant, *The Ship of Fools* (London, 1509), the originally barefoot fool who stands next to the bell with the foxtail-clapper in the illustration to Chapter 41, has been given one shoe – clearly Pynson's cutter felt this was an appropriate addition. In Hans Schäufelein's sheets of playing card designs issued *c.* 1535, the Prince of Bells, who is dressed as a cross between a fool and a morris dancer, similarly wears only one shoe. Thus when Joseph is depicted wearing only one shoe as in the Adoration of the Magi scene on the small Bargello diptych painted *c.* 1390 and attributed to the School of Paris, as well as scratching his head, thus upsetting his cap, 'underscored by a semi-idiotic countenance', we can be sure he is being portrayed – as so surprisingly often in the medieval tradition – as a fool.[62]

A post-medieval parallel, but wonderfully appropriate to the similarly half-shod man 'banging his head against a brick wall' in Bruegel's *Netherlandish Proverbs* painting of 1559, appears in the records of the Spanish Inquisition, referring to events just seven years earlier than Bruegel's picture:

> I saw Sanchez walking with a cap on his head, one shoe on and the other off, and a staff. I asked him why he was walking around with one shoe on and the other off, and he replied, 'Because the world is going topsy-turvy.'[63]

The Fool's Gestures

Finger in mouth

We have already noted the important non-psalter fool to be seen in the mid-thirteenth-century English *Apocalypse* manuscripts: he is the Emperor Domitian's almost naked court fool, who has a distinct tonsure and a decidedly phalliform *marotte*, but the artist has also shown him with his finger in his mouth. Much later, in 1520, on a misericord in Beverley Minster, the carver depicted, as his central subject, another fool with his finger in his mouth, flanked by two goose supporters (Figure 6.8). A homily *Against Contention*, intended for preaching throughout the churches of Henry VIII's realm in 1547, includes the rhetorical question, 'Shall I stand still, like a goose or a fool, with my finger in my mouth?' This quotation significantly combines all three of the elements which go to make up the misericord and constitutes valuable proof that its goose supporters are not merely whimsical, decorative additions – the goose has been a proverbially foolish bird since about 1500, at least.

The finger in the mouth gesture perhaps originally betokened the drooling of the 'natural' fool, the village idiot, rather than the 'artificial' fool or jester. From the date of the *Apocalypse* manuscript, however, the motif is relatively common in the atheistic fool of the *Dixit insipiens* psalter initials, but is also found in other media; for example, in a German mural of a fool-bishop painted in 1486,[64] and on the Flemish bronze statuette now in the Bargello, referred to above.

Figure 6.8

Girning

On another Beverley misericord, we are presented with the head and shoulders of a man pulling the corners of his mouth apart in the grimace known in German as a *Gähnmaul*.[65] In place of the usual fool's hood, however, he seems to wear a hat or cap with, instead of the fool's ass's ears, lappets that flop forwards, rather in the manner of dog's ears. I am inclined to believe that these derive ultimately from some indistinct model which in fact depicted the usual fool's eared hood, the more so as it is possible to point to examples of this same gesture performed by traditionally hooded fools, most notably on one of the Westminster misericord supporters – if we can assume that, like his opposite number, he too is intended as a fool. There can be no doubt, however, about the two fools' heads carved by Jörg Syrlin on misericords at Ulm in 1474; as well as pulling the sides of their mouths apart, these fools in eared hoods also stick out their tongues for good measure.[66] The Beverley grimacer is flanked on either side by lion-mask supporters, a common enough motif in the corpus of misericord carvings as a whole, but these lions also stick out their tongues, as if in gestural support of the grimace of the central carving. Though not indicated as a fool as such, the man who makes the girning gesture in one of the two interior scenes on a painted diptych in Liège (Colour Plate 12), is clearly regarded as the facial semantic equivalent of the bottom-baring of the neighbouring scene.

Lateral mouth-pullers not indicated as fools certainly occur elsewhere in English woodwork, a particularly impressive example can be seen on a misericord at Sherborne Abbey (*c.* 1440, perhaps inspired by the late fourteenth-century stone roof corbel in the south transept), and there are two at Winchester, *c.* 1308; at Finchingfield in Essex is a one-handed example of thirteenth-century date who pulls his mouth downwards. There are also examples in stone from the corbel-tables of Romanesque churches, for example the Herefordshire school piece in the Victoria and Albert Museum collection, and a figure on the façade of the church at Cerne Abbas, while a combined mouth-pull and tongue-out gesture occurs on a figure on the roof screen at Willingham, Cambridgeshire, whose tongue hangs down over the genital area (like some French Romanesque examples).

In scenes of the Passion and Mocking of Christ which, as we have already seen, are so rich in illustrations of often forgotten gestures of derision, the *Gähnmaul* is frequently depicted; on the altarpiece carved *c.* 1510 in the church in Salzwedel, for example, the fool manages to combine the gesture with sticking his tongue out at the Holy Women at the foot of the Cross.[67]

Mooning

Occasionally in scenes of the Mocking of Christ the fool may even expose his bottom at the Saviour, as he certainly does at the saint in Etienne Chevalier's celebrated miniature of the Martyrdom of St Apollonia.

A most important portrait of a jester which resumes several of these iconographical features is attributed to Quintin Metsys (*c.* 1515).[68] He is physically deformed (hunch-backed), has an abnormally long nose, wears a hood through which ass's ears poke and on top of which are the head and neck of a cockerel, has a

Figure 6.9

scalloped edge to his short tunic which is kept in place by a belt hung with bells,[69] and shoulders a *marotte* which terminates in a grinning armless fool who has pulled down his trousers thus exposing his bare bottom at the viewer – and still the picture is not exhausted. The fool himself places his finger on his lips in the familiar gesture of silence, and says mysteriously, 'Mouth shut'! Mezger was the first to note that the apparent bulge visible in his forehead alludes to another well-known motif, the 'stone of folly'. The burlesque operation in which this 'stone', held to be the cause of all the foolishness in the fool's head, is surgically removed, was illustrated by both Bosch and Bruegel, and in the interim appears, for example, on the important Rhenish *Ambraser Narrenteller* painted in 1528 (Figure 6.9).[70]

The Feast of Fools and the Fool-Bishop

The Feast of Fools was an ecclesiastical Saturnalia, celebrated in the late Middle Ages as part of the Christmas festivities, which claimed a biblical justification in the *Magnificat*'s exaltation of the humble, putting down of the mighty, making the first last and the last first. In a cathedral or monastery context this led to a temporary reversal of roles in which the lower clergy assumed authority for a limited period, not dissimilar to the days of Christmas misrule observed in large secular households, and various 'carnivalesque' rites of inversion were practised. Popular throughout continental Europe in the late Middle Ages,[71] the Feast of Fools is somewhat scantily attested in England, except at Lincoln and Beverley, and at Beverley despite his prohibition against clerical celebration of the Feast, even Archbishop Arundel was prepared to allow the continuation of the ancient custom known as *les Fulles*, as one of the Christmas games permitted to the laity. Fool-companies often known as 'abbeys' or *sociétés joyeuses* in France, where they flourished, are similarly rarely attested in medieval England. I fear it would be stretching the evidence to reconstruct such an 'abbey' from the *Pryor of Prikkingham* and his *Convent* mentioned in a stray stanza of a sea shanty jotted in the margins of a late fifteenth-century list of debts by the clerk of the *Tolsey Court Book*.[72]

Fool carvings abound at Beverley, as might be expected historically in the town where the popular medieval Feast of Fools seems to have survived longest in England.[73] A document dated 1391, of great importance for the history of early English drama, exists in the form of a letter from Thomas Arundel, Archbishop of York, concerning the better government of the church at Beverley and forbidding the ancient and customary celebration of the Feast of the King of Fools – though nationally the feast was not formally abolished until a royal proclamation of 1542.[74] Various English cathedral inventories include mention of the props necessary for the Feast of Fools, in particular the fool-bishop's staff: the Salisbury inventory taken in 1222 boasts two (presumably entire) staffs for the Feast of Fools, but the St Paul's inventory, made a generation later, notes that the fool's staff of ivory and horn is missing its head.[75]

The 'fool-bishop' – functionally corresponding to the Lord of Misrule in a secular house – presided over the Feast of Fools, and a unique English depiction of such an anti-bishop is to be seen illustrating the usual *Dixit insipiens* initial of Psalm 52 in a Bible of the first half of the thirteenth century (Colour Plate 10).[76] Wearing a bishop's mitre, he sits on an episcopal throne, his legs crossed in a parody of the *attitude royale*, and as God looms out of a cloud above him, in flat contradiction of his *Non est Deus*, points to his *marotte*, as if in acknowledgement of his atheistic folly. A French manuscript of about 1280 shows the mitred fool-bishop making the gesture of blessing while riding backwards on a donkey,[77] another well-known folly motif as discussed above.[78]

The Fool's Sword and his Relationship to the Vice

John Southworth has rightly pointed out that the term Vice as used to denote a character type in Tudor interludes 'was no more than a synonym for "clever fool"'.[79] A misericord in Beverley Minster carved in 1520 may go some way to corroborating this view. It depicts three dancing fools. The central fool has the usual close-fitting eared hood with cock's comb ridge and scalloped tunic, and holds the hands of the fools on either side of him. The right-hand fool, as well as wearing the traditional fool's costume, holds some sort of sword or dagger behind his head; this is a suggestive attribute as it is not a part of the normal fool iconography – we should have expected to see the familiar *marotte*. The contemporary figure for whom the wooden sword or dagger is a *sine qua non* at this date, however, is the Vice. Late Elizabethan and Jacobean writers were plainly convinced that the wooden sword or dagger was the Vice's characteristic attribute in the earlier drama,[80] and the Vice named Inclination does indeed carry a wooden dagger in the morality play *The Trial of Treasure* (1567). But there is a revealing entry in the Revels accounts for 1551, recording a payment to one Nycolas Germayne for:

> one vyces dagger & a ladle with a bable pendante by hym garnished & deliverid to the Lorde of mysrules foole . . . in december.[81]

This entry proves that although, by 1551 at least, the wooden dagger was felt to belong to the Vice figure, it was also used by the Fool. We know that this was indeed the case on the public stage too, for in Wager's *The Longer Thou Livest The More Fool Thou Art* (1559), although the protagonist Moros (Gk. 'Fool') brandishes both a sword and a dagger, he is given them by the Vice figure, Wrath. The figure of Moros, though ostensibly the fool, is typical of the mid-sixteenth-century hybrid Fool-Vice character. In his last exit, for instance, Moros proclaims:

> If it please the devil me to have/Let him carry me away on his back . . .
> [s.d. exit Moros on Confusion's back],

which in the older morality plays was the traditional way in which the Vice-figure made his exit, and Jacobean writers felt able to adopt a decidedly patronising tone in their references to it:

> It was a prety part in the old Church-playes, when the nimble Vice would skip vp nimbly like a Iacke an Apes into the deuils necke, and ride the deuil a course, and belabour him with his woodden dagger, til he made him roare.[82]

Similarly, in Ben Jonson's play, *The Divell is an Asse* (1616), the Vice named Iniquity recalls that about the year 1560, 'every great man had his "Vice" stand by him, In his long coat, shaking his wooden dagger', in which it is clear Vice is being used as a synonym for household fool. The Beverley misericord carved in 1520 is thus important evidence that the Fool might borrow the Vice's dagger at a time 'when the old Church-playes' in Harsnett's phrase (meaning the moralities) were still a living tradition.

The Fool and the Morris Dance

This same Beverley misericord of the dancing fools has been compared by some commentators to a morris dance, as depicted in one of van Meckenem's two engravings of this subject,[83] though I see it, rather, as depicting an exhibitionist dance of fools in the tradition of the Feast of Fools. If we turn now to the fools carved on the supporters: the right-hand one plays a pipe and tabor, the instruments which do traditionally accompany the morris dance, such as we see in contemporary representations of the dance, though they are not usually played by a man in fool costume.[84] A relevant native parallel is the little-known oak panel carved with an apparent morris dance of probable sixteenth-century date from Lancaster Castle.[85] Again, the dance includes a musician with pipe and tabor, four dancers and a fool with *marotte*, belled costume and hood, and a rather mysterious seventh figure interpreted as the 'Maid Marion' or 'Bessy' (a man dressed up as a woman).[86] It is a great pity we know nothing further of the silver cup carved with a *moreys dauns* mentioned in a will of 1458 from Bury St Edmunds.[87]

The left-hand supporter of this misericord is also of interest; the little fool wears the same scalloped tunic and eared hood as his fellows, but holds in his right hand a stick from which a decidedly phallic bladder(?) dangles. With his right hand he points upwards with his index finger.[88] Certainly, what I term 'commentary' fools do point out scenes of folly for us (especially in the graphic arts), and there is just such an ass-eared fool with pointing index finger on the sixteenth-century Hemingborough panel also in the same county – though he points only at the neighbouring scenes of monsters fighting.[89] Especially given the form of the bladder and the pelvic thrust of this small fool, however, which has the effect of emphasising his codpiece, I believe his erect finger may rather have been intended as an insolent phallic suggestion.[90]

It has also been intimated that this seat might represent another well-attested motif, the dance around the Lady (whether Frau Venus, Frau Minne, or some other anonymous but equally beguiling Lady) who offers the best dancer a prize (such as an apple or ring): the absence of such a Lady on the present misericord seems to me to rule this out. There is certainly other contemporary evidence for this sort of courtly game, however, as in the moresque staged at the young Henry VIII's court in 1514, which featured two ladies, called Beauty and Venus, dancing to minstrelsy in an interlude with six men, one of whom was dressed as a fool.

Commentary Fool

An important aspect of fool iconography is the figure's commentary function. If the subject of a composition is not signalled as a fool by the placing of an ass-eared hood on his head, then his folly is often quite literally pointed to by an accompanying fool. In a woodcut sheet by Erhard Schoen issued *c.* 1530, for example, the fool suggestively points his plainly phallic *marotte* at the old man caressing the young woman in the tavern, unaware that her 'minder' has already purloined his purse. This is a classic example in which the deliberately phalliform *marotte* serves to underscore the fool's commentary function – here it is both the pointer and the point, it points our gaze to the central action, but also implies what it is that has brought the male lover to the folly of mercenary love.

Stultorum Infinitus est Numerus

In late medieval art the fool is ubiquitous, not just in the graphic arts, but in every conceivable applied or decorative art. An inventory of Thomas Cromwell's possessions taken in 1527 includes among the items listed in the parlour adjoining the kitchen, 'An image of a fole to hold a towel, painted.' Sadly this decorative towel-rail has not come down to us – it need not have been English, of course, given the great volume of carved woodwork and other furniture then being imported from the Low Countries. A roughly contemporary and very fine wooden towel-rail in the form of a fool embracing a buxom young woman carved by Arnt van Tricht in Kalkar in the late 1530s has survived, however, and is reproduced at Colour Plate 9.[91]

Fools appear on ornamental garden fountains, municipal fountains (Ettlingen's 'Narrenbrunnen' of *c.* 1540, for example), bronze candelabra (superb examples of these also by Arnt van Tricht), jewels;[92] and – like the Wild Man, a figure almost as popular – as finials and feet for precious vessels. But they also appear decorating the humblest wares in ceramic[93] and brass. Another dubious representation on a hammered brass dish of the fool lying at the feet of a woman, who is naked except for an extravagant feathered hat and tickling her genitals with a carnation was copied from an anonymous woodcut. In 1520 the Abbot of the Heribertkloster in Köln-Deutz even had a silver crozier made, the crook of which was decorated with a fool's head in the usual belled hood.[94]

A few important relics of fool societies survive: the fifteenth-century wooden sceptre of the Infanterie Dijonnaise is topped by a bird's nest in which newly hatched fools are being given wine from a flagon by Mère Folle herself – the fool-as-nestling motif in France is probably to be connected with the etymology of one of the words for 'fool' and 'foolish', *niais*, which originally meant 'nestling'; the semantic development is via 'new-born and hence inexperienced, naive' to 'foolish', and is paralleled by the surname of one Jehans Pau Couves (*c.* 1275), that is, Jean Scarcely Hatched.

I hope sufficient evidence has been brought forward here to endorse my estimate of the fool-figure's significance in understanding the late medieval *mentalité*. An avowed outsider who yet has access to the most powerful, in reality as in art, he is the era's commentator *par excellence*, a persona of many facets whose manifold follies are ours. For the fool is both an individual and a type; the monarch's court jester, the nobleman's household fool, and the representation of the folly of humankind. He is the bitter fool, the scourge who lashes our follies; the clownish fool, whose slapstick buffoonery is too silly for us grown-ups; the witty fool, with repartee and punning, pointed and poisonous, too acerbic for our taste; the *all-licens'd* 'commentary' fool, the Everyman of our own foolishness.

SEVEN

SHOEING THE GOOSE: THE REPRESENTATION OF PROVERBS AND PROVERBIAL FOLLIES IN ART

The representation of proverbs and proverbial phrases in art may be conveniently divided into pictorialised collections or 'anthologies', such as Bruegel's famous *Netherlandish Proverbs* painting of 1559 (Colour Plate 6), which it is convenient to see as the culmination of this tendency in medieval art, and the occurrence of individual motifs in every conceivable artistic medium.

PICTORIAL PROVERB ANTHOLOGIES

The earliest pictorial proverb anthology is not a manuscript, painting or print, but an enamelled silver pot, known to history only as item 69 of the 1364 inventory of the plate of Louis, Duc d'Anjou – a timely reminder that the record of survival is as partial as the survival of records. It appears as:

> a silver pot with six gold-enamelled panels, on the cover of which are the six months of the year, with an enamelled knob on top, and, on the body of the said pot are several proverbs, the contents of which are portrayed in images with the inscriptions below.[1]

It is important to note that this perhaps hexagonal vessel had each of the pictorialised proverbs represented identified by inscriptions.

A little-known proverb-illustrated vessel which has survived from the same era is a silver bowl preserved in the St Annenmuseum in Lübeck (Figure 7.1). A blue-enamelled

Figure 7.1

silver disc set inside the bowl illustrates the four proverbially wonderful things from the biblical *Book of Proverbs* [30, xviii–xix]:

> There be three things which are too wonderful for me, yea, four which I know not: The way of an eagle in the air; the way of a serpent upon a rock; the way of a ship in the midst of the sea; and the way of a man with a maid.

The enthroned King at the centre of the composition is the reputed author of the Old Testament Book, the proverbially wise King Solomon. The same composition is also to be seen on a North German painted table top executed *c.* 1400, now in the Musée du Moyen Age in Paris,[2] and as an illustration to the 1532 Augsburg edition of Petrarch's *Von der Artzney Bayder Glueck des Guten vnd Widerwertigen,* in a woodcut made *c.* 1520 by the so-called 'Petrarch-Master', usually identified with Hans Weiditz.[3]

The Narrenschüssel

Unaccountably neglected since its original publication over a century ago,[4] the late fifteenth-century *Narrenschüssel* preserved in the Germanisches Nationalmuseum features sixteen proverbial 'follies' (Figure 7.2), but in the main, they are follies in

Figure 7.2

the same sense as those depicted in Brant's *Narrenschiff* of 1494, that is, vicious follies, as the text of the quatrain inscribed beneath each image makes clear. The sixteen men representing the individual follies, together with the captions elucidating their particular weaknesses, are painted around the central motif of an enthroned king whose banderole invites them to introduce themselves. It has been suggested – but on no substantial grounds that I am aware of – that this king is King of the Twelfth Night revels, King of the Beanfeast.

The fools, or perhaps better, rogues, who accordingly introduce themselves, cheerfully admit to various vices. They are temporisers, siding now with this party, now with that, as symbolised by the man who carries his burden on both shoulders. They are quite literally 'turncoats', changing their opinions and allegiances like the man shown shifting his coat from one side to the other as the wind veers. They are practised in flattery, removing feathers from the clothing of the rich and powerful, and their deceitfulness is signalled by looking through their fingers, stroking the foxtail, turning the grindstone, blowing with flour in their mouths, and quite frankly, by downright lying. The liar is shown with a beam in one hand that his outrageous lies have cracked.

The Flemish Proverb Tapestry

The portion of a late fifteenth-century tapestry preserved in the Isabella Stewart Gardner Museum in Boston,[5] is a priceless witness to the Flemish tradition of the anthologisation of pictorialised proverbs before Bruegel (Colour Plate 2). It is also a sadly fragmentary reminder of the importance of this medium for the illustration of proverbs, as for so much other secular iconography. This unique proverb tapestry, in its present state, features eight complete representations and part of a ninth, including belling the cat and falling between two stools, as well as the famous *Blauwe Huycke* or blue-cloak motif, in which the wife puts the blue hooded cloak round the husband's shoulders, symbol of her infidelity and his cuckoldry. Almost all nine tapestry proverbs extant may be seen again in Bruegel's painting of 1559, and individually in the corpus of Netherlandish misericords.

Baude's Dictz Moraulx Pour Faire Tapisserie

The French poet Henri Baude, who died *c.* 1500, composed a series of *Dictz Moraulx* (moral verses) which are versified proverbs, intended, according to the majority of surviving manuscripts, *pour faire tapisserie* (for the making of tapestry) – another manuscript adds 'or window-panes'.[6] Although some of these manuscripts include drawings executed according to the rubrics at the head of each versified proverb, until recently there was, in fact, no known surviving example of any tapestry woven according to Baude's verses. In 1987, however, Paul Vandenbroeck published a photograph of a fragmentary early sixteenth-century French tapestry, present whereabouts unknown, which had been sold by an art dealer in New York, and which depicts three separate proverbs, and employs at least one of Baude's quatrains, divided between – as the rubric puts it – 'a man who pokes a sleeping dog with a stick' and the said dog.[7] The richly dressed, if proverbially foolish, man says:

> Master Dog you sleep too much
> and sleeping is not in your nature,

to which the dog not unreasonably replies:

> If I sleep, what's it to you?
> You are wrong to wake me.

This particular proverbial folly is also illustrated in the Walters *Proverbes en Rimes* manuscript.

Sala's Enigmes de l'Amour and 'Currying Favour'

A miraculous survival from the late Middle Ages is the tiny gem of a manuscript, a love-gift entitled *Enigmes de l'Amour* (Riddles of Love) illuminated by Pierre Sala in Lyon *c.* 1500,[8] and presented to the woman who was later to become his wife, in which some of the same series of verses by Baude are copied and illustrated – for example, the expression referring to flatterers as those who 'curry Favel'. The description of the tapestry for which these particular Baude verses were intended as a caption, is simply, 'a horse being curried', and Sala's miniature, in accordance with the second line of the quatrain, depicts two men currying a horse, one in front and one behind. In full, the verse reads:

> I am Favel who desires all the time
> to be curried both before and behind;
> those who do not know the way to curry me
> waste their time at court and labour too much in vain.

This expression which, due to popular etymology, has been reconstituted in English as 'to curry favour', is based on the proper name of a horse, in origin one of the fascinating colour terms referring to horses, *Favel* or *Fauvel,* a chestnut-coloured horse.[9] In 1314, Gervais de Bus completed his *Roman de Fauvel,* the hero of which is a horse named Fauvel, a powerful and villainous lord who is surrounded by a court of flatterers with names like Pride, Hatred, Flattery, Covetousness, Carnality and so on, not forgetting Vainglory, whom he marries (albeit 'left-handedly').[10] Gervais, in true medieval fashion, gives us his etymologising of the hero's name thus:

> Fauvel
> signifies a vain thing
> the deceit and falsity of the world,
> also, etymologically,
> one can know what it signifies:
> *Fauvel* is composed of *faus* [false] and *vel* [old].[11]

The story must have struck a chord with its medieval audience, judging by the speed with which the expression seems to have entered other European languages and become established: already by about 1330, it appears in the English poem, 'A Peniworth of Witte',[12] and is also found early in Provençal.[13]

Gervais himself tells us that he was first prompted to compose his *Roman* by the frequent sight of murals depicting the Wheel of Fortune surmounted by the wily, irrepressible Renard, the figure of Orgueil mounted on a warhorse to his right, and Dame Guile on her mount, *Fauvain* (a variant of *Fauvel*) to his left. A mid-fifteenth century German woodcut sheet seems to continue the tradition of these early fourteenth-century wall-paintings. It is an iconographically complex Wheel of Fortune surmounted by Reynard dressed as the Pope with triple crown and sceptre, and labelled *Fuchs Reynhart*. The Fox-Pope is flanked by a wolf in the robes of a Dominican friar and a bear in those of a Franciscan, their banderoles shamelessly proclaiming their lust for money. Behind the wolf rides a man whipping a prancing steed which is labelled Pride; his counterpart riding behind the bear, is depicted as a woman on a more humble mount identified as representing Hatred and Sloth.[14] The blindfolded figure who turns the wheel is labelled not Fortune, but Patience. A man with a sickle – that proverbially crooked instrument – sitting on one of the spokes within the wheel, identifies himself as Falseness, declares himself Reynard's servant and vows to do harm to Constancy, represented by a naked man at the bottom of the wheel. He is opposed by a parish priest, bearing host and chalice, identified as Belief in God but who is clearly on the way down. Before the wheel sit two figures, a male who seems to represent Charity, and a female identified as Humility. This sheet, as so often, has manuscript antecedents,[15] and it was the great French scholar, Gaston Paris, who first noted that it was at the end of manuscripts of Jacquemart Gelée's 'spin-off' from the beast-epic proper, *Renart le Nouvel* (*c.* 1288), that these reynardian wheels of fortune occur.

In recent years small lead badges, in the shape of a miniature curry-comb on the body of which the name *fauel* is clearly legible, have been found (see chapter ornament). Clearly, these fifteenth-century pieces must embody the expression 'to curry Favel', but what can their function have been? Under what circumstances can such a badge, with its connotations of self-seeking flattery and hypocrisy, possibly have been worn? I can only suggest that these were not badges intended to adorn the person, but are to be interpreted rather as decorative harness fittings, a coded message that the owner of this particular horse is worldly-wise and aware of the dangerous vanity of being susceptible to flatterers. Could they further have had an almost apotropaïc function, perhaps showing that the horse's owner, in the contemporary words of the author of *Jacob's Well*, was aware that 'The tunge of the flaterere harmyth more than the swerd of the smytere'?[16]

An awareness of this symbolic significance of the curry-comb is essential to appreciate its appearance in an illustrated manuscript of Lydgate's *Pilgrimage of the Life of Man*, produced in England 1430x50;[17] on the counter of Hagiography's shop are, as the text puts it:

> Kombes (mo than nyne or ten)
> Bothe ffor horse and eke ffor men;
> Merours also, large and brode . . . [22341–3][18]

Why on earth are there curry-combs for sale in this shop along with the combs and mirrors? This is no ordinary shop, as can be seen from the fact that the mirror the tonsured Pilgrim looks into is no ordinary mirror – it is called *Adulacyon* – for it reflects back a very curly, youthful head of hair. It is a flattering mirror, and that, of course, is why the curry-combs are there too – to signal to the viewer that such worldly merchandise is a trap for the pilgrim. In the lines which follow, Hagiography embarks on a disquisition on the evils of flattery, especially the flattery of lords by their hangers-on (22411ff.).

A remarkable public gesture involving the symbolic presentation of a curry-comb had occurred a generation earlier in London in 1406. A Lollard priest named William Thorpe had objected to a passage in a sermon delivered by the preacher Richard Alkerton and later abused him to his face as a false flatterer. Robert Waterton, a privy counsellor and friend of Henry IV, who was also present, ordered one of his servants to carry a curry-comb to Alkerton 'as if to indicate that he was fawning upon the prelates of the church'. Archbishop Arundel was informed of the insult and acquainted King Henry with it, who at first found it amusing, but subsequently acceded to the Archbishop's demand that Waterton should apologise in Parliament. Waterton's servant, however, fared rather worse, being obliged to parade naked for a number of days carrying the curry-comb in one hand and a candle in the other.[19]

Van Meckenem's Proverb Print

Also from around the same time, as the illustrated proverb manuscripts described above, at the end of the fifteenth century, dates the earliest known proverb print, by Israhel van Meckenem (d. 1503),[20] featuring the biblical King David and four scenes of proverbial, secular activity, provided with banderole inscriptions from the Psalms in Latin above, and proverbial identifications in Low German below (Figure 3.3). The first figure is identified as a judge by the inscription which says he wears the judicial scarlet, but it is clear that he is a corrupt judge, for he is shown hammering a straight length of iron on an anvil into the distinctive crooked shape of a sickle. The caption reads:

> The straight I make crooked
> therefore I wear scarlet.

The crooked judge in the Van Meckenem print is paired with an arrowsmith sitting on a bench testing by eye the straightness of one arrow-shaft, while others lie on the bench before him. His caption reads:

> My things I make straight and true
> therefore I remain a poor man.

The third of van Meckenem's figures enacts two proverbs simultaneously, both of which we have already encountered on the *Narrenschüssel*:

> I grind, I turn,
> and turn my cloak according to the wind.

The final print figure is a fool whose face is being licked by a cat. The legend reads:

> And protect yourself from cats
> that lick your face and scratch your back.

As we have seen in Chapter 3, this last proverb is found several times elsewhere in art.

Entremets *at the Banquet du Faisan (Lille 1454)*

While not quite an anthology in the sense that I have used the term above, I should like, nevertheless, to look at a collection of representations in one of the most transient of artistic media, one-quarter of which are pictorialised proverbs.[21] One of the lavish banquets so typical of the French courts of the late Middle Ages (compare with that of the Swan Knight given only a year earlier by the same patron, alluded to in Chapter 9) the so-called *Banquet du Faisan* (Feast of the Pheasant) included an extravagant number of *entremectz* (table decorations). Like the snow sculptures made in Arras in 1434, in a medium equally evanescent, these assemblages of imagery may serve as a representative sample of the current iconographic repertoire, in which the proverb is well represented. The feast in question was given by Philip the Good of Burgundy at Lille in 1454, and the banquet itself was set out on three tables. The medium-sized ducal table bore four *entremectz*, the smallest table three, and the large table no fewer than nine such decorations. Of these sixteen, four can certainly be regarded as illustrations of proverbs, and in one case, the reporter to whom we owe the most detailed record of these decorations, Olivier de la Marche, helpfully spells it out for us.

On the large table, one of the *entremectz* depicted a windmill on a hill, to the uppermost sail of which was tied a mast with a magpie perched on the top of it,[22] and all sorts and conditions of men were shooting at the bird with bows and crossbows. La Marche glosses this as 'it is the common occupation of all men to shoot at magpies', in which some commentators have detected a democratic message. A representation of this same proverb a century later (*c.* 1566), however, is a satire on the Inquisition.[23]

The neighbouring *entremect* was also apparently proverbial. It took the form of a vineyard in which lay a cask containing two sorts of wine, one good and mellow and the other bad and sour, and sitting on the cask was a finely dressed man holding a placard aloft proclaiming 'Let him who wants some help himself', which sounds like a convivial commonplace.

The third proverb representation on the same table depicted a man with a pole beating a bush full of little birds, while, in the orchard nearby, enclosed in a bower of roses, sat a knight and a lady eating the birds he had dislodged. Furthermore, the lady was shown pointing at the man with the pole to indicate that he laboured in vain and was wasting his time. The same proverb is illustrated as no. 102 in the late fifteenth-century Walters *Proverbes en Rimes* manuscript, where it takes the form:

> He completely wastes his time
> who like a fool
> beats the bush
> while another gets the birds [from it].

A celebrated quotation of this very proverb had occurred fifteen years before the banquet, during one of the most significant moments of the Hundred Years' War, the taking of Orléans in 1429. Philip the Good of Burgundy proposed to the Duke of Bedford that in return for assisting the English with the siege he should get to keep the city, but Bedford replied that he 'would be infuriated to have beaten the bushes from which others should have the birds'. The proverb was well known to the English, the poet Gower managing to deploy it in English, French and Latin!

The final proverb representation, one of the three *entremectz* on the small table, depicted a lion tied to a tree in the middle of a field and a man beating a dog. 'Beat the dog in front of the lion' was a saying used to mean to rebuke a person in front of another of higher rank, but in such a way as to show that the admonishment is intended for the latter. It too is illustrated in the *Proverbes en Rimes* (no. 157) and related manuscripts, but it was popular with visual artists throughout Europe. It was illustrated in Villard de Honnecourt's thirteenth-century sketchbook (*c.* 1240), and sculpted in stone at Chartres in the 1230s, and on one of the portals of Notre Dame in Paris in the early 1260s,[24] and by Niccolo and Giovanni Pisano on the fountain in Perugia in the late 1270s where the Latin form of the proverb is inscribed: *SI VIS UT TIMEAT LEO; VERBERA CANEM.* Exceptionally it is used in place of the appropriate Labour of the Month to illustrate July, when the sun is in Leo, carved on an oak panel (1325x50) perhaps from the French convent of Freckenhorst.

Two early manuscript instances can be found in the *Psalter* and *Hours of Joffroy d'Aspremont and Isabelle de Kievraing* illuminated in Metz *a.* 1302,[25] and very shortly afterwards it is found in the early fourteenth-century English *Queen Mary's Psalter.*[26] Much later, but still in England, it was used by Thomas Palmer for the 147th emblem in his manuscript emblem book *Two Hundred Poosees* (*c.* 1565) to illustrate the maxim, 'Lerne by other mens harmes to beware'. The picture was to be *A whelpe beaton withe a wande before the grate* [cage] *of the lions.*[27]

INDIVIDUAL PROVERB REPRESENTATIONS

It seems as though the late fifteenth century was an era in which the representation of proverbs became a Northern European enthusiasm, one which seems to have culminated in the anthologies of pictorialised proverbs in manuscript, early printed books, and – as we have seen – in less durable media too. The representation of individual proverbs had a rather longer history.

The Ass and the Stallion, or, the Grass is always Greener . . .

The fortieth of Baude's *Dictz* is a warning against giving in to the lure of the apparently greener grass on the other side – to employ a contemporary English idiom. It concerns a pair of animals who are not infrequently coupled in proverbs, the lowly ass and the proud stallion. The ass is depicted happily munching away at a patch of thistles in the open, while the fatally curious horse has just impaled himself on one of the sharp fence posts which bound his lush paddock. One manuscript labels the animals 'the wilful horse' and 'the peaceable ass'.[28] The *dict* appears to be advising a cautious approach to life, implying that while the adventurous life may look glamorous, a humbler life has its advantages. But Baude was not the first to find this topic worthy of illustration: in a Book of Hours of Metz Use produced some time during the first half of the fourteenth century, the artist has painted a bleeding horse similarly impaled on one of the posts of the fence which surrounds his paddock. This time there is a banderole inscribed:

> he who covets more than he ought
> that coveting will deceive him.[29]

The Elizabethan writer Thomas Nashe was clearly familiar with this apparent fable of the ass and the horse, for he has Ver relate it in *Summer's Last Will and Testament* (1592):

> What talk you to me of living within my bounds? I tell you, none but asses live within their bounds: the silly beasts, if they be put in a pasture that is eaten bare to the very earth and where there is nothing to be had but thistles, will rather fall soberly to those thistles and be hunger-starved, than they will offer to break their bounds; whereas the lusty courser, if he be in a barren plot and spy better grass in some pasture near adjoining, breaks over hedge and ditch, and to go, ere he will be pent in, and not have his belly full.[30]

It would be a mistake to think that the proverb is inevitably a form which urges caution (as seen in the example of the impaled horse) and encourages mere acceptance of one's lot, and of life's injustices – let us recall the revolutionary watchword of John Ball and Jack Straw in the Revolt of 1381 'when Adam delved and Eve span, who was then the gentleman?'. And several of Baude's *Dictz*, at least by implication, criticise injustice; nos 14 and 15, for example. The former depicts a courtier staring thoughtfully at a spider's web full of flies, who says:

> I'm thinking about spiders' webs
> which are like our laws
> the big flies get through
> everywhere, the little ones are caught.

A peasant, labelled *laboureur*, and given a spade in one illustration, an axe in another, further drives the message home:

> The humble people are subject to the laws
> which the powerful make in their own image.

Only a generation or so later this was the subject of a German single-sheet print issued *c.* 1535 which illustrates the 'proverb of the spider's web'.[31]

Loyalty is Dead

A particularly interesting pictorialisation of a proverb with accompanying inscription is found on a late fourteenth-century leather-covered casket made in

Northern France.[32] The lid bears a scene of St George and the Dragon; the back, an armed merman confronting a mermaid; and the front a clearly allegorical scene. Within a walled garden a woman, apparently asleep, is observed by a man who leans over the wall and a group of three people who look on and say 'Loyalty is dead'; but the man gestures them to be silent saying, 'Speak softly, Loyalty is sleeping', while Loyalty herself replies, 'I am not dead nor asleep but none of you is concerned about me.'

A century later the Walters *Proverbes en Rimes* manuscript illustrates its 112th proverb:

> Lady Loyalty sleeps
> and Truth is dead

by a prone woman lying at the feet of another who sleeps in a high-backed chair.[33] Its companion-piece, on the folio opposite, depicts a man bowed down so that he almost stumbles from the weight of a woman he carries on his shoulders, which the cynical verse explains thus:

> He is worse than mad
> who bears Good Faith
> for she breaks the neck
> of him who carries her.

Scenes involving the same or very similar allegorical personages are also described in the opening half of a quatrain recorded in a contemporary manuscript of *Les diz et proverbes des sages*, designed for learners of French and written in England:

> Loyalty is asleep and Right is dead
> And Truth breaks the neck of him who carries her.[34]

The Crowned Ass

It was a commonplace of the Latin Middle Ages that an uneducated king was like a crowned ass – *rex illiteratus asinus coronatus*. According to a passage in the *Secreta Secretorum*, the English King Henry I used often to quote this proverb to his father and brothers. It is attested in most European vernaculars by the late Middle Ages, but Yonge's early fifteenth-century English version, 'a kynge unletterid is lyke an hornyd asse', looks like a mistake, translating *coronatus* (crowned) as if it were *cornutus* (horned)![35]

Another early fifteenth-century German painted table top in the Musée du Moyen Age in Paris includes the picture of an ass(?) sitting up in a bed of state attended by two noblewomen and a male petitioner – but although the scene has been interpreted as a representation of this proverb, the animal does not appear to be wearing a crown.[36] Though there is no readily visible curry-comb either, I am rather inclined to suggest that this is another image of Favel waited on hand and foot by his courtiers. Otherwise, the first unequivocal depiction of a crowned ass I am aware of is a miniature in a late fifteenth-century Austrian manuscript treatment of the symbolic figures of the Liberal Arts.[37]

Biblical Proverbs

A popular biblical proverb – to judge from the number of early sixteenth-century representations – was that concerning the mote in another's eye compared to the beam in one's own [Matthew 7.5; Luke 6.42]. Curiously, the earliest examples I am at present aware of occur in secular manuscripts – though there is surely some earlier example in an illustrated Gospels somewhere. It decorates the initial W in a fourteenth-century manuscript of *Parzival*,[38] but occurs again as one of the *Proverbes en Rimes* in the British Library's manuscript of that collection.[39] Engraved versions proliferate in the early decades of the sixteenth century and, on one of the misericords in the church at Hoogstraeten (1532x46), it achieved three-dimensional representation.[40]

PROVERBIAL FOLLIES

Just as the 'number of fools is infinite',[41] according to the apocryphal text which was so popular during the late medieval European craze for fool-literature and -imagery, infinite too is the number of their follies. To attempt a taxonomy of such multifarious absurdities probably deserves to become a proverbial folly in its own right, but, nothing daunted, that is exactly what I propose to do next.

For the most part, proverbial follies are found singly or in small groups, and the suspicion must always be – as accompanying verses often make explicit – that they are to be read morally. For the Middle Ages, folly is not merely foolish, it is morally vicious. The fools aboard Brant's ship are not just amusing clowns, they are flawed human beings sailing to perdition, and their various follies are indicators, not of their simple-mindedness, but of the parlous state of their souls.

Figure 7.3

The representations of folly shade into those of proverbial impossibility, and such impossibilities into the images of the *monde renversé* – the boundaries of the absurd are fatally fluid. Whether identified by cap and bells as such or no, proverbial fools commit such ultimate inversions as wearing gloves on their feet or shoes on their heads (Figure 8.3) as in the *Proverbes en Rimes* manuscripts.[42] But, for me at least, flying pigs and birds carrying sacks to the mill are proverbial absurdities, *impossibilia* or *adynata* rather than follies, while a proverbial folly implies a proverbial fool, that is, a proverbially foolish human agent. Two such agents are the subject of a Bristol Cathedral misericord carved *c.* 1520 (Figure 7.3).

Whipping the Snail

Let us first describe exactly what the carver has represented here. A slug with a pack across its back is being thrashed or whipped by a man with the threshing implement which used to be called a flail, while the other is, according to earlier descriptions, leading the animal on a leash (which has since broken off). Firstly, it is important to realise that the distinction between *slug* and *snail* was not made in English before about 1700, so that writing in 1633, Bishop Hall could still say, 'See there two snails. One hath a house, the other wants it; yet both are snails.'[43] Once we realise that in early sixteenth-century nomenclature this is a *snail*, a word which rhymes with *flail*, instinct suggests a possible popular poetic source, and such, indeed, is to be found in two couplets precisely contemporary with this carving. In the Tudor interlude *Gentylnes and Nobylyte* we read:

> In effect it shall no more avayle
> Than with a whyp to dryfe a snayle . . .

while the indispensable John Skelton – whose work is one of the most in tune with the spirit of the popular imagery of this 'Ultimate Medieval' era – reels off a whole string of nonsense couplets in his characteristically vigorous doggerel in the poem 'Colyn Clout', of which these are two:

> What can it avayle
> To dryve forth a snayle,
> Or to make a sayle
> Of a herynges tayle?[44]

What indeed! It is, however, a proverbial folly the Jacobeans were willing to elaborate. In Webster's *Duchess of Malfi* Ferdinand in his madness says he is studying the art of patience, and proposes as an experiment:

> To drive six snails before me, from this town to Moscow; neither use goad nor whip to them, but let them take their own time . . . and I'll crawl after. . . .[45]

Some twenty years ago, a small mid-fifteenth-century bronze figure which probably came from an ornamental fountain somewhere in Flanders resurfaced at the sale of

the celebrated Robert von Hirsch collection (Figure 7.4).
This figure, too, is shown with whip upraised in a vain
attempt to drive the snail crawling across his other
hand.[46]

Worried That the Ducks Might Drown[47]

The folly of attempting to drive another
inappropriate animal is attested in the person of one of
the characters mentioned in Robert Copland's burlesque *Jyl of
Breyntford's Testament* (*c.* 1563), whose name is Sir John
Whipdoke, or Whip-duck.[48] And yet we have already seen St
Werburgh's servant incredulously driving wild geese prior to
confining them in a pen open to the sky, as what is folly to
the worldly, the saint, as 'God's fool', triumphantly achieves.

Fools and their follies naturally passed into the
repertoire of emblem books and in the sixty-seventh
emblem in Book II of Rollenhagen's *Nucleus emblematum*
(Arnhem, 1613), engraved by Crispin de Passe and family,
another fool, this time costumed as such and identified
as the earlier German court fool, Claus Narr, is shown
mid-steam carrying two goslings in one hand and with a

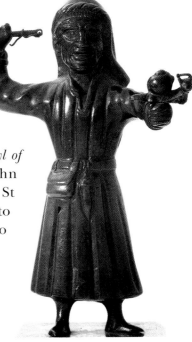

Figure 7.4

further five hanging by their necks from inside his belt. But this is a traditional
folly, entered as J 1909.7 'Fear that frog or duck may drown' in Stith Thompson's
encyclopeadic *Motif Index of Folk Literature*,[49] which means it is a staple of fool
stories and attributed to various named and unnamed fools at various periods.

Good Enough to Eat?

In similar fashion, in the *Memorials of the Holles Family* we hear of 'a naturall foole'
named John Oatesborne kept by Sir William Holles (d. 1590) of Houghton,
Lincolnshire. The writer claims 'to have seene many stories of him in print and
many more I have heard related of him from others' and, indeed, he is at least
mentioned in a book entitled *Foole upon Foole* (1600) by the professional fool,
Robert Armin, under the name Jack Oates.[50] But the writer goes on to give one
such example:

> A gentleman (having brought his hawkes to Houghton to fly at the brooke) was in
> dinner time commending a falcon (that stood upon the perch in the hall) to Sr Wm
> Holles for the sweetest, delicatest and best condition'd bird that ever he was maister
> of. The foole, hearing him, goes out and worries the hawke and returned into the
> dining roome with his lips all bloudy cursing the hawke for the worst meat that ever
> he eat in his life; the gentleman, (suspecting what was done), starts up from the table
> and found his hawke's limbes and feathers scatter'd up and downe the hall flore, wch
> was recompensed to him by another hawke given him, and the poore foole's
> whipping.[51]

Given the circumstantial detail, it comes as something of a shock to learn that this too is a traditional folktale motif, 'The falcon not so good as represented'. As well as being found in Bebel's Latin *Facetiae* (1508) and Pauli's German *Schimpf und Ernst* (1521), it occurs in such fifteenth-century collections of *exempla* as *The Alphabet of Tales*, as well as in earlier anthologies.[52]

Sawing Through the Branch on Which One Sits

According to a Lancashire local tale, Tom Skelton (d. 1668), the household fool of the Penningtons of Muncaster Castle, Cumbria, would sometimes climb up onto the branch of a tree and, after amusing the crowd with his antics, would make his exit by sawing through the branch between himself and the trunk.[53] This visual joke is still a staple of children's comics and cartoons, and even the adult political cartoon. It is possible Skelton may really have done this, of course, but once again, we should restrain our credulity, for it is not difficult to find seventeeth-century and, indeed, medieval illustrations of this particularly popular folly. In Henry Peacham's emblem book *Minerva Britanna* (1612), for example, a costumed fool is depicted doing just this, and again, the fact that it is a recognised folktale motif 'Numskull cuts off tree-limb on which he sits', must give us pause. In a lengthy passage detailing some twenty applied emblems to be seen in various media in a (probably fictional) inn chamber from a work entitled *A Dialogue of the Fever Pestilence* (1564), author William Bullein describes one such as:

> The foole, that stand[eth] vpon the tree, and cutteth the arme therof a sonder, whereupon he standeth, with a sharpe axe, and is fallyng doune hymself.

This particular emblem is interpreted by Civis as signifying:

> all traitors against princes: children against Parentes, seruauntes againste Maisters, poore against riche, tenauntes against their lordes, &c. wherupon thei do liue, and haue their staie in this worlde, and will seeke their hurtes, whiche in deede is their owne decaie, losse, and destruction in the ende.

But, like so many Renaissance emblems, the branch-cutting motif can be traced back further still. On one leaf of Pierre Sala's gem-like *Enigmes de l'Amour*, the artist has painted a fashionably dressed young man hacking with an axe at the branch on which he stands, so that he is on the point of plunging into the river beside which the tree grows.[54] As we have seen above, some of the verses in this manuscript (though not this one) are taken direct from Baude's *Dictz Moraulx pour Faire Tapisserie*, which must have been composed shortly before 1500, and two manuscripts of Baude's work illustrate this same scene according to the rubric, 'A man who has his eyes bandaged standing on a branch which he is cutting with an axe'.[55] But the joke, before it was given a moralising application, is older still. There are many marginal examples in medieval manuscripts (mostly unremarked), for the foliage which luxuriates in the borders of these pages is ideally suited to the presentation of this scene. In the celebrated Flemish *Romance of Alexander*

Figure 7.5

manuscript, for example, on one folio a man takes an axe to the branch on which he stands, while on another, a man and woman saw together at the tendril junction on either side of which they sit.[56]

Trying to Get the Plank Through the Door Crosswise [57]

A recent work on the iconographically rich Danish church wall-paintings describes two late twelfth-century details in the church at Mårslet (Figure 7.5) thus:

1. A man who lifts an entire tree with its crown and roots.
2. A man who lifts a horse with harness and saddle by its tail so that it hangs vertically with its head downwards.

   . . . Subjects 1 and 2 are incredibly well preserved so there can be no doubt about what they depict. By contrast, their interpretation is quite unknown. One might guess that the pictures are intended to express strength.[58]

In fact, I believe the second image is the *monde renversé* motif of the man carrying the horse rather than the horse carrying him. This then provides us with some orientation regarding the first image, for we should identify a motif by the company it keeps – 'birds of a feather flock together'! It is clear from the reproduction of the first image that the man holds the tree transversely across the frame of the archway he is trying to get it through, which is surely the proverbial folly of 'Trying to get a beam through a door crosswise . . .'.[59]

As early as 800, in the *Life* of the Greek Saint Arsenius, the hero sees in a vision two horsemen trying to get a beam through a doorway in this idiotic fashion. The story is found in several later medieval *exempla* collections.[60] A later version slightly elaborated relates how the builders of churches at Domburg in the Netherlands and Ulm in Germany, for example, were struggling to get beams laid across a wagon through the town's narrow gate when they noticed a bird building its nest in a thin aperture in the town wall taking in a stalk at right-angles to the opening! This particular piece of *blason populaire* purports to explain why the people of Ulm are known as 'sparrows', and how Domburg got its name when the builders exclaimed 'What stupid ("dumb") burghers we are indeed!' A mid-seventeenth-century engraved emblem after a drawing by Adriaen van der Venne shows a boy similarly trying to get a long pole through a house doorway.[61]

THE 'WISE' MEN OF GOTHAM

Every country, every county, indeed, picks on some region or village, the inhabitants of which are regarded as proverbially foolish; in Germany it is the villagers of Schilda; in England, the earliest list we have, of late twelfth-century date, attributes to the people of the county of Norfolk several follies which are, in fact, popular international motifs.[62]

By the late Middle Ages, the list of the proverbial follies of the people of Norfolk had been transferred to the inhabitants of the Nottinghamshire village of Gotham. They were evidently already famous as prototypical village idiots as early as the mid-fifteenth century to judge from a passing reference in one of the Towneley Plays to 'the foles of gotham'.

Although the earliest folly to be attributed to the ironically styled 'Wise' Men of Gotham – the argument over which shepherd's as-yet-unbought flock shall have precedence across the narrow bridge[63] – first appears in *A Hundred Merry Tales* (1526),[64] the earliest extant book devoted entirely to the *Merie Tales of the Mad Men of Gotam* was published *c.* 1565, though it is unlikely to have been the first edition.[65] Their most enduringly famous folly, giving rise to numerous field names, was to attempt to pen the cuckoo, in order that she might sing all year round and thus prolong the springtime indefinitely – in Chapter 2 we noted how the saint, as God's fool, was paradoxically able to achieve this proverbial folly. But we know, from onomastic evidence, that the proverbial folly of trying to pen in a bird was current much earlier in English folklore, in the shape of one Henry nicknamed *Pendecrowe* (= Pen-the-crow) who crops up in a late thirteenth-century Staffordshire Assize Roll.[66]

The Humane Rider

Another folly attributed both to the twelfth-century Norfolk fools and, in the earliest printed anthology of their doings, to the villagers of Gotham, is that which I term the 'humane rider' – the rider who thinks to save his horse some of the burden by carrying the sack on his own back.[67] Again this has its own Motif no. (J 1874.1 'Carrying part of the load') and, though often overlooked,[68] is one of the most widely represented proverbial follies in art, found in a wide variety of media and, curiously, with surprising frequency in Norfolk. There is a roof boss of this subject in Norwich Cathedral cloister carved in 1415,[69] and it also features as one of several such follies engraved on a mid-fourteenth-century monumental brass of Flemish manufacture, now in the church in King's Lynn, Norfolk.[70]

A miniature in the *Luttrell Psalter* of the 1330s shows how a sensible person transports his sack of grain to the mill – he sits on it, of course, using it as a saddle. The foolish rider, however, carries the burden on his head, as seen in two fourteenth-century Flemish manuscripts,[71] on fifteenth-century Dutch lead badges (Figure 7.6),[72] a thirteenth-century stone carving at Rouen Cathedral, and an early sixteenth-century Somerset bench-end.[73] As we might have guessed, the motif is also found on misericords of fifteenth- and sixteenth-century date, for example at San Salvador de Celanova in Galicia,[74] at La Guerche de Bretagne, and (now destroyed) at Corbeil in France. In the English corpus it is found on one of the important series of misericords in Bristol Cathedral carved in 1520, though there is reason to believe that this particular example – like several other misericord designs in the cathedral – derives from a series of ornamental metal-cuts which appears in the margins of early sixteenth-century Parisian books of hours, motifs which are of great but still unrecognised importance in the history of the transmission of continental designs to English art.[75]

Figure 7.6

The Hare Messenger

Another 'Gothamite' folly – included in Odo of Cheriton's thirteenth-century fable collection, where it is attributed to the villagers of Wilby (also in Norfolk!)[76] – concerns the payment of the villagers' rent. In danger of being late with it, they catch a hare, an animal proverbially fleet of foot, of course, put the money in a purse tied

around the hare's neck and release it, with strict instructions to run post-haste to their landlord. The hare with the purse round its neck, playfully alluding to this 'noodle-tale', is depicted in the margins of at least three late medieval manuscripts; one illuminated in England in the thirteenth century, and two decorated in Flanders in the early fourteenth century.[77]

Figure 7.7 shows a contemporary stone sculpture of the same hare messenger on an impost in St Mary's Church, Beverley. Some years ago I read this in the church guide:

A legend has grown up that this statuette became the model for the White Rabbit in Lewis Carroll's *Alice in Wonderland*. Lewis Carroll's grandfather was a customs officer in Hull and it is likely that they visited Beverley, and therefore St Mary's, in the nineteenth century. Furthermore he had no qualms about sending an artist from the magazine *Punch*, Sir John Tenniel, to all parts of the British Isles before the illustrations for his

Figure 7.7

book were finally produced. There is certainly a remarkable similarity between Tenniel's drawings of the White Rabbit, and the statuette in St Mary's.[78]

In fact, to my mind at least, there is *not* much similarity between Tenniel's White Rabbit and the Beverley statue, but there does seem to me to be a real resemblance to the hare in *Alice Through the Looking-Glass*, named *Haigha* – 'He pronounced it so as to rhyme with mayor', writes Carroll – the only textual hint that this so-called 'Anglo-Saxon Messenger' is indeed a hare. At one point:

> the Messenger, to Alice's great amusement, opened a bag hung round his neck, and handed a sandwich to the King. 'There's nothing but hay left now', the Messenger said.

It appears from Tenniel's illustration of this scene that, whether directly from the author or not, he clearly understood that Carroll was alluding to the proverbial folly of the hare messenger that the Beverley statuette embodies.[79]

The hare messenger was another popular international motif reflecting on the foolishness of those who despatched it[80] and hence its appearance in the top left-hand corner of the title-page woodcut of a book published in Florence in the early sixteenth century, the *Historia di Campriano Contadino*. The lengthy title summarises the contents of Campriano's exploits:

> The tale of the peasant Campriano who was very poor and had three daughters to marry off, and who artfully made an ass which he possessed shit coins, and sold it to certain merchants for 100 pounds, and afterwards sold them a cooking-pot which boiled without fire, and *a hare which knew how to carry letters* and a trumpet which revived the dead, and in the end he threw the merchants into a river.[81]

The moral being, I suppose, that if you are so foolish as to believe that such things exist, you deserve all you get – or, *caveat emptor*!

Hunting Hares with a Tabour

The hare features in several proverbial follies, perhaps because of its own associations with folly (cf. *mad as a March hare* . . . and note that sometimes the hare's ears replace those of the ass on the fool's hood). It is clearly foolish, for example, to beat a drum while hunting such a proverbially timid animal, 'to hunt a hare with a tabour', as the English proverb, attested from the early fifteenth century puts it.[82] But such folly may be witnessed in the late fifteenth-century Walters *Proverbes en Rimes* manuscript and in the margins of at least two other fourteenth-century French illuminated manuscripts.[83]

The One-legged Man Shears the Running Hare[84]

In the twelfth century there was something of a vogue for 'amusing' scenes featuring men with wooden legs.[85] The man with a wooden leg shown on a medallion inset into a decorated initial on the second folio of the contemporary *Bury St Edmunds*

Bible (Figure 7.8)[86] might at first seem just another instance of this simple, if regrettable, sense of humour, but closer inspection shows that he is attempting (with, one suspects, little success) to shear a hare in full flight. This ambitious feat has parallels for, once again, it is a traditional folktale folly motif. In the Grimms' tale *The Three Brothers*, a father tells his three sons that his heir will be the one who can give the best demonstration of some newly learned trade. One becomes a barber, and on the day appointed for their demonstrations of skill, as they sit, a hare suddenly comes bounding across the field:

Figure 7.8

'Why,' said the barber, 'he's just what I wanted.' And taking his bowl and his soap, he prepared a good lather as the hare approached, then lathered its face as it ran by and trimmed its beard for it too, while it was still running at full tilt, and all without cutting it or hurting it in the slightest. 'I like that,' said the father.[87]

Collected in the early nineteenth century, the story can be traced back in literature only as far as a French version published in 1579,[88] but Master Hugo, the illuminator of the *Bury Bible*, testifies to the existence of a probably similar tall story over four centuries earlier with, in his case, the additional absurdity that the barber has a wooden leg. This is an important image because it is the earliest proverbial folly to be depicted in a medieval manuscript.

Perhaps we might term this newly acquired skill 'hare-cutting'? That my pun is perhaps not quite as silly as it might seem is suggested by a little image from a margin of the early fourteenth-century *Gorleston Psalter* in which a hare pokes its head through the top of a man's hood, playfully alluding to the Middle English proverb, expressive of poverty, 'his hair grows through his hood', very popular in the latter half of the fifteenth century, in particular.[89]

Planting Needles in the Hope they will Grow into Steel Bars

Though it does not seem to be included in the earliest collections of their follies, the proverb scholar James Howell alluded in 1659 to 'the men of Gotham, who sowed needles, hoping they would grow to bars of iron'.[90] It is yet another traditional folly, catalogued in Thompson's *Motif Index* as 'Sowing needles [like seed]', under the more general heading, 'Absurd disregard of natural laws'. The illustration (Figure 7.9) is taken from the late fifteenth-century *Proverbes en Rimes* manuscript where it is no. 17, depicting the man who plants needles to get stakes of iron.[91] I am reminded of a parental 'put-down' I heard some years ago, very much in

Figure 7.9

the same tradition as this medieval proverbial folly, and again demonstrating, I believe, the longevity and orality of the transmission of such essentially popular formulae. In response to a child who had committed some misdemeanour and began to defend itself with 'But I thought . . .', the parent cut in brusquely with, 'You know what Thought did, don't you? – Planted a feather and thought it would grow into a hen!'

Proverbial Follies from the Narrenschiff

We have already referred several times to that literary landmark of the late Middle Ages, Sebastian Brant's *Narrenschiff*, originally published in Basel in 1494 and profusely illustrated with woodcuts by Dürer and other artists, illustrating the various follies excoriated by the author.[92] The cut to Chapter 32 (designed by Dürer) represents the pointlessness – the proverbial foolishness, indeed – of 'Guarding Wives'. Above the motto 'guard closely', a smiling wife observes three fools practising proverbial follies, only two of which are, in fact, mentioned in Brant's epigrammatic caption, the man who superfluously 'adds water to the well',[93] and the fool who attempts to 'shepherd the grasshoppers' in the sun. This latter motif was recalled in a print popular in the decades around 1600, in which the jealous husband's folly at securing his wife, as he thinks, into a chastity belt at his departure, is pointed up by the depiction of a fool in the foreground, trying in vain to keep the 'grasshoppers' from jumping out of a basket.[94]

The third proverbial folly depicted in the woodcut – not mentioned in Brant's text – illustrates the pointlessness of 'washing a tile/brick', an idiom inherited from classical times, as indeed, were the two variant versions. The first of these variants, 'washing an Ethiope (white)', as the earliest English versions have it,[95] passed via Erasmus's *Adagia* into the emblem books, including the very first and most influential such book, Alciato's *Emblematum Liber* of 1531. Interestingly, the cut from the 1542 edition of Alciato was pasted into the manuscript of Thomas Palmer's *Two Hundred Poosees* (c. 1565).[96] Line 4 of the text Palmer provided to this woodcut reads, 'thow labourste all in vayne', and 'The Labour-in-Vain' was the name of at least four London inns which issued trade tokens in the seventeenth century, the obverse of which depicted two women washing a black man. Inn signs depicting the same scene survived into the nineteenth century.[97]

Washing the Ass's Head

The other variant proverbial 'washing' folly is that of washing an ass's head – it too is pictorialised in the late fifteenth-century *Proverbes en Rimes* manuscript. A maiolica dish made in Deruta and dated 1556 portrays the same scene, though

Figure 7.10

adds to the absurdity by seating the ass in a throne-like chair. It is inscribed 'whoever washes the head of an ass wastes all his efforts', and may well derive from a lost Italian print recorded as being in the print collection of Ferdinand Columbus (d. 1539) (Figure 7.10).[98]

Shoeing the Goose

One of the ways in which Rabelais's infant Gargantua amused himself was by shoeing cicadas,[99] though the more usual version of this popular absurdity is to attempt to shoe the goose, a proverbial folly found represented as early as *c.* 1340 in the margins of Flemish manuscripts.[100] On a late fourteenth-century capital in the choir of York Minster is a carving of a goose in a frame, being shod just like a horse

and, incidentally, providing a pictorial antedating of a proverb not found in the literary record in English until Hoccleve's *Oldcastle* of 1415.[101] It is also found carved in wood on misericords at Beverley (*c.* 1520) and Whalley (*c.* 1430); exceptionally, at Whalley (Figure 7.11) the motif is provided with a rhyming couplet as caption, which helpfully points the application of the proverb:

Figure 7.11

> *Who so melles hym of yat al men dos*
> *Let hym cum heir and shoe the gos.*
> [Whoever meddles in everyone else's business,
> let him come here and shoe the goose.]

Elsewhere in Europe it is found as a misericord motif at St Martin-aux-Bois in fifteenth-century France, and at Walcourt in Belgium *c.* 1520.[102] Randall records five marginal examples of this scene, all in manuscripts dating from the first half of the fourteenth century, and of Picard or Flemish provenance,[103] and I believe that this was one of several motifs to have become familiar in England from the repertoire of Flemish artists.

The expression is also significantly attested in the texts of at least two *sotties* (fool-plays), and in the *Sottie des sots qui corrigent le Magnificat*, the pedant Dando enters carrying a goose in his arms, for his speciality is said to be 'shoeing geese'[104] – a timely reminder that proverbial follies may also be enacted on the stage. In late medieval Paris we learn too of a house sign near the Chappelle de Braque which depicted 'The Nun who Shoes the Goose'.[105]

Attention has recently been drawn to six examples in Danish church murals of a man hammering a horseshoe onto the paw of a cat,[106] but the author in question seems to me to be unreasonably reluctant to interpret them as a Danish variant of the commoner European proverbial folly of 'shoeing the goose'. We have already noted the infant Gargantua's attempts to shoe cicadas, and French alone affords further non-anserine variants. Late medieval Parisian documents preserve the sur-/nicknames (which presumably also refer to this topos) of Ami *Ferre-coc* (Shoe-the-cock; 1292, Tax-Roll), and Jacques *Ferre-bouc* (Shoe-the-goat), a printer active 1492–1530, whose rebus device depicts a blacksmith shoeing a goat (*bouc*) in a shoeing-frame.[107]

THE SCHILDBÜRGER, THE 'WISE' MEN OF SCHILDA

The village of Schilda in Germany, corresponds to the English Gotham, similar 'noodle tales' being known as *Schildbürgergeschichten*, and two further such follies associated with building a house are most familiar as part of the story of the construction of the Schildburgers' town hall, first told in full in the *Lalebuch* published in 1597, but earlier related in a *Schwank* composed in 1558 by Hans Sachs (and set in Switzerland), entitled *Die Lappenhawser pauern*.[108] After felling the necessary timber in a hilltop forest and carrying it down to the valley below, the final log breaks free and 'delivers itself' to the bottom of the hill. When the Schildburgers see to what unnecessary toil they have been put in carrying the timber downhill, they feel very foolish, and haul it all back to the top of the hill again, so that they can then let it roll back down by itself![109]

Having finally managed to deliver the timber to the building site, the Schildburgers built their council house, but it turned out to be very dark because they had neglected to put in any windows. In order to illuminate the council chamber they hit upon the remedy of introducing daylight in sacks, baskets and whatever other vessels were to hand (and when this operation proved to be unsuccessful, they gradually pulled down more and more of the building in order to let the light in).[110] One of the several puzzling details in Bruegel's *Netherlandish Proverbs* painting is a man carrying a large basket full of what looks rather like steam, who appears to emerge from a brightly lit interior (Colour Plate 6). Bruegel based his composition on an etching made in 1558 by Frans Hogenberg, who helpfully labelled his proverbs so that we should know that the man carrying the apparently empty basket, 'carries the day(-light) out in baskets', (that is, he is performing the Schildburgers' folly in reverse!).[111] Semantically, this is closely related to the folly of trying to brighten the day with a light, as one of the fools in the *Narrenschiff* woodcuts tries to do, and it is one of the many colourful idioms which express superfluity and labour-in-vain.

But it is also possible that Bruegel's man with his apparently steaming wickerwork basket alludes to the folly of carrying any liquid in a basket, like the man in the 105th proverb in the late fifteenth-century Walters *Proverbes en Rimes* manuscript who has just filled a basket with hot soup from his cauldron. I am reminded of the witticism 'Soup-in-the-basket' heard some years ago in a pub serving 'basket-meals', but this sort of absurdity also recurs as one of the traditional tricks played on apprentices or gullible new employees, where the hapless individual is sent to fetch, for example, a bucket of steam.

Throwing the Baby Out With the Bathwater

While the follies of proverbial fools may be infinite, unfortunately I do not have an infinite space in which to discuss them, so I close this chapter with one of my favourites, the startling image representing the folly of throwing the baby out with the bathwater (Figure 7.12) – note the foolish mother's ass-eared and belled hood – one of the woodcut illustrations to Thomas Murner's *Narrenbeschwörung* of 1512. Interestingly, the proverb does not seem to have become current in English before the nineteenth century.

The decades either side of the year 1500 seem to have been the era in which enthusiasm for the proverb reached its height. While literature in manuscript, and increasingly in printed form

Figure 7.12

(including Erasmus' ever-expanding *Adagia*) collected texts of proverbs, other illustrated works and even such non-text media as tapestry and paintings anthologised pictorial representations of them. Individual proverbs had long been and continued to be represented in every known medium, but neither should we forget – in an age that relied so heavily on authority – the ubiquity of proverbial inscriptions, similarly appearing on a wide variety of artefacts, several of which are noted throughout this book.[112]

Eight

NONSENSE, PURE AND APPLIED

In this chapter I examine the multifarious illustrations of the absurd in late medieval art and thought, from the apparently meaningless grotesques which inhabit the margins of illuminated manuscripts, via the mostly satirical *impossibilia* in a variety of media, to the nexus of such motifs which make up the World Turned Upside Down, and its sensual manifestation, the Land of Cockaigne.

It should not surprise us that, in an era that revelled in such literary genres as the French *fatras* and the German *Lügengedichte*, the same spirit should be abroad in pictorial art. It is a commonplace of the study of such 'nonsense' literature, however, that not all of it is irredeemably nonsensical; but can the same be said for 'nonsense art'?

The question of the meaningfulness or otherwise of the 'Images in the Margins of Gothic Manuscripts' is one which has long vexed art historians, some maintaining that such images are merely whimsical grotesques, the *jeux* of some often rather dubious *esprits*, 'emptily' amusing *drôleries* (however inappropriate to our modern sensibilities such decoration may seem in a prayer book), mere *babuineries*[1] monkeying about in the margins. But others have argued – sometimes in a decidedly contrived manner, with the excess of zeal characteristic of those trying to overturn a prevailing orthodoxy – that almost all are somehow meaningful, if not in an immediately direct way, then tangentially. As so often, the truth would appear to lie somewhere inbetween these two extremes. The passage of the centuries has undoubtedly obscured many allusive pictorial–textual relationships which may sometimes be recovered by industrious iconographers, but, just as certainly, many marginal grotesques stubbornly remain no more than decorative doodles, and we are in danger of falling into the trap, ever open for even the most cautious iconographer, of 'enquiring too curiously' – in the words of Horatio's gentle criticism of Hamlet's fantasising.

In the World Turned Upside Down, of course, *impossibilia* become possible, pigs do fly, and predators become prey. Sometimes there is reason to believe that the World Turned Upside Down is merely comical in its depiction of obvious reversals, in much the same way that many verbal jokes depend on simple reversals of expectation for their humour, but perhaps more usually the World Turned Upside Down is a morally negative state, indicative of the terrible, unnatural situation into which this post-lapsarian world has fallen. There is one species of the World Turned Upside Down, however, that is always joyous, and that is the sensual Utopia known as the Land of Cockaigne in England and in the Romance area as *Schlaraffenland* in German, and as *Luilekkerland* in Flanders, and it is there that we find we have landed.

THE LAND OF COCKAIGNE

The Land of Cockaigne represents an ancient[2] secular, paradisal inversion of life's harsh realities. In this hedonist's heaven food and drink present themselves already prepared – pigs, for example, trot up ready-roasted, the carving knife already lodged in their sides, spitted geese fly about advertising themselves, and ready-roasted larks fly into the mouth! The very buildings are constructed from food – roofs are thatched with pancakes, fences made of sausages. But the way thither is sometimes extremely daunting – in the Anglo-Irish poem of *c.* 1300, one must 'wade seven years through pig-shit up to one's chin'. It is pre-eminently a glutton's paradise. In an era of always precarious food supplies, that is perhaps not too surprising. But the sin of sloth is also well in evidence, for sleeping is paid, and according to the French poem, 'He who sleeps till noon will earn five-and-a-half sous'!

Curiously the vice of lechery is usually conspicuously absent – except in the Anglo-Irish poem, in which the flying 'monks' who inhabit this land are summoned back to earth by their 'abbot' beating out the landing signal on the bared upturned buttocks of a maiden – this brings them down in a hurry, and they all flock around her (and join in the slapping). According to the Anglo-Irish poem, the young 'nuns' of the nearby 'nunnery' like to go skinny-dipping, whereupon the 'monks' each seize one and bear her off to their 'abbey', where they teach the nuns an 'orison' (prayer) with 'legs in the air, up and down'; and the monk who is a good 'stallion' is promised of right, twelve 'wives' each year, 'for to do himself solace'.

Although I know of no English examples, the manner in which the flying monks are brought back to earth by their abbot is somewhat reminiscent of a popular sixteenth-century visual motif in which a fowler within a hide catches flying men in a clap-net by means of setting out an attractive woman as decoy. A drawing of the 1521 Nürnberg *Schembartlauf Hölle* (carnival-float) shows a fowler within a hide operating a clap-net, in the middle of which stands a naked woman (holding symbolic fools' hoods), while fluttering down all around her are the winged heads of various ranks of male society, including cardinal, bishop, monk, burgher, and nobleman.[3] A woodcut of 1534 by Niklas Stoer illustrating a lost poem by Hans Sachs, entitled 'The lovers' snare', depicts essentially the same scene but here the clap-net has closed, trapping several men, and there are two (fully clothed) decoy women; but other men are still coming flying in, and the net is operated by an old crone (procuress?) with the assistance of the Devil.[4]

The earliest European evidence for the existence of this fabulous land, however, is onomastic, rather than literary. Although a place named *Cuccagna* is attested in Italy as early as 1142, Italian stories employing this name are not found before the fifteenth century. When the fabulous land appears in Boccaccio's *Decameron* (1349–51), it is named *Bengodi*, and located in the Basque country. Earlier than the Anglo-Irish poem, and almost as early as the allusion to the abbot of Cockaigne in the *Carmina Burana* (c. 1164), we learn of a place in Essex in 1228 named *Cockaynes*, and thus of presumably legendary fertility. As a surname, however – probably originally a nickname suggesting 'one whose habits and manner of life suggested he had come from [that] fabulous land' – it is found as early as 1193 in Warwickshire (William *Cocaine*, compare Jehan *Coqaingne* [Paris, 1292]).[5]

After the Anglo-Irish poem there is a considerable gap in the English literary record and, extraordinarily, the Cockaigne topos is not found again in our period. As far as I am aware, at least, the next – and still little-known – sighting of the fabulous land in English literature is to be found in Hugh Plat's 'Merrie tale of Master Mendax to his friend Credulus' from his *Pleasures of Poetrie*, printed with *The Flowres of Philosophie* (London, 1572). The relevant section opens, 'There is within Eutopia,/a house all tylde with tarte . . .' attesting to a quite unwarranted Elizabethan confusion with More's political vision. From at least the closing years of the sixteenth century, however, the name *Lubberland* comes to replace Cockaigne; the Christmas revels at St John's College, Oxford in 1607, for example, included an *Embassage from Lubberland*.

The Isle of Lasye

For the earliest depiction of the whole country of Cockaigne we are once again beholden to Hans Sachs, whose poem *Das Schlaweraffenlandt*, was issued as a broadsheet headed by an influential woodcut illustration by Erhard Schoen (c. 1530).[6] The image includes the food-house, the sausage-fence, the man with open mouth waiting for the ready-roasted bird to fly into it, the ready-to-carve pig, the horse which excretes baskets of eggs, and a Fountain of Youth (really an independent motif but also found in the Middle French poem). Although the sixteenth century popularity of this motif in European prints is beyond the scope of the present survey, it is perhaps worth noting that Pieter Baltens's engraving, which served as the model for Bruegel's more famous *Luilekkerland* painting of 1567, has recently been discovered in an English copy issued before 1653 by the print-seller Peter Stent, who entitled it 'The mapp of Lubberland or the Ile of Lasye'.[7] Some of the constituent motifs of the Land of Cockaigne exhibit astonishing longevity, however, turning up in nineteenth-century recordings of English mummers' plays and folktales.

THE WORLD TURNED UPSIDE DOWN

The Land of Cockaigne is really only a special, joyous case of the World Turned Upside Down, for the *mundus inversus* is more usually regarded as the *mundus perversus* by moralists, and it is symbolised by the world-orb (customarily surmounted by a cross), literally inverted, as perhaps most notably, at the end of our period, in the 'sign' of the 'noodle village' painted by Bruegel, whose inhabitants act out so many proverbial follies.

The constituent motifs which are subsumed within this complex represent, in essence, reversals of the status quo. Depending on one's perspective, they may be seen as positive or negative, revolutionary portents of a new order to come, or chronic, unnatural symptoms of a world in terminal decline. Biblical authority meant that reversals of the 'natural order' were not inevitably seen as negative, for Isaiah proclaimed fierily that 'The Lord maketh the earth . . . waste, and turneth it upside down', and was it not Christ himself who preached that the last shall be first, and the first last? And as we have noted in Chapter 6, the *Magnificat* lines, 'He hath put down the mighty from their seats, and exalted them of low degree' [Luke 1:49 (AV)], were eagerly seized on by the lower clerical orders as a biblical justification for the inversions of the Feast of Fools.

The motifs which go to make up the *monde renversé* are usually simple, literal inversions. There are as many conceivable types of reversal as there are relationships: between animals and humans, for example – the horse is carried by the man, the bull milks the woman, the hares roast the huntsman, the ox slaughters the butcher;[8] between animals, especially predator and prey – the hare hunts the hound, the mice hang the cat, the geese hang the fox; between men and women – most notoriously, the woman 'wears the trousers' and the man spins with her distaff, that quintessentially female implement; between social groups – the pupils flog the master (as on a Spanish misericord), the priest ploughs while the peasant celebrates mass (Figure 8.1), and so on.

The World Turned Upside Down in terms of gender roles is a common late medieval and early modern fear, classically expressed in the popular

Das erste Capitel von der veerendering aller stende der Christenheyt/die mag bewert werden auß den sichtbarn zeychen des himels.

Figure 8.1

images of the woman pulling on the breeches while her husband spins with her distaff – a variant is the Hercules and Omphale type, in which she wields his massive club (with its transparent phallic symbolism), and watches while he spins. A significant exchange in which gender attributes are all-important, occurs in Chaucer's *Canterbury Tales* when the Host's wife, angry that he has not shown himself quick enough to leap to the defence of her honour, screams at him, 'By corpus bones, I wol have thy knyf, And thou shalt have my distaf and go spynne!' Even worse humiliated husbands are threatened by their wives while washing the clothes, or beaten on the bare bottom with a switch or foxtail. The foolish Aucassin (held to be a wise man in the topsy-turvy land of Torelore) finds the king lying in childbed, and his queen leading the country's army into the field. But I shall have more to say on this particular variety of the World Turned Upside Down imagery in Chapter 11 on gender roles.

The *monde renversé* is the natural habitation of all unnatural elemental reversals, where, for example, fish fly in the air – a frequent *adynaton* used (in Archer Taylor's phrase) as one of the many colourful 'locutions for never'. It figures, for example, in Caxton's *Jason* (*c.* 1477): 'Certes that shal not be unto the tyme that the fishes flee in the ayer. And that the byrdes swymme in the water' and – a typical context – in a medieval Latin misogynist couplet: 'He who labours to find loyalty in woman, should look for fish in the woods and bees in the sea'. Such expressions are sometimes invoked to convey the perdurability of legal agreements, treaties, and so on. According to *Nestor's Chronicle*, when King Vladimir of Kiev made peace with the Bulgars in 985, it was stipulated that this peace should endure 'until stones start floating on water and hops sink to the bottom'. But they are also the stuff of lovers' vows, of course, as in Burns's 'till all the seas gang dry and rocks melt in the sun' (from 'My love is like a red, red rose'), as they are, less charitably, of the disappointed lover's cynical despair of ever finding, in Donne's words, 'a woman true and fair' (from 'Goe and catch a falling star').

Rats v. Cats

The relationship of the cat with the mouse or rat is one of those paradigmatic relations that function as unconscious measures of normality, of the immutable order of the natural world, and the reversal of such a natural power relation is unthinkable. But the topos of the *monde renversé* was invented to free artists to think the unthinkable, and to invert the normal power relations by which the weak and the meek are held in bondage by their oppressors. The motif of the cats' castle besieged by the rats/mice is a venerable one which is attested in art as early as the twelfth century in Austria, in a mural on the south wall of the nave of the St Johanniskirche, Pürgg in Obersteiermark, and found again in that country (in a less surprising, secular context) in the Jagdzimmer of Schloss Moos-Schulthaus zu Eppan, painted *c.* 1400.[9]

The inversion of predator and prey was always popular, and the cat hanged by the rats/mice was a subject found in the earliest English manuscript to contain such marginal imagery, the *Rutland Psalter* of *c.* 1260,[10] but is also found on fourteenth-century painted Spanish ceiling-panels,[11] and carved on misericords at Great Malvern in Worcestershire (*c.* 1480) and at Talavera de la Reina in Spain.

Hare and Hound

A dog, paws bound behind his back, is pulled by hares in a tumbril towards a gallows in a *bas-de-page* of the fourteenth-century *Smithfield Decretals*[12] and, as with proverbial follies, the most popular World Turned Upside Down images also seem to have involved hares, especially the role reversal in which, instead of being pursued by him, the hare (often blowing a hunting horn) rides the hound, a motif found in a variety of small-scale media especially. It is found, for example, on tiles from the late thirteenth-century priory in Derby (Figure 8.2), and on a number of personal seals of early fourteenth-century date, some bearing the hunting-cry *SOHO*, and the name of the hound (*ROBEN*, for example), others the legend, *ALONE I RIDE A RIVER*, where the final words presumably represent French *à revers* (topsy-turvy). On a Manchester misericord (*c.* 1506) it is the fox who rides the hound; another hare rides the hound on a Worcester misericord (*c.* 1379) where, here at least, it would appear to have a commentary function. It flanks the Labour of the Month for June (three men mowing with scythes), but its opposing supporter depicts a preaching fox standing behind an altar on which what appears to be a sheep's

Figure 8.2

head rests – there can be little doubt that in this latter popular motif we see symbolised the familiar satirical attack on the rapacity of the mendicant orders, nor that this example of the topsy-turvy sinful world in which the pastor feeds off his flock rather than nourishes it, is signalled by the World Turned Upside Down motif of the hare riding the hound.

Hare Hunts Huntsman

A celebrated misericord in Manchester Cathedral carved *c.* 1506 depicts a huntsman being spit-roasted by hares while four of his hounds are stewing in cooking pots. Importantly, as is apparent from the unmistakable, detailed resemblances (such as the hare who reaches into the salt box for some seasoning to add to one of the dogs seething in the pot), it was clearly an engraving by the copyist, Israhel van Meckenem (d. 1503), whose oeuvre so perfectly sums up the spirit of the *ausgehendes Mittelalter*, that the carver of the Manchester seat had before him as his model – an unequivocal instance of the direct influence of 'Germanic' prints on English woodwork design.[13] This or a related image was doubtless also the source underlying the small detail carved by German craftsmen *c.* 1490 as part of a frieze decorating the Toledo Cathedral stall-work, where we see a gleeful hare similarly attending to a hound boiling in a pot.[14]

As early as 1509, the Emperor Maximilian granted the *Hasenhaus* in Vienna's Kärntner Strasse to his hare-warden, Friedrich Jäger, the façade of which was painted with thirty-two separate scenes, including the hares' victorious war against the hunters (Jäger) and their hounds. Also early in the sixteenth century, the main council chamber of Basel town hall was decorated with carvings depicting hares dragging the hapless hunter in fetters and roasting him on a spit.[15] The Flemish folklorist, Maurits de Meyer, described this particular scene of the 'rabbits' revenge' as 'the oldest and best loved World Turned Upside Down motif',[16] and indeed, it is found carved in stone on Romanesque churches at Konigslütter and Murbach as early as the mid-twelfth century.[17]

A classic constituent of this complex, which often appears alone, simply depicts the hunter dangling from a stick shouldered by the hare: examples can be found in one of the lower border miniatures in a fourteenth-century Flemish manuscript (Bodley 264, f. 81v), and on the Hell panel of Bosch's *Garden of Earthly Delights* triptych (*c.* 1510). In the scene painted by Albertus Pictor in 1482 on the ceiling of Kumla Church in Sweden, however, the captured hunter is slung from a pole shouldered by two hares. The twelfth-century sculptures on the exterior of the apse of the church at Konigslütter first depict the hunter carrying a hare dangling from a stick over his shoulder, but then show him lying on the ground being bound hand and foot by two hares. The popularity of the image of the hunter hanging from the hare's stick was doubtless reinforced by the episode in the influential early thirteenth-century French beast-epic, the *Roman de Renart,* in which the hare Couard captures a peasant and transports him in this manner.[18]

The World Orb and Standing on One's Head

As the name of the topos might suggest, the World Turned Upside Down was often presented literally in the form of an inverted globe. A pig with wings which balances tipsily on a toppling world orb (Figure 8.4), clearly signals by means of that symbol the wider *monde renversé* theme. We have already seen it used as a 'sign' both literal and metaphorical in Bruegel's *Netherlandish Proverbs* of 1559, but it can be found earlier in the Netherlands where the inverted globe features on several misericords at Hoogstraeten (1532x48), for example. As early as 1507, the Parisian printer Olivier Senant used as his device a design which incorporated a shield bearing the inverted orb and the accompanying legend, 'Alas, World, perchance you will turn again'. In several late medieval French *moralités* a character named *Monde* (World) appears, and in one, he is re-dressed so that he wears his clothes back to front and is then obliged to wear the costume of a fool over his reversed garments.

Dressing Upside Down and Inside Out

The 'classically' attired fool perhaps sports the most obviously symbolically disjunct costume, but whether identified by his motley as such or no, such vestimentary reversals or disjunctions are always iconographically significant. In 998, the anti-pope Johannes Philagatos was punished by being mutilated and then made to ride backwards on an ass (see Chapter 5) wearing his vestments turned inside out. Like the symbolic World-Fools of the French plays, a costumed German fool is shown standing on his head in a cart *before* which horses have been put, in the title-page woodcut of a poem printed in Basel in 1498 by the *Narrenschiff* author, Sebastian Brant.

In the well-known passage of advice to his son, Polonius notes that 'the apparel oft proclaims the man' (*Hamlet* I.iii.72), but Peter Idley had said the same to his son

150 years earlier, 'clothyng ofte maketh man',[19] and, indeed, it is a commonplace, the Latin form of which, *vestis virum facit*, was discussed by Erasmus in his *Adagia*. If it is symbolic of the inversion of sapience for *homo sapiens* to stand on his head, then to the extent that the apparel proclaims the man, to invert vestimentary norms by wearing a shoe on your head, as does the costumed fool in the British Library manuscript of the *Proverbes en Rimes* (Figure 8.3), or a glove on your foot, as does a man in another image from the Walters manuscript, identifies you as an inhabitant of the World Turned Upside Down.

Given the prevalence of the body politic metaphor, it was natural that the proper places of feet and head in relation to the human body should be extended to the proper relations between the individual members of the body politic (specifically, the peasantry and the ruler). Exchange of their natural places showed up the unnatural nature of revolution, as in Lydgate (*a.* 1430):

Figure 8.3

Thanne al ylyche . . .	[Then all [would be] alike
The ffoot as good as ys the hed;	The foot [would be] as good as the head
A knave also, by hys werkyng,	A commoner by labouring
Sholde ben Egal wyth the kyng	would be equal with the King]

– a topos found more frequently in the succeeding century. We may laugh at the ape painted in the margins of a French manuscript who teaches a man to stand on his head,[20] but it is doubtful whether Lydgate would have found it amusing.

POLITICAL, SOCIAL AND RELIGIOUS APPLICATIONS

Even when no particular political revolution was in the author's mind, the constituent motifs of the World Turned Upside Down nexus were pressed into the service of social commentary in that ever-popular genre, the complaint on the times. Woodcut illustrations to Hans Vintler's *Pluemen der tugent* (Augsburg, 1486) include servants riding fine horses while their masters go on foot, a bishop playing with a top, monks riding on horseback and engaging in archery, nuns riding to court, and a man spinning, while it is left to his child to spear a bear.

Less than a generation later, however, it must have been apparent that rebellion was in the air, and a printed prognostication first issued in Nürnberg in 1508 predicted 'the alteration of all estates of Christendom which may be verified by visible signs in the heavens', with as its title-page cut, a priest guiding a plough, while a peasant-farmer celebrated mass inside a church which the artist showed inverted – it was re-issued in Leipzig in 1522, just two years before the start of the upheaval of the Bauernkrieg (Peasants' War) (Figure 8.1). Nor were the Bauern themselves oblivious to this *monde renversé* imagery, for the temporarily victorious peasants who invaded the house of the Teutonic Order at Heilbronn in 1525 compelled the knights to serve them at table, while they themselves dressed in knightly costume and mimicked knightly rituals, declaring that 'Today, little nobles, we are the Knights of the Order!' Significantly, Wat Tyler's rebellious peasants, who invaded the Tower of London where Richard II and his household were staying in 1381, according to one chronicler, 'went in and out like lords'.

It was inevitable too that the imagery of the World Turned Upside Down should as much pervade the annals of witchcraft and heresy, as it does those of insurrection. In his attack on the Waldensians written in the 1460s, Johannes Tinctor predicted that through the effect of the *maleficium* of the heretics, 'Friends and neighbours will become evil, children will rise up against the old and wise, and villeins will engage against the nobles'.

By the time that Ulrich Tengler's *Neu Layenspiegel* was published in Augsburg in 1511, the mounting witch-craze hysteria was such that the woodcut depicting the evil deeds of witches included a scene of a devil copulating with a witch, 'naturally' with the far from hag-like young witch on top.[21] Just as witchcraft represented an inversion or perversion of the natural order, so the sexual proclivities of the witch herself are portrayed as similarly inverted and, indeed – in the world of orthodox late medieval misogyny – perverted. Relations between men and women seem to have been particularly strained in the late medieval era and there was a particular fear (or delightful *frisson* in the fear?) of women getting 'the upper hand', of being 'on top', not just in terms of gender roles and social position, but quite literally, in terms of sexual position. The idea of the 'woman on top' during intercourse was denounced, of course, by all right-thinking theologians. According to the sixteenth-century writer, Thomas Sanchez:

> This position is absolutely contrary to the natural order . . . if the man is beneath, by the very fact of this position, he submits, and the woman plays the active part, and it is obvious how much Nature herself abhors this reversal.[22]

Indeed, it was precisely because 'women [had] gone mad and abused their husbands in this way', that God had sent the Flood to destroy humanity.[23]

In similar vein, in his *Life and Death of Cardinal Wolsey*, alluding to events *c.* 1530, prior to the Dissolution of the Monasteries, Cavendish reported a prophecy notable for a similar sexual inversion, that:

> whan the Cowe ridyth the bull
> than prest beware thy skull

which was popularly interpreted to have come true upon Henry VIII's marriage to Anne *Bull*eyn.

But on occasions, the heretics turned this same imagery back on the orthodox. Luther's attack on the Papacy significantly drew on the ready-made Christian tradition of the Antichrist, identifying the Pope with this *monde renversé* Christ, above all in the *Passional Christi und Antichristi* of 1521. There are several contemporary broadsheets which strikingly exploit this graphic World Turned Upside Down tradition; one depicts wolves, identified in the accompanying text as Catholic priests, monks, etc., hunted down by Reforming sheep,[24] while another includes a monk and priest among those hunted and captured by the hares-turned-hunters. Luther also accused the rebellious peasants of turning the world upside down in the Bauernkrieg, but was himself accused of this by Catholic polemicists. Thomas Murner, the only really influential contemporary Catholic apologist, writes in his new song of the decline of Christian faith of 1522: 'The stools stand on the benches, the cart before the horse, religion will indeed go under.' The former World Turned Upside Down motif of the chairs on top of, rather than under, the table, had already been illustrated in Murner's own *Narrenbeschwörung* (1512), where a fool is shown placing two stools on top of a table.

The Fauna of the World Turned Upside Down

Pigs Might Fly but they are Very Unlikely Birds

During the Gulf War of 1991, a cartoon appeared in the *Guardian* newspaper which set me thinking about the history of this particular proverbial absurdity. A common derisive response in contemporary Britain to an unlikely speculation is 'Pigs might fly!'[25] In the vernacular literary record this now popular absurdity can apparently be traced no further back than the early seventeenth century, where it makes its first appearance in the 1616 edition of John Withals' dictionary, in the form 'Pigs fly in the air with their tails forward',[26] though it seems to be adumbrated in Peele's *Old Wives Tale* a generation earlier, where it is perhaps part of the English Land of Cockaigne topos, here called *Catita*.[27] The earliest occurrence of this particular *adynaton* that I am aware of, however, is in the mid-thirteenth-century *De Mundi Vanitate* (On the Vanity of the World) by the English Latin poet, Walter of Wimborne. In a lengthy list of the impossibilities which will come to pass when the poor man finds friends, the penultimate absurdity is that 'the winged pig will fly'.[28]

Figure 8.4

In French literature, however, the flying pig motif is certainly found in Rabelais' *Quart Livre* published in 1551, in Chapter 41 of which 'a big, fat, great, grey pig with huge long wings' suddenly appears flying towards Pantagruel and his companions and bombs them with mustard-pies! The Rabelaisian flying pig would appear to be male, a boar, as indeed is the woodcut example reproduced in Figure 8.4, probably issued in the 1530s by the Dutch artist Cornelis Anthonisz – significantly, it clearly associates the flying pig with the *monde renversé*, here represented by a symbolic world orb, the World Turned, if not entirely Upside Down, then, at least, On Its Side![29] From Coquillard's long satirical poem, 'Les Droitz Nouveaulx' (1480), however, it would appear that in late fifteenth-century Paris there existed at least one tavern called *La Truye vollant* (The Flying Sow),[30] but the animal depicted in a little contemporary lead badge, barely an inch wide, recovered from the Thames foreshore in London seems to be a flying boar (see chapter ornament).

Figure 8.5

Wrens Carry Sacks to Mill

The proverbial absurdity which is the subject of Figure 8.5 involves more ordinary winged creatures, but performing an absurd task. Some years ago I was able to identify the subject carved on this supporter to one of the late fifteenth-century misericords in St George's Chapel, Windsor.[31] Reading my way through the relatively small corpus of surviving nonsense verse in Middle English, I was struck by a line in a misogynist carol which advises (men, presumably) only to put women 'in trust and confydens' when the various *impossibilia* listed come to pass; 'when spawrus byld chyrchys on a hyth' (height), for example, and 'wrenys cary sekkes onto the myll' – and here they are, though these look more like sparrows than wrens, flying towards an undoubted mill and bearing sacks across their backs! Importantly, this little carving seems to confirm that the line in the nonsense verse was no mere arbitrary formulation – as might otherwise all too easily have been assumed (and doubtless has been hitherto)[32] – but had indeed achieved a fixed and sufficiently recognised proverbial status to be represented in three dimensions. It proves that even this subsidiary carving was no mere whimsy of the craftsman, but a recognised literary figure of speech, and makes us wonder how many more such remain unknown to us, dismissed as mere *drôleries*. The sting in the tail of this identification, however, is that, in the verse, at least, the application of this *adynaton* is in the elaboration of the theme of misogyny.[33]

Visual nonsense, 'nonsense for nonsense's sake', as it were, is perhaps most clearly to be identified in the form of the many grotesques which inhabit marginal areas of the medieval world, though even here – as these wrens carrying their sacks to the mill on the Windsor misericord demonstrate – we cannot be entirely confident that their grotesqueness is entirely empty of meaning. It is always possible to argue that the innumerable hybridised creatures which crawl along the margins of manuscripts are intended as a hellish foil to the heavenly host and characters of sacred story who inhabit the interior of the page framed in miniatures and letters. Indeed, Michael Camille has argued precisely this, seeing such marginal 'images on the edge' as consciously constructed signs of incoherence and disorder on the edges, crucial to the construction of coherence and order at the centre.

It is certainly possible so to argue, then, but I do not know of any contemporary textual evidence to support such a thesis. Indeed, we have St Bernard of Clairvaux's famous and oft-quoted denunciation to suggest the exact opposite – if such a famous exegete, a near-contemporary of this grotesque imagery, could make no obvious sense of it, who are we, some 800 years later, to claim that he did not understand the artistic intentions of his own era?

> Here's a quadruped with a serpent's tail and there a fish with a quadruped's head. Here's a beast with a mare's forequarters dragging a half-goat behind it and there a horned beast with the hindquarters of a horse. In fact, so multifarious are the divers shapes everywhere that we would rather study the sculptures than our books and spend the entire day gawping at them rather than meditating on God's law. For God's sake! If we are not ashamed of these monstrosities, why at least do we not shrink from the expense?

It is perhaps as well St Bernard died when he did, a century before the exponential growth of such material in the margins of Gothic manuscripts!

Animal Musicians

Animal musicians (animals playing musical instruments such as we would expect to see only human musicians play), were a commonplace of late medieval *drôlerie*, though even here, it is possible to make out some method in the apparently arbitrary madness.

A misericord in Beverley Minster carved in 1520 has as its central subject a cat catching mice and, as one of its minor 'supporter' carvings, a cat playing the fiddle to four smaller animals, which some have seen as her kittens and others as mice, but it is the 'cat and the fiddle' combination which most concerns us here. The very fact that we have this ready-made oral formulation in English should give us pause; for we traditionally associate the cat with this particular instrument and no other. And so do the French, and what is more, it is an association of venerable antiquity in both languages. An English document dated 1361 mentions a tenement (probably an inn) named 'le Catfithele',[34] and in medieval Amiens there was similarly a house called *le Cat qui vielle* (the cat who fiddles) in the Rue des Orfèvres,[35] while just over a century later, in 1501, we hear of a London inn called 'Le Catte cum le Fydell' in Bucklersbury.[36]

Iona Opie notes that although 'Hey! diddle, diddle, the cat and the fiddle' is 'Probably the best-known nonsense verse in the language, a considerable amount of nonsense has been written about it. One of the few statements which can be authenticated is that it appeared in print *c.* 1765.'[37] She goes on to compare a couplet from Preston's *Cambises* (1569) as 'possibly' referring to the nursery rhyme, but while it mentions a new dance called 'hey-diddle-diddle' – a typical nonsense refrain – and rhymes it with 'fiddle',[38] there is a fatal absence of cat! Whatever the literary history of the nursery rhyme, however, the fiddling cat is undeniably attested in the artistic record of late medieval England, so that a history of stringed instruments in the Middle Ages, can state that '*c.* 1300 the predominant animal fiddler became the cat'.[39] In fact, the motif can be found a century earlier, for it occurs in two English psalters of the first quarter of the thirteenth century – at the centre of a C-initial filled with foliage in one manuscript a cat fiddles to its kitten, while in an English manuscript of Peter Lombard's *Commentary on the Psalter* executed *c.* 1200, it appears as part of one of the terminals of the *Dixit insipiens* initial.[40] On the *Beatus* page in a border surrounding the B-initial in the other English psalter, eight animal jugglers and musicians perform, including a seated cat playing the vielle, and the ever-popular topos of the ass on the lyre (see next).[41] The cat and the fiddle is also found several times in English woodwork, both on misericords and elsewhere. On two roughly contemporary fourteenth-century misericords at Wells (1335x40) and Hereford (*c.* 1340–55) the cat fiddles, alone at Wells, but in the company of a goat lutenist at Hereford. A well-known bench-end carving of an animal, assumed to be a cat, fiddling to two similar but smaller animals, assumed to be its kittens – and which has sometimes been advanced as illustrating the nursery-rhyme, or even as its origin, and of similar date to the carving at Beverley – is to be seen at Fawsley, Northamptonshire. An example in another medium is a fragment of ?mid-sixteenth-century wall-painting in a house at Fenny Stratford, Buckinghamshire, which depicts a cat fiddling to birds within scrolls of foliage.[42]

Ass Plays Lyre, etc.

Of all animal musicians, the ass is the most proverbially incompetent, and it was the late classical philosopher Boethius who seems to have coined the expression of ridicule, 'like an ass playing the lyre'. But he is also sometimes found playing the organ as on the fourteenth-century stall-work of the St Marienkirche in Lübeck where he is accompanied by three songbirds,[43] and in a circular Flemish pen-and-ink drawing of *c.* 1480 now in the Ashmolean Museum, Oxford, (perhaps the design for a glass roundel), the bespectacled asinine organist is shown playing while being fed a thistle by a man who may perhaps be his teacher (Figure 8.6).[44] Ferdinand Columbus (d. 1539) owned a print which featured the ass playing the organ accompanied by a pig standing on a bench and singing from a sheet of music, as well as another Italian sheet of the ass playing the bagpipes.[45] An anonymous late fifteenth-century Master also made a circular engraving of a bagpiping ass, and a later engraving preserves the appearance of the no longer extant gravestone of Iohannes Lange and children formerly in Hamburg dated 1537, inscribed, 'The world has become so topsy-turvy that I, poor ass, have learned to pipe . . .', significantly associating the animal musician with the World Turned Upside Down.

Figure 8.6

Musical Pigs

Another misericord at Beverley Minster (appearing slightly earlier at Manchester) features musical pigs. The central carving depicts a sow bagpiping to its four piglets, while on the right-hand supporter another sow plays on the harp. The sex of the animal is important. This bagpiping sow is also to be seen on a late fifteenth-century misericord at Ripon (but with only two piglets and with conventional 'rose' supporters – is there a suggestion there of the biblical proverb variant, '[casting] roses before swine'?) and elsewhere. Also relevant here, one of the wooden roof bosses in St Mary's Church, Beverley, depicts a pig playing the bagpipes which can be dated to the early 1520s; doubtless the 'W. Hal Carpenter' who signed one of the bosses, had had a good look at the newly installed Minster misericords.

The bagpiping pig is also very common in contemporary continental stall-work, appearing at Kempen and Kalkar on the Lower Rhine, Breisach in Germany, Lausanne in Switzerland, Champeaux and St Martin-aux-Bois near Paris, and Ciudad Rodrigo and Sta Maria la Real de Najera (Logrono) in Spain,[46] while at Oviedo, two pigs copulate to the music of a porcine bagpiper.[47] In other media, there are several (ithyphallic) bagpiping boar lead badges of fifteenth-century date from Flanders, as well as examples in Flemish manuscripts,[48] in a fourteenth-century English manuscript of Aristotle, where the bagpiping pig is found next to a most interesting ithyphallic fool (Figure 6.6), and at least three English examples in stone, including a gargoyle at Melrose of 1450.[49] We may therefore safely conclude from this list that the bagpiping pig was a commonplace of late medieval *drôlerie*. The bagpiping boar was also one of the border ornaments featuring in early sixteenth-century Parisian printed books of hours, appeared as a binding stamp on a book bound in Portugal, *c.* 1534, and on a contemporary book printed in Lyons, where it was given a banderole inscribed *FACIO SOPOR[EM]* – the ironic 'I produce drowsiness'.

But what was the original meaning of this widely attested motif? An early twentieth-century art historian thought it was possibly 'a skit on the unmelodious squealing of pigs which was held to resemble the tones of bagpipes, and then was extended to pipes in general and other musical instruments, such as the fiddle and the harp'.[50] And no evidence has yet been produced to contradict this 'common-sense' opinion.

The harping sows of the Beverley and Manchester misericord supporters, however, are another matter, and are otherwise only found in English woodwork on a Windsor supporter where there is an audience of three dancing piglets, a bench-end finial at Stowlangtoft in Suffolk and, once again, on a roof boss in Beverley parish church.[51] The only other instances of this motif I am at present aware of, are a marginal drawing in a manuscript of Froissart's *Chroniques* dating to the second half of the fifteenth century,[52] in which a sow on stilts and wearing a henin with veil plays a harp, though a boar playing the harp while a bear tumbles also appears in the same early fourteenth-century English hours in which we have already noted a cat and fiddle.[53]

We are fortunate, however, to have contemporary literary references to the harping sow in late fifteenth-century English nonsense verse. It is a commonplace that 'pure' nonsense is very difficult to write – not least, because it would be very difficult to read. However nonsensical a piece as a whole may be, it will often be found to be composed of individually meaningful units, for example, collocations which the writer has been unable to avoid and which are to be found elsewhere. In other words, nonsense – literary nonsense, at least – has its own clichés. As we have seen above, the birds on the Windsor misericord which fly with the sacks on their backs towards the mill are not a merely arbitrary piece of *drôlerie*, but an established literary figure of impossibility. That is, while in itself it might be nonsense, it is not, as it were, an original piece of nonsense.[54] Another verse from the same nonsense-poem in which the 'wrenys cary sekkes onto the myll', opens with a line which is highly appropriate to these porcine harpists – 'Whan swyn be conyng in al poyntes of musyke' – but another nonsense-poem actually uses the image of the harping sow itself. In a passage featuring nine animal musicians, the cacophonous concert is introduced by the line, 'The sowe sate on hi benche, and harppyde [a tune/ballad called] Robyn Hoode'. Then we are told that:

> The shovelard[55] made a loud noise on a shawm, the turbot played the trumpet, the rat played the rebec, the fox fiddled, the cat played the clarion.[56] The snipe played on a symphony, the lark played on a lute, the humble-bee played on a hornpipe – her fingers were small.[57]

It will be observed that each animal musician has been allotted an instrument that alliterates with its name, except that is, for the sow. In the two known independent texts of this poem, the line is the same, the alliterative connexion between instrument and animal is broken only for the sow-harpist. This is all the more significant in that, had the author wished to preserve the alliteration and also retain the porcine theme, the word *hog* was available or, alternatively, the sow could have been allotted an alliterating instrument. I believe the inescapable conclusion must be that the harping sow was already a well-established collocation which the author could not lightly avoid or adapt.

The Animal as Instrument

On occasions in late medieval art, the animal becomes itself the instrument. On the right-hand supporter of one of the misericords at Beverley Minster (1520), for example, and seemingly having nothing to do with the main carving, an ape 'plays' a dog as if it were a bagpipe. This motif is found twice elsewhere on English misericords, a generation earlier at Lavenham in Suffolk, where the animal-bagpipe is a pig, and in 1390 at Boston in Lincolnshire, a particularly attractive composition, depicting two fools in ass-eared hoods and with bells on their sleeves and shoes, biting the tails of two cats in this manner.

Of roughly the same date as the Boston seat, an illuminator in the Boucicaut Workshop chose to illustrate the opening words of Psalm 52, 'The fool hath said in his heart there is no God', with this motif.[58] With his club over his shoulder, bells on his eared hood and round his waist, and torn shoes, the unbelieving fool contrives to hold the dog by its front legs while biting its tail. To his right, two well-dressed men point at him, clearly discussing his folly, perhaps, indeed, the illuminator intended this representation as an example of the 'abominable iniquity' which the Psalmist attributes to those fools who have denied the existence of God.

Can we assume that such animal musician and animal-as-musical-instrument images have a satirical function? And if so, then who or what is being satirised? One Victorian cultural historian had this to say about the bagpiping and harping sows:

> These have evidently sarcastic reference to the decline of minstrelsy, and the degradation of the minstrels of the period, in which the harp . . . was either neglected for the bagpipes or tabor, or borne by unworthy disciples of the lyric art. . . . These may also have covert reference to the Guild or Brotherhood of 'Mynstrells', which had extensive influence at the time; though nothing now remains to keep in memory the ancient fraternity except a few of its documents, a carved pillar in the Church of St Mary, Beverley (presented by the Guild in the reign of Henry VII [1486–1509]), and such covert allusions as these carvings.[59]

Regarding the Cat and the Fiddle nursery rhyme, Iona Opie has suggested that the motif might conceivably have its origin in a sort of cruel joke, an allusion to the use of catgut for stringed instruments.[60] In similar vein, the nineteenth-century iconographer Druce attributed the popularity of the representation of the bagpiping pig in woodwork to a certain similarity between the sound made by the instrument and that made by the animal. In his chapter on pig musicians, however, Schouwink rejects the notion that such carvings could have had any moral purpose in the Middle Ages; rather, he believes the porcine musician to be an example of a pictorial motif which by this date had lost any moral connotations it might originally have had, and become simply an amusing grotesque as an independent free-floating motif.[61] His conclusion is the common-sense one (it seems to me) that, whether or not such humorous motifs as the animal musicians began life with a moral purpose, as intentional satires, for example, certainly by the time the late medieval choirstalls were carved, they are devoid of any such serious moral purpose, and are merely representatives of a traditional repertoire of 'emptily' amusing images. That said, the ass who was shown playing the bagpipes on the tombstone in Hamburg dated 1537 makes an explicit statement to the contrary, significantly associating at least this asinine musician with the World Turned Upside Down.

Fighting the Snail

On one of the Beverley misericords of 1520 the left-hand supporter shows a man spearing a disproportionately large snail, and the right-hand one a man apparently crawling into a sack; the two are thematically related, as we shall see.

Figure 8.7

To begin with the snail: from about the mid-thirteenth century (the earliest example known to me is in Villard de Honnecourt's sketchbook), the motif of a fully armed warrior attacking a snail – as on this fourteenth-century draughtsman in the British Museum (Figure 8.7) – or even begging the animal for mercy and surrendering his sword, becomes increasingly popular as a manuscript ornament; as an added refinement, some show a woman imploring the warrior not to risk his life in combat with the horned monster.[62] Many other variations are known, as has been demonstrated in two wide-ranging studies,[63] and the theme can be traced both visually and verbally for several centuries. One of the earliest literary snail combats is that reported in a branch of the *Roman de Renart* which can be dated to 1179, where the 'heroes' mocked by the author, are peasants with flails, among other things, as their weapons.[64]

The tradition was still very much alive in the nineteenth century, in the form of humorous folktales about peasants terrrified at meeting a snail in the road, and children's rhymes from France, Germany and Britain describing battles between snails and humans, the latter being generally cowardly, as well as depictions of tailors dropping their work to flee from an outsize snail.

In the decades around 1300 the motif was understood to refer specifically to the Lombards, who had a long-standing reputation for cowardice, and were particularly disliked at that time because they increasingly acted as usurers and pawnbrokers throughout Northern Europe. When the motif 'reappears' at the end of the fifteenth century in the enormously popular printed *Shepherd's Calendar*,[65] it is no longer linked to specific national satire. The hesitant attackers are anonymous men at arms, led by a valiant woman, with the snail, according to one authority, representing the 'insolent and rebellious' common people.[66] The best-known appearance of the motif in English literature is in the Tudor interlude *Thersytes*. In the central episode, the *miles gloriosus* or braggart soldier, Thersites, despite his outrageous boasting, dares not fight the snail single-handed. When he first comes on stage, one of his boasts is that:

> . . . when I am harnessed well,
> I shall make the dasters to renne into a bagge   [dastards]
> To hyde them fro me, as from the devyll of hell.[67]

Here, then, is the explanation of the other supporter of the Beverley misericord; it too represents cowardice, by the image of a man hiding himself in a sack. The main carving of this misericord is a man combatting dragons, and so may be seen as representing the virtue of Courage, while both supporters display the antithetical vice of Cowardice.

The Terrifying Hare (and the Tailor)

A precise semantic equivalent to the flight from the snail is the flight from the hare. As we have noted above, the hare is a proverbially cowardly animal throughout European tradition;[68] indeed, Couard is the name of the hare in the influential medieval *Roman de Renart* epic.[69] In the early thirteenth-century text of the *Roman*, however, he appears to belie his name by capturing a peasant, whom he carries over his shoulder dangling from a stick, in the motif we have already met with above. If the animal really is such a coward, however, then it follows that the armed man who drops his sword at the mere sight of a hare is some sort of super-coward, and indeed this scene is made to symbolise the vice of Cowardice (Ignavia), and is juxtaposed with a confidently seated warrior representing the virtue Courage (Fortitudo), on thirteenth-century French cathedral façades, in the contemporary rose-window of Notre-Dame, and on several little fourteenth-century lead tokens.[70] Middle English nicknames of the *Stickehare*, *Pykhare* type might also belong to this tradition if, as nicknames seem so often to have been, they were applied ironically.[71]

A more directly insulting application is reflected in the Middle High German 'send a hare's tail', presumably recalling – somewhat analogous to the giving of the white feather centuries later – the actual practice of sending a coward a hare's tail as a symbolic insult,[72] and Röhrich notes that calling someone a 'hare' is already forbidden in the early medieval *Lex Salica*. A letter written *c.* 1060 by Meinhard of Bamberg in which he refers scathingly to Gunther, Bishop of Bamberg, uses the expression 'helmeted hares' to mean cowardly soldiers:

> You ask what our master does? What battles does he wage with his army of helmeted hares? What victories do they celebrate? Great gods, that is a collection of mice not men![73]

The cowardice of the hare is proverbially contrasted with the valour of the lion, especially in fourteenth-century England, in the ironic observation that men talk big in the safety of home, but are cowards on the field of battle: 'Nu ben theih liouns in halle, and hares in the feld.'[74] In Trevisa's late fourteenth-century translation of Higden's Latin *Polychronicon* the same sentiment is expressed with similar stylistic bravura: 'In the mouth he is a lyoun, and in the herte an hare.'[75] And 'hare-hearted' is indeed the polar opposite of 'lion-hearted', a compound for which there is evidence in medieval German and in the Norse sagas (*hèra hjarta*). A thirteenth-century Arras source lists one *Car de lion*, more familiar as the sobriquet of the English King, Richard *Coeur de Lion* or the Lion-Heart, but what are we to make of another Arras resident, one *Car de veel* (1255) (Calf-Heart)? As with 'hare-hearted', the implication is surely the exact opposite of Lion-Heart; these are nicknames which imply cowardice.

Nine Tailors Make a Man

Doubtless because he sews clothes – traditionally, 'women's work' – the tailor has long been regarded as an unmanly man, and a figure of fun in European tradition. It is no accident that the tailor in Shakespeare's *Midsummer Night's Dream* is named Starveling, or that his fellow in *Henry IV Part 2* is named Feeble.[76] In the recruiting scene, Falstaff says ironically to the tailor, 'Well said, courageous Feeble! Thou wilt be as valiant as the wrathful dove, or most magnanimous mouse, and later, for a retreat, how swiftly will this Feeble the woman's tailor run off!'[77] Clearly on the man/mouse spectrum – a comparison not noted in English before *c.* 1540 (but see Meinhard of Bamberg's striking early use of it above) – Feeble inclines to the latter end. The Swiss poet, Heinrich Wittenwiler, in his burlesque epic poem, *Der Ring* (*c.* 1400), cites the Roman military authority Vegetius to the effect that tailors (and weavers) make poor soldiers. The tailor's traditional unmanliness has become proverbial, but has also suffered from inflation, for whereas according to *Tarlton's Jests* (*a.* 1600) 'Two tailors goe to a man', by 1607 Dekker records that 'They say three Taylors go to the making vp of a man',[78] while by the mid-century it was 'Nine tailors make a man', as it has been ever since.

Graphic illustration of the feebleness of the tailor cowed by a hare is to be found in the marginal *drôleries* of at least two Flemish manuscripts illuminated *c.* 1300. In the *Metz Pontifical* a hare carrying a shield pierces a tailor in the breast with his spear causing him to drop onto one knee and let fall his shears (Figure 8.8), and in British Library MS Yates Thompson 8 he kneels before a hare wielding a club and surrenders his shears.[79]

The Seven Swabians and the Hare-Dragon

Another similar human confrontation with a hare from the other end of our period was painted in 1568 in a room of the 'Hasenhaus' (Hare-House) in the Schloß Augustusburg near Chemnitz by Heinrich Göding, and is the earliest extant illustration of the famous 'noodle tale' of the *Seven Swabians* (as later collected by the Grimms), which was popular in German applied art from this period on, who thought the hare was a monstrous dragon and cautiously made to prod it, all seven holding a long boar-spear. The present example is also the earliest-known version to

Figure 8.8

use the now canonical seven Swabians, the earlier poem by Hans Sachs had featured nine. The same extraordinary murals, incidentally, include another noodle tale,[80] which must similarly be the earliest-known depiction.[81]

Absurd Mounts

While it may be theoretically possible to ride a cow or a pig – for which activity we should perhaps rather use the term 'proverbial folly' – it clearly is impossible to ride a goose or a lobster. But for convenience I discuss all such non-equine mounts here.

Riding the Lobster

Brant's *Narrenschiff*, in its numerous editions, translations and adaptations, created images of proverbial folly and absurdity that were to reverberate down the centuries. The fool who illustrates Chapter 57 is mounted on a lobster, referred to as a 'crab' in the motto, an animal which proverbially walks backwards and is thus a symbol of inversion. Making use of the same proverbial image of retrogression, the youthful Hamlet tells the aged Polonius that 'yourself, sir, shall grow old as I am – if, like a crab, you could go backward',[82] combining the notion of going backwards in time with that of going backwards in space. As Polonius rightly remarks, 'Though this be madness, yet there is method in't', and the task of all iconographers is to find the method in the apparent madness! But, in addition, Brant's fool absurdly relies for support on the proverbial 'broken reed' of Isaiah 36.6, and further opens his mouth in the foolish hope that a ready-roasted dove will fly into it (as the infant Gargantua had also done) – something which can only happen in the topsy-turvy world of *Schlaraffenland* or the Land of Cockaigne, to which topos this motif belongs.[83]

In early seventeenth-century emblem books the world itself is sometimes depicted on the back of a lobster, implying that our comfortable notion of progress is an illusion, that we are, in fact, retrogressing.[84] A typical instance of the influence of the *Narrenschiff* illustrations is afforded by the re-use of the lobster-rider image as the model for a small South German wooden platter painted *c.* 1520.[85] The young male rider indicates an inscribed scroll, which reads:

'Often my affairs go backwards – look!
Then I can't go forwards . . . – look!'

Riding the Goose

One of the Bristol misericords carved in 1520 depicts a sort of parodic joust in which a woman mounted on a pig (only her weapon's shaft remains) rides against a man mounted on what appears to be a goose, a broom couched under his arm. The goose and the sow seem to have been the most popular absurd mounts, and German writers, in particular, had a fondness for the former. Before 1260 one of Reinmar von Zweter's *Lügengedichte* (lying-poems) begins 'I came riding into a country on a goose . . .', and the text of Murner's *Von dem grossen Lutherischen Narren* (1522) includes a knight similarly mounted, and thus a woodcut illustration, which seems to have provided the hint for a similar cut in Wickram's *Losbuch* (1539).[86]

The goose is a proverbially foolish bird,[87] and was thus early adopted by the folk as the favourite bird of the *monde renversé*. J.B. Smith has drawn attention to the extraordinary folk-idiom used as a 'put-off' – 'whim-whams for a goose's bridle'.[88] A *whim-wham* is not anything definite, indeed its function is precisely to denote something indefinite, but clearly the notion of bridling, as of saddling geese (or shoeing or milking them, for that matter – for which, see below) is absurd, but it is a notion of surprising antiquity.[89]

There is, for example, a Middle English nickname, *Sadilgos* (Saddle-goose), which has been glossed, 'one who tries the impossible, an utter fool',[90] and in Stephen Hawes' *Passetyme of Pleasure* (1509), the fool's grandfather is significantly named Sym *Sadlegander*,[91] while in the Tudor play *Misogonus* (*c.* 1570) one of the rustic characters says, 'Cha bene sadlinge my gose. . . .'[92] The goose's popularity as an absurd mount is confirmed by the name of Rabelais' Judge *Bridoye* and his use of the expression *oyson bridé* (bridled goose), which appears in both *Gargantua* (1534) and *Pantagruel* (1532). In the former book, moreover, the infant Gargantua poses an 'unpleasant choice', a genre of oral game still popular with children, in these terms: 'which would you rather – ride a goose or lead a sow on a leash?'[93] A precisely contemporary parallel appeared on a *Renndecke* (cloth horse-trapper) of *c.* 1535 on which Fortuna standing on a crab led a pig on a leash.[94]

Riding the Sow

Gargantua's latter option, brings us on to the notion of riding a sow. In a Boschian *Temptation of St Anthony* attributed to Aertgen van Leyden and painted in the 1520s, a small serious monster leads a saddled pig on a leash, ridden by another monster[95] (the pig, of course, being St Anthony's attribute). Earlier English possessed a proverbial simile, 'as meet as a sow to bear a saddle', first attested in Heywood's proverb collection of 1546;[96] so that the misericord supporters at Manchester

Cathedral and Beverley Minster (carved *c.* 1512 and *c.* 1520 respectively), which clearly depict a saddled pig, provide pictorial antedatings of this motif.[97]

Riding the Cow

For the sake of completeness, I should perhaps mention another proverbially absurd mount, the cow. Palsgrave's 'It becommeth hym as wel to do, as to see . . . a cowe to beare a saddel' (1530) presumably derives directly from Erasmus's enormously influential *Adagia:* 'Clitellae bovi sunt impositae'. By the date of publication of the play *New Custom* (1571), however, it has a much less obviously learned air, especially as it appears in the company of another well-known absurd motif, 'As fit a sighte it were to see a goose shodde, or a sadled cowe.' A mid-fifteenth century English poem, however, provides evidence of pre-Erasmian usage 'Now trewly yow becometh al your gere As wel as Cowe a sadel to bere. . . .'[98] Though I know of no pictorial use of this figure in our period, it does provide part of the satirical humour of a fascinating Elizabethan political cartoon in which Philip II of Spain is depicted as the rider of the Cow of the Netherlands.[99]

Putting the Cart Before the Horse

But perhaps the crowning absurdity, or anthology of absurdities, is the title-page cut to the Basel 1498 edition of Brant's poem 'De corrupto ordine vivendi pereuntibus', further improved for Geiler von Kaysersberg's *Narrenschiff*-derived 'Navicula sive speculum fatuorum' (Strasbourg, 1510), as if summing up the manifold follies to follow within. The woodcut artist has presented us not only with the famous proverbial folly of putting the cart before the horse, but the animals are being urged on by a fool who follows them (rather than sits on one of them), holding his whip by the wrong end of the handle and incidentally hitting himself on the head with it, not to mention wearing his spurs at his toes instead of his heels.[100] The whole is symbolised by the uppermost coat of arms featuring the retrogressive 'crab', but also by the ultimate human inversion in which *homo erectus* stands in the cart not on his feet, but his head. In the later version the retrogressive nature of humanity is further elaborated by the motif of putting the cart's wheels on at right angles to the direction of travel.

In England the best-known depiction of this particular folly is on one of the Beverley Minster misericords of 1520. What has not been remarked before, however, is that positioned directly above the seat in question, as a corbel-supporter on one of the shafts which buttress the overarching canopy of the stalls, the carver has placed a grinning fool's head – surely a deliberate signal of the folly to be seen below. The Beverley misericords are not exceptional in displaying several fools who, I argue, have such a 'commentary' function (see Chapter 6 above). Coincidentally, the proverb is first attested in English in the selfsame year that the Beverley carving was made. In Whittinton's *Vulgaria* (1520) we read that:

That teycher setteth the cart before the horse that preferreth imitacyon before preceptes, and it is next noted twice, *c.* 1530, in the works of Sir Thomas More.[101] Under the significant headword, 'arsy-versy', the *OED* gives as its earliest citation of that word, the following from Richard Taverner's 1539 edition of Erasmus's *Adagia:* 'Ye set the cart before the horse . . . cleane contrarily and arsy versy as they say.'

A generation after the date of the misericord, the Marian Catholic, John Christopherson, in a book written immediately after the suppression of Wyatt's Rebellion in 1554, and entitled, 'An exhortation to all menne to take hede and beware of rebellion', made good use of a passage of World Turned Upside Down imagery, and one which is well worth quoting in full in order to convey the very serious purposes to which this topos was often put:

> dyd [not] children order their parentes, wyves their husbandes, and subjects their magystrates: So that the fete ruled the head and *the cart was set before ye horse* . . . was not al thinges through it brought so farre out of order, that vice ruled vertue, & folishnes ruled wisdome, lightnesse ruled gravitie, and youth ruled age? So that the olde mens saying was herein verified, that when Antichrist shuld come, the rootes of the trees shulde growe upwarde.[102]

It is possible, chronologically at least, that Christopherson could have known the *monde renversé* broadsheets of the type represented by an Italian example, probably Venetian and of the 1560s,[103] but this sheet includes the usual continental version of this folly which puts the cart before the *oxen.*

Milking Non-mammals

It will be observed how a common factor in many of these absurdities is a basic misunderstanding of the natural world, especially of the animal world. If ignorance of the natural world and its processes is one of the unifying themes of the World Turned Upside Down, the attempt to milk birds or any non-mammalian animal, is a classic expression of it.

On the Beverley misericord of putting the cart before the horse, but long unrecognised, the left-hand supporter depicts a milkmaid who foolishly attempts to milk a bull. The standard catalogue of English misericords describes it as a girl milking with a pail with three hoops. The girl is there certainly, as is the milking pail with its three hoops, of traditional stave-construction, and with the contemporary handle on one side only (unlike the modern semi-circular handle attached at two points) – indeed, there is such detailed attention to the everyday minutiae that it is curious the carver seems to have forgotten to provide the 'cow' with an udder! The udder is surely the *sine qua non* of the medieval, as of the modern cow – this milkmaid is attempting to milk a bull, and thus invokes the same degree of disorder as the man who is attempting to put the cart before the horse in the main carving. She was obviously unaware of Motif no. H.1024.1 Milking bull is impossible task.[104] For all that, however, it was not beyond the miracle-working powers of certain early Celtic saints, being managed by both the Irish saint Fechin and the Scottish saint Columba – who but a saint or a simpleton would attempt such a task?[105] One simpleton who certainly did, was memorialised

14 Cassandra of the Nine Female Worthies: oil on panel, Lambert Barnard, Amberley Castle, 1530s.

15 Solomon and Marcolf: manuscript miniature, *Ormesby Psalter*, English, early 14thC.

16 Riddle, test of resourcefulness: manuscript miniature, *Ormesby Psalter*, English, early 14thC.

17 Petrified maidens' dance: manuscript miniature, *Marvels of the East*, English, early 12thC.

18 Lovers grafting clasped hands of fidelity, and 'daisy oracle': tapestry (detail), Strasbourg, *c*. 1430.

19 Love-magic Ritual (*Liebeszauber*): oil on panel, Cologne, late 15thC.

in rhyme for his folly, in the late sixteenth-century ballad, 'Martin said to his man, "Who's the fool now?"' which contains the line, 'I saw a maid milk a bull, every stroke a bucketful. . . .'[106] The salutary lesson to be learned from this tiny wood-carving on the Beverley misericord is the importance of looking closely at what we think we see.

Christa Grössinger has drawn attention to one of the playing card designs of Hans Schäufelein (*c.* 1535), the 8-of-Bells, which is very similar to our carving, and it seems conceivable that the hair hanging down her back from under the cap of the Beverley milkmaid may be a reminiscence of some lost earlier version of the pigtails of Schäufelein's milking crone.[107] The possibility that the Beverley carver may ultimately owe the inspiration for this supporter to a playing card design is far from unlikely and, indeed, the certain dependence of late medieval English wood-carvers on such sources has been demonstrated elsewhere.[108] We may feel the ultimate has been reached in this kind of natural reversal, in the marginal image of an early fourteenth-century Flemish book of hours in the library of Trinity College, Cambridge, which depicts a bull milking a naked woman.[109]

Milking Birds

In England, however, more popular than the notion of milking male animals was that of milking birds. A good literary example is a fifteenth-century schoolboy's facetious reply to his teacher's enquiry as to why he is late for the lesson. The master asks, 'Wher hast thou be, thow sory ladde?' to which the boy replies, 'Milked dukkes, my moder badde' (My mother said I had to milk the ducks) – whereupon he was soundly birched for his impudence.[110] Another contemporary poet, John Skelton – whose work is so much in tune with the spirit of the sort of art in which this book is interested – seems to have been much taken by the ridiculousness of the notion of trying to milk ducks, and called one of the 'gossips' who frequent Elynour Rummynge's ale-house 'Margery Mylkeducke', re-using the name in his play *Magnyfycence* (both works *c.* 1520).[111] In one of the East Anglian *N-Town Cycle* mystery plays, *The Trial of Joseph and Mary*, some thirty-four characters are summoned to appear before the ecclesiastical court, and in the dubious company of Letyce Lytyl trust (Little Trust) and Symme Smalfeyth (Small Faith), appears one Malkyn *Mylkedoke* (Milk Duck).[112] A real-life example of such a name was borne by Herueus *Milkegos* (Milk Goose) who features in an entry dated 1288 in the *Norwich Leetbook*.[113]

It is clear that the milking of birds was a popular *adynaton* throughout the European Middle Ages; there is talk of milking cranes, for example, in the mid-twelfth-century Flemish Latin *Ysengrimus*,[114] but the motif is certainly already present in classical texts, for example in the expression 'rarer than birds' milk' in Aristophanes' *Wasps*. In a *fastnachtspiel* (carnival play) of 1478 Hans Folz uses the phrase 'old goose milk' as one of the typically dubious ingredients listed in an example of that well-loved genre, the burlesque prescription, an ingredient which, together with hawk's milk, is found in English medieval Latin as early as the twelfth century, in the burlesque prescription to lengthen the ass's tail in Nigel Longchamps' *Speculum Stultorum*.[115]

Brooding and Hatching Eggs

There are occasions when the depiction of a folly is intended as a satire directed at a particular target – we have already noted the use of the 'snail-combat' motif as a derisive attack on the Lombards. In a number of Northern French and Flemish manuscripts of the late thirteenth and early fourteenth centuries, recurs the image of a man sitting on a nest of eggs and holding one up to the sun as if candling it, or checking its readiness to hatch.[116] By the late sixteenth century the motif is merely a general allusion to the foolishness of individuals, as can be seen from a Flemish engraving showing a fool in costume with bauble, sitting on eggs, and labelled 'Here's one sitting on eggs'. In the earlier manuscript marginal illustrations, however, the fools are not identified necessarily by their costume, only by their action, and there is good reason to believe that these egg-hatchers are intended as satirical hits at the English, whose continental possessions were much resented at the time and place where these manuscripts were produced. In French writings of the thirteenth century, the English were frequently abused as long-tails, and it becomes a common anti-English insult from then on. It was Lilian Randall who elegantly solved this iconographical puzzle (as so many others) by pointing out that in medieval French *couvé* (hatched) and *coué* (tailed) were pronounced alike,[117] so that the tailed English soon became the English who were so foolish that they attempted to hatch eggs.

Threshing the Water

The woodcut sheet reproduced here (Figure 8.9) was issued *c.* 1526, and is an illustration by Hans Sebald Beham of a particular kind of German proverbial verse known as a *Priamel*. It might be entitled 'Labour in Vain' or 'Wasted Effort', and although it looks sensible enough at first glance, it is clear, from the verse at least, that the man on the right is threshing water, and his companion trying in vain to make his hurdy-gurdy heard above the deafening din of the water-powered mill as it grinds corn:

> That man who threshes in the weir
> and fishes in the woodland wild
> and plays the 'lyre' in a flour-mill too
> and courts a lovely lady
> and in the springtime sows the salt
> and pebbles mows in August
> and tries to dry snow in the sun
> and pours the water in the well
> and greases [too] the fat sow's arse
> and shaves a bald man's head
> and tries to wash the raven white
> and heat a room with ice
> and brings a dead man to a dance
> his labour's quite in vain.

Figure 8.9

This is full of proverbial follies and *impossibilia* and several of the constituent lines may be found in other *Priameln*, including those attributed to the Nürnberg poet Hans Rosenplüt (d. *c.* 1470), while the seventh and ninth lines were recorded as still current in the German Alps in 1890.[118]

Catching the Wind in a Net

Many of these *Priamel* verses are 'elemental follies', yet another species of absurdity demonstrating fundamental ignorance of nature, as did those Officers of the

Quintessence in the *Cinquième Livre* who were attempting to 'catch the wind in a net', as a fool depicted in La Perrière's emblem book *Le Théâtre du Monde* (1539) had tried to do, with equal lack of success, one suspects, a generation earlier.[119]

Figure 8.10

Now We Are Seven?

The French woodcarving of probable early sixteenth-century date in the Musée de la Chartreuse in Douai, depicts three foolish-looking humans singing from a book and three creatures (Figure 8.10), and yet the plinth is puzzlingly inscribed *NOUS SOMMES SEPT* 'We are seven'. If we can assume that this was the original title of the piece, it appears to be the earliest version of a popular European joke at the viewer's expense which depicts a group of *six* foolish animal and human figures, leaving the puzzled viewer by his enquiry to make himself the seventh. By the seventeenth century the usual version shows three foolish-looking men seated on three asses, and it is this type which is found painted on one of the *caissons* of the (?)early seventeenth-century painted ceiling of the Château d'Oiron also labelled, 'We are seven', and which first appears in England on the title-page of *A pamphlett called wee be seauen* by John Taylor the Water Poet, first issued in 1637, but only preserved in a later edition which claims to be for sale 'at the signe of the 7 Wise-men of Goatham'.

In retrospect it seems more than a little absurd to have spent so much time in attempting to construct a taxonomy of absurdity, to have made such heavy weather of nonsense. It is an enterprise fraught with self-evident dangers and results, perhaps, in another volume fit only for the shelves of the Library of St Victor – indeed, I hate to think what Rabelais would have made of it! And perhaps a fitting reward would be one of those oddly poetic mock-compensations[120] from medieval law, such as a sieveful of oats and an eggshell (*Cyfraith Hywel Dda*), or the shadow which the wronged minstrel is entitled to (*Sachsenspiegel*).[121] And yet I hope at least to have shown that this pictorial nonsense is rarely unmotivated, rarely pure, more often applied to some satiric purpose, especially in the nexus of inversions that constitutes the World Turned Upside Down, and that even when we might be tempted to think it at its purest – as in the images of the wrens flying with sacks to the mill, or the harping sow – further research reveals that *though this be madness yet there is method in't*, that whether meaningful or not, these are still only the clichés of nonsense.

NINE

NARRATIVES – HEROIC AND NOT SO HEROIC

Even before the Renaissance and its revival of classical learning there was
already a basic familiarity with the principal motifs of Greek and Roman
stories, such as the heroes of the Trojan War[1] and the pseudo-history of
Alexander the Great,[2] as well as such 'set-piece' subjects as the Judgment of Paris –
this last scene sometimes an excuse to introduce a definite touch of the erotic.

The indigenous heroes of the Middle Ages – however much their pedigrees can
be seen to go back ultimately to antiquity – were the chivalric heroes of vernacular
verse romances and foremost among them, of course, was King Arthur.[3] Within the
vast orbit of the Arthurian cycle, are other heroes almost as popular, most notably
the lovers Tristan and Isolde, for example, and Ywain/Gawain. In those cases where
only a single allusion is made to a romance, it is of interest to note which scenes the
artists chose as representative of the stories of the particular heroes.

In France the heroes of the Charlemagne cycle rivalled those of the Arthurian
cycle in popularity, including Roland,[4] undoubtedly, and the Four Sons of Aymon
who feature in the romance of *Regnault de Montauban*.

In Germany[5] native romances were popular. Such was *Der Busant* (The Buzzard),
an early fourteenth-century love story composed in Alsace, but whose protagonists
are not German at all. The hero is an English prince who has gone to study in Paris
and falls in love with the French princess. As she is to be married off to the King of
Morocco in a diplomatic alliance, the couple elope. While in the forest, a buzzard
steals her ring. The prince pursues the bird but gets lost, fails to find the princess
and finally becomes a madman, very much in the tradition of the Wild Man of the
woods (see Chapter 3). The princess finds shelter with a miller who lodges her in
his house. The prince is eventually discovered by hunters in the forest who take him
back to Burg Engelstein, where he is restored to his senses, but not his memory.
While out hunting one day his hawk catches a buzzard which he proceeds to tear
apart in an unconscious frenzy, and in so doing recalls all the events which led to his

original madness. He subsequently recognises his beloved, who is by now a guest in the same castle. There is the traditional happy ending. The story survives in a number of late fifteenth-century Alsatian tapestries woven in Strasbourg. The beautiful but fragmentary tapestry reproduced here (Colour Plate 11) shows the princess leading her lost love's horse out of the forest, encountering the honest miller, who has respectfully doffed his hat, and asking him for shelter. Significantly the prince, depicted on all fours and covered in the shaggy hair of the Wild Man (but still wearing his crown!), has lost the power of speech and thus has no banderole. He is accompanied by a unicorn and – almost as if mocking him – at the far left-hand edge of the fragment we can see the eponymous buzzard with the princess's ring in its mouth.

Let us now turn to look at a few other representative romance heroes and the depiction of their stories in late medieval art.

HEROES OF ROMANCE

Guy of Warwick

Apart from being the legendary progenitor of the house of Warwick, Guy was a very popular and quintessentially English hero with a strong patriotic appeal, since he was regarded as having saved England from the Danes. The Guy of Warwick tale was so popular in England and, indeed, in continental Europe, that in the latter years of the fifteenth century, it has been said that 'No legend . . . of all those then in circulation was more widely familiar.'[6]

Figure 9.1

Perhaps the earliest visual evidence for Sir Guy's popularity in England appears in two roughly contemporary manuscripts, both probably illuminated in the 1330s, the *Smithfield Decretals* and the *Taymouth Hours*,[7] and both examples of that surprisingly common phenomenon, *bas-de-page* illustrations bearing no relation to the text of the manuscript. What is unique about the latter manuscript, however, is that many of its scenes include identifying inscriptions in Anglo-Norman. But a climactic moment in the tale also appears as a silver print set in the base of a mazer bowl of the first half of the fourteenth century, also with an Anglo-Norman inscription, depicting Guy's rescue of the lion from its fight with the dragon (Figure 9.1),[8] inscribed 'Guy of Warwick is his name who here kills the dragon'. In 1394 'Guy's Tower' at Warwick Castle was completed, but four years later Thomas Beauchamp, Earl of Warwick, was obliged to forfeit an arras of the history of 'Guy of Warwick' which adorned his castle. In 1400 the Earl made his will in which it is not too far-fetched to see further evidence of a family cult of the heroic Guy.

Certain romance heroes, notably those of the Arthurian cycle and especially King Arthur himself, of course, had by this time begun to acquire relics, as if they were secular saints.[9] In Beauchamp's will of 1 April 1400, he bequeathed to his son Richard, Guy's sword, coat of mail, harness and 'ragged staves' these last being part of the arms of Warwick.[10] Guy of Warwick's alleged sword and cooking pot, still in the castle today, were shown to the diarist Evelyn in 1654 – the latter is a probably a post-medieval bell-metal pot. Richard is also bequeathed by the same will some uncertain object wrought with the arms and story of Guy of Warwick, and the talismanic 'cup of the swan' discussed below.

One of Guy's legendary feats was to slay the Dun Cow of Dunsmore Heath near Dunchurch, a fairy cow milked dry by human greed and thus transformed into a marauding monster – her relics, in particular a rib over six feet long and nine inches in circumference, were shown to a Dr Caius at Guy's Cliffe, Warwick, in 1552.[11]

On one of the late fourteenth-century misericords in Worcester Cathedral, a knight fighting two 'griffins' and bearing a shield on which is a bear *sejant*, is probably intended to be Guy, as the bear was his badge.[12] Another Worcester stall features a lion–dragon combat which, far from being a commonplace of romance or artistic whim, was part of Guy's legend, in particular, for it was rescuing the lion from the dragon – as depicted on the mazer print – that earned Guy its undying gratitude.

Bevis of Hampton

The hero Bevis of Hampton is especially dear to Southampton, his birthplace (formerly known merely as Hampton), and from at least the sixteenth century, two panels painted with images of Bevis and his giant adversary and later companion Ascupart, hung on the Bargate, symbolically protecting one of the principal entrances to the city. The panels are 'unique survivors of a class of artefact known to have played an important role in pageantry designed to enhance civic pride and prestige during the fifteenth and sixteenth centuries'.[13] A recent study of the heavily repainted panels has concluded that the visit of the Holy Roman Emperor Charles V to Southampton in 1522, from Winchester where King Arthur's celebrated Round Table had just been repainted for his benefit, provides the perfect occasion for their original production. They are recorded as having been repainted in 1594, on the occasion of a similar visit by Queen Elizabeth.

Bevis of Hampton's exploits are also recorded in the *Taymouth Hours*,[14] and from an inventory of his 'tappis a ymages' (illustrated tapestries) taken in 1408, it is known that Valentine of Orléans owned a tapestry of *Beuvon d'Hantonne*,[15] and the English king Henry V had two, according to the inventory made in the year following his death in 1422:

> 1 old piece of arras with inscription beginning, *How Bevis of Hampton.*[16]
> 1 very old Arras tapestry with inscription beginning *How Bevis of Hampton asks Josiane.*

According to the romance, Josiane was a heathen princess who fell in love with Bevis after his wicked mother had sent him to be sold abroad as a slave. After the usual adventures, including another dragon-slaughter, they returned to England where they lived adventurous lives until, together with Sir Bevis's valiant steed, Arundel, they all died within minutes of each other. A carved medallion of the 1530s at the back of the provost's stall in King's College Chapel, Cambridge, has assimilated the episode of the lion carrying off a baby proper to Bevis's story into its depiction of St George's legend.[17]

Bevis also has at least one relic, his famous great sword 'Morglay' (from Celtic elements meaning 'great sword' – compare, in reverse order, *claymore*). It is preserved as a relic of the hero in the armoury of Arundel Castle in West Sussex.[18]

Knight slays Wodehouse who Abducts Woman ('Sir Enyas and the Wodehouse')

The *Taymouth Hours* also preserves what seems to be the fullest version extant of an *exemplum* in which the key moment is the rescue by an old knight, here named Enyas, of a lady abducted by a wodehouse. She, however, turns herself into an example of 'female ingratitude'[19] by going off with a young knight who suddenly appears on the scene – unlike Enyas's dog who does not succumb to the blandishments of the young man. The knights joust and the younger man is killed, whereupon Enyas and his faithful hound depart, leaving the 'lady alone on account of her unnaturalness', or – in the *Smithfield Decretals* version – alone with two bears who eat her! The manner in which the *damoysele* was expected to show her gratitude to the *viel chiualer* is nowhere spelled out, but may perhaps be imagined.

The central incident of the rescue from the clutches of the Wild Man was a popular subject in a variety of fourteenth-century media. Exactly contemporary with the manuscript illustrations is a small probably English enamelled ?amulet-case, which has been thought to refer to this episode.[20] In the Bodleian *Romance of Alexander* manuscript illuminated *c.* 1340 in Flanders, the Wild Man brandishing his club at the mounted knight who pursues him, abducts the lady on a stag. This abduction similarly appears on French ivory caskets, a silver-mounted ivory horn now in the Treasury of St-Servais in Maastricht, and on a painted leather ceiling in the Hall of Justice of the Alhambra (1380x1400), while Louis Duc d'Anjou's 1364 inventory records two cups and a basin with base enamels which also appear to represent this scene.

Figure 9.2

Tristan and Isolde

The entire Tristan and Isolde romance is told in a lengthy series of mid-thirteenth-century tiles made in Chertsey and now in the British Museum, but was popular throughout Europe in all media.[21] One of the climactic moments of the romance, however, and one which was frequently chosen to represent the story, was the lovers' tryst beneath the tree from which King Mark spies on them, as on misericords in Lincoln and Chester Cathedrals, and on thirteenth-century hand-mirror frames in lead which have recently come to light in London, Regensburg and Perth.[22]

The Perth example illustrated here (Figure 9.2) shows Tristan holding aloft the cup of love potion beside Isolde and her maid, while King Mark approaches them on horseback with upraised sword. The two groups are separated by an ambiguous column that could conceivably have been intended as the trysting tree, but is perhaps more likely to be a fountain and laver before a tree, as in other comparable illustrations of the romance. I read this mirror's scenes as a conflation of romance episodes, allowing the artist to put all the main characters on stage at once – even Tristan's faithful hound, Husdent, who appears in the lowest register. The three protagonists are labelled, and an additional perimeter inscription in Anglo-Norman, somewhat garbled as so often in such castings, reads 'Whoever carries/wears me will have no lack of joy, I am well loved', in the well-attested idiom of courtly love to be found on rings, brooches, amulets and so on (see Chapter 10). This piece is a notable example of the trickle-down of courtly love iconography to the masses and consistent with other examples on the lead badges (of identical manufacture).

Ywain

Apart from illustrated manuscripts of his story, Ywain's adventures were also illustrated in fresco cycles at Rodenegg in South Tirol and Schmalkalden in Thüringen, as well as in other media;[23] but in England it is the misericord corpus which provides a climactic scene, apparently unique. Ywain is in hot pursuit of the guardian of the fountain who nevertheless manages to escape into his castle and lower the portcullis onto his pursuer, narrowly missing our hero himself, yet slicing his horse in half.[24] Ywain is captured and imprisoned, but later helped to escape by Lunete. No fewer than five extant English late fourteenth-

Figure 9.3

century misericords are carved with this scene – at New College, Oxford; Boston; Chester; Lincoln and Enville in Staffordshire (Figure 9.3); and it seems also to have been represented among the lost misericords of St Peter-per-Mountgate, Norwich.[25]

The Swan Knight

The name of Wagner's hero Lohengrin is a contracted form of earlier 'Loherain Garin' (Garin of Lorraine) one of the heroes of the *Geste des Loherains*[26] and, with a

fair degree of variation, his name is to be recognised in several of the fourteenth-
and fifteenth-century inventories of the tapestries owned by the great magnates of
France. Valentine of Orléans had a 'tappis a ymages . . . appele Loheranguerin'
according to his inventory of 1408, and Philip the Good of Burgundy, an 'ystoire
Lorens Guerin' according to his of 1420 (for whose interest in the legend, see
further below) – we can assume that these tapestries included images of the Swan
Knight. Wynkyn de Worde's *Elias, Chevalier au Cygne. The Knyght of the Swanne*
appeared in London in 1512, translated from the French text by Robert Copland,
and including ten large designs copied from the *editio princeps*, a *Godeffroy de Boulion*
printed for Jean Petit in Paris in 1504.[27]

According to the legend, Godfrey of Bouillon, the hero of the First Crusade and
thus made one of the Nine Worthies, had for a grandfather a mysterious Swan
Knight who had rescued his grandmother, the widowed Duchess of Bouillon, from
the threatened usurpation of Renier, Duke of Saxony, arriving in a boat drawn by a
swan. Various important European families claimed descent from Godfrey, and thus
ultimately the Swan Knight, and used a swan as one of their heraldic badges; in
England, the Bohuns and the Beauchamps, earls of Warwick, were two of the most
prominent. As early as *c.* 1190, in his history of the First Crusade, William of Tyre
refers to the 'story of the Swan' from which bird, 'according to vulgar report',
Godfrey and his brothers were descended.

In the English tradition, as recorded in his history of the Beauchamp family,
written and illustrated *c.* 1484 by John Rous, the family's chantry priest at Guy's
Cliffe, Warwick, the legendary swan ancestor is named Eneas, and is the eldest of six
brothers and sisters (sextuplets), the rest of whom were changed by magic into
swans, with collars and chains of gold, by their evil grandmother Mattabrune. It was
from these gold collars and chains, Rous tells us, that the Beauchamps' 'cup of the
swan' – which sounds very like a family talisman of the sort familiar from such
vessels as 'The Luck of Eden Hall'[28] – was made. It was this 'cup' which, as we have
seen, Thomas Beauchamp bequeathed to his son in his will of 1 April 1400, and
which Rous tells us was in his day kept in the treasury of Warwick Castle, and from
which he had himself drunk of the best wine in the castle. In the so-called *Rous Roll*,
this 'cup', held in Eneas's right hand, is depicted in the shape of a fifteenth-century
mazer bowl ?enamelled with a *semée* of hearts inside and the Sacred Monogram in
the base, while a golden chain is wrapped round his forearm.

It is clear from casual visual allusions that the characteristic scene used to refer to
the legend as a whole was that of the swan pulling the knight in his boat, and it is
found in manuscript margins,[29] and as the subject of one of the earliest English
misericords (*c.* 1240) in Exeter Cathedral (see chapter ornament). Similarly, at a
magnificent banquet in Lille in 1453, given by Philip the Good of Burgundy, the
centrepiece of the principal table was the Knight in his boat, and the swan drawing
the boat by the long chain which attached to his gold collar. Also part of the earlier
festivities, had been a joust at which the prize for the knight who performed best
was a golden swan jewel on a golden chain terminating in a ruby.

Excavated at Dunstable in 1965 the beautiful white-enamelled gold swan jewel
with its gold chain attached to a coronet around its neck, must surely have been just
such another deliberate recalling of the details of the legend, and noting how the

swan became a Lancastrian badge after the marriage of Henry of Lancaster to Mary de Bohun in 1380, John Cherry has argued convincingly that the exquisite Dunstable Swan Jewel must have been made in this late fourteenth-century English milieu. Carved bone panels from an early fifteenth-century Italian ivory casket also survive in the British Museum depicting the earliest episode in the story just prior to the transformation of the children into swans by the wicked Mattabrune,[30] but the complete story of the *Chevalier au Cygne* is portrayed in a set of tapestries woven in Tournai *c.* 1460 which survives in St Catherine's Church, Cracow.[31]

It can be regarded as virtually certain that any late medieval tapestry that featured the hero Godfrey of Bouillon would have made some visual reference to his legendary ancestor, the Swan Knight. Louis, Duc d'Anjou had at least four such tapestries in 1364, and Charles V of France (1379) and Margaret of Flanders (1405), two more, while in his château at Pleshy in 1397, Thomas, Duke of Gloucester had another, and Henry V of England (d. 1422), a tapestry depicting the Voyage of Godfrey of Bouillon.[32]

Four Sons of Aymon

This is one of those images one has to look at twice, to see not one, but four riders on the same horse – a medieval version of Tom Pierce's grey mare! It seems to have been a story and an image popular and instantly recognisable to rich and poor alike from at least the beginning of the fourteenth century.[33] The most famous of the Four Sons of Aymon was Regnaud de Montauban, by whose name their late twelfth-century romance was also known. He it was who killed Charlemagne's nephew, but managed to make his getaway, together with his three brothers, on Bayard the wonder-horse. After a penitential pilgrimage to Jerusalem he met his death while helping, as a humble labourer, to build the shrine of St Peter in Cologne, and thereby achieved canonisation. The nineteenth-century literary historian Roquefort noted that on the walls of the nunnery of St Reynold in that city was a painting of the four *paladins* mounted upon Bayard, with the canonised Reynold distinguished from his brothers by a halo.[34] In similar vein, a detail from a painting by Pieter Saenredam of Haarlem (d. 1665), shows a graffito drawn on a wall of the four mounted on Bayard, with a chalk inscription which appears to include the date 1644,[35] though an earlier representation may be seen in Pieter van der Borcht's *St Georgsfest* of 1553.[36]

If the image was popular enough to be scrawled upon walls, it was also common on more formal inn- and shop-signs. In France we learn of a shoemaker's shop at the sign *Aux Quatre Fils Aymon* in Amiens in 1318,[37] and a bath-house or 'stews' so named in Arras in 1434 (*une estuves nommeez les IIII fieux Emon*).[38] Beauvais Museum still has a fifteenth-century inn-sign bearing the name *Aux Quatre Fils Aymon*,[39] and the four-on-a-horse image is found as a personal seal as early as 1313 in Ghent,[40] and a contemporary lead badge recently turned up from Ypres. Yet again, fourteenth- and fifteenth-century tapestry inventories mention the heroes: Louis, Duc d'Anjou had two such pieces in 1364, 'a tapestry of the IIII sons of Aymon fighting against the army of Charlemagne', and 'a tapestry of the four sons of Aymon, how they were attacked near to Valcouleur'. As he is the most prominent of the Four Sons, we can assume that the tapestries recorded simply as *Regnault de Montauban* (inventory of Valentine of Orléans (1408)) and *l'istoire du duc Regnault de Montaban* (inventory of Philip the Good of Burgundy (1420)) portrayed the same story.[41]

I have not noted any medieval English tapestry of this subject and yet we know that there was medieval literary interest in the Four Sons in England. A mid-fifteenth-century illuminated manuscript of the romance in the British Library includes the arms of John Talbot, first Earl of Shrewsbury, while from an inventory taken in 1466 of the almshouse at Ewelme, Oxfordshire, we learn of a roughly contemporary, but presumably less sumptuous, 'frensh boke of quater fits Emundis',[42] and before the century was out, Caxton had printed his own unillustrated translation of the work as *Foure Sonnes of Aymon* (1489). When his successor, Wynkyn de Worde, printed his edition some sixteen years later, however, woodcuts were added, copied from a French edition.[43] Though the title-page is missing in the best available copy now in the Huntington Library in California, we can assume it bore the famous image that appears on the title-page of the 1554 edition issued by Copland, who re-used many of de Worde's old cuts. In 1602 the upper chamber of the Chelmsford barber, Hugh Barer's house, was 'hung around with painted cloth whereon was described the history of Hammon and his sons': Emmison interpreted *Hammon* as 'Amon of Judah', adding that 'such biblical scenes were common enough', but the biblical Amon (about whom the Bible has little to say) appears to have had only one son (Josiah), so that we may be certain that this Elizabethan tapestry must rather have depicted the Four Sons of Aymon.

The Nine Worthies

Somewhere between the heroes of the romances and those of the *exempla* are the exemplary heroes of biblical history, classical antiquity and medieval Christendom, known collectively as the Nine Worthies (*Neuf Preux*). Their numeration as a triad of triads – three Pagans, three Jews, and three Christians[44] – satisfied that part of the medieval mind that liked to classify by numbered groups such as the Five Senses, Seven Ages of Man, and so on.

It seems to have been in Jacques de Longuyon's 'Vows of the Peacock', composed in 1312 that the Nine Worthies were first enumerated. The vows in question were made at a Peacock Feast, a magnificent banquet at which a peacock was the principal dish. Just such a Peacock Feast, perhaps recalling that of Longuyon's romance, is depicted at the foot of the lavish monumental brass of Flemish manufacture commemorating Robert Braunche (d. 1364) and his wives in the church at King's Lynn, Norfolk.[45] Once again, Louis, Duc d'Anjou had 'two large tapestries of the Vows of the Peacock' according to his 1364 inventory, as well as another of the Three Christian Worthies.

The Worthies seem to have been particularly popular in tapestry, and are well represented in French noblemen's inventories, and a fragment representing Arthur and Caesar from the set owned by the Duc de Berry and mentioned in his 1416 inventory, is preserved in the Metropolitan Museum, New York. A perhaps corresponding set (for they bore the arms of Berry) depicting the Nine Female Worthies (*Neuf Preuses*) – a somewhat later invention – is recorded in Charles VI's inventory made shortly before 1422. A locally woven late fifteenth-century fragment also survives in Basel Museum, but such tapestries are recorded in contemporary England too. According to the inventory of his effects taken in 1422, Henry V died possessed of '1 hanging of "gold" arras of the IX Powerful Ones, the text of which begins . . .'.[46] and Sir John Fastolfe's inventory taken in 1459 records his 'clothe of ix conquerouris',[47] while in his will dated 1454, Nicholas Sturgeon bequeathes his brother 'the hallyng with the ix wurthy',[48] and in 1483 John Dyghton gave to the Grey Friars of Norwich 'a stained cloth with the 9 worthies'.[49] In his *Life of St Werburgh* (*a.* 1513) Bradshaw describes a tapestry of the Nine Worthies he had seen hanging in the hall of Ely Abbey.

The Nine also put in an appearance at spectacles of one kind or another, at royal entries, for example, as in a pageant at Henry VI's coronation in Paris in 1431, or at humbler civic celebrations as recorded in Coventry in 1456, 1474[50] and 1498.

The Nine Worthies were soon joined by Nine Female Worthies whose personnel fluctuated much more than that of their somewhat earlier male counterparts. As we have seen, the inventory of Charles VI of France taken shortly before 1422, includes a set of tapestries of the *Preuses* bearing the arms of Berry,[51] and it would seem that the presence of the Female Worthies usually implies the presence of the male series. About the year 1404 a celebrated illuminator known as the Master of the *Cité des Dames* illustrated Thomas de Saluce's *Le Chevalier Errant* with miniatures of the *Neuf Preux* and the *Neuf Preuses* on facing pages,[52] probably from just such a tapestry model – though only a few years later in Thomas's home-town of Saluzzo in upper Piedmont both sets were painted in fresco *c.* 1420–30 by Jacques Iverny on the walls of the Sala della Manta in the Castello.[53] Philip the Good of Burgundy's inventory of 1420 records *Ung tapiz ouvre des IX preux et neuf preuses*, but significantly, in 1402 Louis d'Orléans had a new chimney-piece installed in his Château de Couci carved with images of the *Neuf Preuses* to complement an existing set of the *Preux*.

In England, unaccountably neglected, are the superb eight surviving Female Worthies (all nine male Worthies have disappeared) painted on panels *c.* 1530 in Flemish style by Lambert Barnard for the Great Chamber of Amberley Castle, home of Robert Sherborne, Bishop of Chichester (Colour Plate 14).[54] The surviving verse captions have a definite relationship to an anonymous poem, 'The ix ladyes worthy' found only in a manuscript of *c.* 1500 in Trinity College, Cambridge, but later published as a Chaucer apocryphon in John Stowe's appendix to the second edition of the poet's *Collected Works* (London, 1561).[55]

FOLK HEROES

Robin Hood

Since Joseph Ritson's pioneering application of rigorous historical method to the hero and his legend at the end of the eighteenth century, one of the most hotly discussed topics in Robin Hood studies has been his very historicity – was there ever a real, historical, flesh-and-blood medieval original, or is he merely a hero of story, an embodiment of wishful thinking, a sort of Marxist brigand who, as the popular formula puts it, 'stole from the rich and gave to the poor'?

As recently as 1984 David Crook published his discovery of the record of a Berkshire fugitive named William Robehod in 1262, the same man being earlier referred to as William son of Robert le Fevere, proving beyond peradventure that *Robehod* was in use as an appropriate nickname for a robber by that date. Any 'original' Robin Hood must therefore have lived at least a generation or two before 1262, in order to have become sufficiently notorious for his name to be attached in this jocular generic fashion to some other robber not originally so named. In fact, *Robinhood* as a nick-/surname has now been found a further six times before the end of the thirteenth century, twice in Huntingdonshire, twice in Hampshire, and once in both Suffolk and Essex, and in five out of these eight cases, the men so named were 'suspected or outlawed criminals'.[56]

We thus infer the earliest existence of Robin Hood, from the generic appropriation of his name, in much the same way that we infer the existence of that other, equally elusive English hero, King Arthur, from the stanza praising the otherwise unknown Gwawrddur in the B-text of the early medieval Welsh 'Gododdin' poem who, in what must surely be one of the earliest-known back-handed compliments in the literature of these islands, is said to have 'glutted black ravens on the rampart of the stronghold, but was' – almost proverbially, it would appear – 'no Arthur'.

For a hero whose exploits enjoyed such popularity, it has always seemed strange to me that Robin Hood makes such a very late appearance in art. The Yeoman woodcut from Pynson's edition of the *Canterbury Tales* (1492) was pressed into service in one of the earliest prints of the *Gest* of Robin Hood – a common enough practice in book illustration at this date – but it makes this earliest extant 'portrait' quite anomalous in depicting 'Robin' on horseback. De Worde's slightly later edition of the *Gest* (1506?) is similarly unoriginal in using a factotum block of a youth holding his sword by its tip over his shoulder – he carries no longbow! – to serve for Robin. There are now known to be no fewer than five English editions of the *Gest* published in the years 1500–15 (one of them in Antwerp), and then no more until *c.* 1560. At least the broadsides of the later seventeenth century are illustrated with what was probably a custom-made archer!

All these, though, are text-bound images. For early freestanding images we have once again to turn to the invaluable evidence of inventories, where we learn of two 'painted cloths', the poor man's tapestries in which images were literally painted onto canvas, and of which very few survive. Hanging in his parlour in 1492, so at least as early as any of the unoriginal woodcut images, Robert Rychardes of Dursley had just such 'a paynted cloth of Robyn hod',[57] while a century later, in late Elizabethan Essex, Thomas Shouncke of Havering also had a Robin Hood cloth hanging in the hall.[58] Such inventory evidence is invaluable in allowing us to 'correct' the surviving iconographic record.

The Man in the Moon

It is probably a universal in human cultures to discern a face or figure of some kind in the moon. In English, the Man in the Moon is the subject of one of the *Harley Lyrics* of the early fourteenth century.[59] The poem opens by describing its subject in mid-stride, carrying a bundle of thorns on a wooden fork, but as early as the late twelfth century, the English writer Alexander of Neckham recorded the belief that the Man in the Moon is a peasant banished thither for having stolen thorns or brushwood. Other European folk traditions (the German, for example) add that this theft took place on the sabbath, and connect the Man in the Moon with the sabbath-breaker of Numbers 15, 32 ff. who was stoned for gathering sticks on the Lord's Day, and there is a late fifteenth-century engraving of this Old Testament tale by Israhel van Meckenem. He was also sometimes identified as Cain – by Dante, for example – but Reginald Pecock writing *c.* 1449 was having none of this superstitious nonsense:

Figure 9.4

> Vntrewe . . . is this opinion that a man which stale [stole] sumtyme a birthan [burden]of thorns was sett in to the moone, there forto abide for euere.[60]

The most interesting and valuable piece of pictorial evidence of this tradition in England is the seal of Walter de Grendon (a village in Northamptonshire), appended to a document dated 1336, and thus exactly contemporary with the Harley manuscript poem (Figure 9.4). It is inscribed with a rhyming Latin legend, which in translation reads:

> I will teach you, Walter,
> why I carry thorns in the moon

and bears the image of a hooded man carrying a double bundle of thorns hanging from a stick over his shoulder inside a crescent moon, with a little dog at his feet in front of him and two stars.[61]

There is no obvious reason why Walter chose to have such a seal engraved – how much more appropriate it would have been for the Richard *Moneshine* whose seal is dated 1394 and whose surname, incidentally, represents the earliest-known appearance of the word *moonshine* in English. Richard's nickname may suggest, indeed, that the still current figurative sense of *moonshine* as 'an appearance without substance; something unsubstantial or unreal' may be at issue here and – as so often with nicknames, a still undervalued resource – significantly earlier than the dictionaries' first examples. An alternative possibility is that Richard, like the tailor Starveling in Shakespeare's *Midsummer Night's Dream*, had once 'presented' the moon in some play or pageant 'with lantern, dog, and bush of thorn' as Quince describes him in his Prologue [V.i.134], confirming incidentally the traditional presence of the Man in the Moon's dog as on Walter's seal.

A second medieval representation of the Man in the Moon carrying his thorns is to be found painted on the ceiling of Gyffyn Church near Conway in North Wales, and certainly by the sixteenth century there were inns named 'The Man in the Moon' to be found in England, which would doubtless have been provided with suitable signs. It has been suggested that the English surname Moon may sometimes be a locative 'sign-name', that is, the person so named will have lived *atte Mone* 'at the sign of The Moon', and such a hostelry is attested in fifteenth-century London.[62] But already in 1369 in Paris we learn that the English students of the Faculty of Arts were accustomed to meet in *hospicio Lunae* in the English quarter – and here too we may assume an appropriate sign.

Commoner, however, than the image of the peasant with his bundle of thorns, is the shorthand representation of the moon (and, indeed, the sun) as a disc presented frontally, or as a crescent in profile, bearing human facial features. This is a type of venerable antiquity, and in the medieval period perhaps most familiar in

Figure 9.5

the form of the twin luminaries which appear above the transom on either side of Christ's head in images of the Crucifixion, in the mid-thirteenth-century English *Amesbury Psalter*, for example, presumably on the authority of Matthew 24.29.

This simpler facial image is well exemplified by a misericord at Ripple of late fifteenth-century date, a ?male face seen in profile within a crescent (Figure 9.5). Of similar date (1477) is the three-dimensional moon carved by Erasmus Grasser just three years before his famous morris dancers and, like them, intended as part of the programme of

sculptural decoration for the old Town Hall in Munich, though here it is a decidedly female wimpled face seen in three-quarter profile which he has placed within a hollowed crescent.[63] The femininity of Grasser's moon harks back, of course, to the traditional genders of the masculine sun and feminine moon in classical art, but was also undoubtedly influenced by the popularity of the image of the Virgin standing in a crescent moon, as in the several versions engraved by the Master ES.

Lazybones

The Dutch lead pendant reproduced as Figure 9.6 which was cast about 1400 is a tiny minor masterpiece, just 44 × 57 mm. It bears the legend LEIIAERT (modern *luiaard*), meaning Lazybones. Despite the bagpiper playing just above the head of the young man (whose fashionable dress includes a girdle of 'folly bells'), and the similarly clad youth who brings him a tankard of ale and takes his hand as if to help him up, the supine Leiiaert cannot be induced to rise.

Figure 9.6

A fascinating print issued *c.* 1550, engraved by Peter Baltens after Cornelis Massys, pictorialises proverbs on the subject of laziness in a village setting. They are numbered one to nine and identified in both Flemish and French, with eighteen lines of Flemish verse below. Undoubtedly the oddest proverb represented is the fourth, the old woman who sows buttocks in the street, but directly above her head is the sign of the inn which dominates the foreground of the composition. It depicts a large man reclining in a comfortable armchair, and bears the name of the tavern – also bilingually – as *Au Parasseux* and *Op Den Lvyaert*. In a song in the contemporary *Antwerp Song-book* published in 1544, the Lazybones appears canonised as St *Luyaert*, together with St *Noywerc* (Neverwork). For his native home, the Land of Cockaigne, later dubbed in English, 'the Ile of Lasye', see Chapter 8.

Nobody

Thanks to the bureaucratic habit, lists of animals' names are occasionally preserved in late medieval sources – significantly, as early as 1526, a Brunswick archive records a presumably tricksy horse named *Ulenspeygel*, for example.[64] But it is thanks to a great shooting festival held in Zurich in 1504 and, specifically, to the lottery organised on that occasion, for which participants subscribed not only their own names, but also those of their dogs, that some eighty Swiss dogs' names are preserved for us from that year.[65] There are grandiose names from romance such as *Artus* (Arthur) and *Melesinn* (Melusine), even classical names such as *Venus* and

Fortuna. The commonest name (eight examples, amounting to 10 per cent of the sample) was *Fürst(li)* (compare modern English *Prince*). There were 'exotic' Oriental names such as *Turgk* and *Soldan*, and colour names too, of course, such as *Mörli*, still used in modern German for a black dog, while the dogs named after the materials *Dammast* and *Sattin* presumably had smooth, shiny coats. An interesting group bear names related to the occupations of their owners, for example *Stosel* (Pestle), the apothecary's dog, *Hemmerli* (Little Hammer) the locksmith's, and *Speichli* (Little Spoke) the waggoner's dog.

But another fascinating group bear facetious names designed to tease the enquirer. Such are *Wass du* and *Wie du*, both approximating to 'You what?', and *Werweisd* (Who knows?) – an equivalent English example, though in French, as Lord Lisle was appointed Lord Deputy of Calais in 1534, is his wife's dog *Purquoy* (Fr. *pourquoi*, 'Why?'), mentioned in one of the *Lisle Letters* for that year.[66] But it is another name in this same riddling tradition that is of most interest to our present investigation, that of the dog at the shooting festival which belonged to Uoli Hunenberg von Surse, for he was called *Nieman* (Nobody), and the clerk also recorded the reason why – 'and everything bad that happens, he did it'. What is so significant about this entry is that it is evidence to show that this joke was current some years *before* publication of the various *Niemand* broadsheets introduced this richly folkloric figure to a wider audience.

In his discussion of the appearance of the figure on the famous painted table in Zurich, previously erroneously attributed to Hans Holbein, Lucas Wüthrich re-examined the accepted dates of publication of these earliest *Niemand* broadsheets, and concluded that it is not possible to establish priority between the High German version published by Kunne in Memmingen, and the Low German *Nemanth* published by Winter in Magdeburg, both around 1510.[67] Be that as it may, the idea was instantly and enthusiastically taken up by no less a writer than the humanist Ulrich von Hütten, on the title-page of the 1510 *editio princeps* of his *Nemo* published in Erfurt.[68] Another very early *Niemand* (dated by Wüthrich 1500x1511) is that painted on the outer surface of the door to the famous *Grüne Saal* in Burg Reifenstein near Sterzing in the Italian Tirol. It is accompanied by the inscription: 'Nobody I'm called, whatever's done (wrong) it's put down to me',[69] very reminiscent of the explanation of the dog *Nieman*'s name, but – from a comparison of the legends alone – almost certainly derived from the Kunne broadsheet on which *Niemand*'s banderole reads, *Niemants hais ich was ieder man tut das ziicht man mich*.

The *Niemand* who appears on the Zurich table (now shown to be the work of Hans Herbst) is securely dated 1515, and a banderole above him (despite his padlocked lips) is inscribed:

> I'm called Nobody. Everything that's broken, I must have done it.
> It grieves me that I cannot exonerate myself from it [that is, the false charge].

The next appearance of our hero known to me, just two years after the table-top, is on one of the biscuit-moulds inventoried by Claus Stalburg with which we began: '1517. The 8th stone(-mould) is Nobody with his household-utensils and a rhyme above. . . .' The classic portrayal of Nobody is that established by the Kunne and Winter broadsheets, a man standing or walking across a floor strewn with a large number of broken household objects. Sometimes he is shown seated amid them, as on the Zurich painted table and on a mid-seventeenth-century Swiss biscuit-mould, which probably gives a close enough idea of what Claus Stalburg's *Niemansz* mould must have looked like some 150 years earlier. In the Kunne version of the sheet only, Nobody's clothes are ragged, but both sheets agree in giving him pattens, a walking-stick, and a peculiar, apparently winged hat (though only one wing is visible in Kunne's version), giving him a superficial resemblance to the Roman god Mercury. The most important feature of his iconography, however, is the padlock which keeps his lips shut – the texts explain that this is so he cannot protest his innocence when careless servants, children and others, in response to the question, 'Who broke that?' reply, 'Nobody!'

The great success which the image of *Niemand* enjoyed in the second decade of the sixteenth century meant that it was inevitably pressed into the service of the Reformation, and in 1533 a lightly adapted version of Kunne's woodcut was issued in Strasbourg, but with the key difference that *Niemand*'s mouth is now unlocked, so that he is able to state his blatantly Protestant message. An English-language version was issued in London *c.* 1550, and the banderole above the strange figure in the woodcut now reads: 'Nobody is my name that beyreth euery bodyes blame'. A tapestry woven in Flanders and clearly based on this particular image was recently published as dating from the 'late fifteenth century/*c.* 1500', but its unrecognised dependence on this Strasbourg second edition puts it, rather, at about 1533.[70] Strangely, the tapestry designer has discarded all the broken household objects and the domestic setting in favour of a rabbit-populated *millefleurs* sward, and the swirling tail of the banderole held by the woodcut *Niemand* has metamorphosed into a horn! And yet he retains a broken flask which, together with his staff, gives this protean figure the air of a pilgrim, or even the Wandering Jew – 'I wander from place to place' says the Nobody in Kunne's model for the Strasbourg sheet.[71]

The Ideal Servant

Padlocked lips and ass's ears are also part of the make-up of the strange allegorical figure I shall call the Ideal Servant. Because, according to some texts, the ass is long-suffering, portraits of the Ideal

Figure 9.7

Servant give him ass's ears, and various other animal attributes appropriate to his duties, such as a pig's snout, to show he is not fussy about his food, and deer's hooves to denote his swiftness about his master's errands.

The earliest extant image of such an Ideal Servant is a French print entitled *Le Bon Serviteur* which was issued 1558x75 (Figure 9.7).[72] Though sadly not extant, it is known that 'The pourtraiture of A trusty servaunt' was licensed to Henry Bamford in 1577, having been sold to him by William Hoskins,[73] but a still extant mural of the figure with accompanying descriptive Latin and English verses was painted on a wall outside the kitchens of Winchester College by a scholar named John Hoskins (possibly the nephew of William) in the early 1580s.[74] Recently, however, on the basis of similarity to the extant French example, from the very detailed descriptions given in his inventory, I was able to recognise two prints of this subject in the collection of Ferdinand Columbus (d. 1539):

> A man, on the right shoulder is a pole with a pot at each end, in his left hand he holds a shovel and a taper, below one of the pots, and he has a very large nose [a snout] and ears like an ass, his legs are stretched out/astride, and from the left hangs a rosary of 14 beads from which hangs a cross, and above his left leg are banderoles in 'Flemish'.[75]

Contemporary with the last years of Ferdinand's collecting, the *De Officio Famulorum* (Paris, 1535) written by Gilbert Cousin (Cognatus) notes that in France such figures were painted in houses. The following quotation is from the English translation, published eight years later, entitled *Of the Office of Seruantes*:

> The image or portraiture of a good seruant, accordinge as the frenche men haue the same paincted in their howses, and that in this wyse. Furste sholde he haue a skarlette bonet apon his heade, with a faire shurte on his backe, but in steade of a nose, they make him a hogges snowte, with asse eares, and hertes feate [that is, hart's feet], holdinge vp his right hande stretched fourth, and apon his left shoulder bering a cowlestaffe [pole] with two pailes of water, one before, an other behinde. Last then, holding in his lefte hande a shouell full of quicke coles, signifienge by theise deuices, as towchinge the fayre cappe, and shurte, howe a seruant should go netely apparellyd, by the hogges snowte was mente, he sholde nat be lykerous, or ouerdayntie mowthed, but content with al meates. the asse eares pretended, that he also should haue pacient earis, in suffrynge what euer his maister should roughly say vnto him. So lyke wyse his hand holden vppe warned him of vprightnes, in handlynge his maisters goodes. The hertes fete betokenid quykenes in dispatchinge lightly what euer he went abowt, and so by the two pailes, and the fyre was vnderstode both deftenes, and good conueyaunce in bringinge many thinges at ones to passe.

The literary tradition, however, certainly goes back to the Middle Ages proper. It is first found in English in the *Castell of Labour*, first printed by Vérard in Paris, *c.* 1503, and then in London in 1505 and 1506. But the *Castell* is a translation of Pierre Gringore's *Chasteau de Labour* (Paris, 1499), though the passage concerning the Ideal Servant's animal attributes is, in fact, derived from a much earlier, rambling allegorical poem by Jacques Briant, entitled 'La Voie de povrete et de richesse', written in 1342. Joan Evans noted that in the painted window-glass of Jacques Coeur's house at Bourges, built in the 1440s, a man was portrayed with padlocked mouth and a scroll inscribed with the proverb, 'En bouche close nentre mousche' (No fly enters the closed mouth), and alongside him another man with ass's ears whose scroll was inscribed *Taire* (Be Silent).[76] As we have seen, both padlocked lips and ass's ears are the attributes of the Ideal Servant, and such Jacques Coeur undoubtedly aspired to be to his royal master Charles VII – here were the reassuring symbols that this servant knew both how to hear his master's confidences, but also how to keep his mouth shut.

EXEMPLA

The *exemplum* is hard to define satisfactorily, for it is something of a catch-all category which includes, for instance, saints' stories, fabliaux, fables and Bestiary beliefs. The 'ideal' *exemplum* was a reasonably short anecdote or mini-narrative, that could be told, usually at the end of a sermon, as a means of diverting the congregation, but it is also, of course, a moral tale, even if at times the preacher had to expend considerable and often unlikely ingenuity in discovering and expounding that moral. The story, when 'moralised', provides an *example* of good Christian conduct to be followed, or an illustration of sinful behaviour to be shunned, so that the listener may learn, by *example*. The *exemplum* sugars the bitter pill of moral instruction. It is hardly to be distinguished from the parable and, indeed, it is that term that Caxton chose to render the *exemplum* of the serpent's judgment by the fox discussed below.

It is rare for the manuscripts which collect the texts of *exempla* also to illustrate them. One such early exception is a Northern French *Vie des anciens peres*, compiled in the 1220s, in which *exempla* are drawn inside initial letters, with which – though not an *exemplum* collection as such – the *Rothschild Canticles* may be compared, made in the same region *c*. 1300, in which thirteen miniatures of moralised tales are set in small square frames within the text area.[77] More frequently, *exempla* are illustrated in the margins of books to which they have no obvious direct relevance, often in ones and twos, occasionally – as with the *Smithfield Decretals* (*c*. 1330–40) – in a much more voluminous, almost programmatic fashion.[78]

Many scenes painted in the margins of late medieval manuscripts still remain to be identified, among which we may reasonably estimate a fair proportion to be unrecognised *exempla*. Occasionally one distinguishes a pictorial detail from such a story, and several such are discussed elsewhere in the present book, such as the hare with the purse round its neck, despatched by the proverbial fools, in Chapter 7. Typical of such unrecognised *exempla* is the *bas-de-page* scene on f. 110 of the English *Rutland Psalter* (*c*. 1260) (Colour Plate 13).[79]

Serpent Judged by Fox; Snake Bites Liberator

On a grassy mound, a man is shown reclining and wearing only a cloak wrapped loosely around him; he gestures at a snake beside him and appears to be watched by a fox or wolf. The story which this image illustrates is listed as no. 4262 in Tubach's motif index:

Serpent judged by fox: a man releases a snake from a trap, but the latter wraps itself round his leg. A fox [to whom the man appeals for judgment] tricks the snake into returning to the trap.

It appears in the Middle English *Alphabet of Tales*, where it is attributed to Petrus Alfonsus (d. 1108), in whose *exempla* collection, the *Disciplina Clericalis*, it is Tale no. 5,[80] and is, indeed, to be found in the fifteenth-century Middle English translation of that work, as Tale no. 24.[81] It enjoyed great popularity on the continent,[82] and was twice printed by Caxton, as the 'fable of the dragon and of the kerle' (churl) in his *Aesop* of 1484, and in Chapter 30 of his *Reynard* (1481), translated from the Dutch, as 'A parable of a man that delyverd a serpent fro peryl of deth'. The *Rutland Psalter* illustration thus importantly antedates any extant literary telling of the *exemplum* in England.

The Petrified Maidens

There are several prehistoric stone circles in Britain and on the continent to which a petrifaction legend is attached. The usual version is that a group of people were dancing a ring-dance (*carol, chorus*) on the Sabbath, and despite warnings from a priest to stop, would not, and so were punished by being turned to stone where they stood for their profanation of the Lord's Day.[83] The classic medieval account is located at modern-day Kölbigk near Bamberg in Germany and appears, for example, in William of Waddington's Anglo-Norman *exempla* collection, *Le Manuel des Pechiez* (*c.* 1270), and thence – though considerably amplified – in Robert Mannyng's English adaptation, *Handlyng Synne* (1303).[84]

Surprisingly, none of the folklorists who have studied this motif were aware that tacked onto the end of an early twelfth-century manuscript of *The Marvels of the East* are three such petrifaction stories with an illustration that appears to conflate all three (Colour Plate 17).[85] The three stories are set respectively in Brittany, England, and a third unnamed location. M.R. James suspected that the third and shortest account was 'the earliest form of [the Kölbigk] legend', which he saw as a later elaboration of the present account, which merely reads (in his translation):

Upon certain others the sentence of a curse was laid for a year. . . . From the dance of these women one man tried to detach his sister, but her arm remained in his hand – she apparently taking no note of it. At the end of the year however all of them died.

In fact, an account of the Kölbigk legend even earlier than this appears in the Latin *Life of St Edith of Wilton* by Goscelin, *c.* 1080, but in any case, the Kölbigk legend lacks the picturesque circumstantial detail of the torn-off arm.

The first legend, located in Brittany, describes a round-dance of seven women with the soil sinking beneath their feet in the form of a circle. They were six sisters with their mother dancing on a feast day, who failed to stop when twice rebuked by a priest named Urri, who was about to celebrate mass, so he prayed that they might never leave off dancing, and thus they have remained. There is one empty place in the ring where the mother tore herself away at the moment of the curse.

The second English legend concerns a similar dance of girls or maidens, one of whom, when similarly twice rebuked by a priest with the distinctly post-Conquest Norman name, Odo, turned the curse back on him, praying that he might never stir from the spot till Doomsday, whereupon he too was rooted to the spot, and can still be seen holding his book to his breast. Though this is quite illogical in terms of narrative motivation, it is easily explicable in terms of megalithic ground-plans, where stone circles often feature an 'outlier'. The gap in the circle in the first legend, occasioned by the mother's last-minute flight, is similarly to be explained in terms of a missing, fallen or destroyed, megalith.

As James pointed out, the early twelfth-century illustrator of Bodley 614 has ingeniously combined elements from each of these three versions of the petrifaction legend for his miniature. The six maidens, and the gap in the circle at the left representing the absent seventh, are taken from the Breton story, as is the sunken ground which, as James noted, may refer to the half-buried condition of the stones, or to a trench surrounding them, and the tonsured priest holding his book at the extreme right is clearly taken from the English legend, while the man holding an arm at the extreme left of the circle, just as clearly derives from the third, unlocalised legend.

The manuscript locates none of the three circles precisely, nor is any of them given a name, but one involves a dance of seven women and another of maidens. Use of the word 'dance' is reminiscent of the earliest name for the Stonehenge monument, which in Geoffrey of Monmouth's contemporary pseudo-chronicle, *Historia Regum Britanniae* (*c.* 1136), is called the Giants' Dance, hinting perhaps at some similar petrifaction legend. As early as 1584 in his *Topographical and Historical Description of Cornwall*, John Norden noted that the megalithic stone row at St Columb Major was known as 'The Nine Maids or Nine Sisters' and that 'the country people will tell you [they are] so many maids turned into stones for dancing on the sabbath day'; significantly, one of the nineteenth-century names for an outlier here is 'The Fiddler'. The present 'Merry Maidens' stone circle, also in Cornwall, has outliers documented in the eighteenth century as 'The Blind Fiddler' and the 'Two Pipers'.[86] In similar vein, the Stanton Drew stone circle was referred to as the 'Wedding' from at least 1644, and the explanation offered that the wedding party had impiously continued their Saturday night celebrations into Sunday morning.

The Old Woman, the Devil and the Shoes

In this tale, frustrated at being unable to sow discord between a happily married couple, the Devil enlists the aid of an Old Woman, promising her a pair of shoes if she is successful. When she triumphs easily in this piece of wickedness that was beyond even the Devil's capacities, he is obliged to hand over the reward, but is so afraid of her that he can only proffer the shoes on the end of a stick held out at arm's length. (For further examples of the traditional sexist fear of the Old Woman, see Chapter 11.)

As ever with such motifs, unless one already knows the story, the image is quite meaningless. It was painted on the very first folio of *Jan Olbracht's Gradual* made for the Polish King *c.* 1500,[87] but seems to have been especially popular in late medieval

Sweden. No fewer than eighteen Swedish churches contain wall-paintings of the motif executed between the 1450s and 1520s, suggesting the *exemplum* must have had some sort of didactic function – perhaps as a pictorial warning to the congregation against the sin of calumny.[88]

The Wife-hanging Tree

In a nastier tale, also found in the *Gesta Romanorum* and in Gringore's *Fantasies*,[89] where it is illustrated by a woodcut, a man tells another how his three wives have all hanged themselves on a tree in his garden – the other man asks him for a cutting.

RIDDLES

The riddle, like most other genres of popular orality, is not one we look on with much favour today, yet riddle collections were printed in England as early as Wynkyn de Worde's *Demaundes Joyous* of 1511 (though much of it was translated from a late fifteenth-century French collection), and it contains all the usual obscenity and curiously post-modern wit associated with the genre. For example, 'Whiche was fyrst ye henne or ye egge?' The answer to this truly old riddle is 'The henne whan god made her.'

Some time in the early 1530s George Puttenham, author of *The Arte of English Poesie* (1589), was told a riddle by his nurse – judging from its content, she might find it difficult to get a job nowadays. In his discussion of the riddle genre he recalls how:

> My mother had an old woman in her nurserie, who in the winter nights would put vs forth many pretty ridles, whereof this is one:
>
> > I haue a thing and rough it is
> > And in the midst a hole Iwis:
> > There cam a yong man with his ginne   ['engine', that is, tool, instrument]
> > And he put it a handfull in.
>
> The good old Gentlewoman would tell vs that were children how it was meant by a furd glooue (that is, that the solution was 'furred glove').

He then goes on to say, presumably disingenuously:

> Some other naughtie body would peraduenture haue construed it not halfe so mannerly. The riddle is pretie but that it holdes too much of the Cachemphaton or foule speach and may be drawen to a reprobate sence.

But that it 'may be drawen to a reprobate sence' is, of course, the whole point! Puttenham was born about 1529, so we may imagine his nurse putting this *prety ridle* to her charges some time in the 1530s. By coincidence, this same riddle must also have been the very first printed in a riddle book which survives only as a sad fragment, published by Rastell *c.* 1530, but now containing only four of the original one hundred riddles, and four solutions – but not to the surviving riddles, unfortunately! 'The solucyon of the fyrst ryddyll' reads '[fu]rred gloue. But this ryddyl must be put by a wo[man] it is not proper.' Quite! Yet this particular indecency can be traced back to the earliest English riddle collection of all, the hundred found in the late Anglo-Saxon *Exeter Book*.[90]

Riddles have always gone in for the risqué and the scatological:

> Whiche is the moost cleynlyest lefe amonge all other leues?
> It is holly leues for noo body wyll not wype his arse with them[91]

and riddlers seem particularly to enjoy the 'catch riddle', in which the guesser is embarrassed into refusing to offer the indecent solution, only to be rebuked by the riddler, who offers some innocuous answer, for being so dirty-minded. Another instance of this favourite stratagem is to be found in a typically unhealthy erotic exchange between Ferdinand and his sister, the Duchess of Malfi, in the eponymous play written by Webster in 1614:

> Ferdinand: Women like that part, which, like the lamprey, Hath nev'r a bone in't.
> Duchess: Fie, sir!
> Ferdinand: Nay, I mean the tongue . . . Farewell, lusty widow.

Extraordinarily, this appears to be an erotic motif of Indo-European antiquity, for Hesiod's 'boneless', traditionally interpreted as an octopus or snail, is paralleled by a passage in one of the Sanskrit hymns of the *Rig Veda*, and the 'boneless member' is similarly found in Old Czech, in Old English – another *Exeter Book* riddle alludes to the penis as a 'boneless bird' – and in Middle French, in one of the late fifteenth-century *Adevineaux Amoureux* (where the pretended solution is 'mole'). Ferdinand's (apparently boneless) lamprey is merely the Jacobean variant.[92]

The Clever Daughter or Peasant Girl

Some years ago I was able to increase the number of known depictions in medieval art of another *exemplum*, known to folklorists as 'The Clever Peasant Girl'. The central motif is the bizarre image of a semi-naked person riding a goat and holding a rabbit, but is, in fact, the solution to the riddle of how to appear neither naked nor clad, neither riding nor walking, neither barefoot nor shod. It is posed almost incidentally in some

Figure 9.8

manuscripts of the *Gesta Romanorum*, as an elaboration of the riddling task set the dutiful son by the tyrannical emperor.[93] By the date of the early fourteenth-century *Ormesby Psalter*, at least, the motif had been brought into the orbit of the Solomon and Marcolf tale, and it is in this context that it appears on misericords in Beverley parish church and in Worcester (Figure 9.8) and Norwich Cathedrals.

The *Ormesby* image is actually a compressed narrative (Colour Plate 15). Reading from right to left, we see Solomon seated on his throne debating with Marcolf, counting on his fingers in the familiar gestural convention evolved by medieval illuminators to convey a *disputatio*. The central scene shows Marcolf, naked except for a cowl and one shoe (which does not touch the ground), riding on a goat which bestrides a ditch and proffering a rabbit in his raised hand. The left-hand scene shows King Solomon pointing at this bizarre apparition from the gateway of his palace, as does one of his servants, who threateningly holds on a leash two dogs who have also spotted the goat-rider.

Significantly, this image appears on the folio on which Psalm 52 begins, where we have come to expect images of the fool (see Chapter 6) – though Marcolf is more trickster and boor than fool – but I believe there was another, punning motivation here. The Latin text of Psalm 52 opens, *Dixit insipiens in corde suo non est Deus* (The fool has said in his heart there is no God), where *in corde suo* means 'in his heart', but I suggest this brought to the artist's mind the words *in corda sua* or *in cordis suis*, that is, 'in his cord(s)', conjuring up exactly the sort of string body-stocking which the goat-riding Marcolf wears in a somewhat earlier image in the margin of an English register of writs manuscript now in the Pierpont Morgan Library in New York; here the bizarre rider is actually labelled *Marculf*, and the miniature shows him with one foot significantly poking out of the network, and a rabbit in the crook of his elbow.

Test of Resourcefulness: Carrying Wolf, Goat and Cabbage Across Stream[94]

Pictorialised riddles are not always easy to spot. Also in the *Ormesby Psalter*, a few folios further on from the Marcolf-as-Clever-Daughter image, the artist for no apparent reason, unless to exhibit his natural playfulness, has depicted a 'classic' riddle (Colour Plate 16). The modern French proverbial idiom, *ménager la chèvre et le chou* (manage the goat and the cabbage) alludes to the same situation. In the present miniature the goat's part is taken by a sheep and although the artist has painted the other animal to look more like a fox, for the purposes of our riddle we must regard him as a wolf, for the logic of the riddle requires that he will eat the sheep if left alone with it. Similarly the sheep and cabbage cannot be left alone together while the man is ferrying the wolf across, and only one item may be taken across in the boat at a time – it is soluble!

The Queen of Sheba's Riddles

Probably the most popularly depicted riddles in the fifteenth and sixteenth centuries were those posed to Solomon by the Queen of Sheba who, in order to test his already proverbial wisdom, came, in the words of the Authorised Version, to 'prove him with hard questions', or *aenigmata* (riddles), according to the Vulgate text. She asks him to judge whether the two children who accompany her, dressed identically in long gowns, are of the same sex or not, and whether the flowers she has brought are artificial or real.

On a cushion cover embroidered in Strasbourg in the final decade of the fifteenth century and now in the Metropolitan Museum in New York, she stands before the youthful king seated on his throne and holds up two flowers; her banderole reads 'Tell me, King, whether the flowers and the children are alike or unlike in their kinds.' Between the monarchs the two children are collecting up apples which Solomon has thrown, one of them (evidently the girl) kneeling and gathering them in the fold of her dress – an intriguing observation of socialised gender behaviour. A bee is also visible making towards the flowers held out by the Queen. Solomon's banderole expounds his pragmatic solution of the riddles: 'The bee does not miss a real flower, kneeling shows the female kind.'

Several other sixteenth-century German tapestries of the subject are known, the earliest dated 1506. There is also a contemporary engraving of this Testing of Solomon's natural powers by Israhel van Meckenem (d. 1503), but this time there are four boys and four girls and four flowers held aloft. Near the flowers a Latin banderole reads, 'He who painted the flower did not paint the flower's scent.' One of Solomon's retainers releases a hive of bees which make for only two of the flowers, while another attendant empties a basket of apples onto the ground and the King and Queen watch the children's reactions.

FOLKTALES

Fables

By *fables* I intend principally those stories whose actors are animals in the main, and which are popularly and traditionally referred to as Aesop's.[95] People in the Middle Ages owed their familiarity with this corpus of material not to the 'original' classical collection – in so far as that can be reconstructed – but to the post-classical verse versions of Babrius and Phaedrus (both equally shadowy) and, in particular, to early medieval prose versions of the latter known as *Romulus*. Many fables early achieved a proverbial status ('sour grapes';[96] 'dog-in-the-manger'; 'lion's share') and some of this type are therefore discussed in the chapter on the representation of proverbs (for example, 'the grass is always greener on the other side').

It still seems little appreciated that the so-called *Bayeux Tapestry*, usually ascribed to the 1090s, includes numerous fable representations in its borders, anticipating the practice of later Gothic manuscript illuminators.[97] The fables whose identity we can be sure of include the fox, the raven and the cheese; the pregnant bitch; the wolf and the lamb; the wolf and the crane; the mouse, the frog and the kite; and the lion's share.[98] Some of these even occur more than once. But again there is the problem of how we should interpret their presence here; one eminent scholar was of the opinion that 'these fables serve a purely decorative purpose and cannot be related to the main scenes', while more recently, other scholars *have* detected some relevance, even if of quite conflicting types!

The pregnant bitch occurs for the second time on the *Tapestry* placed beneath the scene of William exhorting the Norman knights to fight valiantly against Harold, a man whom he claims is an ungrateful perjurer in illegal possession of his land. As Bernstein notes:

> Since the pregnant bitch's actions seem to fit comfortably as a metaphor for Harold's ingratitude and guile when making promises, and then for his use of force to retain his possession, this . . . fable would appear to be anti-Harold.[99]

The fable of the fox, the raven and the cheese occurs not twice, but three times:

> What are we to make of the fact that the Tapestry's creators thrice repeated this tale of a foolish creature who lost a prize by opening its mouth, within one narrative unit – the Normandy expedition – and moreover flagged its importance by placing it as the first and the last of the fables around that part of the story?[100]

After careful consideration of all three examples, Bernstein is inclined to see Harold as the foolish conceited raven and William as the cunning fox, in much the same way as the Canterbury historian Eadmer portrays the protagonists; Eadmer also suggested that William coaxed the oath out of Harold's mouth involuntarily. Such an interpretation is neither exactly for or against either Saxon or Norman, but then, as Bernstein cogently puts it:

> How often in world art has a subject people been called upon to make a monument depicting the events that led to their own enslavement, and, in the eyes of their victorious patrons, legitimised that victory?

The Fox-Friar/-Bishop Preaches to Birds

As early as the thirteenth century, Gautier de Coinci lamented that the clergy were less interested in statues of Our Lady than in representations of *Ysangrin et sa fame* from the beast-epic Reynard the Fox,[101] and it will not have escaped notice how many of these popular fable representations feature the fox, the archetype of cunning, as protagonist. But for a full account of that animal trickster's exploits I refer interested readers to Kenneth Varty's recent *Renart, Reynard, Reinaert*.

A hugely popular animal cleric was the Fox-Friar or Fox-Bishop who is seen preaching to a congregation of birds, especially geese – cf. the wolf who preaches to the sheep on an English painted glass panel (Figure 1.5) – his duplicity pointed up by the bird he has already bagged hidden in his cowl, or dangling from his belt behind his back. I discuss it here though there does not seem to be any extant fable or literary anecdote as such which puts it in a narrative context.[102] It was certainly, however, already a proverbial scenario in English and other vernaculars by the fifteenth century:

whanne the fox prechyth, kepe wel yore gees [*Castle of Perseverance a.* 1425]
Quant oyez prescher le renard, pensez de vos oyes garder [Charles d'Orléans] *a.* 1465.

The motif is found in every conceivable medium: in manuscripts, of course (the *Smithfield Decretals*, London, *c.* 1330–40),[103] and the famous Franco-Flemish *Black Hours* of *c.* 1470,[104] on misericords in Boston (*c.* 1390), Ely (1338 – for further English examples, see below), Basel, Bardowiek, Minden, Kempen, and Kappenberg, and carved on the pulpit in the church at Huckarde near Dortmund.[105] The range of media include a fourteenth-century wall-painting in a house at Krems in Austria;[106] fifteenth-century German tapestry and biscuit-moulds; floor tiles excavated from Christ Church Cathedral, Dublin and a former monastery at Eldena near Greifswald,[107] a fourteenth-century leather strap,[108] and lead badges, such as the one from Salisbury. The inventory of the plate of Louis d'Anjou (1364) includes a fox-bishop with mitre and crozier, and another preaching to geese, while that of Charles V records an ebony fox dressed as a friar kept in his study at the Hotel St Pol.[109]

Figure 9.9

As often as not, however, the scene of the rapacious vulpine preacher was accompanied by that of his comeuppance, and he is seen dangling from a gallows while the birds on which he preyed pull down on the rope. Such is the case on a late fourteenth-century English choir-stall desk-end now in Haddon Hall near Bakewell,[110] on contemporary bench-ends at Brent Knoll in Somerset (Figure 9.9), and on paired misericords at Ludlow (*c.* 1415–25), Bristol Cathedral and Beverley Minster (both *c.* 1520), and paired roof bosses at Bury St Edmunds (1430), and Worcester Cathedral (late fourteenth century), and in several German cathedrals (Brandenburg; Katharinenkirche, Lübeck), while the fourteenth-century Lübeck altar-cloth similarly includes both scenes.

Stories, their heroes, and allusions to them serve many different purposes – entertainment, of course, but also moral instruction, and sometimes, satirical attack, as in the case of a Catholic priest in Annaberg in Saxony who in 1524 found a drawing of a fox in priest's habit left in his pulpit.[111] Narrative is more normally an oral or written medium, so stories represented in art are often concentrated down to a single episode which must stand for the whole, like Gawain's unhappy horse severed in two by the portcullis or King Mark in the tree spying on Tristan and Isolde, and unless we know the story already, there are many medieval and later images we shall miss. Undoubtedly there are many anecdotes and *exempla* still to be recognised in the margins of manuscripts and elsewhere, for the 'Ocean of Story' is vast, and we have but dipped a toe in it here.

TEN

HEARTS AND FLOWERS AND PARROTS: The ICONOGRAPHY OF LOVE

The iconography of love as opposed to sex (and in so far as the two can be separated) was not all 'hearts and flowers', though it certainly was that too, of course, as I shall hope to show. At times, however, when the course of true love did not run smooth, the disappointed lover was at pains to advertise that disappointment by 'wearing the willow', every bit as much as his more fortunate colleague was ready to 'wear his heart on his sleeve'.

SAYING IT WITH FLOWERS

Wearing the Willow

It is a commonplace of Elizabethan literature that, as Drayton put it in *The Muses Elysium* [IV. 1509f.]:

> In love the sad forsaken wight
> The willow garland weareth,

and in *The Faerie Queene*, Spenser similarly referred to 'The willow worne of forlorne paramours' [I.1.v.9],[1] and it is clear that actual garlands or sprigs of willow were demonstratively worn by such disappointed lovers.

Although the proverb dictionaries only attest the expression from the mid-sixteenth century,[2] it is certainly considerably older. A late fifteenth-century poem known variously as 'The Cuckolds' Dance' or 'Sir Corneus', refers to the typical cuckold in the lines 'Garlandes of wylos schuld be fette [fetched] /And sett vpon ther hedes',[3] and more than a century before that, the following poignant couplet is all that survives of a vernacular song recorded in the Anglo-Irish *Red Book of Ossory* (*a*. 1360), where it owes its survival to the fact that it serves as an indication of the tune to which the Latin hymn it prefaces is to be sung:

> Gayneth me no garlond of greene,
> Bot hit ben of wythoues ywroght
> [No garland of green becomes me,
> unless it be made of willows].[4]

The convention was current also in mid-fourteenth-century Wales. In his poem *Siom* (Betrayal), Dafydd ap Gwilym tells how his friends gave him a willow hat to wear as a visible sign of his betrayal by Morfudd.[5] In German the currency of the willow as a symbol of sorrow (not necessarily of disappointed love) is said by Grimm to be dependent on Luther's translation of Psalm 137, and there may well be such biblical influence ultimately behind the European convention. Be that as it may, in Clara Hätzlerin's earlier *Liederbuch*, written in 1471, in a fascinating section entitled 'What various leaves signify', restricted in the main to their significance for lovers, we read this of the willow:

> He who wears willow by his own choice signifies he is lonely and wretched! To him who is instructed to wear it, however, it is a comfort and an earnest confirmation of love. For the willow is a comfort to land by water allowing it to take away with it as little land as possible. That is why it is planted next to the bank.[6]

The young man with his fashionably long shoes (*poulaines*) depicted in this late fifteenth-century 'dotted' print (Figure 10.1) is evidently suffering from the pangs of unrequited love, for his banderole proclaims, in terms as extravagant as his shoes:

> Love is a hard pain,
> Who knows it not,
> Ah! he is fortunate.
> Love will kill me.

The somewhat unspecific plant in the background was perhaps intended to symbolise his sorry condition – as frequently in the art of this era – but I cannot identify it.

Melancholy Columbines, Pensive Pansies

For the fifteenth-century poet Jean Regnier, the columbine, from the accidental similarity of its French name, *ancolie*, to *melancolie*, was the flower of sadness and, incidentally, one of the very puns condemned by Rabelais in the 9th Chapter of *Gargantua*. According to his

Figure 10.1

inventory of 1364, Louis d'Anjou had a cup in the shape of a columbine supported by three feet in the shape of bats – in fact, the French word *ancolie* is from the Medieval Latin name *aquilegia*, 'water-collector', on account of the flower's vase-like petals, and is thus a very fitting form for a cup. Louis further advertised his own fashionable melancholy by wearing a red velvet tunic embroidered with no fewer than 516 columbines.[7]

A German brooch of *c.* 1330, formerly in Stettin but destroyed in the Second World War, showed a pair of lovers inside a cinquefoil frame from the angles of which hung bell-like flowers, described by Lightbown as columbine cups. Though I doubt this identification, the perimeter inscription, a couplet in Low German proclaiming that love will keep the wearer true, is worth quoting:

> Love will make me constant
> therefore I must all life long watch over you.[8]

In the famous *Très Riches Heures* manuscript of the Duc de Berry (*a.* 1416), columbine flowers are again used symbolically by the miniaturists, the office for the Fourth Sunday in Lent being bordered with snails for the Resurrection,[9] and columbines for sadness. Similarly, for the border of the Office of the Dead in the Franco-Flemish *Heures de Boussu* (*c.* 1490), columbines figure along with the forget-me-nots of remembrance, and the pansies of thought (*pensées*), and in 1455 Marie d'Orléans commissioned two garters with gold mounts bearing her device of tears, and pansies for sad thoughts.[10] This particular punning symbolism was still in vogue as late as the performance of *Hamlet*, *c.* 1600, where in Ophelia's famous flower-distribution scene she says, 'And there is pansies, that's for thoughts' (IV.v.174), and when the wife in Chapman's *All Fools* (1604) points to a pansy in her needlework, her jealous husband exclaims, 'O that's for lover's thoughts' (II.i.234).[11]

A particularly good example of late medieval pansy symbolism is the head-and-shoulders portrait of a pensive-looking Spanish lady in the Louvre – she is set against a backdrop of pansies and a banderole inscribed 'I remember that one whom I no longer see.'[12] The National Gallery has a superb early sixteenth-century small Flemish panel depicting a man holding a pansy in one hand and resting his other hand on a skull, clearly this is a *memento mori* and this sitter's thoughts have turned to death (Figure 10.2).[13]

Evergreen Love

Evergreen trees also played an important role in popular iconography. Although they are far

Figure 10.2

from constituting a pair – indeed, they could hardly be more different – the following two emblematic 'jewels' will serve to introduce the lore of the holly and the ivy (for fuller discussion see below). A holly sprig from Salisbury belongs to the humblest kind of personal jewellery, the lead badge. Brian Spencer has suggested that such holly badges 'doubtless became magical talismans when worn for the feast of Christmas, combining, as they did, peasant lore and fable with symbols of Christ's passion'.[14]

A gold pendant found on Rocklea Sands near Poole,[15] on the other hand, is fraught with the graceful imagery of courtly love. In the form of a heart, it is engraved on one side with an ivy leaf and the legend *tristes en plesire* (sadness in pleasure), and on the reverse with serried ranks of tears.[16] Though found in England, it is probably French and dates from the third quarter of the fifteenth century.

Comparisons have been made with a gold reliquary pendant in the form of an ivy-leaf now in the Museo Civico, Cividale, probably made for the marriage of Prince Philip of Taranto, son of Charles II of Anjou, to Tamar Angela in 1294. As John Cherry noted, 'through its clinging nature [ivy] was taken to represent fidelity',[17] and I feel sure, in addition, that we may suspect the influence of popular etymology which may well have seen a link between French *lierre* (ivy), and *lier* ('to bind', that is, in wedlock). In this connexion it is significant that a will made in mid-fifteenth-century York names as one of its bequests, '1 belt of silk . . . with leaves and ivy'.[18] Another clinging plant which attracted this same lovers' symbolism was the woodbine/-bind, as in Chaucer's description of Troilus and Criseyde's embrace:

> And as aboute a tree, with many a twiste,
> Bytrent and writh the swote wodebynde,
> Gan ech of hem in armes other wynde.   [III. 1230ff.]
> [And just as with many a twist the sweet woodbine
> encircles and wreathes itself around the tree,
> so they wind themselves in each other's arms].

Posies

Nowadays, the word *posy* means a small bunch of flowers, but as will be seen from its closeness to the old form of the word for *poetry* (*poesy*), there has been a transfer of sense from the verse dedication originally presented with the flowers to the flowers themselves. The short verses inscribed on rings and other love-gifts, however, *are* still referred to as *posies*.

A charming fifteenth-century lead badge recovered from the Seine in the form of a rosebud (Figure 10.3) still retains its posy, inscribed *GENTIL BOTU* (noble bud). Traces of surviving paint (pink on the petals, green on the sepals and gold on the leaves) show that as well as imitating the sentiments of courtly love in such a humble medium, it also aspired to imitate the colouring of more pretentious jewelled and enamelled brooches.

Figure 10.3

The later Middle Ages enthusiastically took up the fashion for wearing posies – also called *words* or *resouns* in Middle English – not only on jewellery but also on clothing, in a manner not so dissimilar to today's besloganed T-shirts. In the *Instructions to his Son*, composed by Peter Idley in the late 1440s, there is mention of a man who 'hadde a ffreshe cote/Was al to-jagged with poisies on euery side'.[19] Such profusion was evidently felt to be a bit over the top, but there is evidence that verses of an amatory nature might be worn decorously enough on the sleeve. In 1404, for example, Charles d'Orléans had a mantle made with the opening words and music of the song, 'Madame, je suis plus joyeulx', picked out in pearls on the sleeves.[20]

Close inspection of Richart's sleeve in a miniature in the late fourteenth-century manuscript of *Richart et Catelle* by Guillebert de Metz, reveals that it bears the legend *mon:♥: espoire*:[21] A similar sentiment is expressed by the posy on a ring from Brighton, *en espoir ma vye endure*,[22] by that on a ring-brooch now in the British Museum, *vie in espoir*, and the equivalent in English on one from Gloucester, 'Y leve yn hope'.[23] Such messages themselves certainly border on the proverbial – for, as Chaucer says in his contemporary partial translation of that classic of courtly love, the *Roman de la Rose*, 'Nere hope, ther shulde no lover lyve' (Without hope no lover could live),[24] but I suggest that it is more the *siting* of Richart's posy which constitutes the proverb here, for does he not, in fact, 'wear his heart on his sleeve'?

To my knowledge, this proverbial idiom has never been properly investigated. The earliest recorded instance I am aware of is a line in one of the English poems of Charles d'Orléans, dated to *c.* 1440, which reads:

> Madame, y wold bi god alone
> How that myn hert were in yowre sleve[25]

where *in* may perhaps allude to the heart's being embroidered into the sleeve, as in the illuminated example just referred to, or, as elsewhere in fifteenth-century English, it may have the modern meaning *on*.

The Dutch lead badge reproduced as the chapter ornament is in the form of a sleeved arm from which a gauntleted hand emerges holding a falconry lure and with a bird perched on the wrist; furthermore, a small heart is literally pinned to the inner sleeve by an arrow.[26] An inscription under the bird's feet is incomplete but originally read *AMOVR*. In English the idiom of '*pinning* one's heart to one's sleeve' is not found before about 1600, though a writer of 1660 – if his evidence is to be trusted – alludes to 'a good saying of Sir Thomas More, "I will not pin my faith upon any man's sleeve"',[27] and More was beheaded in 1535. Curiously, a line from the opening scene of *Othello* is perhaps of particular relevance to this badge:

> I will wear my heart upon my sleeve
> for daws to peck at.   [variant: doves]

Is this Dutch bird just such a predator exposing the lover's vulnerability?

Other sleeves bearing hearts are to be seen on the beautiful boxwood combs carved in France, *c.* 1500.[28] Whenever their first literary attestation, however, the origin of these pinning expressions is presumably to be found in the practice of wearing someone's favours or colours as a declaration, or 'badge', indeed, of one's amorous or party loyalty, pinned to one's sleeve. Charles d'Orléans' recommendation that the courtly lover should send his mistress 'Some hert, or ring, or lettre or device, Or precious stone', perhaps supports the suggestion that such model or jewelled hearts might be literally pinned to one's sleeve in this way. Chaucer's Troilus did not omit to send Criseyde 'a broche, gold and asure, In which a ruby set was like an herte', and the several representations in late medieval art of a lover handing a small heart to his beloved probably record such symbolic gift-jewels, some perhaps to be pinned to the sleeve as visible signs of the acceptance of another's love.[29]

SAYING IT FROM THE HEART

Be My Valentine

There is some evidence to suggest that Chaucer himself (for example in his *Parliament of Fowls* and *Complaint of Mars*), or else his 'circle', may have been responsible for the establishment of the Valentine's Day convention of choosing one's love for the coming year – at least, no other mention of the custom is demonstrably earlier than his, and it has been suggested that it may have been a courtly love game to read Valentine's Day poems, such as is known to have occurred at the *Cour Amoureuse* set up at the French court on St Valentine's Day 1400, complete with charter and 'King'.[30] A perhaps unique depiction of a Valentine's Day game in action is found in the *bas-de-page* scene of the calendar picture for the month of February in the magnificent *Hours of Adelaide de Savoie*, Duchess of Burgundy, illuminated in Paris *c.* 1460.[31] A lady is seated centrally and holds on her lap a basket into which a single man and four couples are putting or are about to put little slips of paper on which, presumably, their own names are written. Subsequently each member of one sex would draw out one (?colour-coded) slip with the name of a member of the opposite sex written on it. As to the date on which the illuminator envisaged this game being played, however, it has to be admitted that Valentine is not one of the saints listed in the Calendar opposite the illumination, although we may perhaps surmise that the name *Valerien* against the 14th day of February (whose feast-day is the 14 April and who is duly calendared in the present manuscript again on the 13th of that month!), was a slip of the scribe's pen for *Valentin*.

Other Courtly Love Games

We know of several other courtly love games, some of them leading to conclusions far from courtly. The title of one of the latest *fabliaux*, 'The Well-trodden Path', by Jean de Condé (fl. 1313–40), is the punchline of a well-known lovers' game which the ladies and gentlemen decide to play, 'The King Who Does Not Lie', in which a 'Queen' asks questions of a gentleman, the 'King', who is honour-bound not to lie. As early as 1240, the ecclesiastical Council of Worcester in the person of the bishop, Walter Cantilupe, had proscribed the playing of this question-and-answer game in England because of the lascivious spirit which it all too often engendered, as indeed it does in Jean's *fabliau*, where equivocal applications are given to well-known proverbs. A young nobleman who, it is said, 'had hardly any beard, indeed it was little more than the kind of fuzz ladies have in certain places'[32] is obliged, by the rules of the game, to answer the question whether he has ever fathered any children, truthfully. He answers in the negative and is all too readily believed by the proud noblewoman playing the 'Queen', who then humiliates him by quoting the proverb, 'It is easy to judge from the state of the hay, whether the pitchfork is any good.' Similarly obliged by the rules of the game to answer candidly, his direct, uncourtly enquiry as to whether she has any hair between her legs, she has to admit that there is none at all, to which revelation he responds with the proverb, 'Grass doesn't grow on a well-trodden path', hinting at her corresponding *over*-experience in matters sexual.[33]

Books purporting to record such erotic question-and-answer sessions were compiled, entitled *Les Demandes D'Amours*, mostly in manuscript (one English translation entitled *The Demaundes off Love* written in 1487 is now known), but also in print from as early as *c.* 1504.[34] To the same genre belongs Martial d'Auvergne's satirical selection of cases tried in Love's court, entitled *Les Arrêts d'Amour*, written in the early 1460s, which includes a cast-off lover's description of a love-token given him by his lady, very close to the Rocklea Sands heart-pendant discussed above:

> a little gold heart decorated with tears, which he had always worn, and still wore, for love of her, between his flesh and his shirt. . . .[35]

Figure 10.4

Another game, the *Ventes d'Amour* or *Venditions en Amour*, was a sort of instant poem competition in which at its simplest, the Lady, for example, began by feeding her lover the opening line 'I sell you such-and-such', and the lover had then to extemporise four further lines, the first rhyming with her opening line, lines 2 and 3 with each other, and the final line ending in a different sound – but his whole contribution somehow alluding to the subject of love in general, or his love for her, in particular. The types of opening subject chosen, tended to be those typical properties of *amour courtois*, flowers and birds (see *papegault* below).[36]

Love-lace

But another very popular type of oral courtly love game was the riddle. Those written and printed alongside the *Demaundes d'Amour* are, for the most part, far from courtly, and have been thoroughly discussed elsewhere,[37] but occasionally we come across rather more delicate, rhymed riddles accompanied by equally delicate illustration; such is the late fifteenth-century pen-and-ink drawing of the lady seated within a circle of interlace while three gentlemen, her would-be lovers, look on admiringly (Figure 10.4). She issues the riddling challenge inscribed above her head:

> He will win my love
> who can cross the 'lace' [*lacz*] to this side
> without knotting or undoing it
> without passing either over or under it.

It has been suggested that the solution to the riddle as to what it is the young men are striving for, depends on the various contemporary senses of *lacs*, which include 'snare' – both concrete and metaphorical – and 'lace, interlaced ribbon, chain, etc.

and, specifically, *lacs d'amour*.[38] A *las d'amors* is defined as 'strands wound into the shape of a recumbent 8', but it might also mean 'a drawing of interlaced initials', and it is this sense which Professor Baldinger proposes as the solution to the lady's riddle. The first suitor to combine her initials with his in a piece of interlaced penwork (?) will win her love, since he will be with her in a *lacs* (that is, *d'amour*), but will not have transgessed the *lacs* which encircles her.

With the same meaning as *lacs d'amour*, *neu d'amour* (literally love-knot), is found contemporaneously in late fourteenth-century France and England: as an ornamental device

Figure 10.5

in a 1388 inventory of the dukes of Burgundy, and as *love-knotte*, the design 'in the gretter ende' (the head) of 'a ful curious pyn' of gold 'for to festne his hood under his chyn', worn by Chaucer's very worldly Monk.[39] A superb fourteenth-century gold ring in the Lübeck Museum für Kunst und Kunstgeschichte (Figure 10.5) has as its central motif a braided love-knot, a *las d'amors* as just defined,

further secured by a tiny padlock (for padlocks, see below),[40] while at the centre
of a very similar English ring in a Viennese collection the padlock is replaced by a
'portrait-head'.[41]

There is an excellent discussion and collection of *lacs* or *noeuds d'amour* often
taking the form of a trefoil with double-stalk (the two horizontal foils looping
round or through the uprights of the letters), in Margaret Freeman's fascinating
book on *The Unicorn Tapestries*.[42] In the latter part of the fifteenth century
especially, so-called 'friars' knots' as symbols of true love were a universally
popular motif for women's chains and collars: in 1469, for instance, Marguerite of
Brittany had a gold collar enamelled black with the letters *M* and *F* (for her
husband, François), plus the ever-popular pansies enamelled in white and violet.[43]

Curiously the pen-and-ink riddle drawing has further implications for our study
of the iconography of love. The literal English translation of *lacs d'amour* is *love-lace*,
and such a word is, indeed, found (seemingly unremarked) in English fourteenth-
century romances. 'He was nomen [caught] wiþ loue las', we read in *Arthour and
Merlin*,[44] but so indeed, more famously, was Sir Gawain, having accepted the
treacherous Lady's love-token, the *luf-las*, a literal 'lace' (belt), in one sense
(supposedly affording its wearer invulnerability), but also a 'love-*snare*', one of the
earliest meanings of *lace*. Clearly *love-lace* was a Middle English compound for a
love-token in the form of a 'lace', whether in the sense still current of a lace to
keep together two portions of a garment, such as a bodice, or in the sense of an
ornamental cord, used as a belt, most of them, presumably, fairly innocent and
without the drastic implications of the two literary examples quoted.

Hearts and Flowers

There is an implicit riddle in the first illustration to be found in the tiny gem of a
manuscript, itself a love-gift, written by Pierre Sala for Marguerite Bullioud who
was subsequently to become his wife, shortly before 1520.[45] On f. 5v is the
quatrain:

> My heart wants to be in this daisy
> it shall be there whatever the envious say
> and my thoughts shall always serve it
> because it is of all flowers the best.

Facing it on f. 6r is the miniature of a young man placing a heart into a half-open
outsize daisy growing amid pansies – clearly, as we have seen elsewhere,
symbolising Pierre's *pensées* which serve 'the best of all flowers' who is Marguerite,
into which he places his heart. The daisy (Fr. *marguerite*) or the pearl (Lat.
margarita) are inevitably the favourite tokens of those whose beloved is named
Marguerite[46] (and the lady's own badge, indeed). Another such lover was Henri II
d'Albret, King of Navarre, who married Marguerite d'Angoulême (sister of
François Premier) in 1527, and a miniature in a manuscript painted the previous
year depicts him standing in a formal garden holding a daisy and pointing to a
banderole inscribed 'I have found a precious pearl and gathered it to my heart.'[47]

The Daisy Oracle

The engraving reproduced in Figure 10.6 by Melchior Lorch dated 1547 depicts an open book on the pages of which capital letters (starting with the alphabet) are being consulted by a blindfolded young woman in what I take to be some divinatory ritual – perhaps she traces the letters of the name of her future husband?

The extraordinary tapestry reproduced in Colour Plate 18 includes the earliest known depiction of the lovers' divinatory game known to folklorists as the Daisy Oracle.[48] Still current, this refers to the practice of plucking the petals one by one from a daisy saying alternately, '(s)he loves me, (s)he loves me not', and its first literary attestation would seem to be in the *Liederbuch* of Clara Hätzlerin of Augsburg (1471):

Figure 10.6

Whoever wears daisies [literally, 'plucking-flowers'] indicates that he is in doubt whether his love truly loves him! But he who wears them already plucked except for two remaining petals, that means that he will obtain complete justice from his beloved. But he who has only one petal remaining, that means an injustice has happened to him.[49]

This is not quite the 'oracular' practice as we know it today, for here the flower is worn in an ostentatious manner in its plucked state, with only either one or two petals remaining, as an advertisement of one's happiness or otherwise in love, but it clearly attests to a related notion.

The present tapestry must antedate this written record by some forty years. Woven in Strasbourg, it is a fragment of a repeating design which shows two pairs of lovers, and it is the right-hand pair who are 'consulting' the oracle. Whether or not the flower was intended as a daisy, it had nine petals originally, but three have already been pulled off and lie on the ground. Given an odd number of petals and assuming the questioning of the flower began as in present-day English with '(s)he loves me', then a happy pronouncement is assured, whether it is the young man alone who seeks this reassurance – he is shown in the act of pulling off another petal – or both lovers taking turns. The unicorn that stands behind the man would appear to be a good omen, given its association with chastity, but the corresponding ape behind the woman is at least equivocal, apes being regarded as lascivious – perhaps the two beasts symbolise the tension in the relationship which has driven the lovers to try this divination in the first place. The tree that separates the two pairs of lovers has clearly recognisable bindweed twining round its trunk – as with the ivy discussed above, this is a good sign, and suggests an intimate closeness and growing together.

But the right-hand couple are also involved in a strange symbolic ritual. The lady is grafting a branch, from which hang three pairs of clasped hands in the well-known gesture of fidelity, to the trunk of an elder tree. She says, 'I graft fidelity onto this elder here', while her partner who seems to point at her act says, somewhat ominously perhaps, 'I hope you will not regret it.' The elder has a symbolic significance here too, for at this period *holder* (modern, *Holunder*) was also used to mean 'lover'.

There seem to be no similarly early references to the 'daisy-oracle' type of love-divination in either English or French, but a similar practice is attested even earlier in the works of the German *Minnesänger*. Both Walther von der Vogelweide, writing *c.* 1200, and Heinrich von Meissen (1250–1318), refer to the practice of measuring a grass-stalk (*halm*).[50] Mieder explains the procedure as 'a children's game which basically consists of measuring off a blade of grass with the thumb and index fingers while alternating the right and the left hand and saying, 'she does [love me], she does not, she does, she does not', etc. A clearly related game existed in late medieval Wales, as poems by Iolo Goch (fl. 1345–97), his slightly older contemporary, Dafydd ap Gwilym, and the fifteenth-century Ieuan ap Rhydderch, testify. It was called 'Nuts in my hand', and whether the number of nuts left in the player's hand was odd or even, decided whether or not the loved one was faithful – only an odd number guaranteed that one was truly loved.[51]

Weighing Fidelity

Last seen before the Second World War, a poignant fragment of Strasbourg tapestry woven *c.* 1500 depicted a young woman sitting in a *hortus conclusus* (enclosed love-garden), wearing a chaplet of bittersweet, the woody nightshade (*solanum dulcamara*), and holding out a pair of scales in the heavier pan of which was more bittersweet, and in the lighter, gold.[52] Although the tapestry had been cut down and the young woman's lover was missing, his banderole was preserved, and read *Je lenger ie lieber bin ich hold*, which might be rendered approximately, 'I love you more each day' but also puns on one of the vernacular names for the bittersweet, *Je-länger-je-lieber* 'the longer the better/more loved', explained thus by the botanist Hieronymus Bock in his herbal of 1531:

> The outer stem of this plant is of such a nature that the more it is chewed in the mouth, the sweeter and lovelier the taste, at first however it is quite bitter and ill-tasting.[53]

The tapestry banderole continues, 'she weighs the silver and the gold'. The woody nightshade is also still known in German as *Bittersüß*, like the equivalent English name *bittersweet* (used first in Turner's *Herbal* of 1568), translating the Latin *dulcamara*, but the fact that its silver flowers outweighed the gold pieces, belied the young man's words and, in this late medieval language of flowers, signalled to us that for her this love would decline into bitterness.

Winged Hearts and Flowers

But to return to Pierre Sala's book; a few pages further on (f. 13r) two women are depicted stretching a bird-snaring net across a clearing in woodland into which winged hearts fly and are thus caught, The quatrain on the opposite f. 12v reads:

> Pleasant Mien and Courteous Manner
> at the corner of the wood have stretched out their net
> waiting for the more attractive hour
> when an unsteady flying heart may pass that way.

The names of the two allegorical ladies and, indeed, the entire quatrain (with minor adaptations) are taken from a verse in that classic of late *amour courtois*, René d'Anjou's *Livre du Cuer d'Amour espris* (1457), a stanza said to have been inscribed at the foot of one of the six tapestries in Venus's chamber.[54] In less courtly art, a decade or so later, German artists use this same motif of the fowling-net beside which a beautiful woman sits as the bait, to lure men or fools to their doom – the contemporary Zurich table-top painted by Hans Herbst is so ungallant as to reverse the sex-roles, showing a male fowler catching women who have been attracted not by his person, but by the coins he has strewn on the ground as bait.[55]

A tapestry which sounds intriguingly similar and must somehow belong in this context is recorded in an inventory of Henry VIII's possessions as being among the 'hangings of tapestry olde and some worne' at his manor of Beddington, thus:

> 1 pece having a Quene in a grene gowne with redde hartes uppon it with a table having a face in it, two fooles, lyinge in a nette.[56]

Of course, one cannot be certain from such a relatively vague description, but the mysterious 'table having a face in it' is perhaps the inventory-maker's attempt at making sense of a shut clap-net lying flat on the ground with the face of one of the ensnared staring up through it; another possibility which might explain why only the *face* is mentioned, and might further suggest some relationship to the winged hearts type, is that the tapestry depicted the men about to be snared in the form of winged heads only.[57]

The earliest manuscript of René d'Anjou's *Livre du Cuer d'Amour espris* is sumptuously illustrated[58] and one illustration depicts Amour, God of Love, plucking the poet's heart from the royal body while he sleeps, which then becomes the personified knight Cueur, and goes on a quest for the lady of René's dreams, Sweet Grace. The illuminator shows us Cueur as a knight in full armour on a steed whose bard is decorated with winged hearts. The knight's shield bears as its device three forget-me-nots, while his helmet crest is another winged heart encircled by a wreath of pansies, the latter, as we have seen, once again punningly symbolising his *amoureuses pensees* (loving thoughts). At one point in his quest he is led by Dame

Melancholy to a narrow bridge, to cross which he must joust against the Black Knight whose helmet-crest, and the device he bears on his shield, is the marigold (*soussye* punning on *souci*, 'sorrow'), while – and we have noted other examples of this symbolism above – his helmet is also wreathed with columbines (*ancolie* for *melancolie*). This same punning 'language of flowers' is employed by a woman abandoned by her lover, who sings a chanson beginning 'If, due to liars I have lost my love' and tells the nightingale to shut up (*Tes toy*), suggesting instead that he bring her *presans De soucy, pensee, encolie* as more befitting her mood![59]

Another significant instance of the winged heart is found on the important Regensburg Town Hall tapestry (*c.* 1390). In one of the roundels a young man holds out a winged heart (his own?), which a woman wearing a crown pierces with an arrow, while the scene is surrounded by an inscription which reads:

> my heart suffers pain,
> pull Love's arrow out of me.

Also of great interest, confirming the suggestion made below as to the erotic milieu in which the bird belongs, adjacent to the roundel in question, a pair of addorsed parrots with 'the long tail split to the base, as it often is in aviaries'[60] and one of which is shown with the distinctive collar, hold a leaf in their beaks, their heads resting beneath a crown – precisely as in the popinjay badges discussed below.[61]

There are also English examples of the winged heart as the symbol of erotic love, in a mid-fifteenth-century manuscript of *The Canterbury Tales*, for example, in which the Virtues and Vices of *The Parson's Tale* are illustrated, and *Charite* (Love), holds a sceptre in one hand and in the other a flaming, winged heart.[62] A small lead badge recovered from the Thames foreshore in the form of a head springing from winged shoulders with arms which hold a crowned heart, is one of those equivocal devices which could quite possibly represent an angel bearing the Sacred Heart, but given the iconography of the winged God of Love, might just as well have been a lover's badge.

The great popularity of the heart as a device even led to the production of heart-shaped manuscripts, of which an illuminated songbook in the Bibliothèque Nationale in Paris is the best known,[63] and a portrait bust of a young man in the National Gallery, London, clearly represents him as a lover, for he is shown reading from just such another little heart-shaped book, undoubtedly a love-gift.[64]

Love-Magic

What must surely be the most spectacular representation of late medieval heart symbolism is to be found on a late fifteenth-century panel painting now in Leipzig, but probably produced in the Cologne region, and usually referred to as the Leipzig *Liebeszauber* (Love-Magic). We see a naked woman striking sparks from a flint, which shower down onto the wax model of a heart inside an opened casket – this ritual of love-magic seems to have had the desired effect, for coming through the doorway behind her is a young man, presumably her longed-for lover, successfully conjured into her presence by the force of the charm (Colour Plate 19).

We learn from contemporary treatises that a woman anxious to know who her future husband will be can, with certain magical rites performed in 'cultic nakedness', make his image appear in the doorway or even summon him in person.[65]

But let us not overlook the central metaphor being enacted here: as the sparks fall onto the wax heart, it melts – 'the heart melts', as we still say. This is sympathetic magic: she performs the ritual, that the heart which was 'hardened against' her, should melt. A contemporary parallel is perhaps afforded by a design on the Duke of Saxony's horse-bard, worn at a tournament in Jena in 1487, depicting an elegantly dressed young woman, left hand upraised in mid-gesture, speaking the ritual words over a heart burning on a fire.[66]

A roughly contemporary late medieval English instance of this metaphor of the heart melting is to be found in Stephen Hawes' *Passetyme of Pleasure* (1509):

> Harde is the heart that no love hath felt
> Nor for no love wyl than encline and melt.[67]

Interestingly, the earliest examples of the metaphor – in English, at least – belong to the language of Christian mysticism, but the image is, of course, much older than Christianity. In the immediately post-classical era, it was St Augustine who described the 'swirling mists' of sexual desire and its power to reduce the human heart to 'molten wax', but something very similar to the subject of our painting is described in Virgil's eighth *Eclogue* (itself based on one of the *Idylls* of the Greek poet Theocritus), where Amaryllis melts wax in a fire and thereby successfully draws home her reluctant lover, Daphnis.

There are at least three examples of other love-magic rituals recorded by Hans Vintler in the extraordinary interpolation of contemporary Germanic superstitions into his translation of Leoni's *Fiori di virtu* entitled *Die Pluemen der tugent* (the Flowers of Virtue) made in *c.* 1411.[68] The woodcut in the early printed edition (Augsburg, 1486) which illustrates the passage '. . . some sorceresses who keep vigil during the time of the star Venus for love',[69] depicts a kneeling man with one arm upraised who looks back over his shoulder – presumably a deliberately magical posture – at the star, though it seems unlikely that the 'evening star' would be known by the Latin name *Venus* to the populace – it is perhaps Vintler's own usage. Another illustration shows a kneeling woman digging up a flower. From the text it is apparent that it is meant to be vervain, but the woodcut artist has signally failed to convey a realistic likeness of that plant:

> Some people have the notion
> that the plant vervain
> makes people fall in love with one another
> if it is dug up at the summer solstice.[70]

Curiously, in England at least, this aphrodisiac property of vervain seems not to be attested before the late nineteenth century: 'In many rural districts, Vervain is still regarded as a plant possessing magical virtues as a love philtre.'[71]

The Tortured Heart – Sacred and Profane Love

Courtly love was, of course, a game that was played with a greater or lesser degree of seriousness throughout our period. The well-known woodcut print designed by Casper of Regensburg *c.* 1485 depicts a young man kneeling before his all-but-naked beloved (who adopts an attitude very similar to the fair magician of the Leipzig panel), surrounded by no fewer than sixteen hearts all undergoing various horrific tortures: pierced by hook, knife, arrow or spear, caught in mouse-trap, lobster-pot or salt-canister, burning on a fire or griddle, pinched by tongs, sawn in half, crushed in a press, etc. A similar conception lies behind a pen-and-ink drawing by the early sixteenth-century Swiss artist Urs Graf, known as *Die Liebesquälen*,[72] in which a naked woman piercing her own breast with a sword, stands on a large heart which is being assaulted in many of the same ways depicted in the woodcut, including being sawn in half.

Although some doubt has now been cast over the authenticity of the entire class of small caskets traditionally known as *Minnekästchen* (love-caskets), a fifteenth-century Swiss example has one of its side-panels also carved with the motif of a heart sawn half through by a two-handed saw. Another contemporary Swiss casket depicts a lady grating a heart into a mortar, while her gleeful banderole reads 'this heart of yours suffers pain', to which the young man looking on can only plead, 'have mercy on me most beloved maiden', while an Alsatian casket carved *c.* 1400 includes the fearsome image of a lady hammering a heart more to her liking on an anvil, as her banderole informs us: 'This I make to my liking.'[73] Precisely the same scene is found on the certainly authentic early fifteenth-century biscuit-mould described in Chapter 1.

I know of two other examples of this gruesome saw image in other media, one of which is religious. A little lead mirror-case found on the site of the Steelyard in London, and probably German, therefore, an accomplished piece of openwork casting, is inscribed *ave maria gracia plena* around the mirror, and is surmounted by an ornamental cresting below which two devils work a two-handed saw into a heart, presumably that of the Virgin – the whole scene topped by a crown.[74] The use of this scene in religious iconography too, hints at a possible derivation, in some cases, from scenes of martyrdom such as that of St Cyricus on the twelfth-century painted altar-frontal in the Museum of Catalan Art, Barcelona, which shows the saint being sawn vertically in half by two men using a similar saw.[75] Of course, Marian iconography itself might be thought to provide a sufficient precedent in illustrations of the Seven Sorrows of the Virgin, particularly the scene of her heart pierced by the symbolic sword as she stands at the foot of the Cross. Evidence of similar cross-fertilisation or, rather, the availability of such iconography to illustrate divine as well as human love, is afforded by a large fifteenth-century woodcut sheet in Berlin which depicts the human heart, from which flowers sprout, burning on a fire stoked by the Virgin and the Eagle of St John. The heart is held in position at the end of a long chain by God the Father, and pierced by an arrow fired by Christ, while two angels hover above it with a crown (for the flowers and crown see further below).[76]

The Heart in the Press

As we have suggested above, it is sometimes difficult to distinguish between the secular and the religious use of some of these lovers' motifs, at least without careful consideration of the context and, specifically, of the other motifs with which they keep company. The well-known and widespread motif of Christ in the wine-press, for example, was borrowed into the world of fool-iconography (albeit in the service of religious polemic) in Thomas Murner's *Von dem grossen Lutherischen Narren*, (Strasbourg, 1522) in the woodcut illustrating lines 2714f., 'How lately . . . double fools are pressed from the great fool.'[77]

The device of a heart being crushed in a press, found as a stamped ornament on early sixteenth-century ceramic wares from the region of Beauvais, has been interpreted as a Christian emblem,[78] but there is no evidence that this was intended as the heart of Christ and, in fact, on closer inspection, what the author saw as the nails of the Crucifixion, depicted above the pressed heart in the roundel on an apothecary jar, can be seen to be crossed *arrows*, a type of missile which does not figure as any part of the *Arma Christi*. Indeed, as we shall see on the boxwood comb discussed below, and as the existence of several lead badges of different sizes depicting a heart (sometimes crowned) pierced by crossed arrows confirms, the motif seems rather to derive from the iconography of courtly love, and the heart-in-the-press also features in the entirely secular context of the tortures undergone by the lover's heart in the Casper woodcut just mentioned. The same author reproduces two French biscuit-moulds of the device, one of which also features a flower beneath the heart and a perimeter inscription (unfortunately illegible),[79] the words of which are punctuated by what are either lovers' knots or stylised quatrefoils. Equally interesting is an impression taken from a similar mould of a heart pierced by crossed arrows through which a two-handed saw cuts and out of the top of which a flower grows,[80] further confirmation that the pressed heart device on these Beauvais ceramics is unlikely to have a religious import.

A superb late medieval pendant of tapering square section found only a few years ago at West Acre, Norfolk, again makes use of the familiar repertoire of courtly love motifs (Figure 10.7).[81] At the thick end it is ornamented with four hearts-in-presses with four stylised quatrefoils beneath (or trueloves – see below), and at the thin end, four stylised tears. A dagger suite, made somewhere in Upper Germany *c*. 1500 and inscribed with courtly love mottoes such as 'I am in pain' and 'Happy in suffering', and ornamented with various engraved and nielloed figures, includes an awl, the handle of which bears on one side a chained heart surmounted by a crown, and on the other a heart pierced by an arrow in a press.[82] A contemporary copper counter issued by Maximilian I also bears on one side a heart in a press surmounted by a crown and under it a lover's knot and the mysterious initials M.H.I.V.F.G., the first of which have been plausibly interpreted as standing for the opening of a courtly lover's lament, 'My heart is . . .'! On the other side is the image of the philosopher Aristotle ridden by Phyllis (see Chapter 11).[83]

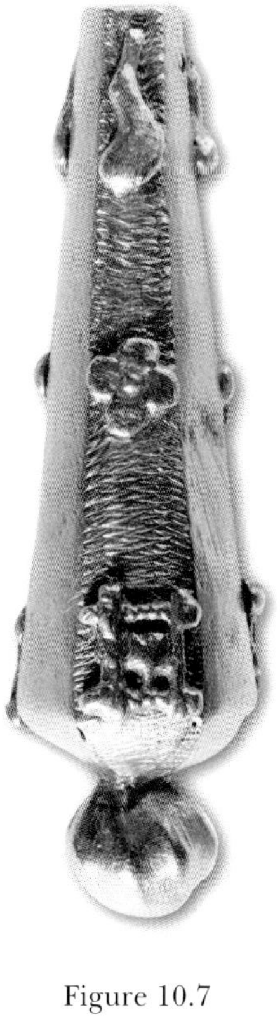

Figure 10.7

The Heart Pierced by the Arrow of Love

Undoubtedly the most common form of heart attack, however, is the still familiar piercing or shooting of the heart with an arrow. In an early sixteenth-century English poem which opens 'Alas, a thousand sith alas',[84] a despondent lover says farewell to the various tokens of love. Among those he enumerates is 'the baw bond and the arow therein', that is, a brooch in the shape of a bent bow with an arrow in it, which suggests that the simple lead badge of a drawn bow found at Salisbury might well be just such a love-token.[85] The version which is augmented by a crowned horseshoe is perhaps an example of adding a good-luck charm to a love token. A delightful instance of this symbolism is an early fourteenth-century North German brooch in the form of a letter 'e' to which is applied a little figure of the God of Love holding arrows in both hands, that in his right hand pointing at the breast of the wearer. Furthermore, the upper surface of the brooch and the figure on it is hinged and lifts to reveal a secret inscription, 'Fair Lady, may I ever be close to thy heart'. Because of the nature of the fastening, this inscription remained hidden except when the wearer was in the act of attaching the brooch to her costume.[86]

The heart pierced by an arrow is found on typical French mid-fourteenth-century *amour courtois* ivories,[87] and the cheap contemporary English and Dutch badges in the shape of two sleeved arms surmounted by a crown and terminating in clasped hands which hold, or are themselves pierced by an arrow which transfixes a heart.[88] Significantly this undoubtedly secular badge yet forms a crowned letter 'M', the emblem of the Virgin Mary.[89] A rather more spectacular case of such parallelism is the crude fifteenth-century silver badge inscribed *AMOVRS* in the form of a crowned 'm' with a man and woman standing under the 'arches' of the letter, found at Nieuwlande in Holland,[90] which may be compared to the magnificent jewel of the same form probably made in France *c.* 1400 belonging to New College, Oxford, depicting the Annunciation, with the Archangel and the Virgin standing beneath the 'arches' of the 'm' and the symbolic lily pot placed on the central minim.[91] But more basic lead badges in the form of hearts pierced by an arrow, some crowned, some not, have also been recovered from the drowned village of Nieuwlande.[92]

The Holly and the Ivy, the Flower and the Leaf (and the Orpine)

The well-known holly and ivy carols have been shown to have been originally examples of a 'game-song' in which holly (with its pricks) symbolised the menfolk,[93] and ivy the women, and which 'strongly suggest a dramatic game during which [the carol] would be sung, and in which the feminine party of Ivy would be excluded from a company representing those in the "hall" and would be grouped by itself "without the door"'. The medieval surname *Ivimey* may recall a maiden (Middle English *may*) who had acted her part (particularly memorably, presumably?) on the side of Ivy in such a game.[94] Stevenson's *The Twelve Months* (1661), still alludes to this traditional gender symbolism in the line, 'Great is the contention of holly and ivy, whether master or dame wears the breeches', with which compare from a fifteenth-century carol:

> Nay, Iuy, nay, hyt shal not be, iwys;
> Let Holy hafe the maystry, as the maner ys.

We might also recall that when the Green Knight gatecrashes King Arthur's Christmas games, he carries his fearsome green axe in one hand, but in the other a holly bough (*holyn bobbe*), which he explains as a sign that he comes in peace. The narrator's seemingly redundant remark, that holly is 'grattest in grene when greuez ar bare' (literally, 'greatest in green when groves are bare'), is no mere piece of alliterative padding, in my opinion, but a deliberate allusion to the traditional Christmas contention between the holly and the ivy – the Green Knight, not surprisingly, being a partisan of holly.[95]

In the light of the two competing teams of participants in this Christmas game, it may well be that the little lead holly badge mentioned above belonged to one of holly's partisans, 'defending' the Christmas hall against the incursion of the female ivy party. A set of tapestries belonging to Mary, Queen of Scots was 'maid with the figures of personnages quha [who] cuttis the holine', according to an inventory of her effects in Holyrood House taken in 1567, and contained no fewer than *14 peces* – the suite presumably depicted the cutting of the holly-boughs for use in just such a ritual game.[96] Once cut and perhaps after playing their part in the game, the boughs were undoubtedly used for decoration – one continuation of the *Brut* chronicle records that in 1445, just after St Paul's steeple was burnt by lightning:

> at the Ledenhall in Cornhill of London, a standard of tre was set in myddys of the pavement fast in the grounde, nayled with holme and Ive, for disport of Cristmasse to the peple of the Cite.

It too was cast down by the storm.[97] Before the advent of the Puritans, even churches were commonly garlanded with holly and ivy at Christmas. The accounts of St Michael's Church in Oxford, for example, record *iid* paid 'For yvy and holy' in 1444–6, and a generation later the parish wardens are still paying the same amount *Pro holy et hyve*.[98]

If human beings might be divided between holly and ivy according to sex, birds were also made to adopt one or the other plant, but they were divided according to species. The fifteenth-century carol quoted above says that:

> Holy hath byrdys, a ful fayre flok,
> The nyghtyngale, the poppynguy, the gayntyl lauyrok.

Against the nightingale, the *popinjay* (probably not 'parrot' here – as the context suggests native woodland species – but the later-attested meaning, 'green woodpecker') and the lark, ivy can only muster 'the howlat, that kreye, "How, how!"' – an early association of the bird and the plant which in the form, 'An owl in an ivy-bush', was soon to become proverbial.[99] The enmity of the owl and the nightingale is, of course, already found in the eponymous early Middle English poem where the owl is also already associated with ivy: she 'sits on old stoc . . . mid iui al bigrowe' (on an old stump . . . all overgrown with ivy).[100] An early sixteenth-century version of the carol written into Richard Hill's commonplace-book, substitutes the *thristilcok* (the thrush) for the lark, and makes no mention of the nightingale – it does, however, appear at first sight, to even up the odds by making the *woode-coluer* (the wood-pigeon), feed off ivy's berries, but then:

> *She liftith vp her tayll, and she cakkes or she go;*
> *She wold not for [a] hundred poundes serue Holy soo.*
> [She lifts up her tail and shits before she goes,
> She would not for a hundred pounds serve holly so.][101]

A much more elevated version of the type of folk-game implicit in the holly and ivy carols was the courtly adherence to the parties of the Flower and the Leaf, apparently imported into England from France, and referred to in passing by Chaucer in the prologue to his *Legend of Good Women*. 'Whethir ye [lovers] ben with the leef or with the flour', and perhaps implicitly in 'The Knight's Tale' (see below), but celebrated above all in the eponymous mid-fifteenth-century poem, 'The Floure and the Leafe'.[102]

Another plant which features on a piece of lovers' jewellery is the orpine. A fifteenth-century ring found at Cawood depicted two orpine plants joined by a true-love knot, with the inscription 'My betrothed is willing'. The stalks of the plants were described as 'bent to each other, in token that the parties represented by them were to come together in marriage', that is, according to the popular belief,[103] and inside the ring were the words 'Joy. Love. Passion'. Last seen in 1801, what may be the same ring is now in a private collection, but if so, the interior inscription reads 'Joy without end'.[104]

The Parrot – Bird of Love?

In one of the famous early fourteenth-century *Harley Lyrics*, known as 'Annot and John', the poet compares his beloved to various birds: she is a *trewe tortle*, but also a *papeiai* (parrot) – a somewhat unexpected lover's bird for us! What was this poet trying to say? The turtle-dove, of course, was renowned for being loyal and chaste, but the medieval encyclopedists, citing Aristotle as their authority, believed the parrot to be 'an excessively lecherous bird', and 'counterfeiting the gestures of a lover, eager for copulation'.[105] At the end of the Middle Ages this tradition was certainly familiar to Skelton who, in his attack on Wolsey of 1521, called *The Popingay* in the poet's own list of his works, makes several references to the bird's lascivious nature.[106] Its dubious reputation as the symbol of erotic rather than sentimental love, is particularly evident in fifteenth-century art.

When Guillaume de Machaut met his beloved for the first time she wore a blue hood decorated with green parrots (the only type known to the Western Middle Ages), and in an era when colour symbolism played a much more important role in life than it does today, he rejoiced because green signified new love.[107] One of the verses in a *Vente d'Amours* (see above) opens, 'I "sell" you the green popinjay', showing once again how the popinjay sprang naturally to the mind of the courtly lover.[108]

Despite their dubious reputation, popinjays were evidently a popular feature of late medieval applied art. In the fourteenth-century romance of *Sir Degrevant*, bed-hangings are described decorated with popinjays and trueloves,[109] and the fourteenth-century poem 'Purity' describes gold cups with embossed lids chased with foliage, 'Pyes and papeiayes purtrayed withinne'.[110] Contemporary inventories and wills confirm the relatively common occurrence of these decorative motifs. An inventory of tapestries in the Flemish castle of Middelbourg taken in 1477 records a set of white damask hangings embroidered with branches and parrots, with a lady in the middle and parrots in a cage.[111] Popinjays were similarly a conventional subject for brooches in late medieval royal circles. The French queen, Jeanne de Boulogne (d. 1360), had a brooch decorated with clusters of three pearls and a lady holding a popinjay at its centre, and in 1400 the English royal jewels included a brooch of a young lady among white flowers holding a popinjay.[112] But humbler, plebeian popinjays are also known.

Several lead badges depict a parrot wearing a collar with a ring and bearing an inscription, one found in Amsterdam, with the identifying inscription *papagaei*.[113] Elsewhere I have reconstructed the legend on the English badges as the courtly French 'Popinjay, jolly May', associating the badge with the month of May, the lovers' month *par excellence*, of course, and it is indeed in French that the best parallels which unite all three elements of this inscription are to be found. A song from a collection printed in Paris 1515x25 which opens *Voicy le may* continues:

> The lovely month of May
> So soft, lively and joyful,
> Sweet and gay,
> Green as a popinjay,
> Loving, gracious.[114]

Another good parallel is afforded by a verse in Maximien's *L'Advocat des Dames de Paris* of *c.* 1500,[115] which opens:

> As for the first of May,
> after we've planted the may
> at our sweethearts' . . .
> whose hearts are gay
> and livelier than a popinjay. . . .

The rhythmical rhyming phrase *Papege, iollys May* on the English parrot badges invites comparison with the similar rhyming legends borne by the more pretentious jewellery and personal seals discussed below.

Other more equivocal parrots accompany the fashionably dressed lady playing the lute in a late fifteenth-century engraving by Wenzel von Olmutz, who sings 'I too long greatly for you, my dear love, believe me', and her contemporary, the entirely naked young woman whom the artist has captured in the middle of carrying out the ritual of sympathetic love-magic in the painting in Leipzig discussed above. On the Leipzig panel the parrot perches on a dish of comfits, but the banderole with which the painter has provided him is unfortunately and frustratingly blank. The connexion of the parrot with love is further brought out by the entry under *Sittich* (parrot) from a contemporary German *Losbuch* (a book which explained the significance of the particular lot drawn), verses 6 and 7 of which read:

Heart and also sense
you have set on Love

You are faithful with constancy
So you must suffer love and pain.[116]

Another extraordinary German production is an embroidery of *c.* 1460, housed in the Germanisches Nationalmuseum, in which a hound on a leash held by a young man blowing a hunting-horn drives a stag towards a young woman.[117] In the four corners of the piece are two dogs and two birds, one of which is a parrot, and all except the stag are equipped with banderole texts. To the boast of the huntsman's bird, 'I am a falcon fair and proud', the lady's parrot replies much more humbly that '(?) the intention before God is what counts'. The more obviously erotic tradition survived into the German Renaissance, however, in a drawing by Virgil Solis dated 1540 depicting a naked woman apparently out hawking but with a parrot instead of a falcon perched on her wrist. It has been suggested that he is pecking at her arm and that she represents one of the Five Senses (Feeling), although the drawing is labelled *DANT*, that is 'a trifle, bauble, geegaw, worthless thing' and also 'idle chatter' – this last especially appropriate to parrots, of course.[118]

The Truelove

A stray, world-weary English quatrain from the fourteenth century, found in a well-known Latin handbook for preachers, the *Fasciculus Morum*, is most interesting testimony to the contemporary practice of wearing these little amatory lead tokens, the disproportionate importance of which, I have been at pains to stress throughout this work:

Trewe loue among men that most is of lette	[of late]
In hattes, in hodes, in porses is sette.	[in hoods]
Trewe loue in herbers spryngeth in May,	[arbours]
Bote trewe loue of herte went is away.	[is turned away][119]

There must be a punning reference here to the plant known as the *truelove* or herb paris (*paris quadrifolia*), given and worn as a love-token, and presumably some, at least, of the quatrefoil flowers found on humble lead badges, such as that from London in the form of a hand wearing a lover's gimmel-ring and holding out a spray of flowers on which one quatrefoil remains,[120] may have had this significance.

The tendency towards 'moralisation' of such symbolic flowers is well illustrated in the case of the truelove. In the romance *Emare* of the late fourteenth century there is a lengthy description of a tapestry portraying four pairs of lovers, heroes and heroines of other romances, which includes the lines:

For they loueden hem wyth honour,	[*for* = because]
Portrayed they wer wyth trewe-loue-flour,[121]	

where the tapestry background, probably 'powdered' with trueloves, is seen as a proof that their loves were true – the presence of such symbolic background flowers is certainly attested in late medieval Swiss tapestry.[122] As Sir Gawain rides out on his quest, the poet notes that part of his *vrysoun* (the band of silk attached to the back of the helm to prevent it from slipping forwards) is embroidered with *tru-lofez*, paired with that other equivalent symbol of faithful love, the turtle-dove.[123]

One of the Paston letters, undated but probably written in 1445,[124] describes the armorial shield of the Catfield family which the writer also draws. The sketch shows what he calls 'iii bukkeles of syluere' with 'floweres of syluer on the bukkelis mad of iiij lyke a trewlove'. This is of interest firstly, in showing that in the mid-fifteenth century, at least, any conventional quatrefoil might be understood as a truelove flower, and secondly, for the design of the *bukkeles* themselves. Although the writer calls them 'buckles', they look much more like ring-brooches, and of a specific, archaeologically recognisable type, popular around 1300 in Northern England and Southern Scotland.[125] Similarly, a man in the late fourteenth-century poem 'The Parliament of the Three Ages' wears a richly ornamented 'chaplet With trayfoyles and trewloves of full triede perles',[126] which also seems to confirm the equivalence, *trewlove* = quatrefoil (and *vice versa*), in the way that mention of the truelove follows on directly from the *trayfoyle* (trefoil).

A fourteenth-century alliterative poem entitled by its modern editors, 'The Quatrefoil of Love',[127] composed originally in Northern dialect, but modernised and 'Southernised' by de Worde, who printed it *c.* 1510, as *The .iiii. leues of the trueloue*,[128] is a Christian moralisation of the courtly lovers' interpretation of the plant as represented, for instance, by the poem which opens, 'I loue so sore I wolde fayne descerne', recorded in a manuscript of the second quarter of the sixteenth century.[129] This secular poem names each of the four leaves in turn as 'desyre of affection, mekenes or elles humylyte, audacyte or boldenes, and kyndnes most pure', but the 'rote wheryn the leves may be fastenyd . . . stydfastnes that ys sure thys rote I may call', whereas the poem published by de Worde interprets the four leaves as representing the three persons of the Trinity plus the Virgin. It is in this context that the extraordinary replacement of the head of God the Father by a veined quatrefoil in the censored image of the Trinity, to be found in Trinity College, Cambridge must be seen (Figure 2.3).

The Flowering Heart and the Forget-me-not

There are many examples now known of a type of lead badge which depicts a flowering heart, a solid or perhaps merely outline heart, from which spring two or more four-petalled flowers, a motif also found on some ten silver finger-rings from the decades either side of 1400 (such as the gimmel-ring referred to above), a device which makes one of its earliest appearances on two of the large number of seals and seal-impressions bearing the motif, dated 1323.[130] As John Cherry notes, this motif 'seems to have been one of those ambiguous medieval devices that could equally represent religious as well as secular love'.[131] A painting by Hans Mielich dated 1545 of the future Duke Albrecht V of Bavaria shows him wearing a pendent locket enamelled with just such a flowering heart held between male and female hands from which forget-me-nots sprout,[132] demonstrating that the type survived into the Renaissance.

The absence of examples of the forget-me-not as a lovers' token in the English Middle Ages is probably due to the fact that the flower (*Myosotis palustris*) was relatively unfamiliar (not being part of the native flora at this period) and, indeed, the modern name seems not to be recorded before its inclusion in an early printed *Introduction to French* (*c.* 1532), where 'A flour of forget me nat' translates *une fleur de ne moubliez mye*, but is far from suggesting that such an English name was current. Although not indigenous, the flower itself was, of course, known to the English; it was, for example, the device of the English king, Henry IV, who bought hundreds of gold forget-me-nots from goldsmiths in the 1390s for use as dress-spangles.[133] The modern English lovers' name for the flower is of continental origin. Grimm quotes a most interesting fifteenth-century text which explains the symbolism of the *vergiz min niht*:

> there is a little flower called forget-me-not, which will recommend itself to him who would be of joyous mood, it is worn by him who at no time wants to forget his love.

From the many examples in 'Germanic' art, I must mention the presentation of the flower by a young man to his beloved in a full-length double portrait painted in Ulm *c.* 1470 – he wears a further spray of the flower in the front of a circlet around his head. This idyllic young lovers' tryst is shockingly, brutally justaposed with a panel, originally on the reverse, of what is presumably the same pair portrayed as living corpses in their winding-sheets eaten by worms, toads and so on. No more shocking *memento mori* could be imagined.[134] Appearing as an infinitely kinder reverse to the portrait bust of a young man painted by Hans Suess von Kulmbach, *c.* 1510, is the young woman – his fiancée? – who with hair unbound sits in an open window with her cat and plaits a garland of forget-me-nots (Colour Plate 20), and says, *ICH PINT MIT, VERGIS MEIN NIT* (I bind (you) with forget-me-not), a poignant and quasi-magical act. In a piece of tapestry woven in Basel in the 1470s, with a similarly ritual feel to it, a pair of lovers meet beneath an elder-tree in full bloom.[135] The young man swears 'My beloved/The elder has possessed my heart, so that now I have forgotten my pain.' The young woman who wears a chaplet of forget-me-not herself, offers one to him with the words, 'If you are able to love, beloved, you should wear the forget-me-not' – with the same pun on the name of the tree that we have noted above. On a cushion cover woven in Strasbourg in the early sixteenth century, another young woman sits plaiting a garland which includes forget-me-nots for a young man. Perhaps somewhat ominously her banderole reads:

> So you may be spared the pain of worldly suffering
> take this garland from me here.

He responds with:

> Tender lady, how may I deserve/be worthy of
> this chaplet for me today?

The vague feeling of unease about this relationship is only strengthened when we notice the bittersweet plant the designer has placed between the two. Similar suspicions must be harboured about the couple from a sadly damaged hanging woven in Basel around 1490. Before a garden wall against which honeysuckles climb, a young man wearing a garland of bittersweet, says 'The honeysuckle/bittersweet stands . . .'. His Lady is now missing, but she still maintains a ghostly presence, as some of her words remain, 'Forget me not, I shall (?Make you) a garland.' Maybe she intended to replace his somewhat equivocally symbolic chaplet of bittersweet with one of forget-me-nots? There is no trace of any such garland remaining, however. But there is punning at work here too, for in this dialectal area the honeysuckle as well as the bittersweet was known as *je-länger-je-lieber* (literally, 'the longer, the better/the more loved').

On the other hand, the young woman who holds aloft a spring flower on the basal print of a sadly fragmentary fifteenth-century silver-gilt bowl now in the Museum of London (Figure 10.8), while she may well have been understood as a lover, is actually one of the so-called 'Labours of the Months', being labelled *apriel*. But that month, proverbially associated with showers, was also associated with love, and Mark Antony combines both suggestions when he says of Octavia, on the point of tears at her brother's departure, 'The Aprill's in her eyes, it is Loue's spring' (*Antony and Cleopatra*, III.ii.43). Indeed, the popular late Elizabethan verse-anthology, Bodenham's *Belvedere* (1600), denied that the more usual May was love's month, rather is it 'dropping April – Loue is full of showers'.

Figure 10.8

But to return to the flowering-heart motif: one of the so-called 'love and loyalty' seals, dated to *c.* 1320,[136] bears the English legend *LOVE ME AND I THE* [sic] and depicts a male and female bust in profile either side of a heart which sprouts a large veined quatrefoil which may well have been intended to represent the truelove. An identical design – for there is plenty of evidence that certain of the cheaper seals were mass-produced – attached to a document of 1334 is surrounded by the slightly variant legend, *LOVE ME AND LYVE*.[137]

Truelove or Four-leafed Clover?

In Chapter 2 I suggested that the little quatrefoil lead badges inscribed with a 't' at their centre were perhaps to be regarded as the traditionally lucky four-leaf clover 're-inforced' by the initial of the miracle-working St Thomas of Canterbury. However, there is also the possibility that these badges are secular lovers' tokens, lead emblems of the truelove, and that the 't' with which they are emblazoned stands for *truelove* rather than *Thomas*, and that they may therefore be examples of that very:

> Trewe loue among men that most is of lette
> In hattes, in hodes, in purses . . . sette.[138]

A personal seal in the form of a four-leaf clover attached to a document in the Public Record Office was perhaps felt to protect the owner's 'signature' magically,[139] but another such seal attached to a document dated 1355 bears the courtly love legend 'From your "friend" . . .'.[140]

Another fascinating fragment refers to the use of the truelove by a medieval lover, Chaucer's Absolon, in 'The Miller's Tale':

> Under his tonge a trewe-love he beer,
> For therby wende he to ben gracious.

The would-be lover sets off to court Alisoun with a truelove under his tongue which he believes will render him *gracious*, a word which editors gloss as 'attractive', though it seems more likely from the fact that he places the leaf under his tongue that he believed it would make him eloquent in his amorous entreaties.

SAYING IT WITH WORDS

Amatory legends on seals, brooches, rings, etc. are legion, and we cannot hope to sample more than a few. The majority of inscriptions on English artefacts are in Latin or French, but from the fourteenth century English legends become increasingly common.

Seals – strictly speaking, seal-*impressions* – are often found on late medieval documents in local and national archives, of course, and while many thousands are extant, their number (even if many are still uncatalogued) is fixed; seal-dies or matrices, on the other hand, are still constantly turning up as archaeological or metal detector finds, especially the cheaper secular sort of seal considered below.

We have seen above the use of the legend *LOVE ME AND LYVE* with a possible conventionalised truelove flower on an early fourteenth-century seal. Equally stylised and 'off-the-peg' in appearance, is a contemporary group inscribed with the legend 'You have a faithful lover', surrounding a variety of motifs: a conventionalised quatrefoil (= truelove?), or clasped hands[141] and bird (= turtle-dove?), while another seal uses the clasped hands motif but is inscribed 'Keep faith' (that is, Be true).[142] The same central motif as on the seal inscribed *LOVE ME AND I THE* is also found with roughly equivalent inscriptions in French: '[you] have my heart, do not deceive it', and 'Love, love me, for you have a faithful lover'; and the last inscription, in its turn, with a different central device, the bust of a young man.[143] A variant inscription on a seal attached to a document dated 1368 is 'Love, love me, you have my heart', but this time the device is an armorial shield.[144]

Many such seals proclaim themselves to belong to lovers, the seals themselves, as it were, speak. In the decades around 1300 the legend 'I am the seal of loyal love' is common. 'I am a handsome seal, gay and loyal' is an expanded version, 'I am a seal good and loyal',[145] somewhat more modest – though note the punning invocation of the name of *Jesus* in the opening words of the French *Ie sus*. Such inscriptions surround various central devices, some of which are not of such obviously amorous import as the hearts and flowers we have been considering, the last-named, for example, bears the device of a bird preying on a rabbit, a device more usually found with the legend 'Alas I am caught!'[146] But this is quite in tune with the imagery of courtly love, the user's heart, represented by the rabbit, is hunted or captured by the predatory lover. The erotic *chasse au connin* (coney-hunt) with its scarcely veiled sexual innuendo is discussed in Chapter 3,[147] and we have noted above, in passing, an embroidered example of the hunt of the Stag of Love, also expressed, however fleetingly, in the legend on an early fourteenth-century seal-die which reads 'I am [the seal] of love', and has a running stag as its central device.[148] In English, long before the Elizabethan era, medieval lovers seized joyfully on the homonymy of *heart* and *hart*, and I know of no better illustration of the pun than a superb boxwood comb of *c.* 1500 now in Birmingham Museum. On one side of the central openwork rosette we see a hart looking back at a heart pierced by crossed arrows on the other side of it, the visual symmetry suggesting the oral equivalence.[149] Such combs were typical late medieval love-tokens and always inscribed with an amatory 'posy', such as one now in Edinburgh which appears to read *du bon du* ♥ *done fera* (? given with pleasure from the heart).

Many rings and brooches, however, 'speak for themselves': 'I am a love-token (*druerie*), don't give me away' is a relatively common inscription. The most famous *drurye*[150] in medieval English literature is the belt of alleged invulnerability given to Sir Gawain by the lady, which he accepts for sound protective reasons (in the same way that his coat armour is decorated with apotropaic devices, the *conysaunce* (badge) of the *pentangel* and *vertuus stonez*),[151] but the narrator knows full well that, from the lady's point of view, it is a *luf-lace* (that is, 'love-lace', in both the literal and metaphorical senses we have noted above).[152]

But there were other possibilities for binding one's lover. A rich hoard of roughly contemporary jewellery buried around 1464 was discovered at Fishpool in Nottinghamshire, and included a unique miniature gold padlock and key, decorated with enamelled flowers and the legend *de tout mon cuer* (with all my heart).[153] The closest analogy known to me is 'a lytell locke of gould' mentioned in a letter dated 20 September 1484, as having been sent to George Cely, a wool merchant residing in Calais, by his wife Margery,[154] but note also the ring now in the Lübeck Museum (p. 203 Figure 10.5).

It is a mistake to regard courtly love as too rarefied, too elevated a convention, to allow the intrusion of a sometimes quite coarse sexuality – one ring-brooch, for example (Figure 10.9), goes so far as to proclaim:

Figure 10.9

IEO SUI FERMAIL PUR GA[R]DER SEIN
KE NUS VILEIN NI METTER MEIN
[I am a brooch to guard the breast,
so that no churl may put his hand there].[155]

In a delightful small panel painting in the National Gallery, London, a young man holds a ring against a background of raining clouds, with beneath each the motto *har. las. uber. gan* (Lord, let (them?) pass over). It is attributed to the 'Netherlandish School' and dated *c.* 1450–60. The emblem and motto, together with the ring he holds (on which 'the letters *i d* are perhaps inscribed') suggests that he is a melancholy lover who prays for the current storm in his relations with his ladylove to blow over.[156]

Amatory 'posies' often appear in the form of rhyming couplets, some more polished than others, but all with a certain charm. I append a selection, inscribed on various objects, not all of them jewellery.[157]

My heart I give you,   (ring-brooch)
both near and far

When God pleases   (ring)
we shall be united

Often I am so ravished by love
that I think I am in heaven   (ring)

Most in mynd and yn myn herrt (signet ring)
Lothest from you ferto deparrt

Figure 10.10

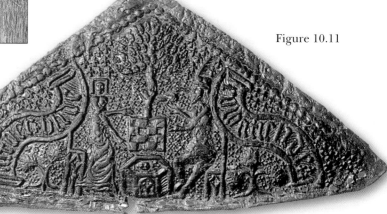

Figure 10.11

To love and be shunned/spurned
is a bitter pain   (1480; wooden capital (Figure 10.10))[158]

Always happy
no matter what I suffer   (*c.* 1400; leather shoe-upper (Figure 10.11))

Perhaps the most popular proverbial amatory inscription was the Latin *amor vincit omnia* (love conquers all): so common, indeed, that one suspects its meaning was known even to those who had no Latin. Chaucer's Prioress had a gold brooch attached to her rosary 'On which ther was first write a crowned A, And after "*Amor vincit omnia*".[159] How much more fitting would have been the poesy, *Jesus est amor meus* (Jesus is my love), which her contemporary, Margery Kempe, tells us in her spiritual autobiography Our Lord had commanded her to have inscribed on a ring (the same legend was also found on a set of beads bequeathed by William of Wykeham to Archbishop Arundel in 1403).[160] The legend favoured by the Prioress, however, is to be found, for example, on two pewter tokens now in the Museum of London,[161] on an early fourteenth-century personal seal,[162] and on a triangle of leather excavated in Bruges,[163] – perhaps part of a shoe like that of late fourteenth-century date with the amatory inscriptions and scenes preserved in the British Museum, which also features this Latin tag, as well as the proverbial *Honny soit qui mal y pense* (Evil be to him who evil thinks).[164] But it was especially popular on ring-brooches; Joan Evans listed five certain examples sixty years ago,[165] but doubtless several more have surfaced since.

The cynical 'Love does much, money does everything' on a mid-fifteenth-century ring in the British Museum,[166] is also found on an enamelled Flemish hat-badge made in the 1520s, which illustrates the mercenary love implicit in the proverb by depicting a young woman standing between a young man and an old man; she has turned away from the young man to face the old man, whom she allows to fondle her breast as her hand reaches into his purse.[167] A precisely contemporary badge of probably much the same origin appears on the hat of a presumably love-sick Portuguese nobleman painted by Jan Gossaert (Figure 10.12); the perimeter inscription reads:

Figure 10.12

QVI PAR TROP ERBRACE [*sic*]   [He who embraces too much
EN VAIN SE[S] BRAS LAC[H]E [*sic*]   in vain, his arms give way]

which is quite possibly related to the proverb *Qui trop embrasse peu estreint* (He who holds too much retains little) illustrated in the *Proverbes en Rimes* manuscript, and

Figure 10.13

the image on the badge is of a young man apparently trying to embrace, or get his arms around, a tower! 'Embrace' is likely to be an amorous pun in the context of the lover's hat-badge.[168]

Another example of an inscription which can be shown, I believe, to be a lover's proverb, is found on one of the lead brooches now in the Museum of London and takes the form of a pair of human arms with clasped hands (cf. *fede* rings and brooches), surmounted by a crown and the legend, 'truthe schall be crownid'.[169] The legend refers to 'truth' between lovers, that is, fidelity (cf. the similarly constructed badges which include a heart pierced by an arrow, discussed above), but also sounds proverbial, and bears comparison with proverbs relating to more existential truth, such as 'Greet is treuthe, and it passith bifore alle othere' (*c.* 1395), and 'Trouth shal surmounte' (*a.* 1420). A beautiful silver-gilt bridal crown made in Southern Germany in the mid-fifteenth century is reproduced in Figure 10.13. The openwork circlet bears the word *trewelich* (truly) – in precisely the same sense which we have been considering – repeated four times and punctuated by pink-enamelled rosettes. There is evidence that such crowns were sometimes those of statues of the Virgin Mary kept in churches and lent to the earthly virgin for the day of her wedding.[170]

A further citation for such 'truth' is the legend *trowthe is fre* found on a bilingual ring in the British Museum, which also bears the motto *Soiez leals en amours* (be loyal in love),[171] seeming to confirm the amatory sense we have suggested for the lead brooch's TRUTH. Another badge from Salisbury, in the form of a hand clasping a heart on which the legend *hert be true* appears has, however, been shown by Brian Spencer from more complete examples to be the hand of God,[172] but once again testifies to the close link between the motifs used for human and divine love. But the famous Regensburg Rathaus tapestry (already referred to above) woven *c.* 1390 includes in one of its twenty-four courtly love medallions two lovers whose clasped hands are positioned beneath a crown, and around the perimeter of the scene, an inscription, part of which reads 'Truth shall be crowned', an exact parallel to our humble lead badge.

I have discussed elsewhere the fashion for inscribing proverbs on almost every conceivable type of artefact including household vessels,[173] but – however incongruous it might seem to us – some also bore amatory inscriptions, such as the late medieval French bronze cauldron in the Metropolitan Museum, New York, which bears the legend:

> I will love all my life no matter who should blame me.[174]

A particularly romantic relic is the spur lost at the Battle of Towton in 1461, inscribed with the words 'in loyal love all my heart',[175] which belongs to the same

Figure 10.14

cultural milieu as the famous contemporary Flemish parade shield in the British Museum depicting a young knight kneeling before his lady, Death standing menacingly behind him, and inscribed 'you or death'.[176]

It may come as something of a surprise to find quite so many of our modern romantic notions and conventions concerning love and courtship already in existence in the late Middle Ages. The giving as love-tokens of flowers and other personal items, principally jewellery, of course, but also things such as combs and mirrors together with accompanying 'posies', is one fashion that endures. Similarly, the heart-symbol is still universally current and understood – we have only to look on the walls of the nearest bus shelter for proof of that.

It is perhaps strange to find a late medieval 'language of flowers' flourishing centuries before the Victorian era, albeit one with several constituent dialects. If courtly love in its visual and verbal manifestations was a game played with greater or lesser earnestness according to taste and period, not all games are mere empty conventions, some have perhaps evolved to enable us to articulate 'thoughts that do lie too deep for tears'. It would be hard perhaps to find a meaner flower than the little lead violet that blows on a grassy bank (Figure 10.14), and yet I find I cannot but be moved by it, and by its inscription, *veolit in maye lady* (violet in May, Lady). For all their apparent mass production (and several examples of this particular badge are now known), it is hard not to believe that many of these poignant tokens, even the humblest lead badges given and received by those poorer lovers who would yet seem courtly, are not, each one, memorials of deep feeling between lovers not unlike ourselves.

ELEVEN

WHO WEARS THE TROUSERS: GENDER RELATIONS

The Virago and the Scold

It is the properte of a woman to vse scoldynge.

This startling sexist observation is the recommended translation of the Latin *Ingenium est mulierem conuicia exercere,*[1] and was part of the everyday reading of the Tudor schoolboy from at least 1509, in Wynkyn de Worde's editions of Stanbridge's popular English–Latin textbook known as the *Vulgaria*. It is in the context of such impressions of women, doubtless unconsciously absorbed by late medieval males, that many of the images discussed below must be seen. It is hardly surprising in a cultural milieu in which every Tudor schoolboy learned to render such sentences into Latin, and in which the virago was a commonplace of both the traditional and the new humanist drama, that such fearsome women should also figure in contemporary media.

Of all the sexist stereotypes in the medieval world, perhaps the commonest and certainly the most derided and feared was the virago, shrew or scold, the woman whose 'unfeminine' aggressiveness was perceived as a direct threat to male authority, who reverses the natural order by domineering, and even physically assaulting her husband, whereas it is he who, according to all legal codes and moral systems of the period, has the right to chastise *her*. Both she and her 'feeble' husband were objects of popular scorn,[2] for the corollary to this anxious attack on the increasingly emancipated woman of the late medieval and early modern era was, of course, a similar holding up to ridicule of the feeble husband, known in contemporary English as a *cotquean*.

THE SPINDLE AND THE SPEAR – GENDER-APPROPRIATE ATTRIBUTES

Eleven hundred years ago, when Alfred the Great drew up his will in his native Old English, he referred in it to the land his grandfather had bequeathed in his will, *on tha sperehealfe naes on tha spinlhealfe* (on the spear 'half' and not on the spindle 'half'). The most recent editors in their note on the line remark that 'this expression means, of course, "in the male line and not in the female line"' – of course – though strangely, modern English has lost this alliterative balance of *spear* and *spindle*, lost *spear* in this symbolically male sense altogether and, indeed, preferred the word *distaff* to *spindle* to symbolise the female half of the family or *distaff side.*

In Lyly's *Campaspe* (1584) the very terms used 700 years previously by King Alfred recur: 'Will you handle the spindle with Hercules, when you should shake the speare with Achilles?'[3] Here Lyly calls to mind the many representations in art of Hercules and Omphale, one of the most striking being the contemporary painting by Bartholomaus Spranger (d. 1611), now in the Kunsthistorisches Museum in Vienna, in which a hefty Hercules, clad in a revealingly slit pink gown, spins with the distaff, while an all but naked Omphale, seen from behind, shoulders a massive club – a striking example of heavy, late Mannerist eroticism.[4] But Lyly's more famous contemporary, whether consciously or not, also made use of these quintessential gender attributes. In a passage of *monde renversé* imagery in *Richard II* (*c.* 1595), Scroope reports that things have come to such a pass that 'distaff-women manage rusty bills' (that is, spears, compare *bill-hook*) against Richard, while in *Cymbeline* (*c.* 1610), the heroic deeds of an ancient warrior and two boys in reversing a British rout were such that they 'could have turned a distaff to a lance', according to Posthumus.[5]

When the early thirteenth-century artist came to illustrate a passage in the *Topographia Hibernia* of Giraldus Cambrensis (1185) concerning an interesting 'bearded lady' in the entourage of the King of Limerick, he naturally depicted her at her distaff (Figure 11.1), in order to point up the contrast, though there is no textual reference to her spinning.[6] Conversely, when some macho hero like Hercules 'mans' the distaff, or the last of the Assyrian kings, Sardanapalus, we may be sure that the artist is signalling in this drastic manner the extent to which the man has been *un*manned and defeated by the woman. That this should feature as one of the fascinating Brussels snow-sculptures of 1511 attests to the contemporary late medieval anxiety over gender roles.[7]

Figure 11.1

So strong were the female associations of the distaff that, as we have seen in Chapter 5, they were exploited as the basis for one of the characteristic medieval punishments by humiliation: in medieval London men convicted of crimes of sex and violence might be paraded in public carrying a distaff.[8]

The distaff, the quintessential attribute of a woman, is usually the symbol of her quiet domestic industry, and so the man who is so *un*manned as to ply the distaff

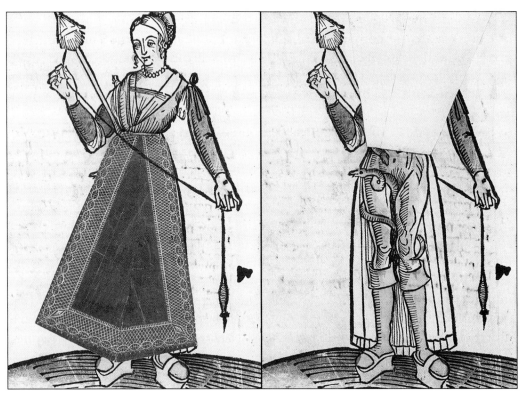

Figure 11.2

instead of his wife, or who allows himself to be ignominiously beaten with it, is a figure of fun, an actor in a scene which, while on one level it partakes of the boisterous farcical reversal of the World Turned Upside Down, is yet inevitably more disturbing than pure fantasies such as hares roasting the huntsman, for it threatens a disruption which *could* conceivably occur, and implies a warning that any relaxation of patriarchal authority could lead to intolerable humiliation of the male.

An extraordinary image executed in a technique which we would now consider appropriate only for very young children is reproduced as Figure 11.2. This startling lift-the-flap drawing, probably copied from a woodcut original, is found in an early sixteenth-century manuscript of German folksong where it ostensibly functions as a *memento mori* device, being accompanied by a verse put into the mouth of the young woman which advises us to think on our end.[9] It appears that with the flap down, the attractive young woman virtuously plying her distaff represents the world, pleasant to look at, but by this *figur* we are to understand that, be we never so good-looking, high-born, young or old, in a short while we will look just 'as you see me under my apron'. I say 'ostensibly' because it is hard for a post-Freudian to view a snake emerging from a woman's crotch as entirely innocent of sexual symbolism. Certainly *memento mori* parallels do exist – the diptych now in Cleveland of the beautiful bridal couple paired with their cadaverous selves in which a toad appears clamped to the woman's crotch, for example – but it is difficult not to see the snake's head emerging from between the quite undecayed thighs of the young woman in our drawing as an example of the *vagina dentata* motif. Certainly this motif was known to the Middle Ages, in *Mandeville's Travels*, for example, composed in Anglo-Norman *c.* 1357, but then translated into other vernaculars as well as Latin, one of the islands under the rule of the fabulous Prester John observes a custom whereby virgin brides are deflowered by a special caste of 'reckless fools' called *cadeberiz*. I quote from a modernised version of an early fifteenth-century English translation:[10]

> And I asked them the cause why that they held such custom. And they said me that of old time men had been dead for deflowering of maidens that had serpents in their bodies that stung men upon their yards, that they died anon. And therefore they held that custom to make other men ordained therefor, to lie by their wives for dread of death and to assay the passage by another, rather than for to put themselves in that adventure.

The fact that the flap lifts at the young woman's girdle puts me in mind of Lear's outburst (IV.vi.120ff):

> . . . Behold yon simp'ring dame,
> Whose face between her forks presages snow;
> That minces virtue, and does shake the head
> To hear of pleasure's name;
> The fitchew nor the soiled horse goes to't
> With a more riotous appetite.
> Down from the waist they are Centaurs,
> Though women all above:
> But to the girdle do the gods inherit,
> Beneath is all the fiend's: there's hell, there's darkness,
> There is the sulphurous pit – burning, scalding,
> Stench, consumption . . .

And she *does* simper!

Just as the distaff and spindle is the gender-appropriate attribute of the woman, the spear or knife is the corresponding gender marker for males – and an obvious phallic symbol to boot. In a domestic context the knife is ever at the man's side, in his belt. A most significant literary passage in which the sexes' traditional roles and attributes are at issue occurs in the Prologue to Chaucer's 'Monk's Tale', where the Host relates how his wife, angry that he had not leapt to avenge what she considered an affront to her status, screamed at him:

> By corpus bones, I wol have thy knyf,
> And thou shalt have my distaf and go spynne![11]

The argument about *maistrie* in marriage, a recurrent theme in *The Canterbury Tales*, is here crystallised, together with the stereotype of the quarrelsome shrew, in a visual image of reversal closely parallel to those found in contemporary art.

Marginal illustrations in fourteenth-century manuscripts, for example, show men being beaten with a distaff,[12] while an influential late fifteenth-century engraving by Israhel van Meckenem shows a man already down on one knee reaching out to reclaim his breech-cloth, while his wife (spurred on by a devil) threatens him with her distaff and, significantly, has already placed her foot over his.[13]

In the domestic scene carved on a late fifteenth-century misericord at Fairford,[14] while the wife threatens the husband with an upraised ladle, he squats before her in a posture of submission and, as I interpret the carving, places his hand under his wife's foot as a token of his submission – a gesture which interestingly explains the Tamed Shrew's notorious recommendation to obedient wives to 'place your hands below your husband's foot'.[15] In a similar manner, the placing of the wife's foot over that of the husband is symbolic of her domination of him, as in the van Meckenem engraving.

Close examination of a misericord in Beverley Minster reveals between the two men performing household chores the (now broken) figure of a woman with a distaff directing operations. In the contemporary early sixteenth-century mystery play from the Digby manuscript, *The Killing of the Children*, the braggart soldier Watkin, 'drede[s] no thyng more thanne a woman with a rokke [distaff]', and later admits that:

> the most I fere is to come among women,
> For thei fight like deuelles with ther rokkes.[16]

The scene on a misericord at Hereford, similar to that at Fairford, is unfortunately damaged, so that it is uncertain whether the ladle is again in play here or whether the wife is not, rather, throwing a dish at her husband, as seems to have been the wife's habit in the fifteenth-century carol whose henpecked author laments that

If I aske our dame fleych	[meat]
Che brekit myn hed with a dych:	[She breaks my head with a dish]
'Boy, thou art not worght a reych!'[17]	[worth a rush]

We learn of a bizarre symbolic gesture which seems to involve both the symbolism of the spindle and the horns of the cuckold (?) in one of the late medieval law cases concerning poaching in the royal forests known as Pleas of the Forest.[18] A nobleman named Simon Tuluse and his companions went on a three-day poaching spree and on the final day Tuluse cut off the head of a buck, and:

> put it on a stake in the middle of a certain clearing . . . placing in the mouth of the aforesaid head a certain spindle; and they made the mouth gape towards the sun, in a great contempt of the lord king and his foresters.

At the inquisition, however, the head was said to have been that of a doe, and the object stuck in its throat a *billet*. Clearly this had some meaning for the perpetrators and it has been claimed, probably rightly, as 'a gross sexual insult [which] took the

20 Girl Binds Forget-Me-Not Garland: oil on panel, Hans Suess von Kulmbach, *c.* 1510.

21 Venus adored by famous lovers: painted birth-salver (*desco da parto*),
Florence, first half of 15thC.

22 Assault on the maiden's castle: pen-and-ink drawing with colour-wash, Flemish, *c.* 1470.

23 Knight of the drooping lance: pen-and-ink drawing with colour-wash, Flemish, *c.* 1470.

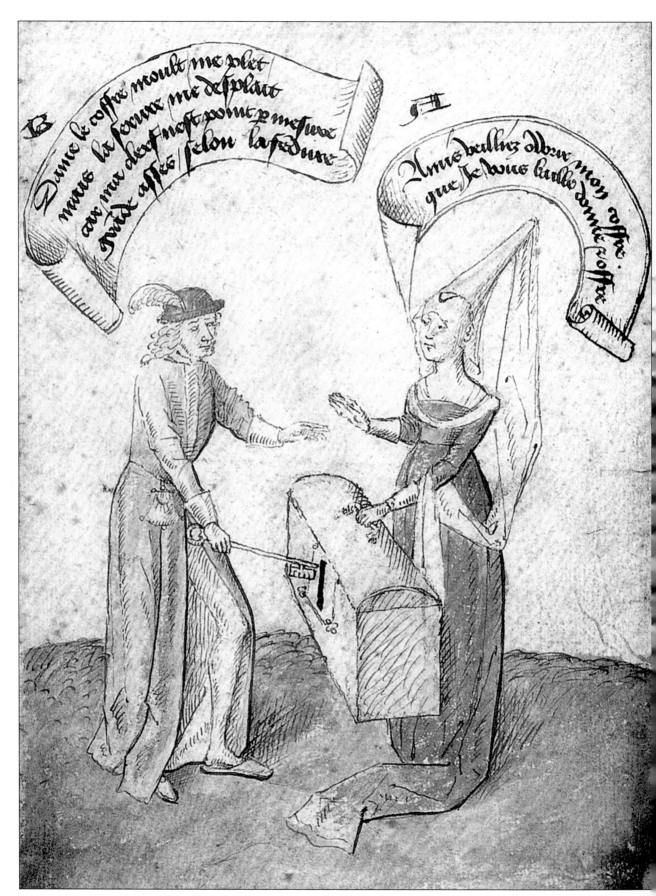

24 His key too small for her lock: pen-and-ink drawing with colour-wash, Flemish, *c.* 1470.

form of a sexual inversion'. If the details of the original report are correct, 'the male animal, had a woman's symbol – a spindle – in its throat' and, moreover, 'the action was premeditated, for no man would have been carrying a spindle . . . on a poaching party'. The most recent interpretation of this curiously ritual act implies that 'the symbolic overtones suggest sexual inversion, with the buck's throat representing the vagina and a female implement the penis. . . . Turning the head towards the sun was also an insult, perhaps their defiance in acting in open daylight rather than under cover of night.' The insult was presumably intended to mock the impotence of the male foresters responsible for policing the King's forests.

Woman Puts on Breeches while Man Spins or Winds Yarn

One of the most influential depictions of this consummation devoutly to be deplored, is another late fifteenth-century engraving by Israhel van Meckenem showing the husband winding thread while his wife threatens him with her upraised distaff and pulls on his breeches.[19] A misericord in Leon Cathedral (1464x1475) similarly depicts a woman pulling on a pair of breeches while she brandishes a distaff at a man winding thread on the neighbouring seat. Given what we now know of the use of print sources by misericord carvers, it seems likely that the Leon carvings are copied from the van Meckenem print.[20]

Perhaps one of the most significant representations of this type is a burlesque coat of arms engraved by the Housebook Master (Middle Rhine, late 1480s). It shows (as a helmet-crest) a woman sitting astride a man's back spinning, while he bends over and holds the base of her distaff, his trousers round his ankles. The device on the shield is a man standing on his head, the implication clearly being that this is a complete reversal of the natural order when the wife dominates the husband in this manner.[21] This or, more likely, an engraved copy no longer extant, was the source for a similar misericord subject in Toledo Cathedral (1489–95) carved by the Fleming Rodrigo Aleman. A slight variant of the motif in which the woman is not shown pulling on the breeches, but belabours her thread-winding husband whose trousers are down not with her distaff but a switch, can be seen, for example, on a brass dish of late fifteenth-century German manufacture (Figure 3.12), where the instrument of punishment is probably a foxtail (for the symbolism of which, see Chapter 3).[22]

The Battle for the Breeches[23]

At its simplest, the Battle for the Breeches involves a husband and wife, perhaps with some weapon in their free hands, pulling in opposite directions at a pair of trousers, such as appears on a misericord in Rouen Cathedral carved 1458x69. This sort of presentation seems to begin in the fourteenth century, the earliest I am aware of being a little marginal drawing in a mid-fourteenth-century Franco-Flemish manuscript of the *Voeux du Paon*, which shows the woman holding the captured trousers with one hand and fending off her husband who makes to strike her, with the other.[24]

From the 1460s there is a fine though little-known and damaged 'dotted print' of the subject by an anonymous engraver of the Upper Rhine known as the

Figure 11.3

Keulenmeister held uniquely in the British Museum (Figure 11.3).[25] The breeches (labelled in the vernacular, *bruch*)[26] hover just above the ground between the two combatants, who are provided with banderole inscriptions in Latin, that over the man reading:

> *Est contra legem*   [It is contrary to law
> *reginam regere regem*   for the queen to rule the king]

and that above the woman,

> *Est tibi iam mirum*   [Here's a wonder for you, then,
> *mulierem regere virum.*   the woman ruling the man!]

The image of the Battle for the Breeches – like the idiom itself – are attested surprisingly late in England. The earliest literary mention I am aware of (antedating the *OED*) is a ballad entitled 'A merie dialogue betwixte Iohn and Ione striuing who shall were the Breeches' included by Hugh Plat in his *The Flowres of Philosophie and the Pleasures of Poetrie* (1572). In the 'merie dialogue' John laments that:

> . . . if thou wilte weare thy husbands gere,
> then shalte thou be aboue me,

but the rebellious Joan goes so far as to envisage a situation in which:

> men must reele, and winde the wheele
> with distaffe in their hande,

undaunted by John's entreaty never again to beat him:

> for feare thou weare the wispe, good wife,   [for the 'wisp', see pp. 92–3]
> and make our neighbours ride.[27]   [ride = perform a skimmington ride]

At present, the earliest English example of a visual illustration of the Battle I can cite is the woodcut heading 'The Jolly Widdower: OR A Warning for BATCHELORS', a broadside ballad printed for J. Blare in London in the 1680s. This must surely be far too late really to be the earliest such depiction, but in fact – entirely in keeping with normal ballad-publishers' practice – the woodcut in question was probably already a century old by this date and may well, indeed, have originally illustrated one of the Elizabethan ballads of similar title recorded in the *Stationers' Registers*.[28] It was also the source (reversed) of the central design on a mid-seventeenth-century dish depicting the Battle for the Breeches in the Glaisher Collection of the Fitzwilliam Museum in Cambridge.

The English proverb 'Most Masters wear no Breech' is first attested *c.* 1500, which is also surprisingly late,[29] and in any case, does not mean quite the same thing – the fact that the masters of most households do not wear trousers (that is, they are women), is not precisely the same as affirming that the women have donned the men's trousers, though clearly they are roughly synonymous. The idiom to *wear the breeches* seems not to be found until the Elizabethan era.

Battle for the Breeches between a Group of Women

The earliest-known version of what was to become a popular design, the Battle for the Breeches between a number of women fighting over a single pair of trousers, is a Florentine engraving of *c.* 1460, but it is certainly derived from a lost German version by the influential Master of the Banderoles. It is a burlesque production: two winged angels (*putti*?) hold aloft a wreath, in the centre of which is a bleeding heart pierced by an arrow, and from which a pair of breeches hang, just above the heads of no fewer than twelve brawling women who punch, scratch and pull each other's hair. They are watched by a costumed fool (a 'commentary fool') playing fife and drum and – more alarmingly – by a skeletal Death with scythe over his shoulder. By the mid-sixteenth century the number of women became fixed at seven,[30] an allusion, it has been suggested, to the haughty daughters of Zion in all their finery and trinkets referred to in Isaiah 3.16–4.1. Coupe has seen this later type as 'an allegory on the plight of women without men and their readiness to fight even for the empty attribute of the male sex',[31] a reading which perhaps receives some support from a Parisian engraving of *c.* 1580 in which the trousers have been transformed into an eel – a pretty transparent visual pun on their principal contents.[32] That it is in fact the male organ for which these unruly women strive, is perhaps suggested by a fifteenth-century Dutch lead badge depicting two standing women flanking a phallus which projects vertically from the waistband of a pair of trousers (Figure 2.8).

The Medieval House-husband

Domestic topsy-turveydom can also be conveyed by scenes in which a man reveals himself as a feeble husband by undertaking household chores. Such a husband wearing an apron is depicted washing-up on one of the Beverley misericord supporters carved in 1520,[33] pointedly mocked by the grin on the face of the small

Figure 11.4

fool's head carved in the stall-elbow spandrel directly opposite him. The central carving shows that he has made the mistake of allowing the dog to steal a joint from the cooking pot, while his wife was warming her hands by the fire (Figure 11.4); significantly, the weapon with which he chases off the dog is her distaff, while on another Beverley seat showing the dog's head still in the pot, she seizes her husband by the hair and turns the distaff on him. Another medieval example of the husband dish-washing occurs in the tale known as 'The Wright's Chaste Wife', in which the husband foolishly undertakes to do all the wife's household chores (and she his) – it was illustrated, together with so many other popular tales, in the lower margins of the *Smithfield Decretals*.[34]

Such a man, who acted what was felt to be exclusively the housewife's role, was known in England from at least the mid-sixteenth century as a *cotquean*. In Middleton and Dekker's gender-role comedy *The Roaring Girl* (1611), the eponymous heroine dresses as a man and acts like one, smoking and bearing weapons, yet does not pretend to be one. She usurps the superficial attributes of manhood in order to enjoy the freedom not afforded the traditionally meek wife. In the same play, Mistress Gallipot berates her husband for fussing over her:

I cannot abide these apron husbands: such cotqueans. . . .[35]

Here we see how pointed is the fact that the earlier carver has given the Beverley washer-up an apron. Though, curiously, the *OED* does not seem to recognise it as such,[36] the apron, certainly in a domestic context, has come to be seen as a pre-eminently feminine garment; as the characteristic garment of the mother, as found, for example, in the idiom, '[being tied to] one's mother's apron-strings', first noted in Udall's translation of Erasmus' *Apothegms* (1542).

That there was, indeed, something of a tradition of portraying such *Pantoffelhelde* (literally, 'Slipper-heroes') in English art and literature, we may infer from several little-regarded works of art,[37] most notably the plaster panel dating from the final decade of the sixteenth century at Montacute House near Yeovil, Somerset, depicting a 'skimmington ride', the occasion for which is clearly represented in the left-hand scene of the panel, where the husband, in the act of feeding the baby, is hit over the head by the wife's slipper/clog (itself reminiscent of the thematically related German expression, *unter dem Pantoffel stehen*, 'stand/be under the slipper').[38] This scene immediately precedes, and is therefore to be read as the proximate cause of the other, in which the husband is made the target of a stang-riding (see Chapter 5).

That the husband should wash the baby's nappies was felt to be equally demeaning, and *c.* 1536 in a woodcut attributed to Hans Schäufelein,[39] we see a man with a washing-beetle doing just this, supervised by his hefty wife who threatens him with a stick. The Schäufelein woodcut illustrates a Hans Sachs poem entitled 'The Nappy-washing Husband', but there is also a German *singspiel* of sixteenth-century type, 'The Nappy-washer' published in the significantly titled *Engelische Comedien und Tragedien* (Leipzig, 1620). Indeed, the possible English source of this *singspiel* is Ingelend's *Disobedient Child* of 1560, in which a shrewish wife forces her husband to wash clothes, a work itself based on a school dialogue, 'The Youth, the Father and the Wife', by the humanist, Ravisius Textor (Jean Tissier de Ravisy, d. 1524), of which an English adaptation known as *The Prodigal Son* (1530x34) is extant in a fragmentary copy.

Groping the Hens

Thomas Nashe's use of the word *cotquean* in his *An Almond for a Parrot* (1590) is found in a significant context which takes us straight back to the satirical world of the earlier misericords, for in it he refers to a husband 'groping his own hens like a cotquean'.[40] The same insulting insinuation – of effeminacy presumably – lies behind Dame Chat's assertion that Hodge came:

> . . . creeping into my pens,
> And there was caught within my house groping
> among my hens,

in *Gammer Gurton's Needle* (ante-1563).[41] A piece of popular literature published in the Netherlands *c.* 1550 was entitled 'Of the "Hen-groper" whose wife went to plough the land . . .', which sounds as if it must be related to Martin Parker's broadside ballad entitled 'The Woman to the plow; And the Man to the hen-roost; OR A fine way to cure a Cotquean' (1629), once again showing that for a man to concern himself with hens and their eggs was felt to be fatally effeminating.

In Flemish art the *hennetaster* (hen-groper) is a type of the effeminate man (and, as we have seen, in the Elizabethan mind too). Such a man shown groping the hen – in fact, to determine whether she is ready to lay – is depicted *c.* 1500 in stallwork at Aarschot, Emmerich and Kempen (see chapter ornament) and, more familiarly, in Bruegel's *Netherlandish Proverbs* painting of 1559 (Colour Plate 6). It is part of this same semantics that *Herr Uber-Sie* (Mister Over-Her) of the early seventeenth-century German broadside engraving,[42] who roams the world in search of a man not ruled by his wife, should lead about with him a magnificent stallion to be awarded to such a man (who, of course, he fails to find), and a coach-load of *eggs*, to be handed out to every husband he meets who defers to his wife in any way (all of them, of course) – for the care of poultry and their eggs is 'women's work'. Indeed, it is notable how so many of these terms concerning dominant and subservient sexual roles revolve around the barnyard relations of the cock and hen (see further the discussion of *Cock* in Chapter 3).

The Feeble Husband as Brooding Hen or Caponised Cock

The late Gothic windows of what is now the conference room of the Stadthof Fetzenreich in Trier (1540s) are divided by uprights, the bases of which are adorned with small figural sculptures. Four of the five are devoted to subjects that illustrate the Power of Women topos (see below), including Virgil in the basket, Delilah cutting Samson's hair, and a woman seated astride her crouching husband's back, belabouring his naked backside with her (skimming-)ladle, but the fourth is, at first sight, something of a puzzle. In the only recent publication I am aware of, it is described as 'a man sitting with his naked backside in a vegetable basket holding up a turnip', and left at that![43] Presumably, some strange personal quirk.

In fact, the same scene can be found elsewhere in early sixteenth-century Germany, in woodcut illustrations to the works of Thomas Murner, for example. The chapter 'Hatching the gowk/fool' from *Die Geuchmatt* (Basel, 1519) and *von dem grossen Lutherischen Narren* (. . . 1522) depict, respectively, a woman (exceptionally) and a man sitting on eggs. It is plainly a fool, however, who sits on the eggs in Urs Graf's signed woodcut illustration to Murner's earlier *Narrenbeschworung* (1512), in the chapter entitled 'Hatching gowks/fools'. In our opening chapter we noted an early sixteenth-century German biscuit-mould on which a man sits on a basket of eggs while his wife holds one aloft,[44] just as the hatcher himself does in the Trier sculpture, a gesture which seems to have been last seen some two centuries earlier.

In a number of Northern French and Flemish manuscripts of the late thirteenth and early fourteenth centuries, recurs the image of a man sitting on a nest of eggs and holding one up to the sun as if candling it or checking its readiness to hatch.[45] By the late sixteenth century it is merely a general allusion to the foolishness of individuals, as can be seen from a Flemish engraving showing a fool in costume with his bauble, sitting on eggs, and labelled 'Here's one sitting on eggs'.[46] In the earlier manuscript marginal illustrations, however, the fools are not identified necessarily by their costume, only by their action, and there is good reason to believe that these egg-hatchers are intended as satirical hits at the English, whose continental possessions were much resented at the time and place where these manuscripts were produced. In French writings of the thirteenth century, the English are frequently abused as long-tails, and it becomes a common anti-English insult from then on (see p. 168).

Ingenious and certainly correct though Randall's interpretation of the significance of this egg-hatching motif is for the decades around 1300, between that period and the sixteenth century, especially in the earlier sixteenth century, there is reason to believe that it was seen as almost the defining posture of the 'henpecked' man dominated by his wife (see also what we have said above about the *hennetaster*). This semantics endures in current colloquial English where a fussy man may be described as being 'like an old broody hen', where the implication of effeminacy is clear. In a German woodcut of *c.* 1520 attributed to Hans Sebald Beham we see a man, trousers down, sitting on a basket of eggs while his crone of a wife pulls his hair and tells him that if he concerned himself as much with the eggs as he does with the tavern, he would be able to hatch more of them out – which also of course, implies that he regularly sits on eggs![47] Another print of this subject must originally have been issued *a*. 1539, as it is now known to have been in the collection of Ferdinand Columbus who died in that year, though it only survives in an impression dated 1588. The man shown seated on the basket of eggs brooding them, holds up one from which a miniature cockerel emerges, and the meaning of his action is made explicit in the caption: 'Hen on eggs/Thus I am a man/who can never leave the house'; he is trapped in the domestic role which earlier centuries regarded as exclusively the woman's.

Old Woman Beats or Binds Devil

A variant of the fear of the virago or shrew is the fear of the old woman – significantly synonymous in this scenario – and so terrible is she that late medieval popular imagery and literature sometimes showed her battling with and overcoming the Devil himself, even binding him to a cushion. In German literature this act is itself the subject of three *fastnachtspiele* (carnival plays), one entitled 'Of three evil women who go cattle-rustling in front of Hell' – see further below – and a poem which was probably first composed *c*. 1400.[48]

As an independent graphic motif, the earliest print I am aware of is a broadsheet issued in Augsburg *c*. 1475 which portrays an old woman who routs an army of devils armed only with a wooden spoon. Barthel Beham's print of *c*. 1532 showing the Devil being worsted by an old woman with a stick was still part of the Danish popular print repertoire some 300 years later![49] In a contemporary engraving by Daniel Hopfer three old hags have beaten a devil to the ground with their wooden washing-beetles, and a lone old woman similarly forces the Devil to submit to the blows of her distaff in an engraving by Jacob Bink.

It seems possible that the motif of binding the Devil to a cushion is in origin a misogynist 'secularisation' of the triumph of St Margaret over the Devil. In the pictorial telegraphese of the Heidelberg manuscript of the *Sachsenspiegel* (*c*. 1330), she is shown binding the Devil (even here, perhaps, to a cushion), merely as a device to symbolise the saint's day on which the corn tithe is payable – St Margaret's Day, 13 July. As an independent motif, the earliest certain depiction of the virago binding the Devil to a cushion appears in a Florentine engraving of *c*. 1460, but is again based on a lost work by the German Master of the Banderoles. Five fearsome women armed with whips and cudgels are shown engaged in chaining the Devil to a tasselled cushion, while a sixth whips another devil off stage right, holding his tail and causing him to exclaim, *OI ME OI ME*! A third devil is hanging by a chain from a gallows, to the uprights of which his hands are also shackled, he exclaims *O MALA CHONPAGNIA* (O evil company), while a fourth squatting devil pulls an ineffectual face against one of the women binding the principal Devil.

Some such similar print model presumably accounts for the popularity of this subject with Flemish woodcarvers, who carved it on early sixteenth-century misericords at Aarschot, Dordrecht and L'Isle-Adam, and there is an early example carved by Pere Sanglada who is known to have visited Flanders (purchasing oakwood from Bruges Cathedral) before embarking on the stalls at Barcelona in the 1390s.[50] Another example features as an armrest on the stalls at Hoogstraeten (1532x48) (Figure 11.5), and the motif appears a little later in two of Bruegel's

Figure 11.5

paintings, the *Netherlandish Proverbs* (1559), and, more importantly, in his *Dulle Griet* (1562/4), where one of Griet's female hell-raiders performs this feat.[51] Significantly, *Griet* is a shortened form of the saint's name *Margaret*, and a play presented at the Antwerp *Landjuweel* festival in 1561 featured a group of wayward women including one 'Griet who plunders in front of Hell'. A book of Dutch proverbs published ten years earlier, records the expression, 'She could plunder in front of Hell and return unscathed', also significantly located among proverbs describing the plight of henpecked husbands.[52] The same idiom was clearly part of the German tradition:

> He who wants to
> plunder in front of hell
> let him take an evil wife with him
> that way he'll come away victorious.[53]

Old Wives' Forge and Furnace

A well-known folktale 'Christ and the Smith' involves the rejuvenation of an elderly wife by reforging her in a blacksmith's forge, in which, after Christ has miraculously made the smith's ancient mother-in-law young again in this manner, the smith tries the same on his wife – who, of course, is burned to a frazzle and has to be restored to life by Christ. William Copland printed a version of this tale *c.* 1565 as *A Treatyse of the Smyth whych that Forged hym a New Dame* with a woodcut on the title-page showing a woman lying on an anvil in front of a forge (Figure 11.6).[54] Copland inherited many of Wynkyn de Worde's titles and blocks, and from the style of the title-page woodcut to *A Treatyse* we can be certain that it reproduces the de Worde edition of *c.* 1505, only a fragment of which survives. A similar, slightly earlier woodcut by Georg Glockendon depicts the same motif, though here it is introduced as a purported explanation of the origin of apes.[55] On 12 November 1608 the *Stationers' Register* licensed to Henry Gosson, 'A fayringe for Women both old and yonge called the blacke Smythes cure ouer A curst Wyfes tonge' – as nothing of this title has survived, it is not possible to say whether this 'fairing' was a ballad or a broadsheet, and whether it concerned our present motif, or perhaps the 'scold's bridle', a real horror which would seem to belong originally to the late sixteenth century.

A woman lying prostrate on an anvil between two men with heavy hammers appears on an early sixteenth-century misericord at Champeaux near Paris,[56] and again as the title-page woodcut to a drama by Hans Hechler printed in Augsburg in

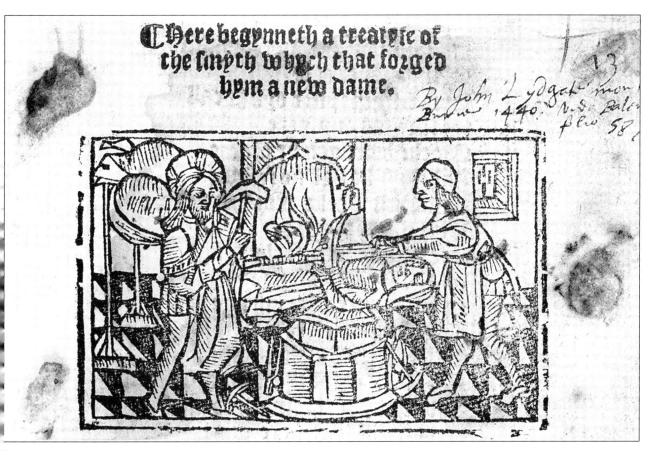

Figure 11.6

1540 (originally played at Utzendorf in Switzerland),[57] and a similar play is recorded from Zurich in 1530.[58]

A variant of the forge motif is that of the furnace, which appears in the 1540s on a pair of woodcut sheets also issued in Augsburg with woodcuts by Anthony Cortoys, one of which, for a change, is devoted to the rejuvenation of old husbands.[59] In Chapter 5 we considered barrowing as a demeaning motif sometimes used as a humiliating punishment, and old women are shown being barrowed towards the furnace on the Corthoys broadside, but probably because they are too frail to walk or are otherwise crippled with age. However, it may be that other scenes of women being barrowed towards an apparent flaming hell-mouth, are in fact examples of this burlesque rejuvenation.

Old Wives' Mill[60]

Another method of rejuvenation was the 'Old Wives' Mill'. This has not been noticed in art before a Dutch woodcut of *c.* 1600, but is known to have been the subject of a *fastnachtspiel* (carnival play) entitled 'how old wives are made young' performed in Thorn in West Prussia as ealy as 1440.[61] As with the furnace motif, a pair of sheets, one of which featured the male equivalent, was issued in Augsburg *c.* 1630 by M.A. Hannas.[62]

In England the motif is attested only late: a chapbook entitled *The Merry Dutch Miller and New Invented Windmill* was printed by E. Crowch, for F. Coles, T. Vere, and J. Wright in London in 1672, and a related ballad entitled 'The Dutch Miller, and New Invented Wind-Miller' was registered on 1 March 1675. The woodcut images which adorned these publications ultimately perhaps lie behind the signs of the inns named *The Grinding Young* at Harold's Cross, Dublin, and *The Mill for Grinding Old People Young* in late eighteenth-century Belfast.[63] There was also a ballad, 'The Miller's Maid Grinding the Old Men Young', known to me only from its publication as the text accompanying the transfer-print of the subject on a Wedgwood teapot manufactured in the late 1770s, which opens with inevitable innuendo:

> Come Old, Decrepid, Lame or Blind,
> Into my Mill to take a Grind.[64]

Of course, such mills might be used for other purposes too. Thomas Murner's *Mülle von Schwyndelsheym*, which ground fools into wise men, was written in 1515, the same year as a windmill carnival float appeared in the *Schembartlauf* procession in Nürnberg, but the mill was earlier a religious iconographic motif (the 'host-mill'), as indeed it was to become again in the sectarian polemics of the Reformation.[65]

Women's 'Sins'

There is no getting round the fact that the late Middle Ages was a misogynist era. Criticism of women already had a lengthy history by this period, a tradition indeed, so that medieval authors could also appeal to the 'authority' of classical writers. These traditional targets for attack included women's alleged garrulity, obsession with dress and personal appearance, lasciviousness, and desire to dominate men – in the words of Chaucer's exemplary Wife of Bath, to have the *maistrie*. So numerous are images of women dominating men at this period, despite the fact that such was obviously the complete inverse of the prevailing social realities, that art historians have coined the collective term 'The Power of Women' to denote these highly popular representations. This topos includes a number of scenes starring biblical and classical heroines such as Judith and Holoferenes, Solomon being persuaded to worship false gods by one of his foreign wives, Samson and Delilah, Phyllis and Aristotle, Virgil and the Emperor's Daughter, and the Battle for the Breeches.[66] Relations between the sexes might almost be summed up by this Power of Women topos. In an era not noted for its championing of women's rights, and in which very few real women held positions of power, it is remarkable to what extent contemporary imagery is dominated by what seems an obsessive fear of women, nor do I believe this is a false impression seen through the distorting-glass of the early twenty-first century. Of course there are portraits of loving couples on an apparently equal footing, but everywhere there are images warning of the disastrous state of affairs that results if men allow women's innate lust for power to be satisfied.

Woman and the Men of the Four Elements

Despite the profusion of such imagery, however, the fact that this desire for dominance is sexually motivated is not usually made explicit.

The fourth of a series of twelve engraved prints satirising relations between the sexes originally offered for sale by Hugh Perry in London *c.* 1628 depicts a fully clothed woman in the centre foreground flanked by two men on either side in the middle distance, one hawking, one fishing, one digging, and one working at a forge.[67] The evidently bowdlerised verses below the similarly inexplicit image read:

> Fyer, Ayre, Earth, Water, represents,
> to thee their sundry Elaments.
> By which thou maist receiue thy fill,
> that powerfull cann preserve & kill:

from which it is apparent that this is no mere genre scene, but that the men are clearly representatives of the traditional Four Elements, even if it is less clear quite how the woman who dominates the scene is to be regarded. The verse is fraught with ambiguity – who is 'thee'? The reader? The woman depicted? In the other plates in the series sometimes the verses belong to the characters represented and sometimes are merely descriptive of the scene. On the whole, the tone is decidedly misogynist, as one might expect – even if the penniless man whose beguiled inamorata presents him with his bastard child is implicitly criticised in one of the twelve – and it is the power of women to ruin men's lives, especially by making cuckolds of them, that is the unifying theme of the series. In this light, we should perhaps understand the present verses to mean that the author compares Woman to the Four Elements, essential to life, but sometimes also the cause of death.

Like so much other Elizabethan and Jacobean iconography, however, this image too has its origins in the late Middle Ages, though immediately it would seem to have been based on an anonymous engraving in the *Nieuwen Ieucht Spiegel* (Arnhem, 1617).[68] In this version the lady is fully clothed but her index finger points to her groin and the German caption to the scene reads in translation, 'Oh you are fools all four, what you're looking for you will find here.' In the 1580s Balthasar Jenichen had executed a woodcut of essentially the same design except that this time the woman is naked but for her coif; she hides her genitals and her right breast with her hands, and her banderole opens, 'Have you never known a woman that you look for her in the Four Elements?' and finishes 'you will find her here'. Quite where 'here' is, is made explicit in the similar version engraved by Jan Wierix (dated 1601),[69] in which the woman points unmistakably to her crotch and the somewhat bald French couplet reads in translation: 'In vain you search in earth, water or fire/for it is only to be found in my lady's hole.' The version of this composition which was owned by Ferdinand Columbus (d. 1539) must have been similar to the woodcut image made *c.* 1521 by Hans Weiditz, in which the lady is once again naked (except for her shoes) and uses one hand to hide her genitals, but the other to point to them.[70]

The motif seems to be suggesting that while it is (literally) through Woman that men of all types are born to pursue their various occupations, all these men feverishly searching in the four elements are actually looking in the wrong place, all their multitudinous strivings are, if the truth were known, but strivings after her sex.

Woman on Top: Phyllis riding Aristotle

The World Turned Upside Down in terms of gender roles was a common male fear in the Middle Ages, the classic expression of which, as we have seen, is the popular image of the woman pulling on the breeches while her husband spins with her distaff. In the topsy-turvy land of Torelore, the king lies in childbed while his queen leads the country's army into the field.[71]

The thought that women might gain the upper hand in the domestic *ménage* was bad enough, but the idea of the 'woman on top' during sexual intercourse was denounced by all right-thinking theologians, for not only was such sexual 'inversion' perceived as demeaning to the male, it was regarded as a 'perversion' of the type which had led God to punish humanity with the Flood, and the sort of position fitting only for such perverters of the Faith as witches (see p. 152).

From the late thirteenth century, the Power of Women topos included countless representations of the courtesan Phyllis riding Aristotle. One of the philosopher's pupils, Alexander, the future The Great, stung by his teacher's rebuke that he had allowed himself to be distracted from his studies by women, determined to have his revenge. The philosopher had foolishly proclaimed his own imperviousness to the charms of women, so Alexander hired a courtesan named Phyllis to seduce Aristotle. The philosopher eventually dropped his guard so far as to allow her to ride him naked around the palace courtyard – where Alexander had gleefully arranged for the unseemly spectacle to be publicly visible.

Images of the riding of Aristotle range from such remarkably delicate renderings as the elegant aquamanile in the Metropolitan Museum, New York (Figure 11.7),[72] to versions such as Urs Graf's drawing dated 1521 which in their emphasis on the

Figure 11.7

whip and bit give the *equus eroticus* motif a decidedly sado-masochistic air,[73] though none ever depicts such a blatantly phallic philosopher as a fifteenth-century lead badge from Nieuwlande.

Somewhat surprisingly – just as we have observed of the Battle for the Breeches motif – there seems to be no certain example of this motif on an English misericord, all the more puzzling, in that in continental stallwork the scene is found on numerous fifteenth- and sixteenth-century misericords, such as the one in Rouen Cathedral probably dating from the 1460s. The earliest English example of the motif known to me is a woodcut illustrating *The deceyte of women* (?1557), but like most of the other illustrations in this book, it first appeared early in the century in one of the Flemish printer Jan van Doesborch's publications.[74] From the end of the Elizabethan era comes another fascinating example functioning as the title-page woodcut to *The Brideling, Sadling and Ryding, of a rich Churle in Hampshire, by the subtill practise of one Iudeth Philips, a professed cunning woman, or Fortune teller* (1595), at a period when 'cunning woman' was more or less synonymous with witch.[75]

Virgil in the Basket

The Middle Ages knew a different Virgil, and had transmogrified the classical epic poet into a great magician.[76] He too was held up as an example of the humiliating Power of Women, for on one notable occasion when he came on a secret nocturnal visit to the house of his paramour Febilla (daughter of the Roman emperor), to whose tower room he was accustomed to be drawn up in a basket, having already tired of him, she had left him hanging helplessly in the basket beneath her window all night, to be exposed to public ridicule in the light of day. Determined in his turn to humiliate her publicly, and by means of his magic, he arranged that the citizens of Rome should only be able to light their torches at her vulva, to which end she was exposed to the sight of all, stark naked on a pedestal in the market-place. Both these humiliating scenes were popular in contemporary art in a variety of media. One version of a Florentine print depicting the key episodes in the legendary Life of Virgil issued in the 1460s had the torch-lighting portion erased on the plate – it must have offended the sensibilities of at least one publisher, or perhaps some public censor. In an era when almost all artists and craft-workers were men it is depressing, but perhaps not altogether surprising, to note how much of the erotic art of the period only serves to reinforce the prevailing atmosphere of misogyny, and yet, if this image was censored on the grounds of its perceived obscenity, paradoxically it seems to me to reveal a grudging acknowledgement of the power of female sexuality. What the vengeful Virgil intended as a demeaning punishment for Febilla, and the publisher perhaps as a piece of lucrative 'soft porn', seems transformed – at least in the uncensored version of the print – into a homage to this incandescent Venus of the market-place.

A curious insult offered to a woman in 1476/7 may perhaps allude to familiarity with this story in contemporary London.[77] Before the commissary court she testified that she had been defamed in these words: 'sche beryth feyre in her ars for every man to lyte his candyll at' – but maybe this was only the equivalent of the abusive epithet, *burnt arse*, which we saw applied to the image of Our Lady of Willesden in

Chapter 2, and similarly implied that the woman was a common whore infected with venereal disease.

In the middle of his sermon, an early fifteenth-century preacher makes this striking allusion to the Power of Women topos:

> Who was stronger than Samson, wiser than Solomon, holier than David? And yet they were all overcome by the queyntise and wiles of women.[78]

Queyntise at this period meant 'cunning' which must be the principal sense at issue here, but also 'elegance of dress', though it is impossible not to suspect that the preacher is further punning on the obscene sense of *queynte* familiar from Chaucer's 'Miller's Tale' ('Pryvely he caught hir by the queynte'), that is, he is maintaining that these biblical strong men were all overpowered by their vulnerability to a woman's sex.

An almost literal illustration of this sentiment, a strikingly overt recognition, celebration indeed, of the power of female sexuality, is afforded by a contemporary Italian birth-salver, a commemorative tray presented to the expectant mother and from which she was served during her confinement. Inside the vulvate mandorla stands the naked Venus flanked on either side by two angel-like *putti*. Beneath her kneel six famous male lovers, her adoring devotees. Rays emanating directly from her vulva enter the eyes of Samson, Achilles, Tristan, Lancelot, Paris and Troilus (Colour Plate 21).

Women's Fashion

Preachers of sermons and other moralists inveighed, predictably, against women's fashions and in Chapter 4 we have already noted an early pictorial satire in the mid-twelfth-century *Winchester Psalter*, in which the devil who tempts Christ is dressed as a woman in the height of contemporary fashion, in a tightly laced gown slit revealingly up the side and with a train and sleeve so extravagantly long that they have had to be knotted to prevent them from trailing on the ground. St Jerome's tale of the devil who settled on the trailing train of an overdressed woman surfaces frequently in medieval *exempla* collections, and appears in manuscript and then early printed book illustrations too.[79]

But it was perhaps the woman's 'crowning glory', her hair, that attracted the most vitriol from contemporary moralists. It was alleged that elaborate coiffures of false hair housed mice and rats;[80] other hairdos were said to make women look like cats, wolves or snails.[81] A fifteenth-century poem called upon Christ to destroy extravagant fashions, particularly women's headdresses:

> Fell dovne the pryde of wommens hornes,
> And suffre hem no longer with longe tayles
> Ne none other vicyous entayles,
> Of nother of males ne femayles,
> Ne hodes, ne tyres lyche carrake sayle.[82]   [Nor headdresses like ships' sails]

The horned headdress, in particular, which became popular in this period, was an irresistible target for both writers and artists. There are several poems about them;

one, the fourteenth-century 'Des Cornetes', complains that women now have 'horns' in order to kill men, who must therefore defend themselves. There is a parallel to this verbal hyperbole on a misericord at Ludlow, dating 1415x25, the central carving of which is a 'grinning, bridled female head a scold, with winged hat and veil', while the right-hand supporter is, significantly, a man carrying a shield.[83] Little devils, themselves horned, were shown peeping between a woman's 'horns', as on a misericord at Minster-in-Thanet of *c.* 1410 (Figure 11.8) – the implication is obvious.

Figure 11.8

Obsession with one's personal appearance was a species of pride, and Pride is one of the Seven Deadly Sins. Thus it is that in one of the woodcuts illustrating *Der Ritter vom Thurn* (Basel, 1493) (Figure 11.9),[84] we see an elegant young woman in the act of combing her hair before her mirror, but to her horror she sees reflected in it not her own beauty, but the image of the Devil's arse, mocking her pride in her appearance.

Gossiping

Another misericord carved *c.* 1365 for the Royal Foundation of St Catherine in Stepney[85] depicts as its central motif a hairy, cloven-hoofed, bat-winged devil hovering above two female busts, one exhibiting a pronounced *décolletage*; it is not just their fashionable immodesty that has drawn this devil's attention, however, but the fact that they are gossiping in church. The left-hand supporter makes this clear: it features a recording demon displaying a parchment on which he has copied down their tittle-tattle. This is a very popular motif found throughout Europe, both in the verbal genres of *exemplum* and folktale,[86] and visually represented in stone sculptures, wood-carvings, wall-paintings and window-glass, as an ever-present reminder to congregations to behave decorously in church. Examples in all these media are known in Britain.[87] The recording demon was a popular figure in contemporary morality and mystery plays too, as well as in sermons and religious poetry. One such poem sums up his function thus:

Von eyner edlen frowen wie
die vor eym spiegel stůnd/sich mutzend/vnnd sy in dem spiegel
den tüfel sach jr den hyndern zeigend/

In ander exempel will ich̄ lich aber sage/vff die meynūg vō

igure 11.9

> Tutivillus the devil of hell,
> He writeth her names, sooth to tell,
> Ad missam garulantes.[88]   [of those who chatter during mass]

The motif was sometimes applied to other sins besides irreverent chattering. On one of the earlier Ludlow misericords (*c.* 1415x25),[89] a recording demon appears as the left-hand supporter to a central carving depicting another stereotype, the 'dishonest ale-wife' (Figure 5.7).

By 1560 at the latest, a broadside print had evolved in France, the earliest version of which is entitled 'The Cackling of Women' which depicts a townscape in which women gossip at the bakery, the bath-house, the laundry, and even in church – note once again the metaphorical use in the title of a term originally appropriate only to hens.[90] But I believe the prototype of this image, which was subsequently to become popular in England, France and Germany, is to be found in a *Proverbes en Rimes* illustration of the simple everyday observation, as Randle Cotgrave was later to point out in the entry at *four* (oven) in his English–French dictionary published in 1611 (with an admirable and anachronistic 'gender-blindness'), that 'while the bread bakes, and the corn grinds, people have some leisure to tell how the world goes'.

Monsters of Misogyny: Bigorne and Chicheface

The various monsters spawned by medieval misogyny included the unholy pair of the painfully thin *Chicheface*, starved for want of faithful obedient wives, its sole diet, and the swollen-bellied *Bigorne*, glutted on a surfeit of husbands complaisant to their wives' wills.

In English the earliest notice of Chicheface is a sarcastic reference in Chaucer's 'Clerk's Tale' (*c.* 1386):

> O noble wyves, ful of heigh prudence,
> Lat noon humylitee youre tonge naille . . .
> Lest Chichevache yow swelwe in hir entraile!

There is no corresponding mention of Bigorne.

The canonical pairing is first found in English in one of the most interesting of Lydgate's early fifteenth-century 'minor' verses, introduced in one manuscript as:

> the deuise of a peynted or desteyned clothe for an halle a parlour or a chaumbre deuysed by Iohan Lidegate at the request of a werthy citeseyn of London.

The surviving verses were the texts which accompanied the painted images described in the rubrics, but sadly, there is no trace of the painted cloth itself. Lydgate's English *device* is certainly dependent on the French tradition of these monsters, and faithfully reflects the historical development of their story, in which Chicheface first appears alone and is only later paired with the complementary Bigorne. The name Chicheface in French exists as a common noun meaning 'starveling' from an early date, and is found as a nickname, for example in one of

Coquillart's late fifteenth-century verses which refers to one *Laurence la grant Chicheface*; and there were also houses so called, presumably from their painted signs, in contemporary Amiens and Paris.

Lydgate's verses are the earliest attestation of the tradition of *graphic* representation of these marital monsters; but from later in the century we learn from another of Coquillart's poems, 'Les Droits Nouveaux' (1480), that Chicheface prints, doubtless accompanied by explanatory verses, were on sale near the Palais de Justice in Paris.[94] Furthermore, he mentions the mythical monster in the context of a new young mother's desire not to see her *tetons* become *tetasses*, hanging down like those of a chicheface – exactly as the monster's pendent dugs are shown in the earliest prints, which seems to confirm that the poet was familiar with precisely the same type. The earliest such print extant seems to have been issued by Guy Marchant in Paris *c.* 1495.[92]

From *c.* 1537 survive unique copies of separate sheets entitled 'Chicheface who eats all good wives', and 'Bigorne who eats all men who do their wives' bidding' probably printed in Lyons. The 1537 Chicheface woodcut and text are both clearly copied from that of *c.* 1495, and the probability that its companion was similarly derived from a no longer extant late fifteenth-century print, is strengthened by wall-paintings of both beasts in the château at Villeneuve-Lembron (Puy-de-Dôme), which are assigned to the first decade of the sixteenth century. A rather similar Chicheface is painted on one of the panels of a coffered ceiling in the château at Plessis-Bourré near Angers, dated 1500x06.[93] It has texts identical to those painted beside the monsters at Villeneuve-Lembron and they are clearly related to those of the 1495 print, as are the portraits of the Chicheface monsters.

Lydgate also gave a speech – in the words of the manuscript rubric – to 'a companye of men comyng towards this beest Bicorne', though such a company is not otherwise attested in graphic representations of the beasts until the standardised Northern European prints of *c.* 1600, which unite them into a single composition. It may therefore be that Lydgate had access to an already unified presentation of this type which has not survived.[94]

'Bi the rode, wimen are wode!' (By the Rood, women are mad!) proclaims the rhyming legend of one fourteenth-century seal, as if to confirm that gender relations were no easier in the late Middle Ages than they are today. If over the past century Western women, at least, have escaped many of the stifling gender-role restrictions of their medieval forebears, a century is not a long time in which to dispel the stereotyping of millennia, and many attitudes regarding appropriate gender relations which reflect medieval and even earlier *mentalités* doubtless persist into the twenty-first century.

I hope to have shown here the history behind some at least of these 'patriarchal' attitudes to gender roles, inescapably 'normal' for the late Middle Ages, and their metaphorical expression in language and art. As ever, our linguistic past lives on to haunt us, and while some of these metaphors may now be dead – and some readers may well feel that some that are not, should be – others linger on in the 'twilight zone' of political incorrectness. It is a commonplace that metaphors construct our thinking, and it perhaps does no harm from time to time to delve into the history and evolution of those we have lived by, in this as in other areas.

TWELVE

WICKED WILLIES WITH WINGS: SEX AND SEXUALITY IN LATE MEDIEVAL ART AND THOUGHT

In this chapter I embark on a whistle-stop tour of late medieval and early modern sexuality as revealed in the art of those eras. The potential field is vast and so, for reasons of space, there is much I have to omit: I cannot here do justice, for example, to the entire area of male and female homosexuality,[1] though in earlier chapters I have been able to touch on other sexual topics, such as the use of images of bestiality in *Schandbilder*, and the public humiliation of 'sex-offenders'. Except incidentally, I am not here concerned with pornography in the modern sense, which I take to begin in the post-medieval era with Aretino's notorious *I Modi* (The (Sexual) Positions), consisting of his sixteen *Sonetti lussuriosi* illustrated by the engravings of Marcantonio Raimondi (from original designs by Giulio Romano), issued, and publicly burned, in Venice in 1527.[2]

In what follows I make full use of the astonishing and often bizarre range of lead badges from the drowned villages of the Schelde estuary. Thanks above all to the publication of two recent catalogues of badges in the Van Beuningen Collection in Rotterdam,[3] these are at last becoming more widely known among cultural and art historians, and necessitate a serious rethink of late medieval popular iconography in general, and especially in the area of sexuality. Let me state at once my continued belief that almost all such sexual badges were not intended as 'erotic' in the sense of provoking sexual arousal, but principally as apotropaic – by the exposure of the genital icon, whether male or female, they were intended to disarm that ever-present yet vague malevolence known as the Evil Eye. However, this is not to say that the precise forms these sexual badges take are random – although in some cases they may well be – for, as I hope to demonstrate, there are perhaps certain cultural universals in human attitudes to sexuality, as to most other matters, and often such unconscious thinking will out.

THE SEXUAL BADGES

Evidence is provided below and elsewhere to suggest that many of the sexual badges incorporate, in whole or in part, metaphors current in the late medieval period relating to the sex organs and sexual intercourse – such explanations, however, cannot tell us what the function of these badges was. Because they are technically identical with the much better- and longer-known 'pilgrim badges', it has not unreasonably been assumed that these badges too were worn on the clothing; but were they worn overtly on the *outer* clothing, or were they worn secretly? If they were indeed worn, we still know nothing about *how* they were worn. In Chapter 10 I referred to Martial d'Auvergne's *Les Arrêts d'Amour* (*c.* 1460) in which he tells of a courtly lover who wore a brooch 'between his skin and his shirt': might not such sexual badges have been worn in similarly secret fashion?

And what of their iconographic forebears? Does the strongly represented phallic presence in this corpus confirm suggestions that these badges are rooted in the tradition of late Roman iconography? Are these sexual badges frivolously 'carnivalesque' in the loose sense in which that word has come to be used – celebratory of that licensed misrule that obtained during periods of carnival and in which brazen sexual display was almost *de rigeur*? Or does their often equivocal humour, rather, have a deeply serious intent? Do they embody just that combination of *bizarrerie* and visceral shock which from Roman times was felt to be the perfect antidote against the Evil Eye, as affirmed by Plutarch?[4] Good and bad luck are but two sides of the same coin; the *apotropaion* which averts and diverts bad luck from the wearer may also come to be considered in a positive sense as functioning to attract good luck. Do these sexual badges have a dual function? On the one hand, the Evil Eye is repulsed, in both senses of that word, by the exposure of the genital icon, or diverted, in both senses of that word, and thus distracted from its malign intentions; on the other hand (on the analogy of coin-filled purse badges), perhaps on the principle that like attracts like, might such badges have been worn by persons of either sex attempting magically to attract good luck in sexual matters? The stark inscription *PINTELIN* which captions the badge of the ambulant phallus approaching a 'standing' vulva (see chapter ornament) might mean either 'little pintle' an affectionate diminutive (as English 'willy'), or be construed rather more urgently (and magically) as 'pintle, in!'

It is precisely because these tiny, seemingly inconsequential badges were mass-produced in the cheapest of materials that they have such a disproportionate significance for our understanding of late medieval popular culture. Indeed, I would go so far as to contend that henceforth any history of late medieval art or culture that purports to describe that era without taking this material into account will be fundamentally flawed.

I believe there are certain unexceptionable – and indeed, unexceptional – conclusions to which the study of this body of sexual iconography as a whole leads, and it may be helpful if I state one such in advance of the discussion of the individual images which follow. I believe that we may be certain that many representations of the human sex organs (sometimes, of the literally dismembered male organs alone) continue to play their immemorial, apotropaic role. Whether pre-Christian in origin or not, there is a surprising wealth of such imagery affixed to the exterior of Romanesque churches and, in my opinion, not every female carving of the drastic type represented, for example, by the famous corbel at Kilpeck on the Welsh border, was intended as a representation of the vice Luxuria.[5] As far as the badge corpus is concerned, I regard the ambulant phallus found at Middelburg, cast *c.* 1400,[6] as key to the understanding of this imagery, for a now headless figure standing on the shaft holds a banderole which reads *DE SELDE-*, which I take to be the Middle Dutch definite article, *de*, followed by the word *selde* meaning '(good) luck'. These sexual icons are, then, lucky charms, amulets to bring good luck, but also *apotropaia* to repulse bad luck, to avert the Evil Eye, in the same way hypothesised for the sexually exhibitionist sculptures of often indeterminate date set into churches and secular buildings alike, that have come to be known by the mysterious Irish name, *sheelagh-na-gig*. Here too, one badge in particular, from Nieuwlande,[7] seems to me to be of special importance; if it were carved in stone and 310 mm high, rather than a mere 31-mm high lead casting, it would be just such a monumental *sheelagh-na-gig* – particularly significant is the clear indication of the figure's ribs, very reminiscent of stone figures from Llandrindod (Figure 4.7) and Cavan,[8] and the sort of crone-like anatomy attributed to such figures as the Scots Gaelic *cailleach*.

The *apotropaion* need not be merely passive and defensive, it may be actively aggressive too. The tri-phallic man of a badge found in Rotterdam brandishes one dismembered phallus in a fairly combative fashion, but I know of no better illustration of this aggressive use of the phallus – much as if it were a pistol – than that pointed at a griffin by a grotesque in the *bas-de-page* of an extraordinarily sexualised Parisian *Roman de la Rose* manuscript of *c.* 1350, which has recently been aptly compared to this sexual badge imagery.[9]

Trimming Her Pubic Hair

The predominantly female exhibitionist carvings known as *sheelagh-na-gigs* are usually interpreted as apotropaic, perhaps the most convincing example of such a function, datable to the twelfth century, is the figure which once stood above the Porta Tosa in Milan. The image is of a woman who has lifted her skirt up, thereby exposing her nakedness, and who is, further, apparently in the process of trimming her pubic hair with a rather alarming pair of shears. A similar though much more crudely carved figure (now known only from a photograph) was found at Egremont in Cumbria, and it has been plausibly suggested that she is 'removing her pubic hair, so exposing her pudendum more completely, in order to ward off bad luck the more effectively'.[10]

Whether these medieval stone sculptures have any relationship with an early sixteenth-century woodcut by Peter Floetner entitled by Geisberg – on what authority I do not know – 'Allegory of Truth', is far from certain. The fool who holds a candle upright between the woman's legs while she plies the shears is, at least, suggestive. Other details seem to invite a satirical reading: the open-air setting seems very odd for such intimate toilet and the flamboyant feathered hat worn by the otherwise naked woman is the sort usually reserved in contemporary art for prostitutes and mercenaries' whores.

There was clearly a certain male fascination with female pubic depilation in the late Middle Ages: one of Poggio's mid-fifteenth-century *facetiae* (*De meretrice conquerente de tonsoris maleficio*), for instance, concerns the shaving of a prostitute's pubic hair, and women's pubic hair, frequently referred to as a woman's 'beard' (compare the male peasant abusively nicknamed *Futzenpart* (Cunt-beard) in Wittenwiler's *Ring, c.* 1400),[11] is often discussed in late medieval French works in particular.[12] In a classic piece of euphemism the Parisian street called in 1292 the *Rue de Poile-Con* (Cunt-Trimming Street) is now the *Rue de Pélican* (Pelican Street)! There are similarly some remarkable yet unremarked minor Middle English place-names which appear to recall the same aspect of feminine toilet: a spring named *Shavecuntewelle* is attested in Kent, and a *Swylcontdich* (Swill-cunt-ditch) in Cheshire from 1396. As in the case of the Parisian street-name the same 'taboo interference' has been at work in the latter instance, which by 1620 had become *Swilckhorne* (*ditch*) and by 1848, *Swillinditch*.

Anasyrma

The simple exposure of the vulva by raising the skirts is a well-established apotropaic gesture, technically known by the Greek term *anasyrma*. The gesture was illustrated in a miniature reproduced (unfortunately without provenance) by Eduard Fuchs with the caption, 'Women mock their fleeing menfolk', from a mid-thirteenth-century French manuscript in which a group of mounted knights are confronted by three women who have raised their skirts thus exposing their pudenda.[13] This medieval miniature is very similar to a late sixteenth-century Dutch painting in the Kunsthistorisches Museum in Vienna,[14] and it may be that both allude to the Persian incident noted by Rabelais. The same gesture is made by the Old Woman of Papefiguière in Chapter 47 of Rabelais' *Quart Livre* (1551), where it has the traditional apotropaic effect of frightening away the Devil, who is under the naive impression (yet traditional for simpletons) that the old woman's exposed pudendum is a 'wound' which her husband, the farmer with whom he has come to fight, inflicted upon her with his 'little finger' – another traditional sexual metaphor.[15] At this point, however, Rabelais shows himself a true Renaissance scholar by finding a classical precedent for the Vieille's unseemly gesture, albeit in its derisive, rather than apotropaic application, by describing it as 'the manner in which the Persian women long ago presented themselves to their children who fled from the battle'. This is likely to derive from Plutarch's *De Virtutibus Mulierum*, but immediately, via Book VI of Erasmus' *Apothegms*, in which he recalls the incident as follows:

> When the Cyperi had been fighting miserably against Astyages the women went out to meet their men as they fled back towards the city, with their bellies exposed: 'Where are you running to, cowards?' they asked. 'Don't you know it isn't possible to come into this vessel [that is, womb] again?

Although it is here used more as an insult to their cowardly menfolk than as a protective gesture, it is still literally an *apotropaion*, in that it has the effect of turning their own retreating troops away from them to go back and rejoin the fray.

A purely insulting use of the same gesture, this time as an insult directed at a male homosexual, is recorded from Dubrovnik at a date roughly contemporary with that

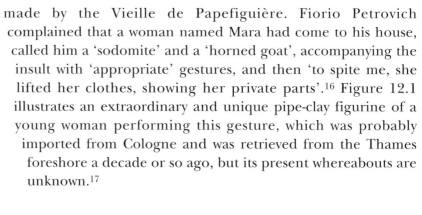

made by the Vieille de Papefiguière. Fiorio Petrovich complained that a woman named Mara had come to his house, called him a 'sodomite' and a 'horned goat', accompanying the insult with 'appropriate' gestures, and then 'to spite me, she lifted her clothes, showing her private parts'.[16] Figure 12.1 illustrates an extraordinary and unique pipe-clay figurine of a young woman performing this gesture, which was probably imported from Cologne and was retrieved from the Thames foreshore a decade or so ago, but its present whereabouts are unknown.[17]

The 'Megaphallus'

The similar use of what have been termed 'megaphallic' sculptures on the façade of the Romanesque church,[18] has been compared with the description of a statue of a boy pulling a thorn from his foot (and thus 'accidentally' exposing his genitals), the so-called *Spinario*, then outside the Lateran Palace in Rome, as recorded by the twelfth-century English tourist, Master Gregory. Locally the figure was known as 'Priapus', which would make sense, as – like the traditional classical statues of that deity – Gregory described it as having 'male parts of wonderful magnitude'. At Orense Cathedral in Spain, however, a dwarfish but disproportionately phallically well-

Figure 12.1

endowed figure (characteristic of dwarves according to Aristotle) has been identified as the trickster Marcolf.[19]

Anthropologists and psychiatrists have understandably been tempted to make much of the development, not to say, the *over*-development, of the codpiece in the late medieval and early modern period.[20] Even before the advent proper of that inevitably puffed-up piece of male finery, however, and if we may trust the poet Hans Sachs (d. 1576), German peasants were accustomed to practise an imposture allegedly not unknown to the modern pop-star:

> the clothing of the peasant lads
> caused great scandal
> because they wore such great codpieces
> on their breeches,
> which were hollow within
> but completely padded out with rags –
> and the devil himself lived in them.
> By such great stuffed codpieces
> many a simple girl was deceived
> who too late regretted it after.

Such *hypocriticques braguettes* (deceiving codpieces) were derided by Rabelais, himself, as he tells us in the eighth chapter of his *Gargantua* (1534), the purported author of a work entitled *De la dignité des braguettes*, but his eponymous hero, of course, had no need of such fraud, his codpiece being truly gargantuan and correspondingly and authentically well filled:

> it was long and capacious, but well furnished within and well 'victualled' [punning on *vit*, 'penis'], in no way resembling the deceiving codpieces of so many gallants which are full of nothing but air, to the great disappointment of the female sex.

But in his *Instructions to his Son* (*c.* 1450), Peter Idley warns him specifically against such women who 'set their myndes galantes to asspye, Beholdyng . . . how the stuffyng off the codpece berys ought'.[21]

Sex and Spinning

As well as with men of different races and monstrous men, exceptional penile length was traditionally associated with certain animals, which are constantly invoked, for example, in erotic verse; the bull, the horse and the ass will spring to mind, but we have already examined this aspect of animal folklore in Chapter 3, as well as the perhaps less obvious baboon.

The lead badge found at Dordrecht of an ass, with an erection, sitting spinning at a distaff[22] is probably to be seen in the light of what we have said about spinning being a quintessentially feminine activity, making this very much a *monde renversé* scene. That an animal should be spinning at all might be thought topsy-turvy enough, but that such a proverbially well-endowed male animal and in such an obvious state of sexual excitement should be depicted spinning is a burlesque overplus. Although a badge of an ape spinning has been found in Konstanz (compare Figure 3.6), by far the commonest animal to be so depicted is the appropriately female sow – *la truie qui file*, as she is known in French – and although no badges of her have yet surfaced, she is depicted in several media including manuscript margins, misericords, woodcut prints and in late medieval house-signs.[23] The late fifteenth-century German print is provided with a satirical text to the effect that human females could learn a thing or two from this sow who spins so industriously with her piglets.

It is also sexually appropriate, if bizarre in the extreme, to find a vulva sitting spinning, as on a badge found near Amsterdam: 'she' sits on a three-legged stool and wears a three-phallus diadem.[24]

Roman Origins?

In his *Quaestiones Conviviales* (V.7.3) Plutarch noted that the Romans believed that indecent or ridiculous images drew the eyes of ill-disposed spirits and men to themselves and thus averted the malevolent gaze of the Evil Eye from the vulnerable, distracted it, 'fascinated' it, indeed. Such amulets designed to do just this were termed *fascina* by the Romans and foremost among them were the small phallus pendants commonly found on Roman sites and the more substantial phallic grotesques hung about with bells known as *tintinnabula* which were suspended from the ceiling.[25] Not only is there an obvious similarity between such pendants and the medieval phallus badges, but the fact that the latter frequently bear a bell around the 'neck' of the phallus, led me to suggest ultimate derivation from just such Roman models, perhaps due to the discovery of a cache of bronzes including *tintinnabula* in the late medieval Netherlands. Late Roman *fascina* in various media include similarly bizarre scenes: the Roman pottery beaker from Saffron Walden depicting a chariot pulled by four phalli, for example, or the terracotta figurine of two phalli sawing through an evil eye, or the popular winged phalli or phallus-birds.[26]

Liberal Shepherds' Grosser Names – the Sexuality of Plants

The Greek word *satyrion*, 'in allusion to the reputed aphrodisiac properties of the plant so named' (as the *OED* notes), was similarly a name given to various kinds of orchid, and thus *Saturia* is rendered *ballokwort* in a fifteenth-century glossary, while in his *Herbal* of 1562 Turner referred to 'Whyt satyrion, or in other more vnmanerly speche, hares ballockes'. For, as the dictionary explains, the plant-name 'orchid' derives from the Greek word for 'testicle', 'so called from the shape of the tubers in most species'. The testicles might be those of various animals, the hare, for example (as above), or the wolf, *wolvys-ballock* being recorded as a fifteenth-century name for the soldier or military orchid (*orchis militaris*).[27] In Lyte's translation of Dodoens' *Herbal* (1578) he mentions *fooles ballockes* as a name for the commonest English orchid, that is generally known today as the Early Purple, but these are also the *long purples* that Hamlet's mother informs us 'liberal shepherds give a grosser name' though with laudable sensitivity, given the context of Ophelia's drowning, forbears from citing (IV.vii.169)!

These 'gross' orchid names perhaps provide a context for the four examples now known of Dutch badges in the form of a gardener who appears to be stroking or planting a phallus which has been placed in the ground;[28] on one a person leans on a spade while another bends down to stroke the phallus, the shaft and glans of which has emerged from the soil, while its – in this context – bulb-like testicles are still rooted below. If we can accept that there may be varying degrees of surreality in this imagery, then we are presumably still in the land of metaphor here. *Semen* is the Latin word for 'seed' and the metaphor is universal in those European cultures that owe their anatomical knowledge to the Graeco-Roman tradition; the notion that the man's 'seed' is planted in the 'fertile soil' of the woman's womb is similarly a commonplace of this procreational discourse. Catherine Johns has drawn attention to a detail of the decoration on a red-figure vase by the Hasselmann Painter (*c.* 430–420 BC) which depicts a woman sprinkling phalli set in the ground with water, as a probable fertility ritual to encourage seed to grow,[29] and we cannot totally rule out such a function for some, at least, of these badges.

Funny Ha-ha or Funny Peculiar?

I believe we are entitled to conclude that some of the sexual imagery in the lead badge corpus is intentionally comic; sometimes, as perhaps when we see a ship 'crewed' by phalli,[30] it is 'emptily' humorous, having no ulterior purpose beyond that of raising a laugh – though even that might perhaps be enough to deflect the malign intentions of the Evil Eye – but in other examples the humour seems to me clearly *satiric* in intent.

The most drastic example I have yet come across of such a presumably satiric intention, which must, I believe, adumbrate the polemics of the Reformation, is a badge in the form of three phalli walking on human legs and carrying a sort of litter on which rides a vulva crowned with a three-phallus diadem (Figure 12.2). Despite the early date of this badge, cast *c.* 1400, I am tempted to suggest this may be seen as a satirical proto-Protestant attack on a Catholic procession in honour of the Virgin Mary, whose image, perhaps in the form of a crowned statue of the Queen of Heaven, and surrounded by a rayed 'glory' or mandorla – itself a vulvate shape, of course – was paraded through the streets on her feast-days. Such parodic *pre*-Reformation processions were not unknown; in 1441, for instance, we hear of a Cologne inn-keeper, Johan van Ghynt, who, with four men and a woman, was punished for parading about the city during the carnival period bearing an imitation reliquary-shrine on which sat a doll with a banneret and *aspergillum*.[31]

Figure 12.2

A century later, however, when the German Reformation proper was in full swing, we learn of *real* mock processions such as that in Hildesheim during the 1543 carnival period, in which relics of the Virgin and the foreskin of Christ were similarly paraded through the streets in a monstrance and mocked and abused.[32] Another procession two days later, parodying the various religious orders and in which some of the revellers sang the *Kyrie* from prayer books that were, in fact, gaming-boards, is very reminiscent of an engraved broadsheet of a *Satirical Procession* by Peter Floetner datable to 1535; it also features two nuns who carry pitchforks from which hang male undergarments, a parody of the customary religious banners and, further, a hit at the sexual improprieties of the clergy.

Depictions of the sex organs have long been used as satirical weapons in themselves, of course: in another *real* candle-lit festive procession at Pamiers near Toulouse some time before 1327, for example, members of the clergy were burlesqued with effigies, lewd songs, boys dressed as women, and banners depicting male and female genitalia, not surprisingly this spectacle was condemned by the local bishop – ironically, as so often, the only reason we now know anything about such incidents![33]

We may similarly assume that the Zurich apprentice who hired a painter to depict four coats of arms featuring male and female genitals in 1455 had some satirical purpose,[34] as the Witshire villager certainly did when in 1616 he set up a buck's horn stuffed with a wisp of hay and 'a picture of a woman's privities' by the roadside to greet the return of a bridal party. Having married a woman of dubious local reputation, Richard Tomes was felt to have thereby made himself a cuckold on the same day.[35]

The inevitability of the French pun on *vit*, 'penis' and *vie*, 'life', besides appearing *c.* 1500 in riddles,[36] and visually in *rébus de Picardie*,[37] was even the subject of another satirical procession in the opening years of the sixteenth century, a daring political *charivari* entitled *Le Vit de François Premier*, in which a gigantic phallus in a pageant car was pulled through the streets of Paris and onlookers invited to come and help flagellate the royal member.[38]

The Sexual Pilgrim – Medieval Sex-tourists?

Figure 12.3

A badge, now known in several examples, depicting a pilgrim as vulva or a vulva on pilgrimage, complete with all the usual pilgrim's attributes, hat, rosary, and suggestively phallus-tipped staff,[39] similarly seems best interpreted as a satirical attack on the dubious motives it was suggested some women had for going on pilgrimage. The notorious Wife of Bath, for example, openly confessed that her motives were not purely devotional, for Chaucer tells us 'she koude muchel of wandrynge by the weye',[40] and we noted in Chapter 2 the sexual abuse directed by Lollards and other Reformers at cult statues of the Virgin visited by pilgrims in England.

A variant of the vulva-as-pilgrim badges adds phallus epaulettes[41] to the standard staff, hat and rosary (Figure 12.3), but if these badges are satirical of women's alleged mixed motives for undertaking pilgrimages, a male 'sex-tourist' is also known in the form of an ambulant phallus with pilgrim's staff and scrip. What is different about this sexual pilgrim, however, is that his 'head' is being literally crowned by a young woman.[42] The Christian saint's spiritual journey often ends with the 'crown of martyrdom' as his reward, and the acknowledgement of having arrived at his heavenly goal – is the designer of this badge making some mischievous satiric point here? Crowning implies consummation, and it is not difficult to imagine a sexual reading of the placing of a circlet over the 'head' of the phallus. This Petrarchan convention of the Passionate Pilgrim, of the lover going on a pilgrimage to the shrine of his saint, underlies that medieval classic of erotic love, the *Roman de la Rose*, and at least one manuscript illustrates the climax of the Lover's pilgrimage in search of the Beloved by a miniature in which the pilgrim Lover suggestively thrusts his staff through the slit in the base of the statue.

This image of the pilgrim's staff, Latin *baculum*, Middle English *burdoun*, brings me to another general conclusion, that is, that the majority of erotic visual imagery proceeds relatively subtly, *by metaphor*. Punning on the sense 'chorus', which *burdoun* could also have in Middle English, and ostensibly describing the duet which the two men sang together, Chaucer hints at their homosexual relationship when he says that the Summoner bore the Pardoner 'a stif burdoun'.[43]

The Amorous Joust

The *Roman de la Rose* miniature is paralleled in one of an important series of six Flemish drawings of sexual metaphors executed *c.* 1470, in which a soldier with a spear tells the chatelaine that he will enter her castle by 'the Lower Court' (Colour Plate 22).[44]

Spearman:	Noble and pure maiden
	I have to conquer your tower;
	at least, sooner or later,
	I will enter by the Lower Court.
Chatelaine:	Gallant, I do not fear your assault
	my castle is very strong and valuable
	it cannot be beaten by any 'engine'
	unless by your battering-ram.

But the spear is also an ancient metaphor for the penis, of course, and like the staff, an unequivocal phallic symbol. In Lydgate's free mid-fifteenth-century translation of a popular late medieval misogynist classic, the *De Coniuge non Ducenda*,[45] for example, which he entitled *The Pain and Sorrow of Evil Marriage*, it is said that the husband will be cuckolded if 'he be no spere-man good'.[46] In similar vein, John Skelton's early sixteenth-century Malkyn is said by her lover to be 'trussed for to break a launce',[47] further hinting that at least some Middle English surnames of the *Brekelaunce* type, are not nicknames of the battlefield or tiltyard, but commemorate more amorous jousts. A fascinating glimpse of an early Jacobean *charivari* in which the metaphor recurs is recorded as part of the Wells May Game of 1607:

> he's growne so ympotent he cannot wield his launce
> nor pike nor scarce can beare his shield
> Butt yet potenciall he can breake his speare
> in venus darlinge with a full Carreare.[48]

The vagina is similarly described as 'A pavys or a target' – both words meaning 'shield' – 'for a sperys heed', in the poem 'Whan She Hath on hire Hood of Grene', formerly attributed to Lydgate,[49] but another of the Flemish drawings (Colour Plate 23) perfectly illustrates such a metaphoric encounter. The Knight of the Drooping Lance, as I shall call him, approaches on horseback a lady who holds a large shield out in front of her at waist-height. His quatrain reads:

> How come, no matter what I do,
> That my thrusts don't strike your shield
> as they should do;
> they're always too high or too low

To which the lady responds:

> The fault is not mine, love,
>   it's because your lance is bending;
> you can't strike it right
>   if your shaft isn't stiffer.

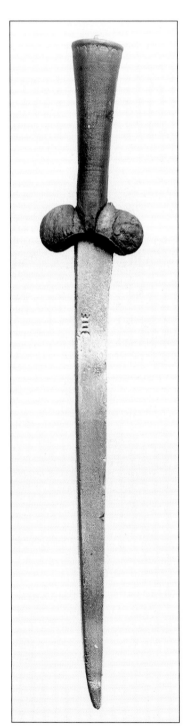

That thrusting weapons such as spears, swords and knives are phallic symbols is not a discovery of modern psychoanalysis. A particularly interesting recognition of this appears in the form of haft borne by a particular type of late medieval dagger, referred to in England, at least, as a *ballok-knyf*, or a *ballok-hefted* knife (Figure 12.4).[50] Attempting to gloss Langland's use of the former in *Piers Plowman* (1377x1379), where worldly priests are satirised for wearing 'A baselard or ballok-knyf with botons overgilte',[51] but unfamiliar with the *realium*, the *OED* unarchaeologically explains this sort of knife as '?one worn at the girdle'. In the London Museum's 1940 *Medieval Catalogue* they are still euphemistically styled 'kidney daggers',[52] but by 1978 A.V.C. Schmidt in his edition of *Piers Plowman* was able to grasp the nettle and provide the gloss, 'A fashionable ornamental dagger or a knife with a knobbed (= testicle-shaped) haft, covered with gilt studs.' Worn at the girdle, the handles of these daggers present an obviously phallic appearance, as sported by the young noblemen who surround the Duc de Berry's table in his celebrated early fifteenth-century *Très Riches Heures*, for instance, or by the jaunty gallant in the foreground of Bruegel's *Netherlandish Proverbs* painted 150 years later (see jacket illustration).

The Sword and the Sheath

In this context it seems highly suggestive that an illustration of a stall selling knives and sheaths in a fourteenth-century English manuscript includes a scene of rape in the foreground, especially as scenes of intercourse of any kind are comparatively rare in medieval manuscripts.[53]

In symbolic terms, the sexual counterpart of the sword or knife is the scabbard or sheath, as attested by the modern medical use of Latin *vagina* (sheath), and the relationship of the two is occasionally spelled out in late medieval literature, as in *Der Kurz Hannentanz*, a fifteenth-century German *fastnachtspiel* in which the maiden says to the young man, 'I am the sheath, you are the sword.'[54] The dream of a husband who feared he was being cuckolded, related in the Middle English

Figure 12.4

version of *Partonope of Blois*, is as transparent to us post-Freudians as it must have been to its original, late fifteenth-century audience:

> He thogte he sawe hys neygbore drawe owte hys swerde,
> And fulle hys scawbarte he thogte that he pyssed.[55]

In another late Middle English poem, 'The Epistle of Othea to Hector' (*c.* 1450), the danger to the male of 'vncouth straung love' is encapsulated in the maxim that, 'Owte of a cankred sweerd is hard to rubbe the rust',[56] and the *rusty blade* which Chaucer's Reeve is said to bear by his side, is perhaps similarly symbolic of his self-confessed lechery and, indeed, his comparison of himself to a rotten fruit.[57]

My, What a Big Nose You Have!

Another metaphorical strategy in the taboo area of sex-organ nomenclature, and hence in that of representation also, is the substitution of an analogous bodily part for the tabooed member. The classic instance of this usage, styled by E.K. Kane, 'the widest spread of any popular erotic belief',[58] is the theory that the relative size of a man's nose corresponds to the size of his penis, or in the words of a precept of the Salernitan medical school, the most famous and respected such school in the Middle Ages, 'It is known by his nose how big a man's "spear" is' – in which once again we note the 'spear' metaphor. This is certainly a belief which goes back to classical times, and thus Sir Thomas Elyot, in his English–Latin dictionary published *c.* 1540, rightly defined one of the senses of the word *nasuti* (literally 'nosed') as, 'men which haue their private members very great'. Even in Roman Britain we find graffiti in which the nose is replaced by the phallus,[59] or as on a cameo of an ithyphallic mime actor, with a second phallic nose.[60] Generous nasal endowment is also one of the aspects of the fool's phallicism, as we noted in Chapter 6.

Another striking Dutch lead badge in the form of a penis projecting from a hood where its owner's nose ought to be, illustrates the equivalence, nose = penis, at its simplest.[61] A particularly grisly instance of this equivalence occurred on the death of Simon de Montfort at the Battle of Evesham in 1265 when his body was mutilated, his genitals cut off, and the testicles hung either side of his nose.[62] Less than a generation later, an erotic Medieval Latin couplet was copied into the margin of a manuscript owned by Ramsey Abbey and also translated into English as a lament by a woman named Rose:

> *I am Rose: wo is me, sutere, that I snete the!*
> *that I wacs, weylawey! Cherles hand me thristet ay.*
> [I am Rose: woe is me, shoemaker, that I 'blew your nose'
> woe is me that I grow big, I was forced by a peasant!][63]

This interestingly combines the female image of the rose with a uniquely elaborated, active use of the male nose image. Vernacular literatures are also perfectly familiar with the erotic convention concerning nose-size, of course; in the late fifteenth-century *Farce joyeuse de Maistre Mimin,* for example, one of the characters says:

> I've heard it said of M. Mengin
> that he has the finest 'engine'
> that ever lad bore;
> you've only got to refer
> to his nose, that'll show you.[64]

And when Gargantua asks Rabelais' womanising Frère Jean why he has such a fine nose, he says it is because he was one of the first at *la foyre des nez* (Nose Fair), and so took one of the finest and biggest on offer, concluding with a deliberately perverted version of the popular medical adage cited above, by punning on the opening of Psalm 122, 'By the shape of my nose it is known how I have lifted up for you.'[65] *Nose-Fair* would be an appropriate alternative title for the woodcut illustration by Hans Sebald Beham of the Hans Sachs poem, 'Der Nasentanz zu Gumpelsbrunn', issued in 1535. It depicts a number of male peasants with large, grotesque noses, cavorting about a central pole from which hang three prizes to be awarded to the three dancers with the three biggest noses. The first prize is a garland, second prize a false nose, while the third prize – which only makes sense if we are aware of the popular equivalence we have just been considering – is a breech-cloth. There *are* hints as to the real nature of the competition in the accompanying verse text, however; for example, one of the types of nose listed as borne by the dancers is described as copper, and this, together with the second prize, a nose-shaped prosthesis, alludes to the practice of wearing false noses made of various metals, in order to disguise or replace syphilitic deterioration of that organ. There is said to be a portrait of the poet Sir William Davenant wearing such a nose (*a.* 1650), and compare the Shakespearian allusion to the practice in *Troilus and Cressida* (1606): 'I had as lieve Helen's golden tongue Had commended Troilus for a copper nose' (I.ii.101), and such false copper noses seem also to have tried the skills of Elizabethan writers of paradoxical encomia.[66] The very title of the Sachs poem offers a much broader hint, however, for the bird-name *gumpel* was also used as a term for the penis.[67] Beham has also carefully contrived to place this second-prize nose on a level with the cockerel on top of another pole in the background, around which other peasants are doing a *Hahnentanz* – itself the occasion for many a bawdy innuendo in the two *fastnachtspiele* so titled[68] – thus Beham establishes a visual equivalence also for the two phallic synonyms. At least two modern commentators have signally missed the point of this piece of bawdy fun, and seen the Beham print as evidence of authentic sixteenth-century German folk custom. Certainly Sachs and his illustrator *are* poking fun at peasant festivities in the poem and accompanying woodcut, but it does not therefore follow that a real 'Nose-Dance' ever took place!

The Flying Phallus

The phallus-bird, as we have noted above, is a peculiarly long-lived motif: two of the earliest known to me are a Greek cup painting, in which the testicles double as the bird's gizzard,[69] and a detail from an early fifth-century BC red-figure vase, showing a girl holding a phallus-bird and uncovering a basket of phalli.[70] I have already suggested that its abundance in late Roman iconography led to its readoption in the late Middle Ages as, for example, in another Dutch badge depicting a predatory phallus-bird preying on a stylised vulva.[71] In a marginal illustration from the opening folio of a *Decretals* manuscript of *c.* 1400, the female sex strikes back, and a deft huntress manages to hit the phallus-bird in flight – again the 'bird' bears a bell round its 'neck'.[72] It is also to be seen, though all but obliterated, on a rare surviving late fifteenth-century Italian copperplate for producing pornographic prints.[73] In 1551 Rabelais tells us that Lent daydreams about penises flying and creeping up walls, not such an entirely arbitrary piece of grotesquerie as might at first have been thought, for Brantôme, recalling the same period, attests the real existence of such wall-paintings in Spain.[74]

The Phallovitrobolus

Drinking from a vessel in the shape of a phallus is a joke – if, indeed, that is what it is (in certain cultures there may well be cult implications)[75] – of some antiquity. The pre-Columbian Mochica culture of *c.* AD 500, for example, produced just such embarrassing drinking-vessels,[76] but the Romans too had such phalliform containers – we even know the technical name for them, *phallovitroboli*.[77] More surprisingly, actual examples in glass survive from the late Middle Ages, such as a German example of about 1500.[78] A rare English depiction, which escaped the destruction visited on several others in the series in the nineteenth century on the grounds that they were obscene, probably because it was mistaken for a musician playing an instrument (as it is still described), is a supporter of one of the Bristol misericords carved in 1520 which, in fact, represents a woman drinking from just such a vessel – careful inspection reveals the everted rim of the glass and its scrotal base (Figure 12.5). We can also be sure that such vessels were known in Elizabethan England, for in 1571 a West Ham brothel-keeper was arraigned before the local ecclesiastical court in Essex, charged with giving her clients to drink from 'a glass like unto a pintle and a pair of ballocks'.[79]

Figure 12.5

Gossip and Dreams

Thus alerted, I took a second look at another Bristol misericord supporter and the (at first sight) innocent snail poking its head out of its shell, began to take on a decidedly phallic appearance. There is a well-represented late medieval poetic genre in which a group of wives sit drinking and gossiping, and in one mid-fifteenth-century English example,[80] they seem to have met only to discuss their husbands' inadequate penile endowment in humorous detail (a similar discussion takes place in a Tirolean *fastnachtspiel* (carnival play) of 1529).[81] The first of the ten English wives estimates her husband's penis at the length of a snail, but as well as the imputation of shortness and limpness, her comparison of his penis to a snail should perhaps be related to the ancient erotic riddle of the 'boneless member', discussed in Chapter 9.

The acknowledged authority for the interpretation of dreams in the late Middle Ages – much of it, like most medieval 'science', a synthesis of earlier, classical work – was the *Somnia Danielis*. The manuscript tradition begins in the tenth century, but there were also five early printed editions by 1508, the earliest-known edition having been issued by Bartholomaeus Guldenbeck in Rome, *c.* 1475. In this edition occurs the following dream interpretation: 'To dream that you have lost your virile member signifies the failure of an undertaking.'[82] There is interesting evidence from elsewhere, however, that penis-loss was a real fear of men in the late Middle Ages, the medium suspected being witchcraft.[83] In the fatally influential treatise on witchcraft, the *Malleus Maleficarum*, first published in Strasbourg in 1487, we read of:

> those witches who . . . sometimes collect male organs in great numbers, as many as 20 or 30 members together and put them in a bird's nest, or shut them up in a box, where they move themselves like living members, and eat oats and corn . . . a certain man tells that, when he had lost his member, he approached a known witch to ask her to restore it to him. She told the afflicted man to climb a certain tree, and that he might take whichever he liked out of a nest in which there were several members. And when he tried to take a big one, the witch said: 'You must not take that one because it belongs to our parish priest.'[84]

Leaving aside the *fabliau*-like gibe at the parish clergy, the disembodied yet evidently still mobile penis seems to have enjoyed a surprisingly eventful independent life. One almost tasteful Dutch badge depicts what is perhaps just such a nest of magically removed phallus-birds. Hans Vintler's *Pluemen der tugent* was printed in Augsburg in 1486 in an edition liberally illustrated with woodcuts.[85] In the main, this work represents an early fifteenth-century translation of Tommaso Leoni's *Fiori*

Figure 12.6

di virtu, but the passage of greatest interest to students of Germanic folklore is a lengthy addition by Vintler concerning the various superstitions current at that date in his native Tirol. Referring to the deeds of the *zaubrerin* (sorceress), he writes 'they will even steal a man's tackle from out of his breeches', though with no further details as to where these misappropriated members are stored, but the woodcut artist has thoughtfully provided a box – just as described in the *Malleus* – and we are shown the witch adding another purloined penis to her collection (Figure 12.6).

The Romance of the Rose

We have examined several of the fauna which symbolised the organs of both sexes in Chapter 3, but when it comes to flora, the flower which above all others symbolises the female sex is, of course, the rose.

The fourteenth-century *Roman de la Rose*, often described as a classic of 'courtly love', has at its heart the far from courtly metaphor of the lover's pursuit of the rose, in which, as Fleming baldly expressed it, 'the only identity the rose has . . . is that of an entirely unsentimentalised and anonymous pudendum'.[86] The metaphor of plucking a flower or, specifically, a rose, is a commonplace of erotic diction, as in this fourteenth-century English quatrain jotted down on f. 1v of Bodley MS Rawlinson D. 193:

> Al night by the rose, rose
> Al night by the rose I lay.
> Darf ich nought the rose stele
> and yet ich bar the flour away.

There is thus reason to believe that the Middle English nickname *Pluckrose*, attested from the late thirteenth century, was sometimes applied to philanderers.[87]

The same imagery, used rather less bleakly perhaps, was also part of the language of late medieval anatomy; the early fourteenth-century physician, Henri de Mondeville, in his book on surgery describes how:

> the cervix in its cavity, between its two openings, penetrates through numerous whorls and folds that fit into one another like the petals of a rose before it opens, or like the mouth of a purse closed by a cord.[88]

Only a decade ago, a previously unnoticed late fifteenth-century engraving in the style of the Master E.S. came to light, pasted between the pages of the much earlier *Northumberland Bestiary* manuscript,[89] and looking very like a late medieval pin-up. The young woman is naked except for a wholly inadequate scarf or stole draped around her shoulders and a pair of shoes; with one hand she modestly makes as if to cover her genitals but only seems to draw attention to them thereby, while in the other hand she holds an opened rose. Unfortunately, the banderole which surrounds her, and would have told us what she was saying, is blank, as is that of her little dog, but luckily a very similar engraving is known in which the shameless woman pretends to cover her nakedness with the rose, and points to a banderole inscribed 'Look everyone where I put this rose', to which her little dog responds censoriously, 'Shame on you, Fool!' Athena in the *Judgment of Paris* engraving by the Master of the Banderoles similarly holds such a strategic rose.

Another significant contemporary use of the rose image is reported by the Dutch poet, Jan Smekens, in his early printed description of the extraordinary Brussels snow-sculptures of 1511. The similarity with contemporary graphic images (down to the suggestively positioned lapdog) in this most evanescent of all artistic media is striking:

> In the Rosendal a wonder was to be seen: a huge plump woman, completely naked, her buttocks were like a barrel, her breasts were finely formed, a dog was ensconced between her legs; her pudendum was covered by a rose; the 'coffer' beneath the rose, once you taste it, causes many a man to lose his silver-plate.[90]

It is thus no accident that in his late fifteenth-century poem, 'Nouveau Calendrier', Jean Molinet pairs the burlesque phallic *sainct Vital* (formed on the standard Middle French word for 'penis', *vit*) with the correspondingly female sexual *saincte Rose*.[91]

Figure 12.7

Erotic Stance

There is some reason for believing that the cross-legged stance of the young woman in the recently discovered engraving from the *Northumberland Bestiary* was considered sexy in the late fifteenth century. While it may have a practical motivation in a rather belated attempt at modesty, it is the stance affected by many of the all-but-naked young women of this period, for example by the 'sorceress' of the *Leipzig Liebeszauber* (Colour Plate 19), the dominatrix of the contemporary print by Casper of Regensburg, by Venus in the *Judgment of Paris* engraving by the Master of the Banderoles,[92] and as exemplified by at least three similarly posed (semi-)naked young women in engravings by the Master E.S., whose folly is importantly signalled not by the device of canine denunciation, but by the introduction of an *actual* fool.[93]

A remarkable engraving by Hans Sebald Beham dated 1529 and known as *Death and the lascivious couple* (Figure 12.7) depicts a young woman who adopts the same stance but has her hand round her partner's tumescent penis and he too seems to be groping in her crotch. More alarmingly, a skinny figure of Death with a skull for his head who stands behind the young man and places his hands on his shoulder and hip, also brandishes an evident erection. The young man's other hand rests on the head of a small boy whose own hand dips into a sack of coins. The picture also bears the caption *Mors vltima linea rervm* (Death is the final end of things) – is this a traditional morality signalling that the fruits of human sexuality lead inevitably to death, or is it as some recent commentators suspect – merely a thinly veiled excuse for a piece of pornography?

Metaphors for Intercourse – Playing the Organ

An art historian should not be too high-minded. It can lead to bathos. But it would seem that many art historians of the old school were just not dirty-minded enough. The great Erwin Panofsky, following Otto Brendel, took Titian's *Venus with an Organist* paintings in Madrid, executed in the late 1540s, to be a 'Neo-Platonic allegory'.[94] But it is clear from a number of less-high-art manifestations that playing on the organ was another relatively common metaphor for sexual intercourse. In an English play entitled *Respublica*, for example, composed less than a decade after Titian's paintings, one of the female characters complains that Piers Pickpurse – and the innuendo on *purse* is also unlikely to be accidental (see below) – 'plaieth att organes vnder my gowne'. It seems likely that this is an equivoque available to most vernaculars; in the sixteenth-century *Proces d'un jeune moine et d'ung viel gendarme*, for example, the young monk is described as being 'equipped with organ instruments, big and ?ready for a plain-chant'.[95] Similarly, I think we are entitled to suspect the same equivocal meaning behind the outwardly decorous mutual organ-playing of a couple in an engraving by van Meckenem, from a series of couples which is imbued with a correspondingly coded eroticism. As both partners are fully clothed, however, it might be felt that I am guilty of over-interpreting the message of this engraving, but in support of my contention, I adduce slightly earlier and, it seems to me, unequivocally erotic examples. Engraved on the side of a mid-fifteenth-century German *Minnekästchen*, for example, we see a naked woman playing on the organ to a clothed man,[96] just as on one of the contemporary biscuit-moulds with which we began, in which he is clothed and plays the lute, while she is completely naked and plays on the organ (Figure 1.2)[97] – a verbal innuendo which works as well in medieval German as in modern English. Under the pseudonym Conrad of Zwickau, one of the 'Obscure Men' whose letters were composed with satirical intent by Ulrich von Hütten and first published in 1515, he writes that in Leipzig that Lent there were festivities held:

> and the Prince himself rode in the Platz, and he had a fine horse, and a fine saddle-cloth too, upon which was painted a woman in brave attire, and near her sitting a youth, with curly locks, who played an organ to her. . . .[98]

We have seen how the act of intercourse is frequently represented by metaphor, but there is not space here to discuss them all,[99] and I simply refer in passing to such equivocal scenes as the ram or unicorn which charges the basket held out by a young woman,[100] or the tinker who offers to stop the leaky cooking pots of *Les femmes qui font écurer leur chaudron* (339f.), which employs an erotic metaphor very similar to that of the *Bellows-Mender* in the painting in Tournai attributed to Pieter Baltens. But to put the key into the lock,[101] is one of the several metaphors (in a useful collection of such) of which the arch-pornographer, Aretino, affected to disapprove, and is nicely illustrated by the Flemish drawing of *c.* 1470 (Colour Plate 24):

> The Lady: Do open my coffer, love,
>   That I present, give and offer you
>
> Gentleman: Lady, your coffer pleases me greatly,
>   but the lock does not,
>   for my key isn't big enough
>   in size for the slot.

Putting the Stone

Another, perhaps unexpected, and certainly by now dead, erotic metaphor, is that of putting the stone, and is to be found represented in a complexly allusive scene of courtly love dalliance in the *bas-de-page* of the *Peterborough Psalter*, one of the famous East Anglian manuscripts illuminated in the decades around 1300.[102] We see the knight at a tryst with his lady; he reclines upon a grassy bank, while she sits before a rose-bush. Behind him, the knight's stallion rears up, ostensibly shying at the rabbit which runs towards them, pursued by a hound. The figure whom I particularly wish to consider here, however, is the man to the right of the couple, in the act of putting a large stone. I suggest this action represents yet another erotic metaphor, for in a late twelfth-century Latin sermon, the preacher quotes the titles of several vernacular love-songs and the opening couplet of another (which a second preacher gives us a little more of, allowing me to complete the texts thus):

> *Atte ston castinges my lemman i ches,*   [I chose my love at the stone-putting
> *and atte wrastlinges sone i hym les;*   and soon I lost him at the wrestling;
> *allas, that he so sone fel;*   alas that he fell so soon; why didn't
> *wy nadde he stonde better, vile gorel?*[103]   he stand up better, bloated wretch!]

There are several familiar erotic *double entendres* in this all-too-short verse: 'wrestling' is fairly transparent, and 'standing' and 'falling' are also well-attested in reference to male sexual performance, all of which suggests that 'stone-casting' involves a similar innuendo, doubtless via *stone* in the common colloquial sense, 'testicle'.

Manipulating the Purse

The first anatomists were also analogists. In their minute investigations of the human body, visual resemblances sprang unconsciously to mind: the tip of the penis was like an 'acorn' (Latin *glans*), the vagina like the 'sheath' of a sword (Latin *vagina*). It was thus natural for Henri de Mondeville in his description of the cervix that we have quoted above, to compare its 'numerous whorls and folds that fit into one another' to 'the petals of a rose before it opens, or to the mouth of a purse closed by a cord'. Curiously, the purse is used as a bisexual metaphor for both scrotum and vagina[104] in several European vernaculars. In the *fabliau Trubert*, for example, the eponymous male hero, disguised as the king's bride, completes his wedding-night disguise by deft manipulation of a real purse in place of the missing pudendum, with great dexterity, tightening and loosening its drawstring mouth at appropriate moments.[105] In recent years the Thames foreshore has yielded a fifteenth-century penis-in-a-purse lead badge from Custom House Quay,[106] and a similar but earlier Dutch example which holds three phalli has surfaced from Middelburg.[107]

The Acorn or Glans

Adjacent to the far-from-subtle image of a standing couple copulating, on a fourteenth-century *Minnekästchen* in the Musée du Moyen Age,[108] is the much more satisfying piece of sexual grotesque wit of a bird pecking at the 'head' of a phallus-animal beneath a stylised oak tree laden with acorns – a pun on Latin *glans*, used to mean both 'acorn' and 'tip of the penis' (a usage which was passed on to some of the vernaculars), and it serves to alert us to the possibility of such visual innuendo elsewhere, so that this is also likely to be the import of another badge recently discovered in Rotterdam, depicting a phallus with human legs on the *glans* of which a bird is perched, pecking at it (Figure 12.8).

I believe we should also be suspicious of the import of a scene on a fragment of early fourteenth-century French tapestry subsequently made into a purse[109] which shows the lover offering his beloved an outsize acorn – what may be the cup from which this particular acorn has come, can be seen directly above the lady's head, and may similarly be symbolic of her sex. In an engraving by the Housebook Master (*c*. 1480) of a young woman playing cards with three young men and, significantly, a fool, the only visible card, 'lying on her lap', is the Ace-of-Acorns – certainly, acorns were a contemporary Germanic card-suit, but it seems too much of a coincidence that it should be this card.[110] In the same way, another of van Meckenem's engraved

Figure 12.8

couples play cards, and the gentleman throws up his hands in horror as the woman triumphantly flourishes a decidedly phallic-looking Ace-of-Cudgels.[111]

Suggestive Leaves

It is to be expected that any flower or fruit vaguely analogous in shape to the sexual organs will sooner or later appear in late medieval art as a literary or visual innuendo, and a telling little marginal painting from a *bas-de-page* in the *Gorleston Psalter* (1310x1325), presumably satiric in intent, illustrates the age-old theme of the elderly man offering the young woman money in exchange for sex.[112] If the actors are intended as monk (or hermit, perhaps) and nun,[113] then we may have another example of anti-clerical satire, but, be that as it may, there is no mistaking the suggestive shape of the erect leaf between the couple; indeed, the illuminator has modified it away from the slightly more naturalistic, hastate shape of the other leaves, and positioned it firmly between the pair.

The *bas-de-page* scenes from a mid-fourteenth-century *Roman de la Rose* manuscript which include a depiction of nuns picking phalli from trees have been several times commented upon in recent years.[114] But the phallus-tree grows on the lead badges too and one such depicts a couple having sex beneath its branches, and incidentally observed by a voyeur.[115] On one branch of the tree, above the real human sex on this badge, a phallus pierces a vulva or vulvate leaf, with above it the legend *AMOVRS*. Another phallus-tree is depicted in a wall-

Figure 12.9

painting in Schloss Lichtenberg in the Tirol,[116] but such trees might also be seen at carnival-time, as in a procession in Nördlingen in 1510 when a tree bearing penises (*zageln*) was carried about the town.[117] A unique late fifteenth-century ?German pen-and-ink drawing of a phallus-tree survives in Istanbul (Figure 12.9). It shows a tree sprouting from a vase bearing from its calices two large and two small phalli (the former with tails), as well as two *putti* similarly emerging from calices who carry phalli and one of whom also appears to hold a ball in his upraised hand.

The Erotic Bagpipe

Along the upper margin, above the text, in the *Psalter of Louis le Hutin* (Tournai, 1315), appears a presumably symbolic confrontation;[118] to the right, a group of three apes, one of which holds up a hood, and to the left, a single ape holding on his knees a bagpipe having a decidedly scrotal-looking bag and 'limp' chanter. It is difficult to avoid the impression that the artist has here presented us with two sexual symbols, the representation of this bagpipe, a common phallic symbol, of course, being particularly suggestive. A slightly later instance is the lead badge from Groningen in the form of a man who plays the bagpipes in apparent innocence,[119] but stands between an unmistakable erect phallus and a flask, the latter, I suggest, symbolic of the female genitalia, and for which a good, if later, parallel is offered by the male and female fools engraved by Hans Sebald Beham in the early sixteenth century (Figure 6.4), the former sporting a plainly phalliform *marotte*, and a large narrow-necked pot standing beside the latter. Another such badge takes the form of a standing Wild Man having intercourse with a Wild Woman; he is shown playing the bagpipes, the chanter of which droops in marked contradistinction to his own outsize erection.[120] Attached to her is a cooking pot which may serve the same symbolic function as that we have just noticed in Beham's engraving – she also holds what appears to be a bell in one hand which would presumably jangle loudly given the vigorous intercourse suggested by the badge! We may perhaps here have to do with yet another metaphor for intercourse – English will not be alone in having an expression 'ring the/someone's bell', meaning 'to bring someone to sexual climax'.

From the multitude of similarly suggestive bagpipe illustrations, I select merely a few of the most interesting.[121] A scrap of late medieval Danish wall-painting (*c.* 1500) in a church at Taning near Skanderborg depicts an ithyphallic bagpiper whose strapped-on phallus projects at an angle precisely parallel to that of one of the drones of his instrument.[122] The suggestive use of the bagpipe is also a familiar aspect of the fool's phallicism and we have already noted examples of it in the relevant chapter. A German circular engraving made in 1600 which depicts a seated couple with the man playing the bagpipe is inscribed with the following dialogue:

> Have you felt my bagpipe?
> Yes, friend, it wobbles and never stands firm.[123]

Model Genitals

Lastly, there is the most interesting example of a Ferrarese engraving of *c.* 1470, cut onto the reverse of the plainly pornographic plate referred to above, which is fraught with phallic symbolism, and includes a bagpiper sitting on a close-stool who has a phallus-pendant hanging from the drone of his instrument. His companion who is 'accidentally' exposing himself, carves wooden spoons, the pair in the foreground forming a particularly suggestive shape, as also does the crown of his baggy hat which flops limply forward. The interesting phallus-pendant is probably a *realium*, a good luck charm made of wax, such as we learn from a letter of Sir William Hamilton were still to be purchased, though here as votives, in honour of Sts Cosmas and Damian, in a church near Naples as late as the end of the eighteenth century.[124]

An unremarked passage in Sir Thomas More's *Dialogue Concerning Heresies* (1528), relates how a newly married English couple visited the church of St Valéry in Picardy, where they found to their astonishment that the preventative against *the stone* (gall- and bladder-stones), locally regarded as infallible, involved the measurement of the sexual organ (*gere*) of the pilgrim in question, for the manufacture of a votive model of it:

> For lyke as in other pylgrymages ye se hanged vp legges of waxe or armes or suche other partes so was in that chapell all theyr offrynges yt honge aboute the walles none other thynge but mennes gere & womens gere made in waxe.[125]

In the Italian context of the Ferrarese engraving, however, there is a most suggestive letter written by the poet, Pietro Aretino, ten years after the scandal caused by the publication of his *I Modi*:

> It would seem to me that the thing which is given to us by nature to preserve the race, should be worn around the neck as a pendant, or pinned onto the cap like a badge. . . .[126]

We must note, however, that Aretino specifically does *not* say that such is, in fact, the fashion, but it seems not unreasonable to suspect that this was indeed the practice in the light of the Dutch badges, the Ferrarese bagpiper and ancient, as well as surviving amuletic practice.

Breasts

Something should be said about the representation of the secondary female sexual characteristic, the breasts, in the late Middle Ages.[127]

One of the most familiar, active images of the breast must have been the *Maria Lactans* type of representation of the Virgin, the Madonna suckling the infant Christ, though even this perfectly natural and familiar activity led some artists to paint breasts that look more like bottles or fruits.[128]

It is significant that when the female breast was deliberately compared to a fruit in medieval (and, indeed, classical) literature, it was compared to the apple and not to any larger fruit.[129] From at least the time of Pliny, who reports that a certain variety of apple was called *orthomastium*, because the apples resemble *mammarum effigiae*,[130] via Isidore's spurious early seventh-century etymology that derived *mamilla* from *mala*, to the later Middle Ages, by which time it had become a commonplace of erotic diction, the apparently natural (male) comparison for the female breast was the apple.[131] The comparison was still commonplace in the Renaissance: although the familiar simile is strangely missing from Marot's famous *Blason du tetin*, for Gratien du Pont in 1534, the ideal *tetins* are still *rondz comme une pomme*,[132] and Alcina's breasts are still described as 'two unripe apples' by Ariosto in *Orlando Furioso* (1516).[133] In his refreshing book on humour in Italian Renaissance art, referring to the woman who holds a bowl of fruit in Dosso Dossi's *Bambocciata*, Barolsky points out how the artist (d. 1542) 'has deliberately painted her breasts as part of the fruit bowl . . . which includes strategically placed apples, below her naked breasts'.[134]

To medieval man, the *mameletes* as sex-objects should ideally be 'small and roundish, a little bigger than apples'.[135] The large bust favoured by some cultures (in post-Palaeolithic times, Bronze Age Mycenae and classical India, for instance), was anathema to the medieval man. In a twelfth-century Latin play of French provenance, *De Tribus Puellis* (The Three Girls), for example, we learn that larger-breasted girls feel obliged to compress their bosoms within their corsets so as not to displease the men.[136] Matthew of Vendôme sketching the ideal woman in his influential poetry manual, the *Ars Versificatoria*, is equally convinced of the necessity for the lady to have 'small breasts', and Chaucer's Criseyde typically has 'brestes rounde and lite'[137] – indeed, it is symptomatic that the Latin word used for breast at this period, *mammilla*, is itself a diminutive of the classical Latin *mamma*, 'breast'.[138] One historian of costume has noted that in our period, 'Heavy breasts are characteristic of ugly women (cf. Leonardo's sketches and the portrait sometimes attributed to Quintin Massys in the National Gallery, London) and witches [Hans Baldung Grien's, for example].'[139]

The fragment of late fifteenth-century Swiss tapestry which is the subject of Figure 12.10 exemplifies this same metaphorics in amusing fashion. A young woman is shown in the act of picking an apple from the tree, but a young man has crept up behind her and has cupped both her breasts in his hands, punningly saying, 'Fair maid, the apple is mine.' Unfortunately, neither the girl's response, nor the observation of the somewhat older woman who watches these goings-on, has been preserved. One surely significant detail, however, is that the young man is depicted wearing only one shoe, a polyvalent motif which we have examined in some detail in Chapter 6, where it was suggested that one of its contextually established implications is lasciviousness, as when, in the frontispiece miniature to a manuscript of Chaucer's *Complaynt of Mars and Venus*, illuminated in England probably in the 1450s, one of the otherwise entirely naked Children of Venus was given only one shoe.[140] A better comparison, however, is with the evidently lascivious young peasant couple in Dürer's drawing of *c.* 1502, now in Milan, in which the young man is shown in the act of pinching the girl's nipple, though here it is she who wears only one shoe.[141]

In keeping with the seemingly universal xenophobia which attributes characteristics regarded as unattractive in one's own culture to those of foreigners,

Figure 12.10

an anonymous fourteenth-century Spanish poem significantly describes a *jolie laide* swineherd whose breasts are so huge that one would have thought her English![142] Similarly, we may be sure that the twelfth-century Bavarian woman nicknamed *Zitzelziege* (Tittygoat),[143] and the thirteenth-century Frenchwoman, Alice *Pis-de-Vache* (Cow's Udder),[144] would not have felt complimented on the amplitude of their bosoms.[145]

The Alma Mater

The fashion for anthropomorphic fountains of the famous *Manneken-Pis* type in Brussels, is well represented in the late Middle Ages, not least by the ithyphallic bronze statuettes which were formerly identified as aeolipiles,[146] but also by female figures whose breasts dispense water or, on great festive occasions such as the triumphal entry of Archduke Charles of Austria (the future Charles V) into Bruges in 1515 – wine.[147]

In his wonderful French–English Dictionary (1611), Randle Cotgrave defines *marmouset* as 'The cocke of a cesterne, or fountaine, made like a woman's dug; any Anticke Image, from whose teats water trilleth. . . .' A fifteenth-century manuscript of the *Roman de la Rose* in the Bodleian Library, Oxford, even illustrates a hermaphrodite fountain from whose penis and breasts the water spouts.[148]

It is notable that, unlike the sex organs, the breasts do not appear in dismembered form on the Dutch badges and only exceptionally elsewhere: a pair of breasts decorate one of the corbels of a Romanesque church at Cortazzone,[149] for instance, and Paul Vandenbroeck draws my attention to the breast-shaped vessel which occupies the centre of the lowest shelf of the sideboard on which the gold and silver plate is displayed – in true anachronistic late medieval fashion – in Bosch's *Marriage Feast at Cana*.[150] Another odd appearance is heraldic: the coat of arms for *Dodge* at the Visitation of Kent and other counties in 1530, included a woman's breast distilling drops of milk – this would seem to be an instance of 'canting heraldry' or *armes parlantes*, the heraldic use of rebus, in which the breast stands for *dug* (compare the Cotgrave citation above), and perhaps hints at the pronunciation of the surname as 'Dudge'.

Although gender and sexuality are almost inextricably linked, I have tried to separate them for the purposes of this discourse. It has not been my purpose to discuss pornography, which in this context I take to mean pictorial material deliberately intended to arouse sexual desire – while many of the above images are certainly sexual, few if any could, I think, be termed sexually arousing or erotic in that sense.

Even the most strait-laced scholar could surely not repress a smile at the bizarre sexual badges which feature literally dismembered sex-organs, and although they still remain more than a little mysterious, I have suggested, indeed, that such an amused response is by no means fortuitous, comedy being one of the weapons in the repulsive armoury of the amulet. But if this *is* comedy, it is comedy with a deeply serious life-preserving mission; for the wearer, these humble leaden icons are a matter of life and death.

There is undoubted comedy too in the multifarious but only rarely original coinage of metaphors for sex and their visual expression – we may perhaps allow ourselves a nervous titter. As with the mysteries of love, the mysteries of sexuality possibly touch us too closely, and are perhaps too important to us, for us ever to feel entirely at ease in considering them, and so, like our forebears, we escape into humour.

THIRTEEN

TAILPIECE: THE USES OF SCATOLOGY

This chapter might perhaps have been entitled 'Scatology, the final taboo', for at the beginning of the third millennium we seem happy enough to talk about sex in all its pleasant and unpleasant manifestations, but we fight shy of – we do not want to dirty our hands, as it were – with scatology. Academically, as far as this particular topic is concerned, we are still toddlers, merely dabbling with it, if not quite in the manner attributed to one of the radical early sixteenth-century continental Anabaptist sects who called themselves 'Like Little Children' and one of whom, according to Bullinger's *Heresiography* (1531),

> having kept his excrements in store many days, powred them out in the street, and turned himself naked into them, saying, 'unless we be made like little children, we cannot enter into the Kingdom of heaven'.

When discussing potty-training in her book *Baby and Child*, the child psychologist Penelope Leach recommends that parents should whisk the used potty away with wrinkled nose:

> You don't have to pretend to share [the toddler's] pleasurable interest – discovering that adults don't play with feces is part of growing up – but don't try to make him feel they are dirty and disgusting.[1]

We understand what she means, of course, but clearly, if we as adults did not in general feel that faeces *are* indeed 'dirty and disgusting', the sort of scatological insults and gestures discussed below would have no force, no power to offend – this the child must also learn. And we adults do, in a sense, 'play with feces', though not usually in such a concrete way as the Anabaptist just mentioned, contenting ourselves, for the most part, with merely verbal games. I don't, of course, want to imply that the Middle Ages was the toddlerhood of the race, or anything of that sort, but a certain 'pleasurable interest', to use Penelope Leach's phrase, in the contents of the medieval potty is, indeed, discernible, and those contents, I'm afraid, we must now go on to examine more closely.

Farting for Pleasure and Profit

> Shall we fart to amuse ourselves?
> I can't think of anything better!

We may feel that humour cannot get much 'lower', yet this somewhat surprising suggestion coming from an adult, accepted with equally surprising alacrity by another, is made by Gautier in Adam de la Halle's late thirteenth-century *Jeu de Robin et de Marion*. It is clear from a number of sources that this accomplishment was also reckoned part of the inferior minstrel's repertoire; indeed, an Old Irish legal tract, *Uraicecht Becc*, even accords a place, albeit very near the bottom of the grades of the 'men of art', to the *braigetoir* (farter), but one of the subdivisions of versified satire in Old Irish was also euphemistically known as *mac bronn*, 'son of womb'. Even in the twelfth century, John of Salisbury had complained that:

> illustrious persons allow buffoons to frequent their houses and perform before the eyes of all disgraceful actions with the obscene parts of their bodies . . . worse still, these fellows are not ejected when in the turbulence of their hinder parts they cause the air to reek by emitting a series of loud noises which add to their deplorable conduct.

Several of the marginal illustrations in the well-known Bodleian manuscript of the *Romance of Alexander* illuminated in Flanders *c.* 1340 seem to feature some sort of anal entertainment performed by these medieval *petomanes*.[2]

But the ability to fart at will could on occasion be profitable even to those who were not entertainers. At much the same time as the French peasant Gautier was making his indelicate suggestion as to how they should amuse themselves, Henry III, King of England, was witnessing a similar performance by one Roland, surnamed *Le Pettour* in Anglo-Norman, *Le Fartere* in English, who held land in Hemingstone, Suffolk, by serjeanty of appearing before the King every year on Christmas Day to do a jump, a whistle and a fart, or as the Latin puts it, rather more sonorously, *unum saltum et unum siffletum et unum bumbulum.*

Clearly Henry was no 'Clerk of Oxenford', whom Chaucer tells us, with apparent surprise, 'was somdeel squamous Of fartyng' (was somewhat squeamish about farting). Attitudes towards this particular bodily function, clearly fluctuated, however: the fifteenth-century *Book of Curtesye* (printed by Caxton *c.* 1477), for example, has this advice on the matter, for when a boy is seated at table:

> Be ware also no breth from you rebounde
> Vppe ne downe, be ware that shamefull sounde.

By the time Erasmus published his *De civilitate morum puerilium* (Good Manners for Boys) in 1530, however, his advice was quite different:

There are those who teach that the boy should retain wind by compressing the belly. Yet it is not pleasing, while striving to appear urbane, to contract an illness. If it is possible to withdraw, it should be done alone. But if not, in accordance with the ancient proverb, let a cough hide the sound.

Among medieval nicknames which frequently immortalise such 'low humour', in addition to the above-mentioned Roland whom we left performing his unique triathlon, we find a *John le Fartere* in Leicestershire in 1327, while fifty years earlier in Oudenaarde in Flanders we learn of the Rabelaisian *Jehan Pet d'Asne* (John Donkey-Fart), presumably a reference to the customary loudness of his farts.[3]

Farting in Earnest – 'Excremental Exorcism' and other Scatological Satire

But farting, however amusing, might also have a more serious purpose, in both positive and negative ways. Luther's penchant for scatology is well known and, if we are to believe his *Colloquia oder Tischreden*, published by his friends and admirers in 1566, twenty years after his death, it was also part of the great Reformer's table-talk. He apparently told the story, for instance, of how a rare female farter had put the Devil to flight with what the Latin text calls a *crepitus ventris*, and as well as having told the story of the 'Bum-in-the-Oven' at a social gathering in Leipzig in 1545, to which we shall turn our attention presently, he also admitted that whenever he had been unable to drive the Devil away with serious words or Holy Scripture, he had succeeded with *spitzige Wörter* (sharp words) and *lächerliche Possen* (amusing tricks) which latter seem to have included saying, 'Devil I have just shit in my trousers, have you smelled it . . .?'

If farting might have a positive, apotropaic function, then, it was also, of course, a time-honoured insult. In 1545, the year before Luther died, a series of broadsides with woodcut illustrations by Cranach was published at Wittenberg entitled *Abbildung des Papsttums* (Depiction of the Papacy). In one of the woodcuts, farts are directed against the Pope as if he is the Devil incarnate, together with the parallel insult of tongues stuck out. It may be, therefore, that some of the marginal illustrations in medieval manuscripts which show men bent over, trousers down, in close proximity to devilish or animal grotesques are examples of what Wentersdorf in a pioneering essay termed 'excremental exorcism'.[4] In one early medieval instance of irreverence to a saint, however, in an unusual case of the punishment being made to fit the crime, a fart *is* the punishment. On a certain Friday a Merovingian woman is told that the body of St Gangolf works miracles, to which she replies, 'and so does my bum' – immediately a loud fart is heard, and thereafter for the rest of her life she could not say a word on a Friday but it was followed by a similar report.

A second sheet from the Lutheran series of 1545, entitled 'The Pope is Adored as an Earthly God', shows men defecating into the inverted Papal tiara, while a third, entitled 'Appearance and Origin of the Pope', depicts a grinning she-devil who gives birth to the pontiff anally. Another such drastic illustration, contemporary with, but not in fact from, that series, entitled 'On the Appearance and Origin of Monks' shows that, according to Cranach, they too are born of the Devil, but again, anally.

Figure 13.1

In fact, the Reformation era was not the first time such scatological imagery was employed to satirise the clergy, and we recall the Prologue to Chaucer's 'Summoner's Tale' in which an angel says to Satan, 'Shewe forth thyn ers, and let the frere se/Where is the nest of freres in this place!' (Show forth your arse and let the friar see where is the nest of friars in this place!) A misericord in the royal chapel of St George's at Windsor Castle, carved 1478x83, depicts a friar evacuating a devil accompanied by another friar and devil (Figure 13.1); this, of course, is, strictly speaking, the reverse of the Cranach illustration, but the effect is much the same. The motif of anal evacuation from a demon can be seen in earlier depictions of hell, such as the late fourteenth-century fresco by Taddeo di Bartolo in San Gimignano Cathedral, or Giotto's *Last Judgment* in the Arena Chapel at Padua, and it was clearly much too good a conception to be allowed to disappear in post-medieval times, being seen again, for example, on the title-page woodcut to John Taylor's *The Devil turn'd Round-Head* of 1642.

(Devilish) Anal Onomastics

There is an interesting clutch of picturesque minor English place-names of the Devil's Arse type. The famous cave at Castleton in Derbyshire's Peak District, formerly one of the topographical *mirabilia* of Britain, is now more genteelly known as the Peak Cavern, though even as I write, I see from my local paper that there is a move afoot to revert to the original and rather more eye-catching name in these tourism-conscious times. The name as recorded in the *Domesday Book* is *Pechesers* (that is, Peak's Arse), and only subsequently the *Devil's Arse*.[5] A place of this name is also attested at Lechlade in Gloucestershire from 1448. A *Fendesers clogh* (Fiend's

Arse Clough) is found in Cheshire in 1407 and a *Trollesers* (Troll's Arse) from as early as 1335 in North Yorkshire – presumably, all are in some way unprepossessing. The *Domesday Book* records a hamlet by the name of *Windesers* or Wind's Arse, in Leicestershire, and a field of the same name is attested in late fifteenth-century Waltham on the Wolds in the same county, explained as 'perhaps used of a conformation of hills resembling buttocks lying in a windy, exposed situation and which funnelled the wind'.[6] The tradition that a violent wind issues from the impressive cave at Castleton is very early and explains its sobriquet. When the engraver of the quirky maps in Drayton's *Polyolbion* (1613x22) came to illustrate the relevant *Song*, as the celebrated cave, is 'of thy blacke Entrance nam'd', according to the poet, he drew a horned devil suggestively bent over.

In his *Testament* written in 1461, Villon left to his adoptive father a sadly lost work of his, *le Rommant du Pet au Diable*, the 'Devil's Fart' being the name of a large boundary-stone – an oddly substantial manifestation for a fart – it seems euphemism was just as active in the late fifteenth century as now! This stone in its turn gave its name to the *Hôtel du Pet au Diable*, a Parisian brothel, but the stone itself gave rise to a series of incidents during the years 1451–3 before being finally removed as a student prank.[7]

Printed on Toilet Paper?

The topos that someone's book is only fit to be used as toilet paper is not new: William Baldwin's *Beware the Cat*, an extraordinary production put into the mouth of a cat named Streamer, was 'answered' by a ballad of *c.* 1570 which includes the couplet

> The boke [of ten leaves] was printed every worde
> Er Stremer saw any pece, to wipe away a t.o.r.d.   [turd]

But earlier in the century polemical Protestant literature had enjoined the use of Papal indulgences as toilet paper. A 1528 pamphlet told how Luther had been sent a copy of a work attacking his marriage in scurrilous terms which was taken off to the privy by various of Luther's supporters in Wittenberg, used as toilet paper, and then sent back to its authors in Leipzig. Similarly the Huguenots of Le Puy protested that devotional woodcut prints of the town's famous Black Virgin were no better than toilet paper, and that it would be a good idea to drag the statue through the town sewage.

In a sermon delivered in 1524, Luther said that the Pope sat in Christ's place in the church, 'giving light like filth in a lantern', a metaphor which seems literally to have been taken up by Protestant artists as in one of the supplementary playing cards to Schäuffelein's series (*c.* 1535), or in Floetner's contemporary satirical attack on Catholic religious processions, *Prozession der Geistlichkeit* (Nürnberg, 1535), which would seem to owe more than a little to an actual parodic procession staged by Protestants in 1524 in the village of Buchholz in Saxony. The local Lutheran preacher, Myconius, provides an eye-witness account from which we learn that the mock relics consisted of a horse's head and two legs, and the jaw-bone of a cow;

these were placed on a dung-carrier (*mistrage*), where they were covered with old bits of fur and dung, then in the market-place a mock-bishop delivered a mock-sermon and holding up the cow's jaw-bone identified it as from 'the holy arse-cheek of . . . St Benno', the translation of whose relics was taking place at nearby Meissen.

One of the relatively few anti-Lutheran publications to survive the triumph of Protestantism in Germany was Thomas Murner's *Von dem grossen Lutherischen Narren* of 1522, and includes a woodcut which shows that Murner would have been quite happy to consign not just his works, but the Reformer himself 'into the shit-house', a motif which is itself also part of the demonisation of one's opponent, for the privy was popularly believed to be the haunt of demons and evil spirits.

'Pancakes' and Other Edibles

Another of Cranach's illustrations to the *Abbildung des Papsttums* of 1545 shows the Pope, riding on a sow, and holding out, in the manner of a carrot before a donkey, a steaming conventionalised human turd, of which pigs seem inordinately fond, at least in contemporary iconography. Interestingly, this was one of the scatological images familiar to the Elizabethan Sir John Harington in his extraordinary work on the flush-toilet, *The Metamorphosis of Ajax*, published in 1586. A Jacobean allusion to this porcine penchant is Puppy's quasi-proverbial 'A turd's as good for a sow as a pancake' in Jonson's masque *The Gypsies Metamorphosed* (1621), in which note the pun on *pancake*, which we shall be meeting again.

Perhaps particularly unpleasant – if, indeed, there can be degrees of unpleasantness in this sort of imagery – is a scatological detail in an earlier production of Cranach's of *c*. 1530, a satirical attack on the Catholic scholar Johann Cochleus, abused in the text accompanying the cut as 'the Devils arsehole'. Cochleus is 'full of shit', as the text tells us – an idiom with a surprisingly modern American ring to it – which he excretes in the form of his books against Luther. But the reason he is so, we are informed, is because the Devil himself defecates directly into his mouth. A drawing by the Swiss artist Urs Graf dated 1516 is inscribed *Ich schis dir ins fud loch*, and there are several graphic illustrations of this regrettably insanitary habit in medieval art proper. An ape is the perpetrator on a tile made at Danbury in Essex *c*. 1300,[8] and in a roughly contemporary illustration of the Tree of Vices from a German manuscript of the *Speculum humanae salvationis*, a devil similarly pollutes a sinner:

'Kiss My Arse!' and other Insulting Invitations

This is a venerable insult. In one of the fifteenth-century *Wakefield Pageants*, when Abel greets his brother courteously with:

> God, as he both may and can,
> Spede the, brother, and thi man,

Cain replies with a brutal 'Com kis myne ars!' That act itself is, of course, a staple of such medieval *fabliaux* as Chaucer's 'Miller's Tale', the Middle English poem concerning one Hogyn (*She torned owt her ars & that he kyst*),[9] and the French *Bérenger au Long Cul*, as well as being depicted in a variety of media, including a fifteenth-century stone corbel in Troyes Cathedral and sundry manuscript marginalia. Reaney showed that the medieval English nickname *Baysers* was a hybrid formed from Middle French *baiser*, 'to kiss', and Middle English *ers* (arse). I have suggested elsewhere that a grotesque in the margin of the early fourteenth-century *Ormesby Psalter* (Colour Plate 15), which points at its own exposed rear with the human hand with which its tail terminates, is the visual equivalent of Cain's familiar invitation. But what are we to make of the man who blows a trumpet at the same grotesque? As a sometime schoolteacher, I became inured to the exclamation that X had *trumped* – a metaphorical usage of the verb which the *OED* traces back as far as *c.* 1425, but for which the *Ormesby* and similar images provide suggestive antedatings.[10] *Trumpas* (that is, Trump-Arse) and his colleague *Vertas* (Fart-Arse) are two of the burlesque authorities cited in the only proper English *sermon joyeux* to have come down to us, in which there is also an anecdote concerning one Kateryn *Fyste* (surnamed after a species of fart). The same sermon further employs the scatological *adynaton* of 'catching a fart in a shove-net' (take a fart in a schowenette),[11] a variant of the more familiar 'catching the wind in a net', which is illustrated by a woodcut in the earliest French emblem book, Guillaume de la Perrière's *Le théâtre des bons engins* (Paris, 1539), no. XXXVI.[12] Luther is playing on the same absurd *adynaton* in his 'as sure as a fart in a lobster-pot'.[13]

The Osculum Infame

In the *Wakefield Pageants*, Cain also suggests that his brother Abel should 'kys the dwillis toute' (kiss the Devil's arse). The motif of kissing the Devil in this manner, however, brings with it the implication of heresy or witchcraft, for that they practised such a rite was one of the commonest allegations made against Cathars, Waldensians, Templars and, indeed, heretics in general. Seemingly first attested in the thirteenth-century writings of David of Augsburg, official sanction was given to the belief that this was an important heretical sacrament in a Papal bull issued in 1233 against the Waldensians by Pope Gregory IX; in another, issued seventy years later, Walter Langton, Bishop of Coventry and Lichfield, was accused of this same practice, and medieval nicknames confirm its popular currency. The Paris tax-roll of 1292 records three separate individuals known respectively as *Bese-Deable*, *Basians-Demonam* and *Demonem Osculans* (all meaning 'Kiss-the-Devil').

Naturally, the charge was soon made that the members of such sects performed this rite on each other – and much later, testifying to the longevity of the gibe, it was depicted on the title-page of a mid-seventeenth-century pamphlet attacking the Ranters. The kissing of animals in this position – when not also a Satanic rite as in the image of the Waldensians worshipping the Devil as goat – is always insulting. A most interesting real-life incident is recorded in early trailbaston proceedings from the Lincoln roll of 1305 in which a certain Philip Darcy was convicted of having removed the wheels from some carts belonging to the Prior of Nocton in Lincolnshire, and further, of having cut off the tail of the horse on which one of the canons was riding. As if this was not enough, he added insult to injury by forcing one of the Priory's grooms to kiss the mutilated horse's hindquarters! Such behaviour has more than a little in common with such classic Trickster figures as Eulenspiegel, for example, whose career we shall shortly be reviewing. Three hundred years after the Nocton incident, in 1610, at King's Sutton in Northamptonshire, a husband and wife were arraigned before the ecclesiastical court for insulting their minister by similarly inviting him to 'kisse his horse under the taile'.

Another context in which this demeaning motif occurs is in representations of the notorious, so-called *Judensau* – as in the late fifteenth-century German broadsheet reproduced as Figure 5.5 – and which, as we have suggested earlier, is taxonomically merely a particular variant of the *Schandbild*, albeit one with a generic application. A frequent component of these paintings is the soiling of the culprit's seal with the dung of some animal, the favourite is the sow, as in the earliest extant example from 1420 (Colour Plate 5), though there are equine variants too: in one dated 1468, not only is the culprit forced to soil his own seal in this manner, but also, incidentally, to ride backwards on the animal – another well-known satirical punishment, as we have seen – and finally a bovine variant from *c.* 1500.

The Dutch municipal lottery tickets to which Herman Pleij has drawn attention constitute a most unusual and fascinating corpus of material. Holders of tickets would attempt to influence Fate by writing messages on their tickets which were either pious platitudes or outrageous obscenities – exhibiting a characteristically schizophrenic attitude on the part of humanity, uncertain whether to cajole or threaten the unknown supernatural force. The tickets of three players who clearly favoured the latter approach come from the 's-Hertogenbosch lottery of 1522: 'Give me something or lick my arse', 'A roast turd in your throat' and 'What shall Martin Shitpot have?' With the second, I compare a line from one of the *sotte ballades* by the fourteenth-century French poet, Eustache Deschamps: 'May shit jump into your throat', and the English exclamation 'A turd in your teeth', attested from the mid-fifteenth century on.[14]

Like the German, the English Reformation also employed scatological imagery in its polemic, of course. Even the saintly Sir Thomas More, admittedly in Latin, and at the instigation of no less a person than the King of England, wrote to Martin Luther in 1523 in response to his scurrilous attack on Henry VIII's *Assertio*, that he considered himself permitted by Luther's own example:

> to throw back into your paternity's shitty mouth, truly the shit-pool of all shit, all the muck and shit which your damnable rottenness has vomited up, and to empty out all the sewers and privies onto your crown.

Mooning

We come now to the time-honoured gesture of baring the buttocks at someone as a gesture of defiance or insult, sometimes termed, in more recent times, 'mooning', although there is an interesting late twelfth-century parallel for this usage in a passage from Nigel de Longchamps' *Speculum Stultorum*, in which a country girl shamelessly relieves herself in the sight of the three Parcae of Roman mythology, who express their outrage that the girl does not know any better than to 'show us the horns of the new moon'.

I illustrate here an early fourteenth-century label-stop in the church at Cley, Norfolk (see chapter ornament), but the gesture is represented in all media including, to cite merely a few examples at random, the margin of a fifteenth-century French book of hours, an earlier *Decretals* manuscript where the gesture seems to have so shocked its victim that it has made his hair stand on end, a Dutch lead badge of *c.* 1400, and a Swiss playing card of *c.* 1530.

The gesture is fairly common on late medieval misericords, especially in France. When it is aimed at no one in particular, it might be interpreted as a general *apotropaion* against the Evil Eye, or perhaps more likely, as a deliberately provocative insult directed towards us, the viewers. The example among the late fifteenth-century Flemish stalls in the church at Aarschot, however, was perhaps motivated by a pun on the first element of the place-name! Just as common as these profile presentations are the contortionists,[15] some of whom are reminiscent of cats washing themselves and recall one of the riddles in the *Demaundes Joyous* (1511):

> What beest is it that hath her tayle bytwene her eyen?   [eyes]
> it is a catte when she lycketh her arse.

The contortionist on the misericord in Stratford-upon-Avon clearly proved too much for some previous incumbent and has been drastically censored, the whole of the front of the carving having been sheared off – a fate that must have been visited on many such images in all media down the centuries and especially in churches where, to modern eyes, they seemed especially inappropriate.

Historical Mooners

Historical instances of the mooning gesture are frequent and recorded throughout the entire Middle Ages. In the late sixth-century *Life of St Paternus of Avranches* a shameless woman who insultingly 'showed her posteriors' to the saint's party was fittingly punished, and the *Life of St Emmeram of Regensburg* records a similar incident in which a woman, 'raising her clothing, displayed her posterior to the saint, behaviour which God on no account allows to go unpunished', and so she was accordingly inflicted with hideous ulcers.

Referring to events of about 1080, the *Gesta Herewardi Saxonis* reported that the Fenland witch 'at the end of her chatterings and incantations thrice bared her arse' at Hereward the Wake and his men. Like some human *Schandbild*, Fromuldus, one of the murderers of the twelfth-century Count of Flanders, was hung up in such a way that his bared buttocks were turned towards his castle 'to the disgrace and ignominy of those traitors'. His contemporary, an Italian nobleman named Alberico da Romano, was so piqued at losing his valuable falcon while out hunting that 'he dropped his trousers and exposed his rear to the Lord, as a sign of abuse and reviling'.

The use of the gesture in wartime is especially interesting: in the Anglo-Scottish wars of the 1290s, the chronicler Pierre de Langtoft records that the English derided the Scots in this manner. Another most interesting instance is depicted in the lowest register of the early fourteenth-century *Roman de Fauvel*, as part of the earliest-known illustration of a *charivari*; of one of the participants it is said he 'showed his arse to the wind' (*vent*), but the illuminator has perhaps anticipated the Champeaux misericord mentioned below, for he seems to have punningly depicted this particular man in a winnowing-fan (*van*). The text goes on to note that other members of this unholy revel-rout threw dung at the spectators.[16]

The man carved on a fifteenth-century stall-end in the French church of Mortemart is so irreverent as to direct the gesture against a kneeling cleric, and is a contemporary of the fool in a well-known miniature depicting a scene from a stage play of the Martyrdom of St Apollonia in the *Hours of Etienne de Chevalier*, who bares his buttocks in derision of the saint. Another fool directs the same gesture against Christ in the engraving depicting the Mocking of Christ in Lucas van Leyden's *Small Passion* series of 1521, and we have already noticed the roughly contemporary painting by Quintin Massys which depicts a fool whose bauble makes the gesture at us, the viewers.

An extraordinary diptych in Liège, probably to be dated to the 1520s, shows on its outer panel a young man leaning out of a window pointing to a banderole inscribed 'Let this board hang closed/or you will see my brown cheeks.' His hand reaches behind him out of sight. Naturally, like Solomon and the oven-door (see below) we cannot resist opening the panel, whereupon we are confronted with a pair of repulsive – in both senses of that word – gestures. The left-hand wing of the interior of the diptych shows the reverse of the image on the outside, the young man's bare bottom staring out at us. There are scabs on the buttocks and, lodged in the underpants at half-mast, a thistle appears to guard the entrance to the anus. The scroll below reads, 'Please don't wish to hurt me – you were warned!' The right-hand wing depicts an elderly man pulling a face in the window frame (Colour Plate 12), making the gesture known in German as a *Gähnmaul* (compare English dialect *girning*), his facial gesture apparently paralleling and equivalent to the anal one, both being intended to shock and insult.

A distinct sub-species of this gesture is performed in the neighbourhood of a mirror, as in the woodcut illustration to an anecdote told in the first German publication of the fourteenth-century French *Livre pour l'enseignement de ses filles*[17] entitled *Der Ritter vom Thurn* and issued in Basel in 1493 (Figure 11.9). An elegant young woman who spends too much time and money adorning herself looks in her mirror and, to her horror, sees reflected not her own beauty, but the image of the devil's arse, mocking her pride in her appearance. Caxton had earlier translated the work into English and published it in 1484 as *The Book of the Knight of the Tower* and it is perhaps to this edition that Skelton owed the line 'Thy myrrour may be the devyllys ars' in his poem 'Agenst Garnesche' written in 1514.[18] The contemporary Scots poet, Henryson, (d. ?1506) seems also to be playing with this image in the punchline of his burlesque prescription, *Sum Practysis of Medecyne*, which proclaims 'It is ane mirk mirrour ane uthir manis erss' (Another man's arse is a dirty mirror). The use of this figure is also attested historically: in 1462 the Viennese rebelled against the authority of the Holy Roman Emperor, Frederick III, and one cratfsman even went so far as to bare his buttocks at the Empress Eleonore and her entourage saying, 'you should look in *this* mirror'. But there is also the possibility of some punning here, as *spiegel* could also mean 'bum' in late medieval German; indeed, it seems that the familiar rebus of Eulenspiegel's name – the owl (*Eule*) and mirror (*Spiegel*) – is a later euphemistic construction, and that the name was originally, and much more appropriately, given this Trickster's decided penchant for scatology, a nickname which meant 'Wipe [my] Bum', just like that of the synonymous *fastnachtspiel* (carnival play) character named *Wissmirdasgesess*.

A further sub-type depicts a man or animal making the mooning gesture at a man who is about to shoot an arrow at, or in some other way attack, the exposed buttocks. Wentersdorf suggested that they had their origin as illustrations of Psalm 77, verse 66: 'And he smote his enemies in the hindquarters, and put them to eternal shame.' Such images are quite common in Franco-Flemish manuscripts illuminated in the decades around 1300, but are also found, for example, in an early fifteenth-century *Hours of Jean Sans Peur* and – deliberately obliterated – in a late fourteenth-century Pisan grammar which we shall consider further below. A late fifteenth-century example is carved on a stone roof boss at Sherborne Abbey. These archers, whether long- or cross-bowmen are clearly made of sterner stuff than the men defending the city of Norwich during Kett's Rebellion of 1549, when, in the words of Sotherton's contemporary history of the rising, the capture of the city was effected not by force of arms but by the gestures of:

vagabond boyes [who] brychles and bear arssyde came emong the thickett of the arrows and did therewith most shamefully turne up theyr bare tayles agenst those which did shoote, which soe dismayed the archers that it tooke theyr hart from them.

Where there's Muck there's Brass – Filthy Lucre?

In the late Jan Verspaandonk's felicitous expression, the notion of excreting coins is 'An easy way of making money perhaps, but not a very likely one.'[19] Be that as it may, on a misericord in the Oude Kerk, Amsterdam, carved in the 1480s, a squatting man achieves this remarkable and lucrative feat, the coins being clearly recognisable as such from the crosses inscribed on them, the *croix* still current in French, corresponding to English *tails* (the reverse of a coin), a usage which recalls a period when French coins were so marked. Another contemporary and famous *Geldscheisser*, is the Goslar *Dukatenmensch* carved in 1494, who supports the statuette of Abundance in the clothiers' guild-house known as the Kaiserworth (Figure 13.2). A pair of early sixteenth-century carved brackets from Stade in Lower Saxony consists of a female *Geldscheisser* and a man who holds out a dish in which to gather the 'newly minted' coins, but cannot help covering his nose with his sleeve.

Figure 13.2

Lilian Randall hesitantly records a couple more such images in a Ghent breviary of the first quarter of the fourteenth century.[20] This identification is perhaps strengthened by evidence drawn from the ever-fruitful corpus of contemporary nicknames. In medieval France we hear of a certain Jehan *Chie-Denier* (John Shit-penny),[21] and there are several persons nicknamed *Couve-Denier* in the Paris tax returns of 1292 and 1313, where *couver*, literally, 'brood, hatch', is probably to be interpreted here as a euphemistic version of *chier*.[22]

Eulenspiegel (Howleglass) and other Scatological Tricksters

It is the Trickster figure Eulenspiegel who above all revels in scatological comedy. It has been established only recently that the first edition of Till Eulenspiegel's pranks was printed *c.* 1510 in Strasbourg in a form codified by Herman Bote of Brunswick – it seems certain, however, that the anecdotes which he recorded had earlier circulated in the oral tradition.

Even as a child, riding behind him on his father's horse, he deliberately exposed his bare bottom to the passers-by who were duly scandalised, but his first recorded exploit as a young man derives from a characteristic linguistic perversion. Commanded by his lord always to defecate on any hemp (*Henep*) he might find growing by the wayside, in order to fertilise this valuable plant from which the ropes that hung thieves were made, he pretends to have become confused and treats in the same manner the mustard (*Senep*) he brings up to the lord's table. There is perhaps an echo of this anecdote in an actual incident which took place during the early days of the Swiss Reformation in 1523, when a mustard-dealer upon arriving in unreformed Zug was told that all his mustard came from Zurich and 'that Zwingli had shit in it', in which remark the Reformer is cast as Eulenspiegel! Till further obtains rewards by eating half of his own excrement, and thus successfully outdoing the King of Poland's court jester who declines to eat the other half, and by substituting his own for that of a constipated child, thus earning the thanks of the duped mother. He tricks a cobbler into thinking frozen excrement is tallow, drives away his employer with a particularly noxious fart, introduces a pile of his excrement into a tavern thereby driving out the company, defecates in a bath-house pretending he thought it was a latrine, imitates the innkeeper's toddlers by relieving himself in the middle of the floor, tricks another innkeeper's wife into sitting on hot ashes with a bare bottom, soils his bed in another inn and claims a priest did it,[23] 'moons' at a messenger, and so on – even on his deathbed the arch-Trickster contrives to fool the avaricious priest who comes to hear his confession into thrusting his hand into a pot full of excrement covered with a layer of coins! It is noticeable, however, that Eulenspiegel's mostly scatological pranks are directed against aristocrats, priests, burghers and tradesmen, but never against the lowliest strata of society to which he himself belongs.

To the Pardoner's displaying of the absurd relic of the 'buttock-bone of Pentecost' in Heywood's *Playe of the Four PP* (*c.* 1520), the Pothecary exclaims, 'Thys relyke hath be-shyten the roste!' and Heywood was to use the expression again in his proverbial *Dialogue* (1546), but the curious idiom is otherwise found again only in a seventeenth-century Scottish proverb-collection (where the unpleasant feat is attributed to 'Jerdan's bitch', who does, at least, have the excuse of being an animal!). The woodcut to episode 69 (72) of Eulenspiegel's pranks, however, depicts him in the very act of 'beshitting the roast', which interestingly suggests that Heywood may have derived the idiom from some German source, even perhaps this very chapter (Figure 13.3).

Figure 13.3

Scatological outrages are to be expected as one of the weapons in the Trickster's armoury – even the contemporary exploits of a cleric, the so-called *Parson of Kalenborowe* as the English translation of *c.* 1520 styles him, obey this rule, as in the chapter entitled 'Howe the parson beshote the clerkes cayes [keys] and the place whereas he sholde sytt in the churche.' In similar vein, Eulenspiegel, as the verger-from-hell, rather too easily tricks a priest into defiling his own church (and wins a barrel of beer thereby).

The scatological *fabliau* in Chaucer's 'Summoner's Tale' is recalled by Eulenspiegel's similar deathbed prank, and its closing riddle, as to quite how to divide the legacy of a friar's fart equally among thirteen of his brethren, was later enthusiastically taken up and (more than) doubled by Robert Copland in his *Jyl of breyntfords testament* (*c.* 1560), where the legacy consists of twenty-six-and-a-half farts.[24]

The Shock of the Pooh

One of the best-known scatological stories of the German Middle Ages and one which seems to have been represented in art several times, is the so-called *Veilchenschwank* (Violet-prank). What two late fifteenth-century preachers refer to as 'Neidhart's Dance' and complain is one of the secular subjects which are replacing the traditional religious mural paintings on house walls, is a heady cocktail of courtly love ritual and peasant scatology. The aristocratic Neidhart sets out one morning to search for the first violet of spring; finding it, he marks the spot by covering the flower with his hat. Unknown to Neidhart, however, whose antagonism towards the peasantry was proverbial, he has been observed, and while returning to summon the duchess and her court, that they may celebrate the discovery with a round-dance, the peasant has plucked the violet and defecated on the spot. The court arrives accompanied by musicians and ready to dance, the duchess herself lifts the hat and the assembled aristocrats receive a doubtless satisfactory shock! The episode is depicted in several extant wall-paintings, the earliest from the first quarter of the fourteenth century, is sculpted on a series of late fifteenth-century stone tablets, and figured in several contemporary woodcut illustrations of the Neidhart material, of which this, representing the climactic episode, is one (Figure 13.4).

Figure 13.4

Marcolf's Pancake Trick and the Mystery of the Bum in the Oven

The use of the term 'pancake' is the *raison d'être* for one of the Trickster Marcolf's pranks, though oddly the pun is not spelled out in the earliest English version of the text, the Antwerp printing of 1492. Solomon imposes the riddling demand that Marcolf's mother should 'sende me of hir beste cowe a pot full of mylke and that the pot of the same cow be coveryd'. She supplies the expected *flawne of the same mylke made* as lid for the pot, but on his way to Solomon's court, Marcolf is overcome by hunger and eats the flan, replacing it with 'a drye bakyn cowe torde' (a cow turd baked dry (by the sun)). Solomon is not amused, though clearly the letter of the condition he imposed has been met! This drastic literalism of Marcolf's is also responsible for the climactic episode in the tale of his dealings with the King, which I have termed elsewhere 'The Bum in the Oven'.[25]

The deeds of Marcolf were known to the illuminators of the so-called 'East Anglian' psalters of the early fourteenth century. One of these manuscripts, the *Douai Psalter*, sadly (and ironically) damaged by damp while in protective storage during the Second World War, includes a *bas-de-page* scene on f. 124v which was described somewhat disingenuously by M.R. James, who saw it before it was damaged, as 'Marcolf bending over: Solomon on horse speaks to him'. Even at this date, however, James described the figure of Marcolf as 'rubbed', and I think we may be fairly certain that this represents an attempt at censorship on the part of some prudish earlier owner, for it is still just possible to discern that Marcolf is – at the very least – exposing his buttocks at the King. Moreover, there may even be a textual prompt for this, given what we know of the whimsical sense of humour of some illuminators, who seem not to have allowed the sacred text to overawe them, and given what we have already said above about the verb *trump*. This particular verso bears the text of the opening verses of Psalm 97, verse 6 of which, written on the recto, opposite our scene, reads (in the Authorised Version), 'With trumpets and sound of cornet make a joyful noise before the Lord, the King!'

In passing, we should just note that scatological, like sexual, imagery, of course, has always been prey to the censor, and together with the Stratford misericord noted earlier, this *Douai Psalter* image of Marcolf is now the second example we have met with. A third instance is another interesting drawing from the lower margin of a grammatical manuscript written in Pisa in the 1390s. A later owner has partly obliterated the scene, but it is clear both from the posture of the left-hand figure,

Figure 13.5

and the way in which the right-hand figure holds his nose with one hand while prodding something with a stick in his other hand, that this was once an illustration of the proverb, first recorded in English in a somewhat euphemistic version from one of Wyclif's late fourteenth-century sermons, to the effect that 'dritte [dirt], yif stired more, is more unsavery' – but Heywood's version is more usual and more straightforward: 'The more we stur a tourde, the wours it will stynke.' Here, a century after the Italian grammar is the same subject depicted as one of the many *Proverbes en Rimes* (Figure 13.5).

In addition to Marcolf's mooning at Solomon in the *Douai Psalter*, we have already noted the grotesque making the obscene suggestion and the trumpeting man placed directly above the figure of Marcolf disputing with Solomon in the related *Ormesby Psalter*. A third scatological jest connected with Marcolf, and the climax, indeed, of his taunting of Solomon appears on a leaf of the contemporary Franco-Flemish *Hours of Marguerite de Beaujeu* in which, bizarrely, a man's naked bottom projects from the opening of a brick-built oven (Figure 13.6). It is all too easy to dismiss this kind of image as mere gratuitous *grotesquerie* when one is unfamiliar with the story, but many years ago now, happening upon the entry in Lilian Randall's *Images in the Margins of*

Figure 13.6

Gothic Manuscripts, catalogued with admirable objectivity as 'oven containing hindquarters', I realised in a flash it could not be anything else! The conjunction of oven and bottom was too much of a coincidence to be mere arbitrary whimsy – but let me explain!

On account of his generally boorish behaviour, Marcolf is formally banished from Solomon's court and specifically the King says to him, 'I never want to see your face again!' Knowing what a keen huntsman Solomon is, however, Marcolf contrives to leave a trail of intriguing footprints which the King follows to an abandoned oven in the woods – naturally he is so curious that he opens the oven door, whereupon he is shocked to find that Marcolf has, in the words of the 1492 English print, 'put downe hys breche into hys hammes that he myght se hys ars hole and alle hys othre fowle gere'. As Marcolf the literalist explains, 'now and ye woll not se me betwyxt myn yes (eyes), ye may se me betwene my buttockys in the myddes of myn arsehole'. Not surprisingly, 'Than was the king sore meovyd' (sore moved, or very angry), and commanded that Marcolf should be hanged from a tree. In typical Trickster fashion, however, Marcolf successfully pleads for the right to be hanged from the tree of his choosing, and equally unsurprisingly, despite being conducted throughout the entire world by the king's servants, is unable to find a tree quite to his liking!

Foul Play

There are also scatological games (for more than one player). The early Tudor interlude *Fulgens and Lucres* includes a parody of chivalric entertainment with a species of joust alarmingly named *farte pryke in cule*

– this has been plausibly interpreted as the game of 'cock-fighting' still being played by public schoolboys in the nineteenth and early twentieth centuries, and which is illustrated on two sets of royal choir-stalls contemporary with the play, carved on misericords in Henry VII's Chapel in Westminster Abbey (*c.* 1512), and in St George's Chapel, Windsor (*c.* 1480) (Figure 13.7).[26] On another Windsor misericord a bizarre scene is depicted in which two men are shown kneeling one behind the other; a scarf attached to the forward man passes round the neck of the following man and has the effect of pulling his nose into the anal cleft of the man in front, whose hose at half-mast have exposed his buttocks. It may also be not without significance that both men have a scalloped edge to their tunics, that is, this may imply derivation from an original design which featured fools in similarly fringed tunics,

Figure 13.7

for there is an undoubted relationship with the identical and plainly scatological antics of the ass-eared fools who inhabit the margins of the 1498 Basel edition of Brant's *Narrenschiff*. As the Windsor stalls were carved at least fifteen years before this, however, the implication must be that the motif was available either in earlier printed book margins or perhaps in the form of a print no longer extant.[27]

Privy Counsel

In Amsterdam in 1481 it was officially declared illegal 'to relieve onself in the street or against walls', but a century later the regulations of the Court of Brunswick (1589) still felt it necessary to declare:

> Let no-one, whoever he may be, before, at, or after meals, early or late, foul the staircases, corridors, or closets with urine or other filth, but go to suitable, prescribed places for relief.

And this in an age before tower blocks and multi-storey car parks! The privy was such a 'prescribed place', of course, and frequently constructed in the companionable three-seater fashion seen on a German playing card of *c.* 1500 – playing cards, incidentally, seem peculiarly prone to scatological imagery.

Construction of the privy over running water as seen in Bruegel's *Netherlandish Proverbs* picture of 1559 (Colour Plate 6) was clearly a sound sanitary practice – the conjoined posteriors which project from his privy, however, also found *c.* 1500 in church woodwork, as on a misericord in Seville and a bench-end at Kappenberg in Westphalia (1509), illustrate the proverbial idiom of being so close to someone that you both 'shit through the same arse'. In one early sixteenth-century French book of hours a naked youth also uses a stream to good effect, though it may come as a surprise to find him decorating the margin of a devotional book. Medieval nicknames once again confirm this particular outdoor practice: in Bruges in 1383 we hear of one Jan, the son of Jan Elux, called *Schijt in de zee* (Shit in the sea) who was perhaps no more than eccentric in this regard, but the fourteenth-century German, *Erhart Schisingarten* (Shit in the garden) was clearly notorious for having fouled his own, or, worse, someone else's, nest. The peasant woman named Jutzin *Scheissindpluomen* (Shit in the flowers) in Wittenwiler's *Ring* (*c.* 1400) would have made a fitting companion, but it is difficult to know quite what to make of the thirteenth-century Johannes *Caca in Basilica*, for *basilica* might mean a number of different things in the Middle Ages, including 'cathedral'!

Listening to the radio recently I heard a resident of a run-down housing estate complain that 'you don't shit on your own doorstep', but this piece of traditional good advice would seem to have been ignored by the man identified as a fool by the eared hood he wears carved on a presumably deliberately mutilated misericord in the church of Sts-Gervais et Protais in Paris. While on the subject of doors, the outside door of a house marks an importantly liminal site, it is thus the location for *apotropaia* such as horseshoes to deny evil forces entrance, but also a potent locus for the working of hostile magic. There is a remarkable record of a private scatological rite which surely smacks more than a little of popular witchcraft, recorded in a fourteenth- or fifteenth-century manuscript preserved in the library of the Abbey of St Florian near Linz:

on Midsummer's Day a certain woman crawled backwards [*ersling*, modern *arschlings*], naked and on all fours, to her neighbour's door. She then walked backwards up the door with her feet, supporting herself on one hand while with the other she cut three splinters from the door and said to the first: 'I cut the first splinter, and may all her milk be lacking', and so also to the second, to the third she said 'I shit on the third splinter, and may all my neighbour's milk be lacking'. Then she went home, again backwards and on all fours.

But to revert to the man fouling his own doorstep, such figures are surprisingly frequent in church woodwork, as on a misericord from Ciudad Rodrigo in Spain, a stall-elbow at Windsor, and a stall partition at St-Claude carved in 1459. The man who deliberately so defiles the world orb on a carved partition of the late fifteenth-century stalls in the church of St Seurin, Bordeaux, is later duplicated in Bruegel's *Netherlandish Proverbs* painting.

Roof-bosses too depict this type of imagery. A man who having just defecated holds his nose, is placed high up on the roof vault in St Mary Redcliffe, Bristol, but another such sited just above the Bishop's Door in the cloister of Norwich Cathedral is unaccountably omitted from the guidebooks, while on one boss in the cloisters of Wells Cathedral we are treated to the sight of three men simultaneously so engaged. In one of the woodcuts in an *Ars Memorativa* published in Augsburg by Anton Sorg *c.* 1470, illustrating the word *Stinckent*, a single-seater privy is depicted with the door open, but presumably on account of the stench within, the man shown in the cut has elected not to venture inside but performs his office outside! The naked man who points to his anus on another Bristol boss, however, is thought to represent the homosexual king, Edward II who was, of course, famously murdered through that orifice.

Does My Bum Look Big in This? – The Naming of Parts

There is evidence that the size of one's bottom was already a concern in the Middle Ages: when the fourteenth-century French poet, Eustache Deschamps, wanted to insult the English enemy in a *rondeau*, he not only availed himself of the venerable *Angli caudati* motif (see Chapter 4), but pointed out that they had bums like barrels, whereas *Les Françoiz* (naturally) 'have small buttocks'.[28] According to the sixteenth-century *Dict des Pays*, however, it is the inhabitants of St Quentin who were noted for big buttocks! But, yet again, the treasury of medieval nicknames has something to offer in this area, and in the year of Hastings we hear of an Anglo-Saxon Alestan, nicknamed *Braders* (Broad Arse). Three and a half centuries later (1421) we hear of Barbelken, a Brabant woman with the unenviable sobriquet, *Groot eers* (Great Arse), while the Paris tax-roll of 1292 lists both a Richart *Gros-Cul* (Big Arse), and an Anes *Cul-Pesant* (Heavy Arse). The late thirteenth-century German, Burchard, nicknamed simply *Burel* (Bum), was presumably not so called on account of the smallness of his bottom, but in French-speaking Flanders (Oudenaarde) an exact contemporary of his, Stevenon *Stroit Cul*, literally, 'Narrow Arse' (?Tight Arse) perhaps was, and Robin *Petit Cul* (Little Arse) certainly was.

A small group of thirteenth-century French nicknames are based on comparisons with the bottoms of animals: a Guillaume and a Johanna *Culdoe* (that is, *cul d'oie*

(Goose Arse)) from Paris, a Martin *Cul d'ourse* (Bear's Arse) from Arras in 1230, and a man named *Cul d'Asne* (Donkey's Arse) *c.* 1275 in Oudenaarde. *Oxan ers* (Ox's Arse) from late Saxon Worcestershire, on the other hand, is not the name of a person, but a local hill. We should probably feel sorry, however, for the Frenchmen Garinus *Torcul,* that is, *tort cul,* (Twisted Arse), and Guillaume *Cul-Percie* (Pierced Arse) (1292), unless the latter is a homophobic sneer, but it is difficult to know quite what we should make of his townsman Drogo *Cul de fer* (Iron Arse). A contemporary Englishman named Cutte *Brendhers* (1279), that is, Burnt Arse, probably also deserves our sympathy, but the sobriquet of the Aalis residing in Arras in 1222 who was surnamed *Hochecul* (Wiggle Arse) probably denotes a bottom felt to be sexually attractive.

A Brussels shipboy named Coppen was called *Vuyleers* (Filthy Arse) by his shipmates and might be compared with the French Guillaume whose nickname in Latinised form was *Culi Putridi.* The late thirteenth-century English miller nicknamed *Scitepilch* (1279) was perhaps merely accustomed to wear a filthy coat caked with flour, but the nickname of his fellow countryman, *Schitebroch* (Shit(ty) Breeches), like that of the Dutchman Jan *Cackebroec,*[29] perhaps alluded to some catastrophic past episode of incontinence which they had never been allowed to forget. It is as difficult to account for Richard *Schittebag*'s sobriquet (1277), as it is to accept P.H. Reaney's insistence that the nickname *Shitface* was complimentary![30]

Enemas

Enemas are still good for a laugh in 'low comedy', but the enema was also a surprisingly popular part of the everyday life of many in our period, administered for purely therapeutic as well as curative reasons. 'A Clyster is a noble remedye to dryue out superfluitees of the guttes', writes Traheron in his 1543 translation of Vigo's surgical work.[31] Representations of such ministrations, however, are almost always humorous in intent – as in literature too, for example in Heywood's *Playe of the Four PP*, where the Pothecary tells his 'lying-tale' of a *glister* he administered to a woman who afterwards farted so forcibly that it destroyed a castle ten miles away – and serious medical illustrations are rare. An example of the humorous type is to be found on one of the misericords at Sts Gervais et Protais, Paris.

What looks like a bladder with nozzle attached seems to be illustrated on a Spanish misericord in the cathedral at Zamora, while funnel delivery is depicted in a serious woodcut illustration of 1515, which is closely related to one of the border scenes on the magnificent Ambraser 'Narrenteller' painted in 1528 (Figure 6.9). A pair of maiolica plates painted by the fifteenth-century Italian artist Gaetano Ballardini depict both syringe and funnel types of enema being administered to men by women. More frequently, however, the instrument chosen to deliver the enema is a type of bellows, as seen in a woodcut by Hans Sebald Beham, a reversed copy of an original composition by Hans Weiditz. The 'doctor' himself is adorned with fool's bells, which hardly signals a serious illustration, and carries a lantern in one hand, while his assistant stands ready with the bellows, rather similar to the scene on a misericord at Diest (1491).

Figure 13.8

What I have elsewhere termed the 'anal bellows' motif, found as early as *a.*-1350 in manuscript margins[32] may sometimes represent an enema, then, but of course, as bellows by definition produce wind, there may often be an allusion to the wind which issues from the buttocks too. This misericord at Great Malvern carved *c.* 1480 (Figure 13.8) has been described as a monk driving away a demon with a pair of bellows, but it seems to me that the 'demon' is in fact a monkey, and if this is granted, it appears astonishingly close to Abraham Holland's illustration in John Davies' *Scourge for Paper-persecutors* of the sort of popular imagery to be found pasted up on walls 150 years later, when as an example of 'an Antique [grotesque] in base postures fall[en]', he cites 'a Frier blowing wind into the taile/Of a Babboone . . .'.

Urinary Motifs

For the sake of completeness I must briefly say something about urinary motifs. The only relevant medieval nickname I have come across is a character in a *fastnachtspiel* (carnival play) named *Saichindenkruog* (Piss in the jug), an act represented on a Swabian playing card (*c.* 1465), a late medieval English earthenware tile and – with the addition of a second jug behind – in a fourteenth-century Flemish marginal drawing.[33] Two Parisian streets mentioned in the 1292 tax-roll, the Rue *Quiquempoist* (Pee-in-the-pot) and Rue de *Quiquentonne* (Pee-in-the-tub), may be compared with London's *Pissynglane* attested from 1425 and the synonymous *Mihindelone* of thirteenth-century Gloucester. London's present Sherborne Lane, incidentally, was *Shitteborwelane* in the late thirteenth century and there were lanes of the same name in contemporary Oxford and Romford, based, it has been suggested, on a facetious formation, *Shiteburgh* being 'a jocular name for a common privy'.[34]

It was Macbeth's porter who sententiously proclaimed that drink 'is a great provoker of three things . . . nose-painting, sleep, and urine', and though not extant, an inventory of the goods belonging to the Gild of St Mary's in Boston, Lincolnshire, taken in 1534 included a mazer bowl with a silver print in the bottom, only revealed, of course, when the cup had been drained, depicting an ape looking into a urine flask with the inscription *THIS WAT' IS FOLOWS* (This is what follows).

Two apes on a panel of a late medieval German *Minnekästchen* on the other hand are themselves gleefully preparing a far from wholesome electuary, however natural the bodily products they are using! A very similar human/ape pair carved in stone humorously served as a contemporary French apothecary's shop-sign, though when a drawing of it was reproduced in a late nineteenth-century book, the artist clearly felt obliged to censor the ape's contribution to the mix in the mortar. The same motif is found on early fifteenth-century English lead badges, but this time the apes who contribute their urine to the mortar stand on fishback. Similar badges are known from the Netherlands. By 1539 in a woodcut illustration to a book issued in Straubing, the apes characteristic of late medieval *drôlerie* have been adapted into the *putti* equally diagnostic of the Renaissance ornamental vocabulary.

Scatology is an important weapon in the armoury of trickster figures and is perhaps a mark of their fundamental antipathy towards civilisation, but the insult that an Eulenspiegel offers to bourgeois civilisation by his very existence is exploited on a smaller scale by individual use of insults, whether verbal or gestural (mooning, for example).

A perhaps necessary socially and culturally conditioned distaste for the subject of the present chapter has led to the general neglect of this inescapable aspect of the human condition, but my own excuse for treating it here must be that without at least some familiarity with this area, our understanding of late medieval culture is incomplete.

CONCLUSION

One thing I hope to have demonstrated in this book, through the use made of inventories, for example, is the apparent paradox that we do not necessarily need visual evidence from the late medieval period in order still to 'see' it. As was noted in the opening chapter, of the thirty-two biscuit-moulds engraved for the Mayor of Frankfurt by the city's assay master, Hartmann Kistener, and so carefully inventoried by their proud owner, only four have come down to us, a survival rate, for these admittedly 'minor' and domestic *objets d'art*, of 12.5 per cent – and even so, probably unusually high. But we have built our histories of medieval art on the tips of such icebergs.

Stalburg's moulds are interesting for the high proportion of non-religious iconography – at least 75 per cent, by my reckoning – that they reveal. Might it be that the Middle Ages was not quite so dominated by religious imagery as we have been led to believe? The winnowing process of the ages is not an equitable, impersonal force preserving for later generations, proportionate and representative corpora of the products of the arts and crafts of our forebears. Much of what has reached us, has been deliberately *selected for preservation* by all too human agents, and is either the inheritance of the elite, the heirlooms of the aristocracy, or the pickings of the connoisseurs. Our knowledge of the content of late medieval visual culture is thus unrepresentative: we have not been well served by these arbiters of taste, these grandees of *gravitas*.

The irony is that that very selection of works of art of an overtly religious content as suitable to be preserved for posterity, betrays an erroneous understanding of medieval *mentalité* – if some of these nineteenth-century connoisseurs on whose *connaissance* our received opinion of the content of medieval art has been based, had troubled to lift up a few misericords in their local parish churches, they would have seen that there was more to medieval art than biblically derived imagery, even where it might perhaps have been most expected.

In recent decades, the democritising science of archaeology has somewhat redressed this imbalance with regard to the availability and study of non-religious imagery, and having myself been privileged to have been in on the exciting 'discovery' (really, of course, the *re*-discovery) of the late medieval lead badges from the Netherlands and, indeed, our own Thames foreshore, will to some extent explain why I have so often cited the evidence of archaeology in the present account of what I understand or, rather, believe *should* be understood, by medieval 'art'.

But it is equally short-sighted to restrict our understanding of medieval 'art' to the 'work of art', to the *thing*, whether the connoisseur's *objet d'art* or the archaeologist's artefact; for, as I hope to have demonstrated in Chapter 5, iconography inheres in acts as well as objects, in ritual and in gesture, whether recorded representationally or not.

Nothing better illustrates the savagery and the symbolism of such immaterial late medieval iconography than the fate of the Scottish Sir Simon Fraser, captured by Edward II's troops at the Battle of Kirkencliff in 1306, and executed with elaborate ritual in London shortly thereafter. A contemporary English poem positively bursting with *Schadenfreude* describes in gleeful detail the horrors to which Sir Simon was subjected in the English capital. Firstly:

A gerland of leves on ys hed ydyht of grene;	[A garland made of green leaves
For he shulde ben yknowe	was placed on his head so that he
Both of heghe ant of lowe	should be recognised as a traitor
for treytour, y wene.	by both high and low].

His legs were fettered under his horse's belly, his hands manacled, and then a garland of periwinkle was set on his head ('A gerland of peruenke set on ys heued').[1]

Following this parodic 'crowning', the wretched Fraser was drawn from the Tower of London through Cheapside to the gallows on a bullock's hide ('Upon a retheres hude forth he wes ytuht'), still in fetters and gyves and wearing his periwinkle-crown, but also in a kirtle of sackcloth (*burel*). Here he was hanged, beheaded and disembowelled. His head was impaled on London Bridge (next to that of Wallace), while the remainder of his body hung in a gibbet, guarded by twenty-four armed men, to prevent its being taken down by Scottish or other sympathisers.[2]

Perhaps the most curious detail of this grisly description is the use of the periwinkle flower as a suitable garland for a traitor, but there are other instances of this symbolism in Middle English verse: in Lydgate's early fifteenth-century translation of Boccaccio's *Fall of Princes*, Fortune congratulates Bochas that he has:

Spared not ther crownys nor ther purpil weedis	[clothes]
Ther goldene sceptris; bot youe to them ther meedis;	[but given them their just deserts]
Crownid oon with laureer hih in his hed vpset,	[laurel set high on his head]
Other with peruynke maad for the gibet.	[another with periwinkle made for the gibbet]

Here laurel and periwinkle are plainly contrasted, as evergreens at opposite poles of the approval/disapproval spectrum, and periwinkle notably characterised as 'made for the gibbet'.

In Jean Regnier's *Fortunes et Adversitez*, written in a Beauvais prison in 1432, however, the green chaplets to be worn at the poet's courtly love-style funeral are also to be made of the 'evergreen' periwinkle, for:

> This periwinkle is of such a nature
> that it is green winter and summer
> And every creature ought similarly
> ever to keep faith.
>
> The green signifies bliss. . . .

If nothing else, this serves to demonstrate that such visual symbols are not univalent – it is naive to think that such-and-such an object 'means' x and only x – and this well illustrates how difficult it is to pin down the symbolism of individual flowers in particular contexts.

In several European vernaculars the periwinkle was given a name that meant 'evergreen' (for example, German *Singrün, Immergrün*) for, although botanically herbaceous, it retains its leaves throughout the winter. Evergreens have long been used to construct wreaths, of course, whether in the *laureate* poet's crown to symbolise his enduring fame (of laurel or bay), or in lovers' chaplets to convey their evergreen *loyaulté* to their loved ones (as in Jean Regnier's directions for his funeral; but also of willow, for the disappointed lover – as we have seen in Chapter 10) or, indeed, in the funerary wreath.

There is ample evidence that the periwinkle was used as a commemorative plant at gravesides in the German tradition, presumably as a tribute to the 'evergreen' memory of the departed, and hence its other German names such as *Totenkraut*, and perhaps also, the synonymous Italian *fiore di morte*. Writing in 1539, Bock noted that the heads of some exhumed corpses had been crowned with garlands of periwinkle and recorded how four years previously he had seen a skull dug up crowned with a garland of the same plant which had also not withered.[3] As we know that the periwinkle was used in funerary wreaths and as a graveside plant in Germany, if the same sort of practice obtained in England, it may well be that to crown a traitor on his way to execution – as in the eyes of the English, the Scottish Sir Simon Fraser was – with a wreath of the plant was, as it were, to anticipate or seal him with the plant of death (*Totenkraut; fiore di morte; peruynke maad for the gibet*). The 'language of flowers' with a vengeance.

A very rare example of a piece of topical verse satire, which from a knowledge of the local history can be dated to *c.* 1485, was discovered on the back of a rent-roll pertaining to Ashford in Kent, and now preserved in that county's Archives Office in Maidstone:

Det peruynkkle hed ykowmbyrght owre town,	[The periwinkle had troubled our
Tyl vs het ybent hys boghe;	town, bent his bow against us;
We han be wendyt yn gret tresoun . . .	??We have been turned in great treason . . .
The brere het ybrowt de wed adown	The briar has brought the weed down
An layd hys leyghuys loywe . . .	And laid his leaves low . . .
Pernk' schel have wel heuyle endyng.	Periwinkle shall have a most evil end.]

Sir John Fogge of Ashford died in 1490 and was buried in the local church, and although his tomb has suffered badly, earlier descriptions of it show that his device was the briar-rose – the *brere* of the poem – and his memorial brass depicted him with a subdued greyhound seated at his feet. On the succession of Richard III, Sir John had repudiated the overtures of the new monarch and in consequence was deprived of all his honours and lands, the latter being bestowed on a certain William Malyverer in 1484. It was inevitable that the herald's taste for punning or 'canting arms' should confer a greyhound badge on Malyverer as if the name contained the French element *levrier* (greyhound), but a mere six months after coming into this undeserved windfall, Sir John was pardoned and most of his lands restored to him. His tomb inscription records him as 'a friend of the common people' and he founded a college in Ashford, as well as paying for extensive restoration to the church.

It would seem, therefore, that the poem in question was written by one of his local admirers and in despite of the treacherous William Malyverer, who must surely be symbolised as the 'weed' periwinkle of the poem, contrasting with Sir John's briar-rose.[4]

Not only, then, may something such as a periwinkle plant have more than one significance at various times and places but, importantly, as we saw in Chapter 3, not *everything* is necessarily a symbol *at all* – sometimes a dog is just a dog, and its presence is not symbolic, unless perhaps as a token of the sheer normality of the scene.

The case of Sir Simon Fraser's grisly ritual demise shows us how much we miss if we rely for our notion of what is medieval art only on the traditionally privileged media. The German *Schandbilder*, those extraordinarily vicious and public shaming-pictures, several of which we examined in Chapter 5, present us with the wishful-thinkings of some very ill-wishers indeed. But while their victims' sufferings might be only proleptically depicted, we know full well, from the historical record, that such gruesome and *degrading* punishments were meted out in reality.

But iconographers must be as alert to the metaphorical nature of languages as to that of images, and analyse their own language with the same perspicacity they customarily devote to analysing a picture. *Degrading*, for example, is another of those words whose etymology we have lost sight of, another 'dead metaphor' we are no longer conscious of. The *OED* defines the earliest, etymological sense of *degrade* as 'To depose (a person) formally from his degree, rank, or position of honour as an act of punishment, as to degrade a knight, a military officer, a graduate of a university.'

The ritual breaking of his sword appears to have been one of the actions performed in the degrading of a knight, as in the following example recorded by Hall for the year 1462/3 in his *Chronicle* (completed *a.* 1532):

These Lordes also tooke by force the stronge castle of Bamborough, and in it sir Raufe Gray, whiche was before sworne to kyng Edward, for the whiche periurie to bothe the princes, he was disgraded of the high ordre of knighthode at Dancastre, by cuttyng of his gylt sporres,[5] rentyng his cote of armes, and breakyng his sword ouer his hed: and finally, there his body was shorted, by the length of his hed and had no more harme, thus was he rewarded for his doble deceipt and manifest periurie.[6]

I hope I have not overemphasised the nasty and brutish aspects of medieval iconography at the expense of the charming and uplifting, in my attempt to describe the 'other half' of late medieval art; but an unwillingness to engage with some of the more distasteful areas surveyed here, the iconography of punishment and scatology, for instance, has contributed to what I argued in my Preface is the prevailing and quite unrepresentative picture we have of the content of medieval visual culture. The aesthetic response is almost always inappropriate to iconographical enquiry – opinion as to the 'quality' of execution of an image should not, to my mind, be part of proper iconographical investigation, and indeed, such sensibilities and sensitivities have long hobbled our study. And folly and filth were as much a part of the human condition in the Middle Ages as were gravity and spirituality – just as much, indeed, as they are today – and we only cloud our view of that era if we ignore these aspects. It is time to take off the blinkers.

I regard art history as a branch of cultural history, not as an end in itself. Or, to look at it the other way round, iconography is cultural history with the pictures added, but with those pictures not merely as *illustrations* of that history but a constituent part of it, and a part of how we know what we think we do about it. It is my hope that the present book will herald a redirection in the thrust of iconographical enquiry into late medieval art, away from the traditional stamping-ground of religious imagery and into the pastures grazed here, still surprisingly new and even, perhaps, greener!

NOTES AND REFERENCES

PREFACE

1. P.D.A. Harvey and A. McGuinness, *A Guide to British Medieval Seals* (London, 1996), p. 78.
2. J. Huizinga, *The Waning of the Middle Ages* (Harmondsworth, 1972), p. 233.

CHAPTER ONE

1. The other two surviving Kistener moulds were not owned by Stalburg. The Stalburg inventory was published by F. Bothe as 'Stein- und Tonmodel als Kuchenformen' in *Repertorium für Kunstwissenschaft* 43 (1922), pp. 80–92. The two most important publications of such moulds drawn on in the present chapter are W. von Bode and W.F. Vollbach, 'Mittelrheinische Ton- und Steinmodel aus der 1. Hälfte des 15. Jahrhunderts' in *Jahrbuch der preussischen Kunstsammlungen* 38 (1918), pp. 89–134, and F. Arens, 'Die ursprüngliche Verwendung gotischer Stein- und Tonmodel' in *Mainzer Zeitschrift* 66 (1971), pp. 106–31.
2. There is reason to believe that the former subject, while undoubtedly biblical in origin, was often an excuse for the medieval equivalent of soft porn, or that the scene owed its popularity to erotic rather than religious enthusiasm; the latter scene was equally popular as a part of the Power of Women topos (see Chapter 11).
3. For this reason, I am suspicious of the popularity of 'tables' of *Lucretia* (at least seven by my count), in the inventory of Henry VIII, as this subject affords the artist an opportunity to display the naked female bosom under the paradoxical guise of exemplary chastity.
4. Also a much later engraving by Hans Sebald Beham made in 1541, itself copied into the *Glockendon Breviary*, *c.* 1542, now in the Stadtbibliothek, Nürnberg. An evidently similar print is described in the Colón inv. no. 2082/3 (*a.* 1539) in which there are two bathing women who try to drag the fool in with them while to the left a man fondles another naked woman.
5. Though not apparently remarked hitherto, this poses a problem in that the inventory is dated 1521! However, as this is the very last of the moulds said to have been engraved by Kistener, I suggest that it was added to the original draft of the inventory at some subsequent date.
6. See Chapter 11.
7. C. de Carli, *I deschi da parto* (Turin, 1997), nos 13 and 43.

8. J.C. Hutchison, *The Master of the Housebook* (New York, 1972), p. 77.

9. I. Mateo Gomez, *'Apostillas iconograficas al Bosco y Rodrigo Aleman'* in *Boletin del Museo del Prado* 6:18 (September–December 1985), p. 133 and fig. 13.

10. A thematically related engraving by Hopfer *a.* 1536 shows a semi-naked (but winged) young woman (?Venus – she is accompanied by a lute-playing Cupid) similarly being used as bait by the Devil who lies in wait half-obscured behind her with the *Kloben*.

11. A drawing of an example from a lost *album amicorum* formerly in the Louvre is reproduced as figure 177 in J.-C. Margolin, *Histoire du Rébus* (Paris, 1986); a mid-sixteenth-century German woodcut version (otherwise unprovenanced) is reproduced in G. Langemeyer *et al.* (eds), *Bild als Waffe: Mittel und Motive der Karikatur in fünf Jahrhunderten* (Munich, 1984), Abb. 191; two examples in Swiss glass-painting are dated 1562 and 1571.

12. M. Jones, 'Seventeenth-century English broadside prints', 1, in *Print Quarterly* 18 (2001), pp. 149–63.

13. M. Jones, 'The Horn of Suretyship' in *Print Quarterly* 16 (1999), pp. 219–28, esp. pp. 226–8.

14. G. Cohen, *La comédie Latine en France au XIIe siècle* (Paris, 1931), pp. 147–9.

CHAPTER TWO

1. See S.A. Callisen, 'The Evil Eye in Italian art' in *The Art Bulletin* 19 (1937), pp. 452–62.

2. R.W. Lightbown, *Medieval European Jewellery* (London, 1992), p. 90.

3. J. Cherry, 'Healing through faith: the continuation of medieval attitudes to jewellery into the Renaissance' in *Renaissance Studies* 15 (2001), pp. 154–71, esp. p. 155.

4. Lightbown, op. cit., p. 237.

5. The identification was made in L. Hansmann and L. Kriss-Rettenbeck, *Amulett und Talisman. Erscheinungsform und Geschichte* (Munich, 1977), p. 224.

6. C. von Heusinger, *'Ein Neujahrsgruss auf das Jahr 1459'* in *Gutenberg Jahrbuch* (1959), pp. 36–40.

7. Schreiber 1454a.

8. See further, J. Berchtold, *Des Rats et des ratières* (Geneva, 1992), but the reference must come with a health warning, the book being described in the publisher's blurb as 'Une étude exceptionelle, réconciliant, une fois n'est pas coutume, le champ des "essentialistes", dénués de base historique, avec celui des travaux d'historien dépourvus de tout pouvoir d'intuition'!

9. L. Carolus-Barré, *'Un nouveau parchemin amulette et la légende de sainte Marguerite patronne des femmes en couches'* in *Comptes Rendus de l'Académie des Inscriptions,* pp. 256–75.

10. D. Bruna, *Enseignes de pèlerinage et enseignes profanes* (Paris, 1997), no. 317.

11. D. Gray, 'The Five Wounds of our Lord' in *Notes and Queries* 4 (1963), p. 165.

12. J. Alexander and P. Binski, *Age of Chivalry: Art in Plantagenet England 1200–1400* (London, 1987), cat. no. 647.

13. Bruna, op. cit., no. 117.

14. J. Evans, *English Posies and Posy-rings* (London, 1931), p. 2.

15. *Archaeologia* 19 (1894), p. 411; cf. a similar legend on a ring in the Victoria and Albert Museum, M287–1962: *qui [me portera]a grant honneur venir.*

16. Lightbown, op. cit., p. 206.

17. *Perceval of Galles* in eds W.H. French and C.B. Hale, *Middle English Metrical Romances* (New York, 1964), II, pp. 589–90, lines 1858–64.

18. MOL cat., 121–2.

19. Admittedly translated from the French *Evangiles de Quenouilles* (1480), but sixteenth-century references confirm it as – at least by then – a native English superstition.

20. I. Gollancz and M.M. Weale (eds), [= EETS OS 195] (London, 1935).

21. Cambridge, Trinity College Library MS B.11.4, f. 119r.

22. Lightbown, op. cit., pl. 57.

23. Lightbown, op. cit., pl. 33.

24. HP1 afb. 962, 963; HP2 afb. 1967, 1968; MOL cat. 319b, 321c, and R.S. Loomis, *Mirror of Chaucer's World* (Princeton, 1978), no. 106.

25. *The Riverside Chaucer*, 3rd edn, L.D. Benson, *The Canterbury Tales*, (Oxford, 1988), General Prologue, lines 160ff.

26. J.R.R. Tolkien and E.V. Gordon (eds), *Sir Gawain and the Green Knight* (2nd edn, N. Davis, Oxford, 1967) lines 626f. The poet claims the pentangle device is known in English as the 'endless knot', though this name for it seems not to have been found elsewhere.

27. Geisberg 1061.

28. HP1 753–6, 918–9; HP2 1842–4, 1974, 2032–5.

29. MOL cat., no. 166.

30. cf. MOL cat., p. 141: a mould for badges from Walsingham depicts the Annunciation as the central device on a six-pointed star.

31. J. Gairdner and R.H. Brodie (eds), *Letters and Papers, Foreign and Domestic, Henry VIII: Addenda, vol. 1 part 1*, no. 29 (cit. Spencer (1998), p. 145).

32. MOL cat., pp. 155–9.

33. Spencer (1990) no. 149 reads *be meri* but the drawing (fig. 195) appears to show *be wari* or possibly *be mari*. For the inscription as read by Spencer, however, cf. a fifteenth-century box for a wine cup in Moulton St Mary Church, Norfolk, covered in leather and stamped with the words *BE MERI MAN* (Be merry, man!).

34. M. Eccles (ed.), *The Macro Plays* [= EETS 262] (London, 1969), p. 168.

35. Wh W223–4.

36. See refs in the *OED*'s etymology paragraph, *s.v. tawdry.*

37. For which one Middle English term is *potence*; Spencer [MOL cat. p. 177] notes that some of these badges bear the Latin words *P[otentia] siue tau* in a curious self-reference to the crutch-like form of the Tau cross.

38. HP1 afb. 35.

39. cit. Spencer, MOL cat., p. 123.

40. For example, those eponyms who owe their existence to folk etymology of the name of the site on which a celebrated church, monastery, etc. now stands.

41. E. Hawkins (ed.), *The Holy Lyfe and History of Saynt Werburghe* (London, 1848), p. 98.

42. These badges depicting St Werburgh's geese in their wattle enclosure are identified as such in B. Spencer, *Pilgrim Souvenirs and Secular Badges* (= Salisbury & South Wiltshire Museum, Medieval Catalogue, Part 2), p. 57.

43. E.R. Henken, *The Welsh Saints A Study in Patterned Lives* (Cambridge, 1991), 158, Motif Index X.B.1.c.

44. MOL cat., pp. 192–5.

45. E. Ettlinger, 'Notes on a Woodcut depicting King Henry VI being invoked as a Saint' in *Folklore*, 84 (1973), pp. 115–19.

46. J. Strachey (ed.), *Rotuli Parliamentorum IV* (London, 1832), p. 232: *Sanctus Edwardus*.

47. First published by E.W. Tristram, 'An English Mid-fourteenth Century Picture' in *Burlington Magazine*, 83 (1943), pp. 160–2.

48. MOL cat., pp. 182–5.

49. MOL cat., p. 195.

50. A facsimile was edited by G.J. Boekenoogen (Leiden, 1903). The most thorough modern study is that by A.R. Deighton, 'The sins of Saint John of Beverley: the case of the Dutch "volksboek" *Jan van Beverley*' in *Leuvense Bijdragen*, 82 (1993).

51. Luther reprinted the earlier *Lugend von Sanct Johanne Chrysostomo* in 1537.

52. Seemingly unknown to E. Wind, 'The Saint as Monster' in *Journal of the Warburg and Courtauld Institutes*, 1 (1937), p. 183.

53. R. Bernheimer, *Wild Men in the Middle Ages* (Harvard, 1952), fig. 4. C.A. Williams discussed the type in two essays: *Oriental Affinities of the Hairy Anchorite* (Urbana, 1925–6), and *The German Legends of the Hairy Anchorite* (Urbana, 1935). The Middle English romance of *Sir Orfeo* is analysed in this light in Penelope Doob's book, *Nebuchadnezzar's Children* (New Haven/London, 1974), p. 164ff.

54. B. Spencer, *Pilgrim Souvenirs and Secular Badges* [= Salisbury Museum Medieval Catalogue, Part 2] (Salisbury, 1990), p. 34.

55. ibid., p. 62.

56. BL MS Royal 10. E. IV ff. 113v.–118v.

57. See n. 50 above.

58. R.A. Skelton and P.D.A. Harvey, *Local Maps and Plans from Medieval England* (Oxford, 1986), pp. 121–6. The map is Cambridge, Trinity Hall, MS 1, f. 42v.

59. Also called St Mildred's Linch (bank) after Mildred, second Abbess of Minster, daughter of Domneva.

60. Henken, op. cit., p. 84.

61. ibid., p. 85. For similar Irish saints, see ed. C. Plummer, *Vitae Sanctorum Hiberniae* (Oxford, 1910), I.58 (St Ailbe sends two to plough for St Squieth), and I.79 (St Carthage arranges for stags to plough for someone who asks to borrow his plough).

62. See G.McN. Rushforth, *The Windows of the Church of St Neot, Cornwall* (Exeter, 1937), pp. 150–90, esp. pp. 181–2.

63. Rushforth, op. cit., refers to S. Baring-Gould and J. Fisher, *Lives of the British Saints* (London, 1907–13), II, p. 225. A Breton hagiographer, Albert le Grand, published a life of Saint Ke in French in 1636.

64. Rushforth op. cit., p. 182. See also F. Bottomley, *St Robert of Knaresborough* (Ruddington, 1993), and his quotation from *The Metrical Life of St Robert of Knaresborough* (Latin text of BL MS Egerton 3143 (*c.* 1250)).

65. Spencer (1990), op. cit., pp. 110–11.

66. N. Pevsner, *North East Norfolk and Norwich* (Harmondsworth, 1962), p. 112.

67. Cambridge, Trinity College Library, MS R.3.14, f. 3v.

68. R. Axton and P. Happé (eds), *The Plays of John Heywood* (Woodbridge, 1991).

69. I. Lancashire (ed.), *Two Tudor Interludes* (Manchester, 1980), p. 220, line 761.

70. R. Axton and P. Happé (eds), op. cit., pp. 153–61.

71. See N.J. Rogers, 'St Sunday: a problem of identification' in *Early Drama and Music Newsletter* (1985), pp. 28–31.

72. Part of the shoulderbone (*humerus*), of the holy Jewish priest, Simeon, was reportedly one of the relics held at Becket's shrine in 1446.

73. The French farce is edited by A. Tissier, *Recueil de Farces*, tome V (Geneva, 1989), p. 243ff.

74. B.B. Adams (ed.), *John Bale's King Johan* (San Marino, 1969), lines 1215ff.

75. Perhaps, like the *Saint Samuell* of *Thersites*, Bale's St Job confirms another strategy for the creation of burlesque saints, that is, the canonisation of Old Testament figures.

76. cit. Harper, op. cit., p. 73.

77. HP1 afb. 328.

78. End of cap. 26. In Pierre Gringore's farce, *Raoullet Ployart* (1512), there is mention of a *Seigneur de Balletreu* who substitutes for the *Prince des Sots* – A. Tissier, *Recueil des Farces*, tome II (Geneva, 1999), p. 242f., suggests that *Balletrou* = Bouche-trou, that is, 'hole-plug'.

79. He also appears in the farce *Les Chambrières qui vont à la messe de cinq heures*, where he is invoked by the suggestively named *Trousse-ta-queue*.

80. J. Koopmans, *Recueil de Sermons Joyeux* (Geneva, 1988), pp. 79–87.

81. J.A.S. Collin de Plancy, *Dictionnaire critique des reliques et des images miraculeuses* (Paris, 1821–2), p. 78f.

82. See K. Schreiner, 'Discrimen veri ac falsi' in *Archiv für Kulturgeschichte*, 48 (1966), p. 37.

83. The *Oeuvres* of d'Aubigné are ed. H. Weber (Paris, 1969); the passage in question is to be found in the *Confession du Sieur de Sancy*, II.ii, p. 633.

84. *The Yale Edition of the Complete Works of Sir Thomas More*, vol. VI.i. *A Dialogue Concerning Heresies*, ed. T.M.C. Lawler *et al.* (New Haven/London, 1981), pp. 228/10–13. A reference I owe to the kindness of Dr Richard Axton.

85. Pierre Viret, the Swiss Reformer, in his *Traicté de la vraye et fausse religion* (1560), VII, cap. 35.

86. Estienne's *Apologie* is ed. P. Ristelhuber (Paris, 1879). The passage in question is to be found in vol. II, p. 321f.

87. ibid.

88. cf. St Ernoul of the *Farce du pâté*, another piece translated into English by Heywood as *A Merry Play Between John John, the Husband, Tyb, his Wife, and Sir John, the Priest*, who also appears earlier, in the *Roman de la Rose*, and in the *fabliaux*.

89. P. Marnix de Sainte-Aldegonde, *Tableau des differens de la religion* (Leiden, 1599), Bk I, Pt v, cap. 10 (modern ed., *Oeuvres*, ed. E. Quenet, Brussels, 1857, II, p. 387) cit. in Ristelhuber's edition of Estienne's *Apologie*, note on p. 322.

90. Ristelhuber, op. cit., p. 323.

91. cit. F. Tupper, 'Chaucer's Sinners and Sins' in *Journal of English and Germanic Philology*, 15 (1916), p. 66f.

92. C.M. Armstrong, *The Moralizing Prints of Cornelis Anthonisz* (Princeton, 1990), p. 41.

93. Spencer, op. cit., pp. 35–6.

94. cit. S. Brigden, *London and the Reformation* (Oxford, 1989), 94 – but she thinks Sampson refers to Our Lady – quoting Foxe, *Acts and Monuments*, IV p. 175, and Guildhall MS 9531/9, ff. 4r–4v and 25r–25v.

95. Brigden, op. cit., p. 94.

96. *Rede Me And Be Nott Wrothe* [= Arber Reprint 28] (London 1871), p. 107; a new edition by D.H. Parker is now published (Toronto, 1992).

97. A woodcut of 'her' by Hans Springinklee was published in 1513, though as St Ontcommer, she was particularly popular in the Netherlands, and there is a miniature of the bearded virgin in a manuscript illuminated by a follower of the Master of Guillebert of Metz *c.* 1430, reproduced as fig. 108 in R.S. Wieck, *The Book of Hours in Medieval Art and Life* (London, 1988), p. 123. Her cult was particularly focused on Steenbergen in Brabant and examples of pilgrim badges showing her crucifixion are known from there – see R.M. Van Heeringen *et al.*, *Heiligen uit de Modder, in Zeeland gevonden pelgrimstekens* (Zutphen, 1987), p. 97f.

98. cit. D.H. Farmer, *The Oxford Dictionary of Saints* (Oxford, 1978), s.n. Wilgefortis.

CHAPTER THREE

1. HP2 afb. 1786 and British Museum, MLA 60, 9–7, 1.

2. Lightbown, op. cit., 166 – though he mistakenly refers to these dogs (Fr. *lévrier* < Lat. *leporarius*) as *leverets* which are, of course, young hares.

3. For the innuendo, cf. *Hamlet*, III.ii.110.

4. G. de Tervarent, *Attributs et symboles dans l'art profane* (2nd edn, Geneva, 1997), *s.v. chien*.

5. Cambrai, Bibliothèque Municipale, MS 87, f. 65 (North-eastern France), Chantilly, Musée Condé, MS 62, f. 170v (Northern France), Oxford, Bodleian Laud Lat. 84, f. 51 (Franco-Flemish).

6. At Kempen, Emmerich, Venlo, Vendôme, Ciudad Rodrigo, and Windsor.

7. Reproduced in J. Simpson, *European Mythology* (London, 1987), p. 88.

8. Geisberg 1154.

9. In editions of the *Seven Wise Masters of Rome*, for example, Purfoot's 1633 edition, Sig. C3.

10. M. Stephens (ed.), *The Oxford Companion to the Literature of Wales* (Oxford, 1986), *s.v. Gelert*, from which the quotations are taken.

11. J.-C. Schmitt, *The Holy Greyhound: Guinefort, Healer of Children* (Cambridge, 1983).

12. In 'Animals in medieval art: the Bayeux Tapestry as an example' in *Journal of Medieval History*, 13 (1987), pp. 15–73, W.B. Yapp convincingly demonstrated that one of the tapestry's border birds derives from a Bestiary *Assida*, and thus – as it is agreed to be the work of late Saxon embroiderers – suggests the probable existence of an illuminated Anglo-Saxon Bestiary. M.R. James published an early list of the books in Peterborough monastic library which also included a Saxon Bestiary – see his *Lists of Manuscripts Formerly in the Peterborough Abbey Library* (= Transactions of the Bibliographical Society Supplement 5), London, 1926.

13. R. Baxter, *Bestiaries and their Users in the Middle Ages* (Stroud, 1998).

14. T.H. White, *The Book of Beasts* (reprinted Gloucester, 1984), p. 62.

15. The story derives from Solinus, as pointed out by D.J.A. Ross, 'A lost painting in Henry III's Palace at Westminster' in *Journal of the Warburg and Courtauld Institutes*, 16 (1953), p. 160 and pl. 22.

16. cit. J.E. McNelis, 'A Greyhound should have *eres in the manere of a serpent*' in L.A.J.R. Houwen (ed.), *Animals and the Symbolic in Medieval Art and Literature* (Groningen, 1997), pp. 67–76, esp. pp. 72–3. Gaston would appear to have taken the story from the *Roman des deduis* by Gace de la Buigne (1359–1370+), but G.E. Brereton and J.M. Ferrier in their edition of *Le Menagier de Paris* (Oxford, 1981), note that it is referred to briefly in the twelfth-century *Chronica Albrici Monachi Trium Fontium*.

17. For a useful essay on the cat in everyday life, see G. Blaschitz, 'Die Katze' in ed. ibid. *et al.*, *Symbole des Alltags Alltag der Symbole* (Graz, 1992), pp. 589–615, here, p. 595.

18. *Gibbe oure cat – Romaunt of the Rose* 'C' (?*c.* 1400), line 6204. L.D. Benson (ed.), *The Riverside Chaucer* (Oxford, 1988), p. 751.

19. J. Scattergood (ed.), *John Skelton. The Complete English Poems* (Harmondsworth, 1983), p. 72, line 27.

20. PRO P756; seemingly unknown to the PRO, in 1888 the gold signet ring which made the impression was in the possession of a Lady Fitzhardinge – see *Proceedings of the Society of Antiquaries* N.S. 12 (1888), p. 97, from which the present chapter ornament is reproduced.

21. To which examples should be added *Gybbe, owre gray catt* in the poem beginning, 'Leve Lystynes' (*a.* 1475), and *Gyb, the catte* in Lydgate's *Aesop* (*a.* 1450), both cit. MED *s.v. gibbe*.

22. The manuscript is Oxford, Bodleian Library, MS Ashmole 1525, f. 39. The motif of the Preaching Fox is discussed in M. Jones and C. Tracy, 'A Medieval Choirstall Desk-End at Haddon Hall: The Fox-Bishop and the Geese-Hangmen' in *Journal of the British Archaeological Association*, 144 (1991), pp. 107–15.

23. G. Dicke and K. Grubmüller, *Die Fabeln des Mittelalters und der frühen Neuzeit* (Munich, 1987), pp. 393–4, no. 341.

24. See D. Gray, 'Notes on some medieval, magical and moral cats' in H. Phillips (ed.), *Langland, the Mystics and the Medieval English Tradition: Essays in Honour of S.S. Hussey* (Woodbridge, 1990), pp. 185–202, esp. pp. 188–9.

25. N.J. Saunders, *The Cult of the Cat* (London, 1991), p. 69. Frontispiece to the Book of Maccabees, f. 350v.

26. Gray, op. cit., p. 189.

27. M. Laird, *English Misericords* (London, 1986), caption to illus. 47, 48.

28. cit. M. Bergenthal, *Elemente der Drolerie und ihre Beziehungen zur Literatur* (Berlin, 1936), p. 156. For citations of the proverb in literature see TPMA *s.v. lecken* 6, which records no examples earlier than the

fifteenth century, nor any from outside the German-speaking region.

29. London, British Library, Harley MS 1807, f. 309; reproduced in S.C. Thorne and J.H.Baker, *Readings and Moots at the Inns of Court. II Moots and Readers' Cases* (London, 1990), p. xlii.

30. With a reference to *Notes and Queries Ser. vi.* VII. 286.

31. E. Dawes, 'Pulling the Chestnuts out of the Fire' in L.A.J.R. Houwen (ed.), *Animals and the Symbolic in Medieval Art and Literature* (Groningen, 1997), pp. 155–69.

32. *De Warachtighe Fabulen* 'appears to be an adaptation of the 1547 edition of Corrozet's *Les fables d'Esope Phrygien*' – see M. Van Vaeck, 'Sixteenth- and Seventeenth-Century Dutch "Emblematic" Fable Books from the Gheeraerts Filiation' in *Emblematica*, 7 (1993), pp. 25–38, esp. pp. 29–30. Several of Gheeraerts' etchings are 'reversed imitations and elaborations' of the woodcuts in *Les fables* – Van Vaeck cites D. Geirnaert and P.J. Smith, 'Tussen fabel en embleem: *De warachtighe fabulen der dieren* (1567)' in *Literatuur*, 9 (1992), pp. 22–33, in this connexion. However, I have not yet been able to establish whether our 'catspaw' illustration is one of them, though in his introduction to the book, Gheeraerts himself remarks on the extension of the Aesopic canon contained within *De Warachtighe Fabulen*. The dedicatory poem is by the artist Lucas d'Heere who had been responsible for designing the pictures for Sambucus' *Emblemata* in which the puppy version of the 'catspaw' fable appears as an emblem.

33. The former title is Walter Gibson's in W.S. Gibson, *Hieronymus Bosch* (London, 1973), the latter, de Tolnay's in C. de Tolnay, *Hieronymus Bosch* (London, 1966).

34. M.C. Seymour (ed.), *On the Properties of Things* (Oxford, 1975), p. 1229.

35. A.V.C. Schmidt (ed.), *The Vision of Piers Plowman. A Complete Edition of the B-text* (revised edn, London, 1982), p. 50, Passus V, lines 254–5.

36. R.L. Greene (ed.), *The Early English Carols* (Oxford, 1935), no. 416.

37. For example, citations in ed. R.E. Latham *et al.*, *Dictionary of Medieval Latin from British Sources* (Oxford, 1975–), *s.v. cattus* (a), *cattinus* (b) and *catulinus*, and Ducange *s.v. catta . . . cattinae pelles.*

38. W. Danckert, *Die Unehrliche Leute* (Bern and Munich, 1963), p. 181.

39. A. Müller, '*Stigma und Stigmatisierungstechniken im Spätmittlealter*' in ed. G. Blaschitz *et al.*, *Symbole des Alltags Alltag der Symbole* (Graz, 1992), pp. 323–47, esp. p. 334, n. 65.

40. C. Grössinger, 'The Misericords in Beverley Minster: their relationship to other misericords and fifteenth-century prints' in *Journal of the British Archaeological Association* (1989), pp. 186–94, here p. 188f., remarks on the apparent fondness of the Beverley carvers for depicting animals scratching their heads.

41. Reproduced in P. Renouard, *Imprimeurs parisiens . . .* (Paris, 1898) as fig. 1033 (*a.* 1526).

42. Reproduced as pls 69 and 70, respectively, in M.B. Freeman, *The Unicorn Tapestries* (New York, 1976), p. 59.

43. ibid., p. 65.

44. C.G.E. Bunt, 'The Lion and the Unicorn' in *Antiquity*, 4 (1930), pp. 425–37, esp. p. 428.

45. P.J.A. Franssen, 'Jan van Doesborch (?–1536), printer of English texts' in *Quaerendo*, 16 (1986), pp. 259–80, cit. 266.

46. See J.W. Einhorn, *Spiritalis unicornis, das Einhorn als Bedeutungsträger in Literatur und Kunst des Mittelalters* (Munich, 1976).

47. J.M. Massing in J. Levenson (ed.), *Circa 1492 – Art in the Age of Exploration* (National Gallery of Art, Washington, 1992), p. 126.

48. cit. *OED s.v. unicorn's horn*, from *Lincoln Diocese Doc.* (1914), p. 51.

49. Lightbown, op. cit., p. 237 and pl. 82.

50. IV.xxiv.70.

51. Fr. *un ours mal léché*; Ger. *ein ungeleckter Bär*; Du. *een ongelikte beer*.

52. cit. *OED s.v. unlicked* and cf. Moryson, *Itinerary* (1618), 'Being drawne to the writing hereof out of a naturall affection to give all the members to this my unlicked whelpe' [iv. (1903) 1]; Burton, *Anatomy of Melancholy* (1621), '"Democritus to the Reader": Enforced, as a Bear doth her Whelps, to bring forth this confused lump, I had not time to lick it into form.' [(1676 edn) 7/2].

53. *Bibliothèque d'humanisme et renaissance*, 22 (1960), pp. 187–8.

54. W. Deonna, *'La boule aux rats et le monde trompeur'* in *Revue Archéologique*, 1 (1958), pp. 51–75.

55. S. Bethmont-Gallerand, *'La Boule aux rats: étude iconographique de la miséricorde'* in *The Profane Arts of the Middle Ages*, 8 (1999), pp. 201–44.

56. BL Add. MS 17297.

57. Part of this manuscript was published with characteristically illuminating commentary by Paul Vandenbroeck as *'Dits illustrés et emblèmes moraux. Contribution à l'étude de l'iconographie profane et de la pensée sociale vers 1500*, (Paris, B.N., MS fr. 24461)' in *Koninklijk Museum voor Schone Kunsten, Jaarboek* 1988, pp. 23–96.

58. A. Regond, *La peinture murale du XVIe. siècle dans la région d'Auvergne* (Clermont-Ferrand, 1983), p. 95.

59. J.-C. Aubailly, *Le Monologue le Dialogue et la Sottie* (Paris 1976).

60. J.-C. Margolin, *Histoire du Rébus* (Paris, 1986), p. 318 and fig. 139.

61. P. Renouard, *Les marques typographiques parisiennes des xve et xvie siècles*, (Paris, 1926), 97, fig. 316.

63. J.E. Salisbury, *The Beast Within: Animals in the Middle Ages* (London, 1994), p. 329.

64. ibid., p. 40.

65. The *Testamentum domini asini* is printed in P. Lehmann, *Die Parodie im Mittelalter* (2nd edn, Stuttgart, 1963), p. 171f.

66. I. Mateo Gomez, *Temas profanos en la escultura gotica espanola las sillerias de coro* (Madrid, 1970), p. 261.

67. J. Scattergood (ed.), *John Skelton. The Complete English Poems* (Harmondsworth, 1983), p. 128, line 163.

68. III.v.32ff. and 128. It is also, perhaps, worth recalling Iago's contemporary triad of lecherous beasts in *Othello* III.iii.409: 'as prime as goats, as hot as monkeys, As salt as wolves in pride. . . .'

69. A.M. Hind, *Early Italian Engraving* (London, 1938), A.I.48.

70. Reproduced as pl. 60 in H. Göbel, *Wandteppiche*, Part 3: *'Die germanischen und slawischen Länder'* (Leipzig, 1934).

71. Heidelberg, Universitätsbibliothek, Bilderhandschrift 438. M.W. Bloomfleld, *The Seven Deadly Sins* (Michigan, 1952), p. 249 – as an American, Bloomfield naturally indexed this particular representation under 'rooster' rather than 'cock'. Lorraine Baird makes the interesting suggestion that it is precisely because of the vulgar sense, that the name *rooster* has replaced *cock* in the US; similarly, it has been my observation, that British English speakers will often use the extended form 'cockerel' to avoid this same embarrassment.

72. A. Walzer, *'Tierkopfmasken in Bild und Brauch'* in *Volksleben*, 18 (1967), p. 255, and Abb. 26.

73. Reproduced as pl. 1b in C. Nordenfalk, 'The Five Senses in Late Medieval and Renaissance Art' in *Journal of the Warburg and Courtauld Institutes*, 48 (1985), pp. 1–21.

74. G. Langemeyer (ed.), *et al.*, *Bild als Waffe: Mittel und Motive der Karikatur in fünf Jahrhunderten* (Munich, 1984), Abb. 236. Others may be seen similarly perched on the shoulders of camp-followers in the baggage-trains of mercenary armies – see the print reproduced and discussed in K. Moxey, *Peasants, Warriors and Wives: Popular Imagery in the Reformation* (Chicago,

1989), fig. 4.11, 82f. Another contemporary image very much in the same tradition is Geisberg 1509, *Woman with Rooster and Maid* by Hans Weiditz, *c.* 1521. She appears to be pregnant and holds aloft in her right hand a cockerel. The accompanying verse oddly makes no mention of the cock, but opens, *Mein Burckhart mit der langen nasen* – this would appear to refer to what must surely be the companion print, Geisberg 1513, *Lansquenet and Stableboy*, whose Lanzknecht is, indeed, well-endowed nasally! (for the history of the venerable folk tradition, *size of nose = size of penis* see Chapter 12).

75. Reproduced in J.M. Fritz, *Goldschmiedekunst der Gotik in Mitteleuropa* (Munich, 1982), p. 319 and pl. 967.

76. Reproduced as no. 35, *Allegorical Genre Scene* in J.O. Hand, *The Age of Bruegel: Netherlandish Drawings in the 16th Century* (Cambridge, 1987).

77. The visual pun has been several times remarked; the earliest notice of it, to my knowledge, was in Edgar Wind's note, 'Dürer's *Männerbad*' in *Journal of the Warburg and Courtauld Institutes*, 2 (1938–9), pp. 269–71. Werner Mezger, *Narrenidee und Fastnachtsbrauch: Studien zum Forteleben des Mittelalters in der europäischen Festkultur* (Konstanz, 1991), p. 547, n. 259, notes a similar visual pun, the cockerel's head sword-pommel like an erect penis worn by a fool in a 1538 engraving by Heinrich Aldegrever. John Cherry published four such bronze cockerel taps of late medieval date in 'Medieval Finds from Lübeck' in *Lübecker Schriften zur Archäologie und Kulturgeschichte*, 3 (1980), p. 175, Abb. 54.7, 54.8, 55.1 and 56.1; see also W. Hering, 'Uber den Zapfhahn und seine Namen in Frankreich' in *Zeitschrift für Romanische Philologie*, 57 (1937), pp. 407–20.

78. The poem is popular with anthologists; for example, T. Silverstein, *Medieval English Lyrics* (London, 1971), p. 129.

79. For example, at Salisbury and London, illustrated as figs 301–2 in Spencer (1990).

80. Mezger, op. cit., p. 547, n. 264; the ritual took place in 1207 and the Pope in question was Innocent III. The Latin original is quoted by Ducange from a manuscript in the church at Cambrai.

81. From a late fifteenth-century manuscript, Paris, B.N. MS fr. 1719, f. 19, section entitled *Pour vous faire aymer aux fammes*, printed in ed. M.M. Schwob, *La Parnasse Satirique: Anthologie des Pièces Libres* (Paris, 1905), p. 63. As late as 1658, the *Rare Verities* tells the story of a man who, usually less than satisfying to his wife, is similarly fed cock's testicles and goes on a sexual rampage – cit. R. Thompson, *Unfit for Modest Ears: A Study of Pornographic, Obscene and Bawdy Works Written or Published in England in the Second Half of the Seventeenth Century* (London, 1979), p. 170.

82. A common enough Elizabethan double entendre; also, see R.W. Dent, *Proverbial Language in English Drama Exclusive of Shakespeare, 1495–1616* (Berkeley/Los Angeles/London, 1984), F 40.11 'To have the falling sickness' (from *c.* 1520), and S 746.11 'To have a spice of the falling evil' (from 1542).

83. Intercourse is described at some length as a ferret's hunting for a rabbit in its burrow in a French *fabliau* ('*connins que li fuirons chace . . .*'); it is also a commonplace erotic metaphor in early sixteenth-century French chanson verse, for example '*Je prins ung petit congnin./Ma dame die: "Il est mien!"; J'ay ung congnin,/Qui est bordé de soye;/Mais mon congnin/Il est frisque et mignon/Pour ces gallans/Qui ont de la monnoye?; "Amye, amye,/Y a il rien en ce buisson?"/La dame tint basse raison/Et luy a dit: "Sauf vostre honneur,/Il gist ung congnin de saison."*' See B. Jeffery, *Chanson Verse of the Early Renaissance*, vol. 2 (London, 1971), pp. 80, 109, 225.

84. cit. *OED s.v. cony*, 5a.

85. cit. *OED s.v. mouse*, 3a.

86. J. Scattergood (ed.), op. cit., p. 220, lines 221ff. Skelton's form is entered at *bonny* in the *Dictionary*. Curiously, the *OED*'s earliest citation of the word as a pet name for a rabbit is from 1690, and Eric Partridge, who made something of a special study of erotic vocabulary, records the sense 'female pudend' only from 1719.

87. A further such list of endearments occurs in the play *Timon* (1603): 'My sparrow, my hony, my duck, my cony', II.i.24. (this is not the play by Shakespeare) – cit. *OED, s.v. honey*, 5.

88. By L.F. Sandler in 'A Bawdy Betrothal in the Ormesby Psalter' in ed. W. Clark *et al.*, *A Tribute to Lotte Brand Philip* (New York, 1985), p. 159, citing R.J. Pearcy, 'Modes of Signification and the Humor of Obscene Diction in the Fabliaux' in T.D. Cooke and B.L. Honeycutt (eds), *The Humor of the Fabliaux: A Collection of Critical Essays* (Columbia, 1974), p. 176, n. 9.

89. *Romeo and Juliet*, IV.iv.II, and *Hamlet*, III.iv.184f., but note in the latter example, that the endearment is peculiarly appropriate to the Queen whose name is Gertrude, earlier regarded as a protectress against mice and rats as discussed in Chapter 2!

90. A. de Montaiglon and G. Raynaud, *Recueil général et complet des fabliaux* (Paris, 1872–90), vol. 4.

91. Reproduced as Abb. 42 and discussed on p. 55f. of C. Andersson, *Dirnen, Kriegern, Narren: Ausgewählte Zeichnungen von Urs Graf* (Basel, 1978).

92. J. Corominas (ed.) (Madrid, 1967), stanza 120c.

93. *The Riverside Chaucer*, 3rd edn, L.D. Benson (Oxford, 1988), p. 26 (lines 191f.).

94. *Faerie Queene*, 1.vi.22.

95. Reproduced as pl. 61 in D.W. Robertson, *A Preface to Chaucer* (Princeton, 1962), 264n, and 113. See also J.V. Fleming's study, *The Roman de La Rose* (Princeton, 1969), p. 186.

96. The manuscript is Oxford, Bodleian Library, MS Douce 6, f. 160v, reproduced as fig. 404 in Randall.

97. The manuscript is Oxford, Merton College, MS 0.1.3, f. 65v, reproduced in ibid., as fig. 405.

98. Reproduced as fig. 71 in P. Webb, *The Erotic Arts* (London, 1975).

99. The pieces are illustrated as HP1 afb. 667 and HP2 afb. 1776, respectively. In L. Hansmann and L. Kriss-Rettenbeck, *Amulett und Talisman: Erscheinungsform und Geschichte* (Munich, 1977), the authors state succinctly that *'Die Muschel wurde von prähistorischer Zeit bis in die Gegenwart immer wieder als Symbol der weiblichen Scham gewertet und getragen.'* Aigremont (pseud.), 'Muschel und Schnecke als Symbole der Vulva ehemals und jetzt' in *Anthropophyteia*, 6 (1909), pp. 35–50, cites no medieval examples of such symbolism.

100. Walter Gibson in *Hieronymus Bosch* (London, 1973), p. 99: 'well after 1500'. Bosch died in 1516. The detail under discussion is also well reproduced in Gibson as fig. 65. In the *Woordenboek der Nederlandsche Taal, s.v. mossel* (1), sense B2 is defined as 'Vrouwelijk schaamdeel', but the sole citation is from a work of the second half of the seventeenth century.

101. Ultimately from Latin *concha*, via an assumed *cocchilla*.

102. According to I. Nelson in *La sottie sans souci* (Paris, 1977).

103. See J. Koopmans (ed.), *Recueil de Sermons Joyeux* (Geneva, 1988), p. 582; text on pp. 440–1, lines 249–52.

104. At least, this would seem to be the implication of the inclusion of this sense of *coquille* in the Larousse *Dictionnaire de l'ancien français jusqu'au milieu du XIVe siècle*, ed. A.-J. Greimas. Huguet's dictionary of sixteenth-century French includes the following citation in this sense from Philippe d'Alcripe's *La Nouvelle Fabrique* (p. 74): '*La chambrière (a qui la coquille*

fretilloit) print le couvrechef de sa teste et avec iceluy empoigna l'instrument dudit taureau.'

105. J. Buchanan-Brown (ed.), *John Aubrey: Three Prose Works* (Fontwell, 1972), p. 254.

106. G.F. Northall, *English Folk-Rhymes* (London, 1892), pp. 153–6.

107. E. Partridge, *A Dictionary of Historical Slang* (abridged edn, Harmondsworth, 1972).

108. Burchard of Worms' penitential, known as the *Corrector*, has long been mined by folklorists and historians of religion as a source for late medieval practices of pre-Christian origin; see, for example, C. Vogel, *'Pratiques superstitieuses au début du XIe siècle d'après le Corrector sive medicus de Burchard, évêque de Worms (965–1025)'* in *Mélanges de Littérature du Moyen Age au XXe siècle offerts à Jeanne Lods*, vol. 1 (Paris, 1978), 751ff. The 'cockle-bread' passage appears under the subheading *'Philtres et sortilèges d'amour'* on p. 755. See also D. Harmening, *Superstitio* (Berlin 1979), esp. pp. 230f.; J.T. McNeill, 'Folk Paganism in the Penitentials' in *The Journal of Religion*, 13 (1933), pp. 450–66; the first chapter of J.A. MacCulloch's *Medieval Faith and Fable* (London, 1932), entitled 'Survivals of paganism', and M. Blocker, 'Frauenzauber-Zauberfrauen' in *Zeitschrift für schweizerische Kirchengeschichte*, 76 (1982), pp. 1–39, esp. 23f.

109. G.L. Kittredge, *Witchcraft in Old and New England* (New York, 1929), p. 104, includes references to most earlier discussions. The Arundel Penitential canon 81 is printed in H.J. Schmitz, *Die Bussbücher und die Bussdichten der Kirche* (Graz, 1958), 1.459.

110. N. Cox, *The Gentleman's Recreation* (1677), *Hunting; Terms of the Tail. Of a Fox, the Brush or Drag; and the Tip at the end is called the Chape*, and cf. Phillips, *Dictionary* (1706, ed. Kersey), *Holy-Water Sprinkle, a Term us'd by Hunters for the Tail of a Fox.*

111. Text printed in W.H. Stevenson (ed.), *Early Scholastic Colloquies* (Oxford, 1929), p. 52, line 8. The paragraph in question contains a most impressive list of mostly scatological insults!

112. *Quand il recontroit quelc'un d'entre eulx par la rue, jamais ne failloit de leur faire quelque mal: maintenant leurs mettant un estronc dedans leur chaperons au bourlet, maintenant leur attachant de petites quehues de regnard ou des aureilles de lievres par derriere, ou quelque aultre mal (Pantagruel, cap. XVI).*

113. C. Andersson, *'Symbolik und Gebärdensprache bei Niklaus Manuel und Urs Graf'* in *Zeitschrift für schweizerische Archäologie und Kunstgeschichte*, 37 (1980), esp. n. 16.

114. Reproduced in E. Fuchs, *Illustrierte Sittengeschichte: Ergänzungs-band Renaissance* (Munich, 1910), pp. 112–13, Abb. 106–7 – not included in Andersson's list. However, there is something of a question mark over this class of historical artefact, as may well be imagined: Timothy Wilson states that 'It is probable that the great majority of examples now existing were made in the eighteenth and nineteenth centuries as curiosities for the prurient, or as jokes for the tasteless.' (Cat. 49 in M. Jones (ed.), *Fake? The Art of Deception* (London, 1990), p. 70). The motif is found on a single sheet of uncertain date from which it was copied onto two sixteenth-/seventeenth-century (gun-)powder-flasks, see W. Harms, *Deutsche illustrierte Flugblätter des 16. und 17. Jahrhunderts* (Tübingen, 1985), I, 103, and Fuchs, op. cit., Abb. 194 and 200. I add a version enamelled onto a Bohemian glass dated 1572 – A von Saldern, *German Enamelled Glassware* (New York, 1965), fig. 155., and P. Vandenbroeck notes another example in a late sixteenth-century *Stammbuch – Jheronimus Bosch: tussen volksleven en stadscultuur* (Berchem, 1987), p. 489.

115. The vulva as 'wound' is a fairly common folklore motif, cf. Tale Type 1095, 'Contest in Scratching Each Other with the Nails': man's wife shows ogre with whom he is to have scratching contest the deep wounds he

has scratched on her body – the ogre departs in terror (see A. Aarne, *The Types of the Folktale: A Classification and Bibliography*, trans. and enlarged by S. Thompson (New York, 1928), p. 153).

116. See *LSR s.v. Fuchsschwanz; einen mit einem Fuchsschwanz schlagen*, which is glossed as to punish someone too mildly.

117. Illustrated as exhibit 73 on p. 65 of the exhibition catalogue, ed. J. Hayward and T. Husband, *The Secular Spirit* (New York, 1975). This dish is now ascribed to Germany by H.P. Lockner in *Messing: Ein Handbuch über Messinggerät des 15. Jahrhunderts* (Munich, 1982).

118. F.C. Tubach, *Index Exemplorum* (Helsinki, 1969), no. 2183.

119. A reference I owe to H. Birkhan, 'Zum Erfolg des Narrenschiffes Sebastian Brant und die Tradition' in eds D. Buschinger and A. Crepin, *La Représentation de l'Antiquité au Moyen Age* (Vienna, 1982), p. 348.

120. S.M. Newton, *Fashion in the Age of the Black Prince* (Woodbridge, 1980), p. 9.

121. I cite the Deschamps passage from J.W. Hassell, *Middle French Proverbs, Sentences and Proverbial Phrases* (Toronto, 1982), sole cit. at Q 7, from *Oeuvres*, IX.119.

122. Reproduced in G. Langemeyer *et al.* (eds), *Bild als Waffe: Mittel und Motive der Karikatur in fünf Jahrhunderten* (Munich, 1984). The squirrel sitting on the shoulder of the Prince of Hearts in Floetner's playing card pack of *c.* 1535 (see M. Geisberg, *The German Single-Leaf Woodcut in the First Half of the Sixteenth Century* (New York, 1974–5)) is perhaps symbolic of his desire, while the creatures seated on the shoulders of the *Mercenary's Whore* are perhaps intended to symbolise both what she desires and what she has to offer in return.

123. J. Alexander and P. Binski (eds), *Age of Chivalry* (London, 1987), p. 395, cat. 450.

124. Reproduced in ibid., p. 360, cat. 367.

125. D.W. Robertson, *A Preface to Chaucer* (Princeton, 1962), p. 191, and fig. 59.

126. L.F. Sandler in 'A Bawdy Betrothal in the Ormesby Psalter' in ed. W. Clark *et al.*, *A Tribute to Lotte Brand Philip* (New York, 1985).

127. Reproduced in Alexander and Binski, op. cit., p. 46, as fig. 17 in Veronica Sekules' essay, 'Women and Art in England in the Thirteenth and Fourteenth Centuries'.

128. See C. Oman, *British Rings 800–1914* (London, 1974), III and pl. 57D. In A. Ward (ed.) *et al.*, *The Ring from Antiquity to the Twentieth Century* (London, 1981), p. 84, in his discussion of this ring, John Cherry notes that 'the verse with its play on grammar recalls fifteenth-century French poetry, particularly that of Charles, Duke of Orleans (1391–1465)'. For a general discussion of this topos, see the section in P. Lehmann, *Die Parodie im Mittelalter*, 2nd edn (Stuttgart, 1963), pp. 107ff. and text no. 13, entitled by Lehmann *'Erotischer Grammatikbetrieb'*; for the topos in troubadour verse, see P. Bec, *Burlesque et obscénité chez les troubadours: pour une approche du contretexte médiéval* (Paris, 1984), pp. 125–30.

129. R.W. Dent, *Proverbial Language in English Drama Exclusive of Shakespeare, 1495–1616* (Berkeley/Los Angeles/London, 1984), N 361.

130. I owe the references to sexual metaphors in the *fabliaux* to an informative chapter entitled 'Sexuality and Obscenity' in C. Muscatine, *The Old French Fabliaux* (New Haven, 1986), pp. 105ff., n. 8.

131. Names from J. Jönsjö, *Studies on Middle English Nicknames, I: Compounds* (Lund, 1979). The first element of *Casnot*, a hybrid name, is OF *casser*, 'crush'.

132. See G.J. Turner, *Selected Pleas of the Forest* (London, 1901).

133. Paris, B.N., MS fr. 616, f. 115v. (1405x1410).

134. British Library, Add. MS 42130.

135. Fundamental to any study of owl iconography is P. Vandenbroeck, 'Bubo significans. I. Die Eule als Sinnbild der Schlechtigkeit und Torheit, vor allem in der niederländischen und deutschen Bilddarstellung und bei Jheronimus Bosch' in *Jaarboek Koninklijk Museum voor Schone Kunsten Antwerpen* (1985), pp. 19–136.

136. B. Yapp, *Birds in Medieval Manuscripts* (London, 1981), p. 37.

137. *LSR s.v. Eule.*

138. See C.J.P. Cave, *Roof Bosses in Medieval Churches* (Cambridge, 1948), p. 73 and pl. 206.

139. H.J. Raupp, *Bauernsatiren* (Niederzier, 1986), p. 85.

CHAPTER FOUR

1. Randall (1966).

2. For example, M. Camille, *Image on the Edge* (London, 1992), and K. Kröll and H. Steger (eds), *Mein Ganzer Körper ist Gesicht* (Freiburg, 1994).

3. For example, HP1 afb. 628 and 924.

4. John Block Friedman, *The Monstrous Races in Medieval Art and Thought* (Cambridge, Mass., 1981).

5. BL Add. MS 28681, f. 9.

6. Westminster Abbey, MS22 (*c.* 1275–1300).

7. BL Maps 184 g.2.

8. iii.xi.20.

9. A.M. Hind, *Early Italian Engraving*, V (1948), pl. 851.

10. See L. Link, *The Devil: a Mask without a Face* (London, 1995).

11. Ed. W.W. Skeat, *The Wars of Alexander* [= EETS ES 47] (London, 1886), lines 4742ff., esp. 4750; Skeat's note is on p. 313. For the euphemism 'extra limb', see MED *s.v. odd*.

12. A. Rapp Buri and M. Stucky-Schürer, *Zahm und wild, Basler und Straßburger Bildteppiche des 15. Jahrhunderts* (Mainz, 1990), cat. no. 31, 'Tugendreiche Dame zähmt Wildmann'.

13. I take *Bild* here to be a short form of *Frauenbild*.

14. See M.O. Renger, 'The Wiesbaden Drawings' in *Master Drawings*' 25 (1987), figs 14 and 15.

15. H.E. Allen and S.B. Meech (eds), *The Book of Margery Kempe* [EETS 212] (London, 1940), II.6. p. 236, line 30.

16. L. Randall, 'A Medieval Slander' in *Art Bulletin*, 42 (1960), pp. 25–40, esp. pp. 33–5. See also Sandra Billington's theories in a paper entitled 'Routs and Reyes' in *Folklore*, 89 (1978), esp. p. 190ff. The subject of horse mutilation, which underlies the saintly involvement in the Kentish Longtail story, I discuss in 'Saints and other horse-mutilators', ed., S. Hartmann, Fauna and Flora in the Middle Ages (Frankfurt, forthcoming).

17. See T. Borenius in *Archaeologia*, 79 (1929), p. 41 and fig. 2 (by Meister Francke, 1434).

18. See D. Brewer, 'Englishmen with Tails: Layamon, "Muggles" and a Transhistorical Ethnic Joke in English' in *The Medieval Heritage* (Ikegami Festschrift) (Tokyo, 1997), pp. 3–15.

19. New Haven, Yale University Library, *Lancelot del Lac*, MS 229 f. 363r.

20. Information from the entry in the *DNB* – but see further *English Historical Review*, 77 (1962), p. 80 and nn.

21. A. Harding (ed.), *Medieval Legal Records Edited in Memory of C.A.F. Meekins* (London, 1978), p. 158. With regard to this latter motif, I note in passing, that 300 years later at King's Sutton in Northamptonshire, a husband and wife were arraigned before the ecclesiastical court for insulting their minister by inviting him to 'kisse his horse under the taile'. This and further examples are listed in the Appendix, 'Kiss my arse', to my 'Marcolf the Trickster in Late Medieval Art and Literature, or, The Mystery of the Bum in the Oven' in ed. G. Bennett, *Spoken in Jest* (Sheffield, 1991), pp. 139–74.

22. R.E. Latham (ed.) *et al.*, *Dictionary of Medieval Latin from British Sources* (Oxford, 1975–), *s.v. curtare*.

23. Reproduced as pl. 108 in A.M. Hind, *Early Italian Engraving* (London, 1938), and text volume, p. 73.

24. See P. Falk, *'Le couvre-chef comme symbole du mari trompé: Étude sur trois mots galloromans (galea, cuppa, cucutium)'* in *Studia Neophilologica*, 33 (1961), pp. 39–67, esp. p. 42. On 65f. he cites the most interesting passage from the Italian Boncompagno writing *c.* 1250 in which he discusses the various horn and horned animal insults. Ducange, *s.v. cucullus*, attests the sense 'cuckold' only from 1350. P. Guiraud's paragraphs *s.v. cocu*, including the one devoted to the *cornes du cornard*, in his *Dictionnaire des Etymologies Obscures* (Paris, 1982), seem to me to be not entirely convincing.

25. The manuscript is Paris, B.N. MS lat. 3898, f. 297, and was first reproduced as pl. ii in A. Melnikas, *A Corpus of Miniatures . . . in the Decretals of Gratian* (Rome, 1975).

26. For this *dextrarum iunctio*, see A. Grzybkowski in *Zeitschrift für Kunstgeschichte*, 47 (1984); see further L.F. Sandler, 'The Handclasp in the Arnolfini Wedding: A Manuscript Precedent' in *Art Bulletin*, 66 (1984), and ibid. in *Art Bulletin*, 68 (1986).

27. cit. *OED s.v. wisp* 2b, with further citations contemporary with the Wiltshire device.

28. cf. the English M Lat. verb *asino* 'to be foolish' (*c.* 1270), and the contemporary marginal insult (written in mirror-writing!) which one cleric directs at another in the *bas-de-page* of f. 37 of the *Rutland Psalter – Tu es asinus* (you are an ass).

29. Oxford, Exeter College, MS 47. Mezger op. cit., p. 241, was able to cite an unequivocal reference to such a fool's hood from a mid-thirteenth-century German poem by Meister Stolle.

30. I base this on C. Löhmer, *Die Welt der Kinder im fünfzehnten Jahrhundert* (Weinheim, 1989), pp. 211–12.

31. Seventeenth-century law books have various corrupt forms of the word.

32. cap. vi, *Lupinum enim gerit caput a die utlagationis sue, quod ab Anglis uulfesheued nominatur.*

33. M. Jones, '*The Lambe Speaketh . . .* an addendum' in *Journal of the Warburg and Courtauld Institutes*, 63 (2000), pp. 287–94.

34. Niedersächsische Landesbibliothek, MS XI, 669, f. 12v.

CHAPTER FIVE

1. R.B. McKerrow and F.S. Ferguson (eds), *Title-page Borders Used in England and Scotland 1485–1640* (London, 1932), figs 77 and 79.

2. But cf. TPMA *s.v. Fliege*.

3. The woodcut illustrating a late fifteenth-century parodic blood-letting calendar by Hans Folz where the flies swarm around the doctor's head; the title-pages of both Murner's fool-books of 1512; and the parodic coat-of-arms of the town of Esellingen (North Netherlands, 1518) – all reproduced and discussed in P. Vandenbroeck, 'Zur Herkunft und Verwurzelung der *Grillen*' in *De zeventiende eeuw*, 3 (1987), pp. 52–84, Abb. 9, 10, 4 and 11 respectively.

4. G. Calman, 'The Picture of Nobody' in *Journal of the Warburg and Courtauld Institutes*, 23 (1960), pp. 66–104, here, p. 82.

5. Anne Matthews 'The Use of Prints in the Hours of Charles d'Angoulême' in *Print Quarterly*, 3 (1986), pp. 4–18, esp. pp. 8–9, 13–15.

6. There is still a considerable semantic field in English awaiting investigation here; it comprises such words as *cricket*, cf. Palsgrave (1530), 'Cricket a worme, cricquet, gresillon' and the anonymous *Image of Hipocrisy* (1533) (ed. Dyce p. 429) which refers to the Pope as 'kinge of crekettes', and *crotchet*, cf. Cotgrave (1611), 'Crochue, a Quauer in Musicke; whence Il a des

crochues en teste (we say) his head is full of crochets.'

7. The beehive + bees are to be found in the Vorau MS 130, the basket of bees in BL Add. MS 15693 (South Germany, 1438), and the nest of bees in Pierpont Morgan Library MS 782 (Augsburg, 1460); it is this last which provided the model for the woodcuts in Baemler's Augsburg 1474 edition of the *Etymachia*.

8. Later in the Middle Ages this phrase was understood to refer prophetically to the Jews in relation to Christ.

9. M. Evans, 'An illustrated fragment of Peraldus's *Summa* of Vice: Harl. MS 3244' in *Journal of the Warburg and Courtauld Institutes*, 45 (1982), p. 27.

10. I say 'ominous', and yet this superstition about the unluckiness of the number 13 is not attested before the eighteenth century according to the indispensable *A Dictionary of Superstitions*, ed. I. Opie and M. Tatem (Oxford, 1989), *s.v. Thirteen*.

11. Interestingly not found as the name for the playing card before the late nineteenth century according to the *OED*.

12. Calman, op. cit., pp. 70–1.

13. cit. *OED s.v. hoop*.

14. See R.L.H. Lops, 'La Huppe: histoire, littérature et légende d'un oiseau' in ed. Q.I.M. Mok *et al.*, *Mélanges de linguistique, de littérature et de philologie médiévale offerts à J.R. Smeets* (Leiden, 1982).

15. F. Merke in *Geschichte und Ikonographie des endemischen Kropfes und Kretinismus* (Bern, 1971).

16. BL MS Add. 34294, f. 208v. He has also been given a 'burst shoe', also a feature of Marcolf iconography.

17. Shakespeare, *King Henry V*, III.vi.57 and 59.

18. R. Mellinkoff, *Outcasts: Signs of Otherness in Northern European Art of the Late Middle Ages* (Berkeley, 1993).

19. W.L. Hildburgh, 'Images of the human hand as amulets in Spain' in *Journal of the Warburg and Courtauld Institutes*, 18 (1955), pp. 67–89.

20. L. Maeterlinck, *Le genre satirique dans la peinture flamande* (2nd edn, Brussels, 1907), p. 36. The manuscript is Ghent MS 22.

21. Mellinkoff, op. cit., p. 203, pls X.23 and I.29, respectively.

22. For example, BL Add MS 50000, f. 11v, reproduced as fig. 250 in N.J. Morgan, *Early Gothic Manuscripts II 1250–1285* (London, 1987).

23. BL Royal MS 10. E. IV, f. 64r.

24. E. Jost, *Bauernfeindlichkeit: Die Historien des Ritters Neithart Fuchs* (Göppingen, 1976), p. 333 and Abb. 8; Jost dates the painting to the first third of the century.

25. A carved stone cross-slab at Drumhallagh in Donegal includes two squatting figures in the upper angles of the cross who appear to me to be thumbing their noses at each other; if so, this would be by far the earliest (?ninth-century) instance of this motif known; positionally the *Oscott Psalter* example in which the two men's heads flank the top of the cross being carried by Christ seems to me to afford a reasonable parallel – see P. Harbison, *BAR 152* (1986), p. 63 for a different interpretation.

26. See the *OED s.vv. prut* and *tprot*.

27. Perhaps a spelling of *wring* here, cf. the *OED*'s earliest, fifteenth-century sense from the Towneley plays, *Bot he that forsake I shall gyf hym a wryng that his nek shall crak*.

28. Mocking verse – an English *Scheltbrief* – sent to Griffith ap David ap Griffith by Lord Grey de Ruthyn in 1400, for which see F.C. Hingeston, 'Letters', Rolls Series (1860), p. xxiii.

29. For a useful succinct discussion of the practice, see David Freedberg, *The Power of Images* (Chicago, 1989), pp. 246–57.

30. Some two hundred years later one of the Royalists' Civil War banners captured at Naseby in 1642 bore the motto *Merces coniuratoris* (The conspirator's reward) and was described by *The Kingdomes Weekly*

Intelligencer when carried with fifty-four other captured colours into London in a triumphant Parliamentarian procession on 21 June 1645, as depicting 'a Souldier in Armour cap-a-pee reversed, his head downwards' – A.R. Young, *Emblematic Flag Devices of the English Civil Wars 1642–1660* (Toronto, 1995), no. 0210.0.

31. That is, openings in the parapet of a fortification – *OED*, *loop* sb.2.

32. ed. F.W.D. Brie, *The Brut*, II [= EETS OS 136] (London, 1908), p. 572.

33. Quoted in Catherine Reynolds, '*Les Angloys, de la droicte nature, veullent touzjours guerreer.* Evidence for Painting in Paris and Normandy, *c.* 1420–1450' in C. Allmand (ed.), *Power, Culture and Religion in France c. 1350–c. 1550* (Woodbridge, 1989), pp. 37–55, esp. pp. 46–8. Of course, the French also used such paintings against fellow Frenchmen: in 1477 Gabriel le Fevre of Evreux was commissioned to paint five portraits of Jean, Prince of Orange *pendu la teste en bas et les pies en halt* (hanging with his head downwards and his feet uppermost) – Freedberg, op. cit., p. 482, n. 32.

34. Otto Hupp, *Scheltbriefe und Schandbilder: ein Rechtsbehelf aus dem 15 und 16 Jahrhundert* (Munich and Regensburg, 1930).

35. Freedberg, op. cit., p. 255.

36. The example in the Visconti-Sforza pack of *c.* 1450 is particularly fine, see M. Dummett, *The Visconti-Sforza Tarot Cards* (New York, 1986), p. 124.

37. W. Brückner, *Bildnis und Brauch: Studien zur Bildfunktion der Effigies* (Berlin, 1966).

38. G. Ortalli, *Pingatur in palatio: La pittura infamante nei secoli XIII–XVI* (Rome, 1979), pp. 87–8.

39. Freedberg, op. cit., pp. 256–7.

40. According to nineteenth-century historians he was depicted hanging upside down from a chain and surrounded by devils – S.Y. Edgerton, *Pictures and Punishment: Art and Criminal Prosecution during the Florentine Renaissance* (Ithaca, 1985), pp. 88–9.

41. I am most grateful to Priscilla Bawcutt for referring me to G. Neilson, 'The Marcher Laws' in *Miscellany*, 1 (Stair Society no. 26), pp. 64–6, section 18, *Baughling*, from which article several of the following references are taken.

42. ed. Ellis (1809), p. 559.

43. *Miscellany One*, [Stair Society, vol. 26], (Edinburgh, 1971), pp. 64–6.

44. (1817 edn, p. 127) the *OED*'s next two citations are also valuable, from Spenser's *Faerie Queene* and a play by Beaumont and Fletcher.

45. Neilson, op. cit., p. 65, citing J. Raine, *North Durham* x, and Armstrong, *Liddesdale*, I, pp. 59–60.

46. Edgerton, op. cit., p. 65, n. 22, and p. 35, fig. 6; in the Prado.

47. MED cites *horned* in the sense 'mitred' from the time of Lydgate (*?a.* 1430), and the DMLBS cites *cornutus* in this sense from the time of Henry II. R. Axton in *European Drama of the Middle Ages* (London, 1974) notes that in Bodel's *Le jeu de Saint Nicolas* (*c.* 1200), the icon of the mitred bishop Nicholas is facetiously referred to as *un mahommet cornu* and *un cornu menestrel*. There is much on this topic in R. Mellinkoff, *The Horned Moses in Medieval Art and Thought* (Berkeley and Los Angeles, 1970), pp. 94ff., 'The Bishop's Mitre', for example, 'from the early part of the twelfth century, the horns of the mitre were very well understood as horns – and were not referred to as points or humps or something else' (p. 100).

48. Copenhagen, Det Kongelige Bibliotek, MS 3384.80f. 301v.

49. Reproduced as the jacket to A. McCall, *The Medieval Underworld* (London, 1979); J.C. Aubailly, *Le Monologue, le Dialogue et la Sottie* (Paris, 1976), p. 70, cites from the *Sermon d'un Cartier de Mouton* (*c.* 1545) the heavily ironic prayer that 'honest' millers '*puissent aller tous mitrés/en paradis à reculons*

(should all go mitred to paradise in reverse, that is, to Hell)'.

50. The image is reproduced in G. Langemeyer *et al.*, *Bild als Waffe: Mittel und Motive der Karikatur in fünf Jahrhunderten* (Munich, 1984), p. 204, fig. 126; the details are taken from Mellinkoff, op. cit., p. 155, and from B.D.H. Miller, 'Dame Sirith: Three Notes: II' in *Notes and Queries*, 206 (1961), p. 414.

51. Miller, op. cit., p. 413.

52. N.Z. Davis, *Society and Culture in Early Modern France* (London, 1975), p. 195. For Italian depictions, see Edgerton, op. cit, esp. p. 65 and fig. 6, and Ortali, op. cit.

53. T. P. Vukinovic, 'Witchcraft in the Central Balkans: I: Characteristics of Witches', in *Folklore*, 100 (1989), p. 10.

54. The resemblance of this instrument to the male genitalia is often exploited in medieval art, for example, the miniature reproduced by Randall as fig. 56. See J. Gagne, *'L'Erotisme dans la Musique Médiévale'* in B. Roy (ed.), *L'Erotisme au Moyen Age* (Montreal and Paris, 1977). For comments on Chaucer's use of the symbolism, see E.A. Block, 'Chaucer's Millers and their Bagpipes' in *Speculum*, 29 (1954), pp. 239–43; K.L. Scott, 'Sow-and-Bagpipe Imagery in the Miller's Portrait' in *Review of English Studies*, 18 (1967), pp. 287–90; R. Boenig, 'The Miller's Bagpipe: A Note on *The Canterbury Tales* A 565–566' in *English Language Notes*, 21 (1983), pp. 1–6, and S. Stanbury Smith, *'Game in myn Hood*: The Tradition of a Comic Proverb' in *Studies in Iconography*, 9 (1984), pp. 1–12. See further, Chapter 12 below, 'The Erotic Bagpipe'.

55. Walter S. Gibson, *Bruegel* (London, 1977), p. 46, notes that when Cock printed engravings based on this drawing the mitre was 'prudently altered to a less distinctive shape, in order to avoid ecclesiastical censure'.

56. P. Hair, *Before the Bawdy Court* (London, 1972), p. 122.

57. Sir John Maclean (ed.), *The Berkeley Manuscripts* (Gloucester, 1883), 2, p. 105.

58. The practice is also referred to in Luther's work.

59. cit. A. Gransden, *Historical Writing in England ii c. 1307 to the Early Sixteenth Century* (London, 1982), p. 382. On p. 278 Gransden further notes that John Hardyng in his *Chronicle* compared Richard's right to the English crown to that of Jesus to be king of the Jews.

60. H.T. Riley (ed.), *Registrum Abbatiae Johannis Whethamstede Abbatis Monasterii Sancti Albani* (Rolls Series) (London, 1872–3), p. 382.

61. R. Mellinkoff, 'Riding Backwards: Theme of Humiliation and Symbol of Evil' in *Viator*, 4 (1973), pp. 153–76, here, p. 159 and n. 27.

62. The subject of an ape holding up a urine flask is very common in manuscript marginalia and in misericords where it is assumed to be satirical of the medieval physician; see Randall, Iconographical Index, *s.v.* 'Ape as Physician', and G.L. Remnant, *A Catalogue of Misericords in Great Britain* (Oxford, 1969), pp. 173–5 and 213 'Animal Satire: Ape with Urine Flask'.

63. The quotation is taken from H.T. Riley (ed.), *Thomas Walsingham Historia Anglicana* [= Rolls Series 28] (London, 1864), 2, p. 63. For the proverb, see Whiting, W 216, and *Oxford Dictionary of English Proverbs* for an earlier French (?AN) example, *s.v. Whetstone*. A 'lying song' was entered into his commonplace-book by Richard Hill at some point in the first half of the sixteenth century with the refrain *I will haue the whetston and I may*. The first verse reads:
I sawe a doge sethyng sowse   [making stew]
And an ape thechying an howse   [thatching]
And a podyng etyng a mowse;   [sausage]
I will haue the whetston and I may.   [if I can]
Such lists of *adynata* relate to the subject of Chapter 8.

64. G.R. Owst, *Preaching in Medieval England c. 1350–1450* (Cambridge, 1926), p. 109;

unfortunately Owst gives no reference for this interesting example, though it presumably falls within the date-range of his book. It would be of interest to discover the original of the word(s) (in whichever language) that he renders 'tall paper hat'.

65. 1364 (AN) Bk G f. cxxxviii.

66. *s.v. Juramentum*; cit. G.R. Owst *Literature and Pulpit in Medieval England* (Cambridge, 1933), p. 421.

67. For further real-life examples, see Ducange, *s.v. scala* 1.

68. BL Royal MS 10. E. IV, f. 94r.

69. A.P. Fox, *Aspects of Oral Culture and its Development in Early Modern England*, unpublished Ph.D thesis, Cambridge, 1992, pp. 222f.

70. H.T. Riley, *Memorials of London and London Life in the XIIIth, XIVth, and XVth Centuries* (London, 1868), p. 473, from Letter Book H, f. clv.

71. BL Add. MS 47682, f. 42v.

72. An English translation of the Latin original is published in Riley, op. cit., p. 319, citing London Letter Book G, f. cxxxvii.

73. cit. MED *s.v. mortar* n (1). 3. In 1468 to *bere the morter* is described as 'the olde custom of this toun'.

74. See article, *anhängen*, in LSR; also, E. von Künssberg, *Über die Strafe des Steintragens* (Breslau, 1907).

75. For further examples and medieval references, see J. Vandereuse, 'Les pierres de justice' in *Folklore Brabançon*, 7 (1927–8), pp. 105–14.

76. See J.W. Spargo, *Juridical Folklore in England Illustrated by the Cucking-Stool* (Durham, NC, 1944); the Tudor citation is given by Keith Thomas, *Religion and the Decline of Magic* (London, 1971), p. 528 (without source). For the continued – and indeed increased – use of these devices at a later period, see David Underdown, 'The Taming of the Scold: The Enforcement of Patriarchal Authority in Early Modern England' in A. Fletcher and J. Stevenson (eds), *Order and Disorder in Early Modern England* (Cambridge, 1985), Chapter 4.

77. BL Add. 62925 (*c.* 1260); the image on f. 86r is reproduced in Randall as fig. 731. The most recent discussion of this important psalter – the earliest English manuscript to feature marginal *drôleries* – is N.J. Morgan, 'The artists of the Rutland Psalter' in *British Library Journal*, 13 (1987), pp. 159–85.

78. M.F. White, *Fifteenth Century Misericords in the Collegiate Church of Holy Trinity, Stratford-upon-Avon* (Stratford, 1974), pl. 22, and J.L. Druce in *Journal of the British Archaeological Association*, 36 (1931), p. 258. In *The World Upside Down. English Misericords* (London, 1997), Christa Grössinger interprets these carvings as carnivalesque expressions and sees the head on the right as biting on a real sausage. She also regards the woman wearing the horned headdress on a Ludlow misericord as bridled, a fact explicitly denied in Owst (1933), op. cit., pp. 402–3.

79. M.Y. Offord (ed.), *The Book of the Knight of the Tower* [= EETS Supp. S. 2] (London, 1971), p. 31; the editor refers to the *OED s.v. wisp*, sb1. 2.b.

80. A. Becker, 'Junggesellen und Alte Jungfern' in A. Becker, 'Junggesellen und alte Jungfern' in T. Kaul, ed., *Aus der Enge in die Weite* (Grünstadt, 1952), pp. 150–62. (1952), pp. 150–62, and H. Moser, *'Städtische Fasnacht des Mittelalters'* in *Volksleben*, 18 (1967), 184–90.

81. Reproduced in N.-A. Bringéus, *Volkstümliche Bilderkunde* (Munich, 1982), fig. 152.

82. G.B. Needham, 'New Light on Maids 'Leading Apes in Hell' in *Journal of American Folklore*, 75 (1962), pp. 106–19.

83. Despite an inscription which mentions this proverbial fate, the Jacobean 'banqueting trencher' bearing the image of the spinster in the set deriving from Sir John Davies' verses does not feature the apes – H. Ellis and J.Y. Akerman, 'Account of Some

"Roundells", or Fruit Trenchers of the Time of James the First' in *Archaeologia*, 34 (1852), pp. 225–30 and pl. XVIII. There is a full discussion of the provenance of these 'posies' in R. Krueger's edn of *The Poems of Sir John Davies* (Oxford, 1975), pp. 225–8.

84. C. Revard, 'The Tow on Absalom's Distaff and the Punishment of Lechers in Medieval London' in *English Language Notes*, 17 (1980), pp. 168–9.

85. Well illustrated in C. Gaignebet and J.D. Lajoux, *Art profane et religion populaire au Moyen Age* (Paris, 1985), p. 53. For the 'hands up' gesture, see H. Demisch, *Erhobene Hände: Geschichte eine Gebärde in der bildenden Kunst* (Stuttgart, 1984). C. Ducange, *Glossarium Novum ad Scriptores Medii Aevi* (Paris, 1766), *s.v. 'Lapides catenatos ferre'*.

86. Paris, B.N. MS lat. 9187.

87. I owe this reference to J.A. Dulaure, *Des Divinités Génératrices, ou du Culte du Phallus chez les anciens et les modernes* ((reprint of 1825 edn), Paris, 1885), p. 272, n. 1; in the same note Dulaure adds that a woodcut illustration of this punishment is printed in *Les Coutumes et établissements du château de Clermont-Soubiran* (Agen, 1596).

88. Paris, B.N. MS fr. 25526, f. 106.

89. F.P. Sweetser (ed.), *Les Cent Nouvelles Nouvelles* (Geneva, 1966), p. 304 (my translation).

90. It is thus peculiarly ironic that the caption to the reproduction of this image in the *Penguin Illustrated Chaucer* (where it accompanies a modern English rendering of 'The Knight's Tale') is labelled 'Here a woman offender is paraded through the streets in an open cart . . .' – testimony to the perils of 'extra-illustrating' medieval texts!

91. A late thirteenth-century illustration from St Omer, Bibliothèque municipale MS 5, f. 13v (Franco-Flemish) – bishop and king – is reproduced in P. Dinzelbacher, 'The Way to the Otherworld in Medieval Literature and Art' in *Folklore*, 97 (1986), 79. In the barrowing miniature placed at the head of the translation of Augustine's *City of God* given to Charles V by Raoul de Presles in the early 1370s, Paris, B.N. MS fr. 22912, the illuminator, the so-called Maître aux Boqueteaux, has given one of the passengers a long pointed hat like a dunce's that is perhaps intended to identify him as a heretic. For a much later English literary reference, cf. from a sermon preached in 1629 by Theophilus Adams: 'This oppressor must needs go to heaven. . . . But it will be, as the byword is, in a wheelbarrow: the fiends, and not the angels, will take hold on him.' Clearly, therefore, 'going to heaven in a wheelbarrow' meant 'going to hell' – cit. *Oxford Dictionary of English Proverbs* 'To go to heaven in a wheelbarrow'.

92. BL MS Yates Thompson 13, f. 139v. As is the practice in this manuscript, such marginal scenes are captioned, this one appearing to read: *Ecy mene le deable humenie feture vers les . . .*

93. cit. M.D. Anderson, *Drama and Imagery in English Medieval Churches* (Cambridge, 1963), p. 155.

94. cit. L. Maeterlinck in *Le Genre Satirique, Fantastique et Licencieux dans la Sculpture Flamande et Wallone: Les Misericordes des Stalles* (Paris, 1910).

95. Oxford, Bodley 264, f. 22. Another barrowload of nuns, but this time bound for hell, appears in the *bas-de-page* of a Last Judgment in a mid-fifteenth-century Flemish manuscript, Berlin, Staatsbibliothek, MS Germ. 8°. 648, reproduced as fig. 83 in L.M.J. Delaissé, *A Century of Dutch Manuscript Illumination* (Berkeley and Los Angeles, 1968).

96. Douai, Bibliothèque municipale MS 193, f. 209v.

97. Princeton MS 44–18, f. 169v–170 (early fourteenth century).

98. Paris, B.N. MS fr., f. 36v. The scene is well reproduced in Gaignebet and Lajoux, op.

cit., with the relevant section from the *Roman*; all treatments of the *charivari* refer to this manuscript, so I cite only P. Fortier-Beaulieu, *'Le Charivari dans le Roman de Fauvel', Revue de Folklore Français et de Folklore Colonial* (1939), pp. 1–16.

99. A cripple in a wheelbarrow is brought to Christ on one of the roof bosses of Norwich Cathedral, see C.J.P. Cave in *Archaeologia*, 83 (1933), pl. 13:5. R.C. Finucane in *Miracles and Pilgrims: Popular Beliefs in Medieval England* (London, 1977), pp. 86 and 228, n. 12, gives references to two medieval cripples pushed in barrows from London to shrines in Evesham and Hereford respectively. Another manuscript illumination from BL Harley MS 3487 (English, 1250x1275), f. 22v of 'a pathetic leper or idiot ringing his bell and pushed in a wheelbarrow' is noted by Michael Camille, 'Illustrations in Harley MS 3487 and the Perception of Aristotle's *Libri Naturales* in Thirteenth Century England' in *England in the Thirteenth Century: Proceedings of the 1984 Harlaxton Symposium* (Grantham, 1985), p. 34, no. 15. A ?crippled/one-legged child asks for alms from a barrow in the *bas-de-page* of the *Luttrell Psalter* (*c.* 1330x40), BL Add. MS 42130, f. 186v; cf. from the mystery-play *Les Miracles de Saint Geneviève* (early fifteenth century): *Pour l'amour du doulz roy de gloire,/Donnez ou denier ou malette/Au povre enfant de la brouette . . .* (For the love of the sweet king of glory give a penny or a halfpenny to the poor child in the barrow), A. Jubinal, *Mystères inédits du XVe siècle* (Paris, 1853), I, p. 281, lines 2617–9 (XIIIe miracle).

100. Maestro Andrea's title-page is reproduced in D. Kunzle, *The Early Comic Strip* (Berkeley, 1973), fig. 9:12.

101. J. Huizinga, *The Waning of the Middle Ages* (Harmondsworth, 1965), p. 176.

102. Numbered 6A in M.R. James, *St George's Chapel, Windsor: The Woodwork of the Choir* (Windsor, 1933).

103. The Bruges carving is well illustrated as pl. 30 in K.J. Steppe *et al.* (eds), *Wereld van Vroomheit en Satire: LaatGotische Koorbanken in Vlaanderen* (Kasterlee, 1973). It is possible, however, that both this and the Windsor carving are examples rather of the motif of rejuvenating the wife in the oven/furnace – for which, see Chapter 11.

104. Paris, B.N. MS fr. 95, f. 24v (Picard), reproduced as fig. 403 in Randall.

105. See J. Grauls in *Onze Taaltuin*, 3 (1934), pp. 111–23, and 4 (1936) pp. 257–68; J.A.J.M. Verspaandonk, *'Die merkwürdigen Hausgenossen der Chorherren'* in *Unser Bocholt* Heft 418, figs 44 (*recte* 45) and 45; H. Arena, *Die Chorgestühle des Meisters Rodrigo Aleman* (Buenos Aires, 1965).

106. The crone is in an engraving by Lucas van Leyden, of 1510. The Flemish print, dated some forty years later, and with the man labelled *desen vloyt den hondt*, is conveniently reproduced in W.S. Gibson, *Bruegel* (London, 1977), fig. 45. The third example is one of the Hoogstraeten misericords (1532x1546) well illustrated in D. and H. Kraus, *The Hidden World of Misericords* (New York, 1975), fig. 158. That English once knew a similar expression related to idleness seems implied in Congreve's (admittedly late) usage: 'Go, flea dogs and read romances!' (*The Way of the World IV*, ix).

107. R. Mellinkoff, 'Riding Backwards: Theme of Humiliation and Symbol of Evil' in *Viator*, 4 (1973), pp. 153–76.

108. See Ducange *s.v. asinus*, citing cases from 1375 and 1383.

109. For the various riding rituals, and charivaris in general, see C.R.B. Barrett, 'Riding Skimmington and Riding the Stang', *Journal of the British Archaeological Association*, New Series, 1 (1895), pp. 58–68; V. Alford, 'Rough Music or Charivari', *Folklore*, 70 (1959) pp. 505–18; N.Z. Davis, *'The Reasons of Misrule: Youth Groups and Charivaris in Sixteenth Century France', Past and Present*, 50

(1971), pp. 41–75; E.P. Thompson, 'Rough Music: le Charivari Anglais', *Annales ESC* 27:2 (1972), pp. 285–312; M.J. Ingram, 'Ridings, Rough Music and the "Reform of Popular Culture" in Early Modern England', *Past and Present*, 105 (1984), pp. 79–113; *idem*, 'Ridings, Rough Music and Mocking Rhymes in Early Modern England' in B. Reay (ed.), *Popular Culture in Seventeenth Century England* (Beckenham, 1985), pp. 166–97; D.E. Underdown, op. cit., esp. pp. 130–3; and a collection of essays by J. Le Goff and J.-C. Schmitt (eds), *Le Charivari* (Paris 1981). There are excellent representations in Gaignebet and Lajoux, op. cit.

110. Oxford, Bodleian Library, MS Bodley 352, f. 6v.

111. C. Zika, 'Dürer's witch, riding women and moral order' in D. Eichberger and C. Zika (eds), *Dürer and his Culture* (Cambridge, 1998), pp. 118–40.

112. Mellinkoff (1973), op. cit., p. 173, n. 104.

113. Note that the backward ride on an ass explains the puzzling line in a fifteenth-century anti-feminist carol that some women *cane sette the moke awrie*, where *moke* means donkey.

114. C. Tracy, *English Gothic Choirstalls* (Woodbridge, 1987), p. xxiii.

115. *Reversatus* in heraldic terminology usually means inverted, and its meaning is succinctly explained in the Chambers *Cyclopedia* of the 1730s: 'In the case of treason . . . the escutcheon is totally reversed, to intimate a total suppression of the honour.'

116. B.D.H. Miller, 'A Primitive Punishment: Further Instances' in *Notes and Queries*, 208 (October 1963), pp. 366–8.

117. The victim was also to be led through the market-place with an inscription about his head in large letters proclaiming, 'This were [wear] I for falsefying the kings letters.'

118. Otto Hupp, *Scheltbriefe und Schandbilder: ein Rechtsbehelf aus dem 15 und 16 Jahrhundert* (Munich and Regensburg, 1930).

119. Mellinkoff (1973), op. cit., p. 156; in n. 12 she remarks that this appears to be a milder version of the punishment of tarring and feathering which was imposed in the contemporary English Royal Navy as early as 1189 as a punishment for theft.

120. J. Misrahi and C. Knudson (eds), *A. de la Salle. Jehan de Saintré* [1476] (Geneva, 1967), pp. 305–6.

CHAPTER SIX

1. Mellinkoff, op. cit., p. 7.

2. ibid., p. 12.

3. ibid., p. 16.

4. See J. Bagnall Smith, 'Votive Objects and Objects of Votive Significance from Great Walsingham, Norfolk' in *Britannia*, 30 (1999), 21–56, esp. 26–8, and pl. III A and B.

5. cf. from a fifteenth-century Vocabulary: *Polimitus, Ray or motle or medlee* in T. Wright and R.P. Wülcker, *Anglo-Saxon and Old English Vocabularies* (2nd ed, London, 1884), pp. 603–46.

6. M. Pastoureau, *'Formes et couleurs du désordre: le jaune et le vert'* in *Médiévales*, 4 (1983), pp. 62–73.

7. S.M. Newton, *Fashion in the Reign of the Black Prince* (Woodbridge, 1980), p. 81.

8. S.B. Meech and H.E. Allen (eds), *The Book of Margery Kempe* [= EETS OS 212] (London, 1940), p. 62, lines 14–17.

9. H.T. Riley, *Munimenta Gildhallae Londiniensis I* [= Rolls Series 12, Part I] (London, 1859), pp. 458–9, and trans. ibid., *Munimenta Gildhallae Londiniensis III* (London, 1862), pp. 180–1.

10. D. Langenfeld and I. Götz, *'Nos stulti nudi sumus – wir Narren sind nackt: die Entwicklung des Standard-Narrentyps und seiner Attribute nach Psalterillustrationen des 12. bis 15. Jahrhunderts'* in ed. W. Mezger *et al.*, *Narren*

Schellen und Marotten: elf Beiträge zur Narrenidee (Remschied, 1984), pp. 37–96, esp. pp. 43–4.

11. Oxford, Bodleian Library, Rawlinson G. 185, f. 43v. (1350x1375).

12. In her will proved in 1448 Alicia Langham of Snailwell near Newmarket bequeathed to her son *unum pannum depictum cum historia Roberti Regis Cesilie* – S. Tymms, *Wills and Inventories of . . . Bury St Edmunds* [= Camden Society, vol. xlix] (London, 1850).

13. F. Lecoy (ed.), *Les deux poèmes de La Folie Tristan* (Paris, 1994), lines 211 and 560 explicitly refer to his head shaven *en croiz*, which modern commentators have taken to mean in such a manner as to leave only a cross of hair on top of his head. Fool tonsure is well treated by Mellinkoff, pp. 186–8, though to my mind she is rather too ready to identify bald-headed or close-cropped mockers of Christ as fools on the strength of their hairstyle alone! She believes *en croiz* must mean 'checkerboard' fashion, the result of shaving the head in strips first vertically and then horizontally, such as is indeed depicted in German fools of the second half of the fifteenth-century.

14. BL Add. 3816, f. 60v, reproduced in Mellinkoff, as pl. I.5.

15. Reproduced as pl. 75 in D. and H. Kraus, *The Gothic Choir-Stalls of Spain* (London, 1986), p. 145.

16. E. Kölbing (ed.) (Breslau, 1889), p. 300, lines 1643ff.

17. Wace, *Roman de Brut*, 9106–8; for a good list of such literary instances, see Philippe Ménard, *'Les fous dans la société médiévale'* in *Romania*, 98 (1977), pp. 433–59, esp. 436f. and n. 1, who notes that the terms *bertauder* and *bestondre* seem to denote a crude irregular tonsure (p. 438, n. 3).

18. F.A. Barack (ed.), (*Des Teufels Netz*) (Stuttgart, 1843).

19. E.K. Chambers, *The Medieval Stage* (Oxford, 1903) vol I., 325.

20. Oxford, Exeter College, MS 47, f. 34 (English, *a.* 1373).

21. Mezger, op. cit., p. 241.

22. Reproduced as fig. 60 in A. Nicoll, *Masks, Mimes and Miracles* (London, 1931); but note that Martial is not describing the man's headgear but his physical appearance.

23. 'Deze zot met zijn marot is de centrale figuur van het middeleeuwse volksfeest' – H. Pleij *et al.*, *Het zal koud zijn* (The Hague, 1980), p. 43.

24. *King Lear*, I.iv.209.

25. For example, the Burrell Collection in Glasgow, the Bargello Museum in Florence, the Louvre in Paris, and the Kunstgewerbemuseum in Berlin, and various fool heads in bronze and other materials, for instance one in the British Museum [reg. no. 91, 4–16, 1], are assumed to be further examples to be attached to staffs. The example reproduced here is from Rowley's House Museum, Shrewsbury.

26. Mezger, Abb. 24 (late fifteenth century).

27. *Coldingham Breviary*, BL Harley 4664, f. 145v.

28. For very similar sexual symbolism, cf. bride going to bed with chamber-pot and candlestick discussed by K. Renger as *'Tränen in der Hochzeitsnacht: das Zubettbringen der Braut, ein vergessenes Thema der niederländischen Malerei'* in L. Griesbach (ed.) and ibid., *Festschrift für O. v. Simson* (Frankfurt/Berlin/Wien, 1977), pp. 310–27.

29. Another example is the *Dixit insipiens* initial in Oxford, Bodleian Library MS Don. d. 85, f. 35v.

30. C. Hayfield and J.G. Hurst, 'Pottery fool's head whistles from London and Tattershall, Lincs.' in *Antiquaries Journal*, 63 (1983), pp. 380–3.

31. Gallo-Roman iconographic parallel to the phallus on the head: two almost identical small Roman bronze heads have been found in Southern England, one from

Margate and the other from Cirencester; both depict a male head entirely shaven except for a small lock of hair (that is, a *cirrus*) at the back of the head and a flat phallus facing fowards on the crown of the head. They are merely the most recent to surface of a group which includes a dozen continental finds, the majority of which come from Northern or Eastern Gaul, such as an example from Trier – one of the three such heads from Bavai on the French–Belgian border provides a very close parallel indeed to the English finds, while another from Mas-d'Agenais and an Italian example now in Naples – from the fact that they feature an erect phallus sited just above the forehead – are oddly reminiscent of the late medieval fool's-head whistles. These heads have, however, been most recently identified by one classical archaeologist (Johns, 1985) as possible amuletic horse-harness mounts depicting the heads of *boxers* – who affected the single lock of hair – with the phallus added to the head to strengthen the apotropaic function of the amulet. A French archaeologist, on the other hand, has identified the Mas-d'Agenais bust as that of a phallic Mercury (Santrot, 1986) or local Gaulish equivalent, and believes that the whole group may be considered as representations of a Gaulish Mercury.

32. H. Arena, *Die Chorgestühle des Meisters Rodrigo Aleman* (Buenos Aires, 1965), pp. 134f.

33. For the fool's foxtail, see P. Vandenbroeck, *Jheronimus Bosch: tussen volksleven en stadscultuur* (Berchem, 1987), esp. pp. 339–41, *'Van volksritueel naar nietvolkse symboliek: de vossestaart'*, and Mezger, op. cit., esp. pp. 258–68, *'Fuchsschwanz und Hahnenkamm'*.

34. For a full discussion of the erotic associations of the foxtail see my 'Folklore motifs in late Medieval art III: Erotic Animal Imagery' in *Folklore*, 102 (1991), pp. 192–219, esp. pp. 203–6.

35. Unfortunately, on close examination, one of Vandenbroeck's instances of the fool's foxtail *marotte*, on an English Dance of Death print of *c.* 1569, turns out to be a bladder.

36. The English tale is not a translation from the French, though the similarities with the French version 'point to a strong common tradition' – Hornstein in *PMLA*, 79 (1964), p. 15.

37. Another manuscript of the work reads: '*Clothed in a lodly* [that is, 'loathly'] *garnement/With ffoxes tayles mony aboute.*'

38. F.J. Furnivall (ed.), *Queene Elizabethes Academy, . . . etc.* [= EETS ES 8] (London, 1869), pp. 77f.

39. cit. from Durham University Library, MS Cosin V.iv.2 by S. Wenzel, 'The Wisdom of the Fool' in L.D. Benson and S. Wenzel (eds), *The Wisdom of Poetry: Essays in Early English Literature in Honor of Morton W. Bloomfield* (Kalamazoo, 1982), pp. 229 and 309.

40. N.J. O'Conor, *Godes Peace and the Queenes* (London, 1934), p. 115.

41. Wenzel, op. cit., Durham University Library, MS Cosin V.iv.2, f. 52r.

42. Reproduced as Abb. 137 in Mezger, op. cit. The fool from the contemporary *Wingfield Psalter* reproduced as the following illustration by Mezger seems to me to be brandishing a bladder on his stick, not a foxtail. The only other certain instance of this foxtail-type *marotte* is late, that is, Vandenbroeck, op. cit., n. 952 – a painting by Vinckbooms (d. 1629) – but note that, in a ballad of 1570, *The xxv. orders of fooles*, it is said of one fool that he must have 'in hand without fayle, A bable, a bell, or els a fox tayle'.

43. Reproduced as Abb. 140 in Mezger, op. cit.

44. Vandenbroeck, op. cit., p. 340 and n. 949.

45. De Pauw de Veen, *'Das Brüsseler Blatt mit Bettlern und Krüppeln: Bosch oder Bruegel?'* in O. von Simson and M. Winner (eds), *Pieter*

Bruegel und seine Welt (Berlin, 1979), pp. 149–58.

46. Note the following from *The Popes Funerall* (1605): 'I shall prove him such a noddy before I leave him, that all the world will deeme him worthy to weare in his forehead a coxcombe for his foolishness, and on his back a fox tayle for his badge.'

47. See the author's photograph of the so-called *Fuchswadel* of the Schomberger Fastnacht, in Mezger, op. cit., Abb. XXXI, p. 268.

48. This must be the original form of *den Fuchsschwanz streichen* (stroke the foxtail), also found contemporaneously.

49. Geisberg 827.

50. LSR *s.v. Halm, Hälmlein – einem das Hälmlein durch den Mund streichen/ziehen* = flatter.

51. Geisberg 1578.

52. cf. from a sermon by Geiler von Kaisersberg: *Christus hat den Juden nit den Fuchsschwanz durch das Maul gezogen . . .* (Christ did not draw the foxtail through the mouths of the Jews . . .), cit. LSR *s.v. Fuchsschwanz*.

53. For which see W. Mezger, *'Steckenpferd – Hobbyhorse – Marotte. Von der Ikonographie zur Semantik'* in *Zeitschrift für Volkskunde*, 79 (1983), pp. 245–50.

54. Bruce Moore, 'The Hobby-Horse and the Court Masque' in *Notes and Queries*, 233 (1988), p. 25.

55. *diutina fatuorum favente demencia per Austriam, Stiriam, Bawariam et Moraviam presul et archiprimas vagorum scoliarum . . . cruda simplicitate et inerti stulticia impellente . . . cit. H. Waddell, *The Wandering Scholars* (London, 1927), Appendix C.

56. Now in the Aachener Münsterschatz, see F. Irsigler and A. Lassotta, *Bettler und Gaukler, Dirnen und Henker* (Cologne, 1984), p. 89.

57. Newton, op. cit., fig. 24(c). The Bible in question is now in Stockholm.

58. Oxford, Exeter College, MS 42, f. 24r.

59. M. Stokstad and J. Stannard (eds), *Gardens of the Middle Ages* (Lawrence, Ks., 1983), pp. 220–1, pls 69a and b.

60. Gift of J. Pierpont Morgan, 17.190.615 a, b. Another fool who seems to have been drawn wearing only one shoe appears on a woodcut title-page frame used by the printer Lazare Schürer who issued, for example, the *Confutation Sophistices* by Brunfels, at Sélestat in 1520.

61. Reproduced as Abb. 29 in E. Meyer, *'Die Gotische Kronleuchter in Stans. Ein Beitrag zur Geschichte der Dinanderie'* in ed. E.J. Beer *et al.*, *Festschrift Hans R. Hahnloser zum 60. Geburtstag* (Basel/Stuttgart, 1961).

62. The quotation is from Martin Walsh, 'Divine Cuckold/Holy Fool: The Comic Image of Joseph in the English *Troubles' Play'* in W.M. Ormrod (ed.), *England in the Fourteenth Century: Proceedings of the 1985 Harlaxton Symposium* (Woodbridge, 1986), p. 281.

63. Sara Nale, 'Popular religion in Cuenca on the eve of the Catholic Reformation' in S. Halicer (ed.), *Inquisition and Society in Early Modern Europe* (London, 1987), pp. 68–9.

64. H.L. Nickel, *'Herleitung und Deutung der Gotischen Drolerie in der Wandmalerei, dargestellt an Beispielen aus dem Gebiet der DDR'* in A. Karlowska-Kamzowa (ed.), *Gotyckie Malarstwo Scienne W. Europie Srodkoko-Wschodniej* (Poznan, 1977), pp. 151–7, reproduced as Abb. 6.

65. There seems not to be any specific English term for this gesture; A. Weir and J. Jerman, *Images of Lust. Sexual Carvings on Medieval Churches* (London, 1986), use the term 'mouth-puller'.

66. Illustrated in C. Gaignebet and J.D. Lajoux, *Art profane et religion populaire au Moyen Age* (Paris, 1985). Another fool in eared hood who simply sticks out his tongue without making the *Gähnmaul* grimace is depicted on a misericord at Levroux.

67. Mezger, op. cit., Abb. 32a and 32b.

68. Mezger, op. cit., pp. 295–7 and Abb. 164.

69. Note how the dangerous madman in the illustrated *Sachsenspiegel* manuscripts is also hung about with bells.

70. W. Mezger, *Welttheater der Narren. Der Ambraser Bildteller und sein Programm* (Stattgart, 2002).

71. On the role of the fool-bishop, see J. Heers, *Fêtes, Jeux et Joûtes dans les Sociétés d'Occident à la Fin du Moyen Age* (Montreal, 1971), pp. 124–7, and L. Lefebvre, *L'Evêque des Fous et la Fête des Innocents* (Lille, 1902).

72. R.M. Wilson, *The Lost Literature of Medieval England* (London, 1952), p. 178.

73. E.K. Chambers, *The Medieval Stage* (Oxford, 1903), p. 321.

74. Quoted, for example, in S. Billington, *A Social History of the Fool* (Brighton, 1984), p. 3.

75. Chambers, op. cit.

76. I owe my knowledge of this to John Southworth's excellent *Fools and Jesters at the English Court* (Stroud, 1998), pl. 11(a). The manuscript is in New College, Oxford, MS 7, f. 142b.

77. Reproduced in Randall.

78. Another fool-bishop is reproduced in the wall-painting dated 1486 in the church at Briesen near Frankfurt-an-der-Oder referred to in n. 64 above.

79. Southworth, op. cit., p. 123.

80. 'It was a prety part in the old Church-plays, when the nimble Vice would skip vp nimbly like a Iacke an Apes into the deuils necke, and ride the deuil a course, and belabour him with his woodden dagger, til he made him roare' (Harsnett, *Declaration of Egregious Popish Impostures* 1603, pp. 114–15).

'. . . this roaring devil i' th' old play, that every one may pare his nails with a wooden dagger . . .' (Shakespeare, *Henry V* (1599) IV.iv.73f.)

'. . . the old Vice . . . /Who, with dagger of lath, in his rage and his wrath,/Cries, "Ah, ha!" to the devil:/Like a mad lad, "Pare thy nails, dad./Adieu, goodman devil!"'

(Shakespeare, *Twelfth Night* (1601) IV.ii.127ff.)

'. . . How like you the Vice i' the Play?'

'. . . But here is never a Fiend to carry him away. Besides, he has never a wooden dagger! I'd not give a rush for a Vice, that has not a wooden dagger to snap at every body he meetes' (Jonson, *Staple of News*, II Interm. (1626)).

In Jonson's play *The Divell is an Asse* (1616), the Vice (named Iniquity) recalls that about the year 1560, 'every great man had his "Vice" [that is, household fool] stand by him, In his long coat, shaking his wooden dagger'. In *Bussy d'Ambois* (1604) Chapman alludes to the jester's 'wooden dagger' and some twenty years later Fletcher and Rowley in *The Noble Gentleman* (a. 1625) similarly refer to the fool's 'guarded coat, and . . . great wooden dagger'.

The last three references are taken from Leslie Hotson's unjustly overlooked monograph, *Shakespeare's Motley* (London, 1952), pp. 58f.

81. A. Feuillerat (ed.), *Documents Relating to the Revels at Court in the Time of King Edward VI and Queen Mary* (Louvain, 1914), p. 73. It also, incidentally, confirms the existence of the hybrid *marotte*/ladle-cum-bladder; in this citation, *bable* must allude to the bladder-type of *marotte*, rather than the fool's-head-on-a-stick type – such a combined *ladle with a bable pendante* can be seen held by a traditionally garbed jester on English wood-panelling of early sixteenth-century date at Abington Hall, Northants., reproduced in a drawing by F. Roe, 'Jesters on Panelling' in *The Connoisseur*, 79 (September–December 1927), p. 196.

82. S. Harsnett, *Declaration of Egregious Popish Impostures* (1603), pp. 114–15.

83. The van Meckenem dances are usefully discussed, with comparative material, by A. Winther, 'Zu einigen Ornamentblättern und den Darstellungen des Moriskentanzes im Werk des Israhel van Meckenem' in ed., ibid., *Israhel*

van Meckenem und der deutsche Kupferstich des 15. Jahrhunderts (Bocholt, 1972), esp. pp. 88–100.

84. For early representations of the morris dance, see D. Huschenbett, 'Die Frau mit dem Apfel und Frau Venus in Moriskentanz und Fastnachtspiel' in Festgabe für Josef Dunninger zum 65. Geburtstag (Berlin, 1970), pp. 585–603. Jelle Koopmans discusses the morris in relation to the sottie in 'Les Sots du théâtre et les sauts de la Morisque à la fin du moyen age' in Les Lettres Romanes, 43 (1989), pp. 43–59.

85. A.G. Gilchrist, 'A carved morris-dance panel from Lancaster Castle' in Journal of the English Folk Dance and Song Society, 1 (1933), pp. 86–8.

86. For the significance of the number seven for a group of fools, see Mezger, especially pp. 327ff., to which may be added a mid-sixteenth-century English example from the royal costume accounts for the Twelve Days of Christmas 1552–3 – see A.J. Kempe (ed.), The Losely Manuscripts (London, 1836), pp. 47f.

87. cit. MED s.v. moreys. P. Glanville, Silver in Tudor and Early Stuart England (London, 1990), p. 286, notes that one of the twenty-nine salts listed in the 1521 inventory of the royal Jewel House was 'the Morris Dance, which was a woman holding a salt'. On the same page, she notes that other salts in Henry VII's Jewel House incorporated figures of fools as their stems, presumably in the same way that similar small fools acted as the feet, etc. of contemporary German silver vessels.

88. A pointing fool, who is himself depicted as phallic, appears on a piece of contemporary Flemish sgraffito-ware – see H. van Gangelen, 'Tot lering en vermaak: een moralistische narren-voorstelling op een Bossche voetschaal van sgraffito-aardewerk uit ca. 1500' in Mededelingenblad Nederlandse Vereniging van Vrienden van de Ceramiek, 135 (1989), pp. 19ff., and afb. 1.

89. Reproduced as fig. 76 in B.D. Palmer, The Early Art of the West Riding of Yorkshire (Kalamazoo, 1990); on p. 255, the author notes that the carved panel derives from North Milford Hall, home of the Leedes family, and dates it to the late fifteenth century. In addition, there is another very fine hooded fool with pendent belled sleeves and fool's-head-topped marotte-staff with apparently pointing finger also from an originally secular context, now preserved in Kirkby Wharfe Church, Yorkshire.

90. Alternatively it is a piece of 'relic' iconography, deriving from the Dixit insipiens initial fools of illuminated manuscripts who point fearfully heavenwards at the God whose existence they deny, looming out of a cloud.

91. See G. de Werd, 'Een handdoekrek door de Kalkarse beeldhouwer Arnt van Tricht (ca. 1540)' in Antiek, 16 (1981), pp. 33–56.

92. For example, the fifteenth-century Von Hohenlohe necklace and pendant, and brooches such as that mentioned in the 1494 inventory of the Guardaroba Estense: facto ala todescha smaltato cum una figura in guisa de bufone.

93. For example, the fool's-head whistles mentioned above, or the sgraffito-decorated bowl which is the subject of H. van Gangelen, 'Een laat-middeleeuwse melkteil van sgraffito-aardewerk met een moraliserende narrenvoorstelling (ca. 1500)' in Antiek, 24 (1989–90), pp. 523–8.

94. cit. H. Jung, Närrische Volkskunst (Duisburg, 1970), p. 50.

CHAPTER SEVEN

1. I am grateful to R.W. Lightbown, former Keeper of the Department of Metalwork in the Victoria and Albert Museum, London, for supplying me with a photocopy of the relevant page of the published inventory of

1364, as referred to in his *Secular Goldsmiths' Work in Medieval France: A History* (London 1978), p. 71.

2. H. Wenzel, *'Eine Sprichwortschale und andere Lübecker Goldschmiedearbeiten'* in *Zeitschrift des deutschen Vereins für Kunstwissenschaft* (1938), pp. 148–58, esp. pp. 148–52.

3. Illustrating the chapter *Vom zweifelhaften Stande.*

4. F. Zarncke in *Anzeiger für Kunde der deutschen Vorzeit* N.F. 6 (1859), pp. 414–16. See also Paul Vandenbroeck, *Jheronimus Bosch: tussen volksleven en stadscultuur* (Berchem, 1987), pp. 271–4.

5. E.S. Siple's original publication, 'A "Flemish Proverb" Tapestry in Boston' in *Burlington Magazine* (1933), pp. 29–31, was expanded by the great Dutch folklorist Jan Grauls in his *'Een Vijftiendeeuwse Spreekwoordentapijt'* in *Artes Textiles*, 3 (1956), pp. 14–26.

6. This important text was edited by A. Scoumanne, *Henri Baude: Dictz moraulx pour faire tapisserie* (Geneva, 1959). Two of the manuscripts containing illustrations are reproduced in J.-L. Lemaitre, *Henri Baude: Dictz moraulx pour faire tapisserie* (Paris, 1988) and, with valuable commentary, in P. Vandenbroeck, *'Dits illustrés et emblèmes moraux. Contribution à l'étude de l'iconographie profane et de la pensée sociale vers 1500 (Paris, B.N. MS fr. 24461)'* in *Jaarboek Koninklijk Museum Voor Schone Kunsten Antwerpen* (1988), pp. 23–96.

7. Reproduced in Vandenbroeck (1987), op. cit., as afb. 46.

8. The verses in 'Les Enigmes de l'Amour' are printed under that title by G.A. Parry in *Revue de Philologie Française*, 22/23 (1908–9), pp. 214–20. The manuscript is BL Stowe MS 955 and features in T. Kren (ed.), *Renaissance Painting in Manuscripts: Treasures from the British Library* (London 1983). J.M. Massing has also pointed out Sala's indebtedness to Baude in *The Book Collector*, 33 (1984), p. 379.

9. The colour term has been retained in English, but its reference is now restricted solely to one species of deer, that is, the *fallow* deer.

10. See L.F. Sandler's note in *Art Bulletin*, 68 (June 1986).

11. We are promised a facsimile edition of this important manuscript, by Nancy Regalado, Edward Roesner and François Avril.

12. Wh F85.

13. In the form *saber de la falveta*; see further, M. Bambeck *'Auf einem fahlen Pferde reiten: Ursprung und Sinn einer alten Redensart'* in *Archiv für das Studium der Neueren Sprachen und Literatur*, 217 (1980), pp. 241–58.

14. W. Harms, *'Reinhart Fuchs als Papst und Antichrist auf dem Rad der Fortuna'* in *Frühmittelalterliche Studien*, 6 (1972), pp. 418–40.

15. A Wheel of Fortune surmounted by a crowned fox is also to be found in the *bas-de-page* of a missal illuminated in 1323, Hague, Museum Meermanno-Westreenianum, MS 78.D.40; the miniature is reproduced as Randall, fig. 684.

16. Wh T395 (*c.* 1450).

17. BL Cotton MS Tiberius A VII, f. 93.

18. Most recently discussed in ed. John Clark, *The Medieval Horse and its Equipment c. 1150–c. 1450* (London, 1995), pp. 158–60.

19. V.H. Galbraith (ed.), *The St Albans Chronicle 1406–1420* (Oxford, 1937), pp. 1–2.

20. Lehrs 487. A reversed version was engraved by Frans Hogenberg, *c.* 1558. An updated and somewhat rearranged version was engraved in Prague by Paul Bayard *c.* 1610 and it is probably this version that Thomas Trevilian is copying in his *Great Book* of 1616, N. Barker (ed.) (London, 2001).

21. J.W. Hassell, 'Proverbs as Table Decoration Motifs' in K.S. Goldstein and N.V. Rosenberg (eds), *Folklore Studies in Honor of Herbert Halpert* (St John's, Newfoundland, 1980), pp. 225–32, and A. Lafortune-

Martel, *Fête noble en Bourgogne au XVe siècle* (Montreal, 1984), esp. pp. 142–5.

22. The 'parrot' is more usual in this role, and I reproduce an early sixteenth-century illustration in my 'Popinjay, jolly May! Parrot-badges and the iconography of May in Britain, France and the Netherlands' in D. Kicken *et al.* (eds), *Gevonden voorwerpen Lost and Found* (Rotterdam, 2000), pp. 214–29, fig. 9.

23. Amsterdam, Rijksmuseum, Rijksprentenkabinet, FM 445-B, reproduced as the frontispiece to A. Duke, *Reformation and Revolt in the Low Countries* (London, 1990).

24. H.R. Hahnloser (ed.), *Villard de Honnecourt Kritische Gesamtausgabe* (Vienna, 1935), pp. 397–401.

25. The manuscript is now divided between Oxford and Melbourne; in the Bodleian Library, it is MS Douce 118, f. 124, and National Gallery of Victoria, Melbourne, MS 1254/3, f. 123; I take the refs from Randall's 'Iconographical Index' where it is described unrecognised under 'Lion chained/tied to post', and also at 'Man and dog, training'.

26. BL MS Royal 2. B. VII, f. 183.

27. J. Manning (ed.), *The Emblems of Thomas Palmer: Sloane MS 3794* (New York, 1988), p. 146.

28. Musée Condé MS 509, f. 9.

29. The MS, noted in Randall's 'Iconographic Index' and reproduced as fig. 575 is New York, Pierpont Morgan Library, MS 88, f. 71.

30. R.B. McKerrow (ed.), *The Works of Thomas Nashe*, vol. 3 (Oxford, 1905), p. 241, lines 241–50 – most unusually, there is no source given in McKerrow's normally encyclopaedic Notes volume.

31. Geisberg 1581.

32. H. Kohlhaussen, *Minnekästchen* (Berlin, 1928), pp. 87f., cat. no. 69.

33. G. Frank and D. Miner, *Proverbes en Rimes* (Baltimore, 1937), p. 65, lines 895ff., and pl. 62.

34. J. Morawski, *Proverbes français antérieurs au XVe siècle* (Paris, 1925), p. 75, no. 235.

35. Wh K60.

36. H. Kohlhaussen, 'Bildertische' from Germanishes Nationalmuseum, Anzeiger (1936–9), pp. 12–45.

37. Vienna, Nationalbibliothek, MS 2975, f. 1v (Austria, 1477).

38. The *Parzival* manuscript is preserved in the Fürstlich Fürstenbergisches Bibliothek in Donaueschingen. I find I have an inadequate reference to another German example depicted on f. 15r of a mid-fifteenth-century manuscript in the library at Montecassino.

39. BL Add. MS 37527, p. 291 (?*c.* 1520).

40. J.K. Steppe, *Wereld van vroomheid en satire: laat-gotische koorbanken in Vlaanderen* (Kasterlee, 1973), where it is reproduced as pl. 25. Other examples: Schäufelein's woodcut to Hagenau's *Teutsch Evangeli und Epistel* (1516); Daniel Hopfer (d. 1536) engraved the scene within the newly built Dominican church of St Magdalene (1513–15), and roughly contemporary (*c.* 1530), is Erhard Schoen's woodcut to the broadsheet *Klagrede der armen verfolgten Gotzen vnd Tempelpilder* (Geisberg 1145) in which it appears as a detail.

41. According to the Vulgate version of *Ecclesiastes* 1.15.

42. Frank and Miner, op. cit., lines 1063ff.

43. cit. *OED s.v. snail*.

44. Both verses are cit. from Wh S420.

45. E.M. Brennan (ed.), *The Duchess of Malfi* (London, 1964), p. 83, V.ii.45ff.

46. Discussed (but misidentified) in *Masterpieces from the Robert von Hirsch Sale at Sotheby's* (London, 1978), p. 101. I am grateful to Dr George Szabo for the opinion that the figure is from an ornamental fountain, and to Sothebys' for permission to reproduce the photograph here.

47. Motif no. J 1909.7.

48. F.J. Furnivall (ed.), *Jyl of Breyntford's*

Testament, by Robert Copland, and other short pieces (London, 1871).

49. S. Thompson, *Motif Index of Folk Literature* (Bloomington, 1966).

50. H.F. Lippincott (ed.), *A Shakespeare Jestbook, Robert Armin's 'Foole upon Foole' (1600)* (Salzburg, 1973), p. 57.

51. A.C. Wood (ed.), *Memorials of the Holles family* [= Camden Society, 3rd Series, vol. 55] (London, 1937), p. 42.

52. F.C. Tubach, *Index exemplorum* (Helsinki, 1969), no. 1968.

53. E.W. Ives, 'Tom Skelton, a Seventeenth Century Jester' in *The Shakespeare Survey*, 13 (1960), p. 97. The motif is Thompson, op. cit., J.133.4 'Numskull cuts off tree limb on which he sits'. See also E.W. Baughmann, *Type and Motif Index of the Folktales of England and North America* (The Hague, 1966), Type 1240, 'Man Sitting on Branch of Tree Cuts it Off'.

54. B.L. Stowe MS 955, f. 15r; reproduced as fig. 22e in T. Kren (ed.), *Renaissance Painting in Manuscripts: Treasures from the British Library* (London, 1983). See also C. King in *Gazette des Beaux Arts*, 112 (1988), pp. 173–84. The manuscript is now properly discussed by E. Burin, 'Pierre Sala's Pre-Emblematic Manuscripts' in *Emblematica*, 4 (1989), pp. 1–19.

55. See A. Scoumanne, *Henri Baude: Dictz Moraulx pour faire Tapisserie* (Geneva, 1959); the Baude manuscript illustrations discussed are Paris, B.N. MS fr. 22461, f. 36, and Chantilly, Musée Condé MS 509, f. 15.

56. Oxford, Bodleian Library, MS Bodley 264, ff. 61r and 63v (*c.* 1340). An example from Copenhagen, Det Kongelige Bibliotek MS 3384 80, f. 37, is reproduced in Randall as fig. 322.

57. Motif no. F 171.6.3.

58. U. Haastrup and R. Egevang, *Danske Kalkmalerier Senromansk tid 1175–1275* (Copenhagen, 1987), p. 70.

59. Motif no. F 171.6.3, but also J 1964 'Tree trunks laid crosswise of the sledge'.

60. J. Bolte and G. Polivka, *Anmerkungen zu den Kinder-und Hausmärchen der Brüder Grimm* (Leipzig, 1913–31), III, pp. 301–3.

61. Dutch Hollstein *Van der Venne* 378 from *Invallende Gedachten*, p. 77.

62. First printed by T. Wright in *Early Mysteries and Other Latin Poems of the Twelfth and Thirteenth Centuries* (London, 1838). The only modern scholarly edition with commentary is in A.G. Rigg, *An Edition of a Fifteenth-century Commonplace Book* (Ph.D thesis, Oxford, 1965), vol. i, pp. 146–56, and ii, pp. 356–70.

63. An incident which occurs in the *First Shepherds Play* of the *Towneley Plays*.

64. Available in ed. P.M. Zall, *A Hundred Merry Tales and Other English Jestbooks of the Fifteenth and Sixteenth Centuries* (Lincoln, Nebraska, 1963), p. 87f.

65. A facsimile text of the earliest extant edition is provided by S.J. Kahrl, *Merie Tales of the Mad Men of Gotam . . .* (Evanston, 1965), pp. 1–20. I discuss the cuckoo-penning further in M. Jones and P. Dillon, *Dialect in Wiltshire* (Trowbridge, 1987), pp. 146ff.

66. See P.H. Reaney, *The Origin of English Surnames* (London, 1967), p. 289.

67. I discuss this particular motif in some detail in ed. M. Twycross, *Festive Drama* (Cambridge, 1996), pp. 242–58, under the title '*Slawpase fro the myln-whele*: seeing between the lines in the Wakefield *Prima Pastorum*'.

68. So that, occasionally, one even sees these 'humane riders' reproduced by mistake in books or articles which purport to illustrate everyday life in the Middle Ages! For the misuse of manuscript images by French medieval historians see F. Garnier, *L'ane à la lyre: sottiser d'iconographie médiéval* (Paris, 1988).

69. See A. Whittingham, *Norwich Cathedral Bosses and Misericords* (Norwich, 1981), pp. 15, 17.

70. H.K. Cameron, 'The Fourteenth Century Flemish Brasses at King's Lynn' in *Archaeological Journal*, 136 (1979), pp. 151–8.

71. BL Stowe MS 17 (?Maastricht, *c.* 1300), f. 89v, and Paris, Bibliothèque de l'Arsenal MS 5218 (Tournai, 1351), f. 20.

72. HP1 afb. 577–580; HP2 afb, 1695, 1698.

73. See P.P. Wright, *The Rural Bench-Ends of Somerset* (Amersham, 1983).

74. See A.A. Rosende Valdes 'The Galician Choir Stalls' in *The Profane Arts*, 6 (1997), p. 196 and fig. 2, where, however, it is misidentified as a monk carrying a wineskin!

75. A topic I discuss at some length in my unpublished Ph.D thesis, 'The iconography and design-sources of the Beverley Minster misericords' (Plymouth, 1991).

76. This is Motif no. J 1881.2.2 'Fools send money by rabbit' and B 291.3.2.(1) 'Hares carry taxes to court'. The story is printed in T. Wright, *A Collection of Latin Stories, Illustrative of the History of Fiction during the Middle Ages* (London, 1842), p. 80.

77. The three are listed in Randall.

78. W.C.B. Smith, *St Mary's Church, Beverley* (Norwich, 1979), p. 14.

79. A similar origin has been proposed for the famous Cheshire Cat, according to a report in *The Daily Telegraph* (6–10 July 1992) entitled 'Riddle of Cheshire Cat solved' by Colin Wright. J. Birenbaum of Chicago sees a resemblance between a small smiling cat on a wall-panel in the church of St Peter in Croft, Co. Durham, the church of which Carroll's father was rector, and where Lewis worshipped as a boy – a reference I owe to my father, Mr S. Haydn Jones.

80. Motif no. J 1881.2.2, 'Fools send money by rabbit'.

81. Reproduced in P. Boglioni (ed.), *La Culture Populaire au Moyen Age* (Montreal, 1979), p. 201.

82. Wh H.125; J.W. Hassell, *Middle French Proverbs, Sentences and Proverbial Phrases* (Toronto, 1982), L 55; first citation from Machaut, *c.* 1352; see also R. Jente, *Proverbia Communia* (Bloomington, 1947), no. 533.

83. Frank and Miner, op. cit., lines 1191ff.

84. Motif no. F 665.1.

85. Such scenes are reproduced in L. Maeterlinck, *Le Genre Satirique dans la Peinture Flamande* (2nd edn, Brussels, 1907), figs 36 and 37, from Douai, Bibliothèque Municipale MS 253, and Valenciennes, Bibliothèque Municipale MS 492 (see also MSS 361, 381, and 460). D. Brewer, 'The International Popular Comic tale' in ed. T.J. Heffernan, *The Popular Literature of Medieval England* (Knoxville, 1985), p. 142, points out Philip Sidney's matter-of-fact observation that 'we laugh at cripples' in his *Apology for Poetry* (*c.* 1580). I contrast the position in Early Irish Law which specifically forbade such mockery – F. Kelly, *A Guide to Early Irish Law* (Dublin, 1988), pp. 93ff.

86. The *Bury Bible* is Corpus Christi College, Cambridge, MS 2 (*c.* 1135). Motif Index no. F 665.1 'The skilful barber shaves the running hare.'

87. Translated D. Luke, *Jakob and Wilhelm Grimm: Selected Tales* (Harmondsworth, 1982), p. 310.

88. See J. Bolte and G. Polivka, *Anmerkungen zu den Kinder-und Hausmärchen der Brüder Grimm* (Leipzig, 1913–31), III, p. 10.

89. The manuscript is British Library, Add. MS 49622, f. 202v. Randall reproduces a group of these hares in hoods images in her figs 219–22. The words *hair* and *hare* were homophones in Middle English only in the precise area in which the manuscript is known to have been produced.

90. cit. M.P. Tilley, *A Dictionary of the Proverbs in England in the Sixteenth and Seventeenth Centuries* (Ann Arbor, 1950), M636.

91. The editors cite a contemporary Spanish parallel from the novel *Celestina* (1499): *meter aguja y sacar reja*, auto iv.

92. An English translation by W. Gillis, *The Ship of Fools* (London, 1971) reproduces all the original woodcuts.

93. Also depicted as a woodcut in Murner's *Schelmenzunft* (1512), it is conveniently reproduced in LSR *s.v. Wasser*.

94. Wh F 265, 'To keep Fleas (or wild hares) in an open lease'. In German works the application of this particular proverbial folly seems always to have been misogynist; see W.H.D. Suringar (ed.), *Heinrich Bebel's Proverbia Germanica* (Leiden, 1879), no. 84, and commentary, pp. 234f. Dutch, French and German versions of the print are known; a German version and its accompanying text attributed to Paulus Furst and dated *c.* 1620 is reproduced in E.J. Dingwall, *The Girdle of Chastity* (London, 1931), pp. 66ff.

95. See 'Wash an Ethiop (blackamoor, Moor), white, To' in *The Oxford Dictionary of English Proverbs*, 3rd edn, rev. F.P. Wilson (Oxford, 1970) – all citations are post-*Adagia*.

96. John Manning (ed.), *The Emblems of Thomas Palmer: Sloane MS 3794* (New York, 1988).

97. The inns so named are listed in J. Larwood and J.C. Hotten, *History of Signboards* (London, 1866), p. 460. The trade tokens may be found in G.C. Williamson, *Trade Tokens Issued in the 17th Century* (reprinted, London, 1967).

98. M. Jones, 'Washing the ass's head: exploring the non-religious prints' in M. McDonald (ed.), *The Print Collection of Ferdinand Columbus (1488–1539)* (London, 2003).

99. *Gargantua*, cap. 11; Bebel, no. 144 (1508) records the expression 'making shoes for lice' used of those who would like to be seen as very learned.

100. R. Wildhaber, 'Die Gänse beschlagen' in T.P. Lucero and A. Domheim (eds), *Homenaje a Fritz Krüger* (Mendoza 1954), II, pp. 339–56.

101. Whiting G 389.

102. The continental misericords are reproduced in D. and H. Kraus, *The Hidden World of Misericords* (New York, 1975), fig. 39, and J.A.J.M. Verspaandonk, '*Het Vreemde Houten Gezelschap*' in *Antiek*, 2 (1974–5), p. 121ff.

103. Two are reproduced as Randall, figs 579 and 580. The *Proverbes en Rimes* example is conveniently reproduced in LSR *s.v. Gans*.

104. This reference I have taken from J.-C. Aubailly, *Le Monologue le Dialogue et la Sottie* (Paris 1976). A final example of this motif appears on one of the fascinating sixteenth-century *monnaies des innocents*, figuring in a rebus of the surname DAVERLOIS, reproduced in J.-C. Margolin, *Histoire du Rébus* (Paris, 1986), as fig. 139 on p. 318.

105. J. Lebeuf, *Histoire de la ville et de tout le diocèse de Paris* (Paris, 1883–90), I, p. 368.

106. S. Kaspersen, '*Körper, Trieb und Leibesdenken; zu einigen Drôlerien der Everlöv-Brarup-Gruppe*' in K. Kröll and H. Steger (eds), *Mein Ganzer Körper ist Gesicht* (Freiburg, 1994), pp. 193–214, esp. pp. 198ff.

107. Renouard, *Les Marques Typographiques*, 97, fig. 316.

108. E. Goetze and C. Drescher (eds), *Die Fabeln und Schwänke in den Meistergesängen* (Halle, 1893), I, no. 199. The tale next appeared in the *Lalebuch* (1597), cap. 8.

109. This is Motif no. J 2165, 'Carrying load up hill to roll it down', and is depicted in a woodcut by the so-called 'Petrarch Master' (Hans Weiditz), published in Schwarzenberg's 1531 edition of *Officia M.T.C.* on p. 26r.

110. Motif no. J 2123, 'Sunlight carried into windowless house in baskets'.

111. Walter S. Gibson, *Bruegel* (London, 1977), reproduces Hogenberg's etching as fig. 43. The central 'Blue Cloak' motif also occurs on the arm-rest of a Toledo stall (1489x1495) carved by a Fleming, Maestro Roderigo Aleman – I. Mateo Gomez, *Temas Profanos en la Escultura Gotica Espanola: las Sillerias de Coro* (Madrid, 1979), fig. 157.

112. M. Jones, 'Proverbial Inscriptions on Medieval Artefacts', unpublished lecture

delivered in October 1992 to The Finds Research Group of the Society of Antiquaries; see now A.G.S. Edwards, 'Middle English Inscriptional Verse Texts' in J. Scattergood and J. Boffey (eds), *Texts and Their Contexts*. (Dublin, 1997), pp. 26–43.

CHAPTER EIGHT

1   On the meaning and exemplification of this term, see J. Evans, *English Art 1307–1461* (Oxford, 1949), pp. 38ff.

2.   The Cockaigne complex is already found in such classical authors as Athenaeus and Lucian.

3.   Nürnberg, Stadtbibliothek, MS Will I, 412.2, reproduced as Abb. 16 in D.-R. Moser, 'Fastnacht und Fastnachtspiel' in H. Brunner (ed.), *Hans Sachs und Nürnberg* (Nürnberg, 1976), pp. 182–218. Another manuscript shows the men, all wearing fools' hoods, already trapped in the net and no woman decoy in evidence. The earliest image of a woman trapping a man in a bird net occurs as a marginal image in Oxford, Bodleian Library, MS Douce 6, f. 83v (Flemish, *c.* 1300).

4.   Geisberg 1357. For the motif of 'Satan the Fowler', see B.G. Koonce in *Medieval Studies*, 21 (1959), pp. 176–83. See further, below, p. 212.

5.   See my article, 'Cockaigne, Land of' in C. Lindahl *et al.* (eds), *Medieval Folklore, An Encyclopedia of Myths, Legends, Tales, Beliefs and Customs* (Santa Barbara, 2000), I, pp. 186–8. The English names material derives from P.H. Reaney, *The Origins of English Surnames* (London, 1967).

6.   In Germanic literature it appears incidentally in fifteenth-century Mercator plays (for example, that from Melk, in which it is called *Leckant*) and the lying-tale *Vom Packofen*, where it is called *Kuckormurre*, the first syllable of which has doubtless been influenced by Latin *Cuccania*, but it is found a century earlier in the form *Gugelmiure* in the mid-fourteenth-century *Wachtelmaere*, which includes a fairly full description of the paradise. Unlike the Anglo-Irish poem, the fifteenth-century Dutch *Cockaengen* appears to be directly dependent on the earliest, thirteenth-century French *Cocaingne*. It has only recently been noticed that the name *Schlaraffenland* which is now standard in German refers to the glutton's paradise as early as *c.* 1400 in Wittenwiler's *Ring*.

7.   See M. Jones, 'Engraved works recorded in the *Stationers' Registers*, 1562–1656: a listing and commentary' in *Journal of the Walpole Society*, 64 (2002), pp. 1–68, esp. pp. 53–4, no. 297.

8.   A Toledo misericord (1489x95) carved by the Fleming Rodrigo Aleman depicts the pig turned butcher with a knife at his belt, while a similar notion is expressed in a ceiling painting of 1437 in the Swedish church of Tensta depicting an ox slaughtering a man.

9.   See M. Jones, 'Folklore Motifs in Late Medieval Art I: Proverbial Follies and Impossibilities' in *Folklore*, 100 (1989), pp. 201–17.

10.   The *Rutland Psalter* is BL Add. MS 62925; another manuscript illustration is found in Karlsruhe Cod. 92, f. 109. In Paris, B.N. MS lat. 1393, f. 136, the cat is grilled by the rats – cf. the fox barbecued by the cockerel in a Flemish book of hours illuminated in 1406, BL Add. MS 29433, f. 59, and another, carved on a late fifteenth-century canopy in Oviedo Cathedral.

11.   In the cloisters at Silos and Teruel Cathedrals.

12.   BL Royal 10. E. IV (*c.* 1330x40).

13.   For further examples, see M. Jones, 'German and Flemish prints as design-sources for the misericords in St George's Chapel, Windsor (1477X84), in L. Keen and E. Scarff (eds), *Windsor: Medieval Art and Architecture of the Thames Valley* (Leeds, 2002), pp. 155–65.

14. Reproduced as fig. 83 in D. and H. Kraus, *Gothic Choir-stalls of Spain* (London, 1986).

15. Other representations of the hares spit-roasting the hunter and boiling his hounds are: one of Erhard Schoen's designs for playing cards of *c.* 1528, the 6-of-Leaves (Geisberg 1308); a marginal illustration by Jorg Glockendon in the *Glockendon Missal* of *c.* 1541 based on an anonymous print; engraved border-strips on the title-page of the *Regula Ordinis Sancti Benedicti* published by Johann Schoeffer in Mainz *c.* 1514x20; and Georg Pencz's woodcut illustration to Hans Sachs's *Die Hasen fangen und praten den Jeger* (1550). The hanging of the hunter from a tree by the hares also features on a German playing card, the 4-of-Leaves, produced by one *Jeronymus* around the middle of the century; somewhat extraordinarily, however, it also appears as part of the title-page decoration of Regnault's Sarum Use *Horae* printed in October 1532. A woodcut attributed to Hans Sebald Beham, *Virgin and Child, with Hares Pursuing a Huntsman*, and dated to the late 1520s, is reproduced as pl. II B in 'Rare Woodcuts in the Ashmolean Museum – II' in *Burlington Magazine*, 63 (1933).

16. M. de Meyer, *De Volks- en Kinderprent in de Nederlanden* (Antwerp and Amsterdam, 1962), p. 429 (my translation).

17. For Konigslütter (Niedersachsen), see *Reallexikon der deutschen Kunstgeschichte* IV (1958), p. 573, Abb. 5; for Murbach (*a.* 1134), see R. Will, *Alsace Romane* (La Pierre-qui-Vire, 1965), p. 130.

18. A variant depicts the hare with a *hound* dangling from the stick over his shoulder, as on f. 161v of the *Gorleston Psalter*, BL Add. MS 49622 (*c.* 1310x25).

19. Wh M 362.

20. BL Royal MS 20.D.IV.

21. A useful discussion of the witch and female sexuality, especially as expressed in the graphic work of the early sixteenth-century German artist, Hans Baldung Grien, is S. Schade, *Schadenzauber und die Magie des Körpers* (Worms, 1983).

22. *De Sancto Matrimonii Sacramento*, not published until 1607 in Antwerp, IX.xvi.I; cit. J.-L. Flandrin, 'Contraception, mariage et relations amoureuses dans l'Occident chrétien' in *Annales ESC* 24 (1969), 1382.

23. Sanchez, op. cit., citing *super Genesium ex Metodio*, cap. 31.

24. The World Turned Upside Down motif of sheep hunting wolves is at least as old as Virgil's eighth *Eclogue* and is also used by Chrétien de Troyes in *Cligès*.

25. In recent years I have noted several examples of the flying pig pressed into the service of commerce, advertising a building society, gas cookers, and most recently, personal computers.

26. M.P. Tilley, *A Dictionary of the Proverbs in England in the Sixteenth and Seventeenth Centuries* (Ann Arbor, 1950), p. 312.

27. 'The land of Catita, where Jack-an-apes flies with his tail in his mouth' in A. Thorndike (ed.), *The Minor Elizabethan Drama. Volume II, Pre-Shakespearean Comedies* (London, 1958), p. 154, lines 701ff.

28. A.G. Rigg, *The Poems of Walter of Wimborne* (Toronto, 1978), 93. 109. 4; a parallel passage in the same author's *De Mundi Scelere* has *uacca uolabit* (the cow will fly), 106.53.

29. For discussion of this particular image see C.M. Armstrong, *The Moraling Prints of Cornelis Anthonisz* (Princeton, 1990), where it is reproduced as fig. 29.

30. M.J. Freeman (ed.), *Oeuvres* (Geneva, 1975), p. 93, line 612. Writing on the illogicality of many contemporary inn-signs in no. 28 of the *Spectator* issued on 2 April 1710, Addison noted that 'Our streets are filled with *blue boars, black swans*, and *red lions*, not to mention *flying-pigs* and *hogs in armour*, with many creatures more extraordinary than any in the deserts of Africa.'

31. M.R. James, *St George's Chapel, Windsor: The Woodwork of the Choir* (1933). The stalls were carved 1477x83.

32. cf. M. Laird, *English Misericords* (London, 1986), p. 30, who thought it 'obviously illustrates some forgotten story or proverb . . . [the sparrows] perhaps having been forced to work for the miller in return for stealing grain?'

33. For literary misogyny, see, for example, F.L. Utley, *The Crooked Rib* (Columbus, 1944), and K.M. Rogers, *The Troublesome Helpmate* (Seattle, 1966).

34. cit. MED *s.v. cat.*

35. A.-A. Dubois, *Les Rues et Enseignes d'Amiens* (Amiens, 1889).

36. B. Lillywhite, *London Signs* (London, 1972).

37. I. and P. Opie, *The Oxford Dictionary of Nursery Rhymes* (Oxford, 1951), p. 203.

38. As, indeed, does Skelton, fifty years earlier, in his *Garland of Laurel*, l. 740f.

39. cit. BL MS Harley 6563, f. 40 (1300x25) as an example – M. Remnant, *English Bowed Instruments from Anglo-Saxon to Tudor Times* (Oxford, 1986). A mid-fourteenth-century example from the margin of a French *Roman de la Rose* manuscript, B.N. MS fr. 25526, f. 151v, is cit. Randall *s.v.* 'cat with vielle'.

40. M. Gibson *et al.*, *Medieval Manuscripts on Merseyside* (Liverpool, 1993) – the manuscript in question is no. 4, Liverpool, City Libraries, MS f. 091 PSA 65/32036.

41. BL Lansdowne MS 420, f. 12v.

42. F.W. Reader, 'Tudor Mural Paintings in the Lesser Houses in Buckinghamshire' in *Archaeological Journal*, 89 (1932), p. 167f., and pl. 22.

43. Reproduced in C.G. Heise, *Fabelwelt des Mittelalters* (Berlin, 1936), as Abb. 112.

44. T.B. Husband, *The Luminous Image. Painted Glass Roundels in the Lowlands, 1480–1560* (New York, 1995), cat. no. 24.

45. See M. Jones, 'Washing the ass's head: exploring the non-religious prints', in McDonald, op. cit. (London, 2003).

46. I have supplemented the list in W. Schouwink, *Der wilde Eber in Gottes Weinberg: zur Darstellung des Schweins in Literatur und Kunst des Mittelalters* (Sigmaringen, 1985), p. 101. In Flanders, there is another example at Hoogstraeten (1532x46), and in England, a carving of a bagpiping pig has been let into the modern pulpit at Ribbesford, while another mid-sixteenth-century example appears on a bench-end at Drax, reproduced as pl. 71 in B.D. Palmer, *The Early Art of the West Riding of Yorkshire* (Kalamazoo, 1990), and another bench-end example at Branston, Lincs., plays not to its piglets but to two women and a non-specific quadruped.

47. D. and H. Kraus, *The Gothic Choir-stalls of Spain* (London, 1986), pl. 28.

48. For example, in two manuscripts of *c.* 1300, cited by Randall, in the Duc de Berry's *Très Riches Heures* of *a.* 1416, and in a fifteenth-century breviary now in Geraarsdbergen Abbey and reproduced as fig. 11 in M. Smeyers, *'Bijzondere randversieringen in een 15de-eeuwse brevier'* in *Spiegel Historiael*, 4 (1969), p. 77.

49. K.L. Scott, 'Sow-and-Bagpipe Imagery in the Miller's Portrait' in *Review of English Studies*, 18 (1967), pp. 287–90, here p. 287f.

50. G.C. Druce, 'The Sow and Pigs; a Study in Metaphor' in *Archaeologia Cantiana*, 46 (1934), pp. 1–6.

51. C.J.P. Cave, *Roof Bosses in Medieval Churches* (Cambridge, 1948), p. 70.

52. BL Harley MS 4379.

53. BL Harley MS 6563, ff. 41v–42.

54. F.L. Utley, 'When Nettles in Winter Bring Forth Roses Red' in *Publications of the Modern Languages Association of America*, 60 (1945), pp. 346–55.

55. That is, spoonbill.

56. That is, shrill trumpet.

57. Printed in T. Wright and J.O. Halliwell, *Reliquiae Antiquae* (London, 1841–3), I, pp. 85f., from the late fifteenth-century manuscript, National Library of Wales,

Porkington MS 10, f. 152; some of these same animal musicians including the sow who harped 'Robin Hood' recur in another contemporary manuscript, Edinburgh, Advocates' Library, MS 19. 3. 1., printed in ibid., p. 81.

58. In the Bible which is now BL Royal MS 15. D. III (*c.* 1415), reproduced in M. Meiss, *French Painting in the Time of Jean de Berry: the Late Fourteenth Century and the Patronage of the Duke* (London, 1967).

59. T. Tindall Wildridge, *The Misereres of Beverley Minster*, pp. 24f. In fact, the famous minstrels' pier in the parish church is to be dated to the early 1520s as it commemorates the money the guild gave towards the cost of erecting this particular pier when the nave was rebuilt after the crossing-tower collapsed onto it in 1520 – see N. Pevsner, *Yorkshire, York and the East Riding* (Harmondsworth, 1972), p. 82.

60. pers. comm.

61. W. Schouwink, *Der wilde Eber in Gottes Weinberg: zur Darstellung des Schweins in Literatur und Kunst des Mittelalters* (Sigmaringen, 1985), p. 101.

62. Randall, figs 307–11; the refinement is found in Paris, B.N. MS lat. 14284, f. 15v (Randall, fig. 311). For English literary references see Whiting S 419 (from 1340); for similar 'overkill', cf. also F20 'To throw a falchion at a fly' (*c.* 1303), from French.

63. The best discussion is L. Randall, 'The Snail in Gothic Marginal Warfare' in *Speculum*, 37 (1962), pp. 358–67, supplemented by R. Pinon, 'From Illumination to Folksong: The Armed Snail, a Motif of Topsy-Turvy Land' in V. Newall (ed.), *Folklore Studies in the Twentieth Century: Proceedings of the Centenary Conference of the Folklore Society* (Woodbridge, 1980), pp. 76–113.

64. cit. Pinon, p. 79.

65. G.C. Heseltine (ed.) (London, 1931). This work is certainly an excellent claimant to the disputed category of 'popular

literature,' for discussions of which at this period see F.B. Brevart, '*Spätmitteralterliche Trivialliteratur: methodologische Überlegungen zu ihrer Bestimmung und Erforschung*' in *Archiv für das Studium der neueren Sprachen und Literaturen*, 224:1 (1987), pp. 14–33, and T.Y. Heffernan, *The Popular Literature of Medieval England* (1988).

66. Pinon, op. cit., p. 81.

67. A convenient, though only partial, edition is to be found in A.W. Pollard, *English Miracle Plays, Moralities and Interludes* (8th rev. edn, Oxford, 1927), pp. 126–45 and notes on pp. 213–8; the lines quoted are 16–18.

68. cf. the following proverbial similes: *arwe as an hare*, *c.* 1300 (*Robert of Gloucester*, line 457); *dredful as a hare*, *a.* 1425, *a.* 1449 [cit. Wh H 111]; *coward as a hare*, 1456 [cit. Wh H 112]; *couard comme lievre*, 1370s (Oresme, *Ethiques*).

69. And note how in *The Huntyng of the Hare* printed in the *Book of St Albans* (1486), E v b, the hare is termed *The coward with the short tayle* translating the Anglo-French *la cowarde ou la court cowe*.

70. Randall, fig. 355: Trinity College, Cambridge MS B.11.22, f. 114v (Flemish, early fourteenth century). The window in Notre Dame is reproduced in E. Mâle, *The Gothic Image* (Fontana edn, 1961), p. 121, fig. 65. For the tokens, see A. Forgeais, *Collection de Plombs Historiés trouvés dans la Seine*, vol. IV (Paris, 1865), pp. 224–7. The Amiens pair is reproduced in Mâle, op. cit., p. 122, fig. 66.

71. J. Jönsjö, *Studies on Middle English Nicknames, I: Compounds* (Lund, 1979), s.n.; cf. also, *Pykhare*, P.H. Reaney, *The Origin of English Surnames* (London, 1967), p. 288. Support for an ironic interpretation is perhaps to be found in the folktale of the Seven Swabians (Grimm no. 119).

72. Nachträge to *Matthias Lexers Mittelhochdeutsches Taschenwörterbuch* (Stuttgart, 1976).

73. cit. R. Axton, *European Drama of the Middle Ages* (London, 1974), p. 44.

74. cit. Wh K 50, from a poem of *c.* 1325 on *The Times of Edward II*, 252 in ed. T. Wright *Political Poems and Songs*, (London, 1859), p. 334.

75. cit. Wh M 751.

76. cf. the following citation from the *OED s.v. feeble*: 1631 T. Powell, *Tom All Trades* (New Shakspeare Society), p. 157: 'The Taylor, who had thrust himselfe in amongst the Nobilitie and was so discovered, and handled from hand to foot, till the Guard delivered him at the great Chamber door, and cryed, "farewell, good feeble!"'

77. Shakespeare, *Henry IV Part 2*, III.2. pp. 156–8 and 262–4.

78. *Northward Hoe* (1607), ii, i.

79. British Library, Yates Thompson MS 8 (*a.* 1304), f. 192; on f. 288 he is depicted borne over the shoulder of a hare.

80. Motif no. J 1754, 'Ass thought to be hare'.

81. See F. Sieber, *Volk und Volkstümliche Motivik im Festwerk des Barocks* (Berlin, 1960).

82. *Hamlet*, II.ii.203f.

83. '*Si les nues tomboyent esperoyt prendre les alouettes toutes rousties*' (*Gargantua*, cap. 11); cf. from Palsgrave's *Acolastus* (1540), 'Do thou but gape, and I shall make larkes fall in to thy mouthe.'

84. For example, J. Camerarius, *Symbolorum et emblematum ex aquatilibus et reptilibus* (Nürnberg, 1604), emblem no. 54 with motto, *Orbis iter*.

85. Reproduced and discussed, but without recognising the image's origin, in a most interesting paper by J. de Coo, 'Die Bemalten Holzteller, Bekannte und Neuentdeckte; ihr Schmuck und seine Herkunft' in *Wallraf Richartz Jahrbuch*, 37 (1975), pp. 85–118. I confess I do not understand the import of the fifteenth-century woodcut of the lobster-rider reproduced as Abb. 5 in J. Knape, '*Der Finckenritter – Text und Untersuchung*' in *Philobiblon*, 35 (1991).

86. Murner, *Von dem grossen Lutherischen Narren*, lines 1961ff., reproduced as Abb. 2 and Abb. 3 in Knape, op. cit.

87. Wh G 27, G 376, G 377.

88. J.B. Smith, 'Whim-whams for a goose's bridle' in *Lore and Language*, 3 (1980), pp. 32–49.

89. For calf-bridles (*brides à veaux*) in Rabelais, see Sainéan, *La Langue de Rabelais* (Paris, 1922), I, pp. 350–2.

90. J. Jönsjö, op. cit., s.n. (*c.* 1346).

91. Ed. W.E. Mead [= EETS no. 173], 135, line 3526.

92. cit. R.W. Dent, *Proverbial Language in English Drama Exclusive of Shakespeare 1495–1616, an Index* (Berkeley 1984), C 758.

93. *Gargantua* (1534), end of cap. 12; other examples of the bridled goose are ibid., Prologue; *Pantagruel* (1532), cap. 29; *Le Tiers Livre* (1546). Cf. John Burningham's delightful children's book, *Would you rather* . . . (London, 1978), where, for example, one set of choices reads, 'Would you rather have . . . a monkey to tickle . . . a bear to read to . . . a cat to box with . . . a dog to skate with . . . a pig to ride . . . or a goat to dance with?'

94. E. Haenel, *Der Sächsischen Kurfürsten Turnierbücher* (Frankfurt, 1910), *Turnierbuch des Herzogs Johann Friedrich des Großmütigen*, f. 146.

95. Reproduced in J.O. Hand, *The Age of Bruegel: Netherlandish Drawings in the 16th Century* (Cambridge, 1987).

96. Wh S 533. Though it is tempting to read *hogge* for *dogge* in the otherwise unique 'It becomyth not a dogge to bere a saddle' in the 1492 printing of the English *Dialogue of Solomon and Marcolph*, the Latin original has *canis*, ibid. D 311 (sole cit.).

97. The *Oxford Dictionary of English Proverbs'* last citation is from Swift in 1738, but the Opies in their *Oxford Book of English Nursery-Rhymes* include a nonsense rhyme beginning 'The sow came in with the saddle, the little pig rocked the cradle . . .', which they date to

c. 1760, and believe 'originated in the recitation of the mummers'; they further reproduce the frontispiece to the 1816 edition of Marshall's *Mother Goose's Melody*, which portrays both the little pig rocking the cradle and the saddled sow, and the motif certainly survived into the nineteenth century, appearing, for instance, in Halliwell's 1849 *Nursery Rhymes and Tales*, in a nonsense tale which begins, 'I saddled my sow with a sieve full of buttermilk, and leaped nine miles beyond the moon into the land of Temperance. . . .'

98. Tilley, op. cit., C.758, and Wh C 501, from a poem of *c.* 1450.

99. M. Jones, 'The Dutch Cow' (Elizabethan political cartoon), Appendix to article by M. Bath, 'Dirtie devises: Thomas Combe and the Metamorphosis of Ajax' in P.H. Daly and D.S. Russell (eds), *Emblematic Perceptions: Festschrift for William S. Heckscher* (Baden-Baden, 1997), pp. 23–32.

100. Reproduced, for example, in H. Pleij, '*De zot als maatschappelijk houvast in de overgang van middeleeuwen naar moderne tijd*' in *Groniek*, 109 (1990), afb. 5. A somewhat more sophisticated version of this woodcut (reproduced in Mezger, op. cit., as Abb. 8) was used as the title-page illustration to the Latin translation of the series of sermons based on Brant's *Narrenschiff* by the famous preacher Geiler von Kaysersberg, *Navicula sive speculum fatuorum* (Strabourg, 1510). Here the horses are more clearly harnessed to the wrong end of the cart and the wheels are shown set at right angles to the direction of travel. In addition, it is clear that in this version, the fool holding the whip by the wrong end of its handle, hits himself on the head with it.

101. Wh C 60.

102. I have been unable to locate 'the olde mens saying . . . that when Antichrist shuld come, the rootes of the trees shulde growe upwarde'.

103. Entitled *Il Mondo Alla Riversa*, the sheet is reproduced in David Kunzle's important essay, 'World Upside Down: the Iconography of a European Broadsheet Type' in B.B. Abrahams (ed.), *The Reversible World: Essays in Symbolic Inversion* (Cornell UP, 1978), where it is reproduced as fig. 11 on p. 44. It should be noted, however, that here it is oxen which are yoked behind the cart – the horse version seems to be peculiar to English. 'A carte and the horse sett behinde to the tayle of the same' is the 107th *Picture*, that is, the emblem proper, in Palmer's emblem manuscript of 1565, published by John Manning as *The Emblems of Thomas Palmer: Two Hundred Poosees* (New York, 1988).

104. In S. Thompson, *Motif Index of Folk Literature* (Bloomington 1966); v. also E.W(ind)., 'Milking the Bull and the He-Goat' in *JWCI* (Journal of the Warburg and Courtauld Institute), 6 (1943), p. 225. The earliest-known English literary attestation of bull-milking dates from *c.* 1548, see M.P. Tilley, *A Dictionary of the Proverbs in England in the Sixteenth and Seventeenth Centuries* (Ann Arbor, 1950).

105. C. Plummer, *Lives of the Irish Saints* (Oxford, 1922), ii.79, and J. Pinkerton, *Scottish Saints* (London, 1789), I, p. 141.

106. The ballad was licensed in the *Stationers' Register* in 1588, but the first extant edition is to be found in Ravenscroft's *Deuteromelia* (1609). In Anton's *Moriomachia* (1613) the Fairy Queen tries to milk the bull Pheander.

107. C. Grössinger, 'Humour and folly in English misericords of the first quarter of the sixteenth century' in D. Williams (ed.), *Early Tudor England* (Woodbridge, 1989), p. 76.

108. M. Jones, 'German and Flemish Prints as Design-Sources for the Misericords in St George's Chapel, Windsor (1477X84)' in Keen and Scartt (eds), *Windsor*, pp. 155–65.

109. f. 118v. Reproduced as Randall, fig. 93.

110. The poem is printed as no. 413A in R.L. Greene, *The Early English Carols* (2nd edn, Oxford, 1977).

111. J. Scattergood, op. cit., p. 225, line 418, and p. 153, line 457, respectively.

112. A.J. Fletcher, 'Line 30 of the *Man of Law's Tale* and the Medieval Malkyn' in *English Language Notes*, 24 (1986), pp. 17–19.

113. P.H. Reaney, *The Origin of English Surnames* (London, 1967), p. 289.

114. J. Mann (ed.), *Ysengrimus* (Leiden, 1987), v. 128; see further, D. Gerhardt, *'Vogelmilch – Metapher oder Motiv?'* in *Semantische Hefte*, 2 (1974–5), pp. 1–50; 3 (1976–7), pp. 81–6.

115. *die Hühner melken wollen*, cit. LSR *s.v. Huhn, Hühnchen . . .* To which one might add, from the Innsbruck Easter Play, the dismissive retort, *get hen, ir sult dy gensse melke!* cit. Gerhardt, op. cit., p. 62, n. 130. For the *Speculum Stultorum*, see J.H. Mozley and R.R. Raymo (eds) (Berkeley, 1960), line 645.

116. Randall, figs 581–4 from, Baltimore, Walters Art Gallery MS 82, f. 179v (Flemish, early fourteenth century); Paris, B.N. MS fr. 95, f. 343r (Picard, late thirteenth century) and New Haven, Yale University Library, *Lancelot del Lac* MS, f. 31r (part of same manuscript); Oxford, Bodleian Library MS Douce 6, f. 93v (Flemish, 1300x1325).

117. L. Randall, 'A Medieval Slander' in *Art Bulletin*, 42 (1960), pp. 25–40.

118. K. Euling, *Das Priamel bis Hans Rosenplüt* (Breslau, 1905), pp. 563–4.

119. Conveniently reproduced from La Perrière in col. 1451 of A. Henkel and A. Schöne, *Emblemata: Handbuch zur Sinnbildkunst des XVI und XVII Jahrhunderts* (2nd edn, Stuttgart, 1976). In F.C. Tubach, *Index Exemplorum* (Helsinki, 1969), *exemplum* no. 4841, from an English *Liber Exemplorum* of *c.* 1275, refers to 'thoughts that cannot be controlled any more than the wind can be caught'. See also Erasmus, *Adagia*, I.iv.63. A well-known literary use of the motif is to be found in Wyatt's sonnet, 'Whoso list to hunt I know where is an hind', which can be dated to 1527 and includes the line, 'Sithens in a net I seek to hold the wind.'

120. For such mock-compensations in medieval law, see R. Stratmann, *Die Scheinbussen im mittelalterlichen Recht* (Frankfurt, 1978).

121. The fiddler in his *mi-parti* points at the man's shadow which is his compensation in the Heidelberg manuscript of the Sachsenspiegel (*c.* 1330), reproduced in W. Koschorreck, *Der Sachsenspiegel in Bildern* (Frankfurt, 1976), p. 97.

CHAPTER NINE

1. See L. Lawton, 'The illustration of late medieval secular texts, with special reference to Lydgate's *Troy Book*' in D. Pearsall (ed.), *Manuscripts and Readers in Fifteenth Century England* (Cambridge, 1983), pp. 41–69.

2. D.J.A. Ross, *Alexander historiatus* (London, 1963); idem., *Illustrated Medieval Alexander-Books in Germany and the Netherlands* (London, 1971); idem., *Studies in the Alexander Romance* (London, 1985). For the most popular motif as seen, for example, on misericords at Beverley St Mary's and at Whalley, see I. Michael, *Alexander's Flying Machine: the History of a Legend* (Southampton, 1974), and C. Settis-Frugoni, *Historia Alexandri elevati per griphos ad aerem origine, iconografia e fortuna di una tema* (Rome, 1973).

3. R.S. and L.H. Loomis, *Arthurian Legends in Medieval Art* (New York, 1938). This great book is now supplemented by Alison Stones, 'Arthurian Art since Loomis' in (1988–9), pp. 21–78.

4. See, for example, D.D.R. Owen, *The Legend of Roland* (London, 1973).

5. H. Frühmorgen-Voss, *'Mittelhochdeutsche weltliche Literatur und ihre Illustration'* in

N. Ott (ed.), *Text und Illustration im Mittelalter* (Munich, 1975), pp. 1–118.

6. *PMLA*, 30 (1915), p. 127.

7. BL Royal MS 10. E. IV, ff. 75–79v, and Yates Thompson MS 13, ff. 12–14, respectively.

8. See A.G. Brodeur, 'The Grateful Lion' in *PMLA*, 39 (1924), pp. 485–524, and additional examples cited by S. Wenzel, 'The Joyous Art of Preaching or the Preacher and the Fabliau' in *Anglia*, 97 (1979), 307. F.C. Tubach, *Index Exemplorum* (Helsinki, 1969), no. 3057.

9. E.M.R. Ditmas, 'The Cult of Arthurian Relics' in *Folklore*, 75 (1964), pp. 19–33, and idem., 'More Arthurian Relics' in *Folklore*, 77 (1966), pp. 91–104.

10. N.H. Nicolas, *Testamenta Vetusta* (London, 1826), p. 154.

11. J. Westwood, *Albion, a Guide to Legendary Britain* (London, 1986), p. 222.

12. In 1414 at Guines in the marches of Calais, Richard Beauchamp, Earl of Warwick, on the third day of a series of jousts, wore the arms of Guy quartered with Beauchamp.

13. A.B. Rance, 'The Bevis and Ascupart panels, Bargate Museum, Southampton' in *Proceedings of the Hampshire Field Club Archaeological Society*, 42 (1986), pp. 147–53.

14. L. Brownrigg, 'The Taymouth Hours and the Romance of *Bevis of Hampton*' in P. Beal and J. Griffiths (eds), *English Manuscript Studies 1100–1700*, 1 (1989), pp. 230–41.

15. Was it perhaps the *Beauve de Hanstonne* commissioned from Nicolas Bataille in the 1480s by Louis d'Orléans-Valois, together with a *Regnault de Montauban*?

16. J. Strachey (ed.), *Rotuli Parliamentorum*, IV (London, 1832), p. 230.

17. *Journal of the Warburg and Courtauld Institutes*, 39 (1976), p. 262.

18. As noted by Westwood, op. cit., p. 82.

19. As expressed by R.S. Loomis, 'A phantom tale of female ingratitude' in *Modern Philology*, 14 (1916–17), pp. 175–9.

20. Most recently by Marian Campbell in her entry to the item (cat. no. 581) in J.

Alexander and P. Binski (eds), *Age of Chivalry* (London, 1987), pp. 458–9.

21. See, for example, H. Frühmorgen-Voss, '*Tristan und Isolde in mittelalterlichen Bildzeugnissen*' in *Deutsche Vierteljahresschrift für Literaturwissenschaft und Geistesgeschichte*, 47 (1974), pp. 645–63; idem., 'Tristan und Isolde in mittelalterlichen Bildzeugnissen' in N. Ott (ed.), *Text und Illustration im Mittelalter* (Munich, 1975), pp. 119–81; D. Buschinger, '*L'iconographie de Tristan*' in *Etudes germaniques*, 29 (1974).

22. D. Fouquet, 'Die Baumgartenszene' in *Zeitschrift für deutsche Philologie*, 92 (1973) p. 360–, and M.A. Hall and D.D.R. Owen, 'A Tristram and Iseult mirror-case from Perth: reflections on the production and consumption of Romance culture' in *Tayside and Fife Archaeological Journal*, 4 (1998), pp. 150–65. I am grateful for Dr Hall's acknowledgement of my own work on this piece prior to his publication of it; my own interpretation of the scene differs somewhat from his in that I see the knight as Mark, not Tristan.

23. J.A. Rushing, *Images of Adventure: Ywain in the Visual Arts* (Pennsylvania UP, 1995).

24. idem., 'The Enville Ywain misericord' in *Bulletin bibliographique de la Société internationale arthurienne* 38 (1986), pp. 279–88.

25. F. Blomefield, *An Essay Towards a Topographical History of the County of Norfolk . . .*, vol. 4 *The History of the City and County of Norwich*, Pt 2 (London, 1806), p. 96.

26. A.R. Wagner, 'The Swan Badge and the Swan Knight' in *Archaeologia*, 97 (1959), pp. 127–38.

27. *The Library*, 14 (1992), p. 292, n. 32.

28. In fact, a thirteenth-century Syrian glass beaker now kept in the Victoria and Albert Museum – see Westwood, op. cit., pp. 303–5.

29. Cambrai MS 103, f. 314, reproduced as Randall, fig. 652.

30. J. Cherry, 'The Dunstable Swan Jewel' in *Journal of the British Archaeological Association*, 3rd Series 32 (1969), pp. 38–53.

31. J. Evans, *Pattern* (Oxford, 1931), p. 132.

32. The two English examples are taken from J. Evans, *English Art 1307–1461* (Oxford, 1949), p. 93.

33. One of the earliest illustrated French manuscripts of the story is Paris, B.N. MS fr. 766, f. 93r (1300x1310).

34. J.B.B. de Roquefort, *De l'état de la poésie françoise dans les XIIe et XIIIe siècles* (Paris, 1815), p. 141 – but date of painting is uncertain.

35. P. Burke, *Popular Culture in Early Modern Europe* (London, 1978), pl. 13.

36. cat. no. 73 in *Die Kunst der Graphik IV: zwischen Renaissance und Barock* (Vienna, 1967).

37. J. Evans, *Art in Medieval France 987–1498* (London, 1948), p. 232.

38. R. Muchembled, *Popular Culture and Elite Culture in France 1400–1750* (English trans., London, 1985), p. 129.

39. Evans, op. cit., p. 231.

40. Attached to a rental of 1 August 1313 in the Rijksarchief Gent, fonds der Rijke Klaren ('Riches Claires').

41. *l'istoire des enfans de Regnault de Montaubant* recorded in an inventory of the Duc de Savoie's Château de Chambery, taken in 1498, is presumably the result of the clerk's momentary confusion.

42. HMC 8th Report, Appendix, item 629a.

43. There were various French editions, including one issued at Lyon *c.* 1480–5, and another printed by Denis Janot in Paris in 1508.

44. Preface to Caxton's *Le Morte D'Arthur* (1485). The heroes in question were traditionally: Hector, Alexander, Julius Caesar (the Three Pagans); Joshua, David, Judas Maccabeus (the Three Jews); Charlemagne, Arthur, Godfrey of Bouillon (the Three Christians).

45. H.K. Cameron, 'The Fourteenth Century Flemish Brasses at King's Lynn' in *Archaeological Journal*, 136 (1979), pp. 151–8.

46. Strachey, op. cit., p. 232.

47. *Archaeologia*, 21 (1827), p. 257.

48. F.J. Furnivall, *The Fifty Earliest English Wills in the Court of Probate, London, A.D. 1387–1439* [= EETS OS 78] (London, 1882), p. 133.

49. cit. C. Woodforde, *Norwich School* (London, 1950), 152 from Blomefield's *History of Norfolk*, iv.110.

50. C. Brown and R.H. Robbins (eds), *The Index of Middle English Verse* (New York, 1943), no. 3881, verses to welcome Prince Edward spoken by the Worthies. For other ME verses on the Nine Worthies see IMEV 1181, 1181.5, 4247.

51. Another such set of *Preuses* is perhaps implied by the existence of a lone Penthesilia in the cathedral at Angers.

52. Paris, B.N. MS fr. 12559, ff. 125r and 125v, respectively.

53. P. d'Ancona, *'Gli Affreschi del Castello di Manta nel Saluzzese'* in *L'Arte*, 8 (1905), pp. 94–198.

54. The fullest account is E. Croft-Murray, 'Lambert Barnard: An English Renaissance Painter' in *The Archaeological Journal*, 113 (1956), pp. 108–25, esp. pp. 118–22.

55. Cambridge, Trinity College MS 599, f. 110v. For another such set of ME verses, see *IMEV* 1016, Oxford, Bodley 6493, f. 38v, *þe neyne worshipfullest ladyes*.

56. J.C. Holt, *Robin Hood* (2nd edn, London, 1989), p. 187.

57. S. Foister, 'Paintings and other works of art in sixteenth-century English inventories' in *Burlington Magazine*, 123 (1981), pp. 273–82, here, p. 277.

58. F.G. Emmison, *Elizabethan Life: Morals and the Church Courts* (Chelmsford, 1973), p. 22.

59. A good study of the poem in question is R.J. Menner, 'The Man in the Moon and hedging' in *Journal of English and Germanic Philology*, 48 (1949), pp. 1–14.

60. C. Babbington (ed.), *The Repressor of Overmuch Blaming of the Clergy* (London, 1860), p. 155.

61. PRO P348.

62. Reaney, op. cit., p. 58.

63. J. Muller-Meiningen, *Die Morisken-Tanzer* (Munich, 1984), p. 679.

64. O. Schutte, '*Braunschweiger Pferdenamen des 16. und 17 Jahrhunderts*' in *Zeitschrift für deutsche Wortforschung*, 13 (1911–12), p. 240.

65. H. Wanner, '*Hundenamen aus dem Anfang des 16. Jahrhunderts [1504]*' in K.F. Müller (ed.), *Beiträge zur Sprachwissenschaft und Volkskunde, Festschrift für E. Ochs zum 60. Geburtstag* (Lahr, 1951), pp. 219–23.

66. M.C. Byrne (ed.), *The Lisle Letters* (abridged edn, Harmondsworth, 1985), pp. 197f.

67. L. Wüthrich, *Der sogenannte 'Holbein-Tisch'* (Zurich, 1990), pp. 108ff.

68. G. Calmann, 'The picture of Nobody' in *JWCI*, 23 (1960), pp. 66–104.

69. cit. J. Weingartner, '*Die Profane Wandmalerei Tirols im Mittelalter*' in *Münchener Jahrbuch der bildenden Kunst N.F.* 5 (1928), p. 54.

70. Failure to spot this derivation has led Paul Vandenbroeck uncharacteristically astray in his otherwise superb exhibition catalogue, *Beeld van der Andere, Vertoog over het Zelf* (Antwerp, 1987), pp. 139–40.

71. There is a Parisian single sheet of the Wandering Jew in the style of the Rue de Montorgueil dated 1616, published by Nicholas de Mathonière and signed by A.C. in the Collection Hennin (vol. 20) of the Cabinet des Estampes of the Bibliothèque nationale in Paris.

72. First reproduced and discussed by R. Saulnier in 'Le Bon Serviteur' in *Dawna Sztuka*, 1 (1938), pp. 193–208.

73. M. Jones, 'Engraved works recorded in the *Stationers' Registers*, 1562–1656: a listing and commentary' in *Journal of the Walpole Society*, 64 (2002), pp. 1–68, here, p. 11.

74. See articles by Herbert Chitty in *The Wykehamist*, issues of 19 March and 4 November 1924.

75. See M. Jones, 'Washing the ass's head: exploring the non-religious prints' in McDonald, *The Print Collection*, (London, 2003). The inventory entry quoted in translation is no. 2571.

76. J. Evans, *Pattern* (Oxford, 1931), I, p. 152, n. 3.

77. The manuscripts are BL Add. MS 32678 and Yale University, Beinecke Rare Book and Manuscript Library MS 404, respectively; both these examples are cited from A. Bennett, 'A book designed for a noblewoman: an illustrated *Manuel des Péchés* of the 13th century' in ed. L. Brownrigg, *Medieval Book Production. Assessing the Evidence* (Los Altos Hills, 1990), p. 168 and n. 30. Bennet suggests a third manuscript, BL Cott. Cleopatra C. XI, in which Anselm's treatise on virtues and vices is illustrated, but these symbolic pictures are not illustrations of *exempla*.

78. BL Royal MS 10. E. IV.

79. BL Add. MS 62925. It is not recognised, for example, in N.J. Morgan, 'The artists of the Rutland Psalter' in *British Library Journal*, 13 (1987), pp. 159–85.

80. See E. Hermes (ed.), *The Disciplina Clericalis of Petrus Alfonsi* (London, 1977), p. 116.

81. W.H. Hulme, *Peter Alphonse's Disciplina Clericalis, English Translation from the Fifteenth Century Worcester Cathedral MS F 172* (Cleveland, Ohio, 1919).

82. To judge from the substantial bibliography devoted to it under Fable no. 512, '*Befreite Schlange, Mann und Fuchs*' in G. Dicke and K. Grubmüller, *Die Fabeln des Mittelalters und der Frühen Neuzeit* (Munich, 1988), pp. 594–7.

83. For a discussion of this specific motif see S.P. Menefee, '*The Merry Maidens* and the *Noce de Pierre*' in *Folklore*, 85 (1974), pp. 23–42. Leslie Grinsell includes a section on *Petrifaction* in his excellent *Folklore of*

Prehistoric Sites in Britain (Newton Abbot, 1976), pp. 54–6. See also, M. Chesnutt, 'The Colbeck Legend in English Tradition of the Twelfth and Thirteenth Centuries' in V. Newall (ed.), Folklore Studies in the Twentieth Century, (Woodbridge, 1980), pp. 158–66.

84. E.E. Metzner, *Zur frühesten Geschichte der europäischen Balladen-dichtung. Der Tanz in Kölbigk* (Frankfurt, 1972).

85. Oxford, Bodleian Library, Bodley MS 614 (*c.* 1120x40). As first pointed out by M.R. James, *Marvels of the East* (Oxford, 1929), pp. 31–2. For a more recent study of this text, see P. McGurk *et al.*, *An Eleventh Century Anglo-Saxon Illustrated Miscellany* (Copenhagen, 1983).

86. Grinsell, op. cit., p. 90.

87. J. Krzyzanowski, 'Two Old-Polish Folktales' in *Fabula*, 2 (1958), pp. 83–93.

88. O. Odenius, '*Hon som var värre än den onde* i svensk tradition' in *Den ljusa medeltiden. Studien tillägnade Aron Andersson* (Stockholm, 1984), pp. 198–218, with English summary.

89. R.L. Frautschi (ed.), *Pierre Gringore's Les Fantasies de Mère Sote* (Chapel Hill, 1962), pp. 185f.

90. It is also found in an early sixteenth-century hand written on the flyleaf opposite the first page of Cambridge University Library MS Dd.5.76 – H.A. Person, *Cambridge Middle English Lyrics* (Seattle, 1962), p. 54.

91. *The demau[n]des Ioyous* (London, 1511), p. 2.

92. See M. Jones, '*Such pretty things would soon be gone*: the Neglected Genres of Popular Verse 1480–1650' in M. Hattaway (ed.), *A Companion to English Renaissance Literature and Culture* (Oxford, 2000), pp. 442–63. The Hesiod passage is discussed by E. Campanile, 'Indogermanische Dichtersprache' in W. Meid (ed.), *Studien zum Indogermanischen Wortschatz* (Innsbrück, 1987), pp. 23ff., where the Sanskrit, Old Czech and Old English examples are quoted. I add the Middle French example

from J.W. Hassel, *Amorous Games: A Critical Edition of Les Adevineaux Amoureux* (Austin, 1974), no. 356. L. Vasvari, 'The battle of Flesh and Lent in the *Libro del Arcipreste*: Gastro-genital rites of reversal' in *La Coronica*, 20 (1991), p. 1ff., gives further references to this international riddle (p. 5).

93. H. Oesterley (ed.), *Gesta Romanorum* (Berlin, 1872), Tale 124. F.C. Tubach, *Index Exemplorum* (Helsinki, 1969), no. 1997.

94. Motif no. H 506.3.

95. See G. Dicke and K. Grubmüller, *Die Fabeln des Mittelalters und der Neuzeit* (Munich, 1988); and for fables in medieval art, D.Lämke, *Mittelalterliche Tierfabeln und ihre Beziehungen zur bildenden Kunst in Deutschland* (Greifswald, 1937), and D. Peil, 'Beobachtungen zum Verhältnis von Text und Bild in der Fabelillustration des Mittelalters und der frühen Neuzeit' in W. Harms (ed.), *Text und Bild, Bild und Text* (Stuttgart, 1990), pp. 150–67.

96. For two fourteenth-century examples of this fable carved in the Polish churches of Gniezno and Tarnowie, see M. Gutowski, *Komizm w polskiej sztuce gotyckiej* (Warsaw, 1973), pls 56–7, pp. 132–3; for examples on Spanish misericords see I. Mateo Gomez, 'Fabulas, refranes y emblemas, en las sillerias de coro goticas espanolas' in *Archivo Espanol de Arte*, 49 (1976), pp. 145–60.

97. Another eleventh-century series of fable representations once adorned the refectory of the monastery of St-Benoît-sur-Loire – the Latin texts of the fables together with their morals are given in J. von Schlosser, *Quellenbuch zur Kirchengeschichte* (Wien, 1896), p. 187.

98. The best study of the fables as a whole is H. Chefneux, '*Les fables dans la tapisserie de Bayeux*' in *Romania*, 60 (1934), pp. 1–35, 153–94, and more recently, W.B. Yapp, 'Animals in medieval art: the Bayeux Tapestry as an example' in *Journal of Medieval History*, 13 (1987), pp. 15–73, who

convincingly demonstrated that one of the tapestry's border birds derives from a Bestiary *assida*, and thus – as it is agreed to be the work of late Saxon embroiderers – implies the existence of an illuminated Anglo-Saxon Bestiary. M.R. James published an early list of the books in Peterborough monastic library which also included a Saxon Bestiary – see his *Lists of Manuscripts formerly in the Peterborough Abbey Library* [= Transactions of the Bibliographical Society Supplement 5] (London, 1926).

99. D.J. Bernstein, *The Mystery of the Bayeux Tapestry* (London, 1986), p. 27.

100. ibid., p. 131.

101. Ed. V.F. Kopnig, *Les Miracles de Nostre Dame par Gautier de Coinci* (Geneva, 1966) Vol. III, p. 30 (line 170).

102. A recent monograph devoted to the motif is K. Rodin, *Raven predikar for gassen* (Uppsala, 1983), with English summary. See also Dicke and Grubmüller, op. cit., no. 616, Wolf und Gänse II, *'Nachdem der Wolf (Fuchs) zu den Gänsen (Hühnern) gepredigt hat, reisst er sie'*; it is noticeable, however, that even this definitive study could only find a single, very late literary account of this episode, long post-dating the representations in art.

103. BL Royal MS 10. E. IV, f. 49v; other examples of the preaching fox in English manuscripts are the *Rutland Psalter* (BL Add. MS 62925, f. 98v (*c.* 1260)), *Queen Mary's Psalter* (BL Royal MS 2. B, VII 5.157v. (1300x25)), the *Gorleston Psalter* (BL Add. MS 49622, ff. 47r and 143v (*c.* 1310x25)), and the *Douai Psalter* (Douai, bib. munic., MS 171, f. 106r (*c.* 1322x5)).

104. E. Trenkler, *Das schwarze Gebetbuch* (Wien, 1948), Taf. 14.

105. Lämke, op. cit., p. 52.

106. ibid., p. 55.

107. ibid., p. 62.

108. ibid., p. 67.

109. J. Evans, op. cit., I, p. 129.

110. M. Jones and C. Tracy, 'A medieval choirstall desk-end at Haddon Hall: the Fox-Bishop and the Geese-Hangmen' in *Journal of the British Archaeological Association*, 144 (1991), pp. 107–15.

111. R.W. Scribner, *For the Sake of Simple Folk: Popular Propaganda for the German Reformation* (Cambridge, 1981), p. 76.

CHAPTER TEN

1. I take the Drayton and Spenser citations from a useful article in *Folk-Lore Journal*, 2 (1884), p. 142ff., entitled 'The Folk-lore of Drayton'; cf., also from the *Stationers' Register*, I.270, a ballad entered to Thomas Colwell entitled, 'I am not the fyrste that hath taken in hande the wearynge of the Willow garlande . . .'.

2. See 'Wear the willow, To' in *The Oxford Dictionary of English Proverbs* (3rd edn, Oxford, 1970), rev. F.P. Wilson.

3. Most recently edited under the latter title by M.M. Furrow in *Ten Fifteenth Century Comic Poems* (New York/London, 1985), lines 58f.

4. R.L. Green (ed.) *The Lyrics of the Red Book of Ossory* (Oxford, 1974), p. xvi.

5. T. Parry (ed.), *Gwaith Dafydd ap Gwilym* (Cardiff, 1952), p. 234.

6. C. Haltaus (ed.), *Liederbuch der Clara Hätzlerin* (Quedlinburg/Leipzig, 1840), pp. 171ff.

7. J. Evans, *Pattern* (Oxford, 1931), I, p. 63. Christine de Pisan avails herself of the same pun in the 33rd of her 'Jeux a Vendre' (see further below): *Je vous vens la fleur d'ancolie./– Je suis en grant melancolie. . . .* See further, A. Planche, 'Le temps des ancolies' in *Romania*, 95 (1974), pp. 235–55 – a reference I owe to J.P. Jourdan, *'Le langage amoureux dans le combat de chevalerie à la fin du Moyen Age* (France, Bourgogne, Anjou)' in *Le Moyen Age*, 99 (1993), p. 83ff.

8. R.W. Lightbown, *Medieval European Jewellery* (London, 1992), p. 151; the inscription is given in J.M. Fritz, *Goldschmiedekunst der*

Gotik in Mitteleuropa (Munich, 1982), pp. 231f.

9. Evans, op. cit. Snails also appear on a jewel placed by Charles V in the oratory at the Louvre described in his inventory thus: 'several snails issuing from large pearls, and above, Our Lord issuing from the tomb'.

10. The manuscript is Paris, Bibliothèque de l'Arsenal, MS 1185. For the garters see Lightbown, op. cit., p. 298.

11. cit. H. Jenkins (ed.), *Hamlet* (Arden edn, London, 1982), p. 538, Long Note to IV.v.173ff.

12. Reproduced in M.B. Freeman, *The Unicorn Tapestries* (New York, 1976), p. 127.

13. inv. no. 1036; M. Davies, *Early Netherlandish School* (London, 1945), p. 89.

14. B. Spencer, *Pilgrim Souvenirs and Secular Badges* [= Salisbury Museum Medieval catalogue, Part 2] (Salisbury, 1990), p. 110.

15. J. Cherry, 'A late medieval love jewel' in *Jewellery Studies*, 1 (1983–4), pp. 45–7.

16. Other objects decorated with tears (as noted by Joan Evans, op. cit., I. 63, n. 11) include: two garters and two collars *esmaillees a larmes et a pensees* (that is, pansies) in the 1455–6 Inventories of the Duke of Orléans; on a flask, a key, and a brooch shaped like a book in the inventory of the Château de Pau taken in 1561–2; the tomb of Sao Francisco do Porto in Portugal (1479) is entirely covered with tears in relief; and in 1455 (Evans, op. cit., p. 145), Charles d'Orléans gave his duchess a gold ring 'enamelled with tears on which is inscribed a song written by him'. Cherry, op. cit., adds O.M. Dalton, *Catalogue of Finger Rings* (London, 1912), no. 943, a gold ring with three rows of tears on the outside and the posy, *Tout a part*, with flowers between on the inside, and compares a passage in Martial d'Auvergne's *Arrêts d'Amour* in which an abandoned lover produces a previous love-gift in the shape of 'a little gold heart decorated with tears, which he had always worn, and still wore, for her love, between his flesh and his shirt' (see further below).

17. Cherry, op. cit.

18. cit. MED *s.v. ivy.*

19. cit. MED *s.v. poesie.*

20. Evans, op. cit., p. 145.

21. The manuscript is Paris, Bibliothèque de l'Arsenal, MS 5070, f. 116, reproduced in E. Vitz, *Women in the Medieval Town* (London, 1990).

22. J. Evans, *English Posies and Posy Rings* (London, 1931), p. 8; cf. Hassell E77, *Espoir le fait endurer* (Deschamps, *c.* 1390).

23. ibid., p. 9; cf. also *IHC HOPE YE BEST* on an English fourteenth-century ring in the Victoria and Albert Museum = Lightbown, op. cit., p. 495 – interestingly, the first word is perhaps deliberately ambiguous, being both a possible spelling of 'I', but also, of course, the Sacred Monogram, the use of which here would be talismanic.

24. Wh H 474.

25. Wh S 381.

26. I first discussed the piece in the closing paragraph of M. Jones, 'The Depiction of Proverbs in Late Medieval Art' in G. Gréciano (ed.), *Europhras 88. Phraséologie Contrastive. Actes du Colloque International Klingenthal – Strasbourg, 12–16 mai 1988* [= Collection Recherches Germaniques no. 2], Strasbourg, 1989, pp. 205–24.

27. ODEP (3rd edn), s. *Pins his faith upon another man's sleeve, He.*

28. E.H. Pinto, 'Hand-made combs' in *The Connoiseur*, 130 (1952), pp. 170–6, no. vii and p. 175.

29. For references see J. Leyerle, 'The Heart and the Chain' in S.A. Barney (ed.), *Chaucer's Troilus: Essays in Criticism* (London, 1980), pp. 181–209, and R.F. Green, 'Hearts, minds, and some English poems of Charles d'Orléans' in *English Studies in Canada*, 9 (1983), pp. 136–50.

30. D. Brewer, *Chaucer and his World* (London, 1978), pp. 162f. See also J.B. Oruch, 'St Valentine, Chaucer, and Spring in February' in *Speculum,* 56 (1981), pp. 534–64.

31. The manuscript is Chantilly, Musée Condé MS 76, f. 2r. J. Bouissounouse, *Jeux et Travaux d'après un Livre d'Heures du XVe Siècle* (Paris, 1925), p. 7f., interprets the scene as an *oral* game of the '*demandes amoureuses, jeux á vendre* or *roi qui ne ment*' type (see below), but is then obliged to suggest (nonsensically!) that the artist has included the *petits papiers* for the sake of making clear the (oral) nature of the game! Otherwise he is prepared to countenance the representation of a mere *conversation galante.*

32. A translation is conveniently available in R. Hellman and R. O'Gorman, *Fabliaux: Ribald Tales from the Old French* (London, 1965), pp. 23–6.

33. See further pp. 254–55.

34. The relevant section of Chantilly, Musée Condé MS 654 (*c.* 1470) is printed in J.W. Hassell (ed.), *Amorous Games: A Critical Edition of Les Adevineaux Amoureux* (Austin, 1974), pp. 5–51; the English version apparently translating a manuscript close to BL Royal MS 16. F. II is now BL Add. MS 60577, and is edited by W.L. Braekman as *The Demaundes of Love: A Middle English Prose Version (1487) of the French Game 'au roy qui ne ment'* (Brussels, 1982); the printed edition is item 117 in H.W. Davies, *Catalogue of a Collection of Early French Books in the Library of C. Fairfax Murray* (1910), but passages of *Demaundes d'Amour* also appear in the incunabulum entitled *Les Adevineaux Amoureux* published by Colard Mansion in Bruges *c.* 1479; for the text of one such passage, see Hassell, op. cit., pp. 200–27.

35. J. Rychner (ed.), *Les Arrêts d'Amour de Martial d'Auvergne* (Paris, 1951), XII, pp. 210ff.

36. See, for example, those printed in Hassell, op. cit., pp. 248–56; A. de Montaiglon notes in his introduction to another selection of these (*Recueil de poésies françoises des XVe et XVIe siècles* (Paris, 1856), pp. 205ff.) that there are several undated early printed copies extant.

37. In Hassell, op. cit., and B. Roy, *Devinettes françaises du moyen age* (Paris, 1977); the earliest English riddle book, *The Demaundes Ioyous* printed by de Worde in 1511, translates some of these erotic riddles.

38. K. Baldinger, 'Le lacs d'amour' in *Travaux de Linguistique et de Philologie,* 31 (1993), p. 37ff.

39. L.D. Benson (ed.), *The Riverside Chaucer* (Oxford, 1988), *Canterbury Tales,* General Prologue, pp. 195ff.

40. A. Legner (ed.), *Die Parler und der Schöne Stil 1350–1400* (Cologne, 1978), II, p. 535.

41. H. Battke, *Geschichte des Ringes* (Baden-Baden, 1953), 57, nr. 70.

42. M.B. Freeman, *The Unicorn Tapestries* (New York, 1976), pp. 156–74.

43. Lightbown, op. cit., pp. 243f. and pp. 290f. My own reservations about the identity of friars' knots with lovers' knots are shared by John Cherry.

44. cit. *OED s.v.*

45. BL MS Stowe 955. E. Burin, 'Pierre Sala's Pre-Emblematic Manuscripts' in *Emblematica,* 4 (1989), pp. 1–30.

46. In 1394, for example, Philippe le Hardi gave brooches of a marguerite symbolising his wife Marguerite of Flanders, Duchess of Burgundy (Lightbown, op. cit., p. 164). Chaucer shows himself familiar with the French genre of *marguerite* poems (as exemplified by Froissart's '*Dittie de la flour de la margherite*' and Machaut's '*Dit de la marguerite*') in the Prologue to his *Legend of Good Women* – see Lowes in *PMLA,* 19, pp. 593–683.

47. See D. Seward, *Prince of the Renaissance, the Life of François I* (London, 1974), pp. 172f. There is presumably a deliberate echo of 'the one pearl of great price' of Matthew XIV. 6 in the first half of this inscription.

48. See W. Mieder, 'Modern variants of the daisy oracle "He loves me, he loves me not"' in *Midwestern Journal of Language and Folklore*, 11 (1985), pp. 65–115, esp. p. 66f. I thank Professor Mieder for an offprint of this paper.

49. See n. 6 above.

50. F. Maurer (ed.), *Die Lieder Walthers von der Vogelweide* (2nd edn, Tübingen, 1962), no. 64 'Halmorakel', pp. 93f. Heinrich's poem is quoted by Mieder, op. cit., from I. Zingerle, *Das deutsche Kinderspiel im Mittelalter* (Innsbrück, 1873), p. 32.

51. See D. Johnston, *Iolo Goch: Poems* (Llandysul, 1993), no. 26 and note.

52. E. Rapp Buri and M. Stucky-Schürer, *Zahm und wild: Basler und Strassburger Bildteppiche des 15. Jahrhunderts* (Mainz, 1990), no. 127, p. 386.

53. cit. ibid., p. 71.

54. Burin, op. cit., pp. 2ff.

55. In fact, this motif – like so many – goes back to the *drôleries* painted in the margins of early fourteenth-century Flemish psalters: a woman has caught a man in a clap-net in the *bas-de-page* of Oxford, Bodleian Library, MS Douce 6, f. 83v, while in British Library, MS Stowe 17, f. 240, it is an ape sitting in a hide.

56. W.G. Thomson, *A History of Tapestry from the Earliest Times until the Present Day* (3rd edn, East Ardsley, 1973), p. 257.

57. As in one of the drawings of the Nürnberg *Schembartlauf Hölle* for 1521 in which the 'decoy' is a completely naked young woman holding a fool's cap in each hand, reproduced as Abb. 16 in D.-R. Moser, 'Fastnacht und Fastnachtspiel . . .' in H. Brunner (ed.), *Hans Sachs und Nürnberg.* (Nürnberg, 1976), pp. 182–218. See above, p. 154.

58. F. Unterkircher, *René d'Anjou: Vom liebentbrannten Herz* (Graz, 1975).

59. G. Paris (ed.), *Chansons du XVe Siècle* (Paris, 1875), no. CXX; see also no. CXXIII.

60. B. Yapp, *Birds in Medieval Manuscripts* (London, 1981), p. 43.

61. For the Regensburg Tapestry, see F.V.D. Leyen and A. Spamer, *Die altdeutsche Wandteppiche im Regensburger Rathaus* (Regensburg, 1910), pp. 2ff.

62. The manuscript is Cambridge, University Library, MS Gg. 4.27, f. 416. See R.S. Loomis, *A Mirror of Chaucer's World* (Princeton, 1965), p. 177.

63. Paris, B.N. MS Rothschild 2973 (?c. 1460).

64. Painting in National Gallery, London, clearly represents him as a lover, for he is shown reading from just such another little heart-shaped book, undoubtedly a love-gift. See National Gallery Catalogue.

65. A. Holtorf, '*Neujahrswünsche im Liebesliede des ausgehenden Mittelalters*' (Göppingen, 1973), p. 124.

66. It is painted on f. 65 of the *Turnierbuch Johann des Beständigen*, Labi Dresden, Hs. J 16, and reproduced as fig. 86 in F. Sieber, *Volk und Volkstümliche Motivik im Festwerk des Barocks* (Berlin, 1960). In the 1520s two separate English noblemen bore as their tournament *imprese* a heart burning on which drops fell from a watering-pot held by a lady's hand – A. Young, *The English Tournament Imprese* (New York, 1988), nos 285 and 334.

67. W.E. Mead (ed.) [= EETS OS 173] (London, 1928).

68. See M. Jones, 'Sex and Sexuality in Late Medieval and Early Modern Art' in M. Reisenleiter *et al.* (eds), *Sexualität – Privatisierung der Triebe* [= *Frühneuzeit-Studien* Bd.1] (Frankfurt, 1994), pp. 187–304.

69. J. von Zingerle (ed.), *Hans Vintler Blumen der Tugend* (Innsbrück) 1874, 7783f.

70. ibid., 7821ff.

71. I. Opie and M. Tatem, *A Dictionary of Superstitions* (Oxford, 1989), s. *VERVAIN, powers of*, citing R. Folkard, *Plant Lore* (1884), p. 575.

72. C. Andersson, *Dirnen, Krieger, Narren . . .* (Basel, 1978), pp. 53f., 58.

73. The Swiss caskets are H. Kohlhaussen, *Minnekästchen* (Berlin, 1928), kat. nr. 112 and nr. 47, p. 81; the Alsatian casket is nr. 61, pp. 85f.

74. B. Spencer, 'Medieval Pilgrim Badges' in ed. J.G.N. Renaud, *Rotterdam Papers: a Contribution to Medieval Archaeology* [= Rotterdam Papers I] (Rotterdam, 1968), p. 142 and fig. 4.

75. Reproduced in M. Thibout, *Romanesque* (London, 1974), unpaginated.

76. Reproduced in P. Kristeller, *Holzschnitte im königlichen Kupferstichkabinett zu Berlin. Zweite Reihe* (Berlin, 1915), p. 180.

77. See the chapter entitled *'Narr in der Torkel und Christus in der Kelter'* in W. Mezger, *Narrenidee und Fastnachtsbrauch* (Konstanz, 1991), pp. 403ff., esp. p. 408.

78. D. Alexandre-Bidon, 'Le coeur du Christ au pressoir mystique: le cas des ceramiques du Beauvaisis au début du XVIe siècle', ed. ibid., *Le Pressoir Mystique – Actes du Colloque de Recloses 27 mai 1989* (Paris, 1990), pp. 155–70.

79. The word which she reads *Deieu* (p. 156), and presumably interprets as *Dieu*, thus confirming her thesis that these are religious emblems, in fact has as its final letter an inverted *V*, which might equally well have been intended as an *A* and thus may not be a reference to the deity at all.

80. An eighteenth-century *Lebkuchenmodel* from Nordmahren which depicts a heart similarly pierced by two arrows and a saw is reproduced on p. 21 of K. Beitl, *Liebesgaben* (Salzburg, 1973); a commemorative wedding jug made in Salzburg and dated 1695 includes another such device as part of its decoration – both hearts are also surmounted by a flaming ?torch.

81. I am grateful to Dr John Cherry, former keeper of the Department of Medieval and Later Antiquities of the British Museum where the piece now resides (reg. no. 1984, 11–5, 1) for drawing it to my attention.

82. At least, this is how I interpret the description in M. Hasse, *Lübeck Sankt Annen-Museum, Die Sakralen Werke* (Lübeck, 1970), p. 217 – a reference supplied to me by the omniscient Christoph Gerhardt of Trier University.

83. C. Hermann, *Der gerittene Aristoteles* (Pfaffenweiler, 1991), pp. 71–3 and Abb. 173.

84. A convenient edition is T. Silverstein, *Medieval English Lyrics* (London, 1971), pp. 159f.

85. Spencer (1990), op. cit., p. 107 and fig. 255.

86. Lightbown, op. cit., p. 187.

87. For example, on one of the two leaves of a writing tablet reproduced in *Les Fastes du Gothique* (Paris, 1981), cat. no. 155.

88. *Schatten uit de Schelde* (Bergen op Zoom, 1987), exhibition catalogue, cat. no. 293. An English mould for making such badges survives on the multiple die-piece discussed below. There is not space here to dilate on the symbol of the clasped hands (but see also the *fede* rings and brooches mentioned below) except to note the fascinating *Minnekästchen* (Kohlhaussen, op. cit., p. 41 (Swiss, *c*. 1400)) one panel of which depicts an 'allegorical hunt' (see n. 119 below) and a hart, between whose antlers the artist has carved a pair of clasped hands.

89. Spencer (1990), op. cit., p. 117.

90. HP1 afb. 967.

91. J. Alexander and P. Binski (eds), *Age of Chivalry: Art in Plantagenet England 1200–1400* (London, 1987), cat. no. 640.

92. HP1 afb. 903 and 905.

93. R.L. Greene, *Early English Carols* (Oxford, 1935), p. xcix. Greene appositely cites Gascoigne on the varieties of holly, in the variant tradition in which 'smooth' holly replaces ivy as the opponent of the prickly holly: 'Mary, there are two kinds of holly, that is to say he holly and she holly. Nowe some will say that the she holly hath no prickes, but thereof I entermeddle not.'

94. E. Weekley, *Romance of Names* (London, 1922), p. 196.

95. See lines 37, 69f., 206ff., 265, and 207, respectively.

96. W.G. Thomson, *A History of Tapestry from the Earliest Times until the Present Day* (3rd edn, East Ardsley, 1973), citing the Inventory of Mary, Queen of Scots published by the Bannatyne Club in 1863, p. 39.

97. F.W.D. Brie (ed.), *The Brut*, vol. II [= EETS OS 136] (London, 1908), p. 487. The continuation in question is found in MS Trinity College, Cambridge, O9, 1, f. 224v. 'The grete shafte of Corneylle' receives incidental mention in the fortune-telling poem known as 'The Chance of the Dice' (line 61), published by E.P. Hammond under that title in *Englische Studien*, 59 (1929), pp. 1–16.

98. cit. MED.

99. See ODEP, s. *Owl in an ivy-bush, An.*

100. E.G. Stanley, *The Owl and the Nightingale* (Manchester, 1972), lines 25ff.

101. Greene, op. cit., no. 136B.

102. D.A. Pearsall, *The Floure and the Leafe and the Assembly of Ladies* (Manchester, 1962).

103. The quotation is from W. Jones, *Finger-Ring Lore* (London, 1898), p. 169. The first attestation of this belief in Aubrey's *Remaines* (1686–7) is admittedly post-medieval, but Lyte's translation of Dodoens' *Herball* (1578) implies a similar practice though not spelled out – see the entry *ORPINE: divination*, in Opie and Tatem, op. cit.

104. J. Boardman and D. Scarisbrick, *The Ralph Harari Collection of Finger-rings* (London, 1977), p. 55, no. 124.

105. D.J. Ransom, *Poets at Play: Irony and Parody in the Harley Lyrics* (Norman, 1985), p. 42. The quotations are from the Englishman, Alexander Neckham, and the Frenchman, Thomas of Cantimpré, respectively; the translations are my own. The standard edition is G.L. Brook *The Harley Lyrics* (4th edn, Manchester, 1968), and the poem in question is no. 3.

106. In line 278 of the poem itself, it is said to be 'namyd the Popagay', but it has come to be called 'Speke Parrot' after the title given it in one posthumous printing. 'Parrot hath a blacke beard and a fayre grene tayle' (84) – the green tail is literally true of parrots, of course, but is also an allusion to the expression 'to have a hoar head and a green tail', that is, to be old and lecherous – see J. Scattergood, *John Skelton; The Complete English Poems* (Harmondsworth, 1983), p. XVIII and notes, and cf. Parott's *lytell wanton iye* (15), and the fact that 'Parrot is a fayre byrd for a lady' (211). Details of the way in which the ladies pet him, for example, 'Bas (= kiss) me, swete Parrot, bas me, swete swete'; 'To dwell amonge ladyes, Parrot, is mete' (104f.) recall the amorous dalliance of that other (traditionally lecherous) bird described by Skelton, Jane Scrope's *Phyllyp Sparowe*, who seems to have been permitted decided liberties: 'he wolde make/Me . . . for to take him in/Upon my naked skyn./God wot, we thought no syn –/What though he crept so lowe? . . . Philip myght be bolde/And do what he wolde; Phillip wolde seke and take/ All the flees blake/That he coulde there espye/With his wanton eye' – the latter part, an interesting anticipation of the only very slightly later vogue for poems on the erotic flea-hunt (for which, see A.N. Gotendorf and H. Hayn, *Floh-Literatur des In- und Auslandes vom 16. Jahrhundert bis zur Neuzeit* (Munich, 1913)).

107. J. Huizinga, op. cit., p. 116.

108. J.W. Hassell, *Amorous Games: A Critical Edition of Les Adevineaux Amoureux* (Austin, 1974), p. 252.

109. L.F. Casson (ed.) [= EETS OS 221] (London, 1949), p. 89 [Cambridge MS, lines 1496ff.].

110. J.R.R. Tolkien and E.V. Gordon (eds), *Sir Gawain and the Green Knight* (2nd edn,

Oxford, 1967), rev. N. Davis, p. 91f. (note to lines 611–12).

111. J. Evans, *Pattern* (Oxford, 1931), p. 67.

112. R.W. Lightbown, op. cit., pp. 157 and 168; it will be apparent from what follows that I have reservations about his statement that 'The parrot . . . and his like were . . . surely intended simply to amuse or delight the eye' (165).

113. HP1 afb. 700. The British Museum possesses a metal die-piece [Dept MLA, reg. no. 56, 7–1, 2242] with multiple designs cut on both faces for making brooches and costume-spangles; belonging to the earliest stratum of its use, around the mid-fourteenth century, is the impression of a crowned parrot with a scroll issuing from its mouth – for a full discussion, see M. Jones, *'Poppinjay, Jolly May! Parrot-badges and the Iconography of May in Britain, France and the Netherlands'* in D. Kicken *et al.* (eds), *Gevonden Voorwerpen Lost and found* [= *Rotterdam Papers 11*] (Rotterdam, 2000), pp. 214–29.

114. B. Jeffery, *Chanson Verse of the Early Renaissance* (London, 1971), p. 179.

115. A. de Montaiglon, *Recueil de Poesies Françoises* (Paris, 1887) XII, pp. 22, 416ff.

116. G. Roth-Bojadzhiev, *Studien zur Bedeutung der Vögel in der mittelalterlichen Tafelmalerei* (Cologne and Vienna, 1985), pp. 89f.

117. See cat. no. 270 in C. Meckseper (ed.), *Stadt im Wandel: Kunst und Kultur des Bürgertums in Norddeutschland 1150–1650* (Stuttgart, 1985), p. 347. This piece clearly belongs in the allegorical tradition of *The Stag of Love* discussed by M. Thiébaux (New York, 1974).

118. H. Geissler (ed.), *Zeichnung in Deutschland. Deutsche Zeichner 1540–1640* (Stuttgart, 1980), cat. no. A 39.

119. See Spencer (1990), p. 119. I suspect the possibility of a pun in the words *of lette*, that is, 'of lead'. I take *went* here as the past tense of *wend*. The final line certainly borders on the proverbial, cf. from Jak

Trewman's letter according to the account in *Knighton's Chronicle* s.a. 1381: 'synne fareth as wilde flode,/trewe love is away, that was so gode . . .'.

120. ibid., p. 118 and fig. 319 [MOL 8741].

121. E. Rickert (ed.) [= EETS ES 99] (London, 1906).

122. A. Rapp Buri and M. Stucky-Schürer, *Zahm und wild, Basler und Straßburger Bildteppiche des 15. Jahrhunderts* (Mainz, 1990), no. 553.

123. Tolkien and Gordon (eds), op. cit., rev. Davis, line 612 and note. This decoration and its symbolism is discussed by E. Porges Watson, 'The Arming of Gawain: *vrysoun* and *cercle*' in *Leeds Studies in English*, 18 (1987), pp. 31–44.

124. See N. Davis (ed.), *Paston Letters and Papers of the Fifteenth Century*, Part II (Oxford, 1976), pp. 25f. The original marginal sketch of the shield is reproduced in ed. J. Gairdner, *The Paston Letters* (Edinburgh, 1910), p. 17.

125. See, for example, J. Alexander and P. Binski (eds), *Age of Chivalry* (London, 1987), cat. no. 652. Dr John Cherry informs me that 'Heralds never seem to use the word *brooch*; for them brooches and buckles are indistinguishable and always referred to as *buckles*' (pers. comm.).

126. Line 113, cit. Davis in Tolkien and Gordon (eds), op. cit.

127. I. Gollancz and M.M. Weale (eds), [= EETS OS 195] (London, 1935) who (mistakenly) understand the four-leaf clover to be the plant intended by the author – oddly the de Worde print was unknown to them. See also H. Phillips, 'The Quatrefoil of Love' in ed. ibid., *Langland, the Mystics and the Medieval English Religious Tradition: Essays in Honour of S.S. Hussey* (Woodbridge, 1990), pp. 243–58.

128. See N.F. Blake, in *Archiv*, 206 (1969), pp. 189–200.

129. From Oxford, Bodleian Library, MS Rawl. C. 813 – published by Padelford and Benham in *Anglia*, 31 (1908), p. 381f.

130. In the case of the seal-matrix inscribed with the name of Christian Sprotforth, dated to *c.* 1330, the device also functions as a rebus, for the flower 'sprouts forth' from the heart! – see Alexander and Binski, op. cit., p. 399, cat. no. 459.

131. Once again, I am grateful to Dr Cherry for the communication of his unpublished note entitled 'The silver ring from the Huntington, Cheshire, coin hoard'.

132. Reproduced and discussed in Y. Hackenbroch, *Renaissance Jewellery* (London, 1979), fig. 326.

133. Lightbown, op. cit., p. 366.

134. See A. Schuttwolf *et al.* (eds), *Jahreszeiten der Gefühle. Das Gothaer Liebespaar und die Minne im Spätmittelalter* (Ostfildern-Ruit, 1998), cat. no. 83.

135. Rapp Buri and Stucky-Schürer, op. cit., cat. no. 34.

136. Alexander and Binski, op. cit., p. 276, cat. no. 199.

137. R.H. Ellis, *Catalogue of Seals in the Public Record Office, Vol. I* (London, 1978), p. 203.

138. See n. 119 above.

139. R.H. Ellis, *Catalogue of Seals in the Public Record Office, Vol. II* (London, 1981), p. 231. In Hans Vintler's *Blumen der Tugend* (*c.* 1411), however, the *vierkle* works much stronger magic, enabling its possessor to see visions or phantasms (*gaugkeln sehen*) – op. cit., Zingerle (Innsbrück, 1874), pp. 7779f.

140. C.T. Clay (ed.), *Yorkshire Deeds*, vol. 5 (Yorkshire Archaeological Society, 1926), p. 111, no. 291.

141. cf. the type of ring-brooch known as a *fede* brooch, a circle which includes a pair of clasped hands – see Lightbown, op. cit., pp. 183f.

142. A.B. Tonnochy, *Catalogue of British Seal-dies in the British Museum* (London, 1952), no. 735.

143. ibid., nos 730, 731 and 733.

144. Ellis, op. cit., p. 386.

145. Tonochy, op. cit., nos 722 and 723.

146. For example, Ellis, op. cit., p. 755.

147. M. Jones, 'Folklore Motifs in Late Medieval Art III: Erotic Animal Imagery' in *Folklore*, 102, ii (1991), pp. 192–219, esp. pp. 195ff.

148. Tonnochy, op. cit., no. 720.

149. E.H. Pinto, *Treen and Other Wooden Bygones* (London, 1969), p. 363.

150. Tolkien and Gordon (eds), op. cit., line 2033, cf. from the fourteenth-century *King Alisaunder: By special messangere, Y wol sende hire love-drewry* (7610).

151. For jewellery and gemstones bearing magical inscriptions, see J. Evans, *Magical Jewels of the Middle Ages and the Renaissance* (Oxford, 1922).

152. Tolkien and Gordon (eds), op. cit., lines 2026f., and 1874, 2438.

153. The hoard is comprehensively discussed and other parallels offered for the padlock by J. Cherry, 'The Medieval Jewellery from the Fishpool, Nottinghamshire, hoard' in *Archaeologia*, 104 (1973), p. 307. Another belt of fifteenth-century date in the Museum of London is stamped with the legend *tout monn cuer* and little dogs.

154. A. Hanham (ed.), *The Cely Letters 1472–1488* (London, 1975) [= EETS OS 273], 223.21.

155. Alexander and Binski, op. cit., p. 484, cat. no. 644. Or, indeed, of scatology: one of the magnificent (early) fifteenth-century ivory saddles listed in J. von Schlosser, 'Elfenbeinsattel des ausgehenden Mittelalters' in *Jahrbuch der Kunsthistorischen Sammlungen in Wien*, 15 (1894), no. 11, depicts a lady and gentleman in amorous dalliance on each side with accompanying and parallel inscriptions – to the courtly sentiment of the right-hand side's *ich hof der liben somerzeit* (I look forward to the lovely summer-time), corresponds the stark observation *in dem ars is vinster* (it is dark in the arse) of the left-hand side.

156. National Gallery 2602. The NG *Netherlandish School* Catalogue notes that the raining clouds emblem also appears on the

sleeve of one of the huntsmen in *The Bear and Boar Hunt* Devonshire Tapestry now in the Victoria and Albert Museum, executed a generation or so earlier.

157. Source for 1–4: J.Evans, *English Posies and Posy Rings* (London, 1931), pp. 4, 12, 14 and 11, respectively.

158. In the Alte Burse of the University, Tübingen. See W. Bosshardt, *'Alte Inschriften in der Burse'* in *Attempto*, 43/44 (1972), pp. 16–23, esp. p. 17. This is proverbial – see TPMA *s.v. Liebe*, no. 1461. The Alte Burse capitals are inscribed with other proverbs too: 'many a bird hates me who is nastier than me', which properly belongs in the beak of an owl; 'he who doesn't have a whore or a knave amongst his friends can rub out this rhyme' – variant of TPMA *s.v. Hure*, nos 3–5, with the word *geschlecht* (ancestry) substituted for *frunden*. For the third inscription, a proverbial *adynaton*, see Chapter 8 above.

159. L.D. Benson (ed.), *The Riverside Chaucer* (Oxford, 1988), *Canterbury Tales*, General Prologue, lines 160ff.

160. See S.B. Meech and H.E. Allen, *The Book of Margery Kempe* (London, 1940), opening of Book 1, Chapter 31, and note thereto.

161. See M. Mitchiner and A. Skinner, 'English Tokens, *c.* 1200 to 1425' in *British Numismatic Journal*, 53 (1984), pp. 29–77, esp. p. 54.

162. P. Nelson, 'Some British Medieval seal-matrices' in *Archaeological Journal*, 93 (1936), no. 77.

163. Spencer, op. cit., p. 118.

164. Most recently published in J. Cherry, *Medieval Decorative Art* (London, 1991), p. 65 and fig. 82.

165. Evans, op. cit., p. 5.

166. Evans, op. cit., p. 6 – dating, courtesy of Dr Cherry.

167. D. Mickenberg *et al.*, *Songs of Glory. Medieval Art from 900–1500* (Oklahoma Museum of Art, 1985), cat. no. 119.

168. Y. Hackenbroch, *Enseignes* (Florence, 1996).

169. MOL cat., 323 and fig. 321j.

170. Schuttwolf *et al.* (eds), op. cit., cat. no. 74.

171. Evans, op. cit., p. 14.

172. MOL cat., 323 and fig. 321d.

173. M. Jones, 'Proverbial Inscriptions on Medieval Artefacts', unpublished lecture delivered in October 1992 to The Finds Research Group of the Society of Antiquaries.

174. J. Hayward and T. Husband (eds), *The Secular Spirit* (New York, 1975).

175. In the collection of the Society of Antiquaries. Discussed in P. Tudor-Craig, *Richard III* (London, 1973), cat. no. 210.

176. Most recently published in Cherry, op. cit., p. 70.

CHAPTER ELEVEN

1. B. White (ed.), *The Vulgaria of John Stanbridge and the Vulgaria of Robert Whittinton* [= EETS OS 187] (London, 1932).

2. A fundamental discussion is D.-R. Moser, *'Schwänke um Pantoffelhelden oder die Suche nach dem Herrn im Haus'* in *Fabula*, 13 (1972), pp. 205–92. See also N.Z. Davis, 'Women on Top: Symbolic Sexual Inversion and Political Disorder in Early Modern Europe' in B.A. Babcock (ed.), *The Reversible World: Essays in Symbolic Inversion* (Cornell UP, 1978), pp. 147–90.

3. M. Rose, 'Sidney's Womanish Man' in *Review of English Studies* NS, 15 (1964), p. 353ff.

4. See P. Barolsky, *Infinite Jest: Wit and Humor in Italian Renaissance Art* (Columbia, 1978), pp. 191ff., for sixteenth-century paintings by Cranach, Dossi and others. For similar depictions of Sardanapalus, distaff in hand, see Herman Pleij, *De Sneeuwpoppen van 1511. Literatuur en stadscultuur tussen middeleeuwen en moderne tijd* (Amsterdam, 1988), pp. 266ff.

5. *Richard II*, III.ii.118, and *Cymbeline* V.iii.33f.

6. BL Royal MS 13. B. VII1, f. 19.

7. Pleij, op. cit., pp. 266ff. There is a miniature of a prone Sardanapalus still clutching his distaff beneath the feet of an enthroned Lady Prudence in a fourteenth-century Italian manuscript in the Galleria Nazionale d'Arte in Rome.

8. C. Revard, 'The Tow on Absalom's Distaff and the Punishment of Lechers in Medieval London' in *English Language Notes*, 17 (1980), pp. 168–9.

9. C. Pieske, *'Die Memento-mori-Klappbilder'* in *Philobiblon*, 4 (1960), pp. 9–10.

10. I quote from ed. M.C. Seymour, *Mandeville's Travels* (Oxford, 1968), p. 221.

11. L.D. Benson (ed.), *The Riverside Chaucer* (Oxford, 1988), *The Canterbury Tales* (*c.* 1386), 'Prologue to the Monk's Tale', 240, VII.1906ff.

12. For example, Cambridge, University Library MS Dd. 5.5 (French, 1325x1350); *Luttrell Psalter* BL Add. MS 42130, ff. 59v–60 (English *c.* 1330x40). For an English misericord example of sixteenth-century date in Westminster Abbey, see M. Laird, *English Misericords* (London, 1986), pl. 20.

13. M. Lehrs, *Geschichte und kritischer Katalog des deutschen, niederländischen und französischen Kupferstichs im 15. Jahrhundert* (Vienna, 1908–34), no. 504. For another example, a century later, see *Mitt Fusstreten Handt drucken vnnd Lachen* – W. Harms, *Deutsche illustrierte Flugblätter des 16. und 17. Jahrhunderts* (Tübingen, 1985), I, p. 92 and note B9.

14. Similar scenes are to be found in Hereford (1340x1355) and Great Malvern.

15. The quotation is from the closing lines of the reformed Katherina's final speech in Shakespeare's *The Taming of the Shrew* (V.ii.178); in his Arden edition (London, 1981), Brian Morris writes of this gesture: 'no precise origin for Katherina's symbolic offer has been proposed'. I thank my wife, Suzanne Alford, for bringing this line to my attention.

16. D.C. Baker *et al.* (eds), *The Late Medieval Religious Plays of Bodleian MSS Digby 133 and e Museo 160* [= EETS OS 283] (Oxford, 1982).

17. R.L. Greene, *Early English Carols* (Oxford, 1935), no. 405 from Sloane 2593, f. 24v (first half of the fifteenth century).

18. B.A. Hanawalt, *Of Good and Ill Repute: Gender and Social Control in Medieval England* (Oxford, 1998), p. 153. The case is taken from G.J. Turner, *Selected Pleas of the Forest* (London, 1901), pp. 38–9.

19. Reproduced as fig. 14 in T. Vignau-Wilberg-Schuurman, *Hoofse Minne en Burgerlijke Liefde in de Prentkunst rond 1500* (Leiden, 1983).

20. Isabel Mateo Gomez seems to have been the first to suggest this derivation in *Temas profanos en la escultura gotica espanola: La sillerias de coro* (Madrid, 1979). There is also a fairly close (reversed) woodcut copy of this van Meckenem engraving.

21. Jan Piet Filedt Kok (ed.), *Livelier than Life: the Master of the Amsterdam Cabinet or the Housebook Master* (Amsterdam, 1985), cat. no. 54.

22. Acquisition no. 64.101.1499 of the Irwin Untermeyer Collection of the Metropolitan Museum of Art, New York (*c.* 1480). See H.P. Lockner in the most recent and authoritative work on such brassware, *Messing: Ein Handbuch über Messinggerät des 15. Jahrhunderts* (Munich, 1982).

23. See L. Dresen-Coenders, 'De Strijd om de Broek', *De Revisor*, 4 (1977), pp. 29–37, 77. I forbear from giving a bibliography for this extremely popular motif here.

24. New York, Pierpont Morgan Library, Glazier Collection, MS 24, f. 30v.

25. Schreiber 2763. C. Dodgson, *Dotted Prints in the British Museum* (London, 1937), p. 32, no. 100.

26. For the breeches as a *realium* but with discussion of their symbolic significance also, see G. Jaritz 'Die Bruoch' in G. Blaschitz *et al.* (eds), *Symbole des Alltags,*

*Alltag der Symbole – Festschrift für Harry
Kühnel zum 65. Geburtstag* (Graz, 1992),
pp. 395–416.

27. The quotations are from pages 127, 131,
and 129 respectively. For the wisp (of straw)
and the (skimmington) ride, see the
section on the iconography of punishment
in Chapter 5. One manuscript containing
the fifteenth-century poem *'Der böse Weib
und die Teufel'* contains the couplet
   an evil woman and a wisp of straw
   they are surely both the Devil's
see H. Niewohner, *'Das böse Weib und die
Teufel'* in *Zeitschrift für deutsches Altertum*, 83
(1951/2), p. 156, lines 99–100.

28. The *Stationers' Register* records two no
longer extant ballads – unless one of them
is represented by Plat's text – which allude
to this idiom: 'a pleasant ballad of a combat
betwene a man and his wife for the breches
(27 August 1591); 'A woman would weare
the Bruches' (November 1629).

29. Wh M 406. The earliest form is 'most
master wears no breech'.

30. For example in an engraving by Franz Brun
dated 1560 (Hollstein).

31. W.A. Coupe, *The German Illustrated
Broadsheet in the Seventeenth Century* (Baden-
Baden, 1966), p. 196.

32. Signed *SB*; Paris, Bibliothèque Nationale,
Cabinet des Estampes, Ea. 17, res. fol.

33. For a contemporary illustration of another
foolish man washing up, see K.O.E Moxey,
'The Ship of Fools and the Idea of Folly in
Sixteenth Century Netherlandish
Literature' in S. Hindman (ed.), *The Early
Illustrated Book: Essays in Honor of L.J.
Rosenwald* (Washington, 1982), p. 92,
fig. 5, frame 2, from the title-page of the
1558 edn of *Van den X Esels* (1st edn
Antwerp, *c.* 1530).

34. BL Royal MS 10. E. IV, illuminated in
England *c.* 1330–*c.* 1340.

35. III.ii.30.

36. But LSR *s.v. Schürze* rightly notes that *'Die
Schürze als ein Hauptbestandteil der*

*Frauenkleidung ist zum Symbol geworden und
steht pars pro toto für die Frau.'*

37. Reproduced and discussed in my *Dialect in
Wiltshire* (Trowbridge, 1987), pl. 33 and
pp. 140–2.

38. LSR *s.v. Pantoffel.*

39. M. Geisberg, *The German Single-Leaf Woodcut
in the First Half of the Sixteenth Century* (2nd
edn, New York, 1974–5), no. 1107.

40. cit. *OED s.v. grope*, sense 3c.

41. V.ii.112f. in F.S. Boas (ed.), *Five Pre-
Shakespearean Comedies* (Oxford, 1970),
p. 262.

42. D.-R. Moser, *'Schwänke um Pantoffelhelden
oder die Suche nach dem Herrn im Haus'* in
Fabula, 13 (1972), pp. 205–92.

43. E. Zahn, *Stadthof Fetzenreich in Trier* (Trier,
1980). I am indebted to my omniscient
friend, Professor Dr Christoph Gerhardt of
Trier University for a copy of this booklet,
as for so much other invaluable
iconographic information.

44. F. Arens, *'Die ursprüngliche Verwendung
gotischer Stein- und Tonmodel'* in *Mainzer
Zeitschrift*, 66 (1971), pp. 106–31, no. 80 –
Städtisches Museum Worms, Alter
Museumsbestand. Inv.-nr. M 1497.

45. Randall, figs 581–4 from: Baltimore,
Walters Art Gallery MS 82, f. 179v (Flemish,
early fourteenth century); Paris, B.N. MS fr.
95, f. 343r (Picard, late thirteenth century)
and New Haven, Yale University Library,
Lancelot del Lac MS, f. 31r (part of same
manuscript); Oxford, Bodleian Library MS
Douce 6, f. 93v (Flemish, 1300x25).

46. L. Randall, 'A medieval slander' in *Art
Bulletin*, 42 (1960), pp. 25–40. For an
example of a costumed fool sitting on eggs
see the woodcut frame to, for example, J.
Eberlin, *Ein getrewe warnung an die Christen
in der Burgawischen marck* (1526 edition),
reproduced as illus. 7 in R.G. Cole,
'Pamphlet Woodcuts in the
Communication Process of Reformation
Germany' in K.C. Sessions and P.N. Bebb
(eds), *Pietas et Societas: New Trends in*

Reformation Social History, Essays in Memory of Harold J. Grimm (Ann Arbor, 1985), pp. 103–22.

47. Reproduced as Abb. 5 in D.-R. Moser, *'Schwänke um Pantoffelhelden oder die Suche nach dem Herrn im Haus'* in *Fabula*, 13 (1972), pp. 205–92.

48. Niewohner, op. cit.

49. Published by Triblers Enke in Copenhagen *c.* 1820 – see V.E Clausen, *Det folkelige danske træsnit I etbladstryk, 1650–1870* (Copenhagen, 1961), no. 505 and fig. 41.

50. Spanish scholars seem to be unaware of the true import of this scene; most recently, Maria Rosa Teres has described it as a 'scene of exorcism' in 'The Choir Stalls of the Cathedral of Barcelona' in *The Profane Arts*, 6 (1997), p. 173. On the authority of the excellent Maria Bergenthal, I add further Spanish (? < Flemish carvers) examples at Tarragona and Saragossa, but I can neither confirm these identifications, nor provide dates – M. Bergenthal, *Elemente der Drolerie und ihre Beziehungen zur Litteratur* (Berlin, 1936), p. 157.

51. Illustrated as fig. 8 in W. Gibson, 'Bruegel, Dulle Griet and Sexist Politics in the 16th Century' in O. von Simson and M. Winner (eds), *Pieter Bruegel und Seine Welt* (Berlin, 1979), pp. 9–16.

52. See W.S. Gibson, *Bruegel* (London, 1977), p. 102.

53. Niewohner, op. cit., p. 156, lines 83–6.

54. STC lists two earlier editions: one of *c.* 1505 by Wynkyn de Worde, and one of *c.* 1510 by R. Pynson, but no woodcut illustrations survive. The furnace motif has been studied by M. de Meyer, *'Verjüngung im Glutofen: Altweiber und Altmännermühle'* in *Zeitschrift für Volkskunde*, 40 (1964), pp. 161–7. I have not seen C.M. Edsman, *Ignis Divinus: Le Feu comme Moyen de rajeunissement et d'Immortalité* (Lund, 1949).

55. Discussed on p. 97 and reproduced as plate XI.c of H.W. Janson, *Apes and Ape-lore in the Middle Ages* (London, 1952).

56. Reproduced in D. and H. Kraus, *The Hidden World of Misericords* (New York, 1975), fig. 74.

57. Reproduced in N.-A. Bringeus, *Volkstümliche Bilderkunde* (Munich, 1982), p. 110, fig. 143.

58. According to Edsmann, op. cit., p. 100.

59. Reproduced in Bringeus, op. cit., p. 110, as fig. 142; cf. the Grimms' story, *Das Jung Geglühte Männlein* (Type 753). A Czech copy based on the *Old Wives Furnace* was issued in Prague in 1594, and Abraham Bach of Augsburg issued another similar pair in the early seventeenth century.

60. A recent work on the mill in art and symbolism is P. Huys, *Molen en molenaar te kijk gesteld* (Gent, 1996).

61. *s.v. Altweibermuhle* in K. Ranke *et al.* (eds), *Enzyklopädie des Märchens*, I (Berlin/New York, 1977).

62. See W.A. Coupe, *The German Illustrated Broadsheet in the Seventeenth Century* (Baden-Baden, 1966), pp. 158ff., and pl. 85 which reproduces the pair.

63. A. Gailey, 'Grinding Old People Young' in *Ulster Folk Life*, 17 (1971), pp. 95 and 97, n. 1.

64. Reproduced as pl. 26 in R. Emmerson, *British Teapots and Tea Drinking 1700–1850* (London, 1992), cat. no. 57. See J. Larwood and J.C. Hotten, *History of Signboards* (London, 1866), p. 461. For the innuendo, see Eric Partridge, *Dictionary of Historical Slang* (abridged edn, Harmondsworth, 1972), *s.v. grind*. See also B. Rowland, 'The Mill in Popular Metaphor from Chaucer to the Present Day' in *Southern Folklore Quarterly*, 33 (1969), pp. 69–79. J.B. Smith draws my attention to the Suffolk saying, 'Go to Bungay and be ground young again' (I. and P. Opie, *The Oxford Dictionary of Nursery Rhymes* (Oxford, 1951), p. 363).

65. For the *Schembartlauf* see S.L. Sumberg, *The Nuremberg Schembart Carnival* (New York, 1941), and H.-U. Roller, *Der Nürnberger Schembartlauf* (Tübingen, 1965). For Reformation sheets, see R.W. Scribner, *For*

the *Sake of Simple Folk: Popular Propaganda for the German Reformation* (Cambridge, 1981), pp. 104ff, and figs 76–8. The whole topos is discussed by P. Heimann, '*Mola Mystica: Wandlung eines Themas Mittelalterlicher Kunst*' in *Zeitschrift für Schweizerische Archäologie und Kunstgeschichte*, 39 (1982), pp. 229–52; and by H. Rye-Clasen, *Hostienmühlenbilder im Lichte mittelalterlicher Frömmigkeit* (Stein am Rhein, 1981). A 1566 example of *Die Pfaffenmühle* in stained glass is reproduced in E. von Witzleben's interesting *Bemalte Glasscheiben: Volkstümliches Leben auf Kabinett- und Bierscheiben* (Munich, 1977), p. 122, pl. XIV. E.M. Ackermann, *Das Schlaraffenland in German Literature and Folksong* (1944), p. 105, notes that Eyering (d. 1578) cites a number of references to the rejuvenation of old women by miraculous means in his *Proverbium Copia* (earliest extant edn Eisleben, 1601). Guy Demerson records several more *moulins-à-hommes* in his edn of *Le Disciple de Pantagruel* (Paris, 1982), p. 65, n. 108.

66. S.L. Smith, *The Power of Women. A Topos in Medieval Art and Literature* (Philadelphia, 1995).

67. Reproduced as fig. 194 in A. Globe, *Peter Stent, London Printseller circa 1642–1665* (Vancouver, 1985), cat. no. 456.iii.

68. Reproduced as fig. 1 on p. 176 of E. De Jongh and G. Luijten, *The Mirror of Everyday Life: Genreprints in the Netherlands 1550–1700* (Amsterdam, 1977).

69. M. Mauquoy-Hendrickx, *Les estampes des Wierix* (Brussels, 1978–83), no. 1700, 'La femme hantise de l'homme'.

70. See *Mitteilungen der Gesellschaft für verfeinerte Kunst*, 50 (1911).

71. *Aucassin et Nicolette*, section 28, *s.v. rex de Torelore*, Ducange quotes a most interesting letter of remission dated 1403 in which the phrase *Roys de Torelore* occurs in a context which implies the meaning 'ineffectual fantasist'.

72. Made in the Mosan region, *c.* 1400; from the Robert Lehman Collection, 1975.1.1416.

73. Reproduced in Andersson, op. cit., as Abb. 43. For a list of such representations in the Middle Ages, see P. Marsilli, '*Réception et diffusion iconographique du conte de Aristote et Phillis en europe depuis le moyen age*' in D. Buschinger and A Crépin (eds), *Amour, Mariage et Transgressions au Moyen Age* (Göppingen, 1984), pp. 239–53, esp. pp. 246–53.

74. R.S. Luborsky and R.M. Ingram, *A Guide to English Illustrated Books 1536–1603* (Tempe, 1998), pp. 325–6.

75. With which cf. the title-page cut of the slightly later German *Imperiosus Mulier das ist Das Regiersuchtige Weib* (*Imperiosus Mulier*, that is, the Domineering Woman) (Magdeburg, 1611).

76. J.W. Spargo, *Virgil the Necromancer* (Cambridge, Mass., 1934).

77. R.M. Wunderli, *London Church Courts and Society on the Eve of the Reformation* (Cambridge, Mass., 1981), p. 80, citing a document in the *Acta quod correctionem delinquentium* of the London commissary court, now held in the Guildhall Muniment Room, MS 9064 series, vol. 3, f. 264r.

78. cit. from BL MS Harley 45 (*c.* 1425), f. 101b, in G.R. Owst, *Literature and Pulpit in Medieval England* (2nd edn, Oxford 1961), p. 385.

79. An example from Paris, B.N. MS fr. 9198, f. 91r (French *c.* 1456), is reproduced as pl. 92 in M. Scott, *Late Gothic Europe, 1400–1500* (The History of Dress Series) (London, 1980), p. 162; two incunabular instances are the woodcut illustrations in the *Seelenwurzgarten* (Ulm, 1483), and Vintler's *Blumen der Tugend* (Augsburg, 1486).

80. Lydgate's *A Dyte of Womenis Hornys* (before 1450), printed in H.N. MacCracken (ed.), *The Minor Poems of John Lydgate* [= EETS OS 192] (London, 1934), II, pp. 38 ff.,

probably owes much of its imagery to Eustache Deschamps (d. 1406), who complains of this fashion in his *'Balade sur l'estrangeté de l'atour et du chief gue plusieurs dames font à present'*. The fascinating parallel with modern urban legends of the 'Beehive Hairdo' was pointed out, together with further related horrors from medieval *exempla*, by S. Marchalonis, 'Three Medieval Tales and their Modern American Analogues', *Folklore Institute Journal*, 13 (1976), pp. 173–84.

81. The chronicler Enguerrand de Monstrelet (d. 1453), referring to the year 1428 when an itinerant Carmelite preacher, Thomas Connecte, persuaded the women of Flanders and Northern France to burn their 'horns', records that their change of heart was short-lived, and that 'very soon they put forth their horns again like snails, every bit as tall as they had been before'. *Le Livre du Chevalier de la Tour Laundry*, written *c.* 1372 as a manual of proper behaviour for the author's young daughters, reports a sermon of 1371 in which a bishop said (in the words of the *c.* 1450 Middle English translation) 'that the women that were so horned were lyche to be horned snailes and hertis and unicornes', as well as 'making horns at' (that is cuckolding) their husbands. J.W. Hassell, *Middle French Proverbs, Sentences and Proverbial Phrases* (Toronto, 1982), F 37, quotes from Coquillart (*c.* 1480): 'As the common proverb has it, a woman is known by her horn(s).'

82. Quoted by V. J. Scattergood, *Politics and Poetry in the Fifteenth Century* (London, 1971), p. 342.

83. This was pointed out by J.R. Owst, *Preaching in Medieval England* c. *1350–1450* (Cambridge, 1926), pp. 402–3.

84. *Der Ritter vom Turn* (Basel, 1493) is a German translation of the work by the Chevalier de la Tour Landry referred to above, illustrated with woodcuts; Caxton's English translation, published in 1484 as *The Book of the Knight of the Tower*, is unillustrated.

85. The central carving is well reproduced in M. Laird, *English Misericords* (London, 1986), pl. 110.

86. F.C. Tubach, *Index Exemplorum* (Helsinki, 1969), no. 1630; A. Aarne and S. Thompson, *The Types of the Folktale* (Helsinki, 1961), no. 826. Discussions include: R. Wildhaber, *Das Sündenregister auf der Kuhhaut* (Helsinki, 1955); P. Halm, 'Der Schreibende Teufel' in *Atti del II Congresso Internazionale di Studi Umanistici* (Rome, 1952), pp. 235–49; H. Hasmussen, 'Der Schreibende Teufel in Nordeuropa', in E. Ennen and G. Wiegelmann (eds), *Festschrift Mathias Zender: Studien zu Volkskultur, Sprache und Landesgeschichte* (1972), I. 455–64; M. Jennings, 'Tutivillus: The Literary Career of the Recording Demon' in *Studies in Philology*, 74 (1977), pp. 1–95; L. Röhrich, *Erzählungen des Späten Mittelalters und ihr Weiterleben in Literatur und Volksdichtung bis zur Gegenwart* (Bern and Munich, 1962), pp. 113–15 and notes on pp. 267–74.

87. The recording demon's sack in which he stashes his sin-laden scrolls appears on a bench-end in Charlton Mackrell Church, Somerset, reproduced in J.C.D. Smith, *A Guide to Church Woodcarvings: Misericords and Bench-Ends* (Newton Abbott, 1974). Other Tutivillus representations in wood are listed in M.D. Anderson, *History and Imagery in British Churches* (London, 1971), p. 155; the nine known instances in English wall-painting, and two in stained glass, are listed by David Parks and Richard Marks in their entries to exhibits 557 and 561 in Alexander and Binski (eds), op. cit. A Corbel in Sleaford church displaying the same motif is fig. 13 in the essay by V. Sekules in *ibid*. Two examples chosen at random are a panel of stained glass from Stanford-on-Avon Church,

Northamptonshire, and a wall-painting inscribed IC EST BELIA DEABOL (This is Belial the Devil), in Melbourne Church, Derbyshire, both belonging to the second quarter of the fourteenth century. For an example in another medium, see the woodcut from *Der Ritter vom Turn* (Basel, 1493).

88. Conveniently available in *The Oxford Book of Medieval English Verse* (Oxford, 1970), p. 484. It is difficult not to believe that there is some relation between the demon's traditional name and the word *tittle-tattle,* together with its cognates in other Germanic languages.

89. I thank Dr Charles Tracy for this dating.

90. It had reached England by the mid-seventeenth century when it was entitled *The Several Places Where You May Hear News,* but a century later it was reissued as *Tittle-tattle; or, the Several Branches of Gossipping.* German versions are also known.

91. *Guillaume Coquillart, Oeuvres,* M.J. Freeman (ed.) (Geneva, 1975), p. 150.

92. F. Geldner, *'Chicheface. Ein unbekannter französischer Einblattdruck'* in *Gutenberg Jahrbuch* (1959), pp. 41–4.

93. A. Regond, *La peinture murale du XVIe siècle dans la région d'Auvergne* (Clermont-Ferrand, 1983), pp. 45–53, esp. p. 52.

94. For full details see A.M. Hind, *Engraving in England in the Sixteenth and Seventeenth Centuries Part II The Reign of James I* (Cambridge, 1955), pp. 210–13.

CHAPTER TWELVE

1. For the representation of male homosexuality in the Middle Ages, see, for example, I.H. Forsyth, 'The Ganymede Capital at Vezelay' in *Gesta,* 15 (1976), pp. 241–6. For a general work concerning the Renaissance, see J.M. Saslow, *Ganymede in the Renaissance: Homosexuality in Art and Society* (New Haven/London, 1986).

2. Study of which can now proceed from the sure base of the recent edition by L.

Lawner: *I Modi. The Sixteen Pleasures: an Erotic Album of the Italian Renaissance* (Evanston, 1989), with a useful introduction by George Szabo, detailing the influence of the engraved postures on contemporary and later art. I know of no surviving precedent for Raimondi's extraordinary engraving of a woman using a dildo, however, partially preserved in the Nationalmuseum, Stockholm. For an interesting visual satirical attack on Aretino, see the Arcimboldesque medals which depict the bust of the poet composed entirely of phalli, discussed in Chapter 4.

3. HP1 and HP2.

4. Plutarch, *Quaestiones Conviviales,* V.7.3.

5. As argued in a thorough survey of these sexual sculptures by A. Weir and J. Jerman, *Images of Lust: Sexual Carvings on Medieval Churches* (London, 1986). See also my articles, 'Sheela-na-gig' and 'Phallic Imagery' in C. Lindahl *et al.* (eds), *Medieval Folklore An Encyclopedia* (Santa Barbara, 2000).

6. HP1 afb. 629.

7. HP1 afb. 619.

8. The former (present whereabouts unknown) is reproduced in R. Bailey, 'Apotropaic figures in Milan and NW England' in *Folklore,* 94 (1983), pp. 113–17, and the latter in M. Jones, 'Sex and Sexuality in Late Medieval and Early Modern Art' in M. Reisenleiter *et al.* (eds), *Sexualität – Privatisierung der Triebe* [= *Frühneuzeit-Studien* Bd.1] (Frankfurt, 1994), pp. 187–304.

9. Paris, B.N. MS fr. 25526, f. 135v (Paris, *c.* 1350).

10. Bailey, op. cit.

11. And the use of *barbau* in a *sotte chanson* – ed. A. Långfors, *Deux recueils de sottes chansons* (Helsinki, 1945), nos 30, 16.

12. The ability to 'shave and clip the vulva' is one of the numerous talents of the eponymous *Varlet à Louer* (servant for hire), as it is of the related 'maid-of-all-work' who

is similarly required to *raser et tondre le cas*, and the practice is also referred to in 'The maids' banquet held at the stews on "Fat Thursday" [that is, that before Shrove Tuesday]' where there is talk of *couper le maujoinct*, as it is also in *Le Rondeau des Barbiers*, the farce of the *Bâtards de Caux*, the prose piece, 'The source and origin of the wild cunts', and the *sermon joyeux* entitled *Barbes et Brayes* (ed. J. Koopmans, *Recueil de sermons joyeux XVe–XVIe siècles* (Geneva, 1988)). See further, M. Schwob, 'Maujoinct' in *Revue des Etudes Rabelaisiennes*, 2 (1904), pp. 138f., and *Klösterliche Sachkultur des Spätmittelalters* (Vienna, 1980), pp. 27f. and pp. 353ff. Predictably, in his opinionated way, Brantôme devotes considerable space to fashions in female pubic hair in the French court around the middle of the sixteenth century.

13. E. Fuchs, *Illustrierte Sittengeschichte vom Mittelalter bis zur Gegenwart I: Renaissance* (Munich, 1909), *Ergänzungsband* (Munich, 1928), Abb. 16.

14. E. Kislinger, '*Anasyrma. Notizen zur Geste des Schamweisens*' in G. Blaschitz *et al.* (eds), *Symbole des Alltags, Alltag der Symbole: Festschrift für Harry Kühnel zum 65. Geburtstag* (Graz, 1992), pp. 377–94, supersedes all other discussions of this motif. To his examples may be added the episode recorded in the third-century *Acts of Paul and Thecla* (condemned by Jerome as apocryphal) in which the first-century virgin, St Thecla of Iconium, sentenced to die by wild beasts in the Colosseum, repulsed a lion by exposing her vulva – an incident alluded to by St Ambrose in his *De Virginibus* of 377, Lib III, cap. 19.

15. Kislinger, op. cit., pp. 379ff., discusses the various versions of this alleged incident in the works of Plutarch and others.

16. B. Krekic, '*Abominandum crimen*: Punishment of Homosexuals in Renaissance Dubrovnik' in *Viator*, 18 (1987), p. 342, n. 24.

17. I owe my knowledge of this extraordinary piece to Brian Spencer who also refers me to R. Neu-Kock, *Heilige und Gaukler – Kölner Statuetten aus Pfeifenton* [= *Kölner Museums-Bulletin, Berichte und Forschungen aus den Museen der Stadt Köln, Sonderheft 1*] (Cologne, 1988).

18. Weir and Jerman, op. cit., esp. pp. 91ff.

19. I examine these statues in some detail under the heading 'Marcolf as Spinario' in M. Jones, 'Marcolf the Trickster in Late Medieval Art and Literature, or, The Mystery of the Bum in the Oven' in G. Bennett (ed.), *Spoken in Jest* (Sheffield, 1991), pp. 139–74, esp. pp. 157ff.

20. G.Q. Vicary, 'Visual Art as Social Data: the Renaissance Codpiece' in *Cultural Anthropology*, 4 (1989).

21. cit. MED *s.v. galaunt*.

22. HP1 afb. 670.

23. See, for a by no means exhaustive list, M. de Meyer, *De Volks- en Kinderprent in de Nederlanden* (Antwerp and Amsterdam, 1962), 'Spinnende Varkens', pp. 417–21.

24. HP2 afb. 1775.

25. For *reliable* general treatments see, for example, the articles *fascinum*, and *phallos* in G. Wissowa (ed.), *Paulys Real-Encyclopädie der classischen Altertumswissenschaft* (Stuttgart, 1894ff.), and the work cited in n. 29 below. For the situation in Britain, see, for example, P. Turnbull, 'The Phallus in the Art of Roman Britain' in *Bulletin of the Institute of Archaeology*, 15 (1978), pp. 199–206, and 'Phallic Vessels' in 'Deities and Religious scenes on Romano-British pottery' in *Journal of Roman Pottery Studies*, 2 (1989), p. 9f.

26. For winged phalli in the late medieval lead badge corpus, see HP1 afb. 634–40, 646–8, and HP 2 afb. 1757–9, 1761, and A. Forgeais: *Collection de Plombs Historiés trouvés dans la Seine*, IV (Paris, 1865), pp. 257–70. There is no evidence for the inference that a thirteenth-century token decorated with such a design found in London is a 'brothel

token', as described in M. Mitchiner and A. Skinner, 'English Tokens, *c.* 1200 to 1425' in *British Numismatic Journal,* 53 (1984), p. 54 and pl. 5.

27. Tony Hunt, *The Plant Names of Medieval England* (Cambridge, 1989).

28. HP2 afb. 1746–9.

29. C. Johns, *Sex or Symbol: Erotic Images of Greece and Rome* (London, 1982).

30. HP1 afb. 642.

31. Paul Vandenbroeck, *'Jheronimus Bosch' Hooiwagen: enkele bijkomende gegevens'* in *Koninklijk Museum voor Schone Kunsten Antwerpen Jaarboek* (1987), pp. 107–42, esp. p. 135.

32. Details of this and the following procession from Bob Scribner, 'Reformation, carnival and the world turned upside-down' in *Social History,* 3 (1978), p. 303ff., esp. pp. 306 and 309. The gaming-boards as religious books motif is also to be found in contemporary literature: at the end of *Gargantua* (1534), Chapter 22, Rabelais refers to *'les beaux Evangiles de boys, c'est a dire . . . tabliers'.* The Floetner woodcut was discussed by C. Dodgson, 'Rare Woodcuts in the Ashmolean Museum – IV' in *Burlington Magazine,* 66 (1935), p. 91, and pl. II, A, B.

33. The full text was first published under the title *'Le Jeu des Cent Drutz dans le Diocèse de Pamiers'* in *Romania,* 22 (1893), p. 274f.

34. cit. H. Kühnel, *'Die städtische Fasnacht im 15. Jahrhundert'* in P. Dinzelbacher and H.-D. Muck (eds), *Volkskultur des Europäischen Spätmittelalters* (Stuttgart, 1987), p. 116.

35. M. Ingram, 'Ridings, Rough Music and Mocking Rhymes in Early Modern England' in B. Reay (ed.), *Popular Culture in Seventeenth Century England* (Beckenham, 1985), p. 170.

36. I take this opportunity of thanking Professor Kurt Baldinger here for a copy of his highly informative study of obscene punning in the late Middle French riddles, 'Homonymie- und Polysemiespiele im Mittelfranzösischen' in *Zeitschrift für Romanische Philologie,* 100 (1984), pp. 241–81, and see also his article immediately following, *'Zum Wortschatz der Rätselfragen im 15. Jahrhundert'.*

37. See J.C. Margolin and J. Céard, *Rébus de la Renaissance* (Paris, 1986).

38. *Kryptadia,* 3, p. 395.

39. For another phallus-tipped staff (one upright phallus flanked by two inverted) held in the hooves of the King of Goats (*I re de bechi*), see the most interesting late fifteenth-century Florentine Satire on Cuckolds engraving = A.M. Hind, *Early Italian Engraving* (London, 1938), A.ll.23. It cannot be mere coincidence that the speech put into the King's mouth begins with the word, *Fallo* (though meaning 'let'), positioned immediately next to the phallus-staff. Further confirmation of this widespread phallic understanding of the pilgrim's staff in the Middle Ages is afforded by M Lat. usage: in the mid-twelfth-century *Ysengrimus,* for example, *baculum* is used to refer to the horse's penis, and in the late twelfth-century *Speculum Stultorum* there is a pun on *baculum,* ostensibly meaning 'pastoral staff' (line 2397); the derived verb *baculare* is used to mean 'copulate' in the *De Coniuge Non Ducenda* (see n. 45 below).

40. *The Canterbury Tales* (*c.* 1386), General Prologue, line 467. For references to the allegedly dubious motives many women had for going on pilgrimage, see ed. Benson, op. cit., p. 818, n. to lines 463ff., and H. Bredekamp, 'Wallfahrt als Versuchung: San Martin in Fromista' in ed. Fachschaft Kunstgeschichte München, *Kunstgeschichte – Aber Wie?* (Berlin, 1989), pp. 221–58.

41. HP2, afb. 1774.

42. HP2, afb. 1752.

43. L.D. Benson (ed.), *The Riverside Chaucer* (Oxford, 1988), *The Canterbury Tales,* General Prologue, line 673. See further, P.R. Orton, 'Chaucer's General Prologue A 673 *burdoun* and some sixteenth-century

puns' in *English Language Notes*, 23 (1985), p. 3f.

44. They were first brought to public attention by J. Becker, *'De duystere sin van de geschilderde figueren: zum Doppelsinn in Rätsel, Emblem und Genrestück'* in H. Vekeman and J. Muller Höfftstadt (eds), *Wort und Bild in der niederländischen Kunst und Literatur des 16. und 17. Jahrhunderts* (Erftstadt, 1984), p. 27, n. 19, but fully published by K. Baldinger as *'Six dessins dialogués à double sens'* in *Travaux de Linguistique et de Philologie*, 31 (1993), pp. 7–36. The drawings are now in a private collection in Brazil.

45. A.G. Rigg (ed.), *Gawain on Marriage. The Textual Tradition of the De Coniuge Non Ducenda* (Toronto, 1986).

46. H.N. McCracken (ed.), *The Minor Poems of John Lydgate* [= EETS OS 192] (London, 1934), II, p. 459, line 78.

47. Scattergood, op. cit., p. 57, *The Bowge of Courte*, line 410. The identical idiom also exists in Middle French (*rompre une lance*).

48. C.J. Sisson, *Lost Plays of Shakespeare's Age* (Cambridge, 1936), p. 185.

49. Published in J.O. Halliwell (ed.), *A Selection from the Minor Poems of Dan John Lydgate* (London, 1840), p. 204. The thirteenth-century German romance, *Der Vrouwen Turnei*, describes how a group of women dress up as men in order to participate in a joust and ends with an elaborated sexual innuendo in these terms – ed. F.H. von der Hagen, *Gesamtabenteuer. Hundert altdeutsche Erzählungen*, I. (Darmstadt, 1961), pp. 371–82. For a recent article discussing the sexual badges in the light of the Middle High German Schwänke, see J.H. Winkelman, *Naturalia et Pudenda. Erotische Insignes uit de late Middeleenwen en hun literaire achtergronden* in Amsterdamer Beiträge für ältere Germanistik 55 (2001) 223–38.

50. The *OED* cites *unum dagar ballokhefted* from a York will of 1438, while MED *s.v. ballok* 2a adds citations from 1423 and 1442.

51. *The Vision of Piers Plowman* B-text (1377x1379), Passus XV. 124. The fifteenth-century carol entitled by the editor, *The Braggart and his Baselard* is very much to the point – see R.L. Greene, *The Early English Carols* (2nd edn, Oxford, 1977), no. 417.

52. p. 47 and pl. IX, no. 1.

53. BL MS Egerton 1894, f. 17 – redrawn as fig. 38 in J. Cowgil *et al.*, *Knives and Scabbards* [= Medieval Finds from Excavations in London 1] (London, 1987).

54. A. von Keller (ed.), *Fastnachtspiele aus dem fünfzehnten Jahrhundert* (Stuttgart, 1853), II, p. 717, line 17.

55. A. Bodtker (ed.), *Partonope of Blois* [= EETS ES 109] (London, 1912), lines 1772f. Compare the practice recorded by J.-B. Thiers in his *Traité des superstitions* of 1679 in which the newly wed husband would urinate into the keyhole of the church in which he had just been married, in order to counteract any spell put on him to prevent him fulfilling his conjugal duties – cit. R. Muchembled in J. Bremmer and H. Roodenburg (eds), *A Cultural History of Gesture from Antiquity to the Present Day* (Oxford, 1991), pp. 139f.

56. J.D. Gordon (ed.), *The Epistle of Othea to Hector* (Philadelphia, 1942), p. 136.

57. L.D. Benson (ed.), *The Riverside Chaucer* (Oxford, 1988), *The Canterbury Tales*, General Prologue, line 618. See further, B. Moore, 'The Reeve's "Rusty Blade"' in *Medium Aevum*, 58 (1959), pp. 304–12.

58. *Modern Language Notes*, 45 (1930), p. 106, n. 11.

59. Two British examples known to me are: on a pottery sherd dated stratigraphically to *c.* 130–60 AD, for which see 'The Roman Amphitheatre at Caerleon' in *Archaeologia*, 78 (1928), p. 188 and pl. XXXIII 4; and another sherd 'of Trajanic-Hadrianic date' from London, for which see 'Roman Britain in 1970' in *Britannia*, 2 (1971), p. 299, no. 62; see J.N. Adams, *The Latin Sexual Vocabulary* (London 1982), p. 35, n. 2 for

further phallus noses elsewhere in the Roman Empire.

60. M. Henig, 'A cameo from Barnoldby le Beck, Humberside, depicting a mime actor' in *Antiquaries Journal*, 67 (1987), p. 371 and pl. XXXVa, dated to the first century AD.

61. HP1 afb. 628.

62. C. Bemont, *Simon de Montfort Chronica Maiorum et Vicecomitum Londoniarum* (Oxford 1930), p. 243, n. 2.

63. A. Barratt, 'I am Rose Restored' in *Notes and Queries*, 235 (1990), p. 270.

64. A. de Montaiglon, *Ancien Théâtre Français* (Paris, 1854), II, p. 339.

65. *Gargantua* (1534), end of Chapter 40.

66. cf. William Webbe's complaint in his *Discourse of English Poetrie* (1586) that 'euery one that can frame a Booke in Ryme, though for want of matter, it be but in commendations of Copper noses or Bottle Ale, wyll catch at the Garlande due to Poets'. Nashe's list of paradoxical encomia in his *Lenten Stuff* of 1598 includes an English writer who 'of an enflamed [zeal] to coppersmith's hall, all-to-berhymes it of the diversity of red noses' which, although red noses are generally associated with drunkenness, also sounds as if it refers to the same pamphlet or ballad. For paradoxical encomia in general, see H.K. Miller, *Modern Philology*, 53 (1956), pp. 145–62.

67. A most useful list of such sexual metaphors is to be found in K. Filzeck, *Metaphorische Bildungen im älteren deutschen Fastnachtspiele* (Würzburg, 1933), pp. 43ff. On the widespread use of the word 'bird' or the name of a particular bird-species for 'penis', see E. de Jongh, *'Erotica in Vogelperspectief: De dubbelzinnigheid van een reeks 17de eeuwse genre voorstelingen'* in *Simiolus*, 3 (1968–9), esp. p. 26f.

68. See A. von Keller, *Fastnachtspiele aus dem fünfzehnten Jahrhundert* (Stuttgart, 1853).

69. Reproduced as fig. II in H. Hoffmann, *'Hahnenkampf in Athen: zur Ikonologie einer attischen Bildformel'* in *Revue Archéologique* (1974), p. 195ff.

70. Reproduced in one of the best books on classical erotic art, C. Johns, *Sex or Symbol: Erotic Images of Greece and Rome* (London, 1982).

71. HP1, afb. 638–40.

72. Paris, B.N. MS lat. 4014, f. 1.

73. See J.A. Levinson *et al.*, *Early Italian Engravings from the National Gallery of Art* (Washington, 1973), p. 526, Appendix A.

74. Rabelais, *Quart Livre*, Chapter 32. Writing in the 1580s, Brantôme refers to winged phalli painted on the wall of a Spanish banqueting hall, as recalled from her girlhood by a woman described as still alive – *La Vie des Dames Galantes. Premier Discours*, trans. A. Brown (London, 1961), p. 91.

75. See, for example, D. Wortmann, 'Ein phallisches Priap-Rhyton aus Neuss' in *Bonner Jahrbücher*, 167 (1967), pp. 280–4.

76. V.L. Bullough (ed.), *Sexual Variance in Society and History* (New York, 1976), p. 41.

77. H. Herter, *De Priapo* (Giessen, 1932), pp. 166f., and cf. Juvenal, *Satires* II.95 (*vitreum Priapum*).

78. E. Baumgartner and I. Krueger (eds), *Phoenix aus Sand und Asche: Glas des Mittelalters* (Munich, 1988), cat. no. 530 and refs there.

79. Quoted in F.G. Emmison, *Elizabethan Life: Morals and the Church Courts* (Chelmsford, 1973), p. 21.

80. Published in F.J. Furnivall, *Jyl of Breyntford's Testament and Other Poems* (London, 1871), pp. 29ff.

81. Entitled *Eine Ehescheidung* by E. Fuchs, *Illustrierte Sittengeschichte vom Mittelalter bis zur Gegenwart I: Renaissance* (Munich, 1909), *Ergänzungsband* (Munich, 1928), pp. 28f.

82. See S.R. Fischer, *The Complete Medieval Dreambook, a Multilingual, Alphabetical 'Somnia Danielis' Collation* (Bern/Frankfurt, 1982), p. 150, *s.v. TWIG*, as the author has not understood that in this combination (that is, with *virilis*), *virga* means 'penis'.

83. On the related castration anxiety in the Middle Ages, see comments on the *fabliau* Trubert in K. Gravdal, *Vilain and Courtois: Transgressive Parody in French Literature of the Twelfth and Thirteenth Centuries* (Lincoln, Nebraska, 1989), p. 134.

84. I quote from Part II, Question 1, Chapter 7, in the translation by M. Summers (London 1971), pp. 267f.

85. ed. I. von Zingerle, (Innsbrück, 1874), p. 268, lines 799 ff.

86. J.V. Fleming, *The Roman de la Rose* (Princeton, 1969), p. 133.

87. cf. PRO Rolls of Gaol Delivery, 18 Edward I (= 1290). See further, W. Ross, 'Rose und Nachtigal: Ein Beitrag zur Metaphorik und Mythologie des Mittelalters' in *Romanische Forschungen*, 67 (1955), pp. 55–82.

88. E. Nicaise (ed.), *Chirurgie de Maitre Henri de Mondeville* (Paris, 1893), p. 75, and translated thus in D. Jacquart and C. Thomasset, *Sexuality and Medicine in the Middle Ages* (Oxford 1988), p. 204, n. 71.

89. Sold at Sotheby's, London, on 25 June 1991, lot 74.

90. H. Pleij, *Die Sneeuwpoppen van 1511* reprints Smekens' text as *Bijlage I*. The passage in question occupies lines 317–24.

91. N. Dupire (ed.), *Les Faictz et Dictz de Jean Molinet* (Paris, 1937), II, pp. 540ff.

92. M. Lehrs, *Der Meister mit den Banderollen* (Dresden, 1886), III.6.

93. A convenient edition is that by Horst Appuhn (ed.), *Meister E.S. Alle 320 Kupferstiche* (Dortmund, 1989), p. 237 [Lehrs 208], p. 238 [Lehrs 213], and p. 239 [Lehrs 225].

94. Cited in David Freedberg's refreshing and important book, *The Power of Images* (Chicago, 1989), p. 17. Titian's erotic paintings are discussed in one of the essays in C. Ginzburg, *Myths, Emblems, Clues* (London, 1986).

95. cit. B. Bowen, 'Metaphorical Obscenity in French Farce, 1460–1560' in *Comparative Drama*, 11 (1977), pp. 331–44, here p. 335.

96. H. Kohlhaussen, *Minnekästchen* (Berlin, 1928), nr. 88.

97. See F. Arens, 'Die ursprüngliche Verwendung gotischer Stein- und Tonmodel' in *Mainzer Zeitschrift*, 66 (1971), pp. 106–31, 115, no. 18 (*c.* 1420); 122, no. 43; 126, no. 63; 127, no. 66; 130, no. 90.

98. F.G. Stokes (ed. and trans.), *Epistolae Obscurorum Virorum* (London, 1925), I.xiii.

99. For a most useful list of such metaphorical expressions, see A. Tissier, 'Invocation et représentation scénique de l'acte sexuel dans l'ancienne farce française' in M. Chiabo *et al.* (eds), *Atti del IV Colloquio della Société Internationale pour l'Etude du Théâtre Médiévale* (Viterbo, 1983), pp. 521–47, esp. pp. 526f. For a useful study of a particular erotic metaphor, I single out B. Rowland, 'The Mill in Popular Metaphor from Chaucer to the Present Day' in *Southern Folklore Quarterly*, 33 (1969), pp. 69–79. Another excellent short article is that by B. Bowen cited in n. 95 above.

100. Randall, figs 307, 712 and 713; the motif is discussed by P. Verdier, 'Women in the Marginalia of Manuscripts and Related Works' in R.T. Morewedge (ed.), *The Role of Women in the Middle Ages* (Binghampton, 1975), p. 137. H. Kohlhaussen, *Minnekästchen* (Berlin, 1928) describes the same motif on a late fifteenth-century South German casket, nr. 89. To Verdier's discussion should be added the fifteenth-century French idiom, *faire le heurte belin* (make the ram's charge).

101. cit. David Frantz, *Festum Voluptatis* (Columbus, 1989), p. 75, where the *chiave nella serratura* is one of the many metaphors in the passage cited; and also J. Becker, 'De duystere sin van de geschilderde figueren: zum Doppelsinn in Rätsel, Emblem und Genrestück' in Vekemann and Muller Höfftstadt, op. cit., p. 27, n. 23.

102. The manuscript is Brussels, Bib. Royal MS 9961-2, f. 74. For a similar analysis of a scene in a *bas-de-page* of a related

manuscript, see L.F. Sandler, 'A Bawdy Betrothal in the Ormesby Psalter' in W.W. Clark *et al.* (eds), *Tribute to Lotte Brand Philip: Art Historian and Detective* (New York, 1985).

103. I quote the text as given in R.M. Wilson, *The Lost Literature of Medieval England* (2nd edn, London, 1970), p. 162, from Cambridge, University Library MS Ii. 3. 8. Note that in the famous *Manessische Liederhandschrift*, the Burggraf von Luenz is also depicted putting the stone on f. 118r.

104. cf. the character punningly named Piers Pickpurse, mentioned above.

105. For a study of this most interesting trickster *fabliau*, see Gravdal, op. cit.

106. Reproduced as fig. 39 in M. Jones, 'Sex and Sexuality in Late Medieval and Early Modern Art' in M. Reisenleiter *et al.* (eds), *Sexualität – Privatisierung der Triebe* [= *Frühneuzeit-Studien* Bd.1] (Frankfurt, 1994), pp. 187–304.

107. HP2, afb. 1768.

108. See E. Haraucourt, *Catalogue des bois sculptés et meubles du Musée des Thermes et de l'hôtel de Cluny* (Paris, 1925), B.457; the pun seems first to have been noted by G.J. Witkowski, *L'Art Profane à l'Eglise* (Paris, 1909), p. 32.

109. See C. Gomez-Moreno (ed.), *Medieval Art from Private Collections* (New York, 1968), cat. no. 198.

110. For the oeuvre of the Housebook Master, see J.P. Filedt Kok *et al.*, *'s Levens felheid – de Meester van het Amsterdamse Kabinet of de Hausbuchmeester* (Amsterdam, 1985).

111. Lehrs, op. cit., p. 510.

112. BL, Add. MS 49622, f. 115. On this January and May theme, see Alison Stewart's essential *Unequal Lovers: a Study of Unequal Couples in Northern Art* (New York, 1979).

113. Lilian Randall, in the 'Iconographical Index' to her *Images in the Margins of Gothic Manuscripts* (Berkeley/Los Angeles, 1966), describes them as 'Cleric offering heavy purse to nun'.

114. The manuscript is Paris, B.N. MS fr. 25526, ff. 106v., 160v. and 196r. Most recently by

J. Koldeweij, *'Erotische insignes en een Roman de la Rose-Handschrift'* in HP1, 110–14, and M. Camille, *Image on the Edge: The Margins of Medieval Art* (London, 1992), pp. 148f. and fig. 8 1.

115. HP2 afb. 1724.

116. A reference I owe to Christoph Gerhardt.

117. H. Moser, 'Städtische Fasnacht des Mittelalters' in H. Bausinger *et al.* (eds), *Masken zwischen Spiel und Ernst* (Tübingen, 1967), p. 176.

118. S.S. Smith: '*Game in myn hood*: the Traditions of a Comic Proverb' in *Studies in Iconography*, 9 (1984), pp. 1–12. Another, more standard presentation of the confrontation of symbols representing the organs of both sexes in the unequivocally sexual context of the wedding night, where the bride is shown carrying candle and jug/chamber-pot, known from 1529 on, is discussed by K. Renger, *'Tränen in der Hochzeitsnacht: das Zubettbringen der Braut, ein vergessenes Thema der niederländischen Malerei'* in L. Griesbach (ed.), and ibid., *Festschrift für O. v. Simson* (Frankfurt/ Berlin/Wien, 1977), pp. 310–27.

119. HP2, afb. 1743.

120. HP2, afb. 1738.

121. See J. Gagne, 'L'Erotisme dans la Musique Médiévale' in ed. B. Roy, *L'Erotisme au Moyen Age* (Montreal/Paris, 1977), esp. pp. 91ff.; G.F. Jones, 'Wittenwiler's *Becki* and the Medieval Bagpipe' in *Journal of English and Germanic Philology*, 48 (1949), pp. 209–28; E.A. Block, 'Chaucer's Millers and their Bagpipes' in *Speculum*, 29 (1954), pp. 239–43; and 'History at the Margins: Bagpipers in Medieval Manuscripts' in *History Today*, 39 (1989), pp. 42–8.

122. See S. Kaspersen, *'Bildender Kunst, Theater und Volkstümlichkeit in mittelalterlichen Dänemark'* in F.G. Andersen (ed.), *Popular Drama in Northern Europe in the Later Middle Ages* (Odense, 1988), pp. 248f.

123. This composition is found as early as the 1520s in the form of a circular engraving by the Master IB [Bartsch 36].

124. See Johns, op. cit., pp. 24f. See also K. Sudhoff, 'Antike Votivgaben, die weiblichen Genitalorgane darstellend' in *Monatsschrift für Geburtshilfe und Gynäkologie*, 38 (1914), pp. 185–99.

125. T.M.C. Lawler *et al.* (eds), *The Yale Edition of the Complete Works of Sir Thomas More*: vol. VI.i, *A Dialogue Concerning Heresies* (New Haven/London, 1981), pp. 228/10–13. A reference I owe to the kindness of Dr Richard Axton.

126. E. Camesasca (ed.) *Lettere sull'arte . . .* (Milan, (n.d.)), pp. 110f., no. 68; translation adapted from T.C. Chubb, *The Letters of Pietro Aretino* (Yale UP, 1967), p. 124, no. 58, *To Messer Battista Zatti of Brescia*, 11 December 1537.

127. Like all areas of research into sexuality, the available bibliography is very uneven, beginning with G.J. Witkowski's quirky two-volume *Tetoniana* (Paris, 1898), and including, more recently, but hardly more usefully, M. Lévy, *The Moons of Paradise. Some Reflections on the Appearance of the Female Breast in Art* (London, 1962), and J.-J. Pauvert, *Mythologie du sein* (Paris, 1965).

128. See, for example, the breast offered to the Child in the fourteenth-century stained-glass panel in the church of St John the Baptist, Fladbury (reproduced as pl. 26 in J. Baker, *English Stained Glass of the Medieval Period* (London, 1978).

129. The conventional comparison of the breasts with apples is discussed in D.J. Ransom, *Poets at Play: Irony and Parody in the Harley Lyrics* (Norman, 1985), p. 61 and n. 33.

130. *Natural History*, XV.15.51. Grimm also cites Aristophanes' use of the apple metaphor.

131. The sexual-parts-as-food metaphor – also implicit in the apple image – is well illustrated in German *fastnachtspiel* (carnival play); cf. 'whether he too would like to eat apples', cit. K. Filzeck, *Metaphorische Bildungen im älteren deutschen Fastnachtspiele* (Würzburg, 1933), p. 53.

132. A. Saunders, *The Sixteenth Century Blason Poétique* (Bern, 1981).

133. Canto 7, 14.

134. From an early fourteenth-century poem entitled *'La lande dorée que le vicomte d'Aunoy fist'*, Saunders, op. cit., p. 54. An earlier instance occurs in Chrétien de Troyes' *Philomena*, pp. 161f.: *'Autressi come deus pomettes/ Estoient ses deus mamelettes'*. For further examples, see P. Menard, *Le Rire et le Sourire dans le Roman Courtois en France au Moyen Age (1150–1250)* (Geneva, 1969), p. 260.

135. *Ubera sepe suis zonis strinxere puelle/Turgida namque nimis displicuere uiris – De Tribus Puellis*, lines 45ff. (and cf. 257f.), P. Maury (ed.), in G. Cohen, *Etudes d'Histoire du Théâtre en France au Moyen Age et à la Renaissance* (8th edn, Paris, 1956), pp. 95f.

136. *Troilus and Criseyde*, III, p. 1250.

137. *Ars Versificatoria*, 1.56; cit. D.S. Brewer, 'The Ideal of Feminine Beauty in Medieval Literature, especially *Harley Lyrics*, Chaucer, and some Elizabethans' in *Modern Language Review*, 50 (1955), p. 257ff.

138. Anne Hollander, *Seeing Through Clothes* (New York, 1975), p. 99.

139. Oxford, Bodleian Library, MS Fairfax 16 (3896); reproduced as pl. 40, cat. no. 83 in J.G. Alexander and C.M. Kauffmann (eds), *English Illuminated Manuscripts 700–1500* (Brussels, 1973).

140. Mellinkoff, op. cit., p. 202 and pl. X.20.

141. Poem beginning, *'Mentre per una ribiera . . .'*, lines 10f.

142. C. Baumann, 'Die Spitznamen in bayerischen Traditionen des 12. Jahrhunderts' in *Blätter für Oberdeutsche Namenforschung*, 24 (1987), p. 38.

143. J. Blottière, *'Surnoms et patronymes du Xe au XIIe siècle dans le Vexin français, le Pinserais et le Mantois'* in *Revue Internationale Onomastique*, 25 (1973), p. 34.

144. Grossness as well as shrivelled condition is implied by Deschamps' description of the old woman's breasts in Ballade 804: 'your tits are like bellows that are closed' – cit.

J.C. Rault, *'Les poèmes grivois d'Eustache Deschamps'* in *Le Moyen Age*, 85 (1979), p. 275ff.

145. P. Barolsky, *Infinite Jest: Wit and Humor in Italian Renaissance Art* (Columbia, 1978), p. 192 and fig. 8–5.

146. W.L. Hildburgh, 'Aeolipiles as Fire-Blowers' in *Archaeologia*, 94 (1951), pp. 35–55. I am grateful to Dr George Szabo for his opinion that these bronzes should rather be seen as fountain figures. See also K. Ranke, 'Manneken Pis und verwandtes' in W. van Nespen (ed.), *Miscellanea K.C. Peeters* (Antwerp, 1975), pp. 576–81.

147. In general, see W. Deonna, 'Fontaines Anthropomorphes: La Femme aux Seins Jaillissants et l'Enfant *Mingens*' in *Genava*, 6 (1958), esp. p. 258ff. For the Bruges *entrée*, see the facsimile edition with this title with introduction by S. Anglo, (Amsterdam/New York, n.d.), woodcut.

148. Oxford, Bodleian Library, MS Douce 195, f. 146r, reproduced as fig. 99 in J.V. Fleming, *The Roman de la Rose* (Princeton, 1969). See further the discussion of 'cock' in Chapter 3, Dürer's *Männerbad*, Schoen's *Jungbrunnen* fool, etc.

149. Reproduced in C. Gaignebet and D. Lajoux, *Art profane et religion populaire au Moyen Age* (Paris, 1985), p. 197.

150. Van Lennep's Alchemy Exhibition Catalogue, however, cites L.S. Dixon Water, p. 95, to the effect that this is an alchemical vessel termed a *mastarion*.

Chapter Thirteen

1. P. Leach, *Baby and Child from Birth to Age Five* (2nd edn, London, 1988), p. 325.

2. For example, that on f. 90v.

3. See also the amusing Carolingian tale of the 'musical donkey' in *MGH Poetae*, III 362, no. 161.

4. K.P. Wentersdorf, 'The symbolic significance of the *figurae scatologicae* in Gothic manuscripts' in C. Davidson (ed.), *Word, Picture and Spectacle* (Kalamazoo, 1984), pp. 1–20.

5. The *EPNS Derbyshire* volume's first citation at 1630 is absurdly late. Because it is one of the ancient *Mirabilia* of Britain, a traditional listing which goes back to the ninth century, Welsh manuscripts are also interested in this English place-name – NLW Peniarth MS 163 (1543), for instance, notes that the English call it *Tin diawl* (that is, Devil's Arse) or *[Tin] pek* (Peak's Arse).

6. B. Cox, *The Place-Names of Leicestershire Part 2: Framland Hundred [EPNS, vol. 78]* (Nottingham, 2002), p. 281.

7. In the thirteenth and fourteenth centuries, Paris could also boast a scatological street-name, the *Ruelle de Cul-de-Pet.*

8. For another contemporary Flemish example, see New York, Pierpont Morgan Library Glazier Collection, MS 24, f. 47v, reproduced as Randall, fig. 529.

9. C. Brown and R.H. Robbins (eds), *The Index of Middle English Verse* (New York, 1943), no. 1222.

10. But anal 'trumpeting' is a common enough image in Medieval Latin as well as the contemporary vernaculars, for example, Matthew of Vendôme's *'tuba ventris'*, and Dante's *'del cul fatto trombetta'* [*Inferno* XXI.139].

11. See M. Jones, 'The parodic sermon in medieval and Early Modern England' in *Medium Aevum*, 66 (1997), pp. 94–114. The manuscript clearly reads *-nette*, for 'shove-net', see MED *s.v. shouven* 1 (b), though Wright and Halliwell, and thus MED, *s.v. scopet(te*, read *-pette*. which is thus a ghost.

12. The earliest English *literary* instance I am aware of is to be found in Wyatt's translation of a sonnet by Petrarch, 'Whoso list to hunt . . .', usually dated to *c.* 1527, which includes the lines, I 'leave off therefore/Sithens in a net I seek to hold the wind' – K. Muir and P. Thomson (eds), *Collected Poems of Sir Thomas Wyatt* (Liverpool, 1969), p. 5.

13. cit. TPMA 135 *s.v. Furz*, no. 62.

14. M. Jones, 'Marcolf the Trickster in Late Medieval Art and Literature, or, The Mystery of the Bum in the Oven' in G. Bennett (ed.), *Spoken in Jest* (Sheffield, 1991), pp. 139–74, esp. p. 170, Appendix 1, 'Kiss my arse'.

15. As found on a late fifteenth-century misericord at Aosta and as a contemporary stall-elbow at Saint-Claude.

16. The same manuscript also includes a song about the *baise-cul* (arse-kisser).

17. Composed by the Chevalier de la Tour Landry, *c.* 1372.

18. Wh M 580.

19. J. Verspaandonk, *Amsterdam. de koorbanken van De Oude Kerk* (Amsterdam, 1984), p. 80.

20. That is, BL Add. MS 29523, f. 41v and f. 410v reproduced in Randall.

21. A. Darmesteter, *Traité de la Formation des mots composés* (Paris, 1875), p. 186.

22. R. Pachnio, *Die Beinamen der Pariser Steuerrolle von 1292* (Paris, 1909), p. 48.

23. This is perhaps the subject sculpted on a corbel in the staircase tower of the Hôtel de Ville in Noyon – G.J. Witkowski, *L'Art Profane à l'Eglise* (Paris, 1909), fig. 382.

24. The redoubtable Jyl is alluded to in Shakespeare's *The Merry Wives of Windsor*.

25. M. Jones, 'Marcolf the Trickster in Late Medieval Art and Literature, or, The Mystery of the Bum in the Oven' in G. Bennett (ed.), *Spoken in Jest* (Sheffield, 1991), pp. 139–74.

26. The game and its misericord representations are discussed by M. Twycross in Medieval Theatre (forthcoming).

27. M. Jones, 'German and Flemish Prints' in Keen and Scarff, op. cit., pp. 155–65, esp. 162–3.

28. Rondeau 671.

29. *Sorgheloos* (1540).

30. Like several others of the names above, this is taken from P.H. Reaney, *The Origins of English Surnames* (London, 1967), p. 294, 'Obsolete nicknames'.

31. cit. *OED s.v. clister.*

32. For example, the *Metz Hours*, New York, Pierpont Morgan Library, MS M 88, f. 173v.

33. Randall, fig. 532.

34. E. Ekwall, *Street Names of the City of London* (London, 1954), pp. 155–6, and he notes that 'many streets were named from such houses [of public convenience] in old Danish and German towns'.

CONCLUSION

1. There is some reason to believe that the periwinkle was classed as an 'evergreen' in the late Middle Ages; although *sengreen* (= evergreen) is agreed to specify the plant known as houseleek (*Sempervivum tectorum*), Grigson records the name used for the periwinkle in modern Somerset and the Isle of Wight (295), and it is the plant identified by the German cognate *Singrün*, but which is more commonly known in Germany as *Immergrün*, that is, 'Evergreen'. If this identification can be accepted for the English late Middle Ages, then it may be that the placing of the periwinkle on the traitor's head was a symbol that his treachery would remain evergreen in the minds of the population.

2. T. Wright (ed.), Revd E. Goldsmid, *The Political Songs of England* (Edinburgh, 1884), III, p. 65–79.

3. cit. H. Marzell, *Wörterbuch der deutschen Pflanzennamen* (Leipzig, 1943 – Stuttgart, 1979), 1147 – a reference I owe to the kindness of the encyclopedic J.B. Smith.

4. R.L. Greene (ed.), *Early English Carols* (2nd edn, Oxford, 1977), pp. 257 and 471–3, where all the relevant information is collected.

5. The same incident is referred to in Speed's, *History of Great Britain* (1611), ix xvii. (1632) 869. *He was first solemnly disgraded, his guilt spurs cut from his heeles by the Master-Cooke.*

6. 1548 (*a.* 1532) Hall *Chronicle* (1809 edn), pp. 260–1.

INDEX